Refugees in the Age of Total War

Also from Unwin Hyman

POLITICAL CHANGE IN THE THIRD WORLD
Charles F. Andrain

AN INTRODUCTION TO DEVELOPMENT ECONOMICS
Second edition
Subrata Ghatak

THE ECONOMICS OF INTERNATIONAL INTEGRATION
Second edition
Peter Robson

RICH AND POOR COUNTRIES
Third edition
Hans Singer and Javed Ansari

THE PRICE OF WAR
Urbanization in Vietnam 1954–1985
Nigel Thrift and Dean Forbes

Refugees in the Age of Total War

Introduction by
MICHAEL R. MARRUS

Edited by
ANNA C. BRAMWELL
for the Refugee Studies Programme,
University of Oxford

London
UNWIN HYMAN
Boston   Sydney   Wellington

This volume was prepared, proofed and passed for press by the Refugee Studies Programme, University of Oxford.

Unwin Hyman Ltd
15/17 Broadwick Street, London W1V 1FP, UK

Unwin Hyman, Inc.
8 Winchester Place, Winchester, Mass. 01890, USA

Allen & Unwin (Australia) Ltd,
8 Napier Street, North Sydney, NSW 2060, Australia

Allen & Unwin (New Zealand) Ltd in association with the Port Nicholson Press Ltd,
60 Cambridge Terrace, Wellington, New Zealand

First Published in 1988

British Library Cataloguing in Publication Data

Refugees in the age of total war.
  1. Refugees, 1900–1984
  I. Bramwell, Anna
  325'.21
  ISBN 0–04–445194–6

Library of Congress Cataloging in Publication Data

Refugees in the age of total war / edited by Anna C. Bramwell;
  with an introduction by Michael R. Marrus.
      p. cm.
    Includes index.
    ISBN 0–04–445194–6 (alk. paper)
    1. Refugees—History—20th century.   Bramwell, Anna.
  HV640.R434 1988   88–14015
362.8'7—dc 19   CIP

Typeset in 10 on 11 point Times
and printed in Great Britain by Biddles of Guildford

Contents

List of contributors

Adelman, Howard, a Professor of Philosophy at York University, was the founder of York University's Refugee Documentation Project in Toronto. Professor Adelman has prepared an index of UNRWA archives and is currently overseeing an international team of scholars involving Egyptians, Palestinians and Israelis, as well as scholars from Britain, the United States and Canada on the genesis and early years of the United Nations Relief and Works Agency for Palestine Refugees in the near East.

Boshyk, Yury, author, consultant and Adjunct Professor in the History Department, York University. He is the editor of *Ukraine During World War II: History and its Aftermath* (Edmonton, 1986), and (with Boris Balan) *Political Refugees and Displaced Persons, 1945–54: A Select Bibliography and Guide to Research* (Edmonton, 1982).

Bramwell, Anna, Research Fellow, Trinity College, Oxford, author of *Blood and Soil: R. Walter Darre and Hitler's 'Green Party'* (Bourne End, 1985), articles on modern European History, and, forthcoming, *A Political Theory of Ecology: Land and Man in European Thought, 1880 to the Present.*

Cels, Johan, studied at Louvain, Johns Hopkins University, Ohio University, currently completing a doctorate at the University of Nôtre Dame, contributor to several studies of refugee law and other refugee issues.

Fox, John P., Fellow of the Historical Society, British Editor of *Akten zur deutschen auswartigen Politick 1918–1945*, author of *Germany and the Far Eastern Crisis 1931–1938: A Study in Diplomacy and Ideology* (Oxford University Press, 1982; Pbk. 1985), 'The Jewish Factor in British War Crimes Policy 1942', *The English Historical Review*, January 1987, and other articles.

Hirschfeld, Gerhard, Fellow of the German Historical Institute, London, has published widely on the history of the Second World War, on political violence and on the emigration from Nazi Germany, among others *Exile in Great Britain* (1984) and *Nazi Rule and Dutch Collaboration* (1978).

Lanphier, C. Michael, Professor of Sociology and Director, Refugee Documentation Project at York University, Toronto, Canada. He has written several monographs and articles on Canadian immigration and refugee issues. His study of refugee resettlement policy, 1981–1982, compared Indochinese refugee resettlement in Canada, the United States and France. He is currently working on governmental and NGO perspectives on refugee movements. Professor Lanphier obtained his doctorate in Social Psychology from the University of Michigan and his BA degree from Harvard University.

Loescher, Gil, Associate Professor of Government and member of Kellogg Institute for International Studies at the University of Nôtre Dame, author of *Calculated Kindness: Refugees and America's Half–Open Door*, (New York and London, 1986) and co–editor with John A. Scanlan of *The Global Refugee Problem: U.S. and World Response* (Beverly Hills and London, 1983).

Marrus, Michael R., Professor of History at the University of Toronto, and a specialist in modern European history. He received his MA and Ph.D. degrees from the University of California at Berkeley, and has been a Guggenheim Fellow, a visiting fellow of St. Anthony's College, Oxford, and the Institute for Advanced Study of the Hebrew University in Jerusalem, and a visiting professor at UCLA. He is the author of a number of books, among them *The Unwanted: European Refugees in the Twentieth Century* (1985).

Melander, Göran, Assistant Professor of International Law, University of Lund, Sweden. Director of the Raoul Wallenberg Institute of Human Rights and Humanitarian Law. Author of several monographs and articles on refugee law, e.g. *Refugees in Orbit* (1978).

Moro, Daniele, Journalist with the Italian State Foreign Services TV-Radio, contributor to *South–East Europe after Tito*, ed. D. Carlton and C. Schaerf (London, 1983), and Head of the Military Department of the Italian Socialist Party in Rome.

Morris, Benny, Diplomatic Correspondent of *The Jerusalem Post*, and author of *The Birth of the Palestinian Refugee Problem, 1947–49* (Cambridge University Press, 1987).

Nichols, Bruce, Director of Studies in Ethics and Foreign Policy, Carnegie Council on Ethics and International Affairs, New York, author of *At Home in No Man's Land: Refugees, Religion and US Foreign Policy* (Oxford, 1987).

Persson, Hansåke, Research Associate at the Department of History and the Center for the Study of International Conflicts, University of Lund, Sweden. He is currently preparing *Caught in the Middle: Britain and the German Expellees*.

Prazmowska, Anita J., historian. She is the author of articles on British and Polish foreign policy during the 1938–39 period, as well as *Britain, Poland and the Eastern Front, 1939* (Cambridge University Press, 1987).

Roseman, Mark, Lecturer in the Department of Modern Languages, University of Aston, Birmingham. Author of a forthcoming study on refugee miners in the Ruhr area in Germany after the Second World War.

Sayigh, Rosemary, anthropologist and journalist, living in Beirut. Presently working for *Middle East International* and reading for a doctorate at Hull University. Author of *Palestinians: From Peasants to Revolutionaries*.

Sword, Keith, Research Fellow at the School of Slavonic and East European Studies, University of London. He is currently preparing a study on Polish resettlement in Britain, 1945–50. Also working on a research project which investigates the fate of Poles deported to the Soviet Union during World War II.

Walker, Christopher J., freelance writer and author of *Armenia: the Survival of a Nation* (London, 1980) and *The Armenians*, Minority Rights Group Report, 1977.

Zayas, Alfred de, Centre of Human Rights, UN, Geneva, lawyer and historian, author of *Nemesis at Potsdam* (London, 1977), *Die Wehrmacht Untersuchungstelle* (Munich, 1984), *Anmerkungun zur Vertreibung der Deutschen aus dem Osten* (Stuttgart, 1986), contributor to *Encyclopaedia of Public International Law*.

Preface

In the twentieth century, tens of millions of people have been uprooted and forced to flee their homelands. The largest forced movements of population were in Europe and the Middle East and followed both world wars. Over the past two decades, the number of refugees has once again risen from hundreds of thousands to millions. This book results from an international symposium which was held in Oxford in 1985. It brought together scholars from various disciplines who are researching refugee movements in Europe and the Middle East to share knowledge and broaden their understanding of the issues.

Refugees are largely a twentieth century phenomenon, and until the 1950s they were largely European in origin. Today, however, most of the world's refugee populations are to be found in the poorest countries of the world which depend on humanitarian assistance to cope with the enormous burden of assisting the uprooted. To those who flee from war and civil strife are added the unknown but probably the greater numbers of people who are uprooted within their own homelands because of environmental degradation and the consequent threat of starvation. Development policies devised by many governments may also require the massive displacement of peoples. Unless due consideration is taken to address the social requirements of such communities, such policies may also result in creating refugee-like conditions for those who are affected.

Does such a book on refugees which examines the period following the Second World War have any relevance for the understanding of present day refugee issues? Although it is a popular belief that the political turbulence which is being experienced today in many developing countries is similar to that of Europe in the Middle Ages, there are startling parallels between what is happening now in Africa, Asia, Central and Latin America and what was occurring in Europe as recently as in the period leading up to, and following World War II.

At the end of the Second World War large areas of Europe lay in ruins. Production was interrupted and all the other ingredients of the contemporary situation were also present: famine conditions, large numbers of refugees, and low income countries. Political considerations influenced the decision as to who received assistance; refugees were forcibly repatriated, opportunities for resettlement were often selected on the basis of an individual's qualifications rather than on genuinely humanitarian grounds, and, as is more frequently the case today, the motives of some European refugees were questioned - many then were also labelled 'economic refugees'.

There are other striking similarities. The origins of the refugee problems in Europe and the Middle East were rooted in the nationalities question, a characteristic prevalent in many current refugee-producing situations.

The influence of cold war politics was also present as it is in most refugee situations today.

Europeans have a tendency to forget their own recent history. Still in 1959 there were thousands of people languishing in camps in Europe. It was this grave situation which prompted Timothy Raison, then a journalist with *New Society*, to promote the idea of a UN 'World Refugee Year' as a way of encouraging member nations to resolve this problem by resettling them.

Today, however, there are not only differences in scale and locality, but also in the attitudes of the wealthier host and donor nations. Then, countries outside Europe were willing to receive large numbers of refugees, and vast amounts of capital were poured into Europe itself to promote its rapid recovery. A further important difference between post-war Europe and many refugee-producing parts of the world today, was the promise of political stability which encouraged massive investment in the rebuilding of Europe.

Europe no longer produces significant numbers of refugees. The Middle East is now experiencing similar developments as Europe has over the past fifty years. Though the origins of the major forced movements of people has now shifted, can something be learned from past refugee movements in these areas which is applicable to Asia, Africa, and Central America today?

Humanitarian agencies often lament their own lack of an 'institutional memory' and their tendency is to re-invent the wheel each time they are called upon to respond to a new refugee emergency. It is the view of the organizers of the symposium that it is only through an analysis of past mistakes and successes that progress can be made. Academics have generally neglected the study of forced migration; they have not provided practitioners with a source of information on the lessons which have been learned. It is hoped that the case studies included in this book will point the way to more co-ordinated studies in this inter-disciplinary field.

This book focuses on a series of case studies of the creation of refugees and their treatment in host countries. As will be seen, rather than lofty humanitarian principles, internal politics and economic considerations have been decisive in determining refugee policies over much of this century. Since the creation of the United Nations and its refugee agencies, the development of inter-governmental measures has taken on an increasing importance, as has the role of voluntary and religious institutions.

The 1985 symposium was co-sponsored by the Refugee Studies Programme, Oxford University, and the Refugee Documentation Project, York University, Canada. Twenty-eight papers were presented by historians, lawyers, anthropologists, sociologists, political scientists, and agency personnel. The venue was Somerville College, Oxford. Professor Joseph Fraenkel, Emeritus Professor, University of Southampton, delivered the opening address. Official representatives from both UNRWA (United Nations Relief and Works Agency) and UNHCR (United Nations High Commissioner for Refugees) attended the symposium as did representatives from various embassies.

Members of the committee responsible for overseeing the publication of this book were Howard Adelman, Anna Bramwell, Yury Boshyk, Michael Lanphier, Hansåke Persson, and Barbara Harrell-Bond. The Refugee Studies Programme, the York Refugee Documentation Project and the editorial committee are especially grateful to Professor Michael Marrus for kindly agreeing to write the introduction; he is one of the pioneers in this new field of studies, and his book, *The Unwanted: European Refugees in the Twentieth Century,* is a landmark in drawing together the widely dispersed sources on European refugees. His work inspired many of the contributors to this volume to investigate further the primary sources on this subject.

Several groups and individuals also deserve special mention for their help. Financial support for the symposium came from the British Council, the Economic and Social Research Council and Oxford University Press. John Defrates, Hansåke Persson, Cyprian Blamires, and Angus Stevenson gave much assistance to the editor. Thanks are also due to the many scholars who commented on the papers included in this book and especially to Ann Taylor who typed and re-typed the manuscript.

Barbara Harrell–Bond

List of abbreviations

ACVA	American Council of Voluntary Agencies for Foreign Service (New York)
AFSC	American Friends Service Committee
CRS	Catholic Relief Services, USA
HIAS	Hebrew Immigrant and Sheltering Aid Society, USA
IGC	Inter-Governmental Committee for Refugees (Evian, 1938)
NCC	National Council of Churches, USA
NCWC	National Catholic Welfare Conference
NGO	Non-Governmental Organisation
PACPR	President's Advisory Committee for Political Refugees (USA, 1938)
UNRRA	United Nations Relief and Rehabilitation Administration
UNHCR	United Nations High Commissioner for Refugees
WRCB	President's War Relief Control Board (USA, 1942)
WRS	War Relief Services, later Catholic Relief Services

Introduction

MICHAEL R. MARRUS

No one knows for certain how many refugees wander the world today, languish in camps without a permanent place of settlement, or survive illegally, in constant fear of being discovered and driven once again to seek safety and shelter. According to the *World Refugee Survey* for 1986, the total number of "refugees in need of protection and/or assistance" approaches 11,698,000.[1] But this total does not include the millions of "internally displaced persons" – refugees in the most common understanding of the term, whose circumstances of uprooting, suffering and the chaos of their lives include every burden carried by refugees except that they have not crossed internationally recognized frontiers. Nor do these numbers take account of the many hundreds of thousands in "refugee-like circumstances" – a designation widely used to denote people torn loose from their homes but who may fail to meet the formal criteria for asylum in the countries where they find themselves, or who for any number of technical reasons lie outside the mandate of international refugee organizations.

However assessed, practically everyone contends that the problem is growing, beyond anyone's prediction a generation ago and far beyond the capacity of present national or international institutions to reduce within a short time. The situation, it is often said, is unprecedented. And it is all the more fearsome because, unlike previous experiences of refugee waves, there appears to be no end in sight to the increase of refugee masses. In the statements and speeches of those responsible for refugee assistance, the tone struck is often one of helplessness in global terms, or despair at the long term prospects. Throughout the Western World, the climate of opinion seems to be turning against refugees. In Western Europe, where the overwhelming majority of incoming refugees had always been of European origin, the significant development of the present decade has been the appeal for asylum from large numbers of outsiders – mainly from Africa, Asia, and the Middle East. During 1986, several European countries appeared to be tightening restrictions on foreigners seeking admission and asylum. A common pattern is that machinery to process applications for refugee status is proving incapable of dealing with the volume of requests that are filed, the numbers of applicants has increased significantly, and public protests against improper granting of refugee status are contributing to the drafting of ever more restrictive measures. In Switzerland, proposed changes in the mechanisms for receiving refugees have provoked intense debate and controversy throughout the past year; in France, widespread antipathy to foreigners in a time of economic difficulty has led to extensive popular support for anti-refugee measures.

In Canada, the recipient of the Nansen Medal for services to refugees for 1986, the government has issued new regulations, widely interpreted as restrictive, fearing an onslaught of Central American refugees as a result of newly imposed restrictive measures in the United States.

Strikingly, the debates over refugees in each of these countries echo the controversies of times past. In this respect, remarkably little seems to have changed. "Restrictionists" argue that charity begins at home, that obligations extend first to local poor and unemployed, and that procedures for receiving refugees must be drafted with an eye to discouraging unmanageable numbers of unwanted applicants who might come in the future. Refugee advocates, on the other hand, champion enlarging possibilities for asylum, assert the economic value of refugees to countries that receive them, and insist on collective responsibilities, both national and international, to solve refugee crises and to shelter the homeless.

Can the work of scholars of refugee movements – necessarily concerned with what has been – help us to understand and address contemporary refugee problems? I believe so. Seen in historical perspective, many of the concerns and fears of present-day policy makers appear highly exaggerated, or without foundation. Moreover, resettlement on a large scale has been undertaken in the past, and is likely not impossible in the future. It makes sense to see our current problems of homelessness in the context of a century of upheaval, denoted here as "the Age of Total War," in which the impact of uprooted and homeless people has in particular circumstances and at various times been even greater than that which we face today.

I have argued elsewhere that refugees present a distinctively modern problem – one that has emerged in the course of the nineteenth and twentieth centuries. Before then there were certainly refugees – people driven by war or persecution to leave their homes and seek refuge abroad. But "abroad" was not necessarily another state, and even when it was those who ruled such jurisdictions frequently had attitudes and interests strikingly different from those that prevail today. This is not to say that such societies were necessarily more humane by our own standards. Prior to the emergence of the welfare state, most refugees had to rely upon the charity proffered by the church, municipalities, or princes. Refugees were lucky if they received such support, and usually perished if they did not. But although conditions varied widely, one can venture the generalization that premodern statesmen tended to view populations as an asset, rather than a liability. Broadly speaking, rulers tended to favour the controlled movement of people into their jurisdictions, expecting thereby to add to the producers of wealth, the community of taxpayers, and those who could be made to serve in local armies. As a result, those expelled from one place could often find refuge in another.

Examples abound. Jewish expellees from the Iberian Peninsula at the end of the fifteenth century were received by Muslim countries, Italian city states, and eventually the Netherlands, often making distinguished contributions to the life of the places that received them; Muslim expellees who followed them out of Spain realized similar achievements in North

Africa a few years later. Following the religious Peace of Augsburg of 1555, with its formula *Cuius regio eius religio* (He who owns the land determines the religion) giving princes the right to order local religious affairs, the displaced sorted themselves out within the vigorous new centres of religious commitment under new political protection. Hundreds of thousands of Protestants fled the French kingdom after Louis XIV's revocation of the Edict of Nantes in 1685, eventually providing distinguished service, among other places, to the emerging Hohenzollern state of a fellow Protestant, the Great Elector Frederick William of Brandenburg.

Permanently displaced persons, such as we have come to know them in our own era, were practically unknown in premodern times. There were no camps to keep people in a suspended state between full admission and the flight from their original homes. Although local jurisdictions sometimes opposed receiving newcomers, seeking to protect markets and limit their responsibilities, central governments tended to encourage or even force the admission of outsiders. In addition, premodern military practice militated against the creation of large numbers of refugees. Armies were heavily dependent on the local population to produce the food and provide the services that the soldiers required. In consequence, commanders required the local population to stay put, rather than flee to somewhere else. Particularly in the era of siege warfare, in the late seventeenth and eighteenth centuries, when large armies remained relatively immobile, it made no sense to turn the occupied population into refugees. Finally, the material resources of premodern societies were simply incapable of sustaining large masses of uprooted and unwanted people. When significant numbers were displaced, as sometimes happened, no level of government or social group necessarily assumed responsibility for them. Such refugees might therefore wander for a time, but unless they quickly found some home they generally could not survive.

Four factors contributed to the change in the social position of the refugee during the course of the nineteenth and early twentieth centuries. First, the emerging consciousness of national identity, familiarly traced to the French Revolution, defined broad categories of people as belonging to the nation state and relegated others to the role of outsiders. Nationalist ideologies now cultivated the view of refugees as inimical to the health of the nation – a threat to its security, cultural cohesion, or way of life.

Second, in an age of revolutions refugees could be seen as the carriers of alien doctrines, often highly subversive of local interests and institutions. Nineteenth-century political upheavals invariably produced waves of refugees, many of whom went abroad as proud representatives of a temporarily defeated cause. To a remarkable degree, European states received these political exiles, exercising a degree of tolerance and indulgence toward them that seems unusual from our vantage point. But restrictions were imposed, grew stronger after 1848, and intensified further at the century's close when a wave of anarchist attacks posed a fearsome threat in many societies.

Third, the growing obligation assumed by states and other institutions for the indigent and the helpless within them meant that refugees could become a burden hitherto undefined in European societies. Princes or municipal councillors in premodern times could turn a blind eye to those who perished of exposure in the woods or by the roadside, who starved on the outskirts of cities, or who appealed for help on the docks when they disembarked. But in societies sensitized to humanistic obligations by Enlightenment ideals, rendered less tolerant of the coarse realities of death of fellow creatures, such reactions became impossible. As well, there were fears of disease. The modes of transmission of such ills as cholera and typhus may have been mysterious for much of the century, but people worried greatly about infection, and did their best to protect themselves from that menace. Much of the opposition to refugees was therefore expressed in terms of public hygiene, the protection of which required not only the exclusion of unwanted strangers, but many other protective measures as well.

Fourth, the scale and destructiveness of international conflict have grown enormously in the past two centuries. Military operations became increasingly industrialized, and less dependent upon the logistical support once provided by local inhabitants. Railways could now bring food to encamped armies, where once only the local peasantry could provide sustenance. As a result, strategists have waged war not only against opposing military formations, but also against enemy civilians as well. Aerial bombardment, the great innovation of twentieth-century warfare, produced a large proportion of refugees in modern conflicts, sometimes even eliminating in practical terms the distinction between combatants and non-combatants. Many more refugees than ever before were forced to move when great masses of men and machinery collided in modern battles, causing ever widening circles of devastation, and the uprooting has extended far beyond the cessation of hostilities.

The cumulative result of these factors was a vast increase in the number of refugees on the European continent. Hundreds of thousands roamed the Balkan peninsula in the decade or so before the First World War, and that great upheaval prompted an even greater exodus. The postwar settlements formalized the collapse of four European empires – Hapsburg, Hohenzollern, Romanov and Ottoman – and along with the political realignments of their territories many thousands more were made homeless. Hundreds of thousands fled the political earthquake that destroyed the Tsarist Empire; and the aftershocks of civil war, the Russo-Polish War, and the Soviet famine of 1921 sent countless others fleeing abroad. An estimated half a million Armenians became refugees from massacre and deportation in Turkey, most of them clinging to life in the short-lived Armenian Republic, while others found refuge in the Middle East, the Soviet Union, or the West. Hundreds of thousands were caught in the bitter quarrel between Greece and Turkey, leading to the forced exchange of population between these two countries, formalized in the 1923 Convention of Lausanne. In all, an estimated 1.5 million had to leave their homes in that cataclysm.

Europeans only just managed to settle the refugees from the First World War when they had to contend with a new exodus that foreshadowed the upheaval of the Second. Refugees from fascism strained the fragile international institutions spawned by the League of Nations in the 1930s, particularly under the stresses caused by the Great Depression. The Second World War itself flooded the world with refugees, with close to thirty million forced to move within Europe, according to one student of the problem.[2] And even more were to come. Close to one quarter of the population of the former German Reich was made up of refugees when the fighting ended in 1945, and Allied armies counted some 14 million European refugees, east and west. Postwar conflicts generated millions of additional fugitives, most notably close to 12 million Vertriebene, ethnic Germans driven out of the countries of eastern and central Europe who surged westwards, the great majority ending up in what became the German Federal Republic.

As has been pointed out often before, present-day definitions of refugees arise from the postwar European context, when Western countries sought a formula to designate the many thousands of uprooted East Europeans who refused repatriation to their homes, which had come under Soviet domination. Göran Melander explains further in this volume, how a concern for their plight gave rise to the definition found in the 1951 United Nations Convention relating to the Status of Refugees: a refugee is "any person who . . . owing to well-founded fear of being persecuted for reasons of race, religion, nationality, membership of a particular social group or political opinion, is outside the country of his nationality and is unable or, owing to such fear, is unwilling to avail himself of the protection of that country; or who, not having a nationality and being outside the country of his former habitual residence as a result of such events, is unable or, owing to such fear, is unwilling to return to it."

To rehearse this history, even in a much abbreviated way, is to survey a series of refugee crises that diminish, somewhat, our own claims to live at a time of unprecedented refugee problems. Europeans, at least, have faced such things before. Most of the essays in this volume chart their responses, together with those of other societies, to waves of refugees from Europe and the Middle East. Significantly, they tend to suggest that refugee crises *can* be solved, given a will to do so within the national and international communities.

It may be worthwhile pointing out the obvious fact that our contributors are overwhelmingly *sympathetic* to refugees. I would suggest that this is not only due to the humanitarian ethos of international civil servants, journalists or academics, who have written the bulk of the papers in this volume. I think it also springs as well from an encounter with the concrete realities refugees experience – cast adrift in a world where they are often rejected everywhere, for reasons that have little or nothing to do with what they have done, and everything to do with what they are. Drawing on her own experience, which included a stay in the notorious French camp of Gurs, the late political philosopher Hannah Arendt wrote feelingly about the humiliation and rejection she felt as a refugee: "once we were somebodies about whom people cared, we were loved by friends, even known by landlords as paying our rent regularly." There was no greater contrast, between the secure world of German Jewry which she had known before 1933 and the Jews' experiences under Hitler. Under Nazism these fugitives, like so many refugees, endured the anger and helplessness of those who are victimized by powerful, impersonal forces. "Contemporary history," Arendt wrote, "has created a new kind of human being – the kind that are put in concentration camps by their foes and internment camps by their friends."[3]

Finally, our contributors relate again and again the exaggerated, unfounded fears of refugees and exploitation of their uprootedness – whether Spanish republicans, detested as revolutionary firebrands in France; German refugee scholars in the United Kingdom, put behind barbed wire in 1940 when the government feared they might join the invading Wehrmacht; demoralized and uprooted Ukrainians, sent forcibly to the Soviet Union after 1945; Italian fugitives, cast into deep gorges to their deaths by the thousands to avenge Fascist misdeeds in Yugoslavia; postwar Polish refugees, rejected by many trade unionists fearful of unemployment in Britain; or Palestinian Arabs, maintained in squalor to satisfy others' geopolitical goals. In each of these cases, an examination of the context suggests that there were alternative strategies to cope with the refugees, that perceptions about them were highly coloured by circumstances that had nothing to do with the individuals concerned, and that more could certainly have been done to relieve the extraordinary human suffering their uprooting entailed.

Notes: Introduction

1   *World Refugee Survey, 1986 in Review* (New York, 1987), 36-7.
2   Eugene Kulischer, *Europe on the Move; War and Population Changes, 1917-47* (New York, 1948), 305.
3   Hannah Arendt, *The Jew as Pariah: Jewish Identity and Politics in the Modern Age* (New York, 1978), 56, 60.

1 The concept of the term 'refugee'

GÖRAN MELANDER

Though refugees have always existed, mankind has never been faced with refugee problems of such formidable dimensions as during the present century. A large-scale influx was caused by the Russian revolution, when millions of people were compelled to leave their home country. At present the total number of refugees is estimated at some ten to fifteen million people throughout the world.

It has been affirmed in various contexts that the refugee problem is international in scope and character and that the responsibility for the international protection of refugees rests with the international community.[1] International bodies have been established for the purpose of providing material and legal assistance to refugees.[2] The legal protection has been complemented through treaties concerning the status of refugees.[3]

There have been various attempts to produce a legal definition of what is a refugee. Between the two world wars international instruments on refugees contained *ad hoc* and generalised definitions of the term. The important criterion was that the person came from a certain state or that he or she was lacking the protection of that state. Refugees were identified by reference to a certain nationality. Implicitly it was indicated that political events in the named country had forced the person to escape. A typical example can be found in the 1926 *Arrangement modifying and completing the Arrangements concerning the Issue of Certificates of Identity to Russian and Armenian Refugees dated 5 July 1922 and 31 May 1924*, in which a Russian refugee was defined as follows: 'Any person of Russian origin who does not enjoy or no longer enjoys the protection of the Government of the Union of Socialist Soviet Republics and who has not acquired another nationality'.[4]

In 1936, when the *Provisional Agreement concerning the Status of Refugees coming from Germany* was adopted, the same course was followed: the term refugee covered all persons coming from Germany.[5] However, when the provisional agreement was replaced by a permanent treaty in 1938, a minor but fundamental change was made. A person was excluded from refugee status, if he had left Germany 'for reasons of purely personal convenience'.[6]

The exclusion clause had consequences in several respects. Although still an *ad hoc* definition it was now necessary to look into the underlying reason for a person's flight. For the first time it also became necessary to determine refugee status on an individual basis. And from the *travaux préparatoires* it appears that a substantial change was intended. During the

1938 Diplomatic Conference the new additional paragraph was commented upon in the following way: 'The text . . . implies a criticism – a perfectly well-founded criticism – of the Government of the Reich: it undoubtedly was not fair that a country which did not desire to have certain categories of persons residing in its territory should compel other States to take charge of them'.[7]

The refugee problem was a subject of constant concern for the Allied Powers during the Second World War. At the Bermuda Conference in 1943 it was decided that protection should be given to persons who, 'as a result of events in Europe, have had to leave, or may have to leave, their countries of residence because of the danger to their lives or liberties on account of their race, religious or political beliefs'.[8] Through its general wording it was still an *ad hoc* definition in so far as a geographical limitation was included. In practical terms the purpose was to protect refugees from Germany, Italy and Spain.[9] The exclusion clause in the 1938 Convention had been rephrased and the causes for leaving a country were explicitly enumerated. Refugee status should be determined on an individual basis.

The main task of the United Nations Relief and Rehabilitation Administration (UNRRA), which was established in 1943, was to assist so-called displaced persons, i.e. 'victims of war in any area under the control of any of the United Nations'.[10] At the first session of the Council of UNRRA the mandate of the new organization was described as 'assistance in caring for, and maintaining records of, persons found in any areas under the control of any of the United Nations who by reason of war have been displaced from their homes and, in agreement with the appropriate governments, military authorities or other agencies, in securing their repatriation or return'.[11] There were, however, persons who refused to be repatriated and this problem led to an open conflict between the Soviet Union and the Western Allies, who maintained that there were persons who, for reasons of race, religious or political opinion, had legitimate reasons not to return to their country of origin. This view was contested by the Soviet Union, which argued that all displaced persons were to be repatriated. Finally it was agreed that the Administration should assist those having 'valid reasons' not to return. Initially, in respect of these persons the mandate was limited to six months,[12] but this period was later extended.[13]

In 1946 UNRRA was replaced by the International Refugee Organization (IRO), which became responsible for both displaced persons and refugees.[14] In the IRO definition of the term 'refugee' the important part of the Constitution prescribed that a person could refuse repatriation, provided he expressed valid objections to return to his country of origin. Valid objections included 'persecution, or fear based on grounds of persecution because of race, religion, nationality or political opinions, provided these opinions are not in conflict with the principles of the United Nations, as laid down in the Preamble of the Charter of the United Nations'.[15] By now the phrase 'danger to their lives and liberties' in the Bermuda declaration, had been replaced by the criterion 'persecution', which term for the first time was used in an international instrument in order to describe a refugee.

The IRO definition of the term 'refugee' was also an *ad hoc* definition. The intention was to protect persons from countries under communist domination and the definition was meant to describe the situation in those countries. A strong political element had been inserted in defining the term 'refugee'.

In this context it should be noted that the IRO was established as a UN specialized agency, i.e. an autonomous, intergovernmental organization having its own constitution, members, budget, etc. It is a notable fact that only few states became members of the IRO, although quite a number contributed to the IRO budget. One explanation for this anomaly may be the fact that the definition of the term 'refugee' was aimed at describing asylum seekers from Eastern Europe. One may speculate that the majority of states were not prepared at this stage to take sides *vis a vis* the Soviet Union.

In 1950 the UN General Assembly established a new organization in favour of refugees, the Office of the United Nations High Commissioner for Refugees. The following year, 1951, the Convention relating to the Status of Refugees was adopted.[16] The term 'refugee' is in all essentials described in the same way in the two instruments. A refugee is a person who, owing to well-founded fear of being persecuted for reasons of race, religion, nationality, membership of a particular social group or political opinion, is outside the country of his nationality and is unable or, owing to such fear, is unwilling to avail himself of the protection of that country. There is, however, an important difference between the mandate of the UNHCR and the Refugee Convention, as the latter contains a date-line. The cause of a refugee situation must have taken place prior to 1 January 1951, while the High Commissioner's mandate covers also future groups of refugees.

The definitions were worked out in the period 1949–51, i.e. at a time when the cold war had reached its height and when in fact the Eastern Bloc boycotted the United Nations. The Korean War started during this period. It was mainly in Europe that refugee problems existed and the refugees emanated almost exclusively from East European states. [The Korean war produced two million refugees, Ed.]

Because of the boycott by the East European states of the organs of the United Nations, the Statute of the Office of the UNHCR and the Refugee Convention were drafted by Western states only. It was quite natural to claim persecution in the country of origin. All the refugees emanated from East European states. Countries of asylum, i.e. Western states, were not obliged to take any political considerations into account. The relations between Eastern and Western states at that time could hardly have been worse.

It is also interesting to note that the Office of the UNHCR is established as a subsidiary organ under the UN General Assembly. Accordingly, the statute of the UNHCR is not a treaty which should be ratified by member states. It is annexed to a resolution, adopted by the General Assembly under the ordinary voting rules of the UN.

The 1951 definition of the term 'refugee' functioned well for about ten years. However, when in the 1960s new refugee problems arose, it was impossible to consider the refugees to be within the 1951 Refugee Convention. The date-line was felt to be a serious obstacle in providing international protection to refugees. Accordingly, a new international agreement was adopted, stemming from the ECOSOC resolution of 18 November 1966 and a resolution of 16 December 1966, which entered into force in October 1967 as the *Protocol relating to the Status of Refugees*,[17], an instrument which can be seen as an amendment to the 1951 Refugee Convention by which the date-line has been deleted.

As stated before, the definition of the term 'refugee' in the Statute of the UNHCR and in the 1951 Refugee Convention/1967 Refugee Protocol is generally considered to be a product of the cold war. It is also looked upon as a European definition, applicable first and foremost to asylum seekers coming from socialist countries. Simultaneously it must be underlined that the definition is a product of a continuous development, starting with the 1938 *Convention concerning the Status of Refugees coming from Germany*. Group determination was repealed and refugee status had to be decided on an individual basis. The various definitions since 1938 also contained a criterion which implies a condemnation of the situation in the country of origin.

The final definition of the term refugee was not established by the adoption of the 1967 Refugee Protocol, which created a more or less complete correspondence between the mandate of the UNHCR and treaty law. Already by the late 1950s, groups of refugees were assisted by the UNHCR outside its mandate. By various resolutions adopted by the UN General Assembly, the High Commissioner was authorized to lend his 'good offices' in respect of refugees who do not come within the competence of the United Nations'.[18] Originally the so-called good offices resolutions applied to refugees in Africa. Later refugees in Asia and Latin America were also assisted and entitled to protection by virtue of similar resolutions. It has been increasingly common to name this new type of refugee as (external) *displaced persons*. It should be noted that the new category of displaced persons has little in common with the displaced persons after World War II.

An important element with regard to the new refugees is the large-scale influx, thus making any attempt to decide refugee status on an individual basis virtually impossible. Furthermore the admittance of refugees does not imply any form of condemnation of the country of origin. A third difference is the lack of the persecution criterion. In fact, the great majority of the displaced persons would not be granted refugee status, should their applications be considered under the 1951 Refugee Convention/1967 Refugee Protocol. The former High Commissioner, Mr Felix Schnyder, has stated that the absence of political considerations is all the more conspicuous in that, with respect to 'other' refugees, the General Assembly did not lay down any definition connecting a given group of refugees with some political event. By the good offices procedure, the United Nations had created an apolitical instrument for coordinating international action on behalf of new groups of refugees.[19] The good offices function of the Office of the UNHCR has made it possible for the Office to assist refugees without making an evaluation of the political conditions in the country of origin.

From a legal point of view, only the African states and the Organization of African Unity have drawn the conclusion that it is necessary to adapt the definition of the term 'refugee' to present needs. A definition is contained in the 1969 *OAU Convention Governing the Specific Aspects of the Refugee Problems in Africa*.[20] Its first part (Article I, paragraph 1) outlines the term in a way similar to the 1951 Refugee Convention/1967 Refugee Protocol. Its second part (Article I, paragraph 2) describes a refugee in the following way: 'The term "refugee" shall also apply to every person who, owing to external aggression, occupation, foreign domination or events seriously disturbing public order in either part or the whole of his country of origin or nationality, is compelled to leave his place of habitual residence in order to seek refuge in another place outside his country of origin or nationality.'

The detailed wording of the definition may be open to criticism. On the whole it covers, however, the actual need and it is an attempt to describe in legal terms the refugees/displaced persons, assisted through the good offices of the UNHCR.

It is obvious that the large-scale influxes of new refugees has once again made group determination necessary, as was the case between the two world wars. However, this is not the only similarity between the displaced persons of today and the Russian, Armenian, etc. refugees. The reasons for the fleeing are also similar. For instance, the causes that impelled the waves of Russian refugees to flee after the First World War were not only political. There were economic reasons, including the Russian famine of 1921.

It was found impossible at the time to differentiate between the various categories of refugees from the Soviet Union. This aspect was discussed at a Diplomatic Conference in 1922, and in a resolution it stated: 'In view of the close connection between the question of relief work proposed by the Powers in favour of the starving population in Russia, and the question of Russian refugees abroad, the Conference considers it would be desirable to co-ordinate the two activities.'[21]

This is equally applicable today. And in domestic legislation there are definitions of the term 'refugee', in which the method and principles used in the earliest agreements are used again. For instance, in Tanzania a refugee is described as a person of a certain origin (i.e. Rwandese) who has entered Tanzania after a certain date.[22]

It seems possible to identify two categories of refugees. The first group consists of persons who, owing to well-founded fear of persecution are forced to leave their country of origin. They arrive individually and their asylum request is determined on an individual basis. The second group consists of persons who are forced to leave their country of origin because of political or other events in that country. They arrive in large groups which makes group determination necessary. It is, however, not possible to draw a distinct line between the two categories, because among the latter group there are individuals who have left their country of origin owing to well-founded fear of persecution.

During the past few years the concept of the term refugee has become even more confusing by the introduction of the term *de facto* refugees. Since the 1960s a considerable number of aliens in Western European states have been granted a status similar to that of a Convention refugee. In most cases it is said by the aliens authorities that these aliens do not have a well-founded fear of persecution within the Convention definition, but that they cannot be returned to their country of origin because of political disturbances there. On other occasions, political obstacles preclude identifying a person as a Convention refugee. In addition some countries apply a restrictive interpretation of the term refugee in the Convention, but do not return or expel those denied Convention refugee status. Sometimes potential countries of asylum are confronted with a new situation in which the traditional definition is considered to be inadequate. One difficulty is the lack of detailed information about the country of origin, which is sometimes far away. Also, the number of asylum seekers from one specific country may be small, adding to the difficulty of evaluating the information provided by the applicant.

The development can be illustrated by the legislation in Sweden, which was the first Western European country to legislate on this new category of refugees. In an amendment to the 1954 Aliens Act, introduced in 1975, a special category of asylum seekers was granted a limited right to enter and to remain in the country.[23] According to the law, a person in this group is described as 'an alien . . . who, although not a refugee, is unwilling to return to his home country on account of the political situation there, and is able to plead powerful circumstances to this effect . . . '. In the present Aliens Act of 1980 the new group of persons in need of protection is described in a separate section (section 6). Thus, the Swedish Aliens Act provides for a certain protection in favour of the *de facto* refugees (or B-refugees) as opposed to the Convention or political refugees. Similar legislation has been enacted in Denmark and the Netherlands, while in other European countries an expanded definition is based on administrative practice.

Thus it may be concluded that the widened definition is meant to cover a second group of refugees, as described in Art. 1, para 2, of the 1969 OAU Convention or by the General Assembly 'good offices' resolutions. It is true that in most cases this category of asylum seekers are granted a residence permit. However, the expanded definition has had consequences in other respects. Once again, the Swedish experience is illustrative. When the new category of refugees was added to the Swedish Aliens Act in 1976, a more restrictive practice regarding the interpretation of a Convention refugee seemed to follow. The restrictive practice could be directly connected to the insertion of the new refugee category into the law.[24] Such a development is certainly unacceptable. When the new category of refugees was introduced in the Aliens Act, the intention was only to legalize the then already existing practice, i.e. to protect refugees from war and war-like situations. The reasons for the subsequently restrictive practice is difficult to understand. An explanation – but not an excuse – is that a Convention refugee has a right to broader protection than a *de facto* refugee, with the result that authorities prefer not to grant Convention refugee status unless absolutely necessary. To the aliens authorities the most important consideration is to permit the asylum seeker to remain in Sweden. However, to the asylum seeker the distinction between being recognized as a Convention refugee or a *de facto* refugee may be important.

It has been argued that any mention of an additional definition of the term 'refugee' in national aliens legislation is counter-productive. Consequently, the whole problem could be solved by applying a more liberal interpretation of the Convention definition. The UN High Commissioner's Executive Committee expressed a similar view in 1974 and 1975, when the concept of *de facto* refugees was discussed at various meetings. The debate was summarized by a staff member of the Office of the UNHCR as follows: 'With regard to *de facto* refugees, delegations hoped, as did the High Commissioner, that the 1951 Convention and the 1967 Protocol would be interpreted liberally. A number of delegations had expressed that the existing international legal instruments in favour of refugees, supplemented if possible by a convention on territorial asylum, constituted an adequate legal framework for the protection of refugees, provided that those instruments were effectively translated into national laws and regulations and that, in their day-to-day activities, the administrative authorities concerned with refugee problems faithfully observed the spirit and the letter of the law.'[25]

Should that statement be correct, the problem of *de facto* refugees, as in Sweden, could be solved by the deletion of the present Section 6 of the Aliens Act. Such an amendment would not, as is often believed, lead to a decrease of the number of refugees being granted residence permits. The consequence would most likely be a more liberal interpretation of the Convention definition. The number of decisions to return or deport asylum seekers would not increase.

On the other hand, a liberal interpretation of the 1951 Refugee Convention would not completely solve the actual problem. There are still groups of refugees from war or war-like situations (displaced persons) who do not fall under the 1951 Refugee Convention. They are covered by Article I, para 2, of the 1969 OAU Refugee Convention, which has meant an enlargement of the term 'refugee'. They are also covered by the above-mentioned 'good offices resolutions' which sometimes have the title 'Assistance to refugees outside the mandate of the United Nations High Commissioner for Refugees'. It is important that this category of refugees are protected by clear provisions in domestic legislation. It is, of course, also desirable – but currently difficult to achieve – that they are protected by a universal treaty.

Notes: Chapter 1

1   See, *inter alia*, United Nations General Assembly Resolution 319 (IV), 3 December 1949; 1951 Convention relating to the Status of Refugees, Preamble; 189 United Nations Treaty Services 150, signed in Geneva 28 July 1951.

2 The first international body dealing with protection of and assistance to refugees was the High Commission for Refugees, which operated between 1921 and 1930. It was followed by the Nansen International Office (1930–38), the High Commissioner's Office for Refugees coming from Germany (1933–38), the High Commissioner's Office for all Refugees (1938–46), the Inter-Governmental Committee of Refugees (1938–47), the United Nations Relief and Rehabilitation Administration (1943–48), the International Refugee Organization (1946–51), and finally the United Nations High Commissioner for Refugees, whose activities started in 1951.

3 The previous international agreements were: Arrangement of 1922 with Regard to the Issue of Certificates of Identity to Russian Refugees (3 *League of Nations Treaty Series* 237); Plan for the Issue of a Certificate of Identity to Armenian Refugees (League of Nations, Document C.L. 72 (a), 1924); Arrangement of 1926 relating to the Issue of Identity Certificates to Russian and Armenian refugees (89 *League of Nations Treaty Series* 47); Convention of 1933 Relating to the Status of Refugees (159 *League of Nations Treaty Series* 199); Provisional Arrangement of 1936 concerning the Status of Refugees coming from Germany (171 *League of Nations Treaty Series* 75); Convention of 1938 concerning the Status of Refugees coming from Germany (192 *League of Nations Treaty Series* 59); London Agreement of 1946 relating to the Issue of a Travel Document to Refugees who are the Concern of the Inter-Governmental Committee on Refugees (11 *United Nations Treaty Series* 73).

4 89 *League of Nations Treaty Series* 47.
5 171 *League of Nations Treaty Series* 75.
6 192 *League of Nations Treaty Series* 59.
7 League of Nations Document Conf.C.S.R.A./P.V.4., p.10.
8 Cf . . . United Nations, *Study of Statelessness*, p. 38.
9 J Vernant, *The Refugee in the Post-War World* (1953), p. 28.
10 Agreement for the UNRRA, Art. 1, para 2 (a).
11 UNRRA Council Resolution No. 1. Part II, para 2.
12 UNRRA Council Resolution No. 71.
13 UNRRA Council Resolution No. 92.
14 18 *United Nations Treaty Series* 3.
15 UN General Assembly Resolution 428 (V) of 14 December 1950.
16 189 *United Nations Treaty Series* 137.
17 606 *United Nations Treaty Series* 267.
18 UN General Assembly Resolution 1388 (XIV) of 20 November 1959.
19 Report of the Fifth session of the Executive Committee of the High Commissioner's Programme, in UN General Assembly, Sixteenth session, Supplement No. 11, Report of the United Nations High Commissioner for Refugees, p. 35.
20 Organization of African Unity, Doc. CM/267/Rev.1.
21 Conference on the Question of Russian Refugees, 22 to 24 August 1921, Resolution XI.
22 See, for instance, The Refugees (Declaration) Order, 1966.
23 Government Bill 1975/76:18.
24 Weibo, 'De fato flyktigar Sverige', in Melander (ed.), *Flykting i Norden*, p. 49.
25 UN Doc. A/AC.96/514.

2 A historical survey of twentieth century expulsions

ALFRED-MAURICE DE ZAYAS

There are too many homeless in our world. It is one of the purposes of this historical survey to recall their experience in as concrete and tangible a manner as possible. Indeed, it is not possible to perceive existentially a statistic of 5 million, 10 million, 15 million refugees and/or expellees, except by visualizing the half-starved mother and child, the broken old man with vacant eyes and bundles holding his last belongings – and not just once, but millions of times. It is this picture of human misery, the sum total of individual tragedies, that must be balanced by politicians and policy-makers who contemplate the collective expulsion of aliens or even nationals. Too many politicians in the past have mistakenly considered expulsions as a permanent solution of social or economic problems. They have preferred the apparent expediency of population transfers to the challenge of living together and striving toward genuine brotherhood. Various justifications have been advanced – arguments of State sovereignty, domestic jurisdiction, social imperatives, economic sabotage – but one aspect has been neglected: the moral aspect. Are mass expulsions ethical? An affirmative answer to this question is hardly possible. And that is why politicians prefer not to pose the question.

It was Albert Schweitzer who sought to remind politicians of that inescapable ethical component when he focused on the fundamental right of peoples to live on their native soil. It was not the 'how' of population transfers that concerned him as much as the 'why'.

At the Nuremberg trials Hitler's mass deportations were rightly condemned as war crimes and crimes against humanity. But after the Second World War even greater deportations were in progress. It is good to recall that memorable speech given by Schweitzer in Oslo on 4 November 1954 upon receiving the Nobel Peace Prize. It was a strong appeal to the conscience of mankind to repudiate the crime of mass expulsions:

'The most grievous violation of the right based on historical evolution and of any human right in general is to deprive populations of their right to occupy the country where they live by compelling them to settle elsewhere. The fact that the victorious powers decided at the end of World War II to impose this fate on hundreds of thousands of human beings and, what is more, in a most cruel manner, shows how little they were aware of the challenge facing them, namely, to re-establish prosperity and, as far as possible, the rule of law.'[1]

And, indeed, if the Allies fought against the Nazi enemy because of his inhuman methods, were they entitled to adopt some of those same methods in retribution? Who was it then who succeeded in imposing his methods on the other? Whose outlook triumphed? It is worth while rethinking the political scenario that led to such expulsions.

Historical Survey

Throughout history the causes of mass expulsions have been varied. In the age of awakening nationalism, expulsions – primarily of ethnic minorities – reflected the affirmation of cultural identity and frequently followed territorial expansion. In the age of religious turmoil from the 15th to 18th centuries, expulsions were motivated by a striving for religious homogeneity. Thus it was that the Kingdom of Spain in 1492 expelled tens of thousands of Jews who refused to be baptized. Spanish Moslems who similarly would not convert to Christianity were expelled in 1502, but many of these 'Moriscos' underwent merely a pro-forma conversion while continuing to speak Arabic and to practise their religion in private. As many as 150,000 were ultimately expelled to North Africa in 1609/10, to the great detriment of Spain's economy, since the Moors and the Jews were skilled farmers, artisans and merchants. Considerable economic damage to the Austrian Empire also resulted from Maria Theresa's decision in 1744 to expel some 20,000 Jews from Bohemia.

Religious intolerance in France led to the forced migration of many Protestants, especially after the Saint Bartholomew's Day massacres of 1572, when several thousand Huguenots were slaughtered in Paris and in the Provinces. The religious pacification of France was marked by the Edict of Nantes, proclaimed in 1598 by the new French King Henry IV. But when Louis XIV revoked the Edict in 1685, some 400,000 Protestants fled from France, many of them emigrating to America, while others sought refuge in Prussia at the invitation of the Protestant Frederick William, Elector of Brandenburg and Duke of East Prussia. Again, in 1731 it was Prussia that welcomed more than 20,000 Salzburg Protestants expelled by the Catholic Archbishop Leopold von Firmian, who exercised the expulsion right founded on the old rule *cujus regio, ejus religio* established at the Peace of Augsburg (1555) and reaffirmed at the Peace of Westphalia (1648).

Meanwhile in the New World the British Governor of Nova Scotia, Charles Lawrence, decided in 1755 to remove the 15,000 French-Acadian farmers from their hundred-year home on Nova Scotia, because he considered them to be less-than-loyal subjects of the King of England. Uprooted and forced into different ships, husbands were separated from wives, mothers from children. The ships unloaded their sad human cargo throughout the British North American colonies and many spouses never saw each other again.[2]

But in the New World, it was primarily the autochthonous population that had to suffer. In the United States, for instance, the policy of 'manifest destiny' resulted in the gradual displacement of the American Indian and in the deportation of the remaining tribes to special government reservations. One of the worst chapters of America's Western expansion was the compulsory transfer of the Cherokee Nation from Georgia to Oklahoma from 1835–1838. Over a quarter of the expelled Cherokees did not survive the ordeal. Other tribes similarly suffered decimation and forced resettlement.

These uprootings of populations occurred in a period of history when the rights of man were hardly recognized, either in international or in national law. The problem to be examined in this essay, however, is that such uprootings still occur in our times. It would seem that only when the world community perceives that population expulsions cannot be an acceptable solution of demographic problems, only when politicians discard this inhuman measure from their possible options, only when the right to one's homeland is recognized and respected as a fundamental human right, will this tragedy cease to repeat itself.

Let us turn to the earliest involuntary migrations of our century and briefly examine each of them, in chronological order, up to the present.

The Exchange of Minorities in Bulgaria, Greece and Turkey

The awakening nationalism of Bulgarian, Greek and Serbian populations in Turkish-dominated Thrace and Macedonia at the turn of the century led to their joining forces against the Ottoman desire for the 'Turkification of the Empire'. In the first Balkan War in 1912 Turkey lost practically all its European Territories except Constantinople. The conflict over the division of the conquered territory brought on the Second Balkan War of 1913, this time between Greece and Bulgaria. The struggle continued during the First World War, with Serbia and Greece on the Allied side, Bulgaria and Turkey on the side of the Central Powers.

This troubled situation in the Balkans was accompanied by migratory movements of the populations affected by war operations or by territorial changes. For instance, in 1913 some 15,000 Bulgarians from Macedonia followed the Bulgarian army in its retreat: 10,000 Greeks left the parts of Macedonia awarded to Serbia and Bulgaria by the Treaty of Bucharest; 70,000 Greeks were forced to emigrate from Western Thrace; 46,786 Bulgarians left Eastern Thrace and emigrated to Bulgarian Western Thrace under the Treaty of Constantinople; 48,570 Moslems emigrated to Turkey from Western Thrace under the same Treaty.[3] In 1914 some 115,000 Greeks were expelled from Turkish Eastern Thrace and sought refuge in Greece; 85,000 Greeks from the same region were deported by Turkey to the interior of Asia Minor; 150,000 Greeks were driven from the coastal regions of Western Anatolia and migrated to the Greek peninsula; meanwhile 115,000 Moslems left Greece with a view of taking the place of the Greeks expelled from Turkey and a further 135,000 Moslems migrated from the other Balkan countries to Turkey. During the world war the Turkish government continued the deportation of Greeks to the interior of Anatolia, many of whom perished from the vicissitudes and privations of the transfer. After the war the migrations began again, being now mostly a return to their homes of populations deported or expelled.

At the Paris Peace Conference politicians thought that one of the ways of achieving a more durable peace in areas where the population was ethnically intermingled would be to disentangle them by reciprocal migration. Article 56, paragraph 2 of the Treaty of Peace between Allied and Associated Powers and Bulgaria, signed at Neuilly-sur-Seine on 27 November 1919, provided that 'Bulgaria undertakes to recognize such provisions as the Principal Allied and Associated Powers may consider opportune with respect to the reciprocal and voluntary emigration of persons belonging to racial minorities'. A special Convention concerning Reciprocal Emigration was signed on the same day by the Greek and Bulgarian plenipotentiaries. A Mixed Commission was established according to article 8 of the Convention and it functioned largely independently with the occasional assistance of the Council of the League of Nations.

It appears from the statistics of the Mixed Commission that practically all the Greeks in Bulgaria, some 46,000, declared their intention to emigrate and left Bulgarian territory in the years 1923 to 1928. And of the 139,000 Bulgarians living in Greek Macedonia and Thrace in 1920, some 92,000 availed themselves of the possibility of emigrating.[4] During these years the Mixed Commission established property rights over immovable property left by emigrants and accepted applications for liquidation through 1928. The Commission also determined the disposition of community properties and had recourse to the Permanent Court of International Justice on the question of communities.[5] In the light of the atrocities endured by the Greek and Bulgarian populations during the Balkan wars and during the First World War, the régime established by the Convention on Reciprocal Emigration was relatively humane and the exchanges took place largely on a voluntary basis. For those Greeks that chose not to emigrate, the Treaty of Neuilly contained provisions for the protection of minorities. The Bulgarians still remaining in Greece benefited in turn from the provisions of the Treaty concerning the Protection of Minorities signed at Sèvres on 10 August 1920.

Unfortunately the Greek-Turkish exchange did not run as smoothly. As a sequel of the world war, Greece had occupied Smyrna and Western Asia Minor at the behest of the Allies. In the autumn of 1922, however, the Greek army was defeated by the Turks and nearly one million Greeks from Western Asia Minor fled to Greece. Peace negotiations at the Conference of Lausanne were difficult and the victorious Turks insisted on compulsory instead of voluntary population exchanges. Dr. Fridtjof Nansen, who had been entrusted with the question of relief for the refugees from the Greco-Turkish war, was formally invited by the Conference to endeavour to reach an agreement, but he opposed both the compulsory nature of the exchanges and the inclusion of the Greeks of Constantinople. According to the minutes of the meeting held on 14 December 1922 under the presidency of the British Foreign Minister, Lord Curzon, the Turkish representative charged 'that the minorities, by continual and persistent misuse of the privileges granted to them and by making themselves the instrument of foreigners, had brought about the deplorable results which had ensued'.[6] The Greek Delegation observed that 'both Greek and the Turkish populations involved in the compulsory exchange are protesting against this procedure. Stirred by the instinctive feeling of attachment to the land and homes where their ancestors have lived for centuries, the people who have already left refuse to believe that they may be severed from their native soil for all time, while those who may be compelled to leave display their reluctance and dissatisfaction by all the means at their disposal.'[7] Lord Curzon, aware of the responsibility devolving on politicians engaged in peace negotiations 'deeply regretted that the solution now being worked out should be the compulsory exchange of populations – a thoroughly bad and vicious solution, for which the world would pay a heavy penalty for a hundred years to come'.[8] In spite of the serious ethical reservations expressed by Lord Curzon and Dr Nansen, the Convention of Lausanne and its Protocol were signed on 30 January 1923. Article 1 laid down the principle of compulsory exchange by providing as follows: 'As from 1st May, 1923, there shall take place a compulsory exchange of Turkish nationals of the Greek Orthodox religion established in Turkish territory, and of Greek nationals of the Moslem religion established in Greek territory'. A Mixed Commission to supervise and facilitate the implementation of the Convention was constituted, as provided in article 11, with its seat in Athens, later moving to Constantinople. Great difficulties ensued, since no preparatory work of any kind had been done either by the delegations of the countries or by the respective governments. Since religion was used as criterion for exchange, there were numerous cases of change of religion in order to avoid being transferred. Turkish authorities also undertook forcible expulsions of Greeks without consulting the Commission and in other cases interned Greeks in concentration camps pending embarkation. As to the Greek inhabitants of Constantinople an advisory opinion was sought from the Permanent Court of International Justice, which held that the Mixed Commission was 'alone competent to investigate in each individual case, whether a Greek inhabitant of Constantinople was "established" in conformity with Article 2 of the Convention and could be exempted from the compulsory exchange'.[9]

The statistical data collected by the Mixed Commission indicate that in the years 1923–1926 a total of 189,916 Greeks and 355,635 Moslems[10] were transferred under the auspices of the Commission. These figures, however, do not reflect the hundreds of thousands of persons (mainly Greeks) who fled or were expelled before the setting up of the Mixed Commission or who left Greece or Turkey on their own initiative and by other means of transportation than those placed at the disposal of the Mixed Commission by the two governments.

Like the Greek-Bulgarian agreement, the Mixed Commission here was responsible for assessment and liquidation of movable and immovable property of emigrants. But the settlement of property matters eventually proved unworkable so that the Convention was abandoned and all accounts were liquidated in a wholesale fashion.

The removal of the Greeks from Asia Minor did not take the orderly character which marked the departure of the Moslems from Greece. There were many irregularities, as those reported by the Sub-Commissions of Mersina and Samsun to the Mixed Commission, indicating that Turkish authorities either issued orders for the immediate and precipitate departure of the Greeks or prevented the departure of other Greeks who were employed on public works. The order for immediate departure usually resulted in the Greeks having to leave behind their movable property; moreover, they were not admitted to the courts to collect their debts. Thus the Greeks who left Asia Minor after the constitution of the Mixed Commission carried with them little more than the destitute refugees who swarmed into Greece in the last months of 1922.

It is interesting to note that at the time only a handful of politicians realized the dangerous precedent that was being set. This compulsory population exchange was not seen by the international community as the brutal uprooting of hundreds of thousands of persons from their homelands; instead it was hailed by many as a legal measure intended to bring peace on the basis of an international treaty and under the auspices of the League of Nations. Thus, State interests were given priority over human rights and mass expulsions gained international respectability as a legitimate solution of demographic problems; in fact, the principle of compulsory population transfers was seen by many as a panacea, a final solution to the troublesome minority problem. More and more politicians in countries with ethnic or religious minorities invoked the precedent of the Convention of Lausanne as a way out of continued internal unrest. This was especially the case in countries which at the Paris Peace Conference of 1919 had been required by treaty to agree to the protection of the rights of their minorities, which was entrusted to the League of Nations as guarantor.[11] These countries resented the restriction of their sovereignty in this respect and considered the petition system of the League of Nations a particularly nasty form of interference in their internal affairs. Thus, a too optimistic appraisal of the results of the Greek-Turkish population exchange under the Convention of Lausanne led both the politicians and world public opinion to exhibit a peculiar euphoria over the conceptual simplicity of the solution. Demographers were soon at work placing arrows indicating the possible destination of prospective expellees.

Hitlerite transfers

Hitler himself became one of the leading advocates and practitioners of the principle of population transfers. Having conquered Poland and re-annexed the pre-Versailles German provinces of Posen and West Prussia into the Reich, he needed Germans to settle the new *Lebensraum*. On 6 October 1939, Hitler announced that there would be 'a new order of ethnographical conditions, that is to say, a resettlement of nationalities in such a manner that the process ultimately results in the obtaining of better dividing lines'.[12] This meant drawing upon the several million *Volksdeutsche* (ethnic Germans) living in the various countries of Eastern and Southeastern Europe. On 7 October 1939, he signed a decree transferring to the Reich all Germans who were 'threatened with de-Germanization'. On 15 October 1939 the Reich concluded an agreement with Estonia involving the transfer of 12,900 'splinters of the German nationality', followed on 21 October 1939 by an agreement with Italy involving 185,365 Southern Tyrolians, on 30 October 1939 an agreement with Latvia involving 48,600 Baltic Germans, on 3 November 1939 an agreement with the Soviet Union involving 128,007 Germans from Volhynia and East Galicia, and others.

These treaties were so-called 'option' treaties, giving the *Volksdeutsche* an opportunity to say 'no' to Hitler's *Heim ins Reich* policy. Over 70,000 Baltic Germans decided that they would rather stay in the Baltic States, where their ancestors had settled in the late Middle Ages. But after the Soviet Union invaded and annexed Lithuania, Latvia and Estonia in 1940, the majority of these *Volksdeutsche* preferred to be transferred to Germany. A new option treaty had to be negotiated, this time between the Reich and the Soviet Union, and was signed on 10 January 1941, five months before Hitler's attack upon the Soviet Union. By the summer of 1941 fewer than five thousand Baltic Germans remained.

These population transfers were 'legal' in the sense that, as in the case of the Convention of Lausanne, sovereign States had decided what to do with their subjects. Admittedly, Hitler's treaties had an 'option clause', but the record shows that manifold pressures were brought upon the persons concerned so as to persuade them to exercise their option in a certain way.[13]

This right of option, however, was only offered to ethnic Germans. Other Nazi population transfers were unilateral expulsions or forced resettlements without treaty or right of option. Hitler thus expelled over one million Poles from the areas of the Warthegau (Western Poland), which were destined for the resettlement of the *Heim ins Reich* Germans from the Baltic and Eastern Europe. And after Hitler's invasion of France and occupation of Alsace-Lorraine, he proceeded to evict 100,000 French Alsatians into Vichy France.

These latter expulsions were not only inhuman but also illegal because they were unilateral acts in no way covered by a Convention. They were arbitrary actions by a belligerent occupant in violation of Articles 42–56 of the Hague Regulations, annexed to the 1907 Hague Convention IV on the Laws and Customs of War on Land. As early as 24 September 1941 at the Inter-Allied meeting in St. James's Palace in London the issue of Nazi expulsions was discussed and the Acting Minister for Foreign Affairs of the Polish Government in Exile said:

'The Polish Government is confident that none of the illegal acts perpetrated by Germany on the territory of Poland shall be recognized by the victorious democracies . . . In particular, the Polish population of the Western provinces, so ruthlessly transplanted, must be given the possibility of an immediate reintegration in the land of their ancestors and the German settlers, installed in Polish homesteads, sent back to the Reich.'[14]

The Allied Declaration on German War Crimes, adopted by the representatives of nine occupied countries in London on 13 January 1942, read in part: 'Whereas Germany, since the beginning of the present conflict . . . has instituted in the occupied countries a regime of terror characterized in particular by . . . mass expulsions . . . The undersigned Representatives... place among their principal war aims the punishment, through the channel of organized justice, of those guilty and responsible for those crimes.'[15]

Article 6 (b) of the Charter of the International Military Tribunal at Nuremberg defined war crimes to include 'murder, ill treatment or *deportation* to slave labour or *for any other purpose* of civilian population of or in occupied territory ...' (author's emphasis) Article 6 (c) defines 'crimes against humanity' to include 'murder, extermination, enslavement, *deportation* and other inhumane acts committed against any civilian population *before* or during the war'. (emphasis added).

Count 3, section J of the Nuremberg indictment charged:

'In certain occupied territories purportedly annexed to Germany the defendants methodically and pursuant to plan endeavoured to assimilate these territories politically, culturally, socially and economically into the German Reich. They endeavoured to obliterate the former national character of these territories. In pursuance of these plans, the defendants *forcibly deported* inhabitants who were predominantly non-German and replaced them by thousands of German colonists.' (emphasis added).

On 17 January 1946 François de Methon, Chief Prosecutor for the French Republic, asserted against the accused: 'Persons who appeared recalcitrant to Nazification . . . became victims of large-scale expulsions, driven from their homes in a few short hours with their most scanty baggage, and despoiled of their property . . . this inhumane evacuation of entire populations ... will remain one of the horrors of our century.'[16] On 26 February 1946, L.N. Smirnow, Assistant Prosecutor for the Soviet Union, stated with respect to the deportations in Poland: 'Locality after locality, village after village, hamlets and cities in the incorporated territories were cleared of the Polish inhabitants. This began in October 1939, when the locality of Orlov was cleared of all the Poles who lived and worked there. Then came the Polish port of Gdynia. In February 1940 about 40,000 persons were expelled from the city of Posen ...'[17]

The attempts on the part of the Defence to appeal to *ultima ratio regum* failed and the Tribunal found the accused guilty of war crimes and crimes against humanity on account of mass deportations. By resolution 95 (1) of 11 December 1946 the United Nations General Assembly 'reaffirmed' the 'principles of international law recognized by the Charter of the Nuremberg Tribunal and the judgement of the Tribunal'.

Post World War II Expulsions in Europe

The Germans from the Eastern German Provinces and Czechoslovakia

Through the Nuremberg principles the Allies seem to have committed themselves to a humane policy of recognizing a universal right to the native soil, the right of the Poles to live in Posen and Gdynia, the right of Frenchmen to live in Alsace – in other words, their right not to be expelled from the land of their ancestors. The Nuremberg principles represented a reaffirmation of natural law and ethics, more particularly of the fundamental human right to life and the right to liberty, in the name of which the war against Nazism had been fought.

The Anglo-American peace programme as set forth in the Atlantic Charter of 14 August 1941 recognized, like President Wilson's Fourteen Points during World War I, the right to self-determination. Looked at more closely, this right reveals a compelling logical nexus to the right to the native soil mentioned above. Indeed, before a people can exercise the right to self-determination in freely choosing a form of government, they must first have the right to live on their own soil. In this sense too we should understand the commitment undertaken by Prime Minister Churchill and President Roosevelt in point 2 of the Atlantic Charter to oppose 'territorial changes that do not accord with the freely expressed wishes of the peoples concerned', which expresses the same concept.

Four more years of war and the unparalleled Nazi crimes in Eastern Europe led the Allies to retreat from their own moral commitments and to discard the Atlantic Charter with respect to the Germans. Just as the Nazis had disregarded the right to self-determination of the Czechoslovaks, the Poles, the Yugoslavs, the Russians – to name a few – so too would the victorious Allies ignore the right of the German people to self-determination. All in all fourteen million Germans would lose their homes in East Prussia, Pomerania, East Brandenburg, Silesia, Sudentenland and in countries throughout Eastern Europe. Over two million Germans would perish in the course of their displacement to the West.

In view of the magnitude of the expulsion, it appears worth while briefly to outline the reasons that led politicians ostensibly committed to human rights to consent to the transfer. First, they remembered the post-First World War I problems associated with the presence of German minorities in Eastern European countries, the frequent disregard of the minority protection treaties by the host States, the failure of the Council of the League of Nations to protect the rights of the German minorities effectively, and finally the political radicalization of members of these minorities and their exploitation by Hitler as a 'fifth column'. Secondly, they were committed to giving Poland a fair deal at the end of the war, but Stalin had insisted at the Teheran Conference (1943) on keeping the 70,000 square miles of pre-war Poland that he had annexed pursuant to the Ribbentrop-Molotov Pact; thus the issue of territorial compensation for Poland arose, and obviously Poland could only be compensated in the West at the expense of Germany, and since the Eastern German Provinces were relatively densely populated, the population would have to be transferred. Thirdly, while they were prepared to accept the principle of population transfers, they intended to limit the numbers of persons affected and envisaged a transfer of three to four million persons; furthermore a 'Population Transfers Commission' was to supervise the transfers and make arrangements for indemnification for movable and non-movable property left behind. Fourthly – and this general feeling played an increasingly important role as the war wore on – they saw the German population as being collectively guilty and meriting collective punishment. As Clement Attlee said in the House of Commons: 'They have broken down the old barriers, and therefore I say that they cannot appeal to the old Europe. If they have to yield, to make restitution, they are not entitled to appeal on the basis of the moral laws that they have disregarded or the pity and mercy that they have never extended to any others.'[18]

The problem lies in the generalization. Who were 'they'? The expulsion would affect guilty and innocent with equal severity. Nothing would protect the Social Democrats or the moderates of Brüning's Zentrum Party from Nemesis's fury. Nemesis was free to smite the East Prussians, the Pomeranians, the Silesians, the Sudentenlanders. 'They' had no rights.

Ostensibly, the legal foundation of the expulsions was article XIII of the Potsdam Protocol, which provides in part:

'The three Governments, having considered the question in all its aspects, recognize that the transfer to Germany of German populations, or elements thereof, remaining in Poland, Czechoslovakia and Hungary, will have to be undertaken. They agree that any transfers that take place should be effected in an orderly and humane manner.'[19]

But the expulsions had been going on for several months and they were anything but 'orderly and humane'. As one of the drafters of article XIII, Sir Geoffrey Harrison, explained in a personal interview with the author, the purpose of this article was not to encourage or to legalize the expulsions, but rather to provide a basis for approaching the expelling States and requesting them to co-ordinate transfers with the Occupying Powers in Germany. The expulsions, which had been preceded by a mass flight of four to five million Germans, were far too advanced and there was no time to plan a gradual exodus. The *fait accompli* was there and the crisis called for emergency measures. Thus, the first concern of the Western Allies was to call a moratorium on the expulsions. Article XIII goes on:

'Since the influx of a large number of Germans into Germany would increase the burden already resting on the occupying authorities, they consider that the Allied Control Council in Germany should in the first instance examine the problem with special regard to the question of the equitable distribution of these Germans among the several zones of occupation. They are accordingly instructing their respective representatives on the Control Council to report to their Governments as soon as possible the extent to which such persons have already entered Germany from Poland, Czechoslovakia and Hungary, and to submit an estimate of the time and rate at which further transfers could be carried out, having regard to the present situation in Germany. The Czechoslovak Government, the Polish Provisional Government and the Control Council in Hungary are at the same time being informed of the above, and are being requested meanwhile to suspend further expulsions pending the examination by the Governments concerned of the report from their representatives on the Control Council.'[20]

But even this appeal was not sufficient to stop the on-going catastrophe. Expulsions from Czechoslovakia slowed down, whereas the massive influx of expellees from the Eastern German provinces and Poland continued unabated. All the memoranda and briefing book papers prepared in the British Foreign Office and in the United States Department of State, the plan to establish a Population Transfers Commission, the idea of providing for compensation – all were rendered moot. In retrospect they appear thoroughly utopian.

Churchill was proven wrong by events. On 15 December 1944 he had said before the House of Commons: 'Expulsion is the method which, so far as we have been able to see, will be the most satisfactory and lasting. There will be no mixture of populations to cause endless trouble . . . A clean sweep will be made. I am not alarmed by these large transferences, which are more possible in modern conditions than they ever were before.'[21] By the late summer of 1945 hundreds of thousands of German expellees had perished in the maelstrom of the flight and expulsion. On 16 August 1945 Churchill told the House of Commons: 'I am particularly concerned . . . with the reports reaching us of the conditions under which the expulsion and exodus of Germans from the new Poland are being carried out . . . Sparse and guarded accounts of what has happened and is happening have filtered through, but it is not impossible that tragedy on a prodigious scale is unfolding itself behind the iron curtain which at the moment divides Europe in twain.'[22]

Appalled at what he was seeing every day in Berlin, the American Political Adviser Robert Murphy cabled the State Department on 12 October 1945: 'Here is retribution on a large scale, but practised not on the *Parteibonzen*, but on women and children, the poor, the infirm . . . Knowledge that they are the victims of a harsh political decision carried out with the utmost ruthlessness and disregard for humanity does not cushion the effect. The mind reverts to other mass deportations which horrified the world and brought upon the Nazis the odium which they so deserved. Those mass deportations engineered by the Nazis provided part of the moral basis on which we waged war and which gave strength to our cause. Now the situation is reversed. We find ourselves in the invidious position of being partners in this German enterprise and as partners inevitably sharing the responsibility.'[23]

As one who had participated at the Potsdam Conference and bore part of the responsibility for the decisions taken there, the American Secretary of State James J. Byrnes cabled on 19 October 1945 to the American Ambassador at Prague:

'We should also point out that the Potsdam Agreement only recognized that the transfer of German populations or elements thereof would have to be undertaken. So far as we were concerned we wished to slow down indiscriminate and disorderly expulsions and avoid unnecessary hardships on the transferees and unnecessary burdens on the zones to which transfers were to be made. We recognized that certain transfers were unavoidable, but we did not intend at Potsdam to encourage or commit ourselves to transfers in cases where other means of adjustment were practicable.'[24]

But these considerations were too late. The problem lay in the acceptance of the principle of population transfers at the conferences of Tehran and Yalta. Once the principle was accepted, its application could always be further extended. Originally only the German minorities or *Volksdeutsche* and the *Lebensraum* colonizers were to be displaced. Eventually the expulsion affected millions of *Reichsdeutsche* whose ancestors had lived in East Prussia, Pomerania, East Brandenburg and Silesia for seven hundred years. And as to the 'orderly and humane' language of article XIII, it should have been obvious to every statesman at Potsdam that involuntary transfers carried out by a vengeful soviet-backed Red Army or local population were not likely to be 'humane' in any sense of the word.

In reviewing the catastrophe of the expulsion of the Germans, the International Committee of the Red Cross observed:

'Had it been borne in mind that the repatriation of some 1,500,000 Greeks from Asia Minor, after the first World War, had taken several years and required large-scale relief schemes, it would have been easy to foresee that the hurried transplanting of fourteen million human beings would raise a large number of problems from the humanitarian standpoint, especially in a Europe strewn with ruins and where starvation was rife.'[25]

But the world had seen too much suffering and death. The plight of the German expellees therefore fell on blunted sensibilities and only a few public figures in the United States and Great Britain raised their voices in protest. The incompatibility of these expulsions with the Atlantic Charter and the Nuremberg principles is too obvious to require comment here. But, more fundamentally, these expulsions represent a breakdown or at the very least a malfunctioning of the moral mechanisms of democratic societies. Not without reason the prominent British socialist Victor

Gollancz called his book on the German expulsions 'Our Threatened Values'. He observed:

'If the conscience of men ever again becomes sensitive, these expulsions will be remembered to the undying shame of all who committed or connived at them . . . the Germans were expelled, not just with an absence of over-nice consideration, but with the very maximum of brutality.'[26]

Other Population Transfers in Europe

Among the population-transfer agreements that were concluded at the end of the Second World War were the following: the treaty between the Governments of Czechoslovakia and Hungary of 27 February 1946, which provided for a compulsory transfer of 200,000 Magyars out of Czechoslovakia into Hungary against 200,000 Slovaks out of Hungary into Czechoslovakia; the treaty of September 1946 between Hungary and Yugoslavia, providing for the exchange of 40,000 Magyars against 40,000 Serbs and Croats; the transfer agreements between Poland and the Soviet Union of 6 July 1945 and between Czechoslovakia and the Soviet Union of 10 July 1946.

The fate of the Polish population residing east of the Ribbentrop-Molotov line was particularly tragic. It has already been mentioned that at the Teheran Conference Stalin declared that he would keep that half of Poland which he had invaded in September 1939 and where some 4 million Poles resided. Admittedly, these areas had been seized by Poland during the Russo-Polish war of 1920/21, and in the Treaty of Riga of 18 March 1921 Soviet Russia had yielded to Poland territories that were mainly Ukrainian and Byelorussian in population. Even the British Foreign Minister Lord Curzon had proposed in 1920 a demarcation line running only slightly to the East of the Ribbentrop-Molotov line. Precisely because of the precedent of the so-called Curzon Line, it was difficult for Churchill and Roosevelt to demand from a victorious Stalin that he restore to Poland all occupied Polish territory and recognize the pre-war frontiers. Indeed, they bargained hard to try to reach a compromise, but Stalin did not lower his demands, which he enforced by the persuasive presence of the Red Army. Another issue was, of course, whether the Polish population should be allowed to stay in their homes and given Ukrainian or Byelorussian citizenship, or would they be forced to emigrate? As it happened, 2.1. million Poles were forcibly resettled in Western Poland by 1950 and since then a further 300,000 have been repatriated.

Mass deportations of a political-preventive and punitive character also took place within and into the Soviet Union during and immediately after the Second World War. Following the German attack on the Soviet Union in June of 1941, hundreds and thousands of Soviet citizens of German ethnic origin, who for centuries had been living in the Volga region and around the Black Sea and the Caucasus, were precipitously transplanted beyond the Urals. Numerous non-German groups, including 200,000 Crimean Tatars, 400,000 Chechens, 135,000 Kalmyks, 92,000 Ingush, 43,000 Balkars, 76,000 Karachais and 200,000 Meskhetians, were also deported en bloc from the European part of the Soviet Union to Central Asia. The manner in which these peoples were deported and the conditions in the resettlement areas were such that it has been estimated that over 46% of the Tatars died on the journey or during the first 18 months after deportation.[27] According to one report 50,000 Meskhetians perished in Uzbekistan alone from hunger and cold.[28]

Alexander Solzhenitsyn described these forced resettlements as follows:

'The military units gallantly surrounded the auls, or settlements, and, within twenty-four hours, with the speed of a parachute attack, those who had nested there for centuries past found themselves removed to railroad stations, loaded by the trainload, and rushed off to Siberia, Kazakhstan, Central Asia, and the Russian North.'[29]

It does credit to the Soviet Union that these excesses were openly criticized by Nikita Khrushchev at the Twentieth Party Congress in 1956 and that in 1957 the President of the Supreme Soviet declared that the Kalmyks, Chechens, Ingush and Balkars could return to their former areas. In 1964 the Supreme Soviet decided that the Volga Germans had been unjustly accused of disloyalty, but they have not been allowed to re-establish the Volga German Republic, abolished in 1941. Nor have the Crimean Tatars been allowed to return to their native Crimea.

Displacement of Palestine Arabs

The territory of Palestine was part of the Turkish Empire until the end of the First World War. The Balfour Declaration of 1917 offered a 'national home' in Palestine 'for the Jewish people', without prejudice to the rights of the 'existing non-Jewish communities' in Palestine, and in 1919 Britain was given a Mandate over Palestine by the League of Nations Covenant.[30]

The Moslem Arab population of the region was less than happy with this Declaration, but most did not immediately perceive a danger to their way of life. The Jewish population in Palestine, which comprised 83,790 souls in 1922, increased largely through immigration under the terms of the League of Nations Mandate; for them immigration was a means toward the establishment of a Jewish majority in Palestine as the prerequisite for the creation of a Jewish State. Gradually Arab political leaders began to oppose Jewish immigration and its political implications, and there were anti-Jewish riots in 1920, 1921, 1929, and 1936–1939. The Arab communities, backed by the neighbouring independent Arab States, demanded that all Palestine be converted into an independent State, ruled by its Arab majority. Such a plan was irreconcilable with Jewish aspirations and thus the stalemate continued through the years of the Second World War and shortly thereafter.

Early in 1947 Great Britain announced her intention to lay down the Mandate by 15 May 1948 and this brought the Arab-Jewish controversy over Palestine to a head. In an effort to arrive at a compromise solution, the United Nations on 29 November 1947, by a two-thirds majority, decided to partition Palestine into a Jewish State with a population of 538,000 Jews and 397,000 Arabs and an Arab State with a population of 804,000 Arabs and 10,000 Jews; the enclave of Jerusalem was to be a neutralized international zone with a population of 105,000 Arabs and 100,000 Jews.[31]

Political scientists in Western Europe and the United States also made a case for an Arab-Jewish exchange of population.[32] Such a scheme had already been put forward in 1937 in the report of the British Royal Commission on Palestine under the chairmanship of Lord Peel, which proposed a partition combined with a transfer of population. The. Royal Commission based its proposal on the 'instructive precedent' of the exchange of Greek and Turkish populations after the Greco-Turkish war of 1922. While the British Government endorsed the scheme as 'the best and most hopeful solution of the deadlock' (Cmd 5513), the discussions in both Houses of the British Parliament on 20 and 21 July 1937 revealed that such distinguished representatives of all three parties as Winston Churchill, Lord Samuel, Lloyd George and Lord Strabolgi, sharply opposed the entire partition scheme. Interestingly enough, the transfer issue played a very slight role in the debate. The partition scheme was then extensively discussed by the Permanent Mandates Commission of the League of Nations, which in a 'Preliminary Opinion' submitted to the Council of the League of Nations endorsed the principle of population transfer in application to Palestine, while stressing that the problem was a 'delicate' one and that 'in order to guarantee that the advantages of such a transfer should outweigh the disadvantages, particular care would have to be given to ensure that it was carried out with the greatest fairness'.[33] The British Government then appointed a special Partition Commission, which concluded, however, that there was 'little possibility of the voluntary exchange of population between the Jewish State and the Arab State'. The partition plan was eventually put aside and other schemes, including the transfer of Palestinian Arabs to other Arab States – notably Iraq - were seriously discussed.

After the Second World War there was a renewed proposal to transfer the Palestine Arabs to Iraq and, as a counterpart, to remove Jewish minorities[34] from Arab-speaking countries and transfer them to the new Jewish State in Palestine. One of the advocates of transfer was the former British Foreign Minister Anthony Eden.[35] Yet, every mention of eventual transfer of Palestine Arabs to other Arab countries caused limitless indignation among them. Similarly, the Jewish communities in the Arab States were not enthusiastic about being transferred themselves.

Following the United Nations resolution to partition Palestine, open Arab-Jewish war broke out, which was intensified after the proclamation, on 14 May 1948, of the State of Israel. The question of a population transfer became partly moot, since the military events led to a mass flight of Arab civilians from Jewish-occupied areas to the Arab-occupied portions of Palestine and to the neighbouring Arab States. By the time the truce was signed in 1949, more than 600,000 Palestinian Arabs had become refugees.

The world community responded to the crisis by establishing the United Nations Relief and Works Agency for Palestine Refugees by General Assembly Resolution 302 (IV) of 8 December 1949. The Agency began its operations in 1950, providing essential services for needy refugees living in Lebanon, Syria, Jordan and the Gaza Strip. Then, as a result of the 1967 hostilities, some 500,000 more persons became refugees, thus increasing the number of the Palestinian homeless to well over a million. UNRWA's operations continue to this day and render invaluable services in the many refugee camps established throughout the Middle East. Today the number of registered Palestinian refugees has reached two million.

Displacements in India and Pakistan

Mass flights to escape intolerable conditions are frequently not very different from mass expulsions. In many ways, they are worse, because there is no governmental or international supervision of the 'transfer' and little or no relief prior to reaching a place of refuge.

In many cases religious persecution is at the root of mass flights. A case in point is colonial India, which in 1941 had a population of 389 million, of whom 255 million were Hindus and 92 million Moslems. After Great Britain announced in 1946 that it would grant independence to her former colony, it was proposed to partition India into the Hindu provinces, the Moslem Northwest and Moslem Bengal and Assam. The Hindus under Jawaharlal Nehru opposed partition, while the Moslem League supported their separation from the Hindu provinces but insisted on a unitary Moslem State.

As a corollary to the partition question the issue arose of transferring Hindus from Pakistan to India and Moslems from India to Pakistan. A categorical opponent of this scheme was Mohandas K. Gandhi, the most outstanding spiritual personality in India, who in September 1947 at a prayer meeting in New Delhi said that even at the risk of standing alone, he would oppose it, because 'the transfer of millions of Hindus, Sikhs and Moslems is unthinkable and wrong'.[36] He believed what the leaders in both Dominions declared on Independence Day, 15 August 1947, when they reiterated their guarantees to all minorities that they could live side by side in peace as they had lived for centuries.

Unfortunately for all concerned, communal warfare broke out not only in the Punjab but also in Calcutta, Bihar and other provinces. Expropriations, vandalism, systematic looting and other forms of persecution led to reprisals and counter-reprisals; it is estimated that as many as half a million Moslems and Hindus perished as a consequence of acts of violence. For millions of human beings caught in this vicious cycle of attack and revenge there was only one salvation: flight. The self-evacuation, for which no one was prepared, took place in the simplest and oldest way – on foot.

India's first Prime Minister Nehru observed at a press conference in October 1947 that the Government of India 'had no policy with regard to exchange of population and that there was no talk of it before [Independence Day], although since March about half a million people must have come through the frontiers of the Punjab to the United Provinces and other places . . . None of us envisaged a major transfer of population at any time.'[37] For his part, Liagat Ali Khan, Prime Minister of Pakistan, declared that there was no deliberate transfer of minority populations in the Punjab, but only an organized evacuation 'of those who wish to go'.[38]

In the absence of a governmental agreement regulating the migration of millions of destitute persons, the Indian Army began using tanks to escort long columns of Moslem evacuees moving toward Pakistan through the Hindu and Sikh country of East Punjab. At the same time the Indian Government, with the consent of the Government of Pakistan, sent its own troops across the Pakistani border to protect caravans of Hindus and Sikhs leaving the West Punjab. By 25 September 1947, the Army had evacuated 400,000 Moslems to Pakistan and had 850,000 still to move, while in Pakistan 600,000 non-Moslems were marching toward the border of the Dominion of India. Finally, the two governments made emergency agreements to organize and co-ordinate the evacuations, so as to prevent further violence and to expedite the transfer before famine and epidemics began. Organized transfers affecting a further four million persons took place from October 21 to November 25, 1947.

In all it is estimated that some 14 million persons were uprooted in the course of these population exchanges. On the other hand, it should be noted that today India still has a Moslem minority numbering some 60 million (10% of the population) and Pakistan a Hindu minority numbering some 6 million (9% of the population). These figures show, *inter alia*, that these two religious communities can and do co-exist in spite of their differences.

But tragedy again unfolded in 1971 during the murderous civil war in East Pakistan. Ten million refugees, both Hindus and Moslems, crossed the border of East Pakistan into India in order to save themselves from the genocidal conflict. As a result of the war the former East Pakistan emerged as a new independent State, Bangladesh. A majority of the refugees then gradually returned to their homes.

Mass Expulsions in Africa

In Africa it has been primarily ethnic, not religious persecution that has led tens of thousands of persons to abandon their places of habitual residence and seek refuge elsewhere. Expulsions have also been motivated by economic reasons. In August 1972 President Idi Amin of Uganda announced that all Asians residing in Uganda who were not of Ugandan nationality would have to leave the country within 90 days. Over 40,000 persons were affected. Although the world hardly took note of this crisis, the United Nations High Commissioner for Refugees gave prompt and effective attention to it; over 27,000 Asians were admitted to the United Kingdom, while the remaining thousands were spread among many receiving States including Canada, Denmark, India, Pakistan, Switzerland and the United States. Those Asians not holding British passports were provided with travel documents issued by the International Committee of the Red Cross, which sent delegates to Uganda to assist in the installation and administration of the United Nations departure centres. Surprisingly enough, there was relatively little comment in the press and in international bodies. The United Nations General Assembly, for instance, did not adopt any resolution censuring the expulsions, and a proposal before the Sub-Commission for Prevention of Discrimination and the Protection of Minorities that a telegram be sent to the President of Uganda expressing 'serious concern' at the proposed action was defeated by fourteen votes to one, with six members abstaining.[39]

Numerous other involuntary migrations have occurred in the African continent since the Second World War, including, for instance, that of some 200,000 African aliens who were forced to leave Ghana in November and December 1969 under conditions of panic. In March 1976 the Government of Libya expelled over 20,000 Egyptians and confiscated their property. In July and August of 1978 some 6,000 Benin nationals were expelled from Gabon. In October 1982 some 80,000 persons of Rwandese origin were driven out from the South-Western areas of Uganda, most of them being expelled into Rwanda and the remainder being moved to refugee settlements in Uganda.

During January and February of 1983 as many as two million persons were expelled from Nigeria into neighbouring States, including Ghana, on the grounds that they were 'illegal immigrants'. It appears that this type of 'mass' expulsion, defined in Art. 12 (5) of the 1981 African Charter of Human and People's Rights as 'aimed at national, racial, ethnic or religious groups' continues unabated. The triggering factor, however, has frequently been unemployment and economic crisis in the expelling States.

The list of examples of collective expulsions still occurring in our days could be expanded for several pages, but such events belong more properly in a study of contemporary political developments or of emergency relief actions rather than in this historical survey.

Evaluation

The legal and ethical aspects of mass expulsions were a major concern of the 1952 Siena Session of the Institut de Droit International. The report presented by Giorgio Balladore Pallieri surveyed the various conventions relative to transfer of populations and distinguished carefully between voluntary and involuntary transfers, giving his qualified endorsement to conventions granting the right of option. M. Pallieri cited the Universal

Declaration of Human Rights, article 9 of which provides: 'No one shall be subjected to arbitrary arrest, detention or *exile*' (emphasis added). Art. 13 (2) provides 'Everyone has the right to leave any country, including his own, and to return to his country'. Art. 15 (2) provides: 'No one shall be arbitrarily deprived of his nationality nor denied the right to change his nationality'. It would appear that compulsory transfers would violate these rights.

The presentation by Alfred Verdross best summarizes the issues:

> In the light of the principles of the United Nations Charter and of the Universal Declaration of Human Rights it seems to be well established that individuals are no longer mere objects of the States but that they are persons having individual rights which must be recognized and protected by the States. From this follows the conclusion that States may no longer dispose of men like cattle: a transfer of populations against the will of the individuals concerned would therefore be barred. On the other hand, it has been argued that the needs of peacekeeping may require the transfer of disloyal minorities. But this thesis forgets that the disloyalty of minorities may be the result of the drawing of national frontiers in disregard of the principle of self-determination (recognized by President Wilson in his famous speech of Mount Vernon), or of violations of human rights and rights of minorities by the State concerned.[40]

If this sober appraisal of the problem were shared by more politicians, mass population transfers would probably cease to occur. Yet, some members of the Institut de Droit International expressed the view that the Institut was not entitled to condemn political events from a legal point of view.

On the other hand, it appears that world public opinion is becoming gradually sensitized to the right of peoples to their native soil. This is reflected in the continuing debate over the right of expellees to return to their homeland. With respect to the Palestinian refugees, for instance, the United Nations General Assembly has specifically affirmed their right to return in numerous resolutions beginning with Resolution 194 (III) of 12 December 1948, paragraph 11 of which provides 'that the refugees wishing to return to their homes and live at peace with their neighbours should be permitted to do so at the earliest practicable date, and that compensation should be paid for the property of those choosing not to return and for the loss of or damage to property which, under principles of international law or in equity, should be made good by the governments or authorities responsible'. Many subsequent resolutions have reaffirmed 'the inalienable right of the Palestinians to return to their homes and property from which they have been displaced and uprooted' (Resolution 3236 (XXIX) of 22 November 1974) and most recently in Resolution 38/83B of 15 December 1983. In spite of these expressions of worldwide concern, the right to return to the homeland has not been implemented.

The 14 million German refugees and expellees who poured into the truncated Reich after the Second World War have not been the subject of United Nations resolutions recognizing their right to return, but their representatives have repeatedly affirmed this right, while at the same time renouncing the use of force to achieve it. Obviously, their return to East Prussia, Pomerania or Silesia would be as difficult as the return of the Palestinians to their homeland, since the areas in question are not uninhabited. Since the end of the Second World War two generations of Polish citizens have been born in the former German provinces and thus they have developed a right to their new homeland, as the Israelis, too, have developed a right to theirs. Indeed, there are conflicting interests and conflicting rights, the balancing of which must be undertaken in the name of peace. While no responsible politician would envisage a collective expulsion of Poles from the provinces east of the Oder-Neisse or an expulsion of the Israelis from the West Bank, it would appear that the best and most human solution would be the increased permeability of national frontiers, which would allow the settlement and co-existence of these neighbours.

This historical survey of mass expulsions in the twentieth century has endeavoured to analyze the causes, describe the execution and assess some of the consequences of such displacements. In particular the principle of population transfers and the collected experience of several transfer schemes have been reviewed. The author believes that many important conclusions can and must be drawn from such past experiments. Millions of people have already been uprooted from their homelands; millions have perished in the course of expulsions or as a sequel of ensuing deprivations; millions of expellees have suffered a total dislocation of their lives, or, transplanted into a strange new environment, have endured a form of cultural genocide. The ostensible justification for compulsory population transfers has been the preservation of peace, it being argued that ethnic and religious minorities pose insoluble problems and that peace is best secured by striving for ethnic or religious homogeneity in States. The author does not share this point of view. On the contrary, it is here submitted that mass expulsions constitute a negative approach to the reality of our world, which is characterized by a diversity of races and faiths. The positive approach consists in accepting the fact that we are one human species, regardless of colour or religion. It is this commitment to the brotherhood of man that requires us to reject schemes to separate the races and the religions. Peace is not secured by alienating but rather by uniting. Accordingly, the goal is to learn to live together in tolerance and mutual understanding, to foster a more intimate communion of people. This is the ethical challenge of our age.

From the above it follows that mass expulsions must be seen as an anachronism in the world of today, incompatible with international law and more particularly with the philosophy of human rights that has emerged since the end of the Second World War and has been further developed by organs of the United Nations. Let us hope that although some politicians may still only pay lip service to *dignitas humana*, expulsions will become a thing of the past.

Notes: Chapter 2

1 Albert Schweitzer, Das Problem des Friedens in der heutigen Welt, Speech upon receiving the Nobel Peace Prize, published in German in Verlag C.H. Beck, Munich 1954. English translation quoted in de Zayas, *Nemesis at Potsdam*, p. XIX.

2 In memory of this North American tragedy the American poet Henry Wadsworth Longfellow wrote in 1847 his epic 'Evangeline':

> 'This is the forest primeval; but where are the hearts that beneath it
> Leaped like the roe, when he hears in the woodland the voice of the huntsman?
> Where is the thatch-roofed village, the home of Acadian farmers,
> Men whose lives glided on like rivers that water the woodlands,
> Darkened by shadows of earth, but reflecting an image of heaven?
> Waste are those pleasant farms, and the farmers forever departed!
> Scattered like dust and leaves, when the mighty blasts of October
> Seize them, and whirl them aloft, and sprinkle them far over the ocean.'

3 Stephen Ladas, *The Exchange of Minorities*, New York (1932) p.15.

4 Ladas, op. cit., pp. 122–123.

5 Greco-Bulgarian Communities, Advisory Opinion, Permanent Court of International Justice, Series B, No. 17.

6 British Command Paper 1814, Lausanne Conference on Near Eastern Affairs 1922–23, Records of Proceedings and Draft Terms of Peace. Also cited as British Blue Book, Turkey No. 1 (1923), p. 217.

7 Ibid., pp. 223–224.

8 Ibid., p. 212.

9 Collection of Advisory Opinions. Exchange of Greek and Turkish Populations (Lausanne Convention VI, 30 January 1923, Art.2). Permanent Court of International Justice, Series B, No. 10, p. 22.

10 Ladas, op. cit., p. 438–439.

11 A notable exception was President Thomas Masaryk of Czechoslovakia, who rejected proposals to expel three and a half million ethnic Germans from Bohemia and Moravia, because he did not want to launch his new nation by embarking on a policy of mass deportations of the native population. A. de Zayas, *Nemesis at Potsdam*, p. 27.

12 Wachenheim, Hitler's Transfers of Population in Eastern Europe, 20 *Foreign Affairs*, p. 705 (1942).

13 Dietrick Loeber, *Diktierte Option*, Neumünster (1974).

14 Louise Holborn (ed.), *War and Peace Aims of the United Nations* p. 462 (1943).

15 144 B.F.s.P.1072.

16 5 IMT 410.

17 8 IMT 256.

18 Parliamentary Debates, House of Commons, vol. 408, col. 1617, 1 March 1945.

19 Foreign Relations of the United States, *The Conference of Berlin* (1945), vol. 2, p. 1459.

20 Ibid.

21 Parliamentary Debates, House of Commons, vol. 406, col. 1484.

22 Ibid., vol. 414, col. 83–4.

23 Foreign Relations of the United States, 1945, vol. 2, pp. 1290–91.

24 Ibid., p. 1294.

25 ICRC Report on its Activities During the Second World War, vol. 1, p. 673.

26 Victor Gollancz, *Our Threatened Values*, (1946), p. 96.

27 Minority Rights Group, Ann Sheehy (ed.), *The Crimean Tatars, Volga Germans and Mesketians* (1973), p. 11.

28 Ibid., p. 31.

29 *The Gulag Archipelago*, vol. 1 p. 84.

30 Facsimile reproduction in J.M. Moore (ed.) *The Arab-Israeli Conflict*, (1977), p. 885.
31 General Assembly Resolution 181 (II) Concerning the Future Government of Palestine, 29 November 1947.
32 Joseph Schechtman, *Population Transfers in Asia* (1949), pp. 84–141.
33 Permanent Mandates Commission, Minutes of the Thirty-second Session, Geneva. See also Schechtman, op.cit., p. 89.
34 J. Schechtman, op. cit., pp. 114 et seq.
35 Parliamentary Debates, House of Commons, December 11, 1947.
36 *New York Times*, September 16, 1947, also cited in Schechtman, op. cit., p. 21.
37 Indian Information, November 1 1947. Quoted in Schechtman, op. cit., p. 22.
38 Schechtman, op. cit., p. 24.
39 Report of the Sub-Commission 1972, United Nations document E/CN.4/1101; E/CN.4/Sub.2/332, p. 23. Motion submitted by the British Expert, Mr. Robert James.
40 Annuaire de l'Institut de Droit International, Vol. 44/2 (1952), pp. 186–187 (translation from French by the author of this article).

Bibliography

Académie de Droit International, Recueil des Cours, 1928, lectures by Professor Séfériades.
Aga Khan, Sadruddin, Study on Human Rights and Massive Exoduses, E/CN.4/1503/Rev.1.
American Friends Service Committee, *Report on Conditions in Central Europe*, 'Expellees', Philadelphia (1946) – *The Problem of 12 Million German Refugees*, Boston (1949).
Annuaire de l'Institut de Droit International, Session de Siena, Vol. 44/2 (1952), pp. 138–199.
Bernhardt, Rudolf (ed.) *Encyclopedia of Public International Law*, Vols. 1–8, Amsterdam (1981–1985).
Churchill, Winston, *Closing the Ring*, London (1952), *Triumph and Tragedy*, London (1953).
Claud, I, *National Minorities, An International Problem*, Cambridge, Mass (1955).
Doughty, Arthur, *The Acadian Exiles* (1916).
Elles, Baroness, International Provisions Protecting the Human Rights of Non-Citizens, E/CN.4/Sub.2/392/Rev.1.
Foreign Relations of the United States, 1945, Vol. 2, pp. 1227–1327.
Glaser, Kurt and Stefan T. Possony, *Victims of Politics* (1979).
Gollancz, Victor, *Our Threatened Values*, London (1946). *In Darkest Germany*, London (1947).
Goodwin-Gill, Guy S., *International Law and the Movement of Persons between States* (1978).
Holborn, Louise, The Palestine Arab Refugee Problem, in John Moore (ed.) *The Arab-Israeli Conflict*, Princeton (1977).
Kulischer, E., *Europe on the Move*, New York (1948).
Ladas, Stephen, *The Exchange of Minorities*, New York (1932).
Proudfoot, Malcolm J., European Refugees, *A Study in Forced Population Movement*, London (1957).
Radley, Kurt, The Palestinian Refugees: The Right to Return in International Law, *American Journal of International Law*, vol. 72, pp. 586–614 (1978).
Schechtman, Joseph, *Postwar Population Transfers in Europe*, New York (1962). *Population Transfers in Asia*, New York (1949).
Schieder, Theodor (ed.), *Documents on the Expulsion of the Germans from Eastern and Central Europe*, Bonn (1953–58), 8 Vols.
Schweitzer, Albert, Das Problem des Friedens in der heutigen Welt, Speech upon receiving the Nobel Peace Prize, published in German in Verlag C.H. Beck, Munich, (1954).
Solzhenitsyn, Alexander, *The Gulag Archipelago*, New York (1974).

de Zayas, A., The Legality of Mass Population Transfers: The German Experience 1945–48, *East European Quarterly*, Vol. XII, Nos. 1 and 2, pp. 1–23, 143–160 (1978).
- entries in Bernhardt (ed.) *Encyclopedia of Public International Law*, including 'Population, Expulsion and Transfer', 'Repatriation', 'Forced Resettlement', 'Westphalia, Peace of'.
- *Nemesis at Potsdam, The Anglo-Americans and the Expulsion of the Germans* 2nd revised edition, (London, 1979).
United Nations, *The Right of Return of the Palestinian People*, (New York, 1978) ST/SG/SER.F/2/

3 Armenian refugees: accidents of diplomacy or victims of ideology?

CHRISTOPHER J. WALKER

The situation of Armenian refugees during and after the First World War was complex. It related not only to the military and political situation of the Caucasus and Cilicia, but also to the lengthy and often barren consultations between statesmen at international conferences, and to the charity of individuals in the United States and Europe.[1] If the most powerful factors governing the status of refugees are military and political, those that determined the situation for Armenians in 1915–23 were of a particularly widely spread type; and since the military and political conditions were almost always at variance with Armenian interests, the enormous response of individuals to the Armenian plight did no more than modify it. International charity meant that more than a quarter of a million Armenians lived who would otherwise have starved to death; but the actions (and inaction) of statesmen and diplomats ensured that many would survive only in exile, and left them with the prospect of having their identity diluted and ceasing to be Armenians in a generation or two.

By the time of the armistice in 1918 an estimated half million Armenians were refugees. They were all refugees from the Ottoman Empire, most from the region known familiarly as Turkish Armenia. Most found shelter in the region of the Russian Caucasus which had declared itself the Republic of Armenia in May 1918. Some were in Iraq, under British military supervision; others in Cilicia, initially under the British and later the French; and there were smaller numbers in Egypt, Greece and Bulgaria. Others too were refugees in consulates and buildings belonging to charitable organizations inside Anatolian Turkey itself. Their US and European benefactors were for a time co-ordinated by an American colonel delegated by the Peace Conference; but the most effective relief was undertaken by private organizations and individuals.[2]

To understand why the Armenians had been brought to such a dire plight by 1918, a brief historical resumé is required. The nature and causes of the Armenian situation from 1915 onwards are matters hotly contested in various quarters; but the outline I shall give seems to me to coincide most closely with the versions of impartial observers of the time, especially of accurate and careful eye-witnesses, of whom there were a number, and also to be consistent with a careful attention to chronology, which is vital for any historical understanding, and in which the proponents of alternative versions have shown some serious errors.

The Armenians have existed in their highlands – the lands divided today by the southern part of the Soviet-Turkish border, and at the beginning of this century between the Ottoman and Romanov empires – since about 800 BC; they are mentioned in an inscription of King Darius, and in Xenophon's *Anabasis*. Their political history was often insecure, and almost always turbulent, in spite of which they developed a remarkable culture. Most significant for their long-term survival was their adoption of Christianity, and their invention of a unique alphabet for their language. The larger, western part of their land was first conquered by the Ottoman Empire in 1514; the eastern part was initially Iranian, subsequently Russian. Thus an important imperial frontier has almost always passed through their lands. There was also a significant Armenian population in Ottoman Cilicia, following a migration there and the establishment of an Armenian kingdom in the twelfth century.[3]

Early Ottoman sultans introduced, as a matter of deliberate policy, Kurds into greater Armenia, to guard the frontier against Iran. The existing Armenians, as Christians, were at a disadvantage to the Kurds, who, as Muslims, were permitted to bear arms, a privilege denied to Christians. Nevertheless a certain amount of somewhat unequal coexistence was possible in the centuries which followed. But taxation was burdensome and violently enforced; and certain taxes fell upon the Armenians alone.[4]

The Ottoman Constitution, had it been implemented and made to work in 1876, would have taken away all the grievances of the Armenians in the countryside. However, Ottoman sultan Abdul Hamid II suspended the Constitution in 1878, and for the mass of the people the abuses continued as before, and indeed grew worse. Within the Armenian community committees grew up dedicated first to self-help and later to revolution. An uprising among Armenian highlanders of Sasun in 1894 led to a massive government assault on Armenians throughout the empire. In almost every Armenian location they were looted, persecuted and killed without distinction of age or sex; in one particularly horrifying episode, in Urfa, Ottoman soldiers burned alive several thousand Armenians who had taken refuge in the cathedral.[5]

Many Armenians left their homeland in succeeding years; large numbers were drawn to America, where the annual rate of Armenian immigration stood at 2,500 in the late 1890s.[6] The American connection had been formed as a result of the widespread missionary activity of the US throughout Anatolia and Armenia since the 1830s. Until the 1890s small numbers had been drawn to the US by its opportunities, so it seemed natural for those who wanted to get out following the Hamidian massacres to go there. In view of the conditions that they were leaving behind it might be fair to class them as refugees.

There was a constitutional revolution in the Ottoman Empire in 1908, known as the 'Young Turk Revolution', in the promotion of which Armenians played an active role. Despite their participation, within two years the leading revolutionary Turks had abandoned them. Turkish ideologists had become drawn to the notion of pan-Turkism, which deeply influenced Young Turk ruling circles.[7] This political theory meant turning away from the multi-ethnic, multi-cultural Ottoman Empire as it then existed, and pursuing instead the exclusivist goal of creating a homogeneous Turkish-speaking realm from the Balkans to Siberia, which would eventually become a political entity. Armenia, even as a group of provinces within two empires, was seen to be a threat to this plan, partly since Armenian national feeling, although not highly developed, would not willingly permit the extinction of the nation, and partly because the Armenian people had developed a fund of sympathy and support from Europe and America. The second stage of the pan-Turkish plan, expansion to the Russian Caucasus and Baku, was manifestly a threat to Armenia. Despite the virtual rejection of Ottoman Armenians from their body politic by the Turks and the continuing violence and insecurity for Armenians in the countryside, the Armenians fought bravely in the Ottoman armies in the Balkan Wars of 1912–13. They also enlisted in large numbers in the armies in the First World War, although there were also sporadic incidents of anti-Government defiance. The ruling Turks, for their part, demonstrated their adherence to pan-Turkism in one of six proposals that they put to the German ambassador in Istanbul in August 1914, at the time of the signature of the secret German-Turkish pact. The fifth of these proposals was that 'Germany would assume the responsibility of rectifying the eastern frontiers of the Ottoman Empire in a manner suitable for the establishment of a link with the Muslim people of Russia'. This expansionist theme was repeated in the proclamation of war aims issued by the government after the empire's entry into the war on 30 October 1914; this document spoke of seeking a natural frontier, to include and unite 'all the branches of our race'.[8]

The fate which followed for Armenians in the Ottoman Empire has been disputed in recent years. It has become a matter of current political debate, with the American State Department issuing a 'position' on it, and a United Nations Sub-Commission has prepared a text on it in Geneva. However, in the years during and immediately after the First World War there was little dispute as to what happened to the Armenians, except among some of those directly involved in anti-Armenian measures. The testimonies, many of them eye-witness, of consular officials, German soldiers, journalists, relief workers, missionaries and of the survivors themselves, all concurred. The version to which I give most credence goes as follows: In the last days of March 1915 the Armenian soldiers who had enlisted in the Ottoman armies were disarmed and turned virtually into pack-animals – driven burdened with military supplies across snowy wastes until they dropped. At the same time there was a vast and over-bureaucratic search for arms in all Armenian towns and villages, accompanied by violence, threats and torture, all unprovoked.[9] (They had been permitted to bear arms since the revolution of 1908.) Armenian leaders in Constantinople were arrested simultaneously, held in prison for three days, then taken into the countryside and murdered. When the people were disarmed and leaderless, the deportations began. Armenians in their towns and villages were summoned to report to the authorities. They were then ordered out, *en masse*, usually with the minimum of supplies. In most cases the able-bodied men were shot at the first halt outside town; women, children and the elderly were driven along pre-arranged routes, mostly via Aleppo to semi-desert concentration places in northern Syria and Iraq. Here they were left to the elements to die. Numbers of police and soldiers were deployed along the route to check on procedure. At certain points the deportees were harassed by irregulars, who robbed and murdered them; their actions were in co-ordination with organisers of the deportations.[10] Some deportees were driven to and fro on long detours, apparently to wear them down. The German consul in Aleppo reported that one convoy was driven from Urfa to Raqqa thus: Urfa – Tell Abiad – Raqqa – Tell Abiad – Raqqa, a distance of 338 km., rather than for the direct route, 138 km.[11] Cilicia was emptied in April-May 1915, Great Armenia in May-July, and western Anatolia in August-September. Armenians were saved where there was an energetic governor who opposed the general trend (such as at Smyrna, Marash and Aleppo); and those needed for essential military supplies were not deported.

The orders for deportation were published in the official gazette, and the measures were implemented cruelly at the local level. Although they are known as 'deportations', there was nowhere to deport the Armenians, except harsh, semi-desert regions. Thus it would seem likely, although it is not proven, that the orders for deportation were a cover for orders for death. (This would coincide with the ideas current in Ittihadist [Young Turk] ideology.) Specific orders have been published, showing both that the Turks sought to kill the Armenians, and that they desired to have them well treated while they were being deported.[12] However, none of the humane orders was ever observed to have been carried out.

The picture of the orders (and hence of the responsibility of the central government) which related to the fate of Armenians is of two tiers of orders, one *en clair*, usually outlining the main directions of policy, and the other in secret, making important modifications which sometimes contradicted the open orders. This picture is given substance by the testimony of Lieutenant Said Ahmed Mukhtar Ba'aj, which is in the Public Record Office, Kew. He was stationed in Trebizond in May 1915. In August 1916 he together with three other Muslim Ottoman officers, went over to the Russians at Kermanshah; they were then handed over by the Grand Duke Nicolas to the British, who sent them to London to be interviewed at the Foreign Office by Sir Mark Sykes. Sykes included their accounts in the Foreign Office's *Arabian Report* which he was editing at the time. The lieutenant states: 'In July an order came to deport to the interior all the Armenians in the vilayet of Trebizond. Being a member of the court martial I knew that deportation meant massacre.' He adds: 'Besides the deportation order referred to above, an imperial *Irade* (decree) was issued ordering that all deserters, when caught, should be shot without trial. The secret order read "Armenians" in lieu of "deserters".'[13] His testimony continues by outlining the contrived duplicity of the government – how for instance it opened a school for children of deported parents, before deporting and massacring the children along with the rest of the population. In the light of the evidence of this Ottoman officer, it is hard to advocate the view that the authorities in the capital did not really know what was going on, or if they did, tried to mitigate it, and that any massacres were just due to the excesses of subordinates. His testimony gives substance to the view that the orders for deportation were in fact orders for death.

For the stubborn survivors, there were two main destinations, and the decision as to which they should go to was made near Aleppo, where a large number of Armenians converged in late 1915. Those with skills were sent south, to the relatively mild fate of surviving by their wits in Damascus, Homs, Hama and other Syrian cities. The others – the overwhelming majority – were sent to Deir ez-Zor, and to other bleak and remote locations on the Euphrates, where, without food or shelter, they died in great numbers.[14] These places were actually death-camps. How many died? This matter is controversial. German consular authorities on the spot estimated between 800,000 and 1 million dead. Dr Johannes Lepsius, the German humanitarian, put the figure at 1.1 million in 1919; while in the same year Ernst Sommer, of the Deutscher Hilfsbund, estimated 1.4 million dead. Djemal Pasha put the number deported at 1.5 million, and the number who died at 600,000. One recent estimate, based on Turkish demographic studies, puts the figure of Armenians who perished at around 500,000.[15] What caused the deaths of Armenians and created the refugees in 1915? There are several possible answers. In view of the co-operation of soldiers and police in their deportation and demise, it is impossible to deny that the Ottoman Turkish government was responsible. However, it is not fully clear what constituted the Ottoman government in 1915; whether it was the Cabinet, the Council of Ministers, or the Young Turk party (that is, the Committee of Union and Progress). There is evidence that the Party, even though it was the party of government, had nevertheless set up its own administrative fabric alongside the recognized officials and civil servants, and that it was this para-government which made the real decisions and oversaw their execution. This theory would fit with the idea of two sets of orders, only one of which was to be obeyed. A dispatch by German ambassador Count von Wolff-Metternich gives strong evidence of the presence of Party officials alongside recognized officials.[16] Even so, we may still ask, what motivated the government or the Party to set in motion such a campaign of death and exile? Is the explanation of racism, and hankerings on the part of the Young Turks to create a new imperial order, too simple? I do not think so; and it was widely believed to be the dominant motive at the time. The American Eliot Grinnell Mears wrote in his impartial study, *Modern Turkey*, in 1924:[17]

> The persecution of the Armenians during the late world war was the worst in their history as far as loss of population was concerned. The horrors of the deportations can scarcely be exaggerated. In this case, an underlying motive was the desire of the Ottoman government to coalesce the rising pan-Turanian movement by doing away with the Armenians, who formed a barrier between the Turkish Muslims, of south-eastern Europe and western Asia Minor, and the Tatars and Turkomans of the Caucasus and Central Asia. This idea received

marked support from the Germans during the war, especially because of the failure of the pan-Islamic drive.

Further evidence of the direct involvement of the authorities in the exiling and death of Armenians is shown in the fact that, in a number of locations from which Armenians were being exiled, Turkish emigrants from Thrace (known as *muhadjirs*) were made ready to take over the evacuated property. Moreover the moveable property of the Armenians was sold (usually for the enrichment of party funds), despite laws which on paper guaranteed that it would be preserved and kept safe.[18]

Thus the Armenian refugees of 1915 were in a sense archetypical refugees: an indigenous people driven out of their homes on the orders of their government. Perhaps the only untypical thing was that, for most of 1915 and much of 1916, the intention was to kill them rather than just to expel them. They were the victims of the government's dominant ideology, and official justifications (that they were committing acts of terror, that they had deserted to the enemy, and so forth) magnified small incidents into large plots, in an attempt to divert attention from the government's policy.

The great majority of Armenians were either dead or on the road to their deaths before the end of 1915, that is, before the Russian armies had penetrated any distance into Anatolia. Erzerum was not captured until 16 February 1916, Trebizond in mid April;[19] so for Turkish and other revisionist historians to say that there was a 'limited form of civil war' going on in Anatolia during the period under scrutiny – a parallel has been drawn with Lebanon during 1975–85[20] – is deliberately to confuse the issue and miss the point; during the whole of 1915 the Ottoman authorities were in control through Anatolia and Turkish Armenia, except where a few Armenians made isolated stands of armed self-defence, and during that period the ministry of the interior exercised its power against Armenian civilians virtually unhindered.

Refugees fled in large numbers across the frontier into Russian Armenia quite early on in the war. Already by March 1915 120,000 Armenian refugees from the Ottoman Empire were reported in the Caucasus.[21] They were cared for by five organisations, three local Caucasian charities and two with headquarters in Petrograd and Moscow. By the following December the number had reached 180,000, which included 20,000 refugee children abandoned at the roadside.[22]

In April 1916 the Armenian Refugees (Lord Mayor's) Fund, a British charity founded in 1915, sent a team, led by the Rev. Harold Buxton, of four relief workers and four nurses, to the Caucasus, travelling via Stockholm and Moscow.[23] Buxton reported from Erevan in June on the appalling conditions, and the harrowing nature of the refugees' escape from the atrocities, but noted that 'Once in Russia they were safe from knife and bullet'. Conditions on arrival in Transcaucasia were rough: 'Thousands of women and children, sick, sore and starved, sheltered themselves in old disused buildings, wooden huts, or with scraps of canvas. Thousands more simply squatted down in the open, without shelter of any kind from blazing sun and torrential rain.' The children 'appear to be particularly healthy now, and on the whole have recovered their natural good spirits, though it is really tragic to see the faces of some of the little boys and girls, which are marred and scarred with lines of pain. I suppose nothing will ever remove those outward signs of what they went through.'[24]

The essentials were food and shelter; but not far behind there was an attempt to make life seem as normal as possible in these numbing conditions. Workshops were set up: the girls did needlework, embroidery and lace-making, and the boys made Viennese-style bentwood furniture and learnt carpentry and smithery.[25] However, not all activities were in accordance with traditional gender stereotypes. When an American Red Cross representative, Captain Edward Bickel, needed to reconstruct roads and bridges in Mesopotamia after the war for the distribution of food, he found that there were no men; they were either dead or wounded or serving elsewhere. The women, however, were living in enforced idleness. So, '500 Armenian women joyfully agreed to be enrolled by the Red Cross to reconstruct roads and bridges'. By October 1919 they had restored 150 km. (94 miles) of roads, and rebuilt several ruined bridges on the tributaries of the Euphrates.[26]

This was exceptional. George Hodgkin, one of the members of the British expedition, found that the problems of administering relief were the typical ones: 'How to give material help without demoralisation; how to have warm hearts but cool heads; how to lend money and seed and oxen with enough, but not too much, in the way of guarantees for repayment.'[27] Where possible they were paid for work done. Dr Paul Monroe, of the American charity Near East Relief, noted:

> Refugees employed in rebuilding roads, reconstructing the sanitary systems in towns and villages and in opening up irrigation ditches, in order to bring large areas of added land under irrigation cultivation, were paid for their services in corn grits at the rate of ten pounds of grits a month. Nearly 130,000 people were thus engaged.[28]

Britain was not far behind the local organisations in providing relief. Several charities offered assistance, the chief ones being the Armenian Refugees (Lord Mayor's) Fund, the Armenia Red Cross and Relief Fund, and the Armenian Refugees Relief Fund. In British cathedrals and churches at this time it became the practice to designate a Sunday in February as 'Armenia Sunday', and give the proceeds of the collections to Armenian relief. By the time of the armistice the total receipts for all the charities amounted to approximately £15,000.[29]

At the same time an extensive American relief operation got under way. After receiving a cable from the US ambassador to Turkey in September 1915 a committee made up of missionaries and philanthropists was set up in Boston, calling itself the Armenian Relief Committee.[30] (It was later re-named Near East Relief.) Through the existing network of

American schools, hospitals and American-founded churches, it was able to give relief on the spot in Ottoman lands, rather than to those who had fled to Russian Transcaucasia. $100,000 was immediately appealed for, shortly rising to $5 million, and after the armistice $30 million, all of which sums were raised owing to the immense American sympathy and generosity.[31] In about ten years from the date of its creation the American committee was estimated to have appealed for and spent just under $100 million on refugees, mostly Armenian, in the Caucasus, Greece, Syria and Lebanon.[32]

Within the Ottoman Empire the US vice-consul in Aleppo, Jesse B. Jackson, became a co-ordinator of relief. He estimated that Armenian refugees, as far east as Deir ez-Zor and south to Damascus, numbered 150,000, all of whom were virtually destitute. Another figure was given in December 1918 by British General Clayton; he reported that there were 85,000 Armenian refugees at Homs, Hama and Aleppo, so Jackson's figure is probably about right.[34]

Harold Buxton, reporting just after the armistice, gives the following figures: 300,000 refugees in the Caucasus, 300,000 in Asia Minor, 1 million in Persia (of various nationalities), and 50,000 in and around Aleppo.[35] The 300,000 in Asia Minor were probably in large part Armenians displaced from their towns and villages in Turkish Armenia, too frightened to return, and now living in foreign schools and consulates. They would also include some Muslim refugees. Henry Riggs, of the American missionary family, noted that the Turkish authorities started deporting the Kurds towards the end of the war, and 10,000 reached Kharput, 'and some of them lay sick in our buildings and were cared for by our people'.[36] One of the charities also aided a few thousand Muslim Laz refugees in the north. It is probably impossible to estimate the make-up of the 1 million in Persia, except to say that Armenians, Assyrians (Christians of the East, speaking Aramaic) and Kurds would have made up the bulk of them.

In addition, in August 1918 the British army established a refugee camp at Ba'qubah, 53 km. (33 miles) north of Baghdad, for Armenians and Assyrians. The average total there at any one time was 40,000, about 40 per cent of whom were Armenians.[37]

All relief workers expressed the hope that, with the cessation of hostilities, the refugees would be permitted to return home. Ottoman Turkey had been defeated in war, and had signed an instrument of defeat. The Young Turk government, which all concerned were sure had planned and executed the Armenian persecutions, had collapsed, so hopes were high for a new life and a new beginning for Armenians. However, this was not to be. The Ottoman army was not disarmed, and so it was able to re-group; the Allied occupation of Turkey hardly existed outside the capital, some districts in the west and the areas in the south which their armies had captured; and the Turkish functionaries responsible at the local level for executing anti-Armenian measures mostly remained at their posts. Fears and doubts, too, about the future nature of Russia meant that Britain pursued a virtually self-contradictory policy in the Caucasus; so help for the homeless and starving was conducted on a day-to-day, semi-improvisatory basis. It was not until August 1920 that the Allies agreed on a Turkish treaty, known as the treaty of Sèvres, which did indeed make adequate provision for Armenians, although in other respects it was greedy, imperialistic, and a hang-over from the worst aspects of nineteenth-century diplomacy. Moreover it was unenforceable, since the un-disarmed Ottoman 15th Army had re-grouped, and had received political inspiration from Mustafa Kemal (Atatürk).[38]

Some Armenians, trusting the Allies, did make their way home, especially to Cilicia, which was under the occupation first of the British and latterly of the French. But the powers, especially the French, were inconsistent, bestowing their favours alternately on Armenians or Turks, being mainly concerned with seeking temporary advantage over their rivals; and as a result the Armenians suffered.

Perhaps the fate of one Armenian town in Cilicia, that of Hadjin, about 100 km. north-west of Marash, illustrates the manner in which the fate of the refugees became intertwined with the political indecision of the time. Hadjin's Armenians, in all about 25,000–30,000, had been deported along with many others in May 1915. Most died of starvation or exposure in the death camps along the Euphrates. In the course of the Allied occupation following the armistice about 8,000 were able to repatriate themselves slowly and painfully. For most of 1919 they lived at peace. But in early 1920 the Turks re-grouped, and laid siege to the fortified mountainous town of Hadjin, at this time in an area allegedly under French occupation. However, no French actually appeared to help the defenders; and through a harrowing ten-month siege they fought alone with courage and tenacity, against the encircling Turks, until by November only 430 of them were left, who fled in darkness.[39] Similar stories were repeated in other Cilician towns; in each case the Armenians were forced to go into exile for a second time – an exile which was not on this occasion a march with death its object, but which was nevertheless unquestionably a permanent exile; their condition was that of more conventional refugees, since the authorities were interested in ousting them rather than killing them. In the areas of the Ottoman Empire unoccupied by Allied forces, two years after its defeat a new ruling group had seized the initiative, and was again implacably pursuing anti-minority policies. Some Armenian survivors remained in Cilicia after its Turkish Nationalist re-conquest, but they were subject to such punitive curfews that they grew weak and some died of starvation. Those that could, left within a month or so of final capitulation. In all, about 90,000 Armenians were forced to quit Cilicia for the French-mandated territories of Syria and Lebanon, after two years of a false dawn. Originally the victims of their own government's violent policies, these Armenians were five years later the victims of the self-seeking inertia of the Western powers that had put in a brief appearance in the region.

The reception of the Armenian refugees from Cilicia in the Arab world deserves a study to itself. Apart from one or two incidents, it was characterized by hospitality (according to a British consul, municipal land was given to them for settlement near Damascus); and even after the departure of the colonial power, the Armenians continued to be accepted as an integral part of the tapestry of those lands, in contrast to their experience in Turkey of death or exile either under the Young Turks or Kemalists, both of whom had forcefully adopted policies designed to achieve racial homogeneity. Even though the French enrolled Armenian fighters to suppress, with considerable savagery, the Druze revolt of 1925, there was no long-term ill-will from the host nation. By 1928 Armenians were voting for Arab-Nationalist parties.[40] It was here, and in Iraq (which had 14,000 Armenian refugees), and Greece (which had 45,000, despite her own serious refugee problems) that Armenians found the first real security that they had encountered for a decade. The great powers had given money and food, but it was left to undeveloped nations to provide the basics of security and shelter and a future for Armenians.

Within Soviet Armenia (in the view of many westerners, part of the chief 'uncivilized' power), there was a remarkable co-existence between the authorities and the British and American charities. Near East Relief signed a 23-point agreement with the Soviet government on co-operation and understanding in 1922, and continued its work: 75,000 Armenian children were on the feeding lists, and 30,000 orphans were being cared for in establishments.[41] But all the time their work was diminishing, since homes were being found for orphans, and food was being transported from Russia south across the Caucasus – although the famine in the early 1920s led inevitably to more hunger in the Caucasus. The Near East Relief orphanages became transformed into great training farms; by 1928, that at Polygon, near Leninakan, had 1,200 lads working in the fields. A professor of agriculture from Columbia University went over and gave two years of his time in supervision and advice.[42]

Near East Relief had been permitted to continue its work in the new Turkey, but by about 1923–4 it shifted its operations into Syria and Lebanon. At the same time it reduced the scale of its enterprises, and the giving of Armenian charitable relief became the task of the Armenian General Benevolent Union (which had been founded in Alexandria in 1906). This had been active since the 1918 armistice, but had lacked the international accreditation of the American and British charities. It continued in the task of maintaining orphanages, supplying medicines and to a lesser degree food, and in persuading families to adopt orphans.

In 1923 the Norwegian philanthropist Dr Fridtjof Nansen was asked by the League of Nations to examine the viability of a scheme to settle 50,000 Armenian refugees on a bare patch known as the Little Sardarabad Desert, not far from the Soviet Armenian capital of Erevan, and to secure international support and funding for the project.[43] There was a considerable amount of international goodwill for this, and a number of countries agreed to put up cash, even quite small ones, such as Albania. Britain failed to do so, even though she was only asked for £1 million, to give a moral lead more than anything else. The scheme lapsed. Churchill, at the Treasury, saw it less as a means of assisting refugees after ten years of instability and poverty, than of giving finance to the Soviet state, and as such would not countenance it.[44]

Thus the position for the Armenians in the Near East became set. Eastern Armenia was Soviet; the Western Armenians, together with those from Cilicia, were either refugees or dead. Their homeland was gone. The losses were enormous, and these, together with the international failure to give Armenians any political redress at all, gives substance to Professor M.S. Anderson's statement that 'their fate remains the greatest tragedy of the modern Middle East'.[45]

And, unless one entirely discounts the eye-witness testimony of the period 1915–18, it is impossible to deny that their death and expulsion was a deliberate act of policy. Death synchronized on such a scale, and forced marches to distant locations, are not by-products of policy; when so many soldiers, police and organized 'irregulars' are employed against a population, the actions become the direct result of the policy itself.

As if to point up the deliberateness involved in the creation of Armenian refugees in 1915, let us consider the last encounter of any substance between Armenians and the Turkish state: the dispute over the Sanjak of Alexandretta. In the course of 1938–9 Republican Turkey wrested this district from French-mandated Syria (which had no right to cede it, since authority for that lay with the League of Nations alone). By threatening to join the Axis powers, Turkey gradually persuaded France to cede Alexandretta, first turning it into an 'independent' state named Hatay, and then in September 1939 annexing it outright. It was Kemal's last diplomatic throw, and it was an old-fashioned irredentist land-grab, dressed up with specious historical, legal and ethnic arguments, used both to disguise and give lustre to his political bravado. In the process almost all the 23,000 Armenians of the Sanjak, fearing, not without some reason, Turkish rule, fled south, with what they could carry. Of those who fled, 6,000 were refugees for the second time, having been settled in the Sanjak from Cilicia by Near East Relief. Some of them were refugees from Anatolia, thereby being refugees for the third time in just over twenty years. They were re-settled in Lebanon both at Ainjar, just off the Beirut-Damascus highway, or in two refugee camps in the south, Sour and Ras ul-Ain.[46]

Their departure from the Sanjak was, insofar as any refugee departure is, voluntary; it did not result from physical compulsion, but from anxieties for the future based on past experience. At the local level, the French, in their keenness to speed up the deal, requested certain Armenian community leaders to influence their own people to leave their homes. The Armenians could probably have stayed, although their prospects would not have been very rosy; 570 Armenians do in fact live there today. Seen against the departure of those 23,000 people, the fate of Armenians in 1915 appears in sharp contrast. In the year 1915, their death or exile was central, not peripheral as in 1939, to government policy. The extensive use of the gendarmerie in their demise is sufficient to demonstrate that; and the merciless application of the measures to women, children and the old indicates that the intention was near-total racial obliteration. The half million refugees were escapees from the Ottoman Ministry of the Interior's deadly organization. The fact that, during the years 1918–1926, European statesmen lacked the will and courage to find a permanent and just place for them, and were thus to some extent responsible for their plight, should not obscure the nature of their original expulsion.

Notes: Chapter 3

1 The bibliography is extensive. See especially Great Britain, Parliamentary Papers, Miscellaneous no. 31 (1916), published commercially as *The Treatment of Armenians in the Ottoman Empire* (London, 1916); Johannes Lepsius, *Deutschland und Armenien: Sammlung diplomatischer Aktenstücke* (Potsdam, 1919); Richard G. Hovannisian, *Armenia on the Road to Independence, 1918* (Berkeley/Los Angeles, 1967); Richard G. Hovannisian, *The Republic of Armenia* (Berkeley/Los Angeles, vol. I, 1971, vol II, 1982); Christopher J. Walker *Armenia: the Survival of a Nation* (London, 1980); Permanent Peoples' Tribunal, *A Crime of Silence: the Armenian Genocide* (London, 1985); also bibliographies in works by Hovannisian and Walker.
2 Hovannisian, *Independence*, pp. 78–79; ibid, *Republic*, vol. I, pp. 126–155; James L. Barton, *Story of Near East Relief (1915–1930)* (New York, 1930), pp. 121–124; [H.L. Charge], *Memorandum on the Armenian and Assyrian Refugees at Present in Ba'quba, Mesopotamia* (Baghdad, 1919); Great Britain, Public Record Office, FO 371/3658.47290 and 68107; Walker, *Armenia*, pp. 349–351.
3 Sirarpie Der Nersessian, *The Armenians* (London, 1969); for works which put the Turkish version of events, see Ahmed Rustem Bey, *The World War and the Turco-Armenian Question*, (Berne, 1918); Stanford J. Shaw and Ezel Kural Shaw, *History of the Ottoman Empire and Modern Turkey*, (Cambridge, 1977); Kamuran Gurun, *The Armenian File: the Myth of Innocence Exposed*, (London, 1985).
4 A.O. Sarkissian, *History of the Armenian Question to 1885* (Urbana, Ill., 1938), p. 43; Walker, *Armenia*, pp. 85–89.
5 Walker, *Armenia*, pp. 121–173.
6 Robert Mirak, 'Armenians', in Stephen Thernstrom, ed., *Harvard Encyclopedia of American Ethnic Groups* (Cambridge, Mass., 1981).
7 Jacob Landau, *Panturkism in Turkey: a Study of Irredentism* (London, 1981); Walker, *Armenia*, pp. 189–191.
8 George Young, *Constantinople*, (London, 1926), p. 269 ; Y.T. Kurat, 'How Turkey Drifted into World War I', in K. Bourne and D.C. Watt, ed., *Studies in International History* (London, 1967), p. 300; A.J. Toynbee, *Turkey: a Past and a Future* (London, 1917), pp. 28-9.
9 Henry Morgenthau, *Secrets of the Bosphorus*, (London, 1918), pp. 198–199 and see quotation by E. Sommer in Tessa Hofmann, 'German Eyewitness Reports of the Genocide of the Armenians, 1915–16' in Permanent Peoples' Tribunal, *A Crime of Silence*, p. 71.
10 Great Britain, Miscellaneous no. 31 (1916), pp. 640–650.
11 Hofmann, 'German Eyewitness Reports', PPT, *A Crime of Silence*, p. 74.
12 Lepsius, *Deutschland und Armenien*, p. 87; Aram Andonian, *Documents officiels concernant les massacres arméniens* (Paris, 1920); Kamuran Gurun, *The Armenian File*, (London, 1985), pp. 204–214.
13 Public Record Office, FO 371/2781.264888, Arabian Report, N.S. no XIII, December 27, 1916 (Night), Appendix B, p. 7.
14 Elise Hagopian Taft, *Rebirth* (Plandome, NY, 1981), p. 57.
15 Hofmann, 'German Eyewitness Reports', PPT, *A Crime of Silence*, p. 83; Djemal Pasha, *Memories of a Turkish Statesman, 1913–1919*, (London, 1922), p. 280; Justin McCarthy, *Muslims and Minorities*, (New York, 1983).
16 Lepsius, *Deutschland und Armenien*, p. 277, quoted in Walker, *Armenia*, p. 235.
17 Eliot Grinnell Mears, *Modern Turkey: a Politico-Economic Interpretation 1908–1923* (New York, 1924), p. 519.
18 See e.g. Great Britain, Miscellaneous no. 31 (1916), p. 488.
19 W.E.D. Allen and Paul Muratoff, *Caucasian Battlefields* (Cambridge 1953), pp. 363, 383.

20   See for instance the political advertisements placed in the *New York Times* and *Washington Post* of 18 May 1985.
21   *Ararat* (London), vol. II, no. 21 (March 1915), p. 335.
22   ibid., vol. III, no. 30 (December 1915), pp. 258, 261.
23   ibid., vol. III, no. 34 (April 1916), p. 437.
24   ibid., vol. IV, no. 37 (July 1916), pp. 9-11.
25   ibid., vol. V, no. 50 (August 1917), p. 78.
26   ibid., Vol. VI, no. 67 (October 1919), p. 513.
27   ibid., vol. IV, no. 42 (December 1917), p. 265.
28   Barton, *Near East Relief*, p. 177n.
29   *Ararat*, passim, esp. vol. V, no. 54 (December 1917), pp. 275-6, and vol. VI, no. 62 (December 1918), pp. 249-51.
30   Barton, *Near East Relief*, pp. 4-5.
31   ibid., pp. 9, 47, 109.
32   Bedros Norehad, *The Armenian General Benevolent Union*, (New York, 1966), p. 25.
33   Barton, *Near East Relief*, p. 60.
34   *Ararat*, vol. VI, no. 62 (December 1918), p. 219.
35   ibid., p. 250.
36   ibid., vol. V, no. 58 (May 1918), p. 430.
37   [H.L. Charge], *Memorandum on the Armenian and Assyrian Refugees*, p. 34.
38   Walker, *Armenia*, pp. 291–292.
39   ibid., pp. 297–299.
40   ibid., pp. 363–365.
41   Barton, *Near East Relief*, pp. 132–136.
42   ibid., p. 245.
43   Fridtjof Nansen, *Armenia and the Near East*, (London, 1928), p. 5.
44   Walker, *Armenia*, pp. 350–351.
45   M.S. Anderson, *The Eastern Question, 1774–1923* (London, 1966), p. 397.
46   Peter Mansfield, *The Arabs* (2nd edn, Harmondsworth, 1985), pp. 204–205; Christopher J. Walker, 'Lessons of Turkey's Subtle Land-grab', *The Times*, 5 September 1974, p. 14.

4 Weimar Germany and the *Ostjuden*, 1918–1923: acceptance or expulsion?

JOHN P. FOX

The experiences and treatment of the *Ostjuden* in the Weimar Republic in the years immediately following Germany's defeat in November 1918,[1] i.e. of Jews who themselves came directly from the lands east of Germany or who were descendants of earlier East European Jewish refugees and immigrants,[2] is a practical example of one of the most important aspects of any refugee question: the initial reception and subsequent treatment accorded to refugees or immigrants by the receiving society. But the nature of that reception and long-term treatment in the host society will always be determined by the first question asked of the newcomers: are they to be a permanent addition to that host population, or are they simply 'travelling through' on their way to more permanent domicile elsewhere? The answers to these questions defines the status of the newcomers with regard to that nation's immigration, nationality, and aliens' laws, whether as itinerant refugees or would-be permanently domiciled immigrants. Yet once their initial status has been defined or assumed other questions and issues arise, the outcome of which determines whether permission to remain permanently or only for a short while is forthcoming from the relevant authorities. An associated issue is whether such permission is likely to be rescinded at any time.

Itinerant refugees, i.e. those simply 'passing through', generally received official support and private philanthropic aid in their efforts to travel to other countries. Visa, passport, and even internal travel and accommodation problems were eased in order to speed the newcomers on their way, especially if at the same time some financial profit was to be made out of such 'humanitarian' activity as was the case with the shipping firms who carried the bulk of the post-1881 Russian Jewish refugees to the United States of America.[3] But if such 'refugees' intended or indeed were forced to become permanent 'immigrants', then a whole host of difficult and sometimes intractable legal, political, economic, and sociological questions presented themselves. For example, how does such a development relate to government policy on immigration generally and the granting of citizenship? Or would their particular racial or religious characteristics (assuming their existence) be resented by the native population and cause or exacerbate social tensions in key areas such as employment, housing, education, and religious activity? And, assuming the presence already within that society of others belonging to similar ethnic or religious groups, how are the newcomers to be treated by their own brethren? Finally, how are the newcomers to be treated if government officials begin to have second thoughts about the wisdom of having accepted them in the first place, if their presence is vehemently objected to by politically active elements of the native population, and if they are even rejected or resented by host members of their own racial or religious group?

Those Jews of Weimar Germany classified as *Ostjuden* had all these and other problems to contend with. Their presence in Weimar Germany was constantly surrounded by controversy, but in a sense they were unwilling or unwitting victims of circumstances (however they or their forbears had come to Germany) since post-1918 attitudes towards them were influenced as well by the history of the *Ostjudenfrage* in Imperial Germany. But while on occasions the focus of attention may have been on the *Ostjuden*, the real issue nevertheless was always the so-called 'Jewish Question' of modern times, particularly in central and eastern Europe.[4] As Franz Rosenzweig, the German-Jewish philosopher, wrote in 1916 from Poland, the German anxiety about Eastern Jews did not concern the *Ostjuden* as such but only the *Ostjuden* as potential *Westjuden*, i.e. if ever they became assimilated to German culture. There was not, he concluded, an Eastern Jewish question (*Ostjudenfrage*) but only a Jewish question (*Judenfrage*).[5]

Whilst Jew and Gentile were agreed that the central issue of the *Judenfrage* was the role and identity of the Jews in modern European society, the verbal and physical violence associated with this issue reflected the unceasing conflict as to the means and ends of resolving something which is perhaps essentially unresolvable. The central issue was whether Gentile-Christian society accepted or rejected the Jews as social, economic, or political equals with or without the latter pursuing a specific Jewish cultural or political identity and autonomy.[6] Likewise for the Jews, especially in the politically advanced nation states of Germany and western Europe (unlike in eastern Europe), it was a question of carefully defining and relating concepts such as emancipation and assimilation to the whole question of what it meant to be a Jew in modern post-Enlightenment European society.[7] But all practical questions associated with such issues were often overshadowed by the Christians' own emotional response to the 'Jewish question' and to the individual Jew because of received myths about the Jews[8] and deeply-held religious feelings, instincts, and indeed antagonisms.[9]

The *Judenfrage*, and therefore the *Ostjudenfrage* in all its manifestations, proved to be as much a problem for Germany's democrats of the Weimar era as it had been for the autocrats of the pre-1918 period.[10] This was because the *Ostjuden* of Russia, Poland, Galicia, Bukovina, and Romania before and after Imperial Germany's military defeat in November 1918, saw Germany as the nearest and most convenient transit land on the way to a new life in the United States of America – or as the final object of refuge from the anti-Jewish persecutions and pogroms in eastern Europe at the time. But neither the German authorities or indeed the German-Jewish community approved of either course of action. The practice of 'transit through' entailed the risk that many refugees might decide to 'jump train' and remain in hiding in Germany with their co-religionists, while any philanthropic aid to these refugees cost the German authorities and Jewish aid societies a great deal of money. As to Germany becoming the final place of refuge for the *Ostjuden*, this idea was anathema to the German authorities who had no wish to see the German population increased in this manner with such alien stock. Nor was the German-Jewish community inclined to favour such a development since they feared that a sizeable increase in the number of *Ostjuden* in Germany would have a detrimental effect upon their own position and strivings for assimilation and acceptance in German-Gentile society while at the same time encouraging active and latent anti-Semitism within Germany generally.

The subject of Germany's dealings with the *Ostjudenfrage* as a refugee or immigrant problem is, consequently, a highly complex one but for the purposes of analysis it can be reduced to a few essentials whose practical application in the early years of the Weimar Republic was necessarily influenced by previous experiences and practices. Five considerations at least dominated the practicalities of the subject. Firstly, the size of the Jewish population in eastern Europe; secondly, the numbers of those who might seek passage through Germany or who might wish to remain within her borders; thirdly, the legal and administrative measures that could be used to control the entry of such immigrants; fourthly, the legal and administrative measures at hand to expel those immigrants whose presence was no longer desired or even required; and fifthly, and perhaps most significant of all, the perception of the special nature and characteristics of the *Ostjuden*, by German Gentile and Jew alike.

Before 1914 the Jewish population of eastern Europe was anything between 7 and 8 million souls.[11] Yet because of the pogroms in Imperial Russia which began upon the assassination of Tsar Alexander II in March 1881, by 1914 some two and a half million Russian Jews alone had emigrated westwards, with perhaps half a million others from Austro-Hungary and Romania.[12] From this one can understand why the anti-Jewish climate and actions of eastern Europe before and after 1914–18 caused such dismay and nervousness in Germany where the perennial fear was that the country would be overrun by hordes of east European Jews. Yet by 1910 only 70,000 of Germany's total Jewish population of 615,000 were considered to have originated from the east. When one considers that the population of the German Reich was then estimated to be 65 million,[13] it means that on the eve of war in 1914 the *Ostjuden* constituted some 11.5% of the German-Jewish population but only 0.1% of the Reich's total population. Two points of significance may be drawn from these figures. The first and most obvious concerns the success of the German authorities in limiting the number of *Ostjuden* resident in Germany at any one time, either through immigration controls or expulsions, especially in view of the potential flood from the east that always threatened. The second and perhaps most important point is why this miniscule minority of *Ostjuden* within Germany itself but also as an emotional or intellectual concept should have caused the furore it did.

While the extent of Germany's eastern borders always made it difficult to control illegal entry, immigration policy as such was a State rather than a Reich prerogative so that it was difficult to organise a unified programme to restrict the entry of *Ostjuden*. Nevertheless, the States most concerned with east European Jewish immigration, Prussia and Saxony, applied to the full the various administrative procedures open to them to restrict the number of resident *Ostjuden*, e.g. the grant of residence permits whose expiry necessarily involved the departure of the individual in question. East European Jewish immigration or residence was also discouraged by the manner in which the various States exercised their power over that dream of all refugees and immigrants, naturalisation procedure. This was often exercised in a discriminatory fashion against the *Ostjuden*, so that when (as was most often the case), naturalisation was denied to them they were immediately confirmed in their status as aliens and subject therefore to arbitrary administrative decrees against which they had little legal recourse. That left them completely defenceless against the final weapon of the States system, the policy of expulsion.[14] Prussia was notorious in this respect and as early as 1881–82 began expelling Russian Jews from Berlin. During the following twenty-five years at least 14,000 *Ostjuden* were expelled by the Prussian authorities.[15] Saxony refined this policy of making Germany an inhospitable place for the *Ostjuden* by becoming in 1892 the first and only German State to deny Jews the right of kosher slaughtering by ordering that all animals had first to be stunned.[16]

As it is possible to trace a degree of continuity from Imperial to Weimar administrative practices and policies concerning the immigration of *Ostjuden* into Germany and the handling of those already resident in the country, so too one can see lines of continuity on the vexed question as to why these people caused so much emotion and vehemence after 1918 as before. The reason may be summed up in one simple statement: not only were they Jewish but they were *different*. Heinrich von Treitschke, Professor of History at the University of Berlin had already labelled the *Ostjuden* in 1879 as 'a horde of ambitious, pants-selling Jews whose children and grandchildren were the future controllers of Germany's press and stock exchange'.[17] Yet even Germany's own emancipated and sophisticated Jewish community regarded the *Ostjuden* with something approaching distaste since the latter conjured up the alien picture of the allegedly 'typical' east European ghetto Jew: physically filthy, medieval, unemancipated, and alien in appearance, manner, language, culture, while even their religious forms such as Hasidism were frowned upon by the more restrained western Jews.[18] The young Adolf Hitler in pre-1914 Vienna was not the only one, therefore, to remark upon the 'apparition' that was the *Ostjuden* in his caftan and side-locks as being something entirely different and strange from normal Western society and indeed even posing a threat to it.[19] But while many German Jews helped their less fortunate brethren from the east by facilitating their passage through Germany to the United States of America,[20] altruism was not always the prime motive at work. It was felt that if the *Ostjuden* were allowed to remain in Germany and increase in numbers, what with all their marked differences from German Gentile and Jew alike, the result would be to slow down the pace of German Jewry's own hard fight for assimilation at best and some form of acceptance at worst since *Ostjuden* could often be seen recreating within Germany, especially in large cities such as Berlin, patterns of ghetto life from the past which the emancipated German Jew was trying to leave behind or even deny.[21]

Official German attitudes and policy towards the entry, presence, and status within Germany of east European Jews underwent significant changes during the period of the Great War of 1914–1918,[22] changes which were eventually to confront Weimar policy makers with a German and an east European 'Jewish question' in a highly accentuated form which Adolf Hitler set about resolving in his unique fashion. In part this was due to the *Ostjudenfrage* itself, which changed during the period together with Polish, Russian, Baltic, and Balkan nationalist aspirations, as these emerged during the war to challenge old imperial suzerainties. The sheer size of the east European Jewish population meant that account now had to be taken of the political significance of the Jews as a distinct ethnic national minority. The German authorities at first ignored this by subordinating the national Jewish question to their *Polenpolitik* in a decree of November 1916 which merely recognised Polish Jews as a religious community but not as an autonomous national entity.[23] Any other policy would, of course, have had untold consequences for the further development of the Jewish question within Germany itself since any official recognition of Jewish national autonomy or identity in the east would have necessitated fundamental and far-reaching changes of attitude and policy within the Reich. Nevertheless, official denial of this aspect of the wider *Ostjudenfrage* would not prevent its *de facto* existence from being brought home to German Gentile and Jew alike in other ways.

Not surprisingly, the wartime period was marked by incessant calls from German nationalist organisations and others for the eastern frontiers of Germany to be completely closed against what they felt was an imminent invasion of Germany by the *Ostjuden* whom Georg Fritz described as 'not only millions of poor, physically and morally stunted people but . . . racially foreign Judaised mongols'.[24] His fear, shared by many others, was that an influx of such people would result in the degeneration of the German race, while others, given the revolutionary and socialist activities of many prominent *Ostjuden* – Rosa Luxemburg, a Spartacist leader, imprisoned in Berlin during part of the war and eventually murdered on 15 January 1919, hailed from Zamość in Poland – feared that Germany would be subverted by their revolutionary ideas and movements. As it was, the cause of *Judentum* in Germany generally, let alone that of the *Ostjuden*, would be severely hampered by the 'Red Republic' in Munich in the early months of 1919 because of the clear identification by then of Jewry with Bolshevism.[25]

As it was, Georg Fritz warned Germany's Jews to support calls for border closures against the *Ostjuden* since any substantial increase of their numbers in Germany was bound to open up the Jewish question again and gravely threaten German Jewry whose own emancipation could no longer be guaranteed. In fact, the sympathy extended to the *Ostjuden* by many German Jews, especially to those brought to Germany from the east for war work,[26] was offset by the ambiguity of others who took only too well the points made by Georg Fritz. But while many German Jews privately agreed with nationalist calls for a limitation on the numbers of *Ostjuden* allowed to enter Germany, they were concerned nevertheless at the prospect of any special legislation designed to close the borders specifically against the *Ostjuden* since the word 'Jew' would have to be included in such a legal measure. Their fear was that it would be but a short sharp step from this towards the introduction of directly anti-Jewish legislation within Germany itself. Finally, though, the Prussian government yielded to consistent anti-Semitic pressure and on 23 April 1918 issued order 11.Z.788 prohibiting the entry of Jewish workers from Poland into Germany. While this purely anti-Jewish aliens' order was justified on the grounds that it would prevent typhus from being brought into Germany by the *Ostjuden*, the basic driving force behind the decree was the growing anti-Semitic sentiment which had been steadily building up throughout the final years of the war.[27]

While this order was to remain in legal effect until well after Germany's defeat in November 1918,[28] it appeared that in the summer of 1918 German officialdom, especially the dominant military authorities,[29] even began to extend the policy of 'no more eastern Jews wanted in Germany' to the occupied eastern territories where a spate of regulations was issued prohibiting the entry of Russian Jews fleeing from the chaos and revolution that was post-Tsarist Russia.[30] These particular regulations were probably seen as Germany's first line of defence against the threatening tide of would-be *Ostjuden* refugees and immigrants into Germany because of the unparalleled wave of anti-Jewish pogroms which swept through Galicia, Poland, Hungary, Slovakia, Romania, West Russia, and the Ukraine in the second half of 1918.[31] That situation, and Germany's immigration regulations and procedures, were to determine the fate if not the lives of thousands of *Ostjuden* in subsequent months and years.

As with so many other aspects of public and private life in Germany after the defeat and revolution of November 1918, a mixture of old and new attitudes[32] came to affect German policy towards the some 160,000 *Ostjuden* present in Germany at the war's end[33] as well as towards the *Ostjudenfrage* generally. With Germany by then ostensibly a 'revolutionary Socialist Republic', the new German leaders were only too well aware of what was expected of them by Britain and America so far as the 'democratisation' and 'humanisation' of German society was concerned. But in the mood of extreme bitterness about defeat in 1918 and the Treaty of Versailles in 1919 which gripped so many Germans, the Jews were vilified for having caused both and so became the object of a vicious anti-Jewish campaign which swept throughout Germany.[34] Any tendency towards a more positive or 'democratic' policy towards the Jews in the new Republic had therefore to be tempered by the political and electoral realities of anti-Semitic sentiments within Germany. But when considering external policy towards the *Ostjuden* as potential immigrants or refugees and internal policy towards the alien *Ostjuden* already resident in Germany, German policy makers were also forced to take into account the realities of world Jewry as a new political force in the twentieth century, particularly after the Balfour Declaration on Palestine on 2 November 1917. So far did the Weimar authorities acknowledge this stage of affairs that the Foreign Ministry, the *Auswärtiges Amt*, even gave financial support to a Jewish publishing firm in Berne, Switzerland, as a means of influencing Jewish world opinion.[35] Furthermore, as part of its fight against French aims to crush Germany after 1918,[36] the Weimar Republic cultivated neutral opinion, and the one nation in which great hopes were placed, the United States of America, just happened to contain the largest proportion of world Jewry outside Europe.

Beyond these political imponderables affecting German policy towards the *Ostjuden* at the outset of the Weimar Republic, there was the technical question of the legal means at hand to deal with the whole question of immigration and citizenship. At first sight it appeared as though matters were perfectly clear, since Articles 6 and 12 of the Weimar Constitution gave exclusive legislative power over questions of citizenship, immigration, and emigration to the Reich government, specifically excluding any *Land* (State) legislation on such matters. It was also stipulated that citizenship of the Reich and in the *Länder* was acquired or removed according to the provisions of the Reich law, and that any limitations on the right of *Germans* to travel and reside could only be established by Reich law (Article 111). Nevertheless, it was also possible that the execution of Reich laws could belong to the *Land* authorities (Article 77), and this, together with the uncertain political relationship existing between Berlin and some *Land* governments, meant that the principal powers reserved to the *Land* governments, the administration of the courts and the maintenance of law and order, could often be exercised by them in a discretionary fashion. This meant that on some issues one *Land* government might behave differently from another *Land* regime, so that often there was no uniform Reich policy on a particular issue. As it was, under Article 7 of the Constitution and subsequent regulations it was possible for the *Land* authorities to exercise their discretionary right to expel all immigrants whose entry papers were irregular or even non-existent.[37]

The vicissitudes of Weimar policy on the *Ostjudenfrage*, both at Reich and regional level, nevertheless often concerned issues which went beyond the specific question of official handling of the alien *Ostjuden* resident in Germany and attitudes towards the *Ostjudenfrage* in eastern Europe. To begin with, though, it appeared that after November 1918 Germany policy was inclined to be more flexible and perhaps liberal on the fate of the many thousands of alien *Ostjuden* brought in from the east to work in Germany's war industries and who lost their jobs at the war's end. On 4 December 1918, for example, the Office for Economic Demobilisation (*Reichsamt für wirtschaftliche Demobilmachung*) urged employers not to dispense immediately with their east European workers because transport difficulties made repatriation to the east currently impossible, while it was also suggested that alien Jews should have the right to return by the last transport.[38] The latter clause was a tacit admission by the German authorities that these Jews no longer had a home to go to outside Germany because of the anti-Jewish hostility and pogroms then sweeping throughout eastern Europe. Furthermore, as early as December 1918 Professor Sobernheim, the *Auswärtiges Amt* official responsible for Jewish affairs, began discussions with other Ministries with a view to obtaining the annulment of the frontier orders of April 1918. His purpose was to remove from any administrative order on immigration any specific reference to Jews, while in an attempt to mollify German bureaucratic attitudes he suggested that any annulment agreed to could be accompanied by orders specifying a health quarantine period for any workers intending to cross Germany's eastern frontiers. In March 1919, however, he was informed by the Prussian Ministry of the Interior that his proposals were, in effect, superfluous since the order of 23 April 1918 was only intended for the duration of the war and had in any case been overtaken by administrative orders of January 1919 extending the passport regulations of 24 June 1916 and which effectively closed Germany's eastern frontiers to all comers.[39]

This reply failed to answer Professor Sobernheim's basic point that it was the *Ostjuden* would-be immigrants or refugees into Germany who were being discriminated against. The Ministry of the Interior argued, however, that the new regulations were of general application. Even so, it was also intended to prevent any more *Ostjuden* from entering Germany. But this still left the problem of what to do about the many thousands of alien *Ostjuden* within Germany, both inducted war workers and war refugees who had fled from impossible situations in the east. Many of the latter had in fact entered the country illegally by being smuggled over the border. German officialdom and certain sections of German public opinion were united, however, in wishing to see all these people removed from German territory. While it seemed that the German authorities differentiated on principle between the pre-war aliens and those who had entered Germany one way or another during the war, their intention was that the latter should eventually leave the country – if need be under compulsion.[40] In fact, it was their sporadic expulsion from many German cities from 1919 to 1923 which dominated the subject of the *Ostjuden* in Germany just after the Great War. Yet at the same time as German officials began attempting to reduce the country's foreign Jewish element in this manner,[41] German Jews from the German territories of Upper Silesia, West Prussia, and

Danzig were making representations in the spring of 1919 to Germany and the neutral countries about their strong desire to remain within Germany's jurisdiction. They feared that the territories in question were to be transferred to Poland as a result of that country's pressure on France during the Versailles negotiations. Their fears became even more marked when it transpired that these territories were to be subject to plebiscites to decide their ultimate fate.[42]

While the expulsion of the *Ostjuden* from Germany which began early in 1919 was undoubtedly popular with conservative and anti-Semitic circles, the German government and local officials soon became aware that the policy involved so many legal, political, and social or moral questions that the matter went beyond being an internal German concern alone but was likely to affect Germany's standing in the world at large at a time when she most needed to avoid increasing the odium felt against her. Expulsion orders against alien *Ostjuden* were issued in Upper Silesia as early as February 1919, followed shortly afterwards by preparations for similar measures in Berlin. But the brutal fashion in which these orders were executed led Professor Sobernheim and the Director of the *Nachrichten Abteilung* in the *Auswärtiges Amt*, Victor Naumann, to argue that Germany risked losing the sympathy of influential English and American Jews who might otherwise persuade their governments of Germany's arguments for the retention of what were still, for the moment, Germany's eastern territories. To an extent foreign policy considerations thus came to influence the execution of domestic policy at different times, although the key word here is 'execution' rather than policy, for in his letter of 9 April 1919 to the Reich Ministry of the Interior proposing an inter-Ministerial meeting on the matter, Victor Naumann was at pains to stress that the policy itself was not in question. As he put it, 'a way had to be found which maintained the interests of the State and which avoided harmful repercussions abroad'.[43]

As in all cases where there was a basic conflict of interests between the State that was the 'host society' and the refugees or immigrants then resident within it, the former inevitably came to dominate. Nevertheless, the meeting held on 10 April 1919 in Berlin between various Ministry, police, and Jewish authorities, as well as subsequent developments, helped to clarify a number of the principles then involved in the treatment of alien *Ostjuden* in Germany. For their part the German authorities made it absolutely clear that because of Germany's domestic employment, housing, food, and political situation there could be no departure from the policy of expelling all aliens from Germany, whether they were Jewish or not. They denied, therefore, Jewish accusations that this policy and that of border closures was specifically directed against the *Ostjuden* as yet another element of German anti-Semitism. (Ethnic Germans from non-German territories were also expelled.) But while the Jewish representatives at this meeting failed, as they were bound to, in their efforts to get the policy of expulsions cancelled altogether, nevertheless and quite significantly their arguments and those of Professor Sobernheim for a more humane execution of this policy were taken into account. For the immediate future, then, it was agreed that guide-lines discussed in the *Auswärtiges Amt* on 3 April to this effect should be explored further in a special commission.[44]

There was nothing altruistic in German concessions on this point. On the contrary, as was made clear at this meeting and later, Germany had no other choice at the time but to take world opinion into account in the execution of this part of its domestic policies.[45] Indeed, from this and other sources one senses the frustration of German officials that Germany's position in European and world affairs at the time was such as to prevent them from pursuing the ideal policy of the mass expulsion of all *Ostjuden* from Germany and territories such as Upper Silesia.[46]

Yet while the policy of expulsions proceeded in a fashion,[47] it did appear that the regulations issued on 1 November 1919 by Wolfgang Heine, Prussian Minister of the Interior, went some way towards improving the general climate, it confirmed the policy of expulsions as such, but laid down guide-lines for its more humane execution. This led many Jewish organisations to believe – or hope – that not all *Ostjuden* would necessarily be expelled. These regulations permitted the expulsion of the *Ostjuden* only in cases in which they broke the law or remained perpetually unemployed (and therefore a 'burden' on society). Those against whom expulsion proceedings were begun could be defended by the Workers' Welfare Association of the Jewish Organisations in Germany (*Arbeiterfürsorgeamt der jüdischen Organisationen Deutschlands*), and if their 'offence' was indeed unemployment that organisation was to be given an opportunity to find them work. The number of foreign workers in any one factory was to be limited to ten, while all those who had been arrested or prepared for expulsion were to be released in accordance with the new regulations.[48]

Neither the German authorities nor the Jewish organisations felt that the regulations of November 1919 would really resolve anything since the whole question of the alien *Ostjuden* in Germany was a cul-de-sac from which there was no easy exit for anybody. The pressures from German public opinion even led Minister Heine to declare in the Prussian *Landtag* on 16 December 1919 that he was considering expelling all 'undesirable' *Ostjuden* from the cities and interning them in special concentration camps. On the other hand, he indicated publicly how far international circumstances were influencing German policy since he disclaimed any intention to expel en masse the *Ostjuden* and so deliver them for execution by the Polish and Russian swords.[49] In one respect, of course, this was an admission that Germany was now burdened with an alien *Ostjudenfrage* which it could only resolve in a marginal way. As such, this was a recipe for internal political trouble since the anti-Semitic and nationalist groups constantly focussed on the *Ostjuden* as epitomising the 'Jewish danger' to Germany.

In fact, the anti-alien sentiment, whether directed against alien Jew or Gentile, was not confined to political extremists since from 1920 onwards both Reich and *Land* authorities were determined to remove the *Ostjuden* (among others) from German soil.[50] But while Minister Heine felt impelled to defend at length his order of 1 November 1919 against the charge that he was being too 'soft' on the *Ostjuden*,[51] General von Seeckt signalled the beginning of the German reaction against the *Ostjuden* in the changed political circumstances of 1920 when Germany, as a sovereign State, at least knew where she stood in world and European affairs after the coming into effect of the Treaty of Versailles in January 1920. On 16 March 1920 he demanded that the Prussian government intern all *Ostjuden* found in Berlin, while eleven days later some 250 *Ostjuden* were actually placed in a military camp at Wuensdorf near Zossen. Other expulsions were planned or effected in Upper Silesia during 1920, and in Munich, Düsseldorf and other cities, until November 1923. The attack on the

Ostjuden as an alien minority reached its climax when a pogrom shook the Berlin ghetto.[52]

It was, however, easier to recognise the problem of alien *Ostjuden* in Germany than to deal with it effectively. Essentially, five solutions or problems were recognised. As before 1914, so after 1918 direct encouragement was given to those *Ostjuden* in Germany who wished to emigrate to America.[53] Secondly, the German authorities faced the real problem of what to do about the original nationality of the *Ostjuden* in the light of border and sovereignty changes in the east when the new nation States declined to accept or recognise claims to *their* nationality by alien *Ostjuden* in Germany. Thirdly, there was the complication that even though Germany might decide to expel the *Ostjuden* anyway, the practical implementation of this policy might be difficult or impossible if, for example, Poland refused to accept those concerned. Another solution discussed at great length and partially implemented was the incarceration of the *Ostjuden* in special internment camps or, as the term was actually used at the time, *Konzentrationslager*.[54] Fifthly, and as the Prussian Minister of the Interior Carl Severing made clear in an order of 1 June 1920, one way of dealing with the *Ostjuden* problem within Germany was to ensure the maintenance of strict border controls against the *Ostjuden* as well as against other aliens wishing to enter Germany.[55] Nevertheless, the general climate of official opinion, let alone that of the racist element in Germany, could be gauged by the directive which came from the Reich Ministry of the Interior on 31 May 1920 in which it was emphasised that from then onwards no special treatment or consideration should be given to the *Ostjuden* in Germany. This was yet another attack on Heine's regulations of 1 November 1919, while interestingly enough emphasis was also placed on the fact that the immigration of the *Ostjuden* into Germany was unwelcome from a social point of view since these people 'originated from a less than equivalent culture'.[56] Furthermore, an official policy of the internment of the *Ostjuden* in special camps foreshadowed in Ministry of the Interior orders of 1 June and 17 November 1920 was activated by Carl Severing in an instruction dated 12 January 1921[57] and announced by him in the Prussian *Landtag* on 23 January.[58] Camps at Stagard and Cottbus were employed for this purpose, while the internment order itself was not annulled until 14 December 1923.[59]

Official German attitudes were, however, not the only burdens which the *Ostjuden* had to suffer in the Weimar Republic. As in Imperial Germany, so too in Weimar Germany they were confronted by degrees of friendship, tolerance, ambiguity, and indeed hostility from the native German-Jewish population. It was well known that German Jews preferred to be served by Gentile servants and that the *Ostjuden* themselves were more comfortable as domestic servants in a German Gentile household. It was also significant that many German-Jewish parents considered that marriage by one of their sons or daughters to an *Ostjuden* was something worse than marriage outside the Jewish faith. Local Jewish community services often discriminated against the *Ostjuden* in favour of German Jews, while it was the question of possible voting rights for the *Ostjuden* in community elections which gave most trouble to the German-Jewish community as a whole. Some communities, such as that in Chemnitz, were adamant that no voting rights would be given to the *Ostjuden*.[60] When protests about such actions reached it, the Prussian State government banned them so far as its authority was able to reach in such matters, except that in general the Prussian authorities showed great reluctance to interfere in Jewish internal affairs. In some areas of Germany it was common to require alien Jews to wait ten years before being granted legal membership of the community. It has even been said of some German towns that when *Ostjuden* sat in unoccupied pews of the local synagogue they were handed cards which read, 'if you do not leave the synagogue *immediately*, you will be charged with trespassing and *disturbing holy services*'.[61]

Despite this situation and the fact that discrimination and oppression was the hallmark of most German-Gentile attitudes towards them, for most *Ostjuden* Germany was now their final home. Many were too poor to consider moving elsewhere and had no other choice but to 'stick it out'. In doing so they too became part of the wider German-Jewish problem throughout the life of the Weimar Republic, and as such also suffered during 1923, which saw a rash of anti-Jewish actions throughout Germany in Beuthen, Königsberg, Nuremberg, Saxony, and elsewhere. A climax of sorts to these actions was to be seen in Berlin between 4 and 8 November 1923.[62] But they also continued to suffer specifically as alien *Ostjuden* since in the autumn of 1923 the Bavarian authorities made it clear that they intended expelling a number of them from the Munich area. This led to a flurry of diplomatic activity between Berlin and Munich, and even between Berlin and the Polish authorities in Warsaw, since these events became embroiled in the wider 'tit for tat' actions of Germany and Poland in periodically expelling each other's citizens. But so notorious was this particular case of the *Ostjuden* in Munich that the British Foreign Office in London was made aware of the problem and urged by Jewish organisations there to take some action.[63]

In the short run, any action taken was relatively mild compared to the fate of the alien *Ostjuden* within and without Germany under Nazi rule. In this sense, one could almost say that German treatment of the *Ostjuden* in Imperial and Weimar Germany, particularly the latter, was humane and decent, except that this is to compare something which was full of shortcomings anyway with what was really to be the unthinkable. But if the German treatment of the *Ostjuden* up to 1923 had little to commend it totally, this was hardly surprising given the fact not so much of the German as of the human condition and the inhuman tendencies which seem inevitably to come to the fore when it is a case of 'the strangers in our midst'. So often, nationalist and racialist feelings of hostility towards the foreigners seem to push aside feelings of humanitarianism. While this is bad enough, in a sense such feelings may be tolerated if the political conditions of a society are such as to prevent or limit their extreme application. Looked at from this point of view, those *Ostjuden* who found themselves in Germany up to 1923 could count themselves rather lucky. But when the nature and forms of German political society changed after

30 January 1933, it was not simply the *Ostjuden* who were to suffer from Adolf Hitler's efforts to place no limit on the forces of evil.

Notes: Chapter 4

1 The standard work on the *Ostjuden* in Germany still seems to be that by S. Adler-Rudel, *Ostjuden in Deutschland 1880–1940* (Tübingen 1959). See also, Jack L Wertheimer, *German Policy and Jewish Politics: the Absorption of East European Jews in Germany (1868–1914)*, Unpublished Ph.D. Dissertation, Columbia University, 1978; idem, 'The Unwanted Element'. East European Jews in Imperial Germany', *Leo Baeck Institute Year Book*, XXVI (1981), 23–46 (*LBYB*); Steven E Aschheim, *Brothers and Strangers, the East European Jew in German and German Jewish Consciousness 1800–1923* (University of Wisconsin Press 1982); idem., 'Eastern Jews, German Jews and Germany's *Ostpolitik* in the First World War', *LBYB*, XXVIII (1983), 351–365.

2 It has been suggested that 'when writers used the term *Ostjuden* before the outbreak of the War, they referred to Jews still in the East, but not to immigrants in Germany', Wertheimer, 'The Unwanted Element', op. cit., 24, n.3. For the purposes of this paper the term is used to describe both the eastern European Jews as an entity in eastern Europe and those of such lineage in Germany itself. See also Raymond Pearson, *National Minorities in Eastern Europe 1848–1945* (London 1983).

3 Wertheimer, 'The Unwanted Element', op. cit., 28.

4 For the 'Jewish question' in the uncertain, fiercely nationalistic and anti-Semitic climate that dominated the successor States of 1918 and 1919, see Ezra Mendelsohn, *The Jews of East Central Europe Between the World Wars* (Indiana University Press 1983).

5 Zosa Szajkowski, 'The Struggle for Yiddish During World War I', *LBYB*, IX, 1964, 131–158, esp. p. 147; Wertheimer, 'The Unwanted Element', op. cit., 36; Cecil Roth, Geoffrey Wigoder (editors), *The New Standard Jewish Encyclopedia* (Jerusalem 1975), 1639.

6 For the German side to this question see Hermann Greive, *Geschichte des modernen Antisemitismus in Deutschland* (Darmstadt 1983); Werner Jochmann, 'Struktur und Funktion des deutschen Antisemitismus', pp. 389–477 in: Werner E Mosse, Arnold Paucker (eds), *Juden im Wilhelminischen Deutschland 1890–1914* (Tübingen 1976); idem, 'Struktur und Funktion des deutschen Antisemitismus 1878–1914', pp. 99–142 in: Herbert A Strauss, Nobert Kampe (eds), *Antisemitismus. Von der Judenfeindschaft zum Holocaust* (Frankfurt/Main 1985); Wanda Kampfmann, *Deutsche und Juden. Die Geschichte der Juden in Deutschland vom Mittelalter bis zum Beginn des Ersten Weltkrieges* (Frankfurt am Main 1979); Richard S Levy, *The Downfall of the Anti-Semitic Political Parties in Imperial Germany* (Yale Univesity Press 1975); Michael A Meyer, *The Origins of the Modern Jew. Jewish Identity and European Culture in Germany 1749–1824* (Wayne State University Press 1979); Hans-Gert Oomen, Hans-Dieter Schmid, *Vorurteile gegen Minderheiten. Die Anfänge des modernen Antisemitismus am Beispiel Deutschlands* (Stuttgart 1978); P.G. Pulzer, *The Rise of Political Anti-Semitism in Germany and Austria* (New York 1964); idem., 'Why was there a Jewish Question in Imperial Germany?', *LBYB*, XV, 1980, 133–146; Reinhard Rürup, *Emanzipation und Antisemitismus. Studien zur 'Judenfrage' der bürgerlichen Gesellschaft* (Göttingen 1975), esp. pp. 74–94; idem., 'Emanzipation und Kirche – Zur Geschichte der "Judenfrage" in Deutschland vor 1890'. pp. 1–56 in: Mosse, Paucker, *Juden im Wilhelminischen Deutschland 1890–1914* op. cit.; Reinhard Rürup und Wolfgang Kaiser, 'Sozialismus und Antisemitismus in Deutschland vor 1914', *Jahrbuch des Instituts für Deutsche Geschichte*, Tel Aviv, Beiheft 2, 1977, 203–277; Eleonore Sterling, *Judenhass. Die Anfänge des politischen Antisemitismus in Deutschland 1815–1850* (Frankfurt am Main 1969).

7 For the Jewish experience in Gemany see Walter Zwi Bacharach, 'Jews in Confrontation with Racist Antisemitism 1879–1933', *LBYB*, XXV, 1980, 197–219; Max P Birnbaum, 'On the Jewish Struggle for Religious Equality in Prussia 1897–1914', *LBYB*, XXV, 1980, 163–171; Gordon R Mork, 'German Nationalism and Jewish Assimilation – the Bismarck Period', *LBYB*, XXII, 1977, 81–90; Marjorie Lamberti, *Jewish Activism in*

Imperial Germany. The Struggle for Civil Equality (Yale University Press 1978); idem., 'The Jewish Struggle for the Legal Equality of Religions in Imperial Germany', *LBYB*, XXIII, 1978, 101–116; Stephen M Poppel, *Zionism in Germany 1897–1933. The shaping of a Jewish Identity* (Jewish Publication Society of America, Philadelphia 1976); Sanford Ragins, *Jewish Responses to Anti-Semitism in Germany 1870–1914. A Study in the History of Ideas* (Cincinnati 1980); Jehuda Reinharz, *Fatherland or Promised Land. The Dilemma of the German Jew 1893–1914* (University of Michigan Press 1975); Reinhard Rürup, 'Emancipation and Crisis: the "Jewish Question" in Germany 1850–1890', *LBYB*, XX, 1975, 13–25; Ismar Schorsch, *Jewish Reactions to German Anti-Semitism 1870–1914* (Columbia University Press 1972).

8 See Joshua Trachtenberg, *The Devil and the Jews. The Medieval Conception of the Jew and Its Relation to Modern Antisemitism* (reprint, Jewish Publication Society of America, Philadelphia 1983); Aschheim, *Brothers and Strangers*, op. cit., passim.

9 Uriel Tal, *Christians and Jews in Germany. Religion, Politics and Ideology in the Second Reich 1870–1914* (Cornell University Press 1975).

10 See Sidney M Bolkosky, *The Distorted Image: German-Jewish Perceptions of Germans and Germany 1918–1935* (New York 1975); Ernest Hamburg, *Jews, Democracy and Weimar Germany* (Leo Baeck Memorial Lecture 16: New York 1973); Hans-Helmuth Knütter, *Die Juden und die deutsche Linke in der Weimarer Republik* (Düsseldorf 1971); George L Mosse, 'German Socialists and the Jewish Question in the Weimar Republic', *LBYB*, XVI, 1971, 123–151; Donald L Niewyk, *Socialist, Anti-Semite and Jew. German Social Democracy Confronts the Problem of Anti-Semitism 1918–1933* (Louisiana State University Press 1971); idem., 'The Economic and Cultural Role of the Jews in the Weimar Republic', *LBYB*, XVI, 1971, 163–173; idem., *The Jews in Weimar Germany* (Manchester University Press 1980).

11 Wertheimer, 'The Unwanted Element', op. cit., 24, n.3. See also S. Ettinger, 'The Jews in Russia at the outbreak of the Revolution', pp. 15–29, esp. p. 14, n.1 in: Lional Kochan (editor), *The Jews in Soviet Russia since 1917* (Oxford University Press 1978). For other calculations of the total see S. Adler-Rudel, *Ostjuden in Deutschland* op. cit., 2.

12 Wertheimer, 'The Unwanted Element', op. cit., 25.

13 S. Adler-Rudel, *Ostjuden in Deutschland*, op. cit., 19–23, 164; Wertheimer, 'The Unwanted Element', op. cit., 32; Agatha Ramm, *Germany 1789–1919. A Political History* (London 1967), 391.

14 Wertheimer, 'The Unwanted Element', op. cit., 27–32.

15 Aschheim, *Brothers and Strangers*, op. cit., 43, 61; Schorsch, *Jewish Reactions to German Anti-Semitism*, op. cit., 163.

16 Schorsch, op. cit., 51; Richard S Levy, *The Downfall of the Anti-Semitic Political Parties*, op. cit., 94–96.

17 Jehuda Reinharz, *Fatherland or Promised Land*, op. cit., 17.

18 Aschheim, *Brothers and Strangers*, op. cit., 58ff; Lucy S Dawidowicz, *The Golden Tradition. Jewish Life and Thought in Eastern Europe* (Boston 1968), 14–27.

19 Adolf Hitler, *Mein Kampf* (London 1939), 58–59. See also, J Sydney Jones, *Hitler in Vienna 1907–1913* (New York 1983).

20 Aschheim, *Brothers and Strangers*, op. cit., 35.

21 Ibid., 41, 46; S. Adler-Rudel, *Ostjuden in Deutschland*, op. cit., 26; idem., 'East European Jewish Workers in Germany', *LBYB*, II, 1957, 136–165, esp. p. 137. When Franz Oppenheimer, the German Zionist economist and sociologist, remarked that the basic difference between the *Ostjuden* and *Westjuden* was that 'we are *Nationaldeutsche*; the *Ostjuden* on the other hand, are only rarely *Nationalrussen*. They are *Nationaljuden*, as much as they are *Kulturjuden*', he was admitting in effect that it was perhaps the *Ostjuden* who were holding fast to a truly genuine and separate Jewish culture and identity which was being lost sight of by German Jewry in keeping its distance from this tradition and the *Ostjuden* in its efforts to be accepted, assimilated, and nationalised within German society., Reinharz, *Fatherland or Promised Land*, op. cit., 130–131; *New Standard Jewish Encyclopedia*, op. cit., 1475. Cf. also Stephen M Poppel, *Zionism in Germany*, op. cit., 28; Yehuda Eloni, 'Die unkämpfe nationaljüdische Idee', 658, 683–686 in: Mosse, Paucker, *Juden in Wilhelminischen Deutschland 1890–1914*, op. cit.

See also, Eike Geisel, *Im Scheunenviertel. Bilder Texte, und Dokumente* (Berlin 1981), an account of the *Ostjuden* ghetto in Berlin.

22 See Egmont Zechlin, *Die deutsche Politik und die Juden im Ersten Weltkrieg* (Göttingen 1969), esp. Part II: 'Die deutsche Politik und die Ostjuden 1914–1918'.

23 Aschheim, 'Eastern Jews, German Jews', op. cit., 361; idem., *Brothers and Strangers*, op. cit., 179.

24 Idem., *Brothers and Strangers*, op. cit., 174; Zechlin, op. cit., 267. What also reinforced the previous antipathy to the entry of *Ostjuden* into Germany was the fact that Germany's military operations in the east and the occupation of Polish lands from 1915 meant that 'instead of the ghetto coming to Germany, Germany came to the ghetto'. For many German administrators and soldiers the cultural shock was tremendous and overwhelming since actual experience seemed to prove that 'the ghetto stereotype was confirmed' so that one suddenly 'entered a totally different world, the world of the Orient'. The *Ostjuden* had always been stereotyped as dirty, and what the soldiers found as they entered the ghettos of Poland, Galicia, and Lithuania seemed to vindicate that idea., Aschheim, *Brothers and Strangers*, op. cit., 139, 143–148.

25 Cf. Nora Levin, *Jewish Socialist Movements 1871–1917. While Messiah Tarried* (London 1978); Robert S Wistrich, *Revolutionary Jews from Marx to Trotsky* (London 1976).

26 S. Adler-Rudel, 'East European Jewish Workers in Germany', op. cit., 143; idem., *Ostjuden in Deutschland*, op. cit., 37ff; Aschheim, 'Eastern Jews, German Jews', op. cit., 363; Zechlin, op. cit., 266.

27 S. Adler-Rudel, 'East European Jewish Workers in Germany', op. cit., 147–148; idem., *Ostjuden in Deutschland*, op. cit., 46–47; Aschheim, 'Eastern Jews, German Jews', op. cit., 364–365; idem., *Brothers and Strangers*, op. cit., 175–178; Zechlin, op. cit., 260–262, 267–272, 274–277.

28 Zechlin, op. cit., 277.

29 Cf. Martin Kitchen, *The Silent Dictatorship. The Politics of the German High Command under Hindenburg and Ludendorff 1916–1918* (London 1976), 142, 194, 211.

30 Documents of the German Foreign Office, filmed copies at the Library and Records Department, Foreign and Commonwealth Office, London: L1288/L350408–422, Dr Franz Oppenheimer, President of the *Komitees für den Osten*/State Secretary, *Auswärtiges Amt*, 24 September 1918 (*Politisches Abteilung III: Akten aus dem Nachlass Professor Sobernheim – Komitees fur den Osten*). Hereafter referred to as *AA*.

31 Zechlin, op. cit., 283.

32 Cf. the prescient statement describing the German situation at the war's end, that 'the German kings had departed. The captains had not', Richard M Watt, *The Kings Depart, The Tragedy of Germany: Versailles and the German Revolution* (London 1968), 273.

33 S. Adler-Rudel, *Ostjuden in Deutschland*, op. cit., 60.

34 See Saul Friedländer, 'Die politischen Veränderungen der Kriegszeit und ihre Auswirkungen auf die Judenfrage', 27–65, and Werner Jochmann, 'Die Ausbreitung des Antisemitismus', 409–510 in: Werner E Mosse, Arnold Paucker (eds), *Deutsche Judentum im Krieg und Revolution 1916–1923* (Tübingen 1971). As Leon Poliakov has stated, 'Germany, defeated and disrupted, was infected in a special way, in proportion, one might say, to the extent of the disaster, of the traumatism inflicted on this proud nation', Leon Poliakov, 'The Weapon of Anti-Semitism', 835, in: *The Third Reich* (UNESCO 1955).

35 AA. L1279/L329107–108, Sobernheim/Haniel, 15 March 1920; ibid., L329105–106, Aufzeichnung Stockhammern, 17 April 1920; ibid., L329111–112, Stockhammern/Bern, 27 May 1920; ibid., L329192, Adolf Müller, Bern/Auswärtiges Amt, 19 July 1920 (*Pol.Abt.III. Judisch-politische Angelegenheiten*, Band I).

36 CF. Sally Marks, *The Illusion of Peace. International Relations in Europe 1918–1933* (London 1976); Jacques Bariety, *Les relations franco-allemandes après la première guerre mondiale. 10 Novembre- 1918–10 Janvier 1925. De l'exécution à la négociation* (Paris 1977); Peter Kruger, *Die Aussenpolitik der Republik von Weimar* (Darmstadt 1985).

37 Louise W Holborn, Gwendolen M Carter, John H Herz (eds), *German Constitutional Documents since 1871. Selected Texts and Commentary* (New York, 1971), 21, 103–104, 156; Erich Eyck, *A History of the Weimar Republic. Volume I: From the Collapse of the Empire to Hindenburg's Election* (Oxford University Press 1962), 74; AA.

L1287/L348721–732, Wolfgang Heine, Prussian Minister of the Interior/An das
Staats ministerium, 23 February 1920 (*Pol. Abt.III. Nachlass Sobernheim. Ausweisung
von Ostjuden.*)

38   S. Adler-Rudel, 'East European Jewish Workers in Germany', op. cit., 149; idem.,
Ostjuden in Deutschland, op. cit., 59–60.

39   AA.L1288/L350339, Aufzeichnung Sobernheim, 20 December 1918; ibid., L350337–338,
Sobernheim/von Gerlach, Prussian Ministry of the Interior, 26 February 1919;
ibid., L350309, Lentze, Prussian Ministry of the Interior/ Sobernheim, 7 March 1919
(*Pol.Abt.III Nachlass Sobernheim. Handakten-Ausgänge*).

40   S. Adler-Rudel, 'East European Jewish Workers in Germany', op. cit., 150; idem.,
Ostjuden in Deutschland, op. cit., 62.

41   It must also be remembered that alien Gentile Poles were also included in the
policy of expulsions, cf. Harald von Riekhoff, *German-Polish Relations 1918–1933*
(Baltimore 1971), 57–59.

42   AA. L1288/L350401–405, Aufzeichnung Friedmann (February-March 1919); ibid.,
L350291–293, Sobernheim/Brockdorff-Rantzau, 2 April 1919 (*Pol.ABt.III. Nachlass
Sobernheim. Komitees für den Osten, Handakten--Ausgänge*); Politische Archiv, Aus-
wärtiges Amt, Bonn (PA): *Akten der Geschäftsstelle für die Friedensverhandlungen*,
P10019, Aufzeichnung der jüdischen Gemeinde in Danzig und der Westpreussischen
Synagogen-Gemeinden, Danzig, April 1919; PA. *Akten der Friedenskommission*, Abteil-
ung A, Band 16, Nr. 343, Judenfragen. Bericht Nr. A.141, Helm, Zurich/Auswärtiges
Amt, 8 April 1919 (I am extremely grateful to my colleagues, Dr Theo Gehling and
Dr Peter Grupp, for supplying me with these and other unfilmed documents from the
Politische Archiv of the Auswärtiges Amt, Bonn. I am also grateful to Dr Peter Grupp
for having read this and my second paper and for the observations he made upon them.)
Cf. also Arno J Mayer, *Politics and the Diplomacy of Peacemaking. Containment and
Counterrevolution at Versailles 1918–1919* (London 1968); Harold I Nelson, *Land and
Power. British and Allied Policy on Germany's Frontiers 1916–19* (London 1963); Sarah
Wambaugh, *Plebiscites since the World War* (Washington 1933). See also *Akten zur
deutschen auswärtigen Politik 1918–1945*. Serie A: 1918–1925, Band 1, 9 November
1918 bis 5 Mai 1919 (Götingen 1982)., Band II, 7 Mai bis 31 Dezember 1919 (Göttingen
1984). Hereafter referred to as ADAP.

43   AA.   L1288/L350327–328,   Aufzeichnung   Sobernheim,   27   February   1919;
ibid.,   L350329–330,   draft   letter   from   AA.   to   Reich   Minister   of   the
Interior   (March   1919);   ibid.,   L350291–293,   Sobernheim/Brockdorff-Rantzau,
2 April 1919; ibid., L350286–288, Unsigned Aufzeichnung mit Anlage, 3 April 1919; ibid.,
L1288/L350289–290, draft letter from AA to Prussian Ministry of the Interior; ibid.,
L350278–279, Naumann/Reichsamt des Innern, 9 April 1919. (*Pol.Abt.III. Nachlass
Sobernheim. Handakten-Ausgänge*).

44   AA. L1287/L348710–713, Protokollauszug der Sitzung über die jüdischen Ausweis-
ungen im Auswärtigen Amt am 10 April; ibid., L348582–644, Protokoll der Sitzung .
. . am 10 April 1919 (*Pol.ABt.III. Nachlass Sobernheim. Ausweisung von Ostjuden.*).

45   Even Nazi Germany had to take foreign, i.e. Japanese opinion and susceptibilities into
account with regard to aspects of its internal racial policies, cf. John P Fox, 'Japanese
Reactions to Nazi Germany's Racial Legislation', *Wiener Library Bulletin*, Volume
XXII, Nos. 2 and 3, 1969, 46–50; idem., *Germany and the Far Eastern Crisis 1931–1938.
A Study in Diplomacy and Ideology* (Oxford University Press 1982), 83–93.

46   Cf. *Akten der Reichskanzlei, Weimarer Republik. Das Kabinett Bauer: 21 Juni 1919 bis 27
März 1920* (Boppard-am-Rhein 1980), 227, for the Cabinet meeting of 28 August 1919.
When Otto Hörsing, Reichs-und-Staatskommissar for Silesia and West Posen, raised the
question of the expulsion of all foreigners, the Minister of the Interior spoke resignedly
about the fact that although officials had been preoccupied with the expulsion of Polish
Jews, little could be achieved 'since the frontiers could not be closed and the majority
of passport officials were corrupt. Besides which, many of those expelled to Poland, if
not the majority, were massacred there. Once again this would be used to good effect
by the rest of the world against the German "barbarians". He had to say that at this
moment we were powerless.' See also ADAP, Series A, Band II, 278–281, Unsigned
Aufzeichnung, 29 August 1919, in which this point about it not being in Germany's

interests *at that particular time* to undertake the mass expulsion of the *Ostjuden* is emphasised. See also ibid., 358, fn. 2, for Otto Hörsing's letter of 20 September 1919 to Foreign Minister Hermann Müller complaining about Silesia being inundated with Polish Jews and how necessary it was to arrange their emigration to Palestine or America, especially since expulsion to Poland really meant their deaths. See also ibid., 358, for the reply of 18 October 1919 of Haniel von Haimhausen, Under Secretary of State in the Auswärtiges Amt.

47 For Auswärtiges Amt concern about the intended expulsion of *Ostjuden* from Munich and efforts to persuade the Bavarian authorities about the nuances of Germany's domestic and international position on this issue, see AA.L1288/L350241–242, 243–244, Naumann Geschäftsträger, Munich, 5 June 1919; ibid., L350220–224, Report of a journey to Bamberg, 9–11 June 1919, presumably by Sobernheim (*Pol.Abt.III. Nachlass Sobernheim. Handakten-Ausgänge*).

48 AA. L1287/L348566–567 (*Pol. Abt. III. Nachlass Sobernheim. Ausweisung von Ostjuden*); Aschheim, *Brothers and Strangers*, op. cit., 99–100.

49 S. Adler-Rudel, *Ostjuden in Deutschland*, op. cit., 114; Aschheim, *Brothers and Strangers*, op. cit., 239.

50 AA. L1287/L349549–550, Sobernheim/Stockhammern, 21 April 1920 (*Pol.Abt.III. Nachlass Sobernheim. Ausweisung von Ostjuden*).

51 AA. L1287/L348721–732, Heine/An das Staatsministerium, 23 February 1920 (*Pol.ABt.III. Nachlass Sobernheim. Ausweisung von Ostjuden*).

52 Adler-Rudel, *Ostjuden in Deutschland*, op. cit., p. 115; Aschheim, Brothers and Strangers, op. cit., p. 242–243; Niewyk, *Socialist, Anti-Semite and Jew*, op. cit. p. 97–100.

53 AA. L1279/L329199–200, Freytag/Bern, 11 September 1920; ibid., L329347–348, Aufzeichnung Sobernheim, 3 January 1921 (*Pol.Abt.III. Jüdisch–politische Angelegenheiten.* Band 1, 2); ibid., L1282/L336790–795, AA/Prussian Minister of the Interior, 12 July 1921 (*Pol.ABt.III. Jüdische Angelegenheiten. Passangelegenheiten, Empfehlungen*).

54 PA. Abteilung IV Polen, Innere Verwaltung 13, Ausweisung von Ostjuden aus Deutschland. Aufzeichnung 'Ostjuden', 2 May 1920; AA.L1279/L329360–361, Report of Verhandlungen im Hauptausschuss des Reichstags, (15 January 1921) (*Pol.Abt.III. Jüdisch-politische Angelegenheiten* Band 2).

55 PA. Abteilung IV Polen, Innere Verwaltung 13, Ausweisung von Ostjuden aus Deutschland.

56 Ibid.

57 Ibid. The order of 17 November 1920 in fact contained the official annulment of the anti-Jewish immigration order of 23 April 1918.

58 S. Adler-Rudel, *Ostjuden in Deutschland*, op. cit., 115.

59 Ibid., 117; Aschheim, *Brothers and Strangers*, op. cit., 242. See AA. L1279/L329525, L329526, and L1287/L348530–541 for further Prussian Ministry of the Interior orders of 25 June, 4 July, and 21 October 1921 concerning the expulsion and internment of the *Ostjuden*, although by then, and as far as possible, the tendency was to drop the term *Ostjuden* and replace it by *fremdstämmige Ausländer*. On this particular point of nomenclature, see AA.L1287/L349057–064, Wilhelmlitten/Blücher, 27 October, 1922 (*Pol.ABt.III. Jüdisch-politische Angelegenheiten. Band 2; Nachlass Sobernheim: Ausweisung von Ostjuden., Ukraine*).

60 S. Adler-Rudel, *Ostjuden in Deutschland*, op. cit., 29.

61 Niewyk, *The Jews in Weimar Germany*, op.cit., 118–120.

62 Aschheim, *Brothers and Strangers*, op. cit., 243–244.

63 AA. L1279/LL329957–958, Sobernheim/Staatssekretär, 29 October 1923; ibid., L329963–964, von Schubert/Haniel (Munich), 30 October 1923; ibid., L329976–984, Sobernheim/Staatssekretär Weismann (Staats-Ministerium), 31 Ocober 1923; PA. Abteilung IV, Polen, Innere Verwaltung 13, Ausweisung von Ostjuden aus Deutschland Erlass Maltzan/Haniel, 3 November 1923; *Akten der Reichskanzlei, Weimarer Republik. Die Kabinette Stresemann I u. II, Band 2: 6 Oktober bis 30. November 1923* (Boppard am Rhein 1978), 964 for a copy of the Maltzan Erlass of 3 November but wrongly dated as 4 November; AA. 2945/D571084, Tel. 257, Wallroth/Warschau, 5 November 1923; *Akten der Reichskanzlei*, Bd. 2, op. cit., 974–975 for Preussische Ministerpräsident Braun/Reichskanzlei, 5 November 1923; AA. L1279/L329992, Haniel/AA., Munich

6 November 1923; Foreign Office Correspondence 371 (FO), Public Record Office, Kew, C19234/1043/18, Volume 8776, Joint Foreign Committee of Jewish Board of Deputies/FO, 7 November 1923; AA. L1279/L329970, Tel, 256, Rauscher, Warschau/AA. 9 November 1923; ibid., L329969, Wallroth/Warschau, 10 November 1923; ibid., L329967–968, Aufzeichnung Wallroth, 10 November 1923; 2945/D571093, Tel. 268, Rauscher/AA., 16 November 1923; FO.371, C19809/1043/18, Volume 8766, Joint Foreign Committee of Jewish Board of Deputies and Anglo-Jewish Association/FO, 14 November 1923; PA. Abteilung IV, Polen Innere Verwaltung 13, Ausweisung von Ostjuden aus Deutschland, Tel. 264, Wallroth/Warschau, 15 November 1923; AA. L1279/L330038–039, Bericht 3585 mit Anlage, Sthamer (London)/AA., 16 November 1923; PA. Abteilung IV, Polen, Innere Verwaltung 13, Ausweisung von Ostjuden aus Deutschland, Bericht K.826, Frank (Kattowitz)/AA., 24 November 1923; FO. 371, C20958/1043/18, Volume 8776, report 155, Clive (Munich)/FO, 29 November 1923; AA. 2945/D571132, Tel. 274, Wallroth/Warschau, 17 December 1923.

[Since the original preparation and presentation of this paper, two important studies of the subject have appeared: Trude Maurer, *Ostjuden in Deutscheland 1918–1933*, (Hamburg 1986), and Reiner Pommerin, 'Die Ausweisung von "Ostjuden" aus Bayern 1923. Ein Beitrag zum Krisenjahr der Weimares Republik', *Vierteljahrshefte für Zeitgeschichte*, 34Jhg., Heft. 3. Juli 1986, 311–39.]

5 German and European Jewish refugees, 1933–1945: reflections on the Jewish condition under Hitler and the Western World's response to their expulsion and flight

JOHN P. FOX

Without the policy of the physical extermination of all Europe's Jews which the Nazi regime under Adolf Hitler's leadership attempted to bring about during the Second World War, it is doubtful whether the subject of Jewish refugees from Nazism would have become the burning historical and moral issue it is even today, forty years after Nazi Germany's defeat at the hands of the Allies in May 1945. But it is that policy of the deliberate, systematic, physical extermination of European Jewry on a pan-European scale which has marked out Adolf Hitler's treatment of the Jewish minority in Christian Europe as something supposedly unique in modern European history, if not in the history of mankind itself. Viewed from this perspective of 'uniqueness', it is not surprising that the political, historical, and moral discussion of the fate of European Jewry under Nazism, including that of Jewish refugees fleeing from persecution and worse in their homeland and seeking a safe refuge elsewhere, should be so full of controversy and indeed bitterness since the Nazis succeeded in exterminating between 5 and 6 million European Jews between 1941 and 1944. However, a great deal of this controversy and bitterness is essentially misguided because much of the discussion starts from mistaken premises, proceeds with false arguments, and concludes with emotion and polemic in place of complete objectivity.

Much of the controversy about the response of the non-Nazi world to those Jews expelled or attempting to flee from Nazism may be clarified by dealing first with the somewhat naive question which is always asked in connection with the subject of the Nazi persecution and extermination of the Jews but which actually causes most of the difficulties: how could it have happened? This question ignores a basic fact about man and history that the Nazi *Endlösung der Judenfrage* simply underlined, that it is relatively easy for some groups of human beings to be ordered and organised to kill other human beings within the confines of particular political societies and systems. For what the Nazis managed to 'tap' so successfully – the potential and indeed the propensity for violence and murder within political societies – was not confined in history merely to Germany and Europe of the years 1939 to 1945. What have been described as 'the destructive tendencies in man' have often been organised as 'institutionalised violence' directed against specifically identified groups of people both before 1939 and after 1945. At one level, then, one might say that there was nothing new about the Nazi experiment in mass destruction. If so, why the furore? The shock came, and still comes, from the fact that the crime of the Holocaust happened in so-called 'civilised' Christian Europe, and it is this, more than anything else, which has given rise to the host of historical, moral, and even theological discussions about the nature of modern societies and the 'nature of man' in the post-Holocaust world. Certainly, one does not hear of the same kind of mental anguish being caused by the barbarities of the Pol Pot regime in Cambodia. Or are there other perspectives to the anti-Jewish crime of the Nazis? Does the so-called 'uniqueness' of the Holocaust have as much to do with its scale, and the fact that the total military defeat of Nazi Germany in 1945 enabled its public and private archives to fall into Allied hands, making it possible for a 'unique' record of human destruction to be written?

If, in principle, there was nothing new in history about mass violence against particular groups of people within political societies which the Nazis refined to a particular art, neither was there anything new in the less than enthusiastic response of the rest of the world to the fact of yet another refugee problem, namely the many thousands of Jews who, forcibly or voluntarily, left their homeland in Germany and other parts of Europe to seek refuge from Nazism elsewhere. That less than enthusiastic response manifested itself in a reluctance, at times a downright refusal, to allow Jewish refugees from the Nazi persecutions into other countries. Although the grounds for such reluctance or refusal would be presented in contemporary political, economic, or social terms, it could be argued that more deep-rooted factors also played their part. If one considers the matter within the wider context of the immigration, nationality, and aliens' policies of twentieth-century political societies until even the present day, it may be argued that those Jewish refugees from Nazism seeking a safe haven elsewhere were additionally the victims of the efforts of modern governments and bureaucracies to control with all the means at their disposal the *numbers* and *types* of people allowed to enter and reside in their particular society. So that in this as in the actual causation of the Nazi *Endlösung der Judenfrage*, the element of anti-Semitism comes to be subsumed under other fundamental causes and so ceases to be the single cause *per se*. The only surprising thing, then, about this fact of government control as it applied to the Jewish refugees from Nazism is that it should still be a matter of some surprise. Nevertheless, the subject of immigration controls invoked against these Jewish refugees is given a different dimension by the additional factor of the eventual policy of the mass physical extermination of the Jews by the Nazis.

This point immediately raises the question of responsibility for the fate of European Jewry and the Jewish refugees from Nazism between 1933 and 1945. Much controversy has been generated by the efforts of many authors to widen the scope of 'responsibility' for the crime of the Final Solution to include the Jews themselves as well as the major powers of America and Britain: the Jews for not having escaped or resisted, the major powers for their restrictive immigration policies. Either way, so the argument goes, this left the European Jews in Europe to be murdered en masse by the Nazis. Apart from denying a whole host of basic facts, let alone recognising certain key nuances, about the Jewish and Great Power positions as they were vis-à-vis the role which Nazi Germany occupied in Europe at various times in its twelve-year history, such arguments ignore the question of where ultimate responsibility lay for the Nazi policy of the deliberate extermination of European Jewry. That ultimate responsibility was Adolf Hitler's alone. Without his peculiar political genius German society would never have been transformed in the way it was so that all normal restraints of supposedly civilised society were discarded to allow policies of the mass physical destruction of specific groups of human beings to operate. Not only does this point help to put into proper perspective the relatively minor role of anti-Semitism in bringing about the Holocaust, but by underlining the Nazi responsibility for the initiation and execution of the *Endlösung der Judenfrage*, one can see the helplessness and tragedy of the Jewish victims more clearly and the dilemmas of the Great Powers in a somewhat different light. Without Adolf Hitler there would have been no Second World War in the form it took, nor would there have been any attempt to exterminate the Jews of Europe in the middle of the twentieth century. The basic fact of the matter is that it was the German system under the leadership of Adolf Hitler which organised and executed the death transports and camps, not Jews or Americans, or the British or the Russians.

From this point of view it must be seen that the Jewish condition in Nazi Germany and Nazi Europe, as well as the response of other governments to Jewish refugees from Nazism had to be just that: a response of some kind or the other to Nazi policies. But the precise nature of that Jewish and Great Power response at any one time depended on three conditions: firstly, the specific nature of Nazi Germany's anti-Jewish policies at particular times as these manifested themselves and therefore became known; secondly, the legal and social position of the Jews within Nazi society (both in Germany and Nazi-controlled Europe); and thirdly, the political and military factors influencing western societies towards a more restrictive or liberal immigration policy so far as these Jewish refugees were concerned. Yet whatever these may have been at particular times, the overwhelming cause of later controversy is that Nazi Germany ultimately formulated and executed a policy of the mass physical destruction of the German and European Jews who came under its control as the Nazi empire extended into eastern, western, and Russian Europe. The question is: could or should these Jews have been 'saved' by emigration from Europe and therefore immigration into other societies, or even 'rescued'?

But saved or rescued from what – persecution or extermination? The fact is that a great deal of the discussion on the fate of European Jewry and Jewish refugees at the time of the Nazi regime is predicated upon later historical knowledge of the facts of extermination. In a way this distorts the historical perspective when it comes to analysing those years between 30 January 1933 and 21 June 1941 when no policy of the mass physical extermination of European Jewry was implemented. That policy of deliberate mass extermination of Jews only began on 22 June 1941 when the German armies and the killer squads of the *Einsatzgruppen* made their murderous entry into Soviet territory. Until the Nazi invasion of Soviet territory no Jew or outsider, nor even a *majority* of the Nazi leadership, could have any idea that Nazi persecution of the Jews would actually develop into physical extermination. Given these facts and contemporary perceptions, it is even more unforgivable of those historians who describe the twelve years of the Nazi regime as 'the Holocaust period' when in fact that 'event' only took place between the summer of 1941 and the autumn of 1944. Such emotional ploys have to be discarded if there is to be any hope of approaching even a semblance of historical truth when dealing with this subject as a whole, so that it is at all times crucial to distinguish between the pre-Holocaust period and that of *Endlösung* itself when attempting to assess the Jewish condition under Nazism and the response of the non-German world to the question of Jewish refugees or even so-called 'rescue'.

One cannot, however, separate into neatly divided compartments the three major factors involved in the subject of Jewish refugees from Nazism: Nazi Germany's anti-Jewish policies; the reaction of Europe's Jews as and when each individual country was occupied by the Nazis; and the response of the non-German world to the flight and would-be entry elsewhere of these Jewish refugees. Each factor is necessarily inter-related with all the others, so it was often the case that a policy decision or response in one area resulted from the interaction of a whole complex of factors beyond what might have been the most apparent or obvious. But for reasoned argument to emerge from this subject instead of simplistic and polemical formulae, analysis must go beyond the apparent and obvious.

For a number of reasons Nazi Germany's anti-Jewish policies developed piecemeal and at an uneven rate, certainly between 1933 and 1939. The hallmark of those years was internal persecution and discrimination as well as the encouragement of Jewish emigration from Germany, and Austria after the *Anschluss* in 1938. While the uneven pace of Nazi policy towards the Jews during those years was due to a combination of internal and external factors, some historians make the mistake of arguing that this feature shows that the Nazi leadership had no real idea of what they were about in their Jewish policies at the time, so that one could even go so far as to talk of 'improvisations'. Of course, a great deal depends upon whom one is talking about in the Nazi leadership, since it is quite clear that the *ultimate* intention of Adolf Hitler, if not of Joseph Goebbels, *was* the physical extermination of European Jewry and that this policy would be implemented the moment conditions became absolutely right. Until that ideal moment arrived, the intention was to get rid of as many Jews as possible by forcing them internally out of the normal patterns of German society and externally by 'persuading' them to emigrate. But while Nazi Germany still remained part of the 'open society' that was Europe until war began to engulf the continent as from 1 September 1939, a number of internal and external constraints acted as brakes on Hitler.

What those constraints were may be indicated by referring to the fact that the policy of Euthanasia and *Endlösung*, applied first of all to Aryan Germans, was only put into operation in October 1939 when Germany was in the abnormal state of war and had begun her policy of territorial expansion. Until then, the conversion of the Nazi racial *Weltanschauung* into political fact, on the Jewish question among others, had to contend with all the practical, legal, moral, and social difficulties involved in what amounted to the dismantling of the legal basis of the German State as it had been until 30 January 1933. Even with the tendency towards a system of totalitarianism under the Nazis, which did not become entirely complete, the business of changing the legal basis of modern German society was an extremely complex process which took a long time. Furthermore, the Nazi authorities pushed ahead with their anti-Jewish campaigns only so far and so fast as German and foreign public opinion, as well as the necessity in most cases of maintaining reasonable foreign relations, allowed them. There were also more mundane things like maintaining levels of foreign exchange and trade and hosting the 1936 Olympic Games to think about whenever more extreme policies were being considered.

Despite these constraints which contributed to the somewhat uneven nature and pace of Nazi Germany's anti-Jewish policies between 1933 and 1939, there could be no doubt about two features of this policy: there was never any retreat from a policy or position achieved, one exception being the limited as opposed to the announced extensive boycott of April 1933; while the cumulative effect of gradually forcing Jews out of German society was to push them into a position where they felt they had to flee their own country. By restricting or removing altogether employment opportunities for Jews within Nazi society, as well as by imposing a whole host of other limitations on their civic freedoms which became quite extreme after the pogrom of *Kristallnacht* in November 1938, the Nazi authorities were creating the kind of climate in which many Jews felt they could hardly survive, economically or even physically, if they remained. But as all those concerned soon found out, it was easier to create the climate that inevitably produced would-be Jewish refugees than actually to effect the outward movement of such people towards other countries and other societies.

There were a number of reasons for this. To begin with, until a drastic change in German internal regulations and policy at the end of 1938 and the beginning of 1939, emigration was still theoretically a matter of choice for the Jews of Germany. While the alternative was an increasingly precarious kind of life in a hostile environment brought about by government regulations which came to exclude the Jews from the German civil service, the professions (especially law and medicine), the Universities, business and commerce, the press, radio, etc., still the choice to remain or to emigrate rested largely with the individual. As in all such cases, a whole host of personal and social factors had to be taken into account: where the majority of one's relatives were, the kind of life one could expect to have to endure if one remained to live under the Nazi dictatorship, the chances of employment, food, and housing being provided through Jewish aid societies, the attitudes adopted by German Gentile neighbours, and so on. Above all, though, there were other equally real questions to be faced: could one afford to emigrate, was it possible to obtain visas or entry certificates to other countries or were these being denied or in such short supply as to make their possession almost an impossibility, was one too old or in the wrong profession to start life anew elsewhere, would the climate be suitable, and would the new host population be welcoming or hostile? While some 150,000 of Germany's possible Jewish population of perhaps half a million plus dealt with such imponderables successfully by deciding to leave Nazi Germany by November 1938, the fact remained that under what might be called the 'voluntary' process of emigration the majority of Germany's Jews remained in what was also for them *das Vaterland*. This was because either they felt no inclination to emigrate, or because it was financially and technically (because of the lack of visa etc.) impossible for them to leave. Besides which, many thousands of Jews who had fled into neighbouring countries like France, Belgium, Luxembourg, Holland, Switzerland, and Czechoslovakia actually returned to Nazi Germany after the worst excesses of 1933 and Ernst Röhm and the SA had been dealt with in 1934 because they felt that perhaps then the 'Nazi revolution' had passed its peak and things would 'settle down to normal'.

For these people as for the world at large the question was just that: wild and strange though the Nazi phenomenon might be, it was something that everyone was just going to have to learn to live with. But just as the Jews and Great Powers dealt with the problems of the years 1933 to 1939 as they actually were and unfolded year by year, so it is incumbent upon historians to make their assessments by the same criteria and not be swayed by knowledge of the later Nazi *Endlösung der Judenfrage*. To argue that even more Jews 'might have been saved' from the Nazi Final Solution had more been able to flee during the 1930s and arrive safely elsewhere is, in effect, an historical *non sequitur*. But just as on the Jewish side there were mixed motives about the decision whether to remain or flee and thus become a twentieth-century 'non-person', i.e a refugee, so on the side of the non-German States there were mixed motives about the indirect threat which the Nazi regime posed to their societies in the form of the potential flood of Jewish and Gentile German refugees. Given the basic facts about human nature, it is quite remarkable how much concern is actually aroused in the rest of the world when one country embarks upon a policy of deliberate persecution of a particular segment of its population. From the very beginning of the Nazi regime on 30 January 1933 the world's concern at what was happening inside Nazi Germany to the Jews and others was made perfectly clear to the regime at both government and private level. But while at one level this international and humanitarian response was perfectly natural, at another it had to remain stillborn since what was happening inside Nazi Germany was occurring within the confines of a sovereign national State. So that while foreign governments, even during the 1930s, felt justified in protesting about events inside Germany, particularly so far as these events affected their nationals, the German authorities were perfectly correct from their point of view in rejecting some protests as unwarranted interference in the internal affairs of their own country. In other words, even before the outbreak of war in September 1939 and certainly from the summer of 1940 when for all intents and purposes Europe became an impregnable German fortress, there was very little that the outside world could do to influence or affect the course of Nazi Germany's anti-Jewish policies.

If the years of peace and war produced different means of achieving the Nazi goal of 'destroying' the Jews of Europe, so peace and war produced different problems for, and different reactions from, other countries who were faced with the phenomenon of the Jewish refugee from Nazi persecution. Most governments and peoples were caught between the anvil of common humanitarianism and the hammer of aliens and immigration laws and orders, the health or otherwise of their domestic economies, especially the moot question of the levels of unemployment, the degree of social services available to cope with any large influx of foreigners who would need a great deal of community help, the levels of anti-Semitism thought to exist and whether or not such feelings might be exacerbated by an influx of destitute Jewish refugees from Nazi Germany. There was also the further question of whether the Jewish refugees were to be seen as temporary or permanent residents in the new host society. If they were to be regarded as temporary residents in, e.g. the United Kingdom, where were they to go to next? London bore no responsibility for making immigration policy in the self-governing Dominions of Canada, Australia, New Zealand, South Africa, etc. each of which had its own aliens policy. The British Government did retain authority to promulgate immigration policy in certain overseas dependencies, especially Palestine where the League of Nations Mandate under which Great Britain administered the country specifically enjoined the government to facilitate Jewish immigration under suitable conditions. Until 1937 these conditions were defined in purely economic terms, as the economic capacity of Palestine to absorb new arrivals.

British policy, for example, on the German-Jewish refugee problem was not really different from that of other countries in that the course followed at particular times resulted from a multitude of different factors and considerations. In the years before the outbreak of war in 1939 the Home Office was concerned for the maintenance of Britain's immigration and aliens laws, worried about the unemployment problem being exacerbated by the influx of possible competitors for scarce jobs, and concerned about the possible importation of an undesirable and alien 'racial problem'. For its part, the Foreign Office was always at pains to avoid friction with Berlin and to avoid criticisms from Washington, and later from new allies such as Poland and Romania. The British Treasury was appalled at the spectre of itself and the public services being burdened with an unlimited financial liability for the relief and possible settlement of needy migrants. The Colonial Office, of course, was primarily concerned about the burning issue of Jewish immigration into Palestine within the context of the perennial Arab-Jewish conflict. At the same time there were also broad hints from the Polish government and other east European regimes that an over-generous response on the part of the western democracies to the flight of Jewish refugees from the Third Reich might create a precedent which could inspire them to expel millions, not simply thousands, of totally destitute Jews from eastern Europe. Such a prospect, for any other nation, was truly appalling.

The combination of such factors in the policies adopted by many other countries towards the question of Jewish refugees from Nazi Germany was compounded by yet another which tended to reinforce certain basic inhibitions when it came to the question of liberalising immigration laws. This was a major step of internal Nazi policy towards the Jews, affecting both their status and rights within Nazi society. The Reich Citizenship Act of 15 September 1935 limited citizenship to nationals of German or related blood (a decree of 1 November 1935 declared that 'no Jew can be a Reich citizen'), while the Act for the Protection of German Blood and Honour prohibited marriage and extra-marital relations between 'Jews and nationals of German or allied blood'. By these so-called 'Nuremberg Laws', German Jews were at a stroke turned into persons with lesser rights than those of other people in the German society. They were legally declared to be social outcasts, as well as condemned from a moral point of view. But while this development gave a psychological boost to the Party extremists who were dissatisfied with the rather slow process of the de-Judaisation of Nazi society and paved the way for later more extreme forms of persecution, there were also external repercussions. While many countries might have been willing to offer refuge to Jewish 'refugees' from Nazi Germany, this would have been done on the basis of the original German nationality of such people. For while German Jews still retained their German nationality, there was always the prospect that the new host society had the authority to expel these people back to Germany because of their status as aliens. Likewise, the German authorities, if forced to do so, would have had to accept them, although their immediate response to returning 'refugees', Jewish or otherwise, was to incarcerate them in special camps for political re-education. But once the German Jews lost their German citizenship this meant that the moment they left German soil they became that pariah of the twentieth-century, not merely a refugee as such but a stateless person and therefore, in effect, nobody's responsibility but potentially everybody else's burden.

The manner in which the German-Jewish refugee question worked out during the year of peace between 1933 and 1939 depended, then, on the interaction of three main conditions: the nature and fundamental bases of Nazi Germany's society; the inclination and ability of Germany's Jews to leave their homeland; and the relationship between the legal and administrative structure of the immigration controls of other countries on the one hand and domestic and international politics on the other. Essentially, the rest of the world was having to deal with an abnormal state of affairs, caused by the far from normal or civilised nature of the

Nazi regime within Germany, with sets of laws and regulations designed to maintain degrees of control over those allowed to enter and remain within those other societies but whose individual administration depended entirely upon the politics of the moment. Furthermore, such controls would have originally been formulated on the basis of an assessed expected normal transfer of refugee populations between the nations. So that between 1933 and 1939, despite the obvious abnormalities of German society under the Nazi regime and the consequent actual and threatened increase in the scale of the Jewish refugee problem, that problem was being approached and dealt with legally from what might be called normal perceptions by outsiders and a normal legal system of immigration controls. That the semblance of normality was only slightly threatened by the increasing scale of the problem was also due to the fact that until the *Kristallnacht* pogrom of November 1938 and subsequent measures, Jewish emigration from Nazi Germany was still largely a voluntary process. One has to put it that way, recognising of course the involuntary aspect caused by the hostile environment being created against the German Jews, because until October 1938 when the Germans expelled a large number of Polish Jews across the border (the *Ostjuden* once again) and so in effect brought about the murder of Vom Rath in Paris, and until further regulations early in 1939, there was no official policy of expulsion of German Jews from Germany.

That situation changed as of 24 January 1939 when a directive was issued providing for the establishment of the Reich Central Office for Jewish Emigration (*Reichszentrale für die jüdische Auswanderung*). Operating under the direction of Reinhard Heydrich, the feared head of the Gestapo, its purpose was to promote the emigration of Jews from Germany 'by every possible means'. Those 'means', in effect, could hardly be distinguished from a policy of expulsion, so that it was not surprising that almost 50% of the total Jewish emigration from Nazi Germany and Nazi Austria took place in the last year of peace. This tide of human traffic, however, threatened to strain to breaking point the continuing efforts of governments and private relief agencies to find a solution to this problem, especially since one basic principle was being kept to by other governments: the maintenance, if not tightening, of immigration controls.

The outbreak of European war in September 1939 changed everything for everybody. At a single stroke it meant that any semblance of a 'normal' refugee question, for Gentiles as well as for the Jews, was a thing of the past. This was underlined by three actions of the British government: the state of war existing between it and Germany meant that there could be no contact between the two governments on the Jewish refugee problem as on any others; the Inter-Governmental Committee on Refugees could no longer negotiate with Berlin on the subject; while on 4 September 1939 the British government announced the imposition of a standstill order on the entry to British territory of all aliens from Reich territories, including refugees of all classes. Although a trickle of Jewish refugees still managed to leave Nazi Europe in the early part of the war, and while the majority of these caused headaches to the British authorities by trying desperately to circumvent the restrictions on Jewish immigration into Palestine as set out in the White Paper of May 1939, the fact of the matter is that Germany's actions in 1939 and 1940 relieved the major powers of a Jewish refugee problem as such. In effect it no longer existed, i.e. in its previous and somewhat precariously 'normal' form. The problems associated with some Jewish desires to leave Nazi-controlled Europe and the question of their reception elsewhere, however positive or negative this was, continued to exist but on a vastly reduced scale and in a completely different form.

But if war completely changed the nature of the German-Jewish refugee problem for the outside world, it also – and quite fundamentally – changed the very basis of the European Jewish question for the Nazi leadership and the Jews of Europe and Russia. In a sense both the Jews and the Nazis found themselves caught in a trap. Those Jews still in Germany at the outbreak of war and those about to come under her control as Germany's power extended throughout continental and Russian Europe, found themselves the victims of the Nazi intention to define, disbar, ruin, and eventually exterminate – (or deform, depersonalise, and dehumanise) the Jews. The Nazis were also 'victims' of a kind in the pursuit of their ideological war to destroy Judaism and world Jewry. War increasingly closed the possibility of emigration for German Jews (though some still managed to leave this way), and made it impossible for most others, above all the three million Jews of Poland. The question for all concerned was: what now? One thing above all became absolutely clear: the fate of the Jews of Europe, and indeed that of all other subject civilians, was now determined totally by Nazi Germany's military, occupation, and anti-Jewish policies, the latter being in a criminal class of its own. As in the Great War of 1914–1918, so in what has been described as the 'last European war' of 1939–1945, the German war machine came to the ghettos of the eastern Jews, the *Ostjuden*. But unlike that earlier experience, which by comparison was almost enlightened, the Jewish experience in the east under Nazism was tantamount to a hell on earth. In Poland Nazi policy aimed at concentrating the Jews in the major cities in ghettos which, as time went on, became increasingly 'closed' ghettos shut off from as much contact with the Gentile world as possible. As more and more rural Jewish communities were shut down and their inhabitants herded into the city ghettos, life in those places became a daily struggle for existence amidst overcrowded, insanitary, and starving conditions. But for the Jews of Poland and the Baltic States until the autumn of 1941 it was still exactly that: life.

The situation of military and political control in Europe which the Nazi leadership enjoyed up to and beyond the summer of 1941 offered them the opportunity, if not the necessity, of devising a 'solution' to the 'Jewish question' they now had on their hands. The ultimate answer to this conundrum was the policy of deliberate, mass physical extermination put into operation only as of 22 June 1941, the day of the attack on the Soviet Union. Later in the autumn that policy was extended back (as it were) into Poland and the Baltic States, until from the end of 1941 through to 1942 and 1943 the systematic organisation of that policy of death meant that most of west and east European Jewry had been totally destroyed in the space of two and a half years. There are some who argue that the genesis of the European part of this policy of mass physical destruction of European Jewry lay in administrative difficulties confronting local Nazi leaders in Poland and the Baltic areas, no longer able to cope with the large numbers of Jews being shipped to their localities. But this is to ignore the essential point of premeditation in anything which concerned Hitlers' policy towards the Jews. The discrepancy, then, in the argument of those who ignore this element of premeditation is that while we are asked to believe that the physical extermination of Soviet Jewry, begun in conjunction with Operation Barbarossa, was undertaken for obvious ideological reasons, the extermination of the rest of European Jewry was somehow something separate, ideologically speaking, and was begun simply because of 'administrative inconvenience'. This is, of course, to turn history on its head since the pan-European aspect of the Nazi *Endlösung der Judenfrage* was hardly 'an accident of war'.

If Nazi Germany's physical control of most of Europe's Jews affected the nature of the relationship between German master and Jewish victim, then likewise for the rest of the world this situation completely changed the nature of the German-Jewish problem as they had previously perceived and been confronted with it. One could no longer talk of a 'normal' refugee problem, Jewish or otherwise, since, obviously enough, the conditions of war nullified this in all respects. Instead, while some Jewish refugees tried to make their way out of Nazi-controlled Europe, especially from and through the Balkan countries of Romania and Bulgaria, the vast millions of Europe's Jews had no means of escape at all from Nazi control, and certainly not from the efficiently organised Nazi machinery of death in the extermination camps. The fact that nearly 6 million Jews were deliberately put to death under this system (in addition to perhaps some 6 million of other nationalities) has led some people to raise the question whether 'Europe's Jews' might have been 'saved' or indeed 'rescued' had the immigration policies and other attitudes towards Europe's Jews of the Allied Powers been different. For many people, however, it has not required a quantum jump from raising questions of this kind in the first place to concluding that since the Allied Powers, e.g. Great Britain and America, are to be found lacking in virtually all respects in their policies towards the Jews of Europe, then they too must also stand accused as 'accomplices' of the Nazis in their crime of the genocide of European Jewry.

It goes without saying that Jewish bitterness and disappointment at Allied policy, at the time and subsequently, can be fully understood. But still the historical problem remains: how to evaluate this problem without losing sight of the first and final responsibility of Nazi Germany for the Holocaust? So that instead of continuing to ask the question, what *should* have been done in the given circumstances, one really has to find out what *could* have been done. The short answer to that is quite simple: not much. After all, it took the combined might of several Allied armies and air forces several years to wipe Nazi Germany from the face of the earth. On the other hand, this does lead to the legitimate question whether what was actually done to relieve the Jewish predicament was enough, and why was more not achieved? Unfortunately, the presentation of this subject has come to turn upon semantics and polemic in the place of cool, reasoned, analysis and argument, largely because the initial premiss of the existence of a given international morality from which some authors proceed simply does not exist, and never has, in the real world. That is the concept of 'imperative responsibility' on the part of groups and governments for the fate of specific minority groups in other societies. This simply does not exist. On the other hand, common feelings of humanitarianism do exist, but the question of their application or effectiveness then comes to depend entirely upon what one might term 'pragmatic responsibility', i.e.what is politically and practically possible at any one time to help those in need within the strict limitation that such responsibility can never be universal or total.

The nature of the Allied response to the Jewish predicament in wartime Nazi Europe, however that predicament presented itself, has to be seen from the perspective of this constraint. Specifically with regard to the actual and potential *European* Jewish refugee question as it manifested itself throughout the war, i.e. within the peculiar circumstances of global warfare, a whole range of contemporary national interests took precedence over those of people who simply wished to move from an existing social environment of hostility to a more amenable one. Again it must be said that while there was nothing new about the desire of such people to become refugees, neither was there anything new about the reluctance of the Allied powers and others during the Second World War to create as many barriers and hurdles to immigration into their societies (and Palestine) as possible, but that once such refugees finally arrived at *their* goal the 'host' authorities reluctantly (to put it mildly) allowed them to remain.

However, because of the Nazi *Endlösung der Judenfrage* it has been argued that the Allied Powers *should* have lifted all restrictions on immigration into Palestine and other territories and so brought about the 'saving' of Europe's Jews by enabling them to leave Nazi Europe. The clear implication of this and similar arguments is that the European Jewish question *per se* should have figured high on the list of Allied policy priorities but especially so because of the Nazi Final Solution of the Jewish Question. That the Allies failed to ease immigration restrictions and to consider the Jews as a priority policy issue has been taken as proving the point that the Allies were simply not interested in the fate of the Jews under Nazism and that such actions in fact contributed to the mass of Jewish deaths in Nazi Germany. In this as in all controversy the truth lies somewhere in the middle of the extremes of argument and polemic – but how to reach that point?

The fact of the matter is that it was Nazi policies which totally determined the fate of European Jewry, not those of any other nation. Furthermore, and while the anti-Jewish policies of Nazi Germany in Nazi Europe remained within the limits of what was relatively normal for the Nazi regime, i.e. of brutality and extreme persecution but not yet extermination, the Jewish question in Europe and the Jewish-refugee question (such as it was) were both viewed from the perspective of objectivity by other nations: the Jews of Europe, while they remained in Europe, were not only considered to be the nationals of their individual countries, but like all other occupied civilians would simply have to take their chances under Nazism until the war ended with an eventual Allied victory; none of this was allowed to affect the basic principles of the various immigration controls invoked against would-be Jewish refugees who were still to be found within the confines of Europe, although attitudes changed if they somehow managed to smuggle themselves out of Europe and into Allied territory. In other words, the so-called 'fate' of European Jewry did not figure in the formulation and execution of Allied immigration policy in its various forms because until Germany's invasion of Russia in June 1941 their 'fate' in Europe was seen as indistinguishable from that of other occupied civilians. Although this was not in fact the case, in the circumstances the Allied policy makers felt it would have been immoral to have distinguished the Jews in any way from other European civilians so far as basic attitudes were concerned. And as regards those Jewish refugees who perpetuated a Jewish refugee 'problem', they were simply to be dealt with on the basis of previous practices.

It has also been suggested that during the years 1939 to 1941 the main obstacle to Jewish emigration from Nazi-controlled Europe was not the German government but the reluctance of other countries to admit them. The fact is that the development of Nazi Germany's Jewish policies after September 1938 was not contingent upon developments in British and American immigration policy. This Nazi policy was far from being concerned with Jewish emigration from Nazi controlled areas of Europe *per se*, especially if that meant 'the great majority of Jews'. The outbreak of war brought millions of Jews under Nazi control and this effectively ruled out any such 'orderly' schemes of emigration as were pursued before September 1938 (and those were hardly either orderly or humane). The rather special and Utopian ideas such as the famed Madagascar Plan did not really belong to Hitler's heartfelt desire actually to exterminate European Jewry, and while it appealed to the German bureaucrats it was in any case contingent upon there being an end to the war and one which involved a total German victory. Furthermore, in the period 1939–1940 the Gestapo and Adolf Eichmann were chiefly and primarily concerned only with continued Jewish emigration from Germany itself. So far as the *Ostjuden* of Poland and the Baltic States were concerned, (let alone the rest of European Jewry), their emigration under Nazi authority was a complete non-starter. But even when one considers the period 1939–1941, one rather basic and pertinent question has to be asked: even if the Jews had to remain in Europe and not be 'allowed' to emigrate elsewhere, why did they have to be deliberately done to death on a pan-European scale by the Nazis if not as a direct result of Nazi intentions towards them?

It is only for the period after the autumn of 1941 and 1942, when news of the physical destruction of the Jews became known in the west, that it becomes legitimate to ask the question: now that the Allies knew of this policy of extermination, what did they do, and was what they did sufficient to relieve the suffering of the Jews? In turn, though, it becomes legitimate to ask something else: what were the Allies able to do? By 1942, and certainly for the rest of the war, the Allies saw the question of the 'rescue' of the Jews as being synonymous with the rescue of the rest of the civilian population of Nazi-occupied Europe by means of a total military victory over Nazi Germany. The purely practical difficulties of achieving even that primary task, let alone anything else, may be seen by the slow and difficult progress of the Allied armies after Stalingrad and the invasions of Italy in 1943 and Normandy in 1944, until costly victory was only achieved five months into 1945.

The key question, as always, was to what extent did information regarding the Holocaust become a guide to action, although an associated problem concerned the psychological difficulties in converting knowledge about the Nazi Final Solution into actual belief. But in turn this raises the next problem: what action was possible in the circumstances? *Pari passu* with the knowledge that gradually emerged from occupied Europe throughout 1942 about the policy of extermination, the Allies not only made persecution of the Jews a central theme of their propaganda but began to commit themselves to prosecute those guilty and responsible for Nazi crimes against the Jews. The Allied Declaration of 17 December 1942 on this issue actually helped to pave the way for a change in international law, so that at the Nuremberg tribunals of 1945 and 1946 the new concept of 'crimes against humanity' was introduced.

While this was an important development, it is also true that in other respects little was offered in the way of help. Ignoring for the moment the fact that neither the British or the Americans were operating the gas camps and arranging the death transports on a continental scale, it is a fact that many of the schemes for 'rescue' mooted during 1943 and parts of 1944 were considered by the Allies from the point of view of the priority given to achieving military victory over Nazi Germany; on the basis of the strict maintenance of their previous immigration policies; on the insistence that there were to be no negotiations with the Nazis; no major relaxation of the economic blockade of Nazi Europe; and that no action was to be taken which might promote dissension between the Western Allies and the Soviet Union and so affect adversely the successful prosecution of the war against Nazi Germany. There were three main schemes of rescue which the Allies had to consider in 1943 and 1944, the successful outcome of which would have necessarily involved the Allies in driving a coach and horses through their previous immigration policies: that of the Romanian Jews in 1943, the Horthy offer of July 1944, and the Joel Brand episode, the notorious 'trucks for blood' offer over the Hungarian Jews. While the British rejected the Joel Brand adventure as a case of blackmail, final judgement on the attitudes and policies of the Allies on the other two cases must be reserved; neither scheme went through because Germany refused to sanction the departure of the Romanian and Hungarian Jews. In a sense, then, Nazi Germany finally saved the Allied governments from having to balance humanitarianism against the maintenance of their immigration policies. In any case, and certainly in the circumstances of the time, the Allied governments did not see it as part of their 'responsibility' to aid Nazi Germany in its desire to re-order the ethnic map of Europe by the shipment of Jews from the continent.

It is, therefore, the maintenance of restrictive Allied immigration policies vis-à-vis the Jews of Europe during the Second World War which lies at the heart of the matter. If those immigration policies had been eased, would the Jews have been saved from destruction by the Nazis? In one sense the question is an immoral one since it is not directed to the instigators and perpetrators of the mass murder of European Jewry. The question is also immoral from another point of view: it is generally posed in a blanket fashion for the whole period of the war, yet its intended effect, to shift blame from the Nazis to the Allies, is almost inapplicable to both since *Endlösung* did not exist before 22 June 1941. But yet other questions make their appearance. Even if the Allies had made it easier for those Jews who had actually got to the Balkan countries to leave Europe and enter Allied territories, would this have affected Nazi policy towards the Jews they controlled and certainly towards the 5–6 *million* Jews they actually destroyed? For it was Nazi policy, not Allied policy, which destroyed Jewish life. Given that *most* of Europe's Jews had in fact been destroyed by 1942 and certainly 1943 – the largest remaining community was that of Hungary, and they were shipped to Auschwitz during 1944 – it must be clear that virtually nothing the Allies could have done in the way of military action (beyond them until late in 1944) or easing immigration controls would have halted the *pace* of the Nazi system of death. So that, in the final analysis, any talk of the Allies possibly having 'saved' Jews by any change in their immigration controls would have involved only some thousands more than were actually saved. But to project from this point of view the notion that 'Europe's Jews' *per se* would have been saved by more liberal immigration policies on the part of the Allied powers is not merely an immoral accusation but a *non sequitur*.

Bibliography

Uwe Dietrich ADAM, *Judenpolitik im Dritten Reich* (Düsseldorf 1972).

Yitzhak ARAD, *Ghetto in Flames. The Struggle and Destruction of the Jews in Vilna in the Holocaust* (Jerusalem 1980).

Yehuda BAUER, *The Holocaust in Historical Perspective* (London 1978).

Yehuda BAUER, *American Jewry and the Holocaust: The American Jewish Joint Distribution Committee 1939–1945* (Detroit 1981).

Yehuda BAUER, *A History of the Holocaust* (New York 1982).

Karl Dietrick BRACHER, *The German Dictatorship: the Origins, Structure and Effects of National Socialism* (London 1971).

Martin BROSZAT, 'Hitler and the Genesis of the "Final Solution": an assessment of David Irving's theses', *Yad Vashem Studies*, Volume 13, 73–125, and originally published in *Vierteljahrshefte für Zeitgeschichte*, Volume 25, October 1977, 739–775.

Christopher BROWNING, *The Final Solution and the German Foreign Office. A Study of Referat D. III of Abteilung Deutschland 1940–43* (New York 1978).

Christopher BROWNING, 'Zur Genesis der *Endlösung*. Eine Antwort an Martin Broszat', *Vierteljahrshefte für Zeitgeschichte*, Volume 29, January 1981, 97–109.

Israel W. CHARNY, *How Can We Commit the Unthinkable? Genocide: the Human Cancer*, (Boulder, Colorado, 1982).

John S CONWAY, 'Der Holocaust in Ungarn: Neue Kontroversen und Uberlegungen', *Vierteljahrschefte für Zeitgeschichte*, Volume 32, April 1984, 179–212.

Lucy S DAWIDOWICZ, *The War Against the Jews 1933–1945* (London 1975).

Henry L FEINGOLD, *The Politics of Rescue. The Roosevelt Administration and the Holocaust 1938–1945* (New Brunswick 1970)

Gerald FLEMING, *Hitler und die Endlösung: Es ist des Führers Wunsch* (Munich 1982).

John P FOX, 'Great Britain and the German Jews 1933', *The Wiener Libary Bulletin*, Volume XXVI, Nos. 1/2, New Series Nos. 26/7, October 1972, 40–46.

John P FOX, 'The Jewish Factor in British War Crimes Policy in 1942', *The English Historical Review*, Volume XCII, No. 362, January 1977, 82–106.

John P FOX, 'The Holocaust in Historical Perspective' (review article) *The Jewish Quarterly*, Volume 27, Nos. 2–3, Autumn 1979, 30–33.

John P FOX, *European Studies Review*, January 1980, 138–146: review of Bernard Wasserstein's *Britain and the Jews of Europe 1939–1945*, leading to exchange of correspondence in *European Studies Review*, October 1980.

John P FOX, 'Das Nationalsozialistische Deutschland und die Emigration nach Grossbritannien' in: Gerhard Hirschfeld (editor), *Exil in Grossbritannien. Zu Emigration aus dem nationalsozialistischen Deutschland 1933–1945* (Stuttgart 1983). English version: Leamington Spa 1984.

John P FOX, 'The Final Solution: Intended or Contingent? The Stuttgart Conference of May 1984 and the Historical Debate', *Patterns of Prejudice*, Volume 18, No. 3, July 1984, 27–39.

John P FOX, 'The Holocaust as History: The Issues. A Review Article', *Patterns of Prejudice*, Volume 19, No. 2, April 1985, 44–55.

John P FOX, 'Confronting the Holocaust' (review article), *Soviet-Jewish Affairs*, Vol. 16, no. 2, May 1986, 47–62.

John P FOX, *Hitler and the Jewish Question* (Macmillan 1986).

Saul FRIEDLANDER, *L'antisemitisme nazi. Histoire d'une psychose collective* (Paris 1971).

Saul FRIEDLANDER, 'The Historical Significance of the Holocaust', *The Jerusalem Quarterly*, No. 1, Fall 1976, 36–59.

Martin GILBERT, *Auschwitz and the Allies* (London 1981).

Yisrael GUTMAN, *The Jews of Warsaw 1939–1945: Ghetto Underground, Revolt* (Brighton 1982).

Raul HILBERG, *The Destruction of the European Jews* (London 1961).

Andreas HILLGRUBER, 'Die *Endlösung* und das deutsche Ostimperium as Kernstuck des rassenideologischen Programms des Nationalsozialismus', *Vierteljahrshefte für Zeitgeschichte*, Volume 20, April 1972, 133–153.

Leo KUPER, *Genocide. Its Political Use in the Twentieth Century* (Penguin Books 1981).

Walter LAQUEUR, *The Terrible Secret. An Investigation into the Suppresion of Information about Hitler's 'Final Solution'* (London 1980).

Nora LEVIN, *The Holocaust. The Destruction of European Jewry 1933–1945* (New York 1968).

Heiner LICHTENSTEIN, *Warum Auschwitz nicht bombardiert wurde* (Köln 1980).

Alan MILWARD, 'It Can Happen Here', *London Review of Books*, 2 May 1985, 3–6.

Hans MOMMSEN, 'Die Realisierung des Utopischen. Die *Endlösung der Judenfrage* im Dritten Reich', *Geschichte und Gesellschaft*, No. 9, 1983, 381–420.

Arthur D MORSE, *While Six Million Died* (London 1968).

Monty Noam PENKOWER, *The Jews Were Expendable. Free World Diplomacy and the Holocaust* (Chicago 1983).

Gerald REITLINGER, *The Final Solution. The Attempt to Exterminate the Jews of Europe 1939–1945* (London 1968).

Werner RODER, Die deutschen sozialistischen Exilgruppen in Grossbritannien 1940-1945. Ein Beitrag zur Geschichte des Widerstandes gegen den Nationalsozialismus (Bonn/Bad Godesberg 1973).

Karl A SCHLEUNES, *The Twisted Road to Auschwitz. Nazi Policy Toward German Jews 1933–1939* (Chicago 1970).

William SHAWCROSS, *The Quality of Mercy. Cambodia, Holocaust and Modern Conscience* (London 1984).

A.J. SHERMAN, *Island Refuge. Britain and Refugees from the Third Reich 1933–1939* (London 1973).

Isaiah TRUNK, *Judenrat. The Jewish Councils in Eastern Europe Under Nazi Occupation* (New York 1972).

Herbert E TUTAS, *Nationalsozialismus und Exil. Die Politik des Dritten Reiches gegenüber der deutschen politischen Emigration 1933–1939* (Munich, 1975).

YAD VASHEM, JERUSALEM, *Rescue Attempts During the Holocaust. Proceedings of the Second Yad Vashem International Historical Conference*, 8–11 April 1974 (Jerusalem 1977).

Bernard WASSERSTEIN, *Britain and the Jews of Europe 1939–1945* (Oxford 1979).

David S WYMAN, *The Abandonment of the Jews. America and the Jews 1941–1945* (New York 1985).

Bohdan WYTWYCKY, *The Other Holocaust: Many Circles of Hell* (Washington 1982).

6 Religion, refugees and the U.S. Government

BRUCE NICHOLS

The world of private voluntarism faces a set of perennial issues that have grown out of structures of co-operation with governmental bodies put in place at the time of the Second World War. When looking at the post-war evolution of refugee problems in Europe and the Middle East, these issues (government regulation, coalition building among agencies, excessively close political ties between agencies and partisan politics) are often treated as secondary. In fact, the ties between governmental and non-governmental bodies are an increasingly important topic in any understanding of humanitarian activities today. This study addresses the formative period of this co-operation when the U.S. Government and U.S. religious bodies mobilized to aid European refugees during the Second World War.

The religious agencies were the prime movers and the chief beneficiaries of the first decades of structured private-public co-operation in refugee matters. It was their field work, and it was the refugee populations of interest to them, that made government involvement in refugee care and resettlement feasible. Furthermore, religious factors continue to influence the response to refugees in the United States despite the presence today of many refugee agencies with no explicit religious commitments.

Public support for refugee causes in the United States is grounded in Judeo-Christian values that command special attention to the widow, the outcast, the sojourner. In recent times Jews, Catholics, and Protestants have all institutionalized their responses to what has become a permanent refugee crisis. Their pioneering efforts are still among the most successful of the privately sponsored efforts at refugee care. Religiously grounded agencies still carry the lion's share of field work. Their contributions to refugee work and the nature of their ties to donor governments are of particular interest in understanding today's crises in refugee assistance.

To be sure, religious voluntary agencies face many of the same problems as their secular counterparts. Today, voluntary service abroad is going through one of its periodic identity crises. In 1966 the Carnegie Corporation of New York issued a report entitled 'The Non-Governmental Organisation at Bay', which called attention to some of the established doctrines of government co-operation with non-governmental organizations (NGOs). The NGOs could move swiftly, arrive at a disinterested appraisal of a situation free of political influence, experiment with an open style, and most importantly, make contact with the people at a level well below official governmental contacts. Refugee work was a key field in which NGOs demonstrated their competence and were rewarded with governmental support and patronage.

In the wake of the expanding welfare state at home, the fortunes of the agencies working abroad rose. A common observation from the 1950s and 1960s was that if the U.S. Government were interested in a particular country, so would be Church World Service. (Any number of agencies could be substituted here.) Surveying such situations at home and abroad the Carnegie Corporation asked, 'Is the non-governmental organization of the future to be simply an auxiliary to the state, a kind of willing but not very resourceful handmaiden? Or is it to be a strong, independent adjunct that provides government with a type of capability it cannot provide for itself?'[1]

This question touched on a long-standing debate over whether the legal definition of voluntary action protected only those efforts that sought to *complement* the work of the state, or whether such legal protection also extended to voluntary action intended as an *alternative* to state-sponsored action. In Great Britain, the Nathan Report of 1952 argued for the existence of both these two approaches to voluntarism in the modern world. Under the pragmatic complementary approach, the government divided pieces of a given task between public and private agencies. This pattern accurately described the state of much private/public co-operation in refugee work, but Lord Nathan argued that the more important function of voluntarism was to offer an alternative to state-sponsored action.

The debate over the proper boundaries of voluntary action is active today in the United States, the UNHCR and among refugee advocates and agencies around the world. To understand its importance in refugee work we must return to the Second World War. In the course of little more than a decade the efforts of America's religious communities to serve those in need overseas were rapidly adapted by Washington's foreign policymakers. Future needs dictated that the church and state learn to go abroad *together*, and no endeavour demonstrated that necessity better than refugee work. Yet that togetherness is today frequently a source of acute discomfort to many who long to see refugee work serving refugees rather than the political ends of governments.

The role of religion in the American polity is complex. Religious rhetoric has always been part of American political life, yet there are outcries if government is seen as favouring one religion over another. The so-called separation of church and state is not a constitutional doctrine, but a quotation from a letter Thomas Jefferson wrote a group of Connecticut Baptists early in the 19th century. The expression has stuck in the public consciousness as a convenient shorthand.

Separation of church and state has never been the norm in social welfare, certainly not since the Supreme Court held in 1899 that the U.S. Government could provide funds for a Catholic hospital in Washington, D.C. as long as the hospital made services available to non-Catholics. Under U.S. law refugee work as well as development activity abroad fall under the category of social welfare. Indeed, a more accurate reading of the intention of the religion clauses of the Constitution suggests that the founders sought *independence* (rather than the separation) of the institutions of government and those of religion. Co-operation on shared objectives was acceptable provided religious institutions did not play a divisive role in politics and/or government did not attempt to control religious bodies. Recent Supreme Court judgements call for government to seek a benevolent neutrality[2] that preserves the independence of all parties.

This tradition of keeping church and state independent of one another remains important in understanding current debates over whether voluntarism is free to establish alternatives to state-sponsored action. Presumably, if voluntary action is based on the same religious values protected by law from ultimate state control, it is due the same protection. Without Lord Nathan's presumption that voluntary action is not ultimately controlled or directed by the state, we are left with a strikingly narrowed field of complementary activities.

The dialectic between complementarity and independence is thus central to understanding the relationship between voluntary action and state-sponsored action. Religious bodies schooled in the problem through centuries of experience entered the realm of co-operation with the state in refugee matters in the 1940s with determination. The decade saw a new integration between government policy and religious agencies. The patterns set then still determine to a large extent the structure of government relations with religious bodies and other private groups active in international work.

The foreign affairs power of the Executive Branch in this period expanded greatly, especially as it touches private voluntarism. One of Roosevelt's greatest wartime tasks was to plan a United States-led global post-war coalition of victor nations. This necessitated an explosion of administrative tasks, regulatory groups and structures of surveillance on a scale previously unknown. Such expanded executive power, including military strategy on a global scale, strained the delicate balance of powers between Congress, the president and the courts. No segment of society was left to an autonomous role, as the private voluntary world soon discovered. As in most wartime situations, the autonomy and freedom of religious institutions were curtailed. American religious work abroad had faced few restrictions before the 1930s; now it was asked to take its place in an expanded global ensemble of American services, occasionally under rather strict terms. Essentially, religious relief services abroad could play as a member of the American team or not at all.

Today all parties in refugee assistance, be they governmental, intergovernmental or private, present humanitarian service as their central motivation. To understand the United States' approach, we must return to the Second World War and the relations it engendered between the U.S. Government and the American religious establishment.

Prelude to War

In 1939, the year following Roosevelt's international refugee conference at Evian, refugee problems intensified. Victims of the Spanish Civil War and the Nazi persecutions added to the list of Europe's problems. The handling of the Jewish immigration problem, always a difficulty under the British mandate for Palestine, had intensified in 1931 when the American government refused to guarantee expanded Jewish immigration to the region. In 1939 a British white paper announced that quotas for Jews entering Palestine would remain at the miniscule figure of 15,000 per year.

Voluntary societies, governments and the High Commissioner for Refugees of the League of Nations faced questions. Was migration the best solution for displaced persons? If so, who would take them? Should migration services be differentiated from overseas relief services to those who could not, for one reason or another, migrate? Who spoke for the refugees themselves, and how could effective response be organized? Following Evian, the governments of 32 nations formed the Inter-Governmental Committee on Refugees (IGC). Its initial task was to assist refugees leaving Germany and Austria and to seek avenues of resettlement[3], but for all the support from high places behind its formation, the IGC worked in a political straightjacket. Refugee problems remained of secondary importance to wider issues of impending war.

The great theme of the agencies and various refugee committees was the horror of innocent suffering. The Non-Sectarian Committee for German Refugee Children, quoting 'Suffer little children to come unto me', joined in support of the Wagner-Rogers Bill, which allowed 20,000 non-quota refugee children of all faiths to enter the United States. But despite strong religious support, which included a recitation of Psalm 46 ('God is our refuge and strength, a very present help in trouble') by Rabbi Steven Wise before Congress, the bill did not pass. Isolationist sentiment such as the following carried the day:

> These refugees have a heritage of hate. They could never become loyal Americans. Let us not be maudlin in our sympathies, as charity begins at home. We must protect our own children. No society, no state can successfully assume the tremendous responsibility of fostering thousands of motherless, embittered, persecuted children of undesirable foreigners and expect to convert these embattled souls into loyal, loving American citizens.[4]

Experienced overseas voluntary agencies realised that the United States Government was worried about the political impact of refugee work in Europe and resettlement efforts at home. Much as Herbert Hoover had been at odds with leftist agencies eager to help alleviate the Russian famine of 1921–23, Secretary of State Cordell Hull in the late 1930s feared that partisan agencies would embroil the United States in the Spanish War.

He therefore refused to issue passports to several voluntary medical units operating in Spain, arguing that such controls were necessary to preserve American neutrality.

Following the first Neutrality Act in 1935, agencies active in Spain were asked to register with the State Department; with a strengthening of the legislation in 1939 they were required to submit monthly statements of contributions and expenditures. Thus 'was begun an official supervision of voluntary giving for overseas relief, which was to become a continuing aspect of American policy.'[5]

Hull himself had hoped that such measures would not be necessary, and that the American public would channel their private donations into the two agencies Hull trusted for their nonpartisanship, the American Friends Service Committee (AFSC) and the American Red Cross. This was not what happened. Numerous ethnic committees were formed to aid refugees and the destitute of Europe. Dozens co-operated in efforts to send relief to Poland. The American Jewish Joint Distribution Committee aided Jews fleeing Poland and Czechoslovakia, as well as refugees from Germany inside France.

The American Government, fighting to retain a neutral posture toward the conflict, grew alarmed over the implications of increased private American relief. Officials feared that unwittingly or deliberately, relief workers might be used to draw America into the war. The Neutrality Act of November 4, 1939 extended the neutrality provisions governing the conduct of American relief activities in Spain. It controlled certain forms of relief to nations the President considered to be in a belligerent state, primarily the parties to the most recent European conflicts.

Furthermore, Roosevelt himself had grown concerned over the response to refugee problems, particularly the fact that they involved a disproportionate number of Jews. It was, after all, a time in American history in which anti-Semitic meetings were held on the streets of New York and Boston, and Jews were often harassed and attacked. In the month before the Neutrality Act became law Roosevelt set forth a comprehensive new approach in a confidential memorandum to Secretary Hull. A solution to the 'whole refugee problem,' could be promoted 'on a broad religious basis, thereby making it possible to gain the kind of world-wide support that a mere Jewish relief set-up would not evoke.' Accordingly Myron C. Taylor, former president of U.S. Steel and chief American delegate to the Evian Conference of 1938, was sent to Rome in December 1939 as Roosevelt's special envoy to the Vatican. He was instructed to highlight the Administration's particular concern for Catholic refugees.

Also in late 1939 Roosevelt sent variations of a single letter to Taylor, George Buttrick of the Federal Council of Churches and Cyrus Adler of the Jewish Joint Distribution Committee outlining what he hoped would be a new attitude of co-operation between religious groups active overseas and the U.S. Government. This message to the 'three faiths' of America shows Roosevelt's skill at evoking the parallel duties of the nation's religious leaders (the 'seekers of light') and its elected officials ('seekers of peace'):

I believe that while statesmen are considering a new order of things, the new order may well be at hand. I believe that it is even now being built, silently but inevitably, in the hearts of masses whose voices are not heard, but whose common faith will write the final history of our time. They know that unless there is belief in some guiding principle and some trust in a divine plan, nations are without light, and peoples perish. They know that the civilization handed down to us by our fathers was built by men and women who knew in their hearts that all were brothers because they were children of God. They believe that by His will enmities can be healed; that in his mercy the weak can find deliverance, and the strong can find grace in helping the weak . . .

Because the people of this nation have come to a realization that time and distance no longer exist in the older sense, they understand that that which harms one segment of humanity harms all the rest. They know that only by friendly association between the seekers of light and the seekers of peace everywhere can the forces of evil be overcome . . .

It is, therefore, my thought that though no given action or given time may now be prophesied, *it is well that we encourage a closer association between those in every part of the world – those in religion and those in government – who have a common purpose.* I, therefore, suggest that it would give me great satisfaction if you would from time to time come to Washington to discuss the problem which all of us have on our minds, in order that parallel endeavors for peace and the alleviation of suffering may be assisted.[emphasis added][6]

No clearer offer of co-operation between the government and America's religious institutions could have been made. Unfortunately in 1939 the moral, legal and logistical problems involved in refugee assistance were far from being solved. No credible international organization had been formed to co-ordinate governmental efforts; the U.S. Government spoke eloquently of the plight of European Jews, but its actions indicated a desire to distance itself from politically unpopular efforts to liberalize immigration law or otherwise to expand the number of Jews reaching America.

Though co-operation abroad between religious groups and the government still lay in the future, two decades of *ad hoc* co-operation in refugee and relief work since 1919 had shown that increased religiously based relief was possible. By 1939 the power and scope of this new service-oriented engagement rivalled that of descendants of the largely Protestant missionary movement of the 19th century. The emergence of contemporary approaches to the refugee problem within Catholic and Jewish communities challenged the priority of the Protestant ethos as the ethical backbone of American foreign policy. That that ethos was still dominant in the 1930s is evident from the importance attached to having Protestants at the head of national or interfaith refugee committees and agencies.

Those who followed events in Washington knew that the situation was about to change. Given the refugee and relief crisis of the Second World War, the issue would no longer be limited to assessing the proper morality today in continuity with America's traditions of providing safe haven to the oppressed. It would also have to take into account the size, scale and efficiency of the particular organization, be it Protestant, Catholic, Jewish or secular.

The Government Organizes Wartime Relief

The Second World War began with established service agencies leading the way in overseas humanitarian service. The AFSC was joined in France by the Jewish Joint Distribution Committee, which focused its efforts on 55,000 Jews in the south. The long experience of the older agencies in the refugee and relief field was soon under vigorous challenge by dozens of new committees and agencies. The Bishop's War Emergency and Relief Committee was organized in 1939 to administer Catholic war relief; Jewish, Protestant and ethnic groups all regrouped. Among new agencies, contemporary survivors include the Presiding Bishop's Fund for World Relief (Episcopal; 1938), the Unitarian Service Committee (also founded in 1938) and the Brethren Service Committee (Church of the Brethren; 1939).

With the coming of the war, American voluntarism expanded greatly. The Quakers spent nearly $1,000,000 on war relief in 1940; war relief giving to all agencies the year before was $2.5 million. In 1941, total giving from private sources jumped to $28.5 million. While this record was the pride of the agencies and their supporters, government officials realized that relief work was being conducted on far too small a scale to meet future needs. Not only would relief services need to expand; the government would also have to standardize private efforts and ensure that they did not overlap. Importantly, but almost invisibly as a political factor, humanitarian relief was harnessed directly to the Allied war effort. Once America had entered the war, there was some debate among American relief workers on this issue, but the overwhelming majority believed humanitarian efforts should further the war effort against Germany and Japan.

The U.S. Government, following Roosevelt's lead in asking religious leaders for closer co-operation in fending off a fundamental threat to American society, encouraged them to form relief societies that would both raise funds and, in concert with fellow believers abroad, operate relief programmes where needed. Religious groups constituted the largest segment of private relief contributions, and with some modifications, the patterns of private giving and service and of church/state co-operation set during the war have remained in place into the 1980s.

Since Evian, Roosevelt had realized that refugee problems stood somewhat independent of broader relief questions. They were more emotional, they entailed more political risks. One commentator wrote in 1941 that refugee efforts were 'at best a stepchild in Washington, to be beaten and buffeted, and at worst a football for anti-Semitism and for petty bureaucrats who take delight in sabotaging the President's program just because it is his.' To the government officials a refugee was an 'alien'; to the military a 'secret agent'.[7]

For the most part refugee care would have to rely on the same Jewish and Christian organizations whose help would be needed in the wider problems of wartime and post-war humanitarian assistance. Roosevelt knew that close Jewish and Catholic involvement with government initiatives was potentially politically divisive at home, something he was eager to avoid during wartime. Far from anticipating mass slaughter of European Jews, Roosevelt foresaw a massive influx of refugees to other western nations. The idea that refugees could be resettled at will to third world countries was not at the time an accepted part of government planning on refugee matters. Limited numbers of Jews had been resettled in the U.S., but many were prominent intellectuals and leaders. Many more moved legally and illegally through Zionist networks to Palestine.

Roosevelt lobbied for intergovernmental attention to the refugee dilemma, and continued to insist, against advice from the State Department, that the Inter-Governmental Committee (IGC) established at Evian in 1938 would be the proper forum for such international co-operation (the State Department preferred to reach its own solutions to the problem). Roosevelt favoured the IGC over the office of the High Commissioner of the League of Nations, to which the United States was not a party. In the IGC he could pursue his own visionary resettlement schemes.

However, the IGC had never had any teeth; when Roosevelt called a meeting in Washington of the IGC officers in the fall of 1939, countries were reluctant to send delegates since the Committee had failed to accomplish anything in the year it had existed. Roosevelt encouraged the gathering to consider the feasibility of massive resettlement projects somewhere in the 'many vacant spaces of the earth's surface'. In a striking reference to the words of Emma Lazarus inscribed on the Statue of Liberty, he acknowledged the significance of new settlements, and told the delegates that America would help the refugees, as long as they moved elsewhere. 'Let us lift a lamp beside *new* golden doors and build *new* refuges for the tired, for the poor, for the huddled masses yearning to be free.'[8] The Inter-Governmental Committee typified Roosevelt's rhetorical and bureaucratic evasions of aspects of the refuge dilemma throughout most of the war.

While both governmental and religious agencies preached the importance of neutral humanitarianism in relief services, problems inevitably arose. After the failure of the Wagner-Rogers Bill designed to admit 20,000 refugee children, Roosevelt responded to pressure by authorizing an order by the attorney general which allowed a little over a thousand children into the United States. Under Wagner-Rogers, half of the children would have been Jewish; nearly all those who arrived under the attorney general's order were English.

The Government's early responses to European refugees were cautious, quiet and largely ineffective. It wanted the help of America's religious institutions, but in a way that would not start them squabbling with each other. Therefore, the refugee question was effectively buried in the early part of the war while the government concentrated on organizing religious and other voluntary groups into an ensemble that could work alongside the government's full range of humanitarian efforts overseas.

Early Policy Initiatives

In the early months of 1941 the State Department in Washington, while busy working publicly to keep America neutral in the European conflict, was quietly expanding its reach to accommodate a new role for America in the post-war world. In early March, Secretary of State Cordell Hull wrote to Roosevelt about the role of overseas relief societies. Of these, only the American Red Cross bore the explicit legislative authority of the Congress. The rest were essentially free agents, existing on private funds and accepting government assistance at times of emergency. Their help would be needed to maintain peace in the post-war world.

The time had come, according to Hull, to strengthen the connection between voluntary foreign aid and official American policy. A first step had been taken with the neutrality legislation. Agencies would be officially 'licensed' for operations abroad only if they registered with the State Department. Export of relief goods, already limited by the 1917 Trading With the Enemy Act, would be reported and registered with the Commerce Department. Records today indicate the scope of private giving from the early years of the war. From 1939 to 1941 the roughly 350 agencies that registered sent nearly $175 million in cash and supplies to the needy overseas.

Traumatic events such as the fall of France in 1940 had made it clear to federal officials that active U.S. government relief involvement would be needed to supplement these generous contributions. The task at hand, Secretary Hull advised the president, was to use private agencies to channel government funded assistance as well. Despite cautious reminders from such journals as the Catholic *Commonwealth* that direct government involvement would undermine 'that personal element which imparts to charity its true nature and its characteristic graces,' many agency personnel and government officials were ready to proceed with new arrangements.

Hull offered two arguments for a closer link between private and public activities overseas, both of which made perfect sense at the time and both of which are still essential elements of State Department doctrine in working with private groups. First, a strengthened public authority in this field would help assure that the goals of the agencies were actually met, and that the public would be protected from fraudulent groups. Second, without greater co-ordination, the best efforts would end up in duplication, inefficiency and failure to be evenhanded. While it may not have been stated publicly, officials from the president down anticipated that relief activities after the war would be under the supervision of Allied military governments, and a good working relationship with American civilians in the field would be essential.

Contact with the Vatican never fully met Roosevelt's expectations of full co-operation. The appointment of Myron Taylor as Roosevelt's emissary to the Holy See was directly tied to Catholic participation in solving the refugee problem, and added moral urgency to the refugee issue.[9] However, Pope Pius XII was unwilling to believe early accounts of mass extermination. Furthermore, there were millions of Catholics in Axis-dominated territories. Even after Stephen Wise reported to Taylor in the fall of 1943 that Nazis were deporting Jews from Rome, and the news was forwarded to the Vatican, no official action was taken.

With military reverses in Europe and in the Pacific, the first half of 1942 was no time for the government to encourage random private initiatives abroad. In June of that year, Roosevelt forcefully called for national unity in winning the war.[10]

The peace offensive he promised carried a place for private voluntarism that willingly sought a complementary role to American and Allied prosecution of the war. That same month, at a national meeting of Community Chest organizations, Winthrop W. Aldrich, chairman of the board of New York's Chase National Bank, made the suggestion that overseas relief efforts should be federated. Given America's difficult military position overseas, the suggestion was greeted with enthusiasm.[11]

The President's War Relief Control Board

Nothing, however, had yet come of State Department initiatives to consolidate relief efforts abroad. Refugee relief in particular was limited during the duration of the fighting; Jews and other refugees within the Axis-held territories were considered off limits. Emphasis shifted to relief of the wounded military and civilians under Allied control. Frustrated with the inability of his own State Department to move quickly on such problems, Roosevelt named a civilian committee to investigate possible arrangements between the nation's private relief activities and the government's strategy for victory.

Accepting the committee's conclusion that 'the establishment of a single authority with adequate regulatory and supervisory powers' was needed, Roosevelt issued Executive Order 9205 on July 25, 1942, creating the President's War Relief Control Board (WRCB). Its function of formalizing relations between private and public humanitarian efforts has, in altered form, remained part of government bureaucracy throughout the 1980s. Its beginnings as a presidential advisory group lifted the sights of the private relief community. In a single executive order they were provided with access to the president that circumvented the various cabinet departments and lower bureaucracies.

The Board had considerable powers over voluntary agencies, including authority over 'all solicitations, sales or offers to sell merchandise or services, collections and distribution or disposal of funds and contributions in kind for the direct or implied purpose' of overseas relief and refugee work. Before the end of the process, 596 agencies engaged in foreign relief had registered, and by their own accounting, raised over $597 million dollars, plus countless contributions of clothing, food and other needed wartime supplies.

In exchange for government protection and access to federal assistance, whether administered directly or through the emerging intergovernmental structures of relief such as the United Nations Relief and Rehabilitation Administration (UNRRA), there were various *quid pro quos* for the agencies. For instance, the WRCB asked many agencies to rename themselves so as to include the word 'American'. All agencies that participated in government-sponsored fundraising were required to have governing boards consisting only of American citizens; their programmes overseas were to be conducted 'purely in the American interest'.[12] Decisions on the disbursement of government assistance would be made by executive and budget committees which did not include representatives of the agencies themselves.

The WRCB was given police powers to crack down on agencies that violated regulations on activities abroad, both political and administrative. The use of such powers, however, was generally limited to agencies that served as fronts for shipments of munitions or supplies to political factions, most of which were ethnic rather than religious in origin. The new regulations also included Board control over the timing of agency fund raising appeals and the authority to consolidate agencies that shared similar objectives.

Experience with the Board during the war indicated that it would be useful for the government to continue its functions in peacetime. On May 16, 1946, President Truman changed its title to the Advisory Committee on Voluntary Foreign Aid. Its new purpose was in Truman's words 'to tie together the governmental and private programs in the field of foreign relief.' A State Department official noted that in 1946 61 qualifying agencies 'undertook to record voluntarily with the Advisory Committee the information that they had been required to provide under licence during wartime'.[13] Once an independent presidential committee mediating private and public initiatives, the Advisory Committee was absorbed by the State Department's Agency for International Development in 1979. Its initial function of mediating private and public interests had been independently abandoned.

The National War Fund

The WRCB's major effort at co-ordinating overseas relief was the establishment of the National War Fund, the centralized, government supported fundraising machine that regulated fundraising appeals and divided the funds among selected private agencies based in the United States. It emerged from a December 15, 1942 meeting in the New York headquarters of the Chase National Bank, where Winthrop W. Aldrich gathered five other appointees at the request of the War Relief Control Board. As with the Control Board's policy on deciding fund disbursals privately rather than in consultation with the agencies, agency representatives were not included. Instead the government had taken the prudent course of appointing prominent academics, businessmen and bankers. The resulting plan consolidated local fundraising drives through local and state Community Chests, a wartime United Fund that would then be disbursed by the government to areas of greatest need overseas, using the voluntary agencies that qualified as members.

In a lively memoir detailing his service as general manager of the War Fund, Harold J. Seymour observes that one of the touchiest problems was deciding on who qualified as recipient agencies under the National War Fund. While nearly 600 agencies registered with the Board, only 23 participated in the National War Fund. What principles, then, governed inclusion?

First, registration with the President's War Relief Control Board had quickly become the essential entrée for establishing an agency's credibility and trustworthiness; no agency got anywhere, abroad or with the War Fund, without prior approval of the WRCB. Second, in the interests of efficiency only one agency would be included for a particular area of operation or function – thus the consolidations of agencies around service to prisoners of war, to refugees or to certain countries. The United Service Organization (USO) was the first of several religiously inspired consortia that pooled resources for common tasks. It received more assistance than any other agency that participated in the fund, providing 'rest and relaxation' for American armed forces abroad. Although the entertainment industry has given us the comic song and dance revue image of the USO, the organization itself emerged from a federation of six national agencies, of which five (the YMCA, the YWCA, the National Catholic Community Service, the National Jewish Welfare Board and the Salvation Army) had religious roots.

The third principle for determining the disbursal of funds was a non-discrimination clause, stating that all monies received from the Fund had to be disbursed 'without regard to color, creed, race or political affiliation.'

Specifically, it meant that labour-sponsored projects could not be designed for the relief of labor groups alone, and that no denominational relief programme, to the extent that it was financed by the National War Fund, could confine its work to the adherents of its own faith.[14]

This principle had been accepted as axiomatic to religiously based use of government funding at home. It was now extended to the international sphere on the basis of an administrative decision.

The War Fund did its best, but achieving some sort of governmental even-handedness with religious groups was easier said than done. The touchy question of Jewish activity abroad began with the fact that Jewish fundraising was conducted separately from other appeals, and was primarily spent on Jewish recipients abroad, fulfiling Jewish injunctions to observe primary responsibility for the community of faith. The same was true of Protestants and Catholics, but both of these groups, lacking for the most part a sense that they were persecuted minorities, were in a better position to help all without reference to race or creed.

Furthermore, European Jews constituted a disproportionate segment of the refugee population, and much Jewish giving was focused on Zionist solutions involving massive resettlement to Palestine. With the War Fund's emphasis on non-discrimination, this was sure to cause difficulties. Furthermore, the government's calculated fear of a backlash against giving associated with the cause of Jewish refugees is evident from the fact that no Jewish presence whatsoever is visible from the names of the 23 instrumentalities listed as Fund agencies, despite the fact that Jewish agencies did indeed benefit from the fund.

The question of direct participation of religious agencies was itself a political, if not legal, question. Questions of church and state before the Second World War often revolved around anti-Catholicism; the problem arose again over the Catholic role in the War Fund. Seymour tactfully noted that to list the newly formed War Relief Services of the National Catholic Welfare Conference 'without policy explanation . . . would be to invite question and confusion'. Despite such difficulties, 'everyone wanted to include the Catholic agency, both in the interest of unity and for the practical reason that the world-wide organization of the Roman Catholic Church . . . provided a ready channel for speedy, effective, and economical relief.'[15] Here Seymour was acknowledging a fact well understood by Roosevelt. The Catholic Church offered a global network of services unequalled in the Protestant or Jewish communities.

Seymour did not explain publicly that negotiations were underway in 1942 between the White House and Catholic leaders to explore a closer relationship between the U.S. Government and the Catholic hierarchy in the United States and their superiors in the Vatican. One participant recalled that they were conducted in a spirit that verged on desperation. 'No one knew where the world was going', he said. 'It seemed to all to be a moment of supreme crisis.'[16]

Roosevelt had of course had Myron Taylor at the Vatican since 1939, but the services of American Catholics were now specifically required in the war. The President's goals were twofold. First, NCWC should organize a national organization devoted to overseas relief. The Bishop's War Emergency and Relief Committee, in existence since 1939, was raising comparatively small amounts of private funding and providing limited overseas services. In late 1942, representatives of the President met with leaders of the NCWC; it was noted that in planning the new War Fund, it might be advantageous to organize a 'super agency' that would supersede the Bishop's Committee and preclude applications to the Fund by the 60 or so Catholic charities actively related to service institutions in the war zones. Second, he wanted to open more extensive intelligence contacts with the Vatican on situations inside Germany.

On January 15, 1943, one month after Winthrop Aldrich announced plans for a National War Fund, a special meeting of the National Catholic Welfare Conference's Administrative Board was called to respond to the government's request for a new overseas agency. Government guarantees of funding to supplement private resources were assured. The new agency, to be known as War Relief Services - NCWC, was admitted to the National

War Fund on April 28; two days later, eleven projects budgeted at nearly $2.4 million dollars were submitted to the Fund's Budget Committee. Projects included work with Polish refugees in Mexico and Palestine, Catholic refugees in England and Portugal, prisoners of war and services to seamen. Also included in these appropriations was an initial request to cover the expenses of the Catholic Committee for Refugees, which since 1936 had been assisting refugees coming to the United States.

From May till June 1943, representatives of the new War Relief Services negotiated acceptable conditions under which they would work with government funds. On June 25, Aldrich and a representative of War Relief Services announced a Memorandum of Agreement, which stipulated that government funds would cover 'health and welfare projects . . . as distinct from church and religious activities,' and gave the National War Fund responsibility for negotiating with any foreign agencies that were affiliated with the new American agency. Only then were incorporation papers filed on June 28.[17] As a matter of wartime pragmatism, War Relief Services was, like the USO, given favoured status among the voluntary agencies. It grew like wildfire; by September of 1944, the fledgling agency was active in 33 countries.

Roosevelt's goal of more sophisticated German intelligence through improved links with the Vatican was also accomplished in part through personnel associated with the new War Relief Services. In one of the resulting operations WRS personnel maintained contact with the largely Catholic opposition Centrist Party in Germany, which had been forced underground by the Nazis; this field network of intelligence complemented formal channels of information passed on to the United States through Myron Taylor and two assistants at the Vatican.[18] Thus War Relief Services – today, as CRS, the largest voluntary agency in the world – included intelligence links with the U.S. Government from its earliest days. Participants clearly felt that rendering assistance to the Allies was the only sane route forward, an act of religious and patriotic duty. Though agreements for co-operation in intelligence were not part of the formal agreements between WRS and the Government, the Roosevelt Administration expected and received co-operation.

Smaller Protestant and Jewish relief agencies did not fare nearly as well with government funds. In order to distribute funds raised nationally, the American Christian Refugee Committee (Federal Council of Churches), the Unitarian Service Committee and the International Rescue and Relief Committee (later the International Rescue Committee), an independent organization formed to help Jewish refugees in the early 1930s, were amalgamated into the 'Refugee Relief Trustees.' Similarly, services to prisoners of the War Relief Services of the National Catholic Welfare Conference and of the YMCA were consolidated into an instrumentality known as War Prisoners Aid, Inc. When Roosevelt finally announced the formation of the War Refugee Board in 1944 (designed to carry out rescue operations for Jews and others fleeing the Axis), the government provided only $1 million, insisting that Jewish agencies bear the brunt of fundraising.

The hairsplitting church/state legal decisions of recent years had little place in the administration of government contracts with religious bodies through the National War Fund. Mutual understanding and good will were the true moving forces within the Fund, 'rather than . . . a legalistic basis of binding contracts . . . [which] in themselves were scarcely worth their ink and paper'. Private and public forces worked together not for financial contracts, but through a national covenant for survival and victory in the midst of war. 'Dynamic federation' and 'maximum decentralization' were concepts common to all. The fund sought to dispense 'authoritative advice' rather than 'authoritarian control' over the way the funds were spent.

Such fine distinctions may be lost when agencies see their responsibilities abroad in conflict with governmental 'advice'. Such was increasingly the case with the refugee problem; by 1943 refugee advocates in religious agencies and elsewhere were beginning to realize that the Roosevelt Administration, for all its sympathetic rhetoric, had little intention of taking decisive action. Emphasis was placed on winning the war, and the administration's policies indicated that they kept an ear to the ground at home: no increase of immigration quotas, continued State Department restrictions on visas, no active rescue programme for refugees caught within Axis-dominated territory, continued reliance on the ineffective Intergovernmental Committee of Evian. Within this context, registered agencies were free to pursue humanitarian assistance. In practice, this meant that 85% of all Government resources going to voluntary agencies went to Europe; 15% went to the Far East and less than 1% went to Africa and Latin America combined. Private resources largely followed suit.[19]

The American Council of Voluntary Agencies

The vigorous efforts of the private sector to address questions of refugee relief and rescue exasperated officials at the State Department in charge of the problem, most notably Breckinridge Long, Assistant Secretary of State for Special Problems. Struck by the frequent intervention of Supreme Court Justice Felix Frankfurter on behalf of Jewish refugees, Long called Jewish refugee workers 'Frankfurter's boys'. Against their international sympathies – and by implication, those of other Christian and secular refugee supporters – Long represented an unabashedly nationalist point of view: 'as usual, they (the radicals) espoused some foreign cause to champion rather than advocate the American point of view or propose some practice in our own interests . . . There is a constant pressure from Congressional and organized groups in this country to have us proceed on behalf of non-Americans; so far I have been able to resist the pressure.'[20]

Long determined he would use his post to emphasize the security problems involved in bringing refugees to the United States. There was little doubt that powerful conservative members of Congress, as well as the overwhelming majority of the public, favoured the restrictionist policies he advocated. The importance of security questions in public debate over immigration affairs at this time cannot be overestimated. In 1940, for instance, the Immigration and Naturalization Service (INS) was transferred from the Department of Labour to the Justice Department, where it remains to this day. According to Secretary of Labour Frances Perkins, this was done because the Administration had decided that immigration was primarily a security rather than an economic issue.[21] Spies could be expected to enter the country as immigrants and refugees.

The record testifies to the unpleasantness that arose early in the war between the government and privately organized efforts of citizens committed to helping refugees overseas and at home. Quite unlike the 'three faiths' world of refugee assistance that emerged after the war, existing agencies sending refugee aid abroad from the United States at the beginning of the decade were overwhelmingly Jewish. Most of the existing Protestant and Catholic groups found that they could not raise funds from their constituencies in large amounts, and quietly accepted subsidies from Jewish groups. Long discerned that Catholic and Protestant support was limited at best, and he acted accordingly.

He faced a welter of requests for special attention to particular refugee intellectuals and other prominent refugees. These requests were often supported by the President's Advisory Committee on Political Refugees (PACPR), itself established by Roosevelt before the Evian conference of 1938 to circumvent State Department restrictions and delays. The Committee was neatly balanced between Protestant, Catholic and Jewish leadership, reflecting the government's attention to religious factors. It was an effort to give a unified voice to refugee efforts, much as the National War Fund unified domestic fundraising. To Long and others in the State Department, PACPR typified the unjustified meddling of private citizens in governmental affairs.

When the United States and Great Britain called a conference on refugee problems in the spring of 1943, it was held in Bermuda, partly to exclude private agencies, refugee advocates and the press. As one British delegate recalled years later, the Bermuda Conference was 'a facade for inaction. We said the results of the conference were confidential, but in fact there were no results that I can recall.'[22] There were no clear lines of communication between the voluntary community and the government, and voluntary agencies had virtually no role in formulating action. Looking at the confusing efforts put forth by various Jewish factions in Washington at the time, the *American Hebrew* said, 'The spectacle is enough to make the angels weep . . . many people cannot but come to the conclusions that some of the groups are exploiting the situation for reasons of their own'.[23]

The time was ripe for some new form of co-ordination among the major agencies active overseas. Therefore, in the words of a participant, 'the government gathered the so-called "three faiths" – Protestant, Catholic and Jewish – and drew a roof over them, and that was the beginning of interfaith ecumenism.' That 'roof' became a reality in 1943 through the New York-based American Council of Voluntary Agencies in Foreign Service (ACVA).

Small groups of leaders from various voluntary service agencies had been discussing their relationships with the government since November

1942. It was Dr. Joseph Chamberlain, professor of public law at Columbia and member of the President's Advisory Committee on Political Refugees, who eventually brought the agencies together with each other and with the government. He had previously served on numerous refugee committees and boards of agencies, and knew the personalities as well as the structures of service in refugee assistance.

In late 1942 Chamberlain wrote to the WRCB to explain the functions of agencies involved in overseas service. In November, shortly after President Roosevelt announced the formation of the federal wartime relief administration, the Office of Foreign Relief and Rehabilitation Operations (OFFRO), Clarence Pickett of the American Friends Service Committee wrote to Chamberlain that a member of Assistant Secretary of State Dean Acheson's staff working on OFFRO 'wants to call together members of the private agencies fairly soon'.[24]

By the end of 1942, Chamberlain had circulated drafts of a memorandum entitled 'Private International Service Organizations in Post-War Relief'. Approved by leaders of half a dozen key agencies, the memorandum addressed several issues, including relationships between private agencies and the government. The American-run agencies were praised for their ability to maintain direct contact with the U.S. Government while serving non-political and objective ends. It also noted, however, that they would remain most effective if they were allowed to continue to function as independent agencies. Here again was a logic that had long flourished in the United States, drawing on the Declaration of Independence, the religion clauses of the Constitution and the strength of the traditions of private voluntarism they engendered. The agencies wanted the government to know that they would not automatically cave in to calls for 'complementarity' that did not overlap their own interests. The memorandum circulated in Washington and among agency officials.

Planning for co-operation in relief and rehabilitation proceeded in Washington and New York. In June 1943 Governor Lehman of New York, Roosevelt's choice to head OFFRO, called representatives of the agencies that had participated in the memorandum to Washington. At that meeting, the agencies agreed to give Gov. Lehman detailed information about their plans for post-war relief. In all, 18 of the major agencies eventually responded to questionnaires sent out by Dr Chamberlain.

By August, when agency executives met in New York, concern was growing that uncertainty about government supervision over private relief might leave the agencies in the position of having to accept whatever the army or other government agencies proposed. After all, within a few months, a government licence and review board (the WRCB), a government authority for channelling funds (The National War Fund) and governmental field mechanism for relief (OFFRO) had all come into being. All private funds sent abroad during the war required a license from the Foreign Funds Control Division of the Treasury. The executives were concerned to maintain their independence, reiterating that '. . . private agencies can be effective in building morale only if they are independent and allowed to carry on their work in their own way.' At the end of the meeting, it was agreed that planning for an association of private agencies should begin.

On October 7, 1943, agreement was reached on a co-ordinating council, eventually named the American Council of Voluntary Agencies for Foreign Service. Dr. Joseph Hyman of the American Jewish Joint Distribution Committee stated that 'As I see it, the whole reason for this council is that, wherever we can co-operate in planning and thinking and in common action we should do so.' Dr. Chamberlain was elected chairman; representatives of Jewish and Catholic agencies were elected to the two vice-presidential posts and the head of a Protestant agency was named secretary-treasurer. The first functional committee of the new Council addressed the question of displaced persons.

Dr. Chamberlain reminded the group that one of their immediate functions as a council would be the role of the private voluntary sector in international relief efforts, a topic on the agenda at the forthcoming planning meeting of the United Nations Relief and Rehabilitation Administration in Atlantic City the following month. The *Memorial* ACVA eventually submitted to UNRRA constituted the first public act of the young Council and gave it a chance to set forth its own views on the proper relationship between private and public efforts at international relief.

From the beginning of the government's direct involvement with voluntary agencies abroad, officials promoted the idea of complementarity: 'volagencies,' in the new slang, would work alongside government, complementing and assisting government services. The government would furnish 'primary' supplies for mass emergency relief, but continuation of the voluntary agencies was essential 'not only as an expression of the generous sympathies of the American people but also as a distinctive service that quasi-public and voluntary agencies can render to complement public resources and services', said Gov. Herbert Lehman and two other relief officials in early 1943.[25]

The agencies were advancing new methods of private co-operation with America's civil and military authorities abroad. This was undeniably in the best interests of the country, the religious agencies and the people they served. Furthermore, this co-operation would free both church and state from the stigma of mutual self-advancement by focusing not on political ends or conversion efforts, but on the well-being of the refugee and others in need. This adjustment of goals by both parties managed to merge secular and redemptive ends to the satisfaction of most observers; it also secured public and Congressional support for extending America's help to the refugees. It was a fitting expression of complementarity between public and private authorities.

Despite the agencies' insistence on independence, the notion of 'complementarity' seemed a suitable explanation of the modern situation in which religious and secular authorities found themselves. It certainly captured the more structured hierarchical flow of power from the state to the citizens in voluntary service that evolved during the war. The remarkable partnership of the late 1940s grew in part because the religious agencies came to acknowledge their dependence upon government. The agencies and their sponsoring religious bodies gathered round national policymakers offering partnership, but the focus of their activities – refugees and humanitarian service – left them as perpetual stepchildren in the distribution of power.

New Religious Efforts

The presence of the government in organized refugee assistance – particularly in respect of the possibility of post-war resettlement in the U.S. and Israel – meant that religious bodies were in a good position to take part. To that end, wartime permitted the existing agencies to restructure and expand and encouraged new agencies to arise.

In 1939 Protestants and Catholics had joined Jews to form a coalition known as the National Refugee Service, which addressed both relief and migration issues. This organization performed a valuable function by uniting the major religious efforts into a single administrative forum. (It also covered what had become an embarrassing problem for Christian leaders; according to Clarence Pickett, director of the AFSC, Jewish contributions to the National Refugee Service exceeded two million dollars each year between 1939 and 1942 while the combined expenditures of the Christian organisations totalled only between $300,000 and $400,000 a year during the same period.) [26]

Co-operative involvement between agencies was the necessary forerunner of an organization such as the American Council of Voluntary Agencies. Leaders of the voluntary service agencies had established interfaith working relationships still largely unknown in other areas of religious mission. During the war the Council participated with such religiously inspired agencies as World Relief (a fledgling evangelical Protestant relief body), the Salvation Army, the Hebrew Immigrant Aid Society and the Russian Orthodox-inspired Tolstoy Foundation. The American Council provided the model of federated relief operations for Americans working abroad in Germany, Greece, Italy, Korea and elsewhere. Before the overseas council approach took hold, agencies co-operated on an *ad hoc* basis.

The expert Merle Curti has called Protestant relief efforts of this period 'a jungle.'[27] This sense of confusion over a proper Protestant response to the modern world should not be neglected in histories of the ecumenical movement. The confusion is particularly apparent in the efforts of Protestants in the 1930s and 40s to institutionalize their efforts for refugees and overseas relief.

Its sources were various. Theological differences among Protestants made it difficult to organize unified programmes. Virtually every denomination participating in wartime relief developed factions which emphasized denominational distinctions, and others which emphasized the importance of unified Protestant goals. Equally important, different denominations had their own groups of fellow believers abroad. American Lutherans emphasized work in German-speaking areas, for instance, but had comparatively little interest in Italy. These unequal interests made common planning a constant struggle.

By 1939, Lutherans, Mennonites and Baptists had all begun relief co-ordination outside the Protestant organizational consensus that eventually led in the mid-1940s to the World Council of Churches. These churches have since frequently co-operated with the World Council (and the National Council of Churches in the United States) but have continued their independent efforts at overseas relief to the present day.

A broad mainline Protestant effort in refugee care eventually came together in 1946 as part of the new National Council of Churches (NCC). Protestants tied to the NCC's predecessor, the Federal Council of Churches, formed the American Christian Committee for Refugees (ACCR) in the 1930s, but its early efforts were on a limited scale. During the war, the committee's efforts were so small that as a condition for entering the National War Fund, it was asked to merge with a Unitarian agency and the International Rescue and Relief Committee. After the war, the work of the ACCR was incorporated into the new ecumenical Protestant agency Church World Service (1946). 1945 saw the birth of Lutheran World Relief, a relief and refugee agency representing the major American Lutheran churches. Through difficulties in co-operation and frequent battles over the propriety of accepting government assistance, Protestants squandered their vast overseas assets at a critical moment in the organizing of the post-war world. By 1946 Catholic and Jewish agencies were already ahead.

The relationship between War Relief Service of the National Catholic Welfare Conference and its overseas Catholic affiliates was of critical importance to both the U.S. Government and the Catholic Church. According to Bishop Edward Swanstrom, a participant in the early formation of WRS and later executive director of its successor Catholic Relief Services for 30 years, the war had decimated the ability of Catholic charities such as the CARITAS network and the Sisters of Charity of St. Vincent de Paul in Europe to provide essential services. 'The bishops [of the NCWC] wanted to re-establish the Catholic charities, the CARITAS network, [and] they needed funds to get on their feet.'[28]

The United States Government shared this interest in the work of Catholic charities in Europe. The Roman church had the strongest network of social services, personnel and facilities on the continent, including those of individual governments. It was a resource that could not possibly be matched by individual Protestant bodies such as the Friends, the Salvation Army or even the new Protestant umbrella, the World Council of Churches. From the practical perspective of the Allies, refugees, dislocated persons, orphans and the wounded needed to be tended and kept from clogging critical transportation arteries and population centres. Catholic service groups, many of which had served individuals and communities for centuries, were in a position to provide help, but they were bankrupt. Contracts with the National War Fund helped provide assistance for putting them back on their feet.

Long-standing Jewish agencies such as the Joint Distribution Committee, the Hebrew Immigrant and Sheltering Aid Society (HIAS) and the more recent National Refugee Committee found themselves pulled in different

directions. Though Jewish agencies faced some of the same internal
dissension as their Protestant counterparts, their tremendous ability to
raise funds and their concentration on the problems faced by Jews allowed
them to bring concentrated efforts to bear in particular areas.

Not only was the Jewish community facing its worst crisis in modern
times, it was also facing the growing strength of the Zionist call for
a Jewish state in Palestine. The story of the struggle between those
favouring a strategy of rescue and those who wanted to concentrate on the
question of Palestine has been exhaustively chronicled in recent years.[29]
Ultimately, however, answers to both questions converged on the fate of
the refugees. If European Jews were rescued, where would they go? And
if a Jewish homeland were founded, who would populate it, and how would
they get there?

While conservative and reform Jews worked through the dilemmas
within the established bodies of Jewish philanthropy just mentioned, the
Orthodox began their own efforts, which focused almost entirely on the
rescue question. Many Orthodox Jews during the Second World War were
strongly anti-Zionist, and found the involvement of their fellow Jews in
the Palestine question at that moment of crisis scandalous. The Orthodox
formed their own overseas refugee arm, Vaad Hahatzala, and advanced
its cause in Washington by the successful practice of *bitzuism*, or
intercession with those in power. The Orthodox had refined their direct
approach to the powerful in the earlier decades of the century, and were
duly registered with the War Relief Control Board. Representative Sol
Bloom, a prominent member of the House Foreign Affairs Committee,
ably defended Orthodox rescue efforts in the later parts of the war. Once
Israel was established, all factions of the Jewish community including the
Orthodox rallied to the unified Jewish state.

Clarence Pickett of the American Friends Service Committee has
observed that the involvement between the private and the governmental
agencies after the Second World War was much greater and more highly
regulated than was the case following the First. For one thing, the
American Army in 1945 was an occupying force, responsible for the entire
governance of its occupied zone; this had not been true in 1918. In 1944
U.S. officials planning the postwar occupation of Germany decided against
the presence of American voluntary agencies, a decision that was soon
reversed in Washington.

Second, there was a new form of intergovernmental agency being
assembled that would serve as the channel for the relief funds of a
variety of interested governments. After 1918 the AFSC had 600 workers
in Europe; after 1945 the number was closer to 50. The Friends and the
other voluntary workers in 1945 found themselves face to face with the
intergovernmental relief arm of the Allies, the United Nations Relief
and Rehabilitation Administration (UNRRA), with 5300 of its own international administrators across the continent and in the Far East.[30]

Such was the context in which American religious bodies acted. The
war was indeed a moment of supreme crisis; lives and an entire civilization
were at stake. Saving them involved a complex operation with many

instrumentalities, among which religious bodies were the key element in the voluntary sector, performing vital tasks and extending mercy to individuals in ways the government rightly recognized as beyond its capabilities. 'I always said they could talk about ecumenism in theory all they wanted, but if they wanted to see ecumenism in action, they could go on down to the American Council in those days', said Bishop Swanstrow of Catholic War Relief Services. 'We all believed in God; we were all concerned about suffering among God's children.'[31]

Once the semi-official 'three faiths' policy was publically advanced by the American Council and government officials after the war, the centrality of American religious service ministries abroad – as a complement to official policies – was firmly fixed. Of all private American philanthropy abroad in 1945, less than one third was channelled through sectarian religious sources. Many Americans gave to the Red Cross and national or ethnic funds during the war. Two years later, over 75% was flowing through Protestant, Catholic and Jewish agencies, a ratio that would remain fixed through the 1950s.[32] This shift was no doubt aided by the favoured status shown to religious agencies in the disbursal of governmental relief subsidies.

More could be said about the development of the church/state partnership in refugee affairs between 1939 and 1956. Ahead still lay the rescue operation of the War Refugee Board, the structuring of expanded resettlement in the United States, the formation of strengthened UN refugee bodies, post-war legislation expanding government subventions to voluntary agencies and the strongly anti-Soviet cast of U.S. programmes for Eastern European refugee programmes. Still, by 1945 the basic contours of the partnership between the U.S. Government and U.S. religious voluntary agencies serving refugees had been fixed.

The new language of partnership and complementarity applied to the ties between religious and governmental bodies was accurate as far as it went. What such terms obscure are the limits placed on religious and other privately sponsored missions seeking *independence* from government priorities. When refugee advocates today speak of the 'humanitarian' nature of refugee assistance they are referring to its relative independence from political considerations. Though religious efforts to form agencies to aid refugees during the war were never in lockstep with the U.S. Government, independence hardly seems like an accurate description of the actual working relationships.

To be sure, agencies may fairly claim that their presence has lent a human face to what is essentially a grim task, the provision of care and protection to persecuted victims of war, revolt or external aggression. They have saved and shielded lives of the innocent. By definition, however, the agencies had accepted positions of complementarity to the refugee policies of the U.S. Government. This stance remained the norm until the early 1960s. The refugee dilemmas of the Vietnam War brought some agencies to the point of rejecting a humanitarianism strongly linked to U.S. military and security concerns.

In its 1966 study, the Carnegie Corporation cited three factors it believed were keeping the non-governmental organizations 'at bay.' They were the need to restructure the mechanisms of governmental assistance, the need to secure voluntary efforts from undue dependence on government, and the need to build more effective structures of co-operation in the voluntary community. Not surprisingly each of these issues had already arisen over twenty years earlier during the war; they still touch central issues for those interested in refugees today twenty years later. Let us look at each in the light of the experiences of religious agencies and the U.S. Government during World War II.

1   The *mechanisms of governmental assistance* in place today were originally built for the prosecution of the war. On the positive side the U.S. Government has continued to affirm private voluntarism abroad by expanding the numbers and types of agencies with which it co-operates. In recent years numerous non-sectarian agencies have registered with the Agency for International Development (AID) for government assistance and subsidies. The wartime pattern of governmental use of private non-governmental organizations in overseas activities has become standard peacetime practice within most Western donor democracies.

The major liability of the wartime arrangements is the closer identification of private voluntarism with the interests of the United States. It might be fairly argued that the benefits of this identification have aided more individuals than it has harmed. It is also the case that distinctions between humanitarianism and the national interests of the United States have suffered. Religious and other private voluntary agencies have not, for instance, achieved the transnational reputation for impartiality achieved by a body such as the International Committee of the Red Cross. Some of this may ironically spring from the early willingness of religious institutions to identify with the Allied cause during the war and with anti-communism in the postwar years.[33] The wartime precedent of informing voluntary agencies of policy decisions after the fact rather than engaging them in substantive planning further reinforced the secondary quality of their participation in overseas refugee efforts.

Recent suggestions for altering the means of distributing government aid have included the formation of a separate endowment that would fund private voluntary foreign aid independent of short-term political considerations. This would in effect remove refugee care from the State Department. In a similar vein many voluntary agencies call for increased reliance on multilateral assistance through the UNHCR, despite trends toward increased use of agencies through bilateral agreements in target nations.

2   Efforts to *limit undue dependence of voluntary agencies on government* resonates with the tradition of church/state independence secured in the Constitution. Yet wartime needs dictated that religious bodies and others organize institutions capable of working on a scale that operated efficiently in the context of vast foreign assistance programmes. Such involvement dictates a certain dependence on government. In the early 1960s there was intense debate among Protestants and Catholics over what constituted an acceptable level of government financial and material assistance. Lutherans held that 50% represented a maximum; Church World Service felt 66% was acceptable. Catholic Relief Services felt that

up to 75% of its resources could come from the U.S. government without an undue sense of dependency. By the 1980s each of these agencies had undertaken a gradual reduction in the use of government funds.

Dependency can be understood from a variety of perspectives. During the war dependency was part of the complementarity built between government and private bodies. In overseas operations today it still appears inevitable that American governmental and private operations will be drawn together administratively as well as politically. The most direct form of dependence, the use of government subventions, has its origins in the structuring of the National War Fund (serving agencies operating 'purely in the American interest') and OFFRO, which was eventually incorporated into UNRRA. Even the interposing of the UNHCR as a neutral channel of U.S. funds has not entirely freed private agencies from dependence on governmental sources. The funds for operations required today cannot be entirely raised from private sources.[34] Under these circumstances, and somewhat aside from endless long-term debates over the proper relationship between religion and the state, the invitation to sign a contract powerfully concentrates the mind.

3 Finally, the Carnegie Corporation drew attention to *the need for more effective co-operative structures within the voluntary community*. Largely Jewish-sponsored refugee committees of the 1930s eventually gave way to the broader co-operative setting of the American Council in New York. This too came into being with the active encouragement of Washington. In the postwar period 'three faith' co-operation was actively promoted as the grounding of interagency ties. More than 15 years after the war ended analysts of foreign policy could still speak of the Judeo-Christian moral tradition as 'the central element in the moral consensus underlying American democratic institutions'.[35]

Despite such optimism, co-ordination within the voluntary community is in a state of flux. Again, the roots of several of the difficulties lie in wartime arrangements. At different times Protestant and Jewish agencies have fought the inclusion of agencies maintained by their more conservative co-religionists in the American Council. Protestants and Jews have fought each other over the fate of Palestinian refugees, and representatives of a variety of traditions have expressed concern over close ties between Catholic Church and the U.S. Government. Each of these difficulties was germinating in political and humanitarian decisions made during the war.

The strongest sign that co-ordination among the agencies is changing is to be seen in the demise of the American Council in 1984. For over 40 years the Council stood as a sign that voluntarism was effective. Increasingly, however, agencies found that they could operate effectively outside the Council, through consortia and other umbrella organizations. Many leaders in the voluntary sector and in the State Department pressed for a new umbrella organization that was not as tied to the postwar order as the American Council. Somehow in a field crowded with new non-sectarian agencies the 'three faith' ethos of the Council seemed musty, its traditions often dated. To other observers, the move to a new body (known as Inter–Action) only raised questions about a new expansion of the government's supervision of voluntary foreign aid.

Whatever future directions lie ahead in refugee work, religiously grounded institutions appear certain to play some role. Whether they will retain the central role given them during the Second World War remains an open question subject to the concerns just enumerated. To some degree arrangements may be determined by the outcome of current discussions in the United States of the role of religion in shaping public policy.

The independence of such religious commitments from ultimate control by government is at the heart of American efforts to separate church and state. If by separation we mean just that, the continued establishment of a provisional distance (rather than a more final 'divorce'), it may be that the community of religious agencies, by virtue of their efforts at international democratic humanitarianism dating from the 1940s, stand in the best position legally, politically and historically to lead the American voluntary community through a critical period in its relations with the U.S. Government.

Notes: Chapter 6

1   A Pifer, 'The Non-Governmental Organization at Bay,' *Annual Report of the Carnegie Corporation of New York* (New York, 1966), 3, 10–11, 14.
2   The religion clauses state that 'Congress shall make no law regarding the establishment of religion, or prohibiting the free exercise therof.' (Bill of Rights, Article 1).*Walz v. Tax Commission* (397 U.S. 664, 669) [1970].
3   Louise Holborn, *Refugees: A Problem of Our Time* (Metuchen, N.J., 1975) Vol. I, 18.
4   Susan S. Forbes and Patricia Weiss Fagen, 'Unaccompanied Refugee Children: The Evolution of U.S. Policies – 1939 to 1984,' (Refugee Policy Group, Washington, D.C., 1984). 6.
5   Merle Curti, *American Philanthropy Abroad* (Rutgers, 1963), 395.
6   Cyrus Adler, *I Have Considered the Days* (Jewish Publication Society, Philadelphia, 1940), xv-xvii.
7   Alfred Wagg III, 'Washington's Stepchild: The Refugees', *The New Republic*, Vol. CIV (April 28, 1941), 592–4.
8   Henry L. Feingold, *The Politics of Rescue* (Holocaust Library, New York, 1970), 85.
9   ibid, p. 185.
10   Harold J. Seymour, *Design for Giving* (New York and London, 1947), vii.
11   ibid, p. 3.
12   ibid, p. 94.
13   Arthur Ringland, 'The Development of Voluntary Foreign Aid, 1939–1953', *Department of State Bulletin*, March 15, 1954, 386.
14   Seymour, op. cit., p. 8.
15   ibid, p. 9, 10.
16   Edward M. O'Connor, personal conversation with the author.
17   *Report to the Board of Trustees*, War Relief Services – N.C.W.C., August 1, 1943 – September 30, 1944, Washington, D.C., 1,2,10.
18   Edward M. O'Connor, personal conversation with the author.
19   'Distribution of Foreign Assistance, 1946–57,' chart in the files of the American Council of Voluntary Agencies in Foreign Service, New York, n.d.
20   Feingold, op. cit., p. 135, 138.
21   ibid, p. 140.
22   ibid, p. 225–6.
23   ibid, p. 221.

24 Elizabeth Clark Reiss, 'Beginnings,' *Four Monographs*, the American Council of Voluntary Agencies in Foreign Service, (New York, ACVA, 1986) 7.

25 *Department of State Bulletin*, January 16, 1943.

26 Clarence Pickett, *For More Than Bread* (Boston, 1953), 142–3.

27 Curti, op. cit., p. 513.

28 Bishop Edward Swanstrom, 'Post-War Catholic Relief,' *Newsletter on Church and State Abroad*, No. 4 (Council on Religion and International Affairs, New York, May 1984), 5.

29 David Wyman, *The Abandonment of the Jews* (New York, Pantheon, 1984).

30 Despite the fact that the presence of an international bureaucracy would limit the functions and size of private voluntarism, religious bodies in the United States led the public support for a new United Nations. Since the time of Benedict XV and World War I the Catholic Church had advocated progress toward some form of international governance. Both Protestants and Catholics produced a substantial literature during the war on postwar contributions of religion to the new international order. John Foster Dulles, later Secretary of State under Dwight Eisenhower, spent the war as head of the prominent (Protestant) Commission for a Just and Durable Peace. Jews, while supportive of such developments, continued to concentrate the bulk of their attention on refugees and the question of Israel.

31 Swanstrom, op. cit.

32 Curti, op. cit., 506–7.

33 ibid, 504.

34 An important development in this field is the use of television for relief and refugee fundraising. In the last 10 years the California-based World Vision has inaugurated a sea change through its fantastic success with 'telethons'. Though World Vision is frequently mentioned as a conservative supporter of U.S. foreign policy, its fundraising successes have allowed it to keep its use of government funds to a miniscule 1–2%. This approach to fundraising obviously cuts into older methods of funnelling funds up from local church offerings and is receiving widespread use among older NGOs.

   Recently, church groups have begun to explore funding from multi-national corporations and others as another alternative to government assistance.

35 Victor Ferkiss, 'Foreign Aid: Moral and Political Aspects,' *Moral Dimensions of American Foreign Policy*, Kenneth Thompson, ed., (New Brunswick, 1984), 202.

7 The re-settlement of ethnic Germans, 1939-41

ANNA C. BRAMWELL

This study will examine the transfer and partial re-settlement of ethnic Germans between 1939 and 1941. This took place from different countries, and with governments of varying political complexions. The groups of refugees created by the transfer differed from each other in dialect, urban/rural culture, lifestyles, history and education. Some had been uprooted since the early 1920s, as with the Baltic Germans, especially the large landowners, while three-quarters of a million German farmers had been driven away from the German-Polish borderlands by the newly created Polish state after the Versailles Treaty. Some were in refugee camps in Germany in 1939, while others were unwanted aliens in Poland, Estonia, Lithuania and Latvia. Other groups included the long-standing German colonists of Wolhynia and Bessarabia, apparently secure, but whose homelands lay in the path of the projected Russian occupation of Eastern Poland. Nearly 600,000 people were involved.

The movement of these groups was thus a mixture of chaotic expulsion and forcible but planned transfer. In some cases, the German government sent mixed civilian and military expeditions to organise evacuation. In other cases, it was a question of receiving expellees as they appeared. Elsewhere the expellees were already *in situ*. As far as the Wolhynien and Bessarabian Germans were concerned, the transfer presents a rare picture of co-operation between Germany and Soviet Russia, two revolutionary governments.

This case study presents certain unusual features which will repay further research. The ethnic German colonies resulted from various historical events. Some preceded or accompanied the medieval expansion to the East. Others were called in by Polish and Russian landowners in the nineteenth century. Some, especially the Baltic Germans, were townspeople: traders and professional middle classes. Others were primitive peasants who had coaxed the difficult steppelands into fertility, but whose dialect and customs were centuries old. This kind of patchwork is perhaps unique. Further, the re-settlement only lasted four to five years. The area in which the refugees were settled, the 'incorporated area' of the Wartheland, Danzig West-Prussia and the Zichenau, became Polish and Russian territory after the Second World War. The ethnic German refugees became part of the human horde, the fifteen million Germans who were uprooted again in 1945. Estimates of those who died in this second expulsion range upwards from two million.

The second displacement and disappearance renders an examination of the events of 1939–1941 more difficult. Most of the eye-witness reports which have been collated refer to the events of 1945–7, so that reports for the period 1939–1941 are rare. Material on refugees from Russia became hard to find after 'detente' in the 1960s, as the German government hesitated to publish material which might have re-awakened hostile memories of the Russians. Soviet sources on this topic seem, predictably, to be unavailable, as are those of most Eastern European countries, although recent releases from Polish archives to West Germany contain new material. There are contemporary reports from the International Labour Organisation, the Red Cross, and the American Quakers. The largest source of information remains the contemporary German reports from the planning and re-settlement offices under the aegis of various SS bodies. These German files were sifted by the Allies for use in the Nuremberg Trial, especially Case VIII of the Nuremberg Trials of 1949. They are therefore highly selective. Special interest groups representing particular refugees, such as the Sudeten Germans, the Mennonites and the East Prussians, have published studies, but these usually concentrate on the period 1945-6.[1]

It is hardly surprising that the ethnic German re-settlement has been virtually written out of history (for example, no mention of it is to be found in Gordon Craig's recent history of Germany, 1866–1945). Besides the paucity of material, there is the factor that the aim of demographic *consolidation* which characterised the programme – although implemented on conquered territory – counters the commonly held view of Germany's *Lebensraum* policy. The shortage of internal German manpower for settling the German-Polish borderlands was an embarrassment to the Third Reich, and was not emphasised in public statements. The improvisatory quality of the re-settlement, the general belief by the Germans closely involved that after 1940 the European war would be over, does not fit the theory that all Nazi officials were involved in Hitler's plans for total war from 1937 onwards. The clash of aims and ideals concerning the re-settlement among the officials of the Third Reich suggests some unexpected conclusions. The kind of 'capitalist/colonial' mentality to which some writers attribute imperial expansion proved, in the case of plans for the incorporated areas, to be far more humane than the populist, socialist, reformist aims to 'Germanise' the incorporated area with ethnic German peasant settlers. The strong socialist dynamic behind German plans for re-settlement is awkward for those historians who see the Third Reich as a conservative-imperialist-capitalist aberration, a function of the infantile disorder which prevented Germany following the proper path of Anglo-Saxon liberal democracy.[2]

The re-settlement programme, in fact, appears not only untypical but unexpected in its morphology. While this makes investigation more difficult, it also makes it more worthwhile, and although this investigation can be no more than a brief and preliminary look at the subject, it should open up areas for further research.

Himmler's Fight over Jurisdiction

German expansion to the East had been a constant theme in German politics. In the First World War, Max Sering, for example, widely regarded as a liberal intellectual, and certainly not a Nazi supporter in later years, produced a detailed plan to establish 250,000 German peasant settlements in Courland. Arrangements were made with Baltic landowners to give up a third of their land for this purpose after the war: the loss of what became Lithuania after 1918 ended the programme. In 1917, a League for German Settlement and Expansion proposed settling German peasants from the Russian interior in the Baltic lands then occupied by Germany. One member of the Prussian Agricultural Ministry suggested 'solving the German-Polish problem' by an exchange of populations: Poles in Germany against Germans in what was then 'Russian Poland'. Proposals of this kind were made several times by administrators, and submitted to the Reich Chancellory throughout the 1930s. How did these earlier plans to repopulate the East with German peasants differ from Himmler's proposals of 1939 and 1940? Partly by the vagueness and rhetoric of Himmler's proposals, but mainly the difference consisted of the proposed division of Poland into the *General-Gouvernement* (G-G), a sort of racial dustbin, and the incorporated areas, which were to be German, Germanic, and/or Germanised.[3] The apparent continuity of re-settlement plans of 1939-40 persuaded sincere followers of peasant, anti-colonial, radical beliefs to alter course to follow Himmler the imperialist. It meant that Himmler was subject to populist pressure from his staff on the issue of *völkisch* settlement in the incorporated areas.

The SS-State envisaged by Himmler had moved far from the original image of the NSDAP. Hitler, especially in his speeches, had presented National Socialism as the creation of the Greater Germany, purged of its alien and treacherous elements, a vision which could be perceived as an extension and fulfilment of nineteenth-century nationalism. Himmler's vision of the pan-European state, with a German and Germanised administrative elite, demanded the creation of a new kind of man to rule it. The ideal SS-man would be linked with the land, but would understand technology, and have mastered it. He would be efficient, able and unhampered by ties of class. This plan to create an elite man, which for many people today is synonymous with National Socialism, was different in kind from the cosy *Volksgemeinschaft* image presented by the NSDAP during its early years, and even as late as 1940, Himmler thought it necessary to keep his plans for the 'State within the State' a secret. Himmler's training and organisational methods managed within a few years to create a tightly knit and loyal group of skilled technocrats, together with a disciplined and skilful fighting force in the mature Waffen SS. The imminent arrival of the

Volksdeutsche attracted ambitious agrarian administrators, such as Professor Konrad Meyer, ex-Ministry of Agriculture official and land planning expert, who took over Himmler's land planning office in Berlin for the National Commisariat for the Strengthening of Germanness (RKFDV).

As SS power grew, other agrarian experts were drawn to Himmler's new Commissariat, the RKFDV, hoping to find there the same values that had inspired Darré, the anti-capitalist, 'blood and soil' peasant advocate. Himmler also recruited intellectuals of the traditional German Nationalist variety, men who aimed at 'restoring the pre-1918 status quo'. For them, the *Volksdeutsche* re-settlement was a matter of completing the failed attempt of the Versailles Treaty, to recreate the 23 major linguistic groups stretching from the Baltic to Greece.[4]

Under Himmler's fifty year plan for the conquered areas, 5 to 6 million Poles and Jews were to be evacuated to non-incorporated Poland, the *Volksdeutsche* were to be resettled in the incorporated areas, and the whole of the East was to become a substitute to Germany for her lost colonies. This was announced secretly in October 1940.[5] Yet an analysis of the planning documents and organisational struggles within the SS between 1938 and 1942 demonstrates that while radical Nazi agrarian ideology strongly influenced SS members at middle and lower levels, their attempts to implement peasant settlement were frequently delayed and even halted by Himmler, because he was set on the potential empire in Russia, and subordinated ideological aims to imperial power. He wanted agriculture to play an important role after the war, but his main purpose, to alter the demographic, political and geographic map of Europe, was completely different from the Germanic *Bauernreich* of earlier Nazi ideology.

The first example of SS institutional imperialism at work was the establishment of the Prague Land Office in 1938. Darré, the Ministry of Agriculture and the National Food Estate were all successfully bypassed, and the Ministry of the Interior's objections ignored. The success of a small and hitherto unimportant SS office in gaining control in the occupied territory was a step towards collecting all the racial offices under Himmler's control, which by the end of 1939 was a *fait accompli*. It paved the way for the first massive transfers of land, property and people.

In institutional terms, then, fundamental responsibility for the re-settlement of the ethnic Germans lay with Himmler and the RKFDV. The Ministry of Agriculture, although unconnected with settlement, was involved in the administration of food production in the Occupied Areas. Regional farming advisers, known as *Kreislandwirten* were installed. They were responsible for ensuring food supplies locally, but had nothing to do with the question of land ownership. Within the framework of the Four Year Plan, a Trustee Department for the East was administered by Winckler (who had undertaken trustee work during the Weimar period). In 1942, Darré was replaced by Herbert Backe, ex-State Secretary in the Ministry of Agriculture. This meant that a new phase of co-operation between the RKFDV and the Agricultural Ministry began. Backe made an effort to retain Himmler's favour, while endeavouring to maintain the level of food production in the Incorporated Areas; he may also have supplied an element of factual information for Himmler, whose practical background in agriculture was limited. The net effect of Himmler's by-passing other civil and military authorities in occupied Eastern Europe was that a series of overlapping authorities and conflicting instructions ensued.

Drang nach Osten?

In 1939, the German eastern border was described sarcastically as a *Raum ohne Volk*, instead of a *Volk ohne Raum*; a space without people, rather than a people without space. This was a reference to a best-seller written in 1926, which called for the return of the German colonies. But in October 1939, a Bavarian settlement official wrote that 'no one knows better than we who, day in, day out, have to settle peasants, that we no longer have the blood needed to settle German land with our own strength.' In a conversation between Hitler and von Neurath, Governor of the new Protectorate, Hitler said, 'The settlement of the Protectorate with Germans is not envisaged, because the new German areas must be Germanised, and there are scarcely enough German settlers for that'. The Hitler Youth tried to recruit peasants in the Sudetenland to go East, but this met strong opposition from the local peasant leaders. 'The South would be stripped of manpower if the Hitler Youth had its way', they argued.The thrusting re-settled, militant Polish villages on the German border met a retreating German peasantry. In 1937, one writer had complained that 'Poland settled [with peasants] all her Western border, using every resource and inexhaustible amounts of money. . .It is quite intolerable that now this barrier of clustered settlement villages should confront German farms which are almost empty of people'.[6]

By 1941, only 800 Reich Germans had been settled in the Warthegau, although by then some 200,000 *Volksdeutsche* had been found farms. In February 1940, German settlement was quietly dropped as a war objective at the highest levels. 'The real task of building up and settling the East with Germans will not be considered until after the war', wrote Himmler's personal adjutant to the SS Race and Settlement Office.[7] This demonstrates the very real need the *Volksdeutsche* were to fulfil: to provide a loyal, ethnically German population, who were to fill the gap left by the dwindling German peasantry. Their task was not to be easy.

'To settle the German East, one needs strong fists, a many sided vocational ability, and a German heart,' wrote Herbert Backe in 1942. The propaganda put out by the Ministry of Agriculture to encourage settlers must often have had the opposite effect. Militancy was stressed, and the term *Dorfrüstung*, armed villages, was used. 'Difficulties have not and must not be ignored . . . A determined will is needed . . . We must look facts in the face . . . only weaklings quail,' (etc), appeared in an article on Eastern settlement in 1942.[8] Along with the already existing shortage of German manpower in factories and fields (by 1939 some 250,000 workers had been recruited from other countries), was a reluctance to press East. The Germans had been thrown out of centuries old provinces in 1918: their faith in Hitler did not stretch to a desire to return.

Planning the Incorporated Areas

Goering, whose authority conflicted with Himmler's, planned to hand out title-deeds to this new German county, and some legal preliminaries to this effect were enacted. Poland was to become Prussia: run by efficient, capitalist landowners, with a Polish peasantry. The attitude of the top Nazi leadership was exploitative, yet their solution was more humane than the populist, socialist plan of the middle and lower ranking SS, to change rural Poland into a fully Germanised nation. Relations between the Polish peasantry and the Polish nationalist intelligentsia were strained and hostile, and the Polish peasantry in some areas at first welcomed the German invasion. This would have enabled the German planners to play one group off against another had they not needed to shift the Polish farmers. SS planning offices envisaged a substantial change of population: but not a 100% Germanisation. 50% of the area's population would remain Polish. 'To summarise, no titles to the new land should be handed out because after the war, priority must be to *Volksdeutsche* peasants . . . this is morally right, also the way to produce as much as possible from the land,' wrote the State Secretary for the Ministry of Agriculture.[9]

Thus, there were two quite separate plans for the area. The first, associated with Goering and Himmler, was to use it as a raw material pool cum corn-chamber. The second was the Germanised peasant nation, which was closer to earlier populist Nazism. This uncertainty about the real aims of re-settlement was immensely complicated by the improvisatory nature of everything that took place between 1939 and 1945. As plan succeeded plan, order succeeded order, and reorganisation succeeded reorganisation, one must distinguish between what was actually happening in the Incorporated Areas from what the most recent pronouncement had demanded was to happen. For example, one might well wonder how it was that the *Z Aktion* of 1942 which expelled Polish dwarf farm smallholders from their holdings in the Warthegau, could find any Polish farmers in the area at all, considering that at least three orders had already emerged from various offices to deport them to the *General-Gouvernement*. A year later, hundreds of thousands of Polish farm labourers were deported to Germany as conscripted farm labourers, workers who would not have been available for that purpose if previous deportation plans had been implemented.[10]

Even the exact whereabouts of the border between the new rump Poland and the new German County was a last-minute arrangement. One SS Race and Settlement Office (RuSHA)adviser wrote scathingly to Himmler in October 1939 that the plan to incorporate Kracow, 'the very centre of Polish culture' into a newly created 'German' area was madness, and would only damage Germany's reputation.[11]

The Police Chief at Bromberg complained in November 1939 that room had to be found in his area for another 10,000 Wolhynien Germans, who were to be resettled in the Pomcatowski villages.[12] Himmler and the SS Police Chiefs wanted to house the ethnic Germans as armed settlers to defend the border area against the Poles while the argument in favour of peasant food production came from members of the National Food Estate drafted as agricultural advisers after the outbreak of war. Increasing peasant productivity was a major German strategic aim, both within Germany and in the conquered territories. Members of the RuSHA advisory staff were strongest in their advocacy of deporting and/or Germanising the Polish population, and replacing them with Germans, for racial as well as food production reasons. No one suggested trying to increase food production using existing Polish agricultural organisational methods. Numerous studies of Polish food production between the wars had revealed the fact that production had dropped by between 20 and 40 per cent in pre First World War Prussian areas. Making allowance for some bias in the study, it is still clear that there had been a sharp drop in productivity under Polish farmers. A special study commissioned by the National Statistics Office in July 1939 described Warsaw, Lodz, Silesia, Galicia and Kielce as 'agricultural deficit areas'. Germany had double the number of cattle, and four times the number of pigs and goats per capita, 25 per cent more arable land and 25 per cent less forest.[13]

> More than one-third of the agricultural land belongs to farms of less than 2 ha; some one-fifth up to 5 ha. No surplus worth mentioning could be brought to market – even with sensible management – given these farm sizes. A large part of the remaining ground is forest. An example of what is produced by the larger farms: one 200 ha farm we took over, which on the whole had not suffered from the war, presumably thus not lost any poultry. Some 28 ha of fish pools delivered 8-10 cwt. of fish a year! The rye was enough for the agricultural labourers, and the manager grew his own food. You can see from this example what large and medium farms are going to produce for urban consumers.[14]

Another report to Himmler commented that Polish land was 'uneven, lacking in natural resources, exhausted and extremely wet, with no natural drainage'. Thus, a mixture of contempt for Polish farmers for having fallen behind Prussian standards, and the fact that areas like Galicia were in any case among the poorest peasant farming areas in Europe, led to the decision to deport Polish farmers and substitute 'good German peasants' in their place. A vivid impression of the poverty of the Polish countryside is given in the diary of a Nazi administrator in the Incorporated Areas in 1941: 'Everything is primitive, poverty stricken and filthy. With the German settlers from Russia, things are much cleaner, but otherwise little different . . . I was told that people actually lived in holes in the ground round here. I saw poverty stricken villages . . . unplastered houses, reed thatched roofs, reed and clay walls . . . farmhouses without solid floors or even plaster.'[15]

In fact, the extent to which Poland was virtually an agriculturally undeveloped land was well recognised by local officials. However, the implications of this fact, the resources and effort that would be needed in order to make Poland and the incorporated areas net contributors to Germany's food requirements, were consistently ignored by civil and military administrators in Berlin, where eyes were fixed on the Polish rye exports in the last two decades. The SS RuS report which showed the unfavourable conditions in Polish agriculture compared to Germany pondered on where the 'agricultural surplus area' was in Poland, concluding hopefully that it was in the West. (Unfortunately for the Germans, it was in the area ceded to Russia.) But, 'the [Warthegau] is in its current structure and density of population *a deficit area*, and in no way a corn chamber, the assumption which is heard all over the place in Berlin'.[16]

The Race and Settlement report of 1939 contained a detailed plan to carry out the population transfer which aimed both at turning the incorporated areas into an agricultural surplus area, and settling it with German peasants. It recommended evacuating double the number of Poles and Jews for the number of planned German immigrants; all Jews, and the Polish intelligentsia would be immediately deported, while the 'indigenous population' would be investigated for possible Germanisation. This meant that, as with Meyer-Hetling's plans for Himmler, quite a large number of Polish citizens were envisaged as remaining in the area. Himmler, however, addressing SS leaders in Danzig in October 1939, prophesied that in fifty years' time, some twenty million German settlers would be living in Posen-West Prussia .[17]

While Himmler's plans were grandiose and vague, the RuSHA officials went into considerable and practical detail. Their recommendation that peasant settlement be confined to Western Galicia and the Southern part of Upper Silesia, so that Polish industrial areas should be spared any evacuation measures, made sense, if a viable economy was to be maintained. The Chief SS and Police Leader was ordered to direct all settlers to the South, while lists of firms which were essential to the Polish economy were drawn up. How is one to make sense of the orders for expulsion and the aim to keep half the province Polish? In practice, Poles who had been brought in to settle previously German land after the Treaty of Versailles were expelled to the South, while most of the pre-First World War Polish residents (the minority, after Polish nationalists were expelled) were allowed to stay on.[18]

As the months dragged on and homes had to be found for hundreds of thousands of *Volksdeutsche* refugees, the arguments over the best way to use the new 'colony' continued. One member of the SS Planning Department for land in the East visited Gauleiter Greiser in February 1941 with detailed maps of planned re-settlement in the Warthegau. He argued that even if every centimetre of Polish land were to be farmed by Germans, the population would still be only one quarter German, because 'the removal of the Polish agricultural and urban proletariat will be a much more difficult task than that of peasant settlement', and that unless the existing agricultural structure was changed, the existence of Polish farm labourers made 'a true Germanising' impossible. Greiser objected that 'the task of the Warthegau is to produce grain, grain and still more grain

– a grain factory, and that is why it has been incorporated into the Reich',
(the Goering view) to which the RuSHA adviser replied with arguments
so characteristic of the peasant producer advocate that they are worth
quoting in detail.

> I answered that fats and milk were needed more and peasant farms were
> more productive in these areas. While this was certainly no time to start
> experimenting, there was undoubted evidence that peasants produced
> more than large landowners from the same land, especially with the aid
> of machinery. Only the peasant could make the Warthegau a German
> county – he alone rendered the Polish labourers redundant.

However, Greiser insisted that Goering had expressly ordered grain
production to be the main crop, and that a system of large estates and
Polish labour was to be kept. The aim of 'Germanisation' was excellent
in itself, but would take thirty or forty years. With the ruthlessness typical
of the reformer mentality, the RuS adviser made the counter-proposal
that Polish labourers' families should all be deported to the *General
Gouvernement* in order to induce their menfolk to follow them. Finally,
Greiser's 'reactionary adviser', Siegmund, informed the RuS office that
Goering had ordered that Poland's agricultural structure should remain
unchanged, with the single exception of dwarf farm consolidation. Only
the large estates could produce corn, or breed herds of pedigree cattle.
An agricultural leading class was needed, and furthermore, the demands of
wealthy men who wanted farms needed satisfying – something stressed by
the Wehrmacht. 'It is mere fantasy to talk of 5,000 new farms by 1941. You
yourself know how all these great plans of the RF [Himmler] end up.'

This interchange of opinions, recounted word for word by an indignant
SS settlement officer in a confidential report,[19] tells us several significant
things about the development of settlement plans in the incorporated areas.
First, that even before the invasion of Russia, which put a stop to ambitious
re-settlement projects, very little had been done in the way of Germanising
the Wartheland as originally planned. Second, that Goering's orders as
head of the Four Year Plan, and Minister in charge of the Economy in the
Eastern Territories, were to leave the existing Polish agricultural structure
in place, merely substituting German for Polish landlords. Third, that
Himmler's impressive sounding decrees and plans were widely regarded
as being romantic fantasies, and it should not be assumed that they were
implemented in practice.

For example, in December 1940, one of Himmler's orders stated that
'to create opportunities for settlement, it is necessary in the Incorporated
Areas to give peasant settlers a greater share than before of farms seized
from Polish and Jewish hands – 40 per cent instead of 25 per cent of the
agriculturally usable acreage'. However, analysis of the implementation
of these plans shows that Germanised land in the Warthegau comprised
barely 10 per cent of the agriculturally usable land by May 1941. The
need to ensure that the 'recaptured' province would become and remain
German was stressed in writings of 1940–1.

> The character of this land is not determined by the formal property ownership of large estates and domains, as long as the necessary peasants and agricultural labourers are of Polish blood; a realisation achieved by Wilhelmine Germany far too late.

wrote one agricultural expert, and "Only the 'Re-creation of the German Peasantry" (a German slogan of the time) can neutralise the danger of having to use Polish elements' as agricultural labourers. Many of the writers who had propounded the virtues of peasant production supported 'Germanisation' of the Wartheland for the same reasons. Dr Otto Auhagen, whose dissertation in 1896 had compared the productivity of small and large estates, reported enthusiastically in 1940 on the possibilities of exchanging populations on Germany's Eastern border. He referred to similar plans drawn up during the First World War. Members of the Economic-Geography Institute in Koenigsberg also drafted proposals for settling the 'New German Area' in September 1940, arguing that complete Germanisation could only take place through peasant holdings of 15–25 hectares.[21]

Some saw the specifically productive aspects of the venture as a challenge. One writer described the flat, largely uncultivated plains of the Warthegau, exposed to cold drying winds, and lacking in hedges and shelter belts. The winters were long and cold, while roads, electricity, drainage and schools were largely lacking. But

> With the new land in the East, it will be easier to create new forms than in the *Altreich* . . . a new beginning . . . we do not have to struggle with established habits, as in the old villages of the West.[22]

Seldom can the modernisation drive that ran in tandem with the support for small farms have been so clearly expressed; significantly, this article appeared in *The New Peasant*. However, the resources needed to create a viable, modernised agriculture in a conquered land seem not to have been costed or considered. Because of the emphasis traditionally placed on the shortage of land within Germany, the availability of 'free' land in Poland was seen as a cure-all for all the shortages of capital and manpower that had beset German agriculture.

Re-settling the Volksdeutsche

In September 1939, the ethnic Germans who were to be involved in the re-settlement programme fell, broadly speaking, into two categories. The first was the ethnic Germans who lived well to the east of the incorporated areas, such as the Baltic Germans who had lost their land under the Estonian, Lithuanian and Latvian land reforms of the 1920s, and the Baltic German townsmen. This category included the more pressing problem of the German colonists from Bessarabia and Wolhynia, some

160,000 people who had originally been invited to settle by Russian and Russo-Polish nobles, after 1815 and 1863 respectively. They presented the most serious problem, since, under the Ribbentrop-Molotov Pact of August 1939, Russia had agreed to repatriate these German colonists, who lay in the path of their invasion of Eastern Poland.

The second category was that of the ethnic Germans living *in situ* in Polish and Czech provinces which had been German/Austrian before the First World War, together with the 750,000 or so refugees who had left the Polish borderlands between 1919 and 1930, after their farms had been compulsorily acquired with near-worthless Polish scrip. These latter were considered by Germany to be refugees with a right to compensation by the Poles. Many Polish-Germans had fled to Germany immediately before the German invasion. They returned eager for revenge.[23]

By 1942, it was estimated that some 500,000 people were involved in the resettlement programme. Despite Hitler's well-publicised remarks about the South Tyrolean Germans, for example, just sailing down the Danube to the Black Sea and finding a home there, the thrust of the re-settlement was defensive rather than expansionist, and was seen as a definitive consolidation of German territory. Homes had to be found for hundreds of thousands of ethnic German refugees, and the incorporation of the newly conquered territory in the East was the answer to many problems. There was the hope that it might include part of the ryegrowing area that had contributed to Poland's massive grain exports before the Second World War: the population density was half that of Germany's, which meant, it was thought, free and empty territory for settling farmers; while the *Volksdeutsche* would fill the gap caused by the lack of German emigres from the *Altreich* prepared to go East. They would provide an indisputably German-ised population in land that would now be German forever. Never again could plebiscites and percentages be a weapon used against land colonised by German settlers.

This application of the concept of self-determination and ethnic identity as a basis for nationhood reversed the expansionist liberalism of 1848, that proposed giving German nationality to all Germans anywhere on earth. It was applied in a territory embittered by decades of strife. German claims of ill-treatment of their minorities in the inter-war years were not a figment of Nazi imagination (although, ironically enough, anti-German activities appeared to recede in Poland after the German-Polish Friendship Treaty of 1934). Militant Polish ex-soldiers and members of nationalist fighting units had been given priority as new settlers in the Polish border areas where the Poniatowski villages were formed, a fact that makes the mutual hatred and fear between Germans and Poles on the border easier to understand. These remarks are not intended in any way to excuse either the German invasion or the evacuation measures that followed it, but rather to help explain the attitude of the German planners and administrators of the re-settlement programme. Men who were not monsters implemented a plan that caused endless suffering.[24]

According to calculations made during and immediately after the war by the ILO, the most reliable and comprehensive guide, the following ethnic Germans were involved in the re-settlement:

93,000	Bessarabians
21,000	Dobruja Germans
98,000	Bukovinians
68,000	Wolhyniens
58,000	Galicians
130,000	Baltic Germans
38,000	East Poland
72,000	Sudeten Germans
13,000	Germans from Slovenia
Total	591,000

The total amount of territory annexed to form new German counties in the East was 102,800 sq. km., of which some 75 per cent had been German territory before the First World War. It included 78,000 sq. km. of Danzig West-Prussia, of which 47,000 had been German prior to 1914; 7,800 sq. km. of East Upper Silesia, and 17,000 sq. km. of the Zichenau, which was annexed to East Prussia. German civil law was introduced in January 1940, including the National Food Estate Marketing Law. Approximately 80 per cent of the 12 million population were Polish, 4.5 per cent Jewish, and some 15.5 per cent German. (The proportion of Jews within the population was considerably smaller than in Eastern Poland, as the main area of Jewish settlement lay in regions which had been Russian and Austrian prior to 1918.)[25]

The RKFDV decree of 7 October 1939, which authorised Himmler, as Reichsführer SS to create new settlement areas, protect the *Deutsche Volksgemeinschaft* from 'damaging influences', and above all, organise the return of Germans living outside the boundaries of Germany, was the major legislative instrument. Clause 3 of the decree gave the task of creating 'new peasants' to the Ministry of Agriculture, under the RKFDV's jurisdiction.

Between December 1939 and December 1940, events continually overtook plans, and the re-settlement proceeded cumbersomely, amid complaints that the SS was being starved of funds by the Ministry of Agriculture, and attacks on the Settlement Societies for 'interfering with ethnic German re-settlement'. One SS General apologised to the head of the Race and Settlement Office that only 1000 people a day were being evacuated from Upper Silesia, instead of the planned 4,000. With no central water supply in most of the Polish towns, and the danger of typhus in the summer months, establishing transit camps was itself no easy task. The planned rapid evacuation of Polish farmers was not taking place.[26]

In December 1939, the plan was to evacuate 400,000 Poles to make way for around 200,000 *Volksdeutsche*, of whom some 120,000 were expected immediately, most on foot and some in wagons. Categories for deportation included all Jews, Polish peasants whose land was being taken for the Wolhynien Germans, and any Poles related to those killed in the fighting, who were described as a security risk.[27]

The Wolhynien Germans, one of the largest groups, did not in fact begin to arrive until the spring of 1940, after complex negotiations with the Russians, and the implementation of a refugee treaty concerning those Poles (some 60,000) who had fled to Russian-occupied territory after Germany's invasion, but who now wanted to return. SS Race and Settlement officials went to Russian-occupied territory to oversee the evacuation of the Wolhyniens and Bessarabians. Uncertainty surrounded their removal: Gustav Pancke, RuSHA's head, claimed that he was not told to prepare for their arrival until February or March 1940. However, a search for suitable transit accommodation was under way in November 1939. Summer homes and bishop's palaces were among the buildings appropriated for use. Fifteen hundred members of the NSDAP Land Service were sent to West Prussia at the same time, to help prepare empty farmhouses for the returnees.[28]

The colonists arrived with the minimum of luggage and possessions. They were confined to 50 kilos per family, and had concentrated on bringing with them seeds and farming implements. 'The negotiations with the Soviet Union went without friction; the officials were extremely *korrekt*', commented the SS man in charge of one such evacuation approvingly, although 'It was sometimes difficult to communicate with such completely opposed points of view. Also, one had to get used to the fact that time and punctuality in general meant nothing to the Russians.' The Germans found that they did the actual organising and packing, while apparently demoralised Soviets got drunk. There were hours or days waiting at stations at temperatures sometimes 20 degrees below freezing, while lost train carriages were found. Shortages were so extreme that Soviet officials even had to borrow pencils and paper from the Germans. The implications of this seemed to pass by the members of the Wehrmacht who accompanied the convoy. They were more concerned to describe the wild life than criticise Soviet administration, and spent their spare time bird-watching. However, just as with Nazi Germany in modern historiography, they observed a multiplicity of conflicting authorities and institutions. Conflicts of competence made negotiation difficult in Russian-occupied Poland, and unsurprisingly, they found that the NKVD was the most powerful organ.[29]

Even under war-time conditions, the incorporated area was to be a paradise of plenty compared to areas under Russian rule. However, more panic-stricken confusion awaited the unfortunate *Volksdeutsche* in Germany. No one seemed to be in charge of the project, or to have any idea of how many people were involved. It is hard to establish the feelings of this unfortunate group. Their East Polish home had been overrun by the Soviet Union, and they dreaded collectivisation. Amid the prevailing poverty the Bessarabian Germans seemed well provided with food, although their farming methods were primitive, and their houses simple. The writer of the report claimed that they had virtually created a black earth district out of nothing, through careful farming and manuring and irrigation. He noted that the village halls had two portraits facing each other – one of Hitler and one of Stalin! Although no collectivisation measures had been implemented, the main impression of conditions in Wolhynia and Bessarabia was that of poverty. In Slovakia, however, now a semi-independent, nationalist Republic, one welfare officer involved in re-settling the Slovakian Germans reported resentment and unwillingness to leave on the part of the German peasants.[30]

Pending the provision of suitable farms, returning ethnic Germans were placed in transit camps within the Reich as well as in the incorporated areas. A form of pocket money was paid to adults as well as children in the camps, and Baltic German adolescents and children not in camps also received weekly payments of 5 and 3 Reichsmarks. The Waffen SS, with its chronic shortage of manpower, recruited as many of their youths as possible, while families were sometimes split up as a result of recruitment. by labour organisations to work in the *Altreich*. The National Socialist Welfare Organisation helped with the provision of furniture and clothes, while the RKFDV provided pocket money for those in camps, and other welfare services.[31]

Evacuation orders regarding Polish farmers were strict in their allowances of furniture and livestock. They were allowed to take one wagon per household, bed linen, bicycles, pets, and small items of furniture, and had to take clothing, papers, gold and valuables, washing materials and five day's food. They were forbidden to take heavy furniture, cows and horses, flour, fruit, bees, and agricultural machinery. However, in practice, they seem to have taken all they could with them, while the buildings and crops that remained were often damaged by relatives of the evacuated Poles. In many cases, the evacuees were moved only to the next village along, especially after 1942. The presence of the dispossessed Polish farmers was a constant threat to the resettled Germans. According to post-war eye-witness reports, it frequently led to a sense of guilt at occupying stolen farms. The repatriated ethnic Germans, after all, had no particular axe to grind where the Poles were concerned.[32]

The returnees varied considerably in their experience of farming, their abilities and education. Bessarabian Germans turned out to be especially difficult to settle in farms, and in December 1940 Himmler ordered them to be put into labour battalions instead. Relationships between different groups were sometimes tense, as indeed they were between returnees and the old-established German families in the Incorporated Areas.

Himmler had ordered in January 1940 that 'despite the joy these Germans feel on returning to their homeland, every encouragement must be given in order to make their adaptation to the new surroundings, and the rebuilding of their lives, easier'. But among the substantial element of integrated *Reichsdeutsche*, usually estate owners and managers who had intermarried with Poles over generations, the newcomers were despised rather than welcomed as racial comrades. In the eyes of the SS administration, many of these integrated Germans had 'gone native', and become quite Polish in their lifestyle; they presented a special ideological problem to the administrators of the newly conquered territory. 'Those *Reichsdeutsche* who own or manage large farms have personal friendship with Poles and drink with them. Unfriendliness towards the *Volksdeutsche* is a commonplace.' What was even worse, some Poles were too friendly with the *Reichsdeutsche*. Local NSDAP welfare workers found their sense of nationalist propriety offended when they heard, for example, Polish maids singing German nationalist songs in a *Reichsdeutsche* household. Class loyalty appeared to be a stronger force than racial solidarity in relations between the new immigrants and the old, at least, where large and medium landowners were concerned, while in the small towns, even the tennis-club membership was split down the middle between *Volksdeutsche* and *Reichsdeutsche*. Members of old landowning families often took different sides. In one family, the eldest son was in a camp for having Polish sympathies, while the second son was a volunteer in the Waffen SS. His mother-in-law, an ethnic German herself, was an outspoken critic of the Nazis, and was in and out of concentration camps until 1945. The head of the Race and Settlement Office described another Polish estate to Himmler: the owner, a representative in the Polish senate, had been shot. The son made 'an impression of extremely low racial value, with a mongolian-tartar face. . . speaks only French with his mother'. In this case the German son of the former owner was not allowed to take over the farm, because he was found to have become too friendly with the Poles. 'He wears civilian dress. . and was found eating with Poles at table.' The *Volksdeutsche* who had suffered from Polish militancy between the wars remained hostile. For example, they would not allow Polish nurses to treat them. They also resented the fact that higher official positions were allotted to *Reichsdeutsche* than to the *Volksdeutsche*.[33]

By mid 1940, 35 camps had been established around Lodz and other towns in the Eastern zone of the Incorporated Areas. 120,000 people had passed through them by summer, while by the end of 1940 some half a million ethnic Germans altogether had 'heard the call of the Führer and returned to the Greater German homeland'. Fewer than half, however, had found farms, possibly less still, if the figure given was inflated for publication. None the less, as a report pointed out, that meant that an area of land the size of Oldenburg had been 'Germanised' in West Prussia, Upper Silesia and the Wartheland. Up to this date, the idea of a peasant settlement was still dominant. 'The work has just begun. The external incorporation of land must march together with internal Germanisation . . . *Volk* borders are more decisive than national ones.'

Some ethnic Germans were reluctant to take up peasant life, especially the Baltic Germans, who were of two kinds; either they were large landowners, who were not prepared to accept the conditions of peasant settlements (which would be like suggesting to Thomas Jefferson or 'Turnip' Townshend that they take on three acres and a cow) or they were urban dwellers. Baltic landowners were described by a contemporary observer as resembling Russian emigrés. They dreamed of their estates, of the corn-fields, sleigh-rides, the long family visits. Away from their homes, they pined and talked and drank away the time. Soon planning officials were calling on the evacuation staff not to send them any more Balts, 'We can only settle peasants here'.[34]

The shortage of labour in agriculture and industry – in Germany especially – overtook re-settlement plans by the end of 1941. The transport of Poles to the G-G were suspended in March 1941 because of the shortage of labour, by which time some 400,000 Poles had been evacuated and 167,450 ethnic Germans settled in their place. The SS Planning Staff at Posen called in vain for further evacuations, arguing that after the war was over, American-European relations would be at a low ebb, and that refugee German settlers from North America could be expected to arrive.

The Planning Staff did their best to help the *Volksdeutsche* settle in, providing libraries and language courses for them, and attempting to fit suitable tradesmen to the right jobs. The attitudes of the Poles varied from entirely hostile to passive, with even some active friendliness shown to the new arrivals in their often desperate straits. Greifelt, of the Immigration Office, Lodz, commented, 'In general, the Polish section of the population have not shown themselves to be friendly to the German resettlers and the resettlement commandos, but have also not been directly hostile'. This situation was not to last.[35]

The easiest answer to the joint problems of shortage of labour and Polish returnees (both from the Russian occupied area and the G-G), was to conscript Polish men and women as forced labour, and deport them to the West, to work in Germany and France. Polish dwarf farms provided most of the workers, and the smallholdings that were vacated were then consolidated for German resettlement. In 15 parishes around Lodz, over 500,000 hectares were resettled in this way (half by *Volksdeutsche* peasants, and half by returning Germans from the old Reich). The SS Planning Staff at Lodz complained that this still left 750,000 hectares locally in the hands of Polish smallholders, which could be made into 40,000 medium sized farms, which 'would break the Polish influence', and enable the land to be used for intensive fodder production, more animal rearing, sugar beet and vegetables. But from 1942 on, Polish farmers were rarely moved out of their counties, but from small farms to nearby villages, while small farms were consolidated before being allocated to *Volksdeutsche* farmers.

The implementation of more intensive and modernised farming encountered the problem of land shortage. When the Germans invaded the Wartheland, there were 3.2 million agriculturally usable hectares, but the first priority in a plan drawn up by the RKFDV Land Planning Office was to set aside nearly 500,000 hectares for afforestation, as well as 100,000 hectares for the Wehrmacht. This immediately cut down the available agriculturally usable land to 2.6 million hectares. 800,000 hectares of this was allocated in 1941 to the *Volksdeutsche*, but only some 300,000 hectares of this was ever settled.[37]

By December 1942, only the 35,000 or so new *Volksdeutsche* farms remained of the 'blonde province'. Every aspect of the original plan, save only the increase in food production, had failed. Even racially, 'In exceptional circumstances, persons of mixed race are to be admitted to the Reich'. Germanisation in the Incorporated Areas meant in effect the attempted Germanisation of some 85 per cent of the existing population there, while those *Volksdeutsche* still in transit camps at the end of 1942 were utilised for labour battalions in Germany. Perhaps fortunately, they had developed 'a certain fatalism as a result of war and revolution'.[38]

This necessarily brief look at the *Volksdeutsch* re-settlement programme has obviously ignored many factors which are important in a wider context. One problem is that the welfare aspect of the programme was considerable, and dominates the archival material. As Koehl points out, the picture that emerges from the RKFDV and RuSHA documents is overwhelmingly one of humaneness, with caring personnel distributing pocket money and showing ethnic German wives how to mend clothes. This took place, however, against a background of forced evacuation, dispossession, draconian anti-Polish legislation and racial bitterness that must be mentioned here, if only to clarify the position of the German settlers.

While frequently the subject of personal kindness from the Polish majority, the ethnic Germans were also obliged to build up homes and farms from scratch, in conditions of poverty and shortage. Many no longer spoke fluent German, but were expected to demonstrate the virtues of German culture to their Polish neighbours. Understandably, they were subject to sporadic physical attacks from partisans and Polish villagers. Far from being the new German homeland which they had been promised, the Incorporated Area was an alien territory of flat wastelands, a wilderness stretching endlessly into mournful sunsets, where the unprotected emptiness of the Eastern horizon exacerbated the fundamental agoraphobia of many of the settlers.

It emerges clearly from the reports, diaries and memoirs of the German administrators that the resettled Germans suffered a poverty as great as that of the Polish villagers, despite the efforts of welfare visitors and other officials. Furthermore, many of the new settlers came from farming communities where techniques were primitive. New methods had to be learnt, with concomitant delays in successful production.

For most of these groups, their eventual fate was worse than if they had remained behind, for the end of the re-settlement period was poignantly tragic. Driven West by the advancing Russian army, murdered *en masse* by Polish partisans, subject to every untrammelled atrocity that troops fuelled by years of hate propaganda and reaction to the terror of the *Einsatzgruppen* could devise, the degree of their destruction will probably never be known for certain. Along with the many millions of East Prussians who fled West in 1945, all that was left of the ethnic German returnees at the end of the war was an incoherent, fragmented body of survivors. Not only did several hundred years of European history disappear with their physical demise, but their fate was either ignored or interpreted as the just deserts of German imperialism.

The ethnic German refugees had provided an internal empire for the SS. German agricultural settlement was not an integral part of Himmler's institutional expansion, but was an obsession with his staff, and popular with the majority of SS members. Himmler appears to have seized the opportunities offered in 1938 when settlement ideology was conjoined with the sudden prospect of territorial expansion. Jan Gross suggests in his work on Poland under the Nazis that the Nazi creed was incapable of coping with the concept of Empire, that both Nazi racialism and its emphasis on institutionalised 'personalism' was incompatible with the creation of a real 'New Order'. Himmler's importance lay in the fact that he, almost alone among leading Nazis, was ideologically and temperamentally capable of thinking in Imperial terms. This helps to account for his rapid seizure of power in the Occupied Territories; Himmler was a phenomenon in National Socialism, representing its (perhaps inevitable) transformation into the full Fascist state: imperialist thus anti-nationalist; elitist not populist; seeking the efficient, planned – and rootless – European super state. This dimension helps to account for the fact that by 1944 more than half the Waffen SS were non-German.[40] The role of the *Volksdeutsche* settlement in Himmler's plans was to provide a valuable element of apparent continuity of aim through Konrad Meyer's Land Office; through the appeal to the old German desire to recover its lost emigres and consolidate its frontiers. It helped to camouflage the qualitative distinction between SS hegemony in occupied Europe and previous ambitions, but its real purpose was to open the door to strategic control of a new Empire in the East.

In the pursuit of that Empire, Himmler discovered that racial purity could give way to a supra-racial and supra-national categorisation that magically enabled a vast source of manpower to become available. By re-labelling, people could be drawn into the system and ranked on a scale of Germanism. The concept lost racial and national meaning, and became a means of grading usable human material, and 'began to acquire an achievement dimension'. The *Volksliste* became a sifting procedure to procure potential citizens of the New Order: loyal, healthy, and possessed of five fingers on each hand.[41]

For many SS personnel in Himmler's empire, the well-being of the ethnic Germans had been of intrinsic importance; the correspondence between SS offices stressing importance of settlement as late as January 1945 is evidence to that effect. However, control of the ethnic German re-settlement programme by Himmler played another role in the SS's drive to total dominance; by enabling them to control land use and distribution in the Occupied Territories, it put them in control of possibly the most vital raw material in all the conquered territories – land itself. There was no inevitability about the emergence of this domination, and it is possible that a settlement programme carried out under the anti-capitalist, anti-colonial Darre would have been more thorough and effective. Whether it would have been more humane is hard to judge. In the end, however, there was only chaos.

Acts of revenge taken on Poles who had been members of nationalist groups; the oppression and corruption of a conquered people after an invasion: these also can hardly be laid at the door of the plan to re-settle ethnic Germans in the Incorporated Areas. Yet because of the plan's emphasis on race, as opposed to nationality, it has attracted especial vilification. Clearly, any programme of forced evacuation and dispossession involved great suffering. But whether the programme was inspired by a desire for national expansion, ideological hegemony or racial consolidation (as exemplified respectively by Polish, Russian or German expansion between 1918 and 1945) hardly affects the experience of the event either for those who suffered or for those who survive.

Notes: Chapter 7

1   See T. Schieder, ed., *Documents on the Expulsion of the Germans from East-Central Europe*, 4 volumes, English translation, abridged, (Göttingen, 1961); F.H. Epp *Mennonite Exodus*, Altona, 1966; M. Proudfoot, *European Refugees*, 1939-52, (London, 1957), and D.A. Löber, ed., *Diktierte Option. Die Umsiedlung der Deutsche-Balten aus Estland und Lettland*, 1939-41. (Neumunster, 1972).

2   J. Farquharson, *The Plough and the Swastika*, London, 1976, discusses *Lebensraum* and concludes that Hitler had no specific plans for Eastern German settlement, see Conclusion.

3   K.R. Schultz-Klinken, 'Preussische und deutsche Ostsiedlungs-politik von 1886-1945' *ZAGAS*, 21 (1973), Dr Otto Auhagen's report on resettling German peasants in the incorporated areas, Bundesarchiv (hereafter cited as BA) R49.20, F. Fischer, *Griff nach der Weltmacht* (Düsseldorf, 1967), pp. 104-5, 138-9, 142-3, *passim*, Broszat, *NS Polenpolitik 1939-45* (Stuttgart, 1961), pp. 13-16.

4   Konrad Meyer-Hetling, 'Lebensbericht' (unpublished memoirs), 1970, in author's possession), pp. 95, 108-9.

5   Report of Himmler's speech, marked 'Secret E.P. Madrid', 20.10.40, BA R49/20.

6   H. Grimm, *Volk ohne Raum* (Munich, 1926); representative of Bavarian Staatsministerum to Dr Kurt Kummer, Ministry of Agriculture Settlement Department, 10.10.39, BA NS26/944; Hitler's comment, N. Rich, *Hitler's War Aims* (London, 1974), ii, 36-7; Gustav Pancke, head of the SS Race and Settlement Office, to Himmler, 14.12.39, BA NS2/55; Polish villages, *Deutsche Siedlung*, April 1937.

7   Himmler's personal adjutant to Pancke, 24.2.40, BA NS2/55.

8   Backe, speech at Posen, February 1942, and G. Pacyna, both in *Deutsche Agrarpolitik*, February, 1942.

9   Polish peasantry, W.C. Wisely, 'The German Settlement of the "Incorporated Territories" of the Wartheland and Danzig West-Prussia, 1939-45', London Ph.D. Thesis, 1955, pp 256-7, 263-4. Ed. H. Heiber, 'Das Generalplan Ost' (docs), *VjhfZg* (1958) 6, 289; Willikens, State Secretary of the Ministry of Agriculture, to Himmler, 23.11.39, BA NS26/943.

10   Three orders and the *Z Aktion*, see Broszat, *Polenpolitik*, 85–100.

11   Report by SS SBF Brehm to Pancke, 24.10.39, BA NS2/60.

12   26.22.39, BA R75/13. For details of the Poniatowski villages, which were the Polish equivalent of the *Wehrbauern* villages Himmler envisaged creating on the German-Polish border, see R. Koehl, *RKFDV; German Resettlement and Population Policy* (Cambridge, Mass., 1957), p. 44.

13   42,000 agricultural experts had been drafted for advisory service in the East by 1941, Hans-J Riecke (head of Chefgruppe la Food and Agriculture in the Economic Command Staff East, in 1941), *Deutsche Agrarpolitik*, October, 1942; the July 1939 report is in *Reichsamt für wehrwirtschaftliche Planung*, July 1939, BA R23/788. For the drop in productivity, see K. Brandt, *Management of Agriculture and Food in the German Occupied and other Areas of Fortress Europe; a Study in Military Government* (Stanford, 1953), pp. 36-8, and M Sering, ed., *Agrarverfassung der deutschen Auslandssiedlungen in Osteuropa* (Berlin, 1939), p. 179.

14   SS SBF Brehm to Himmler, 24.10.39, BA NS2/60.

15   Report to Himmler of 18.7.41, quoted in Lee Wheeler, 'The SS and the Administration of Nazi Occupied Eastern Europe, 1939-1945', Oxford D. Phil. Thesis, 1981, p. 133;

A. Hohenstein (pseudonymous), *Wartheländische Tagebuch aus den Jahren 1941-2* (Stuttgart, 1961), pp. 33, 72.

16 Brehm report, *op. cit.* For the wheat surplus, see J. Gross, *Polish Society under German Occupation: the G-G 1939-44* (Princeton, 1979), 93; Brandt, *Fortress Europe*, p. 36.

17 Meyer, 'Lebensbericht', p. 108-9; Himmler's speech, 24.10.39, BA NS2/60.

18 SS GF Hildebrandt, 26.11.39, BA R75/13. S. Bannister, *I Lived Under Hitler* (London, 1957), is an extraordinary eye-witness report of conditions in Danzig and Poland from 1939 to 1942, by an Englishwoman married to a German doctor. See for this reference, p. 84, and also Chapter 7 in A. Bramwell, *Blood and Soil, R. Walther Darré and Hitler's 'Green Party'* (Bourne End, 1985).

19 Report, 12.2.41, BA R49/I/34.

20 Himmler order, 9.12.40, BA R49/4, and report by D.M. Schmidt, *Aussenstelle Ost*, 8.3.41, BA R49/I/34.

21 *Der Diplomlandwirt*, 15.10.40; Dr Kummer to Horst Rechenbach, ex SS Race and Settlement Office, 19.4.40, BA NS26/947: Auhagen report, *op. cit.*, Königsberg Institute, report quoted in appendix to East German dissertation, P.R. Hartmann, 'Die annexionistische Agrarsiedlungs-politik . . . (in the incorporated areas)' (Rostock, 1969).

22 H. Priebe, 'Wirtschaftsziele eines Umsiedlerhofes im Warthegau', *Neues Bauerntum*, January, 1941.

23 Sering, Agrarverfassung, Schieder, Meyer, Proudfoot, all *op.cit.*, Bannister, *I Lived under Hitler*, p. 86, E.M. Kulischer, *The Displacement of Population in Europe*, ILO Studies and Reports, (Montreal, 1941), p. 38.

24 See Broszat, *Polenpolitik*, p. 47, who estimates the total of German victims at six to seven thousand. The Polish official figure, quoted in N. Bethell, *The War Hitler Won* (London, 1972), pp. 84, 143, is 300. For a fuller discussion, see A. Bramwell, 'National Socialist Agrarian Theory and Practice, with Special Reference to Darré and the Settlement Programme', Oxford D. Phil. Thesis, 1982, p. 301.

25 78,000 sq.km. of Danzig-West Prussia, of which 47,000 had been German prior to 1914; 7,800 sq.km. of East Upper Silesia; 17,000 sq. km. of the Zichenau annexed to East Prussia, Brandt, *Fortress Europe*, p. 36. The *St. Handbuch* (1948) gives figures of 90,000 sq.km. and 9.9m. people.

26 Pancke to Hildebrandt, 27.11.39, BA NS2/60, and see Race and Settlement Office to Himmler, undated, BA NS2/56, and SS General von dem Bach to Pancke, 27.11.39, BA NS2/60.

27 These deportation categories are listed in a file note of a report by SS GF Hildebrandt, 26.11.39, BA R75/13, and correspond with the details witnessed by Sybil Bannister, *op.cit.* The figures on Wolhynien evacuation were given by SS SH Hoffmeyer in May 1940, BA R49/20.

28 Pancke to Himmler, 3.7.40, BA NS2/56. It was probably not just an excuse. Himmler talked of 'eventual' resettlement of 150,000 Bessarabian and Lithuanian Germans in February, 1940, six months after the German-Soviet Pact, Koehl, *RKFDV*, p. 82. On the Land Service, see NSDAP Youth Department to the head of the SS Race and Settlement Office, 22.11.39, BA NS2/60.

29 SS Hoffmeyer report, *op. cit.* One interesting picture of the *Volkesdeutche* is as follows: 'The Germans showed him their settlement. They walked with him through pig-sties stirring up one fat pig after another. They caught sheep betwen their legs and parted the wool to show him its thickness. They spread grain over the palms of their hands, and gingerly opened the stables of horses and bulls. Their scarred faces, cruel and clumsy, were sensitive to the nature of fertility. They brought the smell of fertility to his nostrils. Barbarians too, he thought; but belonging to the earth. The barbarity . . . of the Dictatorship of the Proletariat was abstract.

In the evening the Germans put a military march on the gramophone. They all stood up; stiffly, absurdly, spurred heels clicking together, faces obtusely solemn. A barbarism, Wraithby thought, that may, and probably will, make war on civilization. Not, like the Dictatorship of the Proletariat, on life.' (Malcolm Muggeridge, *Winter in Moscow* (London, 1935), p. 245.

30 Anon., report on Bessarabian resettlement, 1940, copy in author's possession; Melita Maschmann, *Fazit; Kein Rechtfertigungsversuch* (Stuttgart, 1963).

31 Maschmann, *Fazit, passim*. See Himmler orders between November 1939, and December, 1942, in BA R49/4; pocket money, BA R49/12: camp life, BA R49/20; labour units, BA R16/174.
32 Gross, *Polish Society*, p. 71; Broszat, *Polenpolitik*, p. 87, evacuation order, BA R75/10.
33 Bessarabian Germans, 3.12.40,BA R49/12, Bannister, *I Lived Under Hitler*, pp. 87-88, Maschmann, *Fazit*, p. 100; Pancke to Himmer on Polish estates, c. August 1940, BA NS2/56.
34 Figures, 'One Year of German Eastern Settlement', Bronia Alix Elsas, SS Staff Office, BA R49/I/34; Balts, Bannister, *op.cit.*; no more Balts, *Landrat* Krotoschin to Governor of Posen, March 1940, BA NS26/943.
35 Wheeler, 'The SS', p. 101; report, 10.2.41, BA R49/I/34; Greifelt, 26.3.41, BA R75/3. Wiseley, 'The German Settlement', pp. 256-7, 263-4.
36 Koehl, *RKFDV*, p. 122; Gross, *Polish Society*, p. 78; Settlement figure, report, January 1942, BA R49/I/35.
37 Schmidt report, *op.cit.*
38 'Persons of mixed race', Himmler, quoted in Wheeler, 'The SS', pp. 96-7: German Settlement Society report of 1950, p. 51.
39 Gross, *Polish Society*, 35-41.
40 Including two Waffen SS divisions of Muslim volunteers. The SS thoughtfully opened two training schools in Dresden and Göttingen for Muslim priests to be trained to service the Turkish and Indian volunteer units, M. Hauner, *India in Axis Strategy*, (Stuttgart, 1981), pp. 354-5.
41 Gross, *Polish Society*, pp. 196-7, W. Struve, *Elites Against Democracy*, (Princeton, 1973), pp. 423-5; Koehl, *RKFDV*, pp. 80 ff.

Bibliography

Unpublished sources

S. Siebel-Achenbach, 'The German Population in Upper Silesia; 1945-9', Oxford D. Phil Thesis to be submitted Michaelmas, 1986.

Published Sources

E. Kröger, *Der Auszug aus der alten Heimat; die Umsiedlung der Baltendeutschen*, Tübingen, 1967.
I. Morrow, *The Peace Settlement in the German-Polish Borderlands; a Study of Conditions Today in the Pre-war Provinces of East and West Prussia*, London, 1936.
R. Muller-Sternberg and W. Nellner, *Deutsche Ostsiedlung; eine Bilanze für Europa*, Bielefeld, 1969.
H.W. Schönberg, *Germans from the East; a Study of their Migration . . . since 1945*, The Hague, 1970.

8 Refugees from the Eastern provinces of Italy after 1943

DANIELE MORO

An objective analysis of the events relating to the exodus from the eastern provinces of Italy after 1943 is still particularly difficult. The study is complicated because, in contrast to the alarming scarcity of official sources (and the unavailability of those which do exist), there exists a large body of books, pamphlets and reports produced by authors who, in many cases (precisely because they were deeply involved in the tragic events) are often very biased in their writings.[1] Even basic data are still a matter of violent controversy. One of the most striking examples of such problems concerns the number of refugees: 350,000 (of whom 300,000 were Italians and 50,000 Slavs), according to many sources linked with the refugee organizations in Italy, went from East to West; 200,000 according to a study of the *Istituto regionale per la storia del movimento di liberazione nel Friuli-Venezia Giulia*[2]; 'more than 300,000 who left Istria', according to a speech by Marshal Tito on 29 December 1972[3].

The same problem applies to data on the *'infoibati'*, people who were thrown, often still alive, into some of the 1,700 *foibe,* the very deep gorges in the Istria region. Here too, according to many survivors, the numbers killed were in the range of many thousands (20-200,000), whilst other sources report 10-20,000[4]; 4,122[5]; or a 'few hundred'[6]. From the Yugoslavian side there is still an embarrassed silence.[7] Forty years later many obstacles stand in the way of a free account of what actually happened.[8] In preparation for this study, which involved many trips to the areas concerned and interviews with people of different nationalities and shades of opinion, the author was requested by many he spoke to not to disclose their names or quote parts of their answers.[9]

Historical Background to the Italian-Yugoslavian Dispute

In Italian-Yugoslavian relations the border issue has always been of vital importance. At the end of the First World War, Italy occupied the city of Fiume and extended its sovereignty to the whole area west of the Fiume-Lubiana line. In 1941, Lubiana province was also annexed to Italy.

Some observers have stressed that, after the Second World War, Yugoslavia was simply repaying Italy in the same kind.[10] It is true that Italian expansionism was one of the reasons for the Yugoslavian attitude after 1943. The fascist regime in Italy was particularly harsh towards Slavs living in the kingdom of Italy. As in other areas of the country (French speaking Valle d'Aosta, German-speaking Alto Adige, etc.) the regime tried very hard to destroy any 'non-Italian' heritage of language and culture. The strongest resistance to this arose from the Slavs and they suffered the most severe repression.

For centuries Italians and Slavs had lived intermingled over a wide area.[11] After the fall of the Austro-Hungarian empire this resulted in great instability. Ethnic differences were not the only cause of conflict; economic and strategic interests were also at stake.

Ethnic Background to the Conflict

The ethnic issue was what gave the whole issue problematic overtones, resulting in very tense Yugoslav-Italian relations. Although after the Second World War Central Europe was devastated by the refugee problem, the issue of Italian refugees in the area concerned caused particularly deep wounds, which are still open today.

The crisis was made even more severe by mistakes and contradictory measures concerning the definition of new borders: it was only in 1975, with the Osimo Agreement, that Italy and Yugoslavia eventually put an end to their border disputes.

The national claims discussed here could have been enlarged to cover a wider area toward the west (Venetian Slavia) as much as to the east (Dalmatia) because of the Slav settlements in the former case, and the Italian ones in the latter. With some exceptions, the two areas have not been affected by the refugee issue.

Although there were about a dozen different nationalities, the largest groups were Italians, Slovenes (in the north-west), and Croats (in the north-east). The Italians were concentrated in the cities, the others in the countryside. East of the Monfalcone-Udine line, there was practically no ethnic homogeneity: some areas populated by Italians were next to others with a large Slav population. This situation frequently went back for centuries. It is hard to determine which group was in a numerical majority, but the question is not important. The various Allied agreements, the UN Charter and humanitarian principles clearly forbade mass expulsion of national groups, not to speak of mass killings of unarmed civilians.

Economic and Strategic Background to the Conflict

Control of the region, especially of the city of Trieste, has always been extremely important, for several reasons. Economically, the harbour, formerly the main base of the Hapsburg navy, had traditionally been a centre of a substantial flow of international trade. Because of its geographic position it had been termed 'a window on the Balkans'; it was a natural route for Western penetration and an invaluable transit-point for trade to and from Central Europe.

That Italy should take a special interest in Trieste is understandable. On the other hand, it was even more important to the Yugoslavians, for whom the harbours of Monfalcone, Pola, Fiume, and Zara (all of which Marshall Tito wanted to capture) would be highly prized as spoils of war. The importance of the five Adriatic harbours to Yugoslavia was enhanced by their well-developed infrastructures and highly skilled working class, along with a long-standing commercial tradition which Yugoslavia lacked.

Strategic considerations for a country which was at the time a close ally of the Soviet Union, meant keeping a strong hold on secure, well-equipped harbours and at the same time permitting easy access to the Italian Po Valley.[12]

Social and political differences intensified the ethnic ones. The Italian community was heavily represented in the bourgeoisie and important sectors of the working class (mainly in the docks), while the Slav community was found chiefly among the peasantry. This phenomenon was exploited by the Yugoslavian Communists to identify the Slav interest with socialism and the Italian ones with imperialism.[13]

From 1943 Fascist and ultra-nationalist policy gave the Yugoslavian leaders solid arguments with which to inflame the Slav population against the Italians. In many cases completely innocent people were made to pay for the crimes of others. Among those who were thrown into the *foibe*, were not only Fascists, Nazis, and collaborators, but women, old men, anti-Fascists, Italian Communists, priests, and, according to some sources, 23 New Zealand soldiers – in their uniforms – who were part of the Allied contingent which liberated Trieste.[14]

The Italian armistice (8 September 1943) and the collapse of the Italian army left a vacuum in the area. The different Slav armies, from the Fascist Ustascia of Ante Pavelic, who had been till the eve of the armistice an Italian 'Quisling', and the anti-Communist partisans of Colonel Dragoliut Mihailović, to the Communist partisans of Marshal Josif Broz Tito, immediately declared their claims to the whole area east of the river Isonzo. As a result, the Italian population living in this area grew increasingly alarmed. The impending danger of a Slav invasion was the main factor behind the change of attitude of many people *vis à vis* the incoming German army. This attitude was in deep contrast with popular feeling in the rest of soon-to-be German occupied Italy, apart from that of the great majority of the ethnic Germans in the north-eastern province of Alto-Adige/South Tyrol.

Some people viewed the German army as a buffer to protect them from the Slavs, while others, like the *Comitato di Liberazione Nazionale (CLN) di Trieste* (the inter-party anti-fascist body in charge of the fight against the Nazis) hoped that no time lag would occur between the German defeat and the arrival of the Anglo-American army. To them the fight against Nazi-Fascists was complicated by the fear of a possible Slav invasion.

This situation led to endless disputes and the decision by the Italian Communist Party (PCI) to split from the Trieste CLN and to join the Titoist comrades. The PCI had supported the annexation of the region by the Yugoslavians (until the Tito-Stalin clash), and found itself in a very embarrassing situation. To add a touch more drama to a very complicated situation the developing cold war was to split the area further.[15] It did not take very long for the people of the region fully to appreciate the meaning of Winston Churchill's speech in Fulton, Missouri about 'an iron curtain running from Stettin in the Baltic to Trieste'. As we will see later, the demarcation line between the Anglo-American zone and the Yugoslav one (a few miles south of Trieste) became part of the Iron Curtain.

The Exodus Starts

It is commonly believed that the exodus involved only Italian nationals and was motivated by the loss of the territories *per se*. However, there were also Slavs who left Italy, and political motivations were more complex. After the collapse of the Italian army, Slavs of different political convictions were able to occupy part of the region. Then the German army quickly established themselves in the area. This was when the refugee problem developed. First came the defeat of the Italian garrison in the Adriatic city of Spalato, and the take-over by Tito's partisans. In Istria (especially in the southern area) the first mass killings of Italians were recorded in September 1943.

The behaviour of Tito's partisans was especially brutal. The Yugoslavian Communists took pride in imitating the harshest Soviet theories (and methods). It is of interest to look at the opinion of an Italian anti-Fascist historian who wrote: 'Without doubt, the main reference point was the Soviet experience, but it was not so much the contemporary experience as that of the first years of Soviet power that influenced the national and revolutionary struggle of the Yugoslavian people.'[16]

The delegate of Tito's partisans at the *Comitato di Liberazione Nazionale dell 'Alta Italia* (CLNAI), Anton Vratusa, said in July 1944: '. . . the individual irregularities which happened in September 1943 have nothing to do with the aims of the Slovene people . . . They are negligible phenomena caused mainly by irresponsible individuals, who joined the Liberation Army just after the collapse of the Italian Army.'[17] A more sincere version came a few weeks later, on 28 August 1944, with a declaration by the 'Italian' section of the Croatian Communist Party (PCC): 'the "reaction" will also try to exploit the "*foibe*", saying that we tried to destroy the Italians in Istria and that this was the proof of Croat nationalism. We know very well that not only were exploiters and Italian Fascist criminals thrown into the "*foibe*", but also those who betrayed the Croatian people, fascist "*ustascia*" and degenerate "*cetniks*" [the anti-Communist resistance fighters].'

The killings in the '*foibe*' were simply the reaction of a people who had been oppressed for years, a reaction which broke out with the characteristic violence of the popular uprising,[18] involving 'popular trials' (at best), kidnappings, tortures, and the deportation to a concentration camp like Borovnica (between Lubiana and Trieste) of thousands of people often guilty simply of not being on Tito's side.

Some of the people who were able to leave in time were in fact Fascists responsible for horrible war crimes (thus the exodus which occurred between 1943 and 1945 was called the 'black exodus'), while others were simply worried by the rumours about purely anti-Italian violence.

Another wave of the exodus was linked with the fate of the Italian city of Zara, (an Italian outlet on the Yugoslavian Dalmatian coast). Starting on 2 November 1943, a year of Anglo-American bombing killed thousands of people, destroyed or severely damaged 85 per cent of the city, and drove almost all the inhabitants out. They left the city forever, and it was occupied by Yugoslavian partisans when the shelling stopped.

To many observers, such heavy bombing of a city like Zara (at that time of no military importance) seemed pointless. The suspicion that the action was aimed at 'cleansing' the area of the only Italian sovereign territory in Dalmatia is quite widespread among the survivors, even if factual evidence is lacking.

As stated earlier, the Italian armistice and the subsequent founding of the Fascist *Repubblica di Salò* in the area of Italy occupied by the Germans gave a different perspective to the region. On 1 September 1943, Friedrich Reiner was nominated High Commissioner for the *Adriatisches Küstenland* (Adriatic Coast), and the provinces of Udine, Gorizia, Trieste, Pola, Fiume, and Lubiana (annexed to Italy in 1941) were put under German administration.[19] In other words this part of Italy was from a formal point of view removed from the (very weak) authority of the *Repubblica di Salò*. According to many authorities, this step demonstrates the determination of the Germans finally to annex the area. Enzo Collotti observed:[20] 'In a wide sense we could say that the Adriatisches Küstenland shows that the Third Reich was ready to annex these provinces.'

For many people in the area the German occupation had at least one positive aspect: it stopped the advancing Yugoslavian partisans. As the Nazi defeat approached the problem arose again. For some time people had hoped for an Anglo-American landing in Istria, which would allow the Western powers to reach Vienna, taking a short cut and out-manoeuvring the Soviets. In fact such a landing never occurred and the only chance of a direct change-over from the Germans to the Anglo-Americans depended on the speedy arrival of the latter from the Po Valley. The problem, therefore, was how to prevent Tito from liberating the Italian eastern provinces. On this issue too disputes will run for years.

Some argue that the Allied forces never gave definite guarantees that the whole of the Italian territory would be held by them (in other words that the Yugoslavians would be prevented from intervening), while others say that secret agreements existed between the Allied forces and Tito. The Trieste CLN decided to break the impasse and call for insurrection on 30 April 1945. Pier Antonio Quarantottie Gambini described CLN intentions as follows: 'We should try to shorten as much as possible the time lapse between the defeat of the Germans and the Anglo-Americans arrival (as we cannot believe that they will not come), and, if possible, we will try to avoid an interim period occurring at all, without giving up the idea of the insurrection, however, because it must be us, not Tito's men or the Anglo-Americans, who start the rising against the Nazis.'21

The Germans took shelter inside strongholds in the city, waiting to surrender to the Anglo-Americans (as in fact happened). But the CLN's hope was very short lived. On 1 May 1945 Tito's partisans arrived in Trieste. The great majority of the Italian partisans fighting in Tito's army were prevented from participating in the liberation of the Italian cities: the action was to be purely Yugoslavian. Meanwhile Lubiana and Zagabria, to give only two examples, were still waiting to be liberated by the partisans.

Many people thought that the Yugoslavians were deliberately avoiding a 'decisive' participation by the Italian partisans in the liberation of Italian territory. They would be allowed to enter the Italian cities, like Gorizia, only after the liberation was successfully accomplished. The Yugoslavians wanted to avoid, therefore, giving any support to the pro-Italian argument in the impending dispute.

On 2 May the Anglo-Americans entered Trieste. The situation became, if possible, even more complicated. Anglo-Americans, Tito's partisans, and the CLN were occupying Trieste. In a few days the CLN had to go underground again. Some of its members escaped through the Yugoslavian checkpoint of Barcola (north of the city), and others chose to become clandestine again.22

The 'forty days' of Trieste, as the population of the city would name them, had started.

Tito's troops immediately initiated the deportation of thousands of people, while the Allies stood by. With two *foibe* near Trieste (Basovizza and Monrupino) the spectre of mass murder raised its head. At the same time the Italian flag was forbidden, the clocks were changed to Belgrade time, and people who protested were arrested and many disappeared.

It was widely felt that the Yugoslavs were trying to go as far west as they could with the aim of taking over more territory, thereby creating a *de facto* occupation. The PCI furthered this plan. To explain the PCI's reasons Mario Pacor says: 'The victories of Tito's army arose naturally from the enthusiasm of the most advanced strata of the working class and the anti-Fascist movement, especially among those who looked with great hope to the Soviet Union and were dreaming of the socialist revolution. In Tito's partisans they saw the intermediaries of the Soviet Union, which was the stronghold of socialism and the vanguard of the socialist word in expansion, and in that expansion they wanted to participate.23

As Bogdan Novak remembers, in October 1944 Togliatti and Kardely, with the help of Dimitrov, reached an agreement which meant the unification of the two partisan movements. Togliatti hoped that the Yugoslavian army would manage to occupy the whole territory. 'This', wrote Novak, 'would have prevented the Anglo-Americans from advancing.' Thus a bourgeois and reactionary regime would not be established. A campaign to build an Italian partisan army as part of the wider Yugoslavian army should have been started. In the following months, until the Cominform break up, many Italian Communists sincerely hoped that a Communist Yugoslavia would rule the territories as an alternative to capitalist Italy. The League of Communists of Yugoslavia (formerly PCJ) depicts the period following the Nazi fall as follows: 'The Western powers tried to prevent the internal and international consolidation of the new state of Yugoslavia, which had laid the groundwork for the new social relations and an independent internal and international policy. Unable to tolerate the fact that Yugoslavia was not included in their 'sphere of influence', the Western powers tried to support the counter-revolutionary forces in Yugoslavia. They applied particularly strong pressure on the border issue. In May 1945 the Western powers threatened armed intervention unless the Yugoslavian army withdrew from Trieste. For the sake of peace, the Yugoslavian army bowed to their demand.[24]

The Yugoslavian occupation of Trieste and Pola added a further disquieting element to the worries of the Italian population, who were only too aware of the precarious situation they were living in now that the CLN was deprived of the strong PCI, the Anglo-Americans were unwilling to extend their presence in Istria, and the Italian government was in a weak position and certainly unable to help the inhabitants of the region. After the Tito-Alexander agreement and the withdrawal of the Yugoslavians from Trieste, Pola, and Gorizia, the situation of many Italians still living in areas where the Yugoslavian authorities could operate freely became very difficult: from that moment no Western army was able to intervene in those areas.

A New Wave of Refugees

After Spalato and Zara it was the turn of Fiume. In two years the city would become almost totally empty of its former inhabitants. Liliana Ferrari writes: 'After Zara became deserted. . . the exodus from Fiume was the first mass exodus from the 'Giulian' region which came to the attention of both Italian and international public opinion.'[25]

The result was soon evident. 'In about one year Fiume became completely a Yugoslavian city.'[26] As Liliana Ferrari wrote, 'During the night of May 3 and 4, 1945, some of the better-known personalities in the city, in several cases innocent of any compromise with Fascism, were killed. The bodies of those killed weren't immediately removed, but were publicly displayed, under the surveillance of the secret police, the OZNA.'[27]

In Pola the situation had been very similar. Tito's troops entered the city on 1 May 1945. '. . . a problem immediately arose regarding the popular attitude toward the liberators and the reactions to the first measures of the new regime. These, as in Trieste and Fiume, were designed to consolidate the annexation of Pola to the new state order: Yugoslavian flags replaced the red ones, and an enormous amount of Croatian graffiti calling for the annexation of Pola to Yugoslavia appeared. . . . All the banks and warehouses were taken over. The purges started immediately.'[28]

Before the arrival of the Anglo-American troops the Yugoslavians started to loot and dismantle some of the industrial machinery in Pola to send it to Yugoslavia. The fate of Pola, however, was even more complicated and ultimately more dramatic than that of many other cities in the region. In accordance with the Tito-Alexander agreement, the region was divided into two areas: A Zone (Trieste, north-west of Istria and Pola), under Anglo-American administration, and B Zone, under Yugoslavian rule. From that moment until 10 February 1947 (the date of the Italian signature of the peace treaty), the city of Pola seemed to recover and the population gradually started to believe that the Western power would not give the city back to the Yugoslavians. Then, a few weeks before the signature of the peace treaty it was made known that Yugoslavian sovereignty would be imposed, and a mass exodus began which almost emptied the city. The Yugoslavian authorities did not particularly desire such a mass exodus. Only if the number of refugees was very limited could the claim that the exodus was of a 'few escaping Fascists' be justified. When the population started to leave in huge numbers it became more and more difficult to dismiss the problem as a 'reactionary movement'.

The Anglo-Americans were not in favour of the exodus either. They were very worried about the possible resettlement of the refugees in Trieste and adjoining areas (still under Allied administration), because they feared that a concentration of 'irredentists' close to the border could further complicate the situation. The Italian government was convinced that the presence of a mass of refugees from the area would deprive it of solid arguments at the forthcoming negotiations. To defend the 'Italianness' of an area almost emptied by the population concerned seemed a very difficult task.

People, however, were leaving in large numbers. They left with the definite knowledge that they were giving up their belongings and their right to return for ever. On this point the Yugoslavian authorities did not leave any room for doubt. Whoever was not prepared to give up Italian nationality (and passport) had to leave. The situation worsened with the 28 June 1948 Cominform decision to condemn the PCJ, which would fully isolate the Belgrade regime and make the internal situation more difficult too, as we shall see. Until then Titoist propaganda insisted on the equation: Italy = Fascism, Yugoslavia = Socialism. The Cominform crisis was soon going to complicate the situation further.

Gianna Nassisi correctly observed: 'Thus, set against the "cleaned up" image of Italy, where it seemed that anti-Fascist feeling was being suppressed, Yugoslavia and its institutions began to be seen as a new USSR, an almost "utopian and universal" model.'[29] Workers were told, up to then, that Yugoslavia was a socialist country which had won the war, was allied with the strongest continental power, the USSR, and was ready to treat the Italian Communists without discrimination, helping them to set up the core of an Italian anti-Fascist army which would liberate Italy from reactionary forces. In Trieste, especially, the arguments used with the businessmen were slightly different: Yugoslavia could give new impetus to the now-declining harbour, and Trieste could become the major trade centre for Central Europe and the Balkans. Neither of these arguments impressed the Italian community very much. It is quite interesting to read what an (anonymous) citizen, presumably with Communist ideals, wrote about the Yugoslavian attitude: '. . . Tito's policy showed its true face as far back as 1945: to denationalize as much as possible. It was not a policy for Communism; had they wanted to create a Communist regime it would have been all right, those who were not Communists could have left, but Tito's policy was aimed mainly at denationalizing us . . . '[30]

The Refugee and the Italian Peace Treaty

With the signing of the peace treaty on 10 February 1947, almost all of Istria (about 4,000 square kilometers) and Fiume were assigned to Yugoslavia. A Zone and B Zone, therefore, disappeared. In the remaining area of Trieste and Capodistria a 'Free Territory of Trieste' (TLT) was constituted. The territory was under Anglo-American administration (A Zone, with Trieste) and Yugloslavian (B Zone, with Capodistria). As Bogdan Novak wrote: 'The creation of the Free Territory was a compromise between East and West to solve the problem of a region having a mixed ethnic composition and with the aim of recovering the Trieste harbour as an important trade point for Yugoslavia, Hungary, Austria, Czechoslovakia, Poland, Switzerland and Italy. Only the latter two countries and some parts of Austria belonged to the West. All the other states were part of the Eastern bloc.'[31]

The project of building up a sovereign state entity, however, soon appeared an impossible task. The two zones became separate realities.[32] Trade with the Soviet bloc was almost impossible, and A Zone (i.e. Trieste) was economically in a very bad situation as compared with its pre-war status.

In the meantime, the Cold War was also influencing the internal state of Italy. The British and Americans were worried at the prospect of a possible victory by the left-wing parties in the April 1948 Italian elections. Less than a month before the elections the Western powers, on 20 March 1948, released the so-called 'tripartite declaration' making public their intention to give back the whole TLT to Italy. It was a clear propaganda move with the aim of helping the anti-Communist parties in Italy (a left-wing victory would of course have invalidated the promise, according to many observers, and from a legal point of view the declaration should have been supported by the USSR and the UN Security Council). Italy, in agreement with the Allied powers, now accelerated measures to re-establish its presence in A Zone. Yugoslavia did the same with B Zone, speeding up its integration into the Yugoslavian system.

The Cominform Resolution and its Effects on the Refugee Situation

Following the 28 June 1948 Cominform resolution against Yugoslavia and 'Titoism', wide repercussions were felt in the region, with direct consequences for the remaining Italian community. The Communist party which had been formed in the TLT (PC TLT) split into two groups, one led by the pro-Soviet Vittorio Vidali, the other by the Titoists. Palmiro Togliatti, then general secretary of the PCI, wrote: 'We have condemned the Yugoslavian leadership because in that kind of militarist organization which they call the "Communist Party" there is no debate, no internal democracy . . . a police regime and a "Turkish" despotism rule' (in *L'Unitá*, 20 July 1948). In B Zone the pro-Soviet PC was immediately banned.

Yugoslavia was now fully encircled by hostile forces. The PCI and the PC TLT of Vidali were now intent on the struggle to overthrow the 'Titoists', and their position on the border dispute changed too. Tito's official biographer, Wladimir Dedyer, spoke of 5,000 border 'incidents' (around the whole country). Francois Fejto, wrote: 'it was clear that the USSR would no longer have supported the Yugoslavian claim on Trieste.'[33] Fernando Claudin added: '. . . Stalin believed that the heretical state, whose position could hardly be more desperate, would soon collapse. Stalin's offensive also coincided with a whole series of provocations by the Western powers. During the first three months of 1948 American planes violated Yugoslavian airspace twenty-one times. During the election campaign in Italy reactionary forces linked with the Americans made allegations that Yugoslavia had built launching sites for V1 and V2 rockets near the Italian frontier and were concentrating troops to attack Trieste.'[34]

The Situation in B Zone after the Cominform Resolution

At the moment of the Cominform crisis, the B Zone was almost fully *de facto* integrated into Yugoslavia. The non-Communist parties had stopped any official activity in September 1945. In the same period, to protest against the introduction of 'Yugo-lira' – substituted for Italian currency – a general strike was called by workers in Capodistria. (In July 1949 the Yugoslavian dinar was finally introduced.)

Various checkpoints between the two zones were temporarily closed and border crossings were unreasonably delayed. Many workers commuting daily to Trieste were put in an impossible position by the Yugoslavian attitude. The position of the Church was particularly difficult too. The 'number one enemy' seems to have been Bishop Antonio Santin, who was in charge of the Trieste and Capodistria diocese (which the Vatican would leave united until 1977) and represented one of the few 'authorities' still in charge of both the zones. Like his colleague, the Gorizia Archbishop Carlo Margotti, who was expelled from his city during the Yugolavian occupation, Santin very soon became a 'symbol of the Italian reactionaries'.

Anti-religious repression, as in Yugoslavia, started very soon in B Zone too. *Vita Nuova*, the official newspaper of the *Azione Cattolica* (the Catholic mass movement) in the Trieste and Capodistria diocese denounced 'the removal of religious books together with the introduction of divorce, acts of violence against priests, and the prohibition of priests taking possession of their churches'.[35]

But what really impressed the public were the attacks against Bishop Santin. On 17 June 1946 he was prevented from confirming some children, when he was 'spontaneously' stoned by a group near Opicina. A year later, he decided to go to Capodistria, and only just escaped death. The following is his recollection of the affair: 'In June 1947 as the Yugoslavian attitude grew harsher, I decided to prepare to visit Capodistra for the Feast of St Nazario, On the 19th in the morning, I left Trieste alone by boat for Capodistria. I knew that some aggression was planned against me. I arrived in Capodistria, where the priests were waiting for me. A woman came up and said: "Your Excellency, you must leave as quickly as possible. . . ."' Bishop Santin decided to stay, and then: 'they found me, insulted me, shouted that I had to leave. And they threw me down the stairs, beating me over the head with fists and sticks. I was covered in blood . . . At one point a man pointed a big kitchen knife at me . . . they came and offered me a boat to return to Trieste. I refused. So they offered to take me by truck. I accepted. The truck was uncovered, and we were surrounded by armed soldiers. Groups of people threw stones at us throughout the journey till we reached the Allied checkpoint.'[36]

In A Zone the conflict between the two Communist factions was settled in a quite orderly way: in June 1949 the Allies organized the local elections and the PC TLT (pro-Cominform) got 42,587 votes out of a total of 181,820, while the PC TLT ('Titoist') scored a very poor 5,344. In the B Zone, however, the split meant a further opportunity for pressure to be exerted on the Italian community, which was seen, at least in part, as an 'unfriendly' group.

In many areas of B Zone the majority of the Communists were on the pro-Cominform side. One Communist from the city of Pirano (B Zone), Paolo Sema, wrote: 'The party declared its support for Cominform, apart from a small group . . . the violence started only later, because initially they [the "Titoists"] had no one with them, or at least very few.'[37] In Isola d'Istria (B Zone) the same thing happened. At the end of August 1948 many leaders of the PCC were arrested. In September a big trial against anti-Fascist leaders started: they were charged with having built a 'clandestine, terrorist, espionage organization' and 'having procured, under orders of foreign agents, arms, explosives, ammunitions . . . all with the aim of violently overthrowing the "people's power"'.

There were also problems in the schools. In the 1950-1 period there were 250 teachers (of whom 49 were foreigners) in the Italian schools in B Zone. In 1951-2 112 of them left. In 1952-3 32 more left. They explained their reasons as follows: 'We Italian teachers . . . declare that we have abandoned B Zone of TLT . . . because our physical safety has been put in danger. . . facing intolerable persecutions.'[38] With economic, political, religious, and, to some extent, school activity in B Zone almost blocked, the exodus reached massive proportions.

By 1956 the great majority of the Italians had fled the area. With the signature of the London Memorandum in 1954, assigning the two zones respectively to the Italians and to the Yugoslavians, the refugee problem became more than one of 'resistance', it became one of resettlement. The signature of the Osimo Agreement on 10 September 1975 officially settled the problem of sovereignty in the region, sanctioning a *de facto* situation which had by then existed for 20 years.

Zara, Fiume, Pola, and Capodistria, as we have seen, were almost emptied of their population, which was mainly Italian. According to a study of the CLN of Istria, the number of people who left Rovigno was 80 per cent, Dignano 90 per cent, Albona 98 per cent, and Parenzo 95 per cent, with 99 per cent from Montona, Gallesano, Sissano and Pinguente. According to Yugoslavian data for 1980, Pola and Capodistria were the only two Istrian cities where the population had increased compared with the 1936 census.[39]

Resistance in the Region

One of the most obscure aspects of the flow of refugees from the (formerly) Italian provinces concerns 'active' and 'passive' resistance. On this specific subject the author found many people on both sides of the border particularly reluctant to speak. A question frequently asked by the author about the apparent lack of widespread resistance against the Yugoslavians elicited from many refugees the answer: 'We are not terrorists.'

It is often argued that the real 'resistance' was the exodus *per se*, while others say that Yugoslavian repression was so strong that it prevented the organization of armed resistance. In reality, a resistance movement (passive and active) had developed in Istria. Four autonomous channels of information from the Yugoslavian-occupied area were available: the workers shuttling every day from the Yugoslavian area to the Allied one (from B Zone to A Zone and back), the refugees (between October 1953 and August 1956 24,597 persons left from B Zone alone), the Church and the Italian intelligence services. Alvise Savorgnan di Brazzà, then working as self-styled 'observer' for two governments, wrote: 'Italy could do very little for Trieste in the immediate post-war period, and had to do that little without a specific allocation from the budget. But not all the treasure of the *Repubblica di Salò* went to Dongo [where Mussolini and his gerarchs were finally captured]; part of the money . . . about 25,000 gold sterling, was allocated to Trieste . . .' £12,000 was given to an unnamed 'patriot' who was presumably coordinating some kind of action 'on the field'. Savorgan di Brazzà was then working in Trieste. By his admission 'he was lucky, and, shortly after having started his job, he knew everything. . . that was happening in and around Trieste, almost everything happening in Carso and Istria, and a lot of what was going on in Yugoslavia'.[40]

Another very interesting account comes from Paolo Venanzi: 'The hesitation and confusion which, at the end of the war, had created embarrassment and crisis among the Italians in the Peninsula were not shared by the few agents of the Intelligence service who . . . were still in the area, decimated but faithful to their orders. We can say, on the contrary, that their brave work helped to strengthen the surviving resistance at the peak of the Slav occupation. . . In Fiume, in the face of the recruitment campaign for the Yugoslavian army, the general registry disappeared, and an 'invisible group', from within the chain of command spared no efforts to block the carrying out of orders. . . Orders and counter-orders led to many arrests not being executed: suspects were helped to escape, incriminating documents were stolen, forged documents were issued, hiding places were found for wanted people. Thus began a resistance with no ideological aims, which was designed to save the greatest possible number of Italians from Slav persecution.

Unfortunately this climate, so full of enthusiasm and sacrifice, didn't last for long: the 'Centre'[41] ordered the 'operatives' to stop any further activities and go home, and said that they should consider themselves on 'unlimited leave'.[42] It is quite clear that the Italian government was behind this. The other organization which was able to collect information and develop some form of resistance was the CLN of Istria (CLNI), (underground) which in some cases gave specific instructions to the population. During the 45 days occupation of Pola by the Yugoslavians, Paolo De Simone wrote that there was 'more active resistance against the Yugoslavian occupying force, with leaflets being distributed and passive resistance organised against the display of the (Italian) flag with the red star [in the middle]; there was also an attempt to start operating a clandestine broadcasting service, which led to the arrest by the Communist police of a group of young people, who were deported to Yugoslavia'.[43]

Then in Pola there were 'reciprocal accusations (Slav nationalism versus Italian Fascism) and also demonstrations, graffiti on the walls, arms caches, and attacks'.[44]

In general the CLNI operated in 'a practical way, trying to organize passive resistance, for example inviting people not to accept occupation currency'.[45] Moreover, it was suggested that people should 'not vote, not go to meetings, not show the tricolour flag with the red star, and should deface notices and posters using eggshells filled with paint or ink. . .'[46] In every centre of the region a clandestine CLN was constituted, connecting the Trieste headquarters with the villages of the Yugoslavian-occupied area.

In Fiume many students refused to learn the Croatian language and left the schools. Professor Burich wrote: 'the political demonstrations which the adults could not stage were organized by the students in the schools. A rebellious attitude spread around, which could be checked by the police in the city, but which in schools could break out more easily.'[47] 'Anti-Fascist workers' were stopping the students from getting inside the school buildings by beating them with clubs. In Fiume, too, 'the CLN decided to start acting again illegally and clandestinely from underground'.[48] An underground newspaper, *La Libertà* (Freedom), was printed, graffiti were put on the walls, and the Yugoslavian flags were hauled down from public buildings. Workers and students organized in action groups.[49]

Bogdan Novak wrote: 'On July 1951 the Yugoslavs . . . accused the irredentists and in particular the CLNI of espionage against Yugoslavian military installations, not only in B Zone but also in Istria. The CNLI was also accused of being involved, on a vast scale, in getting secret information from Italian teachers and local bureaucrats in Zone B and Istria. The Yugoslavian authorities declared that some irredentist agents, who had been captured by the counter-espionage corps, were soon to be put on trial.'[50]

At some point, however, the CLNI wanted to prevent a further exodus from the area (the fate of B Zone was still under discussion) and asked the Italians to stop active resistance so as to avoid giving the Yugoslavians new reason for expulsions.

One of the most striking acts of violence was the killing of the British commander of Pola, R. W. L. de Winton, by the Italian woman Maria Pasquinelli who was 'shocked by the enormous extent of Italian territorial losses' as Bishop Santjn wrote.[51] During the trial which followed it was written: 'The horrible vision of the *foibe*, from which she exhumed the bodies of so many innocent people . . . guided her hand.'[52]

The murder of this British official happened on the day of the signature of the peace treaty which gave away a great part of Istria (Pola included) to Yugoslavia, 10 February 1947. In this context, note should be taken also of the activities of the PCI and the PC TLT (pro-Cominform tendency), notably the infiltration of Italian Communist groups into Yugoslavia with the aim of spying and organizing terrorist strikes. If it is true that such activity was not a direct result of the situation of the Italians (as a national group) living in the area nor of the wider refugee problem, it is quite clear too that many from the Communist side had thought that 'help' in the contested area could easily be found. As in fact it could.

According to Giorgio Bocca, author of one of the most complete (and unorthodox) biographies of the Italian Communist leader Palmiro Togliatti: '. . . Stalin and Yudin [Editor of the Cominform newspaper] . . . have ordered Vidali and the PCI to create an espionage and resistance network inside Yugoslavia, a very unpleasant and compromising task, about which the party has always tried to maintain secrecy. Some of the comrades on whom Vidali can rely are in Yugoslavia. They are Communist workers from Monfalcone, they have gone voluntarily to help the Yugoslavs in the work at Fiume harbour: some of them have been arrested as a precautionary measure by the Titoist police, others remain free and available. Other Slavic-speaking comrades who know the area well, are being disembarked by night . . . The people arrested are tortured for days and then sent to concentration camps.' Pietro Secchia, then head of the powerful Organization Department of the PCI, said: 'It was a painful episode, many comrades didn't come back from the camps or the Yugoslavian prisons.'[53]

A former Italian Communist who in that period was operating in the area at the time with Yugoslavians has reconstructed the situation as follows: 'There were two organizations: one from the PCI, the other from the PC TLT (Vidali). The first was led by Pietro Secchia from Rome and had two bases near the border, Udine (a kind of "headquarters") and Gorizia. Leader of the group was Adriano Dal Pont. Their activity was espionage, not terrorism. The other group depended directly on the Soviets, and was led by Vittorio Vidali and Marina Bernetich and had its headquarters in Trieste. Their activity was terrorism.'

Two examples were given of the operations undertaken by the Vidali network: 'in Autumn 1948 the passenger ship *Partzanska* was sunk in Fiume harbour, and the Fiume oil refineries (ex ROMSA) were set on fire. In Fiume there were about 3-4,000 PCI members who had left Italy for political reasons.'

More than thirty years were to pass before a Communist historian, Adriano Guerra, could write that 'Italian Communists who worked in that period as employees of Cominform or who, being in Yugoslavia, in the majority of the cases as political refugees, had thought they should not only declare themselves on the side of Cominform (and the PCI) but should also organize the struggle against Tito. Some of them were arrested by the Yugoslavian police and punished very severely; some of them experienced the extremely harsh regime of the Goli Otok concentration camp before being released in 1955.'[54]

Although the authors of *Storia di un Esodo* seem to deny that there was any violent resistance,[55] it is worth noting that in the same book Cristiana Columni wrote: 'In reality, however, there weren't any terrorist operations, except for some that were totally isolated from the population.'[56]

The problem is still debated, and the loss of many sources does not help research. In addition, rumours which lasted throughout the sixties regarding certain operations remain unproven.

Refugee Resettlement

Given a figure of 300,000 refugees, which I consider the most reliable approximation, it is interesting to see how the exodus proceeded. According to Mario Dassidovich, who based his study on Yugoslav sources, there were in 1945 100,000 Italians still under Yugoslavian rule; 79,795 in 1948; 35,874 in 1953; 26,615 in 1961; 21,791 in 1971. By the 1981 census the numbers had further decreased to 15,000.[57]

The refugees were put in 108 camps in Italy before being resettled. About 50,000 had to emigrate from Italy. An undefined number didn't go through the camps, thus making more difficult a precise quantification. The *Opera per l'Assistenza ai Profughi Giuliani* (the state body in charge of refugee resettlement closed down in 1978) built about 13,000 apartments in Italy; 25,000 were given by the Italian Institute for Public Housing (IACP). 3,000 state employees were transferred to other state posts in Italy; the same happened to 8,000 local council employees.

The Italian state is still (!) screening refugees' claims for compensation for property lost in territories which now belong to Yugoslavia.[58] It is possible to say, today, that the refugees are fully integrated with the rest of the population, in Italy and abroad. Of course the Osimo Agreement was resented more strongly by them, but the great many refugee newspapers and bulletins seem now to reflect the common feeling that 'what is lost is lost'.

Current Prospects for the Area

Nowadays many refugees bear a strong grudge against the Italian government, which is charged with having sacrificed their land on political, strategic, and sometimes less praiseworthy grounds. The chairman of the *Unione degli Istriani* (one of the leading refugee organizations) said: 'While the Italian Government worked (or, better, didn't work) with the assumption that it had lost B Zone, the Germans were able, in 1955, to get the Saar back . . . the Japanese were able to recover their full sovereignty over Okinawa island [until 1972 under US administration].'[59]

Interestingly, in the context of these considerations, there is an important sector of the refugee community which is asking for new and more positive relations to be established with the Italian community living on the other side of the border. Guido Miglia, for example, in 1956 wrote about 'the need to see them as the "Italian presence" in Istria. There is no problem with them being members of the PCJ; only in that way they can have some power and influence on the political life of Yugoslavia.'[60]

Thirty years ago Guido Miglia was without doubt a voice speaking in the desert. For many refugees the Italians on the other side of the border were betrayers of Italy and worse. Now the discussions over 'reopening the bridge' with the Italians on the other side of the border seem more mature. Luigi Papo has said: 'We must be careful about the numerous Italian communities which have remained in Istria, Fiume and Dalmatia, and at least look for contact with the *Unione degli Italiani dell'Istria e di Fiume* [UIIF, the state associaton for Italians in Yugoslavia].'[61] For those who are aware of the refugees' deep antagonism against the UIIF this statement is of some significance. Within the Italian community in Yugoslavia there also seems to be a definite interest in *rapprochement*. Many of them, in fact, have started to go back as tourists, while others have been able to obtain residence permits without renouncing their Italian citizenship. This is an important aspect of a new Yugoslavian attitude. The Helsinki and Oslo agreements seem to have contributed to an improvement of the situation.

The relieving of tensions between West and East, and in this case between Italy and Yugoslavia, has had some other positive implications: little by little the traditional influence of Italian culture on the Slav community is reappearing; centuries' old mixing of peoples and cultures is on the increase again. This fact, without nationalist implications, may in the long run create a peaceful life among different peoples.

The work accomplished in recent years by the 'Popular University' in Trieste, which is making a great effort to help the development of contacts between the two Italian communities is very valuable. It will indirectly help to defuse the tensions of this sadly troubled area.

Notes: Chapter 8

1   The author has considered three books to be particularly objective regarding Trieste and the exodus. They are listed in the first part of the bibliography. In the second part are listed other sources which have been very useful for an understanding of the period. Some of them, especially those written by people directly involved in the conflict, must be read with particular care.

2   C. Columni, L. Ferari, G. Nassis, G. Trani, *Storia di un Esodo*, Trieste, 1980, p. 571.

3   *La Voce del Popolo*, 1 January 1973, pp. 1 and 4.

4   A. Pitamitz, *La Verità sulle Foibe*, Storia Illustrata, Milan, June 1983, p. 69.

5   G. Bartoli, *Il Martirologio delle Genti Italiane*, Trieste.

6   G. Fogar, *Foibe e Deportazioni in Venezia Giulia*, Trieste, no. 3, 1983, p. 71.

7   According to a conversation with a person who requested not to be identified there is an 'internal debate' among the Croatian Communists on the issue of *foibe*. In the medium term some kind of historical 'revision' may be foreseen.

8   There are many explanations for these wide discrepancies: 1) secret or semi-secret arrests of people; 2) war-time and post-war difficulties in obtaining an accurate report of many events, mainly due to the lack of recognized authorities in the area; 3) the fact that the greatest number of *foibe* were in Yugoslavian areas, therefore preventing a search; 4) as in many other similar situations, the number of those who 'disappeared' is very difficult to establish. In any case the author believes that the *infoibati* numbered some thousands.

9   It is quite shocking that 40 years later many people of different nationalities and political opinions still refuse to answer any specific questions. It may give an idea of how deep was the conflict among many people.

10   The Fascist regime in Italy was particularly keen to persecute Slavs of Italian citizenship. The same happened in other areas of Italy where national minorities were living but the repression of Slavs was by far the worst of all. Luigi Salvatorelli, in his book *Storia d'Italia nel Periodo Fascista* wrote: 'In the period of action of the (fascist) Special Tribunal there were 113 trials against Slovenians and Croatians' (p. 105).

11   It must be stressed, however, that apart from in Istria, nothing similar happened in other areas of the country where different nationalities were living (e.g. Valle d'Aosta where the French partisans were quite strong or Alto Adige/South Tyrol where the majority of the population was of Austrian descent). In Istria and Dalmatia, different nationalities had been able to live together for centuries under different regimes, and no exodus of any sort had happened before.

12   Geographically the present border between the two countries leaves Italy in a strategically undefended position.

13   cf. the Leninist theory that 'the countryside rules over the city'.

14   On this point a deep division developed between Antonio Pitamitz (quoted) and Galliano Fogar. The latter reacted to the Pitamitz report with an article printed in *Qualestoria*, no. 3, 1983 (quoted) where he strongly contested the figures given by Pitamitz, saying that they were greatly inflated.

15   Then a purely administrative line became a frontier between the two blocks.

16   *Storia di un Esodo*, p. 95.

17   Declaration of Anton Vratusa to Prof. Urban, *Archives of the Liberation Movement of Friuli-Venezia Giulia*, July 1946, doc. 242.

18   *Report from the PCC-Italian Section*, 29.8.1944.

19   Therefore this part of Italy was detached by the authority of the *Repubblica di Salò*.

20   E. Collotti, *Il Litorale Adriatico nel Nuovo Ordine Europeo*, Milan, 1974, p. 13.

21   P. A. Quarantotti Gambini, *Primavera a Trieste*, Trieste, 1985, p. 18.

22   G. Cox, *La Corsa per Trieste*, Gorizia, 1985, p. 266.

23   M. Pacor, *Nazionalismo e Neofascismo nella lotta Politica al Confine Orientale*, Trieste, 1977, pp.5-6.

24   Colakovic et al., *Storia della Lega dei Comunisti della Yugoslavia*, Milan, 1965, p. 532.

25   *Storia di un Esodo*, p. 51.

26   *Storia di un Esodo*, p. 51.

27   *Storia di un Esodo*, p. 66.

28   *Storia di un Esodo*, p. 149.
29   *Storia di un Esodo*, p. 100.
30   Anonymous, quoted in *Storia di un Esodo*, p. 134.
31   B. Novak, *Trieste 1941-1954*, Milan, 1973, p. 259.
32   B. Novak, *Trieste 1941-1954*, p. 269.
33   F. Fejto, *L'Era di Stalin*, Milan, 1977, p. 194.
34   F. Claudin, *The communist movement*, Harmondsworth, 1975, p. 508.
35   *Vita Nuova*, Trieste, 1946.
36   A. Santin *Al Tramonto*, Trieste, 1978, pp. 180-1-2.
37   *Storia di un Esodo*, p. 348.
38   *Il Giornale di Trieste*, 8 April 1952.
39   Data quoted in *L'Istria ieri e oggi*, Leopoldo Bari, Trieste, 1984, p.54.
40   A. Savorgnan di Brazzà, *Sa Verità su Trieste*, Trieste, 1980, p. 100.
41   Although it was not clearly stated, there seem to be few doubts regarding the fact that the 'Centre' meant the Italian Intelligence Services.
42   P. Evnanzi, *Conflitto di Spie e Terroristi*, Milan, 1982, p. 155.
43   P. De Simone, *La Ripresa Italiana dopo il Maggio 1945*, Gorizia, 1959.
44   S. Califfi, *Pola Clandestina e l'Esodo*, Monfalcone, 1955, p. 49.
45   *Il Grido dell'Istria*, Trieste, 4 November 1945.
46   *Il Grido dell'Istria*, 19 October 1945.
47   E. Burich, *Fiume*, Trieste, July/December 1964, p. 124.
48   A. Luksich-Jamini, *Fiume*, January/June 1958, pp. 12-13.
49   A. Luksich-Jamini, *Fiume*, January/June 1959, pp. 78 and 80.
50   B. Novak, *Trieste 1941-1954*, p. 356.
51   A. Santin, *Al Tramonto*, p. 174.
52   *Nazionalismo e Neofascismo nella lotta Politica al Confine Orientale 1945-1975*, p. 155.
53   G. Bocca, *Palmiro Togliatti*, Bari, 1973, p. 506
54   A. Guerra, *Gli Anni del Cominform*, Milan, 1977, p. 183.
55   *Storia di un Esodo*, p. 353.
56   *Storia di un Esodo*, p. 395.
57   M. Dassidovich in *Prospettive Italiane in Adriatico*, Trieste, 1980, p. 43.
58   F. Rocchi in *Prospettive . . .* , p. 114.
59   I. Gabbrielli in *Prospettive . . .* , p. 99
60   G. Miglia, *Trieste*, Trieste, November/December 1956, p. 8.
61   L. Papo, *Prospettive . . .* , p. 40.

Bibliography

Cristiana Columni, Liliana Ferrari, Gianna Nassis, Germano Trani. *Storia di un esodo* (Istria 1945-1956). Istituto regionale per la storia del movimento di liberazione nel Friuli-Venezia Giulia, Trieste 1980.

Jean Baptiste Duroselle. *Le conflit de Trieste 1943-1945* Editions de l'Institut de Sociologie de l'Université Libre de Bruxelles, Brussels, 1966.

Bogdan, Novak. *Trieste (1941-1954, la lotta politica, etnica e ideologica)*. Mursia, Milan, 1973.

Other works have been considered very useful for the historical context or specific parts of the work:

Danilo Ardia. *Il Partito Socialista e il Patto Atlantico*. Angeli, Milan, 1976.

Phyllis Auty. *Tito, a biography*. Penguin Books, Harmondsworth, 1974.

Leopoldo Bari. *L'Istria ieri e oggi*. Italo Svevo, Trieste, 1984.

Giorgio Bocca. *Palmiro Togliatti*. Laterza, Bari, 1973.

Zbigniew K. Brzezinski. *Storia dell'URSS e delle democrazie popolari*. Angeli, Milan, 1975.

Pier Arrigo Carnier. *Lo sterminio mancato (la dominazione nazista nel Veneto orientale, 1943-1945)*. Mursia, Milan, 1982.

Hélène Carrére d'Encausse. *Le grand frère*. Flammarion, Paris, 1983.

Jean Chiana, Jean-Francois Soulet. *Histoire de la dissidence (oppositions et révoltes en URSS et dans les démocraties populaires de la mort de Stalin à nos jours)*. Seuil, Paris, 1982.

Fernando Claudin. The communist movement (from Comintern to Cominform). Penguin Books, Harmondsworth, 1975.

Rodojub Colakovic, Dragoslav Jaucovic, Pero Moraca (Editors), *Storia della Lega dei Comunisti della Yugoslavia*. Edizioni del Gallo, Milan, 1965.

Arthur Conte. *L'aprè Yalta*. Plon, Paris, 1982.

Geoffrey Cox. *La cosa per Trieste*. Goriziana, Gorizia, 1985.

Vladimir Dedjier. *Il braccio di ferro (il conflitto sovietico-jugoslavo, 1948-1953)*. La Nuova Italia, Firenze, 1969.

Anton Giulio De Robertis. *Le grandi potenze e il confine giuliano (1941-1947)*. Laterza, Bari, 1983.

Milovan Djilas. *Rise and Fall*. Macmillan, London, 1985.

Jean-Baptiste Duroselle. *L'Europa dal 1815 ai nostri giorni*. Mursia, Milan, 1974.

Francois Fejto. *Storia delle democrazie populari (L'era di Stalin, 1945-1952)*. Bompiani, Milan, 1977.

Gianna Giuricin. *Istria (momenti dell'Esodo)*. Reverdito, Trento, 1985.

Adriano Guerra. *Gli anni del Cominform*. Mazzotta, Milan, 1977.

Norman Kogan. *L'Italia del dopoguerra storia politica dal 1945 al 1966)*. Laterza, Bari, 1974.

Vladimiro Lisiani. *Good-bye Trieste* Mursia, Milan, 1964.

Denis Mack Smith. *Storia d'Italia 1861-1969*. Laterza, Bari, 1973.

Giuseppe Mammarella. *L'Italia dopo il fascismo: 1943-1973*. Il Mulino, Bologna, 1974.

Pietro Nenni. *Tempo di guerra fredda (Diari 1943-1956)*. Sugarco, Milan, 1983.

Pier Antonio Quarantotti Gambini. *Primavera a Trieste*. Italo Svevo Dedolibri, Trieste, 1985.

Luigi Salvatorelli-Giovanni Mira. *Storia d'Italia nel periodo fascista*. Mondadori, Milan, 1972.

Antonio Santin. *Al tramonto*. LINT. Trieste 1979.

Alvise Savorgnan di Brazzà. *La verità su Trieste, LINT,* Trieste, 1980.

Diane Shaver Clemens. *Yalta*. Einaudi, Torino, 1975.

Paolo Venanzi. *Conflitto di spie e terroristi (a Fiume e nella Venezia Giulia)*. L'Esule, no indication of city, 1982.

Nazionalismo e neofascismo nella lotta politica al confine orientale 1945-75. Istituto regionale per la storia del movimento di liberazione nel Friuli-Venezia Giulia, Trieste, 1977.

9 German refugee scholars in Great Britain, 1933–1945

GERHARD HIRSCHFELD

'one refugee is a novelty,
ten refugees are boring,
and a hundred refugees are a menace'

This phrase, quoted from time to time in exile literature,[1] is not just valid as an apposite summary of the personal experiences of countless refugees throughout history. It also applies particularly to the situation of those university teachers and scholars who fled from National Socialist Germany to Great Britain. Whatever its qualitative and innovative aspects, this cultural and academic emigration[2] represents, in the first analysis, a problem of numbers and thus also a social problem. The exact number of German or German-speaking refugees who worked in Britain after 1933 as university professors and lecturers, or as scholars outside the universities, is not known. We are therefore forced to rely upon estimates, although they are reliable ones in this case.

On 9 March 1935 the United Nations High Commissioner for the Refugees from Germany, the American James G. McDonald, produced statistics indicating that, in the first two years of the Nazi dictatorship, 1202 scholars employed at German universities and colleges were dismissed on the basis of the *Gesetz zur Wiederherstellung des Berufsbeaumtentum* ('Law for the Reconstitution of the Professional Civil Service') of 7 April 1933. These included 311 specialists in medicine, 169 chemists and 107 economists.[3] By the summer semester of 1934 alone, the victims of expulsion included 313 full professors, 109 associate professors, 289 non-established additional and 75 honorary professors, 322 *Privatdozenten*, 232 assistants, 42 foreign language assistants, 133 employees of research institutions and 174 academically-trained library and museum workers. The proportion of those expelled from the universities, which reached 16 per cent, was higher than the 11 per cent affected in the Technical Colleges. It should be noted, however, that the figures produced by the Briton Edward Hartshorne and others from the Germany University Calendar up to April 1936, which estimated 1684 dismissals, are not very reliable and lead one to suspect the existence of a considerable number of unreported cases.[4] The dismissed professor of Mathematical Statistics Emil Julius Gumbel also made some contemporary calculations relating to his former University of Heidelberg. Gumbel, who was then Visiting

Professor at Lyons University, estimated that, by 1936, about 25 per cent of the Heidelberg professors (i.e. 56 out of 215) had lost their posts for political (or 'racial') reasons. These figures included no less than 37 per cent of jurists, at the top of the scale, and 20 per cent of the natural scientists, who were least affected. The philosophy faculty, which lost 30 per cent of its professors, and the medical faculty with 29 per cent, came in the middle. Gumbel emphasised that these figures dealt with the minimum number of actual cases as they did not include 'voluntary' retirement or premature grants of emeritus status.[5] In all, it can be assumed that, by 1938, about one third of the entire teaching staff of German institutions of higher education had lost their posts as a result of the coercive measures of the regime. For the majority of them, there remained only one way to secure their professional and personal existence: by emigration. According to post-war estimates, 2120 university and college lecturers had taken this route by 1938.[6] About half of them migrated to Great Britain.

During the first years of German emigration, Britain was certainly not a preferred destination. At the end of the 1937 only about 5500 out of approximately 154,000 people who had fled from National Socialist Germany were living in Britain. Restrictive regulations on immigration and foreign nationals, combined with fears that unemployment would inevitably increase, made the British government refuse to accept significant numbers of German refugees from political and 'racial' persecution. Despite the guarantee of the Jewish relief organisations and communities that the arriving refugees would not be a burden on public funds, this policy of the 'half-open door' was maintained for some time. The British authorities began to relax their entry restrictions only after the pogroms of 'Crystal Night' in November 1938 had revealed the extent of brutal anti-Semitism in Germany and in the wake of the openly annexationist foreign policy of the Third Reich. The number of people seeking asylum thereupon increased dramatically. Shortly after the outbreak of war there were about 55,000 officially recognised refugees from Germany, Austria and the Sudentenland in Britain.[7]

From the outset, two social groups had been excepted from the restrictive regulations on asylum because the British government hoped to obtain direct benefits from their presence. The first group comprised industrialists and businessmen with private fortunes, who could contribute to a reduction in unemployment by establishing new businesses.[8] The second was made up of well-known artists and scholars. As early as 12 April 1933 the British Cabinet accepted that it was in the public interest 'to try to secure for this country prominent Jews who were being expelled from Germany and who had achieved distinction whether in pure science, applied science, such as medicine or technical industry, music or art. This would not only obtain for this country the advantage of their knowledge and experience, but would also create a favourable impression in the world, particularly if our hospitality were offered with some warmth'.[9] At the same time, the government hastened to make it clear that even in such cases, based on carefully considered utilitarian grounds, the allocation of state funds was not intended. Private organisations and individuals were to be encouraged to bear the burden.

The most important relief organisation for refugee scholars was the *Academic Assistance Council*, founded in 1933. Later it was re-named the *Society for the Protection of Science and Learning*. The AAC was established on the initiative of Sir William Beveridge, then Director of the London School of Economics and Political Science, and had the world-famous physicist Lord Rutherford as its chairman. Large numbers of British universities and teachers soon gave it their support. Its advisory committee comprised a number of illustrious academics including Professor A.V. Hill, who like Rutherford was a winner of the Nobel Prize, Sir Frederick Kenyon, Lord Cecil of Chelwood, the former Lord Chancellor Lord Buckmaster and the historian and former Minister of Education H.A.L. Fisher, as well as several Vice Chancellors of British universities.[10] The aims of the AAC were defined as 'the relief of suffering and the defence of learning and science, assisting university teachers and other investigators of whatever country who on grounds of religion, political opinion or "race" are unable to carry on their work in their own country'.[11] These aims were brought to the attention of British public opinion by a mass gathering in the Royal Albert Hall, which was addressed by Albert Einstein, among others.[12]

The AAC soon had over 2000 subscribers, including numerous academics who regularly gave it a part of their income for the support of their refugee colleagues. For example, as early as May 1933, the teaching staff of the LSE had committed themselves to transferring between 1 per cent (in the case of lecturers) and 3 per cent (in the case of professors) of their monthly salary to the support fund. This provided an annual sum of approximately £1,000.[13] Local relief committees were established in many colleges and universities; they made further contributions and often also attended to the selection of the academics in question. In the first two years of its existence, the AAC succeeded in finding permanent posts for 62 university teachers and scholars, and in creating teaching and research positions for another 148 refugees. London University provided no fewer than 54 of these temporary posts, Cambridge 31, Oxford 13, the Scottish and Welsh universities 7 and 3 posts respectively, and the 'Redbrick' universities the remainder.[14] So as not to place too severe a strain on the universities, and to counter any accusations that they were blocking the careers of British academics who were seeking work, the Academic Assistance Council frequently took responsibility for 'paying' the new arrivals. However, these payments by the AAC were modest, at £250 per annum for a married scholar and £180 for a single person.[15] Some universities and institutes arranged additional courses of lectures and special programmes for academics who were otherwise unemployed, with the AAC again taking responsibility for financing them. Thus, for example, the former Hamburg art historian Erwin Panofsky – later Professor at Princeton – gave six lectures on iconography at the Courtauld Institute in London in December 1933. He was paid £30 from the resources of the AAC. Some weeks later it was the turn of Niklaus Pevsner, who reviewed baroque painting.[16] Offers of work also came from a number of influential heads of institutions – such as Professor Lindemann at the Clarendon Laboratory in London - who concerned themselves with the fortunes of well-known German natural scientists. Lindemann also persuaded Imperial Chemical Industries (ICI) to award special research fellowships to refugee physicists and chemists. This chemical concern had been founded as an amalgamation of four previous companies only in 1926 and was naturally very receptive to recent German research. In 1935, 18 scientists were holding ICI fellowships at British universities, although care was taken to establish that the fellows had had no connection with ICI's German counterpart, IG-Farben, in the past, 'as it was particularly wished not to jeopardise in any way the good relations existing between IG and the German government'.[17]

Apart from the academic Assistance Council/Society for the Protection of Science and Learning, a number of other organisations worked to support refugee academics who had not found posts. These included the *Jewish Academic (Professional) Council*, which concerned itself particularly with refugees from the 'professional' classes such as doctors, solicitors and teachers; the *Federation of University Women in England*, which aimed to help women university teachers and researchers; the *International Student Service*, working for the estimated 3,500 students among the refugees and the *Emergency Society of German Scholars Abroad*. The *Notgemeinschaft* and its permanent Secretary Fritz Demuth had moved from Zürich to London in 1936, and its board was composed of prominent German university teachers who were based in England, including Max Born (Cambridge), Moritz Bonn (LSE) and Ernst Cassirer (Oxford). However, its activities were directed more towards universities outside Europe, and it managed to find posts for German scholars in Central and South America, in Asia and, most successfully of all, in the new Turkish universities in Istanbul, Ankara and Smyrna.[18]

As far as funds for refugees were concerned, the High Commissioner for the Refugees calculated that, up to the end of January 1935 and including donations from industry, £68,903 had been raised by the relief organisations active in Britain. The AAC alone was responsible for £28,142 of this. [Internationally, relief funds raised during this period amounted to £252,605/$1,232,535].[19] The significance of the AAC was revealed by its success in acquiring an international profile after the ending of the Refugee Commissionership with the retirement of James McDonald in December 1935. The society had corresponding members in almost every European country, including the Danish physicist Niels Bohr and the Dutch historian Johan Huizinga.[20]

The problems of the Society for the Protection of Science and Learning increased after 1938 with the growth in the number of refugees. The records of the Allocation Committee revealed that, in addition to about 400 Austrian university teachers and researchers dismissed after the Anschluss, the Society was also approached for help by Italian, Czech, Spanish, Portuguese and – from 1936 – Soviet scholars. But the greatest challenge to the Society came in June 1940, when the War Cabinet ordered the internment of almost all the refugees from Nazi oppression, including scholars and university teachers.[21] The SPSL, with many official and personal interventions, worked for the release of its academic protegés, or for their exemption from the deportations which had begun in the meantime. It frequently referred to the important scientific abilities and qualifications of the people in question, which could be harnessed for the war effort. In more than 550 cases, the Society was able to put before the Home Office reports and statements from renowned British scholars, vouching for the integrity of one or several internees.[22] Thus, for example, John Maynard Keynes obtained the release of four economists who had previously been employed at Cambridge.[23] Many natural scientists and engineers were among those refugees who were released early from the internment camps. In accordance with their re-awakened utilitarian thinking, the British authorities subsequently enlisted them to do research and other work for the war effort. Their crucial achievements, particularly in the field of atomic research, have already been analysed in depth and do not require further discussion here.[24] However, the Allied war effort also provided a field of activity for numerous scholars in the arts. They worked, for example, in 'intelligence' (information gathering, analysis of the press) on the psychological conduct of the war, and in propaganda.[25] On the other hand, the proportion of refugee academics serving with regular units of the British army was relatively small. This is not surprising, as most 'enemy aliens' were prohibited from any military service until 1941, with the exception of the unarmed Auxiliary Military Pioneer Corps.[26]

The records of the SPSL for the years 1933 to 1945 contain the names of 2,541 refugee scholars, of whom somewhat over half came from Germany and Austria. In 1946, about 600 of them were still living in Britain, including approximately 400 from German-speaking areas and 309 from the Altreich itself.[27]

A large proportion of scholars travelled on to the United States after a shorter or longer period in Britain. The USA now became the real host country for German-speaking academic refugees, mainly because of its incomparably greater ability to accept them.[28] The motives which persuaded many university teachers and other scholars to turn their backs on Britain and to settle in the USA are not difficult to recognise. They included American immigration conditions, which were relatively favourable to academics, especially after 1938/39; better prospects for employment and education, and the existence of a multiplicity of private and public relief organisations. In addition, many refugees had a strong feeling for security far from the reach of the aggressive Nazi regime; the strength of this emotion should not be under-estimated.[29]

However, other reasons for the re-migration lay exclusively within the British context, and have not been adequately considered. Two factors were decisive in preventing the acceptance of more German scholars into Britain. The first of these related to the relative stagnation of British university life in the 1930s. In 1929/30 there were 45,603 students at the 16 British universities, and 50,002 in 1938/39. They were taught by 3,504 academics in 1935/36, and 3,994 in 1938/39.[30] Real expansion came only with the influx of demobilised soldiers after the war and the development of the Welfare State during the Attlee era, which led to a more active role of governments in higher education. In 1951/52, for example, there were 83,458 students and 8,952 teachers. But this increase occurred 17 years after the arrival of the first refugees. In the decisive years before the outbreak of war, these people had found a very narrowly-based education system which offered few opportunities for them. Secondly, the aims and methods of 'undergraduate studies' were very different in British universities; German humanities scholars and social scientists – provided that they were entrusted with the intellectual training of the future 'national elite' at all – frequently had considerable difficulty in adjusting to them. It was also significant that the field of 'graduate studies' – those specialised courses with which the refugee university teachers had previously been so familiar – was extremely limited in Britain. In 1928/29 there were only 2,100 graduate students, 1,300 of these in the natural sciences.[31] Doctoral examinations and the degrees of Ph.D. had not been introduced into most universities as a separate aim of education until 1917/18, a sign of the belated completion of the professionalisation of scholarship in Britain.[32]

Quite apart from objective facts, subjective impressions were also decisive in persuading many scholars to leave Britain. These included their predominantly negative experience of the English class system; inadequate social and professional integration of many refugees in their new domain; and, not infrequently, a rejection of British appeasement policies towards Nazi Germany. The nuclear physicist Hans Bethe gave up a temporary post at Bristol University as early as 1934 in order to take a post as Assistant Professor at Cornell University although, as he put it, 'I would have preferred to remain in England'. He later described the different attitudes towards the emigrating scholars which he found in Britain and the United States. In the USA 'people made me feel at once that I was going to be an American'; in England, on the other hand, despite the fact that he had initially felt at home there, 'it was clear that I was a foreigner and would remain a foreigner . . . England had been used to having Englishmen and Commonwealth people in their universities. So we refugees were a rather foreign element . . . whereas America had been a country of immigrants from the beginning.'[33] Another to leave was the political scientist Franz L. Neumann. In 1936 he had taken a second degree at the LSE under Harold Laski and Karl Mannheim with a doctoral work on the modern European legal system, and subsequently moved to the Institute for Social Research at Columbia University in New York. He was determined to draw a clear line between himself and the Old World: 'But England was not the country in which to do it. Much as I . . . loved England, her society was too homogeneous and too solid, her opportunities (particularly under conditions of unemployment) too narrow, her politics not too agreeable. One could, so I felt, never quite become an Englishman.'[34] Although motives for renewed migration varied, the major factor in the decision to stay or to leave was usually professional: the refugees needed to make their living, and hoped for an academic career, in their host country. In Britain, though, there were considerable differences between the refugee natural scientists and medical specialists on the one side, and the humanities scholars and social scientists on the other. Because of the international nature of their disciplines and the fact that linguistic skill was not an essential prerequisite for disseminating their researches, the natural scientists tended to be more easily integrated into the British research and education system. Although the level of re-migration – especially to the USA – was comparatively high even here, refugee natural scientists had an extraordinary long-term impact on their subject in Britain, in terms of both quantity and quality.[35] In contrast, most humanities scholars and social scientists – with some highly significant exceptions – were not able to establish themselves in British universities. It must be left to future research to analyse the reasons for this failure more closely.

One of the exceptions mentioned above was in the field of Classical Philology, with the former Freiburg professor Eduard Fraenkel its most significant representative. In 1935, one year after his flight from Germany, he was appointed Professor of Latin at Corpus Christi College in Oxford. It was largely attributable to his influence that four more Classical Philologists made their way to Oxford in 1938/39. The work of Fraenkel and his colleagues played a decisive part in making Oxford the centre of Classical Philology in Britain. They also helped to remodel 'Classical Scholarship', which had previously been based predominantly on textual criticism, in the light of the German *Altertumswissenschaffen*.[36]

The sociologist, Karl Mannheim, who had been a lecturer at Frankfurt University before leaving Germany, was largely responsible for the development of the Social Sciences into a recognised academic discipline in Britain during the 1930s. Mannheim, a lecturer at the LSE between 1933 and 1945, was particularly well-known as the founder and editor of the influential *International Library of Sociology and Social Reconstruction*, although his earlier work on the sociology of knowledge (*Ideology and Utopia*, Engl. 1936) and his later writings on social education, were not at first recognised.[37] (The philosopher Karl Popper, who was also to lecture at the LSE, did not arrive in London until 1946, from New Zealand.)

There were other significant exceptions to the rule that refugee humanities scholars did not establish themselves in Britain. They included the art historians Leopold D. Ettlinger, Nikolaus Pevsner and Ernst Hans Gombrich, who contributed significantly in the 1950s to the establishment of art history as a subject equal to the other historical disciplines in Britain. The London-based Warburg Institute, headed by Gombrich since 1959, also provided impetus in this sphere.[38] Apart from natural scientists, doctors and medical specialists provided a further example of successful integration of refugee scholars into the British teaching and research system. The reasons for this – as in the case of the natural scientists – involve the international nature of their subject and the relatively high standing and development of German university medicine. It must be noted, however, that the undoubted element of xenophobic mistrust and snobbery against the new arrivals which existed in British universities and public life,[39] was more openly expressed in the medical sphere than in almost any other. In November 1933 Lord Dawson of Penn, the President of the Royal College of Physicians, told the Home Secretary, Sir John Gilmour, that the number of German doctors who could be of use, or from whom something could be learned, could be counted on the fingers of one hand.[40] This opinion, however, quickly gave way to a more realistic assessment, though fear of competition and economic anxieties led to occasional outbursts and agitation against refugee doctors from some parts of the British medical establishment.

The proportion of re-migrants among the medical specialists was in fact surprisingly high, with probably half of them departing for the United States. Nevertheless, they constituted one of the biggest groups among the refugee scholars. One of the best-known of them was Ludwig Guttman, former Director of the Neurosurgical and Neurological Department of the Jewish Hospital in Breslau (1933–1939). He is recognised for his pioneering work on the rehabilitation of patients with paralysing diseases, and for founding the National Spinal Injuries Centre at Stoke Mandeville Hospital.[41]

The achievements of the scholars who emigrated to Britain have been recognised and honoured across the world, for example by the award of a number of Nobel Prizes. Such cases do not need to be itemised here. In Britain itself, there were 28 refugee Fellows of the British Academy in 1977 and 53 refugee Fellows of the Royal Society, including 6 from the second generation. All these distinctions, however, reflect the paramount contribution made by the natural scientists and medical specialists among the refugees.[42]

The migration of self-contained groups and organisations is an exception in the history of scholastic emigration from National Socialist Germany. The amalgamation of refugee scholars into groups and the creation of research teams usually happened by chance and was not the result of observations made before emigration took place. Even in the United States, the privately-founded Institute for Social Research, and the *Bauhaus*, which was re-established by Walter Gropius and Laszlo Moholy-Nagy in Harvard and Chicago, were exceptional cases. It is true that some institutions did appear to be self-contained 'exile universities', because they comprised large numbers of refugee researchers and teachers. These included the New School of Social Research in New York with its Graduate Faculty of Political and Social Science; the Institutes of Advanced Studies in Princeton and Dublin; a number of Chairs and Institutes at the Universities of Istanbul, Ankara and Smyrna in Turkey and at the Hebrew University in Jerusalem; the 'Herzlia Technical Institute' in Haifa and the 'Daniel Sieff Research Institute' in Rehoboth. Most of these, however, were national foundations from which the host countries and the refugees derived mutual benefit. The Warburg Institute in Britain, and the New York Institute for Social Research led by Max Horkheimer in the USA, are the most significant examples of the successful transfer of scholastic institutions which had achieved international recognition *before* emigration.[43]

The library of the Jewish Central Information Office, founded by Dr. Alfred Wiener, also deserves mention. The archive, which was transferred to London in 1939 after six years in Amsterdam, contains an extensive collection of books, journals and documents on European fascist movements in general, and German National Socialism; its anti-Jewish politics and the Holocaust in particular. During the war, the Wiener Library provided the British Ministry of Information with useful material for its own propaganda and became virtually a part of it. Since 1945 the Wiener Library – and despite the transfer of a number of early books and archive material to Tel Aviv in 1980 – has remained one of the most important research libraries for all work on modern German and Jewish history.[44] These exceptions – dependent exclusively on private initiatives – apart, there are no further known cases of an entire academic institution being transferred to Britain.

In conclusion, it can be stated that the extent of scholastic emigration to Britain was more modest than the influence of German refugees in many spheres of university and non-university scholarship might lead one to suspect. In fact, such influence has been widely recognised and in some fields over-estimated. The most important reason for the relatively high level of re-migration, especially to the United States, was the difficult employment situation in British universities during the 1930s. However, there was a conspicuous imbalance between the success of natural scientists and doctors on one hand, and humanities scholars and social scientists on the other. Explanations for this phenomenon must be sought in the politics and sociology of academic life. In particular, educational goals and teaching methods in the field of undergraduate studies were so different from those of the refugee country of origin that they proved to be a serious obstacle to the employment of a larger number of emigrants.

Private institutions, true to British traditions, played an important role in the history of the immigration of German scholars after 1933. The academic relief organisations, foremost among them the Society for the Protection of Science and Learning, and the British academic community, with perhaps the exception of the Association of University Teachers (AUT), responded spontaneously and responsibly to the influx of refugee scholars. They revealed an astonishing degree of solidarity with their colleagues and a willingness to offer help which transcended national barriers. However, this involvement was limited by the economic and social barriers created by the labour market, which made long-term employment of the refugees in many disciplines appear almost impossible.

In the official position of the British government, as also in public attitudes, we can detect two contradictory elements which have co-existed in British immigration policy since the nineteenth century: xenophobic restrictions and liberal hospitality. However, it was the second of these which proved to be the stronger, especially in the critical years of 1938/39. Like the other western democracies, Britain did not pursue any real refugee policy, which would have had to be orientated upon the scope and character of the National Socialist persecutions. Instead it merely pursued an immigration policy which was based first and foremost on its own economic and political interests. Those German scholars who emigrated to escape from National Socialism were not spared from personal experience of this important distinction.

Notes: Chapter 9

1   Cf. D.P. Kent, *The Refugee Intellectual. The Americanization of the Immigrants of 1933–1941* (New York, 1953), p. 172; A.J. Sherman, *Island Refuge. Britain and the Refugees from the Third Reich 1933–1939* (London, 1973), p. 13.

2   For a more general account of the cultural emigration see H. Möller, 'From Weimar to Bonn: The Arts and the Humanities in Exile and Return, 1933–1980', in *International Biographical Dictionary of Central European Emigrés 1933–1945*, vol II, 1, The Arts, Sciences, and Literature, Introduction XLI–LXVI (Munich/New York/London/Paris, 1983); J.C. Jackmann and C.M. Borden (eds), *The Muses flee Hitler. Cultural Transfer and Adaption 1930–1945* (Washington, D.C., 1983).

3   *A Crisis in the University World*, ed. by the Office of the High Commissioner for Refugees (Jewish and others) coming from Germany (London, 9 March 1935), p. 5.

4   E.Y. Hartshorne, *The German Universities and National Socialism* (Cambridge, Mass., 1937) pp. 92–98. See also the *List of Displaced German Scholars*, ed by the 'Notgemeinschaft deutscher Wissenschaftler im Ausland' (London, 1936), Wiener Library, London: Microfilm 407» B 671/2, which comprised 1617 dismissed scholars.

5   E.J. Gumbel (ed) *Freie Wissenschaft. Ein Sammelbuch aus der Deutschen Emigration* (Strasburg, 1938), pp. 16–17.

6   C. von Ferber, *Die Entwicklung des Lehrkörpers der deutschen Universitäten und Hochschulen* (Göttingen, 1956), 143.

7   For the official British policies toward refugees see Sherman, *Island Refuge*; B. Wasserstein, *Britain and the Jews of Europe* (London/Oxford, 1979); G Hirschfeld (ed), *Exile in Great Britain. Refugees from Hitler's Germany* (Leamington Spa, 1984), the contributions by F.L. Carsten, B. Wasserstein, L. Kettenacker and A. Glees.

8   Cf. H. Loebl, 'Refugee Industries in the Special Areas of Britain', in Hirschfeld (ed), *Exile in Great Britain*, 219–249; L. Zeitlin, 'They came to England. The Newcomers in Trade and Industry', in Association of Jewish Refugees in Great Britain (ed), *Britain's New Citizens. The Stories of the Refugees from Germany and Austria* (London, 1951).

9   Public Record Office (PRO) Cabinet 27 (33), Conclusion 8, 12 April 1933.

10   For the history of the AAC/SPSL see N. Bentwich, *The Rescue and Achievement of Refugee Scholars. The Story of Displaced Scholars and Scientists 1933–1952* (The Hague, 1953); W. Beveridge, *A Defence of Free Learning* (Oxford, 1959); W. Adams, 'The Refugee Scholar of the 1930s', *The Political Quarterly* 1 (1968), 7–14. (Walter Adams was the first Secretary of the AAC/SPSL. From 1967 to 1974 he was Director of the London School of Economics.)

11   Foundation Appeal, 22 May 1933. Archive of the AAC/SPSL, Bodleian Library, Oxford (Henceforth SPSL-Archive): 1/7.

12   'Science and Civilisation' by Albert Einstein, 3 October 1933. SPSL-Archive, 1/9.

13   Report of Committee of Assistance to Displaced University Teachers, LSE, 18 May 1933. SPSL-Archive, 1/7.

14   AAC-Second Annual Report, 20 February 1935, 12–13. SPSL-Archive, 1/2.

15   Ibid.

16   'Lectures at the Courtauld Institute under the Auspices of the Academic Assistance Council', and letter from J. Constable (Director Courtauld Institute) to W. Adams (AAC), 4 May 1934. SPSL-Archive, 18/8–9.

17   'Memorandum on the Employment of Foreign Scientists' by F.A. Lindemann and W. Rintoul, quoted by P. Hoch, 'The Reception of Central European Refugee Physicists of the 1930s: U.S.S.R., U.K., U.S., *Annales of Sciences* 40 (1983), pp.217–246, here p. 225.

18   Cf. Bentwich, *The Rescue and Achievement of Refugee Scholars*, 15–18; for the emigration to Turkey see H. Widmann, *Exil und Bildungshilfe. Die deutschsprachige*

akademische Emigration in der Türkei nach 1933 (Berne/Frankfurt, 1973); F. Neumark, *Zuflucht am Bosporus. Deutsche Gelehrte, Politiker und Künstler in der Emigration 1933–1953* (Frankfurt a.M., 1980).

19   *A Crisis in the University World*, pp. 8–9

20   List of Corresponding Members Abroad, 12 January 1938. SPSL-Archive: 3/1.

21   Cf. P. and L. Gillman, *'Collar the Lot!'. How Britain interned and expelled its wartime Refugees* (London, 1980); R Stent, *A Bespattered Page? The internment of His Majesty's 'most loyal enemy aliens'* (London, 1980); M. Seyfert, *Im Niemandsland. Deutsche Exilliteratur in britischer Internierung* (Berlin, 1984).

22   Internment Application Statistics. SPSL-Archive: 65/1–4 . SPSL-Central Dept. for Interned Refugees, Corresponence 1940–42. SPSL-Archive: 66/31 .

23   Cf. Bentwich, *The Rescue and Achievement of Refugee Scholars*, p. 30.

24   Cf. R.V. Jones, *Most Secret War. British Scientific Intelligence 1939–1945* (London, 1978); M. Gowing, *Britain and Atomic Energy, 1939–1945* (London, 1964); R.H. Stuewer, 'Nuclear Physicists in a New World. The Emigrés of the 1930s in America', *Berichte zur Wissenschaftsgeschichte 7* (1984), pp. 23–40.

25   Cf. M. Balfour, *Propaganda in War 1939–1945. Organisations, Policies and Publics in Britain and Germany* (London, 1979), pp. 80–102; C. Pütter 'German Refugees and British Propaganda', in Hirschfeld (ed), *Exile in Great Britain*, pp. 129–161.

26   Cf. N. Bentwich, *They found Refuge* (London, 1956); idem, *I understand the Risk. The story of Refugees from Nazi aggression who fought in the British Forces* (London, 1950).

27   *SPSL-Fifth Annual Report*, SPSL–Archive: 1/5.

28   Cf. L.A. Coser, *Refugee Scholars in America. Their Impact and their Experiences* (New Haven/London, 1984); Kent, *The Refugee Intellectual*; D. Fleming and B. Gailyn (ed) *The Intellectual Migration: Europe and America, 1930–1960* (Cambridge, Mass., 1969); H. Pross, *Die Deutsche Akademische Emigration nach den Vereinigten Staaten 1933–1941* (Berlin, 1955).

29   See for some of these motives the article by H.A. Strauss, 'The Migration of Academic Intellectuals', in *International Biographical Dictionary*, vol. II, 7, Introduction LXCII-LXXVII, here LXXIV-V.

30   See Pross, *Deutsche Akademische Emigration*, p. 35. Cf. statistical material 'Students in Full-time Higher Eucation 1900/1–1962/3, Great Britain' and 'Number of university teachers 1900–80, Great Britain' in *Trends in British Society since 1900*, ed. by A.H. Halsey (London, 1972), p. 206 (Table 7.1), p. 211 (Fig. 7.1).

31   Pross, *Deutsche Akademische Emigration*, p. 36.

32   Cf. V.H.H. Green, *The Universities* (Harmondsworth 1969), 129; P. Alter, *The Reluctant Patron. Science and the State in Britain 1850–1920*, (Leamington Spa, 1987).

33   Quoted by Hoch, 'Reception of Central European Scientists'. 227–8; for Bethe see *International Biographical Dictionary*, vol. II, 7, 99–100.

34   F.L. Neumann, 'The Social Sciences', in W.R. Crawford (ed), *The Cultural Migration. The European Scholar in America* (Philadelphia, 1953), pp. 4–26, here pp. 17–18.

35   Cf. G.V.R. Born, 'The Effect of the Scientific Environment in Britain on Refugee Scientists from Germany and their Effect on Science in Britain', *Berichte zur Wissenschaftsgeschichte 7* (1984), pp.129–143.

36   Cf. H. Lloyd-Jones, *Blood for the Ghosts: Classical Influences in the Nineteenth and Twentieth Centuries* (London, 1982), 251-265; W. Ludwig, 'Amtsenthebung und Emigration Klassischer Philologen', *Berichte zur Wissenschaftsgeschichte 7* (1984), pp. 161–178, here pp. 165–167.

37   For Mannheim see *International Biographical Dictionary*, vol II, 2, 775; D. Kettler, V. Meja, N. Stehr, *Karl Mannheim (Key Sociologists)* (Chichester/London/New York, 1984).

38   CF. D. Wuttke, 'Die Emigration der Kulturwissenschaftlichen Bibliothek Warburg und die Anfänge des Universitätsfaches Kunstgeschichte in Großbritannien', *Berichte zur Wissenschaftsgeschichte 7* (1984), pp. 179–194.

39   Cf. B. Wasserstein, 'Intellectual Emigrés in Britain, 1933–1939', in *The Muses flee Hitler*, 249–256.; M. Berghahn, *German-Jewish Refugees in England. The Ambiguities of Assimiliation* (London, 1984), pp. 138–146.

40 Cf. Sherman, Island Refuge, p. 48.
41 For Guttman see *Internation Biographical Dictionary* vol. II, 1, p. 442.
42 Cf. Z.M. Reid, 'Contributions to Science and Art', in Associtionof Jewish Refugees in Great Britain (ed), *Britain's New Citizens*, pp. 36–41; F.L. Carsten, 'German Refugees in Great Britain 1933-1945', in Hirschfeld (ed), *Exile in Great Britain*, pp. 11–28, here p. 25.
43 For the Warburg Institute see Wuttke, 'Die Emigration der Kulturwissenschaftlichen Bibliothek Warburg'; M. Podro, *The critical historians of art* (New Haven/London, 1982). For the Institute for Social Research see M. Jay, *The Dialectical Imagination: A History of the Frankfurt School and the Institute of Social Research 1923–1950* (Boston, 1973); Coser, *Refugee Scholars in America*, pp. 90–101.
44 Cf. H. Auerbach, '50 Jahre Wiener Library', *Vierteljahrshefte für Zeitgeschichte* 4 (1983), 721–724; *History Today* (July 1983), p. 56.

10 German refugees after 1945: a British dilemma

HANS ÅKE PERSSON

In the years 1945–46 the influx into Germany of Germans from Eastern Europe reached its highest volume. Between five and ten thousand arrived every day in the western controlled zones of Germany. By October 1946, according to a census made by orders of the Allied Control Commission, seven million German refugees had arrived in western Germany.[1]

Since the Teheran Conference in November 1943 the Allies had agreed in principle on the expulsion of the German population from the territories to be ceded to Poland. The Allies believed that this would facilitate the settlement of the problem once and for all. Another element which seems to have had an impact on the decision to transfer Germans from Poland was the need to compensate Poland in the west at the expense of Germany. The Allies believed that the transfer could be carried out in an orderly and humane way.[2] This belief was based on historical precedents such as the exchange of populations between Turkey and Greece in 1923, involving two million people, approved by the League of Nations.[3] Finally, the transfer could be seen as an expression of a desire to punish the enemy, the defeated Germans.

The Potsdam agreement of August 1945 authorised the transfer of Germans from the area under Soviet occupation. The agreement was signed by the representatives of the three Great Powers, Prime Minister Clement Attlee, President Harry Truman and Marshal Joseph Stalin. The document was the last to be signed by the Allies. Earlier the expulsions were treated at Yalta in conjunction with the new borders of Poland. However, there were other aspects of the problem. As early as the beginning of the Second World War the representative of the Government of Czechoslovakia Dr Benes, proposed that a future Czechoslovakia should not include a German minority.[4]

The expulsions that followed the Potsdam Conference made for chaos, even though it was one of the intentions of the Potsdam agreement to create the necessary conditions in the occupation zones of Germany to receive refugees from Eastern Europe. In the Potsdam negotiations Great Britain and the USA demanded that the transfer be carried out in an orderly and humane way. It was not only in the name of humanity that this request was put forward. The lack of facilities to receive millions of people in a country that at the end of the war had only limited ability to feed its own inhabitants was the primary reason why Great Britain and the United States asked for a delay in the transfers. However, when neither the letter nor the spirit of the Potsdam agreement was followed by the East European countries, the refugees from the East created an unwanted burden for the occupation authorities.[5]

The purpose of this essay is to discuss British policy on the refugee question. It is to be regarded merely as an introduction to a study of the subject. At this stage, the intention is to describe the events of one year only. The analysis will primarily concern the central British administration and concentrate on the Government and the Foreign Office. A future study will focus on how refugee policy was implemented in the British zone. From a theoretical point of view, it would be fruitful to approach such a study from a conflict perspective. The question is, in what way and to what extent did the German refugees have a part to play in what we today refer to as the Cold War?

Recent literature on the subject has tended to make a moral issue out of the way in which the Western Allies dealt with the German refugee problem. It has been stated that the Russians, the Poles and the Czechs had the major responsibility because they were the ones who insisted upon expelling the Germans. It has also been said that the Anglo-American acceptance of the principle of population transfers made the catastrophe of 1945–49 possible. In this context it cannot be regarded as fruitful to try to lay the blame on either side. The issue is far too complicated. For instance, what role did British security interests in eastern and central Europe play, and which arguments were advanced in the Foreign Office in favour of accepting the transfer of millions of Germans after the war? Did the 'scramble' for Central and Eastern Europe make Britain prepared to let the Germans in Eastern Europe pay the price for British security interests, or obligations, in Poland?

This paper does not set out to prove a thesis or pass judgements. The main purpose is to show possible linkages between a wider perspective and a subordinate problem; between the oncoming Cold War and the handling of the German refugee problem. Therefore it might be helpful to look at different ways of understanding Britain's role in the international society of the early post-war years.

One way to analyse British patterns of behaviour after the war is to propose that the British failed to understand that after the war they were too weak to play an imperial role, which later had consequences for Britain's role in world affairs. Another possible interpretation would emphasize that British political leaders and advisers did realise how weak the country was, but there were still special interests in the fading world-wide empire that had to be protected. It could also be argued that the defeat of Germany created a real power vacuum in Europe, in which Britain had to play a role. The British were, furthermore, politically involved albeit in different ways, with their former comrades-in-arms, the Soviet Union and the United States.

Before Yalta

In July 1944 the British Armistice and Post-War Committee received a long report from an interdepartmental committee on the transfer of German populations. It had been the task of the committee to consider the following questions:

'(i) having regard to the economic position in which Germany is likely to be placed as a result of the defeat, and of the demands of the United Nations for disarmament, reparations, etc. how great will be Germany's capacity, to absorb emigrants from East-Prussia (including Allenstein), Danzig, Upper Silesia, the Sudetenland, and from areas within the Polish frontiers of 1939 and the Czechoslovak frontiers of 1938 (ii) What conditions (both of time and administration) would be required to ensure that the transfers were carried out without undue suffering to the migrants and without serious economic dislocation both to Germany and to Poland and to Czechoslovakia? (iii) What contributions in finance and in personnel would be required from the United Nations to ensure these conditions? (iv) What possibility, if any, existed of settling the migrants in territories other than Germany?'[6]

It must be taken into consideration that the report consisted for the most part of expressions of opinion which could not be conclusive or definite until the three Great Powers had decided their policy in regard to the larger issues.[7]

The answer to the question of Germany's capacity to absorb emigrants was that in a long-term perspective the transfer might be feasible. It might even be of some advantage to all the countries concerned. In a shorter perspective, the view was that the difficulties might cause a complete German economic collapse. It was added that the drain of people from Poland might also be an insoluble problem. Resettlement, retraining labour, raising capital to restart industry and agriculture were some of the problems that post-war Poland would have to face.[8]

The Committee maintained that to ensure 'that the transfer was carried out without undue suffering to the migrants', the transfer could not begin in an organised way until about a year after the end of hostilities. The report underlined the importance of setting up a special transfer authority and not letting the Poles and the Czechs transfer Germans 'as they might think fit'. It was also argued that if a wholesale transfer was regarded as impossible, although it still was considered important to remove all the Germans from the areas ceded to Poland, the area should be smaller. Moreover, it was said that the estimated 10,140,000 immigrants from the territories annexed by Poland and 1,500,000 from Czechoslovakia would increase the population of 'rump Germany' by 15 per cent above the pre-war level and that the amount of human suffering would be very great.[9]

It appears that the Committee on the transfer of German populations did not discuss if the transfer was to take place or not. The Committee's task was to foresee the economic and social repercussions. It was emphasised that the matter was of international concern, and that the acceptance of a total transfer implied that the number of immigrants that the future Germany could swallow should determine future Polish territory. In fact, the work of the Committee was to be interpreted as a recommendation.

In a House of Commons speech of December 15, 1944, Prime Minister Churchill, said: 'It (the Polish territorial settlement) would of course have to be accompanied by the disentanglement of populations in the East and in the North. The transference of several millions of people would have to be effected from the East to the West or North as well as expulsions of the Germans because that is what is proposed: the total expulsion of the German – from the area to be acquired by Poland in the West and in the North.'[10] It was a matter of moving the eastern and western borders of Poland westwards. The Soviet Union was to expand at Poland's expense and Poland was to be compensated for Russian claims at the expense of Germany.

When the representatives of the Soviet Government, the British Government and Mikolaiczyk, the representative of the Polish London Government, met in Moscow, the following provisions were proposed regarding the Polish future borders:

'1) In the West, Germans in the territories to be ceded by Germany to Poland should be repatriated to Germany.

2) In the East, Soviet-Polish agreements would regulate reciprocal transfer and the repatriation of the population of both countries and the release of persons detained.'[11]

The statements from Moscow in October and the Prime Minister's speech of December might be regarded as the basic policy of the time concerning the German population in those areas which after the war would be administered by Poland. The British point of view on the future Polish-Soviet borderline seems to have been that the eastern border was a bilateral problem, while the western border might be regarded as a multilateral problem.[12] However, Poland's changed boundaries would mean that millions of people of German and Polish origin were to be transferred in the coming years.

On September 13, 1945, almost one year after Churchill had proclaimed the policy of the British Government, the new Prime Minister, Mr. Attlee, received a deputation from the churches in England. The deputation drew attention to the difficult situation in Europe. They were particularly concerned about the conditions of the German refugees who had been evacuated from Poland and the German territories handed over to Polish administration.[13]

The Prime Minister pointed out that the German refugees, who were part of the general economic problem besetting Europe, were engaging the Government's attention and that the Government was doing its utmost to overcome the difficulties. He also stated that the British Government was not in any way responsible, and that steps had been taken at the Potsdam Conference to suspend further expulsions pending consideration of the matter by the Control Council in Germany and by the Governments concerned.[14]

Mr. Attlee's statement shows two things about the general policy on the refugee problem after the war. The first thing to note is that, from the British point of view, the responsibility for this 'particular problem' was to be sought elsewhere. Second, the British wanted to find solutions through the inter-Allied administration. This was not because they had a firm belief in this institution, but international realities reduced British power to act independently.

Why did Attlee wash his hands of the expulsion of the Germans from eastern Europe, when nine months earlier Churchill had consented to the idea of a wholesale transfer?

As early as 1942 Dr Benes, the exiled President of Czechoslovakia, was informed that the British approved of transferring German minorities in central and south-eastern Europe to Germany after the war, in cases where such measures seemed necessary or desirable. Later on the Government established more precise commitments to the Polish Government on the subject.[15] In his speech in the House of Commons on December 15, 1944, Churchill stated that Poland would acquire the whole of east Prussia west and south of Königsberg, including Danzig, and that, as far as Russia and Great Britain were concerned, the Poles were free to extend their territory at the expense of Germany. Churchill went on to say that this transfer of territory would have to be followed by the total expulsion of people from the area annexed by Poland.[16] Of course, this was nothing less than an approval of the idea to move people with borders. It is important to give consideration to the context in which this commitment was made. The Soviet Union was still an ally, and the enemy population could not decide their own destiny.

The commitment of December 1944 should be regarded as a statement of principle concerning the people and the borders of a future Germany. In the following months no decision was taken on which areas or people would be involved in a future transfer. The British Government emphasised that they remained uncommitted as to the precise areas from which Germans were to be transferred.[17] On January 23, 1945, the Parliamentary Under Secretary to the Foreign Office said in the House of Commons that the policy of transferring the German population was one of many on which no final decision could be taken at this stage of the war. He continued by pointing to the obvious but nonetheless important fact that this policy was to be determined by a number of Allied Governments, not the British Government alone.[18]

Yalta

The Big Three – Roosevelt, Churchill and Stalin – conferred at Yalta in the Crimea from February 4 to February 11, 1945. At that time the Red Army already controlled almost all of Poland.[19]

When the Soviet Army seized control of German-occupied Polish territory in January, 1944, a Polish Liberation Committee was set up and recognized by the Soviet Union. In the same month the Soviet Union proposed that the new Polish-Soviet frontier should follow the so called 'Curzon Line' . The reaction of the Polish Government in London to the proposal was that they could not participate in unilateral decisions concerning the frontier of Poland. They had to approach the United States and the United Kingdom for mediation. The Polish Liberation Committee, however, was of the opinion that the Soviet proposal was a just basis for a settlement of the boundary problems.[20]

The future of Poland was to become both the most difficult and the most frequently discussed question at Yalta. The attitude of the Western Allies seems to have been that they were more concerned with Poland's political system than with the future extent of the Polish state.[21]

The leaders of the United Kingdom and the United States came to the Yalta Conference with the intention of not recognizing the so called Lublin regime. They wanted a government that represented the majority of the Polish people. It was estimated that the Lublin Committee represented only a small minority of the Polish population.[22] The future Polish Government should 'as soon as possible' be appointed through free elections. In the meantime the West had to accept the Lublin Committee as a temporary arrangement.[23] At the beginning of the Conference the Lublin Provisional Government, which was permitted to participate in the conference, declared that it had taken over the administration of the country up to the Oder and western Neisse, which meant that it was in control of those German areas which were to be discussed at the Yalta Conference.[24]

The eastern borders of Poland were settled at the Yalta Conference. It was agreed that the future border between Poland and the Soviet Union would follow the 'Curzon Line' with the minor modifications in favour of Poland. If this decision were to be carried out it would affect millions of people.[25]

As regards the western frontier, the Yalta agreement said that Poland must be compensated in the north and west. The size of the future Polish western territory was to be determined after a fully representative Polish Government had been elected. It was also added that the final delimitation of the future Polish-German boundary would be decided at the Peace Conference.[26]

Why was the western Polish border not settled at the Yalta Conference? From a British point of view, the transfer of people was not so much a matter of principle as a technical problem. Churchill stated at the conference that he was not afraid of moving people as long as the transfer was proportionate to what the Poles could manage and to what could be absorbed by Germany. The matter required study, not as a question of principle, but as a practical matter.[27] On February 10, the day before the conference ended, a telegram from the British War Cabinet arrived which strongly objected to any reference to a boundary as far west as the western Neisse, stating that the problem of moving the population was too big to handle.[28] The judgement of the British War Cabinet and the statement of Churchill referred to obviously had a certain impact in delaying the decision on the future Polish-German borders.

Another interpretation would be that the question of Polish borders and the consequent mass movements of people were subordinate to the problem of the internal organisation of the new Poland. It might be surmised that the future Polish 'independence' was a matter of political 'system rivalry' between Great Britain and the Soviet Union. When the British accepted the 'Curzon Line' as the border between Poland and Russia, this might have been a policy of consent.[29] However, the British were not yet prepared to consent to the Oder-Neisse line. They still wanted to retain influence in Poland and eastern Europe.[30]

The Yalta Conference closed without an agreement on the Polish-German frontier. Nor were any decisions made with respect to the number of Germans to be transferred, or the time when these transfers were to begin.[31]

Between Yalta and Potsdam

After the Yalta Conference the British view was that the European Advisory Commission would be the proper forum for discussing the German refugee problem.[32]

The European Advisory Commission was established at a Foreign Ministers' Conference in Moscow in October 1943 and came to an end after taking its final decision on the French sector of Berlin in July 1945. The Commission sat in London and one of the articles in Annexe 2 to the Protocol of the Moscow Conference was:

> 'The Commission will study and make joint recommendations to the three Governments upon European questions connected with the termination of hostilities which the three Governments may consider appropriate to refer to it. For this purpose the members of the Commission will be supplied by their Governments with all relevant information on political and military developments affecting their work.'[33]

The German historian Ernst Deuerlein defines the role of EAC as the most crucial instrument for the planning of Allied post-war policy in Germany. However, the Commission did not manage to establish a framework of permanent and rational arrangements for Germany in the post-war period. This was in part due to the fact that East-West tensions were intensified as the war drew closer to its end.[34]

After a delay of two months, the EAC met in April 1945. In the many formal and informal meetings that were held by the Commission one important item on the agenda was the 'Transfer of populations to Germany'.[35]

William Strang (later Lord Strang), the British representative on the European Advisory Commission with the rank of ambassador, said in a draft memorandum that it was important to establish the principle that the transfers, which would be likely to create many complex problems, should be regarded as a matter of international concern. It was, according to Strang, important to prevent an unregulated flow of population. If this did not succeed it would hamper the occupying and controlling authorities in their primary tasks, that is the disarmament of all German armed forces, the dissolution of all Nazi organisations, the repatriation of displaced persons, etc.[36]

In July 1944, the Secretary of State of War, Sir John Grigg, said that as the Russians would probably do most of the moving of populations, he was of the opinion that the British Government should not take the initiative in the matter. The question was still of interest, and William Strang argued that the U.K. delegation to the EAC should refrain from initiating any discussions on subjects such as the areas from which people should be transferred, the numbers to be transferred, and the questions by whom and by what principles the transferees should be selected for transfer.[37]

The British Government was consequently careful not to act unilaterally and stressed that the transfers were a matter of international concern and should be jointly handled by the powers responsible for the occupation of Germany. Apart from the fact that the British Government was heavily dependent on the policy of the other Allied Powers, it felt that it should not force the issue and let the matter be determined before the peace treaty.[38]

While the Foreign Office was elaborating the British strategy on German refugees, the Red Army was advancing to the heart of Germany and, in so doing, created a *fait accompli* in the Oder-Neisse area. As a result of the Soviet offensive, large groups of Germans fled from those parts of Germany overrun by the Russians.[39]

Ever since the Yalta Conference, the claims of the Lublin Committee for territorial compensation at the expense of Germany had bothered the Foreign Office. It was also troubled by the fact that the Soviet Union allowed the Poles to administer the region up to the Oder and the western Neisse. The Foreign Office was in no position to estimate the number of refugees or of those remaining in the region. The fact that the area had been one of the main sources of German grain supply made the problem even worse. The future 'rump Germany' would be an overpopulated area without proper means to feed itself.[40]

The British Policy followed the same lines until the Potsdam Conference. The Foreign Office stance was mainly based on the following assumptions. Firstly, the question of German refugees ought to be treated with great caution, because this would benefit British interests. It might be that the British were not yet prepared to confront their Russian ally. Secondly, as mentioned above, the problem of German refugees was still supposed to be a matter of international concern. It was of the utmost importance to refer all refugee movements into Germany to the Allied Control Commission to prevent an unregulated flow of refugees.[41] If not, the movements would entail a heavy demand for food, transport and shelter, which were needed elsewhere. As the war was coming to an end, the British were gradually coming to an understanding of the likely impact of mass movements on post-war Germany, but this understanding of future consequences did not as yet change the British approach.

However, in an April 1945 analysis of the Soviet foreign policy, the British Under Secretary of State, Orme Sargent, said that the British should openly state that they were of the opinion that the Soviet and British positions on the European scene had altered. It was of great importance to put an end to the present state of paralysis. The prevailing situation would, according to the Foreign Office, only benefit the Soviet Union and put the British into an unfavourable position.[42]

In the months preceding the Potsdam Conference British scope for action decreased. In the middle of June a Parliamentary question was put forward to the Secretary of State for Foreign Affairs, Mr. Eden, as to whether the British Government would intervene with the appropriate foreign powers to prevent the mass deportation of millions of innocent people.[43] The answer, as prepared by a Foreign Office draft, stated that, apart from the transfer of the Sudeten Germans, the British Government had never discussed the question of population transfers in any detail with the other Allied Powers. Concerning the Soviet Ally the following view was put forward: 'Nothing we say or do is likely to have any effect upon what takes place in the Soviet zone.'[44] The answer expressed the hope that the refugee problem, or at any rate that part of it concerned with the ultimate screening and the resettlement in Germany, would probably engage the attention of the Allied Control Council in Germany, adding: 'If that body ever lived to enjoy an effective existence.' In retrospect this statement can be seen as indicating the dawning of the Cold War.[45]

In other words, the hope of future cooperation on German problems was decreasing, and the British had to recognize the military supremacy of the Russians who made no secret of their desire for revenge on Germany after the suffering inflicted upon them since June 1941.[46] However, this did not mean that the question of transfers from Poland and the Polish borders were lost causes from the British point of view. The problem was how to come to terms with the Russians.[47]

The movement of people and the revision of borders in the Oder-Neisse area would mean a potential threat to future Polish-German relations. For the Russians it was a security interest to intensify Polish-German tensions.[48] A future neutralised Germany and a weak Poland dependent on the Russians would mean Soviet domination in a key area of eastern Europe.[49] The Soviet concept of security accordingly implied support of the extreme Polish claims to former German territory, that is to say the claims of the Lublin Committee.[50] In the long run, the Polish administration would involve transfer of the Germans as a result of the Polish struggle for national security.[51]

The new generation of Polish statesmen and scholars stated that their historical role was to make sure that the whole Polish area was filled with

Polish inhabitants, and that succeeding generations were due to maintain that position.[52]

In the spring of 1945, the expulsion of large groups of Germans was carried out without the authorization of the Western Allies.[53] In March the government in Warsaw assumed the formal administration of the 'liberated areas', and the German areas were referred to as the Recovered Territories.[54]

As mentioned above, the cession of the eastern parts of Poland to the Soviet Union entailed transferring a great number of people. The transfer of the Poles living east of the Curzon line became possible when the German territories had been taken over by the Polish authorities. In March large numbers of newcomers were directed to the Recovered Territories.[55] Consequently, the decision at Yalta to change the Polish-Soviet border meant that another push factor was created to drive out Germans from Poland before the allied summit meeting was held at Potsdam.

Potsdam

The position of the British Government before Potsdam was that Germany within the borders of 1937 should be administered by the Supreme Authority of the Allies in Germany. When Churchill came to Potsdam he stated that 'His Majesty's Government did not admit that territory in the east of Germany overrun during the war could now be regarded as having become Polish territory'.[56] According to the Foreign Office memorandum of July 12, intended as a brief for the Potsdam delegation, British acceptance of the Polish claim would mean concessions to the maximum Russian claims. This would be regarded as a sign of weakness and provoke other demands.[57] The Foreign Office was also troubled by the fact that the Soviet Government was to place part of their zone outside the power not only of the Allied Control Council but also of the Soviet Commander-in-Chief.[58] However, earlier commitments at Teheran and Yalta made it hard to alter British policy on the Polish-German border.

In a brief submitted to the Big Three Meeting of July 4th 1945, the British policy on the transfers of Germans was expressed. The proposed formula on the matters was as follows:

'The Three Powers, having considered the question in all its aspects, have agreed that the transfer to Germany of German population from Central and South Eastern Europe is in principle desirable. They have further agreed that any transfers that take place should be carefully supervised and controlled, in order that they may be effected in as orderly and humane manner as possible. They consider that the actual procedure of the transfers of these persons to Germany should be worked out by the Allied Control Council in Germany in consultation with the governments concerned, due regard being paid to the capacity of Germany to absorb them.'[59]

Still the opinion prevailed that the British should refrain from taking the initiative in these matters. According to the memorandum one argument presuming this position was that Britain was the least directly interested among the Three Powers, because the British zone was the furthest removed from the Polish-Czechoslovak frontiers.[60] Although it was said in the proposed formula that transfers were in principle desirable, the British delegation had no mandate but to accept the total expulsion of Germans from the Oder-Neisse area. Discussions were yet to come about the future status of this region. It was admitted in a memorandum that the British were committed to a wholesale transfer of German population from the areas in Germany which were to be placed under Polish sovereignty.[61] The recommendation of the Interdepartmental Committee was still pertinent (wholesale transfer) but the German area ceded to Poland was not yet determined. Nor were the numbers and timetables settled as yet.[62]

The Foreign Office found the situation prevailing in July in Poland and Polish-occupied Germany obscure. They did not know how large a proportion of the German population had fled westward before the Red Army or how many Germans had been deported eastward for labour camps in the Soviet Union.[63] In July 1945 the Foreign Office had to rely on the figures of the Interdepartmental Committee for the previous year.[64] It was at that time estimated that the Germans in Poland and the territories to be occupied by Poland might amount to anything between five and eight million persons. Once again it was emphasised that to avoid an unregulated flow of refugees when the question of principle was settled, the Allied Control Council in Germany would have to decide on methods and the timing of the transfer of expelled German populations to Germany.[65]

At Potsdam the West accepted Russia's demands for reparations and boundary changes. The Conference decided that the Soviet Union should be compensated for war damages by ten billion dollars. It was also stated that the German eastern borders be temporarily fixed at the Oder-Neisse line.[66]

During the conference, the Russians argued that no single German remained in the territory to be given to Poland and that it would be unlikely that the Poles would have them back. The Russian assessment that the Germans had left was, however, disputed by the British.[67] (One might estimate that, in July, four million Germans still lived in these areas.[68])

The British point of view was that Poland should be compensated for the land she had lost east of the Curzon line. But it was stressed that Poland was claiming more than she was giving up. Furthermore, the British said that the idea of transferring millions of Germans to make room for the Poles who were to be moved from east of the Curzon line would cause a reaction from British public opinion. According to Churchill the transfer of eight and a quarter million would be more than he could defend.[69] When Attlee and Bevin arrived at Potsdam in the middle of the conference, it was obvious that the Poles had the full support of the Russians. Bevin was of the opinion that there was nothing to be gained by challenging the Polish claims. It was important, though, to seek in return satisfactory assurances on political developments in Poland.[70]

In fact, when the Polish question was settled, the British tended to be more concerned with practical considerations regarding the concrete problems of post-war reorganisation. The important thing appeared to be to administer the British zone in such a way that it would not become a burden to the British economy.[71] However, the Allies never consented to the Oder-Neisse boundary as a permanent solution. The Polish administration would be only temporary. The fate of the area was to be decided by a future peace conference.[72] This meant that Poland became the fifth occupation power on German territory. Moreover, in article XIII of the Potsdam agreement, the Allies consented to the transfer to Germany of the German populations remaining in Poland, Czechoslovakia and Hungary. It was added that the transfer should be effected in an orderly and humane way.[73] The real consequences of the Potsdam agreement have, however, been clearly stated by Joseph B. Schechtman in his book *Post War Population Transfers in Europe 1945–55.*

The Potsdam decision to allocate these territories to Polish administration inevitably led to the decision of the Allied Control Council to transfer the entire German population from the entire area handed over to Poland. No distinction was made between single provinces of this area: it was to be cleared in its totality of the remaining German population. All Germans who had fled their residence were implicitly prohibited from returning.[74]

British Reaction after Potsdam

To understand the deadlock on the German refugee problem it is necessary to understand the context in which this question was treated. In August the war was over, the enemy was defeated, and common cause had come to its end. Other values and interests would determine the future relations between the Allies. According to the Foreign Office, it was the complete lack of any German or inter-Allied organisation to deal with the problem that made the situation worse in the period immediately following the Potsdam negotiations.[75]

For practical and political reasons it was no longer a question of treating the matter cautiously which had been the British point of view months earlier. The British troops in Germany were faced with a people and country in a devastated condition. The situation in Germany is described in *Die Vertriebenen in Westdeutschland* (Vol. I) edited by Edding/Lemberg:

'In Germany absolute chaos ruled in Spring 1945. 2.5 million dwellings were destroyed. 4.4 million dwellings were badly damaged – more than the total built between 1918 and 1937. Bombing had made roads and railways unusable. Everywhere there was famine, and a total lack of clothing, medicines and fuel.'[76]

The chaotic situation made the British forbid any entrance of refugees into their zone. The barrier was supposed to be lifted when an organised transfer could take place. At the same time, it was estimated that millions of German refugees from the east were drawn together in the Russian zone, which created a pressure on the sealed frontiers of the British and American zones.[77]

During the first post-war years the British-Russian relationship might be described as a mixture of conflict and cooperation. The Russians were, in fact, in control of the Polish administered areas. And whatever the Russian-Polish goals were concerning the transfers of German population, the British had to avoid conflict and seek cooperation, as they had, after all, signed the Potsdam agreement. The British attitude to the Soviet Union on the question of German refugees might, however, be described in Cold War terms, as exemplified by the former Prime Minister Churchill's speech in March 1946, when he said:

'The Russian-dominated Polish Government has been encouraged to make enormous and wrongful inroads upon Germany, and mass expulsions of millions of Germans on a scale grievous and undreamed of are now taking place.'[78]

The so called Fulton speech shows a different attitude from Churchill's statement of December 1944, when he consented to a wholesale transfer. The speech can be explained by the aggravation of East-West relations in Germany from 1946, in which the refugees played their part in a propaganda war between the two sides. It was important for the West to seek the full support of the Germans and, consequently, put the blame on the Russian side.[79]

In order to find the solution to a problem you have to identify its causes. According to the Foreign Office, in August 1945, the problem was created by the Russians. The argument was that the Poles could not have carried out the expulsions without Russian consent. It was said that the Russians must assume almost exclusive responsibility, and the Foreign Office was troubled by the fact, as they saw it, that the Soviet Union had shown no sign of being in the least concerned about the problem.[80] However, putting the blame on someone else did not help the British Forces in Germany, and the Foreign Office found itself unable to draw up a policy that would solve the problem.

It fell upon defeated Germany to take full responsibility for the incoming Germans. It goes without saying that the German authorities were in no position to deal with a problem of this magnitude.[81] The British tried to delay the expulsion of further Germans from the Polish-administered areas, because they were not yet prepared for the array of problems connected with the settlement of refugees.[82] Even though in August and September the refugees had not yet entered the British zone of occupation, the sight of tens of thousands of refugees in the Berlin area made the British delegation at Potsdam aware of the potential threat the refugees constituted. The problem became all the more acute as the British were to occupy the thickly populated and food-importing areas of the Rhineland

and the Ruhr. The question of the numbers to feed was, consequently, a crucial one for the British Government.[83]

The British voiced deep concern about the situation, but they did very little to improve it. The occupation authorities who dealt with the refugees showed an almost fatalistic attitude. They found the circumstances hopeless and were not able to foresee a long term solution. In other words, the main effort of the British administration during the first year of occupation did not aim at constructive resettlement of the refugees, but rather at preventing their future arrival under the Potsdam scheme.[84]

At the same time, a problem of a different kind came to the fore in Britain: the British anxiety on the question of German refugees, as expressed in newspapers, editorials, parliamentary debates, and so on. It was estimated by the Foreign Office that this 'anxiety will no doubt increase as the facts of the situation become further known'.[85] In the aftermath of Potsdam, the British Government found itself under internal and external pressure. Policy on the German refugees would, according to the Political Adviser to the British Commander in Chief in Germany, Sir William Strang (former delegate to the EAC), be directed towards three objectives:

'1. How to prevent further expulsions.
2. How to improve the lot of those refugees who are now in the Soviet zone.
3. How to dispose finally of these refugees.'[86]

Strang's telegram to the Foreign Office of September 2 had no definite answers to the problems. It only stated the fact that the authorities would have to prevent the prevailing anomalies becoming permanent.

As the Allied Control Council met in September under British leadership, it was to a large extent concerned with the mass movements of Germans from the east.[87] However, the Control Council was not yet in a position to work efficiently. As the *Times* correspondent in Berlin put it at the time (11 September 1945): 'But so far its decisions have been more or less academic and they are not likely to have any deep influence on the universal chaos of Germany until Russian intentions become clearer.'[88]

At the same time, in the middle of September, it was the judgement of the Foreign Office, in a memorandum to the Prime Minister, that the Germans were paying in the most dreadful way for their misdeeds of the previous ten years. It was estimated by the German Economic Department in the Foreign Office that if all Germans in eastern Europe were transferred, the total would amount to over 16 million. The total of the evacuated Germans was not known, and the stated numbers were regarded as pure guesses.[89]

According to the memorandum, it was difficult to suggest any effective remedy. The British authorities were arranging accommodation available in the British zone for the reception of a quota of the refugees. But, as was admitted in the memorandum, it was already hard to find sufficient food and shelter even for the present population of the British zone, and it was anticipated that 'there is going to be a fearful disaster'.[90]

It was the task of the Control Commission to examine the German refugee problem with special regard to the question of the equitable distribution of the refugees among the several zones and it was felt that the Soviet representative was deliberately obstructing the work of the Control Commission regarding the German refugee problem. The Soviet purpose, according to the British point of view, was that by the time the Control Commission could make any concrete proposals, the Germans from Poland and Czechoslovakia would have been expelled.[92]

The memorandum also stressed the importance of giving publicity to the refugee question in Britain. The Foreign Office had the impression that 'the anxiety of the British public' could be used as an instrument of foreign policy. It was of great value to show the Russians and the Poles that the British public was agitated over the question, and it would bring home to the public that the British Government was doing its best to diminish the impending disaster. Moreover, the memorandum stated that officially it was crucial to underline that the British Government was not to blame and that it was doing its utmost to diminish the problem, even though the result would not be very great.[93]

It might be that the British authorities in September anticipated that the refugee problem would get out of hand. It was never a matter of confronting the Russians on the subject, as they were, according to the Foreign Office, in full control of the expulsions but left the refugees to fend for themselves. The British had to rely on the Allied Control Council, which was the supreme organ of control of the Military Government of Germany. Of course, when they could use other means in the negotiations, they would do so. However, during the autumn of 1945 the British authorities were still not in the position to take the initiative in these matters, and their policy remained defensive.

Britain's role in international politics in the early post-war years could be interpreted in different ways. However, with the decline and fall of Nazi Germany a power vacuum had been created in Europe. The Third Reich had collapsed without an immediately foreseeable successor. As a great power, Britain wanted to play a part in the destiny of a future Europe. Therefore it was crucial to the British Government not to lose control of their zone. German immigrants from the eastern parts of former German territory constituted just one of many problems that had to be taken care of. The problem of the expelled Germans was, nonetheless, related to the question of a future British presence in Germany.

As mentioned in the introduction, this brief survey of the German refugee question should only be regarded as an introduction to a detailed study of the subject. However, what conclusions can be drawn from the course of events at the end of the war and in the period immediately following the Potsdam agreements?

The question of German refugees in the eastern parts of pre-war Germany has to be related to the British policy on Poland and, consequently, to the British attitude towards the future of eastern Europe. The fact that Poland was situated between Russia and Germany made its political developments of great significance to British foreign policy before, during, and immediately after the Second World War. British policy on Poland should be seen in relation to her policy on Russia and Germany. Great Britain entered the war as a result of the German attack on Poland, and it was hard to accept that the Soviet Union would dominate the area.

In the war against Germany it was important to strengthen the ties with Russia, and British interests in eastern Europe were no longer assigned highest priority. As the war came to its end, it became clear that the Soviet Union was in a position to act as it wished in an area that for Britain was a key area in Eastern Europe. The impression was that if Poland was dominated by the Soviet Union, the rest of Eastern Europe would follow. However, in Potsdam the British Government still thought they could influence the Polish question. They made it clear that there was a connection between the future political system in Poland and the approval of the Oder and Western Neisse line. Therefore the expulsion of people in this area must be regarded as subordinate to British interests in eastern Europe at the end of the war.

The fact that millions of people had been victimized by the German seizure of territories in eastern Europe might be one way of understanding why the British accepted the expulsions. Although the British Government did not accept the principle of collective guilt at the Potsdam Conference, it agreed, in November 1945, to the transfer of large numbers of Germans. On November 20 the Allied Control Council had approved a plan whereby 6,650,000 would be brought to 'rump Germany' and allocated between the four zones. On top of this figure there were the vast numbers of Germans that already had been driven out of Poland and Czechoslovakia.

We started by asking what changes occurred between Churchill's and Attlee's statements. We can at this stage tentatively note that at the end of the war the German refugee problem had a low ranking on the Allies' agenda. However, in the aftermath of the Second World War, the issue grew in importance as the tensions between East and West intensified.

Notes: Chapter 10

1 Persson, Hansåke, 'Tyska flyktingar från östeuropa efter andra rårklsürget', seminar paper, University of Lund, March 1984. According to Schechtman, the number of expellees who arrived in the British zone in a controlled movement known to the British occupation authorities as 'Operation Swallow' amounted by April 1, 1949, to 3,949,700. In addition, 504,000 refugees from the Soviet zone and from Berlin entered the British zone up to April 1 1949.
2 de Zayas, Alfred M., *Nemesis at Potsdam*, (London, 1979), p.2.
3 Ibid. p. 3.
4 Persson, Hansåke, *Tyska flyktingar*, p. 7.
5 Ibid. p.8.
6 Woodward, Sir Llewelyn, *British Foreign Policy in the Second World War*, volume V (London, 1979), p. 211.
7 Ibid. p. 210.
8 Ibid. p. 211.

9   Ibid.
10 FO 371/46810
11 Ibid.
12 Ibid.
13 Ibid.
14 Ibid.
15 Ibid.
16 Ibid.
17 Ibid.
18 Ibid.
19 Ibid.
20 Schechtman, Joseph B., *Postwar Population Transfers in Europe* 1945–1955 (Philadelphia 1962), p. 155 ff.
21 Wiskemann, Elizabeth, *Germany's Eastern Neighbours* (London, 1947), p. 83.
22 Lundestad, 'The American Non-Policy Toward Eastern Europe 1943–1947' (New York 1975), p. 193.
23 Foschepoth, Joseph, *Grossbritannien, die Sowietunion und die Westverschiebung Polens* (Militàrgeschichtliche Mitteilungen 2/1983), p. 76
24 Wiskemann, Elizabeth, *Germany's Eastern Neighbours*, p. 83.
25 Schechtman, *Postwar Transfers*, p. 156.
26 Ibid. p. 155.
27 Foschepoth, Joseph, *Grossbrittannien, die Sowietunion und die Westverschiebung Polens* (Militàrgeschichtliche Mitteilungen 2/1983), p. 77.
28 Wiskemann, Elizabeth, *Germany's Eastern Transfers*, p. 85.
29 Foschepoth, Joseph, *Grossbrittannien, die Sowietunion und die Westverschiebung Polens* (Militàrgeschichtliche Mitteilungen 2/1983), p. 73.
30 Ibid.
31 de Zayas, Alfred M., *Nemesis at Potsdam* (London, 1979), p. X85.
32 FO 371/46810.
33 Nelson, Daniel J., *Wartime Origins of the Berlin Dilemma* (Alabama, 1978), p. 14.
34 Ibid p. 166 ff.
35 Ibid. p. 81.
36 FO 371/46810.
37 Ibid.
38 Ibid.
39 de Zayas, Alfred M., *Nemesis at Potsdam* (London, 1979), p. 65.
40 Woodward, Sir Llewellyn, *British Foreign Policy in the Second World War*, Volume V (London, 1976), p. 410.
41 FO 371/46810.
42 Foschepoth, Joseph, *Grossbrittannien, die Sowietunion und die Westverschiebung Polens* (Militàrgeschichtliche Mitteilungen 2/1983), p. 78.
43 FO 371/46810.
44 Ibid.
45 Ibid.
46 Wiskemann, Elizabeth, *Germany's Eastern Neighbours* (London, 1947), p. 89.
47 Foschepoth, Joseph, *Grossbrittannien, die Sowietunion und die Westverschiebung Polens* (Militàrgeschichtliche Mitteilungen 2/1983), p. 79.
48 Woodward, Sir Llewellyn, *British Foreign Policy in the Second World War*, Volume V (London, 1976), p. 410.
49 Lundestad, Geir, *Ost, Vest, Nord, Sör; international politikk 1945–1985* (Oslo, 1985), p. 40.
50 Woodward, Sir Llewellyn, *British Foreign Policy in the Second World War*, Volume V (London, 1976), p. 410.
51 Buzan, Barry, *People States and Fear*. This is a theoretical work and an in-depth examination of the concept of national security, and of the implications of the security dilemma.
52 Schechtman, Joseph, *Postwar Population Transfers in Europe 1945–1955*. (Philadelphia, 1962), p. 156.
53 de Zayas, Alfred M., *Nemesis at Potsdam* (London, 1979), p. 80.

54 Wiskemann, Elizabeth, *Germany's Eastern Neighbours* (London, 1947), p. 96.
55 Schechtman, Joseph, *Postwar Population Transfers in Europe 1945–1955*. (Philadelphia, 1962), p. 197.
56 Foschepoth, Joseph, *Grossbrittannien, die Sowietunion und die Westverschiebung Polens* (Militàrgeschichtliche Mitteilungen 2/1983), p. 79.
57 Woodward, Sir Llewellyn, *British Foreign Policy in the Second World War*, Volume V (London, 1976), p. 412.
58 Ibid. p. 413.
59 FO 371/46810.
60 Ibid.
61 Ibid.
62 Ibid.
63 Ibid.
64 Ibid.
65 Ibid.
66 Urwin, Derek W., *Western Europe since 1945* (Harlow, 1981), p. 87.
67 Woodward, Sir Llewellyn, *British Foreign Policy in the Second World War*, Volume V (London, 1976), p. 421.
68 de Zayas, Alfred M., *Nemesis at Potsdam* (London, 1979), p. 86.
69 Woodward, Sir Llewellyn, *British Foreign Policy in the Second World War*, Volume V (London, 1976), p. 421. The British estimation of the numbers of Germans in Eastern Germany and Polandd is confusing, due to the fact that at the Potsdam Conference it was not yet settled which areas were to be ceded to Poland. It can also be assumed that British authorities lacked specified demographic data. According to de Zayas, p. xxv, the following figures were involved in the German expulsion.

THE GERMAN POPULATION IN THE AREAS OF EXPULSION

Before Expulsion

German population in 1939

Eastern Areas of Germany	9,575,000
East Prussia	2,473,000
Eastern Pomerania	1,884,000
Eastern Brandenburg	642,000
Silesia	4,577,000
Czechoslovakia	3,477,000
Baltic States and District of Memel	250,000
Danzig	380,000
Poland	1,371,000
Hungary	623,000
Yugoslavia	537,000
Roumania	786,000

(Total*)		16,999,000

Excess of Births over Deaths

1939–1945	+ 659,000

	17,658,000
War Losses 1939–1945	-1,100,000

German Population at the End of the War	16,588,000

* In addition in the Soviet Union 1.5 or 2 million

War Losses	1,100,000
Expulsion Losses	2,111,000
Total Losses	3,211,000

After Expulsion (1945–1950)

Survived the Flight and Expulsion

from the Eastern areas of Germany	6,944,000
from Czechoslovakia	2,921,000
from other countries	1,865,000
	11,730,000

Remained in the Home Area

in the Eastern areas of Germany	1,101,000
in Czechoslovakia	250,000
in other countries	1,294,000
	2,645,000
Presumed Still Alive as Prisoners	72,000
	14,447,000

Dead and Missing During
the Flight and Expulsion

in the Eastern areas of Germany	1,225,000
in Czechoslovakia	267,000
in other countries	619,000
	2,111,000
	16,558,000

Total Number of German Expellees in 1966 (estimated):

in the Federal Republic of Germany	10.6 million
in the German Democratic Republic	3.5 million
in Austria and other Western countries	0.5 million

Source: German Federal Ministry for Expellees, Bonn, 1967. See also Statistiches Bundesamt, *Die Deutschen Vertreibungsverluste*, 1958. From 1950 to 1978 approximately 1,000,000 Germans who had remained in the home areas migrated to the GDR and FRG.

70 Rothwell, Victor, *Britain and the Cold War*, (London, 1982), p. 47.
71 Foschepoth, Joseph, *Grossbrittannien, die Sowietunion und die Westverschiebung Polens* (Militàrgeschichtliche Mitteilungen 2/1983), p. 79
72 Urwin, Derek W., *Western Europe since 1945*, (Harlow, 1981), p. 87.
73 de Zayas, Alfred M., *Nemesis at Potsdam* (London, 1979), p. 83.
74 Schechtman, Joseph B., *Postwar Population Transfers in Europe 1945–1955* (Philadelphia, 1962), p. 191.
75 FO 371/46812.

76 Lemberg, Eugen and Edding, Friedrich, *Die Vertriebenen in West-Deutschlands* (Kiel, 1959).
77 FO 371/46812.
78 Churchill, Winston, *The Sinews of Peace* (London, 1948) p. 100.
79 Bartlett, C.J., *The Global Conflict* (Harlow, 1984), p. 259 ff.
80 FO 371/46812
81 Schwartz, Leo W., *Refugees in Germany Today* (New Haven) p. 36.
82 FO 371/46812.
83 Rothwell, Victor, *Britain and the Cold War* (London, 1982), p. 108.
84 Schechtman, Joseph B., *Postwar Population Transfers in Europe 1945–1955* (Philadelphia, 1962), p. 309.
85 FO 371/46812.
86 Ibid.
87 Ibid.
88 Ibid. and Grosser *The Western Alliance* (London, 1980), p. 46.
89 FO 371/46812
90 Ibid.
91 Friedman, *The Allied Military Government of Germany* (London, 1947), p. 49.
92 FO 371/46812.
93 Ibid.

Bibliography

Unpublished documents

Public Record Office, Foreign Office files: FO 371/46810, FO 371/46812.

Books

Bartlett, C.J., *The Global Conflict, 1880–1970*, Harlow, 1984
Buzan, Barry, *People, States and Fear*, Brighton, 1983
Churchill, Winston, S., *The Sinews of Peace*, London, 1948
Foschepoth, Joseph, *Grossbritannien, die Sowjetunion und die Westverschiebung Polens*, Militärgeschichtliche Mitteilungen 2/1983
Friedman, W., *The Allied Military Government of Germany*, London, 1947
Grosser, Alfred, *The Western Alliance*, London, 1980
Lemberg, Eugen and Edding, Friedrich, *Die Vertriebenen in West-Deutschland*, Kiel, 1959
Lundestad, Geir, *The American Non-Policy Toward Eastern Europe 1943–47*, New York, 1975
Lundestad, Geir, *Ust, Vest, Nord, Sör, Hovedlinjer i internasjonal politikk 1945–1985*, Oslo, 1985
Nelson, Daniell, J., *Wartime Origins of the Berlin Dilemma*, Alabama, 1978
Persson, Hansåke, *Tyska flytingar från Östeuropa efter andra världskriget*, Lund, 1984 (Ms., project paper)
Rothwell, Victor, *Britain and the Cold War 1941–47*, London, 1982
Schechtman, Jseph B., *Postwar Population Transfers in Europe 1945–1955*, Philadelpha, 1962
Schwartz, Leo W., *Refugees in Germany Today*, New Haven, 1957
Urwin, Derek W., *Western Europe since 1945*, Harlow, 1981
Wiskemann, Eliabeth, *Germany's Eastern Neighbours*, London, 1947
Woodward, Sir Llewellyn, *British Foreign Policy in the Second World War*, Volume V, London, 1976
de Zayas, Alfred M., *Nemesis at Potsdam*, London, 1979

11 Refugees and Ruhr miners: a case study of the impact of the refugees on post-war German society[1]

MARK ROSEMAN

It is only fairly recently that historians have begun to investigate the absorption and impact of the expellees and refugees who entered West Germany after 1945. One important result which has already emerged is the degree to which the interaction between refugees and host community varied from region to region.[2] This is not particularly surprising given the variety of regional and social environments within West Germany but it has made clear that an authentic national picture of the refugee experience can emerge only through investigation of these different environments. Although a number of regional studies have already appeared or are under way, they have tended to concentrate on rural areas in the so-called 'refugee states' – Bavaria, Lower Saxony and Schleswig-Holstein.[3] An important element of the German refugee experience, namely the encounter with industrialised regions and with the industrial working class, has thus been neglected and the present contribution represents an attempt to fill this gap.

Beyond introducing the refugee experience of a particular regional community, the main focus of the present investigation is on conflict; on the issues and problems that generated conflict or antagonism between newcomers and residents and on the policies and other factors that dampened or eliminated it. In part, this choice of focus was motivated by the belief that, if refugee studies are to assist those involved in the making of contemporary refugee policy, then the question of conflict limitation takes on a particular significance. A regional or group investigation cannot explain why conflict does or does not take place at the *national* level, but the great advantage of the case study is that it makes it easier to describe and analyse patterns of interaction between the newcomers and the established community; on the one hand, the environment and population will be less heterogeneous than in the nation as a whole and on the other, the limited scope of the study allows diffuse source materials to be evaluated more intensively.

What sort of social environment did the refugees encounter when they entered the Ruhr mining communities? Traditionally they had been homogeneous and close-knit. Many miners lived in areas and neighbourhoods where mining was the dominant industry. Until the Nazi era and to a certain extent thereafter, communal life had been very strong with formal cultural and political organisations and networks of informal sociability both contributing to the sense of cohesion. Certainly not all miners shared the same religion or creed but within individual neighbourhoods most miners tended to belong to the same faith – the Catholics in the west of the Ruhr, the Protestants in the east – and most shared assumptions and perceptions of the society around them. There was, in other words, a very clear sense of identity. Even in the 1950's, miners' autobiographies and other sources suggest that this strong perception of 'us' and 'them' still prevailed.[4]

Into these closeknit communities poured a flood of newcomers and outsiders after 1945. Every year between 1945 and the early 1950's an average of over 20,000 refugees came to the pits, a figure equivalent to between 5 – 10% of the 300,000 strong underground workforce.[5] Not all of them stayed, but by 1950 the refugees made up 17% of the mining workforce overall and very probably nearer 20% underground. (Refugees continued to enter the mining industry in considerable numbers until the collapse of the coal market in 1958 caused the industry to curtail labour recruitment.) In Bavaria, one of the states most burdened by refugees in the early years, the proportion in the population as a whole was not much higher, namely 21% in 1950.[6] Even these figures to not convey the scale of the influx into the Ruhr. A fact of major importance and one which a regional or sectoral analysis is more likely than a national survey to uncover is that the refugees were by no means the only major mobile group in Germany; indeed something like two-fifths of the German population was mobile at the end of the war.[7] This is one of the unique characteristics of the German refugee experience and it means that the impact of the refugees cannot be analysed in isolation. Closer examination of the mining industry, for instance, reveals that the refugees were only one part of a huge group of outsiders entering the mines in this period. These newcomers included former Nazis who had lost their jobs, ex-soldiers without a home, steel makers from blast furnaces that had remained unlit since the war, and craftsmen, students and many other groups who saw no other way of earning a living in the chaotic economy of the immediate post-war years.[8] Some, around 40% of these new miners, actually came from the Ruhr and were simply changing jobs; the remaining 60% came from other regions of Germany, usually from other professions. Overall, including the refugees, some 600,000 new miners entered the Ruhr pits in the 12 years following the war. By 1950 they already made up at least one-quarter of the workforce; by 1958 between one-third and one-half of the workforce were outsiders.[9] These other labour migrants had much in common with the refugees. Often they brought with them the same needs, came for the same reasons and challenged the established community in the same way.

Yet the striking fact is that this invasion took place with the minimum of conflict. Not long ago the book *Hochlamarker Lesebuch* attracted quite a lot of attention in the Ruhr.[10] Based on the experiences of the citizens of Hochlamark, now a suburb of Recklinghausen and, until the pit closures in the 1960's and 1970's, an area dominated by coal mining, the book tries to provide a chronicle of social change in the Ruhr since the end of the 19th century. The post-war era is covered in considerable depth and a number of accounts deal with the impact of the refugees from the viewpoint of both local and refugee families.[11] As such, the book represents an excellent starting point for our investigation. The overriding impression is that serious conflict barely took place between refugees and established community. True, there are the odd bitter overtones and clearly the refugees generated and experienced a number of difficulties, but in general, the refugee invasion seems to have been a most peaceful and uncomplicated one. This is borne out by other sources. All the materials on the Ruhr which exist suggest that conflicts and tensions were transient and limited. Although the newcomers certainly contained groups which found it hard to gain a place in the new neighbourhoods, the dividing line between newcomers and established mining community did not become an abiding new division. Whichever indicator is taken, whether it be violence between local youngsters and outsiders or political polarisation as an expression of local antagonism, the impression remains of a community not deeply divided by the influx. The refugee party, for instance, barely gained a foothold in the Ruhr.[12]

Given what one knows about refugees *en masse* in general and the post-war influx of German refugees in particular, this result seems, at first sight, extraordinary. One of the characteristic effects of an influx of refugees, for example, is the development of tensions and bitterness over the question of how to allocate resources between newcomers and established community. In Germany, after the war, when almost all resources were in short supply, these conflicts could be particularly bitter. Yet, in general, the extent of the allocation problem in the mining areas seems to have been very limited. It is true that there *was* much resentment amongst established miners in the immediate post-war period that scarce supplies of bedding, building materials, work-clothes and strong shoes should be going to the newcomers, when they themselves were experiencing great shortages.[13] Outside the mines too, general shortages due to bombing and years of inadequate supplies made it very hard for locals to accept that the limited stocks of household goods should be reserved for refugees. However, these disputes were very short-lived and by 1948 many observers felt that relations had improved considerably.[14]

Even where it is apparent that very difficult problems of resource allocation remained, conflict and protest were rarely seen. This was particularly remarkable in the case of housing. Many members of the community lived in appalling or cramped conditions for years and many of the refugees endured long years of separation from their families for whom there was no room in the Ruhr. The mines and work councils responsible for allotting mine-owned housing – chief source of accommodation for the miners – were continually faced with difficult decisions. Yet there is no evidence of great bitterness between the newcomers and the established miners on the issue, even though the housing question was of burning importance for both parties.[15]

Another source of conflict is that a large-scale influx of refugees frequently represents a threat to the host community's livelihood. If the newcomers are tradesmen, they may undercut local competition; if they are workers, their desperate state may lead them to work for less pay and inferior conditions in order to get employment, thus undermining the position of local labour, particularly where, as was the case in mining, the job-skills are relatively easily acquired. The result is bitterness and tension. Yet here too, the problems faced by the mining community were restricted and temporary and, even where this was not the case, led to little conflict.

To a certain extent the newcomers in mining *did* directly threaten the livelihood of the established workers and they did this in one of two ways. As inexperienced and sometimes not very motivated workers some of them were responsible for a drop in output. The majority of coal-faces after the war operated a collective contract wage whereby each face workers' wage was calculated as a share of their joint output,[16] and the output of the newcomers therefore affected the earnings of their experienced colleagues. Although a system of adjusted shares was supposed to compensate for the newcomers' inexperience, expert calculations established that, on average, the deductions made from the new miner's wage did not offset his lack of output. However, this only applied to the newcomer's first few months of employment and to a small group who persisted in underworking.[17]

With time, as the new miners acquired more experience, some of them began to threaten the livelihood of the established workforce in a new way, namely by working too hard. The men responsible either were thinking of spending only a couple of years in mining and so were not concerned about long-term effects on their health, or had lost everything in the war or its aftermath and were now hell-bent on building up a home. There were two ways in which this could have a deleterious effect on the earnings of the rest of the workforce. In the first place there was the so called wage-scissors effect: higher output led to renegotiation of the piece-or-contract rate by management so that, in future, earning the same wage would require more effort. Secondly, the other workers on the face came under pressure to fit in with the higher work-pace or to leave the face for lower paid work elsewhere in the pit. Older men in particular faced an agonizing choice between taxing their health by working harder or accepting loss of earnings for the sake of easier work. This naturally aroused resentment against the newcomers.[18] Yet the extent of these problems should not be exaggerated. First of all, it was only certain parts of the community at certain tiiimes who suffered. In general, the post-war period saw a rapid rise in the miners' income. Between 1948 and 1956, miners wages almost doubled. For most miners, the post-war period was therefore one of growing prosperity. It is true that by helping to step up the pace of work, the newcomers made the miners work harder. But on the other hand, wages rose much faster than productivity. The wage-scissors effect was therefore more than counterbalanced by the rise in wage levels. Moreover, not all the established miners resented the increase in pace. As many observers testify. there were also men from the established mining community just as eager to earn every penny they could no matter what the long-term cost to their health.[19]

It is therefore not surprising that the antagonism generated by the issue remained very limited. Records of strikes and stoppages and likewise minutes of works council meetings show that there was very little organised or official protest over the newcomers' impact on pay and working conditions. Even where there *was* deep resentment, it was very difficult to give it official or organised expression. Indeed, a recent oral history project suggests that a number of older miners were so frustrated at not finding any support over the issue that they tore up their union cards in disgust.[20]

Conflicts, tensions and suspicions can of course develop even where no question of wealth or material resources is involved. Simply by virtue of the fact that they were outsiders with different social backgrounds, the refugees might have been expected to have experienced grave difficulties in finding a place in the close-knit mining communities. Certainly differences in behaviour and speech gave rise to insults and tensions; for example, only the very beefiest of expellees would last long in the Ruhr if he violently objected to being referred to as a 'Pollack', a term of abuse for Poles.[21] Tensions developed particularly between the, mostly younger, new miners in the miners' hostels and the local population. The overcrowded hostels, full of young men with little to do outside work (particularly in the early post-war years when services and recreational facilities were very limited) engendered rowdiness and drunken behaviour reminiscent of the Ruhr before the First World War. Since that date general standards of behaviour in the Ruhr had altered considerably and miners now felt their newly acquired status in the community under threat from the new miners' loutish behaviour. For their part, the newcomers were often desperate for contact with the local community, particularly the girls, and tended to feel despised and rejected. Sometimes the new miners aroused suspicion because they were the first importers of the new youth culture. An observer of the Ruhr in the 1950's recalled how a long-established citizen of Dattein had inveighed against the noisy motorbikes of young new miners. In this instance, the noisy motorbikes stopped being so terrible when her son bought one.[22]

Yet these tensions never became so serious that they could be said to have altered the nature of local life. Once a newcomer exchanged the bed in the miners' hostel for private lodgings or managed to secure the affections of a local girl, it usually proved possible to gain access to the local community.[23]

What these examples show is that many of the issues that might well have engendered conflict between newcomers and the local population were of manageable proportions. Even where the problems were severe, the amount of anger and resentment seems often to have been very limited. And even where feelings clearly did run very high, these rarely engendered direct and open conflicts.

Why was this? Perhaps the most fundamental point is that by dint of accident and deliberate policy only certain refugees were allowed into the Ruhr. In the crucial years up to 1950, by which time the vast majority (around 8 million) of the expellees who were to settle in West Germany had done so, the right to reside in the Ruhr – and in a number of other industrial areas – was tightly controlled. This was due to two simple factors: on the one hand, the shortage of undamaged housing in the industrial areas, on the other the decision by German officials and British Military Government to give the needs of industrial reconstruction priority over other considerations. By the end of the war so many houses in the Ruhr had been destroyed that the area could not house even the diminished resident population. Accordingly the authorities sent the refugees into rural areas, particularly Bavaria, Lower Saxony and Schleswig-Holstein. The Ruhr was declared a housing crisis area and people were, by and large, allowed in only if they would be making no additional demands on accommodation. The only exception was in the case of those needed for industrial reconstruction and, because of coal's unparalleled importance for economic recovery, no industry was given greater priority than mining. Even after repairs and other measures created more dwelling space in the Ruhr, the authorities in North-Rhine Westphalia remained adamant that immigration must be orientated towards the needs of industry.[24]

These constraints on entry to the Ruhr not only initially limited the number of refugees in the area but also meant that those who *were* there differed in a number of respects from the group of refugees in West Germany as a whole.

Some of these differences were the direct result of official selection procedures. Because the industry's needs were given priority, young, able-bodied refugees were favoured over other groups. That is why so few elderly people, unemployables, social cases and the like were to be found amongst the newcomers in the Ruhr. The refugees who came to the Ruhr were, by and large, able to look after themselves.

Self selection mechanisms were at work as well. Most refugees who ended up in the Ruhr had made a deliberate choice to leave the place to which they were originally directed and to come to the Ruhr in search of work. It took considerable psychological resources not to stay put in the (admittedly often miserable) conditions to which the refugees had originally been directed and to move to a new area. Those who made that decision therefore belonged to the more mobile and resourceful of the refugees. All the more so since many were moving to types of employment that were unfamiliar to them. 85% of all refugees who went into the Ruhr pits, for instance, had no mining background.[25] The refugees in the Ruhr were thus much more resourceful and adaptable than the average.

The constraints on migration to the Ruhr also affected the way in which the refugees viewed their right to be there and consequently the way in which they impinged on the community. In general, the refugee may well feel some sort of moral claim to assistance from his new hosts particularly when they belong to the same nation as he. This feeling of a right to assistance was especially strong in those areas to which the refugees had been officially directed. The refugee had been placed in a particular area by official decree – now it was up to the officials to see to his needs. In the Ruhr this did not apply since virtually all the refugees had *elected* to go there. The refugees confronted the local residents as voluntary members of the local community.

What is apparent from all this is that refugee migration to the Ruhr resembled traditional labour migration much more than it exhibited the problems and features associated with refugees elsewhere in Germany and internationally. Mass refugee populations characteristically present the host society with the problem of integrating those physically or psychologically unable to adapt to their new environment or those surplus to the needs of the local economy. This was not the case in the Ruhr. The refugees there were younger and more mobile than the average, were able and ready to perform the work which was available for them and had on the whole *elected* to join their new community. This is fundamental to understanding the refugees' impact on the Ruhr.

The admission requirements contrived to limit conflict in other ways as well. By and large the refugees were admitted to the Ruhr for one of two reasons. In the early years a number were given residence permits on the grounds that they had relatives there *if* the applicants could prove that they would not be taking up surplus living space. The only way of doing this was by moving into housing which according to the not over-generous official calculations, was already fully occupied. Often, in such cases, whole families had to occupy a single room. Provided the relatives were willing to accept this, and many were, it was possible to gain a residence permit for the Ruhr. It is impossible to calculate how many of the refugees in the Ruhr were initially drawn by family ties but local surveys indicate that the proportion may have been quite sizeable. The problems thus engendered tended to be carried within the family rather than being off-loaded onto the community. Although the shortage of room and the problems created by the over-use of domestic facilities were severe, conflict did not come out into the open. The extended family was completely overburdened, but the community was protected.[26]

The majority of refugees who gained access to the Ruhr during the years of shortage did so because they could be employed in local industry. Here too, the local community was protected from having to provide resources for unwanted guests since, for the first few months of residence at least, the refugees' permission to stay in the mines was conditional on his remaining in employment.[27]

The Ruhr was thus very fortunate in being able to control the movement and influence the composition of the incoming flow of refugees. It was equally fortunate in its priority with regard to essential resources, again in the interest of industrial recovery and with special consideration being given to the mining industry.

Resources were concentrated on the Ruhr mining industry in the form of incentive schemes for miners and, later, funds to accelerate the housing programme. Many potential conflicts between refugees and established community over the allocation of scarce resources were avoided or ended by the flow of funds and goods to the Ruhr. The bitter disputes in the first couple of years after the war over who should receive scarce supplies of work-clothes and so on were largely eliminated by the introduction of incentive schemes in 1947. In other words, the allocation of resources became less a question of established community versus newcomers than a matter of Ruhr miners, established or new, versus the rest[28] and this is one major reason why material sources of tension within the mining community remained within manageable proportions. Even in the case of continuing shortages, above all the dearth of family housing which bedeviled the mining areas until the mid-50's, perceptions of the problem were doubtless affected by the knowledge that miners had a far better chance of getting a house than almost all other groups in the Ruhr or, indeed, in the rest of the German urban population.

However, the flow of resources to the Ruhr does not explain why the refugees did not threaten the livelihood of the local miners more than they did.

The explanation for this lies above all in the favourable labour market prevailing throughout most of the post-war period.

Given the depressed nature of the economy prior to the currency reform of June 1948 it comes as something of a surprise to learn that in mid-1947 just 3% of the population of working age in the British Zone of occupation was unemployed. One reason for this was that, until the currency reform, money had little value and normal relationships between wages and production figures did not apply. There was no pressure on employers to streamline their workforces and many big industrial companies were hoarding labour in the hope of an imminent resumption of production.[29] Moreover the Ruhr housing shortage and official immigration policy were keeping surplus labour out. On the demand side there were, both before and after 1948, enormous war losses to be filled. Although it was short of shelter, the Ruhr was the 'Land der Arbeit', the land of work. Between 1945 and 1958 the Ruhr mining industry, for example, hired over a million men of whom some 300,000 were newcomers to the region.[30] The experience of the Ruhr mines here typified that of the many industries in post-war Germany which needed to tap new sources of recruitment to achieve recovery and sustained growth. True, the scale of the 'invasion' in the Ruhr mining industry was to a certain extent unusual. Long-term manpower problems in the industry had produced particularly acute labour shortages in the immediate post-war period, thereby creating a massive demand for new labour. Another problem specific to mining was that, during the 1950's, high labour fluctuation resulted in continuing labour shortages despite the fact that the workforce was hardly growing overall. Finally mining was also unusual in that its reconstruction began earlier than most other industries because of its importance for the German and international economies. At a time when the Western occupying powers were still restricting general production levels, strenuous attempts were being made to restore pre-war output in mines. Many refugees entering the Ruhr therefore went, at least initially, to the mines. But the underlying features were not restricted to coal-mining: war losses and dislocations had resulted in a considerable depletion of German workforces which could not be made good from traditional local sources of labour. Even after these losses had been replaced, rapid economic expansion meant that the number of vacancies did not subside so that, although unemployment rose sharply after the currency reform to reach a peak in 1950, it never exceeded 5% in North-Rhine Westphalia and had already fallen well below that figure 12 months later. Because of the speed of economic recovery unemployment in the Federal Republic as a whole fell by almost one-third between 1950 and 1958.[31] For the mining industry in particular this meant that the supply of labour was considerably in excess of demand only for the period autumn 1948 to 1950. By 1951, the mines were no longer finding it easy to expand their workforces.[32] Thus, as far as the miners were concerned, the refugees did not constitute a reserve army of labour large enough to threaten local livelihood.

Next to the privileged status of the Ruhr, it is this pattern of labour demand that explains why conflict and tension remained within limits. The new miners, whose mobility and resourcefulness have already been noted, were well aware that they would find other employment if they left the mines or even the Ruhr and indeed between 1945 and 1953 over a thousand men left the Ruhr pits every week.[33] This indicated that the new miners were not afraid of the consequences of leaving the industry. The employers were never, or only briefly, in a position to exploit the newcomers' anxiety over employment.

These statistics also underline the fact that the absence of serious conflict did not imply that all refugees were smoothly integrated into the local community. Some left the Ruhr entirely and the majority of newcomers who came to the mines did not stay there. What did *not* take place was the growth of a group of embittered and unintegrated outsiders bringing conflict and tension into local life.

Yet it should not be assumed that conflict was avoided simply by encouraging or forcing newcomers to leave who did not find conditions acceptable. Major efforts *were* undertaken to integrate the newcomers and this too is an essential part of the Ruhr experience. Above all the institutions and established organs of interest representation in the Ruhr did not favour the locals at the expense of the newcomers. Take the example of housing: much of the available housing belonged to the mines and allocation was controlled jointly by management and works councils, the latter ensuring that the miners' union also had strong influence on the process. If these institutions had favoured the established workforce in allocating housing stock, the result, despite the other favourable aspects of the Ruhr situation, would probably have been unrest and conflict between newcomers and the rest. Such a bias would have been understandable, given the close contact between members of the establishedd workforce and trades union, works council and management. Yet, whilst the newcomers probably did not always receive their fair share, a number of sources show that the competent new miner who had proved his worth had no difficulty in exerting influence.[34]

Why did trade union, works council and management prove responsive in this way? No doubt love for their fellow man played its part, but there were sound economic reasons too. At least until the early 1950's, the union was nervous that the employers might exploit the newcomers to undermine the living standard of the established workforce. The miners were vulnerable here because unlike some other professions the newcomers could easily acquire their skills and threaten their jobs. Driven by its fear of the creation of a division between the two groups, the union sought continually to integrate the new men; unions and works councillors realised that they simply could not afford to be biased towards the established workforce.[35]

For its part, management recognised the value of capable workers willing to stay in the industry, particularly as the state of the labour market for most of the period in question made replacing them difficult and costly. At the same time, of course, there were sound economic reasons for not ignoring the wishes of the experienced workers for while they might not be so likely to leave, if they grew too resentful of the outsiders, productivity would be affected.[36]

Thus it was in the material interest of both management and trade unions to treat both groups equitably. Only for a brief period was this not the case: in the immediate post-war period, British Military Government saw enlarging the workforce as the sole means to increase coal production and did not believe that the very low productivity of the experienced miners could be raised in the prevailing conditions. Given this, it made economic sense to ignore the demands of the experienced workers and channel all the available work-clothes and so on to the newcomers; the one-sided distribution was a principle reason for the established workforce's great bitterness during this period. The policy was altered when it became obvious that the positive effect of fair distribution on established miners' morale was more beneficial than cramming in as many new miners as possible and many of the conflicts over allocation disappeared. This provides a clear demonstration of the importance of economic pressures in the limitation of conflict between new and established miners.[37]

There was really only one issue which neither the favoured status of the Ruhr, nor the condition of the labour market, nor the economic pressure to meet the needs of the refugees could avert or alleviate, and that was the tension generated by the refugees' demands of compensation for losses sustained in the expulsion. This was also, incidentally, the one issue which did not involve the other new miners. Here, the refugees did not confront the community as homeless and needy workers but as a group with a moral claim on the nation. Conflict could hardly develop over the issue within the community since the question of *Lastenausgleich*, the sharing of burdens, was thrashed out at a much higher political level. But most of the other miners viewed the refugees' claims with scepticism, and some, who had themselves sustained major losses as a result of the war but had received no compensation, were particularly bitter. Nothing else aroused such long-lasting animosity and rancour as the fact that the expellees were able, thanks to compensation payments, to build their own homes while many local miners remained in rented accommodation.[38]

In effect the refugees' claim to compensation manifested the one point where the moral economy of the local population diverged substantially from that of the refugees. In most other respects, the Ruhr miners proved themselves to be a remarkably tolerant and open group, quite unlike the village populations that refugees encountered in rural areas. As one former newcomer to the Ruhr observed in retrospect: 'The ones I really feel sorry for are the unfortunates who came from the East and landed in Holstein or the Münsterland: Münster, now there it's terrible! – There, even today the expellee is often still a second class citizen as far as the locals are concerned. Here in the Ruhr it's not like that.'[39] There were many reasons for this but one which is worthy of mention was the happy accident that many of the Ruhr miners were themselves second generation migrants from the same areas as the refugees. This alone was sufficient to ensure the refugees a much more welcoming reception than the foreign guest workers who succeeded them in the 1960's.

It is evident that many of the conditions limiting conflict in the Ruhr were unique to that area or, at most, applied to certain other industrial areas where housing shortages led to the introduction of similar restrictions and selection. Such areas were favoured at the cost of the 'refugee states' – Bavaria, Schleswig-Holstein and Lower Saxony, which were unable to place restrictions on who crossed their borders and were forced to care for people whom the Ruhr, for example, would not accept. Thus the Ruhr's experience cannot be used as a guide to the level of conflict in the 'refugee states'.

In the long term the Ruhr experience *does* help to explain the lack of conflict in the nation as a whole. First of all, the industries of the Ruhr continued to grow rapidly and absorbed ever more refugees from the other regions so that, in the long term, the refugee states were able to ease their refugee problem by exporting surplus labour to the Ruhr. Secondly, many of the conditions observed in the Ruhr *did* develop in other parts of Germany once economic growth had begun to soak up surplus labour in those regions too. What examination of the Ruhr cannot do is to explain how it was possible, without endangering the development of political stability in West Germany, to introduce the ruthless prioritisation and favouritism upon which the recovery and limited social conflict in the Ruhr depended.[40] There is no doubt in the economic logic behind the decision to protect the Ruhr, a decision which had very positive social consequences for the region and ultimately benefitted the nation as a whole, but there is equally no doubt that behind the success story of the Ruhr there lay the misery of millions of refugees condemned to sit it out in the rural regions of West Germany until the industrial heartland was ready to take them.

Notes: Chapter 11

1   The material for this piece was gained during research work for my PhD, 'New Miners in the Ruhr: Rebuilding the Workforce in the Ruhr mines 1945–1958, Warwick, 1987.

I am indebted to the German Academic Exchange Service, the Leverhulme Trust and the German Historical Institute, London, for enabling me to carry out the field-work in Germany. I am also very grateful to my mother for eliminating some of the gravest stylistic excesses from the manuscript.

2   See for example the studies on North-Rhine Westphalia and Bavaria in Wolfgang Benz (hrsg): *Die Vertreibung der Deutschen aus dem Osten*, Frankfurt am Main, 1985.

3   An important exception to this rule is the ongoing research project at the University of Düsseldorf, headed by Falk Wiesemann, which looks at the refugees in North-Rhine Westphalia.

4   E.g. the autobiographical novel from Hans-Dieter Baroth: *Aber es waren schöne Zeiten*, Cologne, 1978.

5   Author's estimate based on G. Ludwig, 'Der Wandel in der Zusammensetzung der Grubenbelegschaft seit dem Kriegsende ...', in *Glueckauf*, 1949, 85, 35/36, pp. 625-636; H. Croon and K. Utermann, *Zeche und Gemeinde*, Tübingen, 1958, p. 294, Appendix 9; the Volume 'Statistik' of the Mines' Reception Camp, Heisingen, in possession of the Gesamtverband des deutschen Steinkohlenbergbaus, Essen (henceforth 'Statistik').

6   Franz J. Bauer, 'Aufnahme und Eingliederung der Flüchtlinge und Vertriebenen. Das Beispiel Bayern 1945-1950', in Wolfgang Benz, op.cit., pp. 158-172, here p. 166.

7   Manfred Overesch: *Deutschland 1945-1949. Vorgeschichte und Gruendung der BRD. Ein Leitfaden in Darstellung und Dokumenten*, Koenigstein/Ts. & Düsseldorf, 1979; p.41.

8   On the former professions of the new miners see Croon, op.cit., p.296; Ludwig, op.cit., p. 629 and volume 'Statistik', op.cit.

9   Figures based on sources in note 5, also on statistics from the German Coal Board (Deutsche Kohlenbergbauleitung (DKBL)), the Employers' Asociation Statistical Group (Statistik der Kohlenwirtschaft e.V.(St.d.Kw.)), and the Mining Section of Regional Labour Office (Aussenstelle Bergbau des Landesarbeitsamts NRW). A further source for checking the regional estimates were the very detailed figures for the Shamrock mine to be found in Hibernia Konzern (hrsg), *Sozialbericht 1957*, Berne, 1958.

10 *Hochlamarker Lesebuch. Kohle war nicht alles. 100 Jahre Ruhrgebietsgeschichte*, Oberhausen, 1981.

11 ibid., p. 195 ff.

12 Although the refugees made up 1/6th of the population of North-Rhine Westphalia, the State which contains the Ruhr, the refugee party, the Bund der Heimatvertriebenen und Entrechteten (BHE) gained only 4.6% of the votes in that region in 1954 and 2.7% in 1955. Results in Falk Wiesemann: 'Flüchtlingspolitik in Nordrhein-Westfalen', in Wolfgang Benz, op.cit., pp. 173-182, here p. 173.

13 Letter from Direktor, Zeche Gneisenau, to Personalabt., Harpener Bergbau A. G. (HBAG), 1.8.46, betr. 'Arbeitskleidung für Umschüler' (copy) and subsequent letter from Versorgungszentrale des deutschen Steinkohlenbergbaus to HBAG, 12.8.1946, betr. 'Arbeitskleidung für Bergumschüler', both in the works archive of the Zeche Gneisenau, Dortmund (AZG), File : 1 26 'Zuweisung von Arbeitskräften aus anderen Bezirken' 1.11.1945-31.10.1956.

14 A view expressed in 'Drängendes Problem', *Welt am Sonntag*, 23 August 1948, which can be found in the newspaper cuttings archive of the Mining Union, Bochum (Industriegewerkschaft Bergbau und Energie, (IGBE)), File 'Arbeitskräfte für den Bergbau. Neubergleute. 1945-1952'.

15 The records of the works council of the mine Friedrich der Grosse, for example, contain minutes of only one meeting where resentment over housing was voiced. Minutes of meeting on 20.4.1948, in Bergbau-Archiv, Bochum (BBA) File 10/507. Similarly the detailed minutes of the workforce meetings at the Emscher-Lippe mine do not reveal untoward bitterness over the allocation of housing. BBA 35:234-237.

16 In 1949, just over 2/3 of the face workers were covered by group contract wages (Kameradschafts-und Gruppengedinge). Hans Walther: 'Die Entwicklung der Gedinge im Jahre 1954 im Vergleich zu den Jahren 1949-1950 im westdeutschen Steinkohlenbergbau', in *Glückauf* 1955; 91; 9/10; pp. 217-226, here p. 221, Table 10.

17 Roelen: 'Klarheit und Wahrheit in Lohn und Leistung . . . ', appendix to a letter from Walther to Bergwerksdirector Bergwerksassessor Kleine, 10.1.1949, in AZGfl file : 1 13 'Gedinge Regelung 1.1.1945-31.12.1953'; and see letter from Oberbergamt,

Dortmund to HQ North German Coal Control (NGCC) Mines Inspection Control, 10.1.1947, appendix: 'Kurzbericht über die Lage im Ruhrkohlenbergbau für November 1946', in the Archive of the Landesoberbergamt Dortmund (OBAD), File: I 8010, Bd.2. 1.1.1947-30.9.1947, doc. : 8010/28/47.

18 Carl Jantke: *Bergmann und Zeche: Die sozialen Arbeitsverhältnisse einer Schachtanlage des nördlichen Ruhrgebiets in der Sicht der Bergleute*, Tuebingen, 1953; p.46 and p.75; Rudolf Schmitz: *Das Gedinge, seine Bedeutung und seine Wirkung auf die zwischenmenschlichen Beziehungen im Ruhrkohlenbergbau*, Diss. re. pol. Muenster 1952, pp. 160ff; letter from the Direktor, Gneisenau to Harpener, Abt. R., 27.2.47, betr. Arbeitseinsatz und Entlohnung der Neubergleute, AZG, File : I 126 'Zuweisung von Arbeitskraeften aus anderen Bezirken 1945-1956'.

19 See: Europaeiche Gemeineschaft für Kohle und Stahl (HRSG), *Entwicklung der Löhne und die Lohnpolitik in den Industrien der Gemeinschaft 1945-1956*, Luxemburg, 1960, p. 35ff; Carl Janke, op.cit., p.76.

20 The resentment of older miners emerges in Bernd Parisius, 'Arbeiter zwischen Resignation und Integration. Auf den Spuren der Soziologie der Fünfziger Jahre', in Lutz Niethammer (hrsg): *'Hinterher merkt man, dass es richtig war, dass es schiefgegangen ist'. Nachkriegserfahrungen im Ruhrgebiet*. Berlin Bonn, 1983, pp. 107-148; on the lack of protest see the works council records in BBA Files 10/507 and 35/234-237.

21 Interviews Alfons Nowak, Herten. Interview by Ingrid Grundmann in the project Lebensgeschichte und Sozialkultur im Ruhrgebiet (LUSIR) with Paul Scheffler, Tape reference 1,2,65.

22 Croon, op.cit., p. 136-7; *Hochlamarker Lesebuch*, op.cit., p. 212; Conversation with Prof. Dr. H. Croon, Krefeld 9.4.1984.

23 Ingrid Grundmann LUSIR interviews with Hanse-Georg Stasiewsky, Paul Scheffler, Rudolf Sass, Stefan Puhr, Anton Kessner, Konrad Boronski.

24 Falk Wiesemann: 'Flüchtlingspolitik in Nordrhein-Westfalen', in W. Benze (hrsg), op.cit.; p.173-182.

25 See Gertrud Stahlberg: *Die Vertriebenen in NRW*, Berlin 1957,p.90.

26 See Dietrich v. Oppen: *Familien in ihrer Umwelt . . .* , Köln & Opladen, 1958, p. 14ff and Lutz Niethammer; 'Privatwirtschaft. Erinnerungsfragmente einer anderen Umerziehung', in Lutz Niethammer (hrsg): *'Hinterher merkt man, dass es richtig war, dass es schiefgegangen ist'*, Berlin Bonn, 1983; 170107, here p. 38ff.

27 Letter from 'Wohnungsbezirkstelle Ruhr an die Herrn Oberstadt-bzw Oberkreisdirektoren, 1.2.1947 betr. Unterbringung von Bergarbeiterzuführungen', in Hauptstaatsarchiv, Düsseldorf, File NW9:55.

28 Werner Abelshauser: *Der Ruhrkohlenbergbau seit 1945. Wiederaubau, Krise, Anpassung*, Munich, 1984, p. 36ff and p. 75ff.

29 Report by the Zentralamt für Arbeit, in the German Federal Archive, Koblenz (BAK), file 40:308.

30 Estimate based on sources in notes 5 and 9.

31 *Statisches Jahrbuch für die BRD*, vol. 1955; p.114.

32 The Bochum Group of the Gelsenkirchener Bergwerks AG could barely maintain manning levels during the Summer of 1951. See the remarks of Herr Mommerz, Bergausschusssitzung der GBAG, 24.8.1951, in BBA 55:12200 Nr.12.

33 Unpublished materials of the Statistik der Kohlnwirtschaft, e.V., Essen.

34 Interviews Nowak, Kuhn, op.cit.

35 Interview with works councillor Clemens Kreienhorst, Summer 1983.

36 The GBAG, for instance weighed up the chances of sparking off unrest amongst the traditional miners before it participated in the Resettlememt Programme housing scheme for refugees. Bergausschusssitzung der GBAG, 24.10.1951, in BBA 55:12200 Nr.12.

37 'Again and again we hear complaints from our first personnel (established workforce – MR) when we are not able to correspond to their desires concerning allocation of clothing, that the persons in question stress that assigned mining recruits (are) completely clothed (i.e. kitted out – MR) . . . ', in 'Declaration of mines' representatives at mine Gneisenau about the last transport of workers', *Zeche Gneisenau* 3.5.46, in AZG: I 126 'Zuweisung von Arbeitskräften aus anderen Bezirken 1.11.1945-31.10.1956'. What

made the matter worse was that many of those who came were unwilling conscripts and did not work properly if at all.
38 Interview Helmuth Croon, op.cit.; *Hochlamarker Lesebuch*, op.cit., pp. 213-14.
39 *Hochlamarker Lesebuch*, op.cit., p.216.
40 Falk Wiesemann, op.cit. On the role of Military Government in giving the Ruhr priority, see my piece 'Delayed Recovery. British Manpower policy in the Ruhr mines 1945-1947', in Robert Lee, *Industrialization, Industrial Growth in Germany*, Routledge, 1988.

12 Repatriation and resistance: Ukrainian refugees and displaced persons in Occupied Germany and Austria, 1945-1948

YURY BOSHYK

Helping refugees, exiles, and displaced persons return to their homelands has often been seen by national and international agencies as a humane response to their displacement. But there have been moments in history when repatriation has not been desired by the uprooted. One such moment was the period immediately following the Second World War, when more than a million people, mostly from Eastern Europe, refused to be repatriated. Their resistance created for the Western Allies and the United Nations a dilemma that involved choosing between a policy of political expediency or humanitarian concern. For the refugees, it involved several years of steadfast, organized resistance that in the end exacted a heavy toll on their identity and well being. This paper discusses official repatriation policies, with a focus on the methods used by refugees and displaced persons to resist repatriation: it pays particular attention to the case of one of the largest groups of postwar refugees, the Ukrainians.[1]

The greatest mass movement of civilians took place during and immediately after the Second World War. In Europe alone thirty million people were displaced, and by 1945 seven million non-German refugees were residing in Germany and Austria.[2] The Western Allies had foreseen difficulties in repatriating the non-Germans and for this reason had created a special branch within the military (SHAEF) and formed the United Nations Relief and Rehabilitation Administration (UNRRA) before Germany's surrender on 7–8 May 1945. Political agreements with governments-in-exile and others, such as the Soviet Union, were also signed to speed the process of repatriation.[3]

Repatriation efforts were thus organized quickly. Between 1 March and 30 September 1945 just over ten million people in Europe were repatriated. This number included more than two million Soviet nationals from the Western-controlled (SHAEF) areas of occupied Germany and Austria.[4] During May and June, the most active months, the daily rate of eastward repatriation of Soviet nationals amounted to more than 50,000 people.[5]

From the Soviet-controlled areas of Germany and Austria, about three million Soviet citizens were repatriated at this time.[6]

However, despite this mass movement, 1.5–2 million displaced persons and refugees, mostly from Eastern Europe, refused to be repatriated from the Western zones. Among them were at least 500,000 Soviet citizens, as well as Jews, Poles, Hungarians, Ukrainians, Bulgarians, Rumanians, Estonians, Latvians, Lithuanians, Czechs, Slovaks, Serbs, Croatians, and some Western Europeans.[7] Because Ukrainians did not have an independent state before the war, they were not recognized as a separate nationality by either the Western military authorities or by UNRRA officials, since eligibility for repatriation was based on citizenship rather than national origin. Thus, for official purposes, Ukrainians from outside the Soviet Union were considered citizens of their country of origin or residence in 1939 (as Poles, for example). In some cases they were designated as stateless, or as Nansen passport holders (post-First World War Russian refugees who held League of Nations passports). Those from the Soviet Union were classified as Russian or Soviet.[8] Of the almost 200,000 Ukrainians in occupied Germany and Austria who refused to be repatriated, about one third were from the Soviet Union, and the remaining two thirds were from other Eastern European countries, mainly Poland. By the time Germany and Austria were divided officially into U.S., British, French, and Soviet occupied zones (13 July 1945), most of these Ukrainians were in the American zone of Germany.[9]

The main battles on the Eastern front had taken place in areas heavily populated by Ukrainians, which helps account for the 2.5–3 million who found themselves in Germany and Austria at the end of the war. Most (about 2.3 million) were males less than thirty years old who had been taken as forced labourers. Others were post-1917 refugees (Nansen passport holders), concentration camp survivors, Polish and Soviet prisoners-of-war, former *Osttruppen* (members of Eastern European units in the German armed forces), functionaries in the German bureaucracy that administered Eastern occupied territories, and refugees who fled with the retreating Germans from the Soviets, fearing a repetition of the treatment they received from the Soviet Government in 1939–41, when after the Nazi-Soviet pact, Russia invaded Eastern Poland, and political repression, labour-camp deportations, and killings had been widespread.[10]

The postwar repatriation of Ukrainians and some other Eastern Europeans took place in two distinct phases. The first was a part voluntary, in part forced, mass repatriation, from the spring to the autumn of 1945. The second phase began in December 1945 – January 1946, when new criteria for repatriation were announced that excluded Soviet civilians, reaffirmed that no Baltic or Polish citizens would be repatriated, and thus checked the large-scale, indiscriminate repatriation of the first phase. Nevertheless, these civilians still felt threatened by the continued screenings, UNRRA's encouragement of repatriation, the harassment from Soviet repatriation officers, and the increasing hostility of the German population and the American military. The second phase continued until mid-1948, when

Ukrainians, and especially those from the Soviet Union, were finally safe from repatriation.

The First Phase of Repatriation, Spring-Autumn 1945

At the war's end conditions were not always conducive to an orderly and humanitarian treatment of displaced persons. They had been living in almost every village and city of Germany and Austria; their subsequent fate therefore depended on which army, Western or Soviet, had liberated the area first.

The political agreements governing the repatriation of foreigners in Germany and Austria gave responsibility for the refugees both to UNRRA and to the respective armed forces of the occupied zones, but in the spring and throughout the occupation period, the primary responsibility was assumed by the latter. It was not until the autumn of 1945 that UNRRA took a more active part in the repatriation programme.[11]

In the Western zones foreign nationals were placed by citizenship in guarded assembly centres, interrogated by military authorities, issued special identity cards, housed and prepared for repatriation. These centres, usually former army barracks, were not well suited to families and civilian residence. By August 1945 there were a total of 750 centres in the Western zones of Germany: 450 in the British, 250 in the U.S., and 50 in the French zone. There were several Soviet camps in the Western zones as well.[12]

What further distressed the refugees was that under the terms of the Yalta agreement, Soviet citizens were to be returned to the Soviet Union immediately. Although force was not mentioned in the Yalta agreement, when necessary it was used. The problem, however, was that the Soviet Union claimed authority over territories it had annexed in 1939–41, when the Nazi-Soviet pact divided the Baltic states and Poland between Germany and the Soviet Union. Although the United States did not formally recognize Soviet dominion over these territories, its position was not made explicit in the Yalta agreement. This non-recognition was not, however, widely known among the Western military authorities overseeing the repatriation of Eastern Europeans.[13]

A more immediate threat faced by the refugees were the Soviet repatriation teams.[14] The main responsibility of these teams was to identify former Soviet citizens, but they also designated for repatriation individuals who, before 1939, had not resided in Soviet territory but rather came from countries that fell under the postwar control or political influence of the Soviet Union.

Thus, in the first phase repatriation was indiscriminate, affected masses of people and fostered violent resistance. A dramatic example of this resistance took place in Kempten, Germany, in August 1945:

> The soldiers entered the church and began to drag the people out forcibly. They dragged the women by their hair and twisted the mens arms up their backs, beating them with the butts of their rifles. One

soldier took the cross from the priest and hit him with the butt of his rifle. Pandemonium broke loose. The people in a panic threw themselves from the second floor, for the church was in the second storey of the building, and they fell to their death or were crippled for life. In the church were also suicide attempts.[15]

Because of such incidents Western military officials were forced to clarify the eligibility criteria for immediate repatriation. In essence, displaced persons and refugees who were residing outside the Soviet Union in September 1939 (before the Nazi-Soviet pact came into effect) were not considered eligible for involuntary repatriation to the Soviet Union. This category included Baltic citizens, Poles, and Ukrainians who had lived outside the Soviet Union, but still allowed for the forced mass repatriation of Soviet Ukrainians. The military orders, however, were interpreted in many different ways by local military authorities, and even the orders from British and American central officials were sometimes contradictory.[16] As the following incident shows, confusion was widespread, and American officers held different conceptions of their responsibilities and orders.

On July 31 1945 Suzanne Chalfour, a first lieutenant in the U.S. Army stationed in Passau, Germany, wrote a strong letter of protest to the U.S. Army commanding general, 102nd Artillery, about 'the forced departure of Ukrainians for Budweis'. She insisted that the Ukrainians were being sent to the Soviet zone of occupation 'against their own free will', that 'force had been used, against all orders previously given', and that a secret order had been issued stating that 'Ukrainians as well as Lithuanians, Letons [sic] and Estonians [sic] would *not* be forced back into the Russian Zone'. But, as the letter went on to say, the officer in charge of this repatriation action claimed ignorance of this secret order and about another order from (G-5) Third Army that, 'under U.S. protection *no* one could force these people to go into the Russian zone'. Lieutenant Chalfour also added that not only had the Ukrainians been promised that they would not be repatriated but that she also had been unable to prevent their removal. Her letter went unanswered by the higher authorities.[17]

It must be noted, however, that not all British and American officers carried out orders for forcible repatriation. Some, sickened by the sight of the refugees' self-inflicted wounds, suicides and resistance, simply refused to carry out orders. Other local officers gave to displaced persons special passes or documents designed to protect them from arbitrary actions by military officials.[18] But these humanitarian gestures were more the exception than the rule.

Certainly, it is important to understand the motivations of the Western military and UNRRA officials responsible for this first phase of repatriation. Western officials seemed not to have been fully aware why Ukrainians and others did not want to go home, why they did not want to be 'productive citizens' in their own homelands, and that they perhaps wanted to conceal information about their wartime activities. Also, they were concerned for the welfare of Western POWs and personnel held in Soviet-dominated territory and perhaps believed that by adhering to the

Yalta agreement, they would ensure the safety and speedy return of their people.[19] Moreover, Western authorities were not informed about national and political repression in the Soviet Union – the main reasons why these Ukrainians refused to return. Perhaps reflecting generally accepted views and naïveté, the head of UNRRA, Fiorello La Guardia, stated that he did not understand why DPs did not want to return home just because they disagreed with their government, since he often disagreed with his government's policies but this was no reason for him not to return to his country.[20]

On the local level many soldiers were not very sympathetic to the plight of the DPs. Care and supervision of displaced persons and refugees was felt burdensome while the war with Japan was still on, and many soldiers were also hoping to return home as soon as possible. Moreover, the local German population, which was charged with the responsibility of providing housing and clothing to the displaced persons and refugees, resented them and influenced the soldiers' negative views of the DPs. A confidential report from the executive staff of UNRRA in the U.S. zone noted the existence of these negative attitudes towards refugees and displaced persons:

> [The displaced persons and refugees] . . . are held in the greatest contempt by the Germans, who lose no opportunity to discredit them in the eyes of the American Military Authorities. The effect of this derogatory influence has been strong and widespread to the point where it has seeped up from the operating levels to even the highest military echelons. The DP (Displaced Persons) problem has always been a nuisance to the Army. With redeployment, and introduction of new, untrained and unoriented military personnel, there is almost complete lack of knowledge and understanding of the factors which created the DP situation in the first place; and the subjection of the Americans [sic] mind to German influence has been such that there is even less human sympathy and consideration than there is understanding. The DP are generally considered by military personnel as 'lousy Poles' and 'Goddam DP' who should be sent back where they came from whether they like it or not.[21]

Local military officials were also more inclined to listen to the views of the Soviet Union, an official wartime ally, rather than to the views of the refugees. And Soviet propaganda was resolute and relentless. 'Non-returnees' were labelled 'collaborators' and 'idlers' who preferred the relative 'comfort' of the camps.[22] The Soviets insisted that their citizens had to be returned at all costs to undermine any potential anti-Stalinist *emigré* resistance abroad and to protect their citizens from Western influences.[23] All Soviet nationals were to make their way to Soviet repatriation camps by 10 November 1945 or be arrested 'and sent on the road to the police'.[24]

The Western Allies, therefore, did not appreciate the fate that awaited Soviet citizens and other Eastern Europeans. Considered traitors and class enemies for having left the Soviet Union (a treasonable offence under Soviet law) most returnees were harshly punished even though most were the victims of Nazi forced labour policies.[25] The refugees, however, were well aware of the welcome they would receive from the secret police and even from their compatriots, who were led to believe that only collaborators and traitors remained alive in Germany after the war.[26] Those who refused to return tried to defend themselves and to protest as best they could against the use of force and against Soviet activities.

Resistance of Ukrainian Refugees to Repatriation

In the chaotic months of May and June 1945 Ukrainian DPs and refugees formed self-help committees to assist those who resisted repatriation. These committees demanded the formation of separate Ukrainian camps, and their demand met with some success: at the end of May, an unofficial liaison with the Western authorities was created, thus ensuring at least a hearing for Ukrainian DP concerns.[27]

The committees also tried to bring the matter of forcible repatriation to the attention of Western leaderss. The Ukrainian committee in Neubeuern wrote several letters to President Truman, to Herbert Lehman, head of UNRRA in Washington, to the President of the International Red Cross in Geneva, and to General Eisenhower. Unfortunately, their letters were never received, because the UNRRA officials to whom the letters were sent for forwarding did not send them on.[28]

However, Ukrainians in Western Europe and North America proved to be a great source of assistance. In September 1945, when the desperate situation of DPs became widely known, relief committees were organized in Belgium, France, Switzerland, Canada, and the United States to help the DPs and refugees and lobby for their welfare. They augmented the DPs' publishing of anti-repatriation literature and pressured their respective governments to resettle the refugees. Especially effective in this work were servicemen of Ukrainian background in the Canadian and American armies. Religious leaders also helped convince the Vatican to intervene on the refugees' behalf.[29]

At times expressions of protest against repatriation took an especially tragic form: among the so-called 'Easterners', suicide was a common occurrence.[30] Sometimes, the desperate situation led to threats of mass suicide, as is shown in this cablegram from the Ukrainian Relief Committee in Belgium to the Ukrainian Canadian Committee:

> . . . Ukrainian DPs requested the Military Government in Mannheim that they be granted an extension of two weeks, in order to enable them to receive the Holy Sacrament in preparation for mass suicide, upon hearing the order published a day prior, that is, on December 5, 1945, by the Office of Military Government in the American zone (S.P.O. 758), about forcible deportation to the Soviets.[31]

Another way Ukrainians tried to escape repatriation was to live outside the camps. In the American zone more than one fifth of the Ukrainians managed to stay away from the camps.[32] Others roamed from camp to camp, but this was a more dangerous alternative, because the DPs became easy prey for Soviet agents.[33] For Soviet Ukrainians the most common method of defence against repatriation was fabrication or falsification of documents. Overnight, they became citizens of Poland, claiming pre-1939 residence in that country. These false papers were produced on a massive scale by Catholic priests, political groups and enterprising individuals, who most often used cut potatoes or warm eggs for affixing authorization stamps. The scale of this effort is revealed by the following statistic: in June 1949 106,549 Ukrainians claimed Polish citizenship – up from 9,190 in December 1945.[34] In addition to the fabrication of documents, this eye-witness account tells of bolder methods used by the Soviet Ukrainians:

Saved from the 'motherland' were only those lucky enough to be 'recoloured' in one way or another to a Polish or some other colour – even to a Turkish one. . . . I helped about ten people by advising them to leave their personal belongings in the barracks . . . lose or leave behind their documents with the German factory owner; move to the Polish camp and declare themselves as Poles. But to do this was, naturally, difficult and dangerous because the camp literally teemed with Soviet officials and secret Soviet spies.[35]

A price had to be paid for these attempts to create a new identity. During the screening of DPs (which is further discussed in the section on the second phase of repatriation) interviewees were often asked details about hometown landmarks, churches, street names, and, of course, the language of the country of claimed citizenship. Such questioning caused considerable alarm, and DPs became distraught in their efforts to learn everything possible about their newly claimed personal identities.

In their attempts to protect themselves against and identify Soviet spies and collaborators in the camps, Soviet Ukrainians relied on their judgment and personal acquaintances, but they very often had to defend themselves from Ukrainian underground political groups, in particular the Bander and Melnyk factions of the Organization of Ukrainian Nationalists (OUN). First established in the Ukrainian areas of Poland, these groups' main goals were to achieve independence for Ukraine and unite both Western and Eastern Ukraine. These factions became influential among Ukrainians after the collapse of moderate Ukrainian parties during the war.[36] Control over the DP population was part of the OUN's larger scheme to keep morale and commitment high for the anticipated return to Ukrainian territory and confrontation with the Soviet Union. The OUN was convinced that its goal of independence for Ukraine was at hand, since an underground armed struggle, led by the OUN, was continuing in Western Ukraine. The OUN also believed, like some Western military personnel, that war with the Soviet Union was inevitable and that the West would help liberate Ukraine from Soviet rule.[37]

The Bandera faction of the OUN was the most influential political group in the camps.[38] Through its network of conspirators its members were able to take over most of the important positions and functions within the camps – first the internal camp police force, then the food supplies, and finally, the internal camp administration. Since Western authorities allowed the camps to be self-governed, it was relatively easy for these political groups to assume control by enforcing party discipline or by intimidating opponents. The Bandera faction on occasion used force against alleged Soviet spies, Soviet officials, and its own perceived enemies, including members of rival political factions. Some DPs claimed that political murders were committed in the camps against those who dared to speak out against the faction. And individuals were 'terrorized' by the Bandera faction for not giving enough money to the group's fundraising events and collections. The Banderites claimed that this money was for the liberation of Ukraine but never gave any public accounting of these funds.[39]

Needless to say, these tactics exacerbated tensions between Polish and Soviet Ukrainians, but the seeds of mistrust had been sown earlier. Members of the OUN, who were strongly anti-socialist and anti-Soviet, were suspicious of Soviet Ukrainians, believing them to be insufficiently nationalistic and tainted by communism. And although in the camps co-operation between the two groups was a matter of necessity, relations were often tense, leading Soviet Ukrainians to believe they were misunderstood and discriminated against.[40] In one DP camp a leaflet was circulated that protested their treatment by members of the OUN:

> Ukrainians! Enough is Enough! The Galicians (Western Ukrainians) have seized power in all our camps. They pretend to be our older brothers, they take to caring for us and teaching us . . . We extricated ourselves from Stalin and Hitler, and we will not let anyone rule over us. In all camps – Polish, Baltic, and Russian, people live in safety and peace. Only in Ukrainian camps our 'older brothers' have created a system of terror and suffocation. We too want to live under the guardianship of the democratic order. We have had enough of dictatorship. We demand the removal of the Galicians from the Ukrainian camps![41]

The two OUN factions tried to control all Ukrainian organizations in the camps, but while the refugees were united in their resistance to repatriation, most did not join the OUN or the other political groups. Indeed, the majority were less concerned with factional disputes than they were with personal matters. One observer, for example, noted a greater interest in religion and increased church attendance among the refugees.[42] Another commentator noted what he and others termed 'DP apathy': growing demoralization and hopelessness among the DPs that led to a lack of concern with life outside the camps.[43]

Second Phase of Repatriation

The American policy of forced repatriation for *all* former Soviet citizens (and often indiscriminate repatriation of Eastern Europeans) was altered in late 1945 and early 1946 to exclude Soviet civilians.[44] The reasons ranged from an unease with forcible repatriation, the intervention of political leaders such as Eleanor Roosevelt against repatriation, to the realization that the West was not gaining concessions from the Soviets. Forcible repatriation still applied, however, to three categories of Soviet refugees and displaced persons: those who were (a) 'captured in German uniforms: (b) members of the Soviet Armed Forces on and after 22 June 1941 and who were not subsequently discharged therefrom; and; (c) those charged by the Soviet Union with having voluntarily rendered aid and comfort to the enemy...' Perhaps to placate the Soviet Union, the directive reiterated the American determination to repatriate all those who were 'citizens and actually present within the Soviet Union on 1 September 1939' (that is, before the Nazi-Soviet pact), and who did not fall within the three categories. In no uncertain terms, however, were U.S. military personnel to use force to repatriate Soviet citizens, besides those included in the three categories.[45]

The U.S. military command also affirmed that Baltic nationals and Poles were exempt from forcible repatriation.[46] This was of enormous importance to the Polish Ukrainians, who were now much more secure. What also saved Polish Ukrainians who refused to return to their homeland was the Polish government's unwillingness to allow its former citizens of Ukrainian nationality back into the country. This reluctance was not only the legacy of bitter Polish-Ukrainian relations after the First World War, but also of an agreement between Poland and the Soviet Union, made on 9 September 1944, that Ukrainians from pre-war Poland would be resettled in the former Polish lands now part of Soviet Ukraine.[47]

As a result of these changes in American policy the number of repatriated Soviet nationals dropped dramatically. One writer on repatriation claims that repatriations ceased entirely during November-December 1945, increased to 972 in February 1946 but continued at a rate of 11 persons per day for the next eight months in the Western zones of Germany. The figures for Poles were higher, but they were at least half of what they were in October 1945 and repatriation was strictly voluntary.[48]

The new repatriation policy also meant that different strategies had to be initiated for dealing with Polish Ukrainian and Soviet Ukrainian political refugees and DPs. The goal was still repatriation of as many people as possible, but the methods were to be different. The British authorities, on the other hand, adopted the American policy only several months later.[49]

It must be stressed that this change of policy did not mean that Soviet citizens would no longer be encouraged to return to the U.S.S.R., or that co-operation between the Western Allies and the Soviet Union would no longer take place. The new order in January 1946 gave Soviet repatriation teams 'free access' to Soviet DPs, if requested by the Soviets, 'for the purpose of persuading' Soviet citizens to return. Soviet authorities were also permitted to 'furnish lists and addresses of Soviet Nationals who are charged with collaboration with the enemy and who were subject to the provisions' (outlined in the directive of January 1946). On receiving such lists, U.S. Army district commanders were to 'take measures to collect the individuals listed therein and place them in camps, where they will be held pending screening and examination of charges against them'. However, 'if addresses given are erroneous, Military Authorities will not be required to conduct a search'.[50]

This order also instructed U.S. officers to take whatever practical measures were necessary to minimize resistance to repatriation and the dissemination of anti-repatriation propaganda. Among the specific measures mentioned were the 'segregation of known leaders of resistance groups; [and] the separation of existing groups into smaller groups' (that is, movement to other camps).[51] It was further suggested that UNRRA's cultural and educational courses for the DPs should not be developed too well or allowed to become too popular so as not to encourage DPs and Soviet citizens to remain in the West.[52]

To make matters worse for the refugees, President Truman's Secretary of State, James F. Byrnes, announced in March 1946 that the U.S. government was considering closing the camps in August-September 1946. His statement was intended to pressure the DPs into choosing repatriation.[53]

In March 1946 UNRRA also took measures to increase repatriation by stepping up its co-operation with Soviet and Eastern European authorities.[54] At the same time, the American authorities and UNRRA attempted to ascertain more precisely how many of the remaining DPs and political refugees fitted into the new categories mentioned above, how many wanted to be repatriated, and the reasons why so many refused to go home.

In the first two weeks of May 1946 UNRRA conducted a poll among the DPs in its assembly centres in Germany. Three questions were asked: '(1) What nationality do you claim? (2) Do you wish to be repatriated now? (Yes, No) (3) If you answer to 2 is 'no', explain your reasons in the space below.' The results were overwhelmingly against repatriation, and although the Ukrainians were not designated separately in the results, there is no question that Ukrainians (classified as Poles or Russians or Undetermined) voted against repatriation, as did the Balts, only 2 per cent of whom expressed a desire to return home.

What is of interest in UNRRA's report on the poll is the analysis of the negative votes as well as the reasons given for not wanting to return to the 'homeland': ' . . . nationals of so-called Western countries give both personal and economic reasons for not going home now, while the Eastern Europeans generally fall back on political factors as their primary explanation. The Eastern Europeans seem to show a real fear in their replies, the fear increasing the further east the home of the voter.'[55]

This report also was one of the first and most comprehensive attempts to assess why Ukrainian DPs refused to go home:

. . . Like the Poles, they give mainly political reasons for not wanting to return home but they are generally more violent in their attacks on Russia, and expressed fear of forced labour conditions, even 'deportation to Siberia,' should they dare to return. Some give supposed first hand accounts of previous persecution . . . About 10% of the Ukrainians included in their reasons descriptions of the absence of political, cultural, religious and personal freedom at home, while others compared 'Bolshevik totalitarianism' with Nazism. They claim that their country is occupied and since they do not wish to become citizens of the U.S.S.R., they have in effect no fatherland to which to return . . . Ukrainians . . . seem much more concerned over the lack of religious freedom than do the Poles . . . Others merely stated their dislike for a system where there is no private property.[56]

Despite the nearly unanimous refusal by Eastern European refugees to return home, Western authorities and UNRRA continued their efforts to repatriate. As part of this process, widespread screening of DPs was conducted.[57] For the U.S. Army, the main purpose of screening was to determine whether those in the camps and elsewhere were legitimate non-returnees, that is, they did not fall into one of the three categories for forcible repatriation. For UNRRA, the screening process was designed to ensure that the DPs in its care were eligible for assistance.[58]

Screening was intensified after a decision was reached by the United States not to close the camps, as had been previously announced by Secretary of State Byrnes. Instructions to the chief officers of the U.S. occupying forces, Generals Clark and McNarney, stated, 'Indefinite postponement of closing of DP camps necessitates that screening of DPs remaining in centers be intensified rather than discontinued, and that those found ineligible for UN treatment be promptly discharged from assembly centers or placed under arrest or forcibly repatriated in accordance with existing directives'.[59]

Some aspects of these screenings caused great fear among Ukrainian DPs and refugees. The presence of Soviet officials during these screenings was particularly intimidating. The U.S. military seems to have been inconsistent in allowing Soviet participation; for example, in the American zone of Germany, Soviet liaison officers from the Soviet Repatriation Commissions were not part of the screening teams except as consultants. As one report noted: 'DPs are generally suspicious and hostile to liaison officers and experience has demonstrated better results are obtained by excluding them from screening teams.' Specifically, experience had taught them that ' . . . Soviet officers tend to denounce without evidence as collaborators any person who does not demand immediate repatriation'.[60]

The American military was also aware that Soviet repatriation officers were using these screening operations to gather intelligence. At the same time, the generals complained to headquarters that the shortage of American screening officers who knew foreign languages put the Americans at a distinct disadvantage during the screenings and did not allow for a thorough vetting of DPs. General Clark wrote to his superiors about the problem: 'U.S. officers who can speak [the] language must supervise [Soviet] liaison officers to avoid their screening and repatriation activity being used to cloak intelligence work. U.S. officers used to screen independently must have fluent command of languages as well as the ability to detect and evaluate discrepancies in testimony and documents.'[61]

The shortage of qualified officers was so acute that sometimes committees of DPs were used on a limited scale to 'certify others of their nationality', but U.S. authorities found that there were considerable problems with this arrangement. As one officer pointed out, these committees had to be used with 'caution in view of the antagonistic political factions among DPs'.[62] Presumably, members of one faction betrayed individuals from other factions, causing them to lose their DP status and be evicted from the camps. Nonetheless, the shortage of trained U.S. personnel and the sometimes 'casual' screenings saved some DPs from losing their status.

In the American zone in Austria, however, Soviet authorities were allowed to sit on what was called the 'Soviet-U.S. Screening Board'. The French also allowed the Soviets to do the same. These rather flexible arrangements changed over time but perhaps they explain why, in Austria, 730 DPs found to be Soviet citizens in May and June of 1946 were repatriated, while in Germany those found to be Soviet citizens were only evicted from the DP camps but not repatriated.[63]

The DPs being screened would never know in advance what questions would be asked, nor were they told quickly whether they had passed the screening and were still *bona fide* DPs. As late as May 1947 Maria Iurkevych, the wife of the former pre-1917 political activist Lev Iurkevych, wrote to a friend that three months after her last screening, she still did not know the outcome. For a sixty-four year old woman very much concerned with her daily subsistence, this was a very trying experience.[64] To lose DP status was a catastrophe, given the severe economic crisis in the occupied areas, and loss of DP status also made it very difficult to emigrate from Germany.[65] To avoid such a catastrophe, 'Polish, Yugoslav, Russian (and Ukrainian) DPs tended to support each other in opposition to screening by liaison officers regardless of past differences'.[66]

For some refugees, the screening process seemed interminable. A January 1947 report from officials in the American zone in Austria mentioned that the DPs had to go before three separate screening committees, which were conducted by the Soviet repatriation mission, by the Intergovernmental Committee on Refugees, and by an UNRRA official, Dr. Bedo. Many families were separated when the screenings determined that one member of the family was considered ineligible for UNRRA support, and hundreds lost their DP status in 1946-47. Black flags were hung in the camps whenever the results of the screening were announced and hunger strikes were started. Thousands of Ukrainians demonstrated in sympathy and solidarity with those who lost their status, as for example, after a screening at Hindenburg Kaserne, where 230 people were evicted from the camp simply because they were 'Soviet citizens', even though they did not fall into the three categories for repatriation. Thus the ruling was clearly in violation of the new orders of January 1946, but when the error was rectified it was too late to locate the evictees. They had scattered to other camps or found other accommodation.[67]

Other forms of assistance with repatriation were also given to Soviet and Eastern European officials by Western authorities. One new tactic was the so-called '60-day ration scheme'. In October 1946 UNRRA offered each DP willing to be repatriated food rations for sixty days, to be handed over at the frontiers of their country. This programme, however, did not meet with much success despite the general decline in rations – a deliberate gesture intended to encourage repatriation.[68]

It was also a matter of official U.S. Army policy to 'facilitate' direct Soviet contact with DPs of Soviet, Baltic, and 'Ukrainian' origin. Soviet liaison officers could visit the camps and request lists of DPs the U.S. Military Authorities had determined were Soviet citizens: the officers could also interview these individuals or groups (including Baltic nationals) with the purpose of persuading them to repatriate. During these visitations, the Soviet officers were to be accompanied by U.S. representatives, preferably military personnel and guards, and in no instance were threats or force to be used. For their part, the Americans were given full authority to 'control' DPs who 'deliberately wished to instigate hostile or riotous action calculated to interfere with the normal privileged functions of the Soviet Liaison Officer while visiting the camp'. Moreover, U.S. military personnel were to help Soviet officers distribute Soviet repatriation literature, posters, and films in the camps.[69]

This co-operation resulted in considerable psychological pressure on Ukrainian and other Eastern European DPs, as is shown by the following March 1947 report from the Director of UNRRA's Landeck Camp in the French zone of Austria:

> During the visits of the Soviet representatives every effort was made to persuade the people to talk to the (Soviet) officers, to ask questions and to get information. Very little result. No active hostility was shown to the Soviet representatives, but a marked indifference. Soviet literature is available in the library and in addition distributed to each barrack. (The supply being ample). The peasant class are repeatedly informed that they are wanted in their own country and have nothing to fear. The cultivator being the backbone of the country. The professional classes are told that their diplomas are of very little use in any country but their own. Every repatriation appeal is translated, distributed, and broadcasted over loudspeakers. English conversation classes are conducted by all (UNRRA) team members and repatriation is urged and recommended at these classes. The people are repeatedly informed that UNRRA in the camp ceases on June 30th of this year (1947), and that their future after this in Austria is full of doubts.
>
> The UNRRA camp director interviewed personally all displaced persons in the camp who were professionals, to try to persuade them to return. He reported, however, that his efforts to encourage the DP camp leaders to form a repatriation committee met with 'passive resistance'.[70]

Soviet authorities were untiring in their efforts to ensure the return of even those DPs who were exempted from forcible repatriation by the new policy of January 1946. One method was to discredit prominent individuals, usually Ukrainian leaders, by charging that they were Nazi collaborators. Through the press, public forums such as the United Nations, various international commissions, and then through formal submissions to Western military authorities, they tried to influence public opinion against the DPs and were successful in having several people investigated. In the end, however, all that the Soviet efforts and investigations accomplished was harassment of the individuals in question.[71]

The Soviets also complained about anti-repatriation propaganda distributed in the camp by what they called 'fascist' and nationalistic organisations (presumably referring to the OUN and its factions) but U.S. military intelligence replied that it could not find any evidence to support their charge.[72] As for anti-repatriation literature produced by the DPs and by Ukrainians abroad, UNRRA and U.S. military authorities prohibited such material from being disseminated.[73]

Another oft-repeated Soviet charge was that these organisations were forcibly preventing those who wanted to return home from doing so – a charge the Soviets later levelled (and still do) against Western governments.[74]

In their efforts to repatriate Ukrainian DPs and refugees, the Soviet officials resorted to elaborate methods. Soviet sympathizers and local Communist Party members in the West attacked the reputation both of individuals and the refugees as a group. For example, well-known pro-Soviet Ukrainians in Canada, such as Vasyl Svystun, denounced the DPs as war criminals and Nazi collaborators.[75] In the United States some Ukrainian front organizations, such as the Ukrainian-American Fraternal Union, tried to persuade U.S. authorities that many 'Ukrainian war criminals, quislings, and collaborators' were among the DPs and refugees.[76]

Finally, mention should be made of another Soviet method of repatriating Ukrainians – kidnapping. We have already mentioned the kidnappings of DPs from the Western zones of occupied Germany, but as early as 1945 Soviet secret policemen seized Ukrainian *emigrés* living in Czechoslovakia. This action violated international law because those kidnapped (who, for the most part, had participated in the 1917 revolution or, since that time in various Ukrainian-Governments-in-Exile) were Nansen passport holders. These individuals, among them Valentyn Sadovs'kyi, Maksym Slavins'kyi and others, were brought to the Soviet Union and given severe sentences. Being men in their late 60s and 70s, most either died in prison or in concentration camps.[77] In Italy, Soviet agents persuaded the Italian police to arrest five Ukrainians in 1948 who had already boarded a ship bound for resettlement in Argentina, even though these DPs had been screened by Western authorities and were legitimate refugees.[78]

The frustration of Ukrainian DPs with the screening process, the privileges granted to Soviet officials, and the Soviet repatriation teams' tactics, was sometimes expressed in violent ways. Numerous reports speak of physical attacks against Soviet repatriation officers who visited the camps. The following incident took place at the Wiesbaden-Biebrich camp in the spring of 1946:

> . . . two Russian officers accompanied by two interpreters entered the camp on the authority of a letter from 7th Army Headquarters, in order to attempt to ascertain if any of the camp residents were Soviet Nationals. The Russians were attacked and eventually had to run from the Camp to the safety of the nearest Military guard. All four Russians were injured, two received multiple cuts, lacerations and concussion and one was stabbed in the back and in the chest.

At the Mittenwald camp Soviet officers were stoned by an irate crowd.[80] There were many such outbreaks of frustration and anger. This frustration came to head in mid-1948 when DPs refused to participate in any further screenings by UNRRA's successor, the International Refugee Organisation (IRO).[81] A few months later in March 1949 the U.S. occupation authorities closed down the offices of the Soviet Repatriation Commission in Germany.[82]

But in the end what saved the DPs and refugees from repatriation was the change in political relations between the two superpowers, and this in turn made the Western authorities think of resettling rather than repatriating the 'last million', as they were called. The onset of the Cold War in mid-1946 created a climate in which the refugees' reasons for not returning home were given a sympathetic public hearing and ensured their resettlement in the West. Perhaps even more fortunate for the refugees was the growing realization in the West that the displaced persons and refugees were a readily available source of unskilled labour.[83] Thus, political, humanitarian and economic reasons intermeshed to provide for the refugees a long-awaited respite from uncertainty.

Several accounts of this period have stressed how the Western Allies, and particularly UNRRA, successfully repatriated millions of people within a short period. But what this paper has tried to show is that the repatriation process was less than considerate and successful for many hundreds of thousands of Eastern Europeans, especially for those who either lost or, like the Ukrainians, never had their own nation state. For these latter peoples the problems of repatriation was compounded by the lack of official recognition of their nationality, and lack of understanding why they refused to return home.

The remaining refugees and displaced persons, almost all of whom were from Eastern Europe, presented a major political problem for the Western Allies. Caught between East and West, return of the refugees posed a dilemma for Western governments. Their presence also called into question the nature of East-West relations at a time when these relations were being reassessed. As an editorial in the *Economist* expressed it: 'Shall they (the United Nations) bend the residue of the world's homeless and stateless to the will of authoritarians who want them back, or shall they jointly create a new National Home, or shall each liberally offer a fair share of sanctuary?'[84]

This question was posed at the height of the forcible and mass repatriation of millions of Eastern Europeans but it was not resolved until two years later. Offers of resettlement were extended but only when it was politically and economically beneficial for the host countries to do so. For the refugees, resettlement was also a welcome alternative to the psychological pressures of screening boards, resentment and harassment from the local German population, police and American soldiers, and the steady but deliberate decline in food rations.[85]

Ukrainian displaced persons from pre-war Polish territory were, after the initial phase of indiscriminate repatriation, much better off than Ukrainians from the Soviet Union. Not only were Polish Ukrainians exempted from forced repatriation, but Polish authorities also did not want them back. What made matters worse for Soviet Ukrainians, however, was that their reasons for not returning – chief among them the likelihood of imprisonment, deportation or death – were not generally appreciated or understood. Moreover, they themselves found it difficult to understand why the West was eager to assist Soviet repatriation teams, and in the end, believed that the West, and especially the United States, was politically naive about the true nature of Stalin's regime.

In later years, once in the emigration, their belief in the correctness of their political understanding of the Soviet system sometimes bordered on self-righteousness. Like some of the more recent Soviet exiles and political *emigrés*, postwar refugees criticized the moral and political 'weakness' and 'indifference' of the West and saw the world in much the same way as they had in the DP camps – almost exclusively in terms of East-West competition and conflict.[86]

What some of these refugees did not appreciate was the courage and compassion shown by many U.S. officers and UNRRA officials, who, in the face of pressures to do otherwise, took action that proved helpful to the displaced persons and refugees. Similarly, the efforts of Ukrainians living abroad were exceptionally effective in bringing the refugees' situation to the attention of Western governments.

Perhaps the most important resource DPs drew upon to resist repatriation, however, was self-reliance and organization. This became the basis of their ability to survive the present and have hope for the future. Political activity was but one part of an extraordinarily diverse and rich social life in the camps. Hundreds of theatrical groups, newspapers, literary societies, schools, and other cultural organizations were formed in the camps, and these helped restore some of the self-respect they had lost under the difficult and humiliating circumstances they endured both during and after the war.[87] And if Ukrainian refugees and displaced persons seemed to some UNRRA and Western officials to be overly concerned with their national identity, this too was understandable, for their concern helped to restore their sense of dignity. By 1952 most had been resettled in the West. They remained full of animosity for the system they had left behind, convinced of the correctness of their decision not to return, but grateful that their long ordeal had come to an end.

Notes: Chapter 12

1 Western military officials distinguished between refugees and displaced persons, the latter being those who had been displaced from their homeland, and the former who were not outside the national boundaries of their country. For the official definitions, see, Malcolm J. Proudfoot, *European Refugees; 1939–52. A Study in Forced Population Movement*, (London, 1957), p. 115. The United Nations used broader and more traditional definitions. See E.F. Penrose, 'Negotiating on Refugees and Displaced Persons, 1946,' in *Negotiating with the Russians*, edited by Raymond Dennett and Joseph E. Johnson (Boston, 1951), p. 146. This paper makes a distinction between refugees and displaced persons similar to the United Nations', that is, refugees are viewed as those also beyond the borders of their homeland. At the same time, those who were displaced by the events of the war and refused to be repatriated were, in effect, and considered themselves, refugees by November 1945. Among the more recent works on Western repatriation policy after the war, see: Wolfgang Jocabomeyer, *Von Zwangsarbeiter zum Heimatlosen Auslander* (Göttingen, 1985), pp. 123–52; Mark R. Elliott, *Pawns of Yalta: Soviet Refugees and America's Role in Their Repatriation* (Urbana, 1982); Krystyna Kersten, *Repatriacja ludnosci polskiej po II wojnie swiatoweij* (Warsaw, 1974); Michael R. Marrus, *The Unwanted: European Refugees in the Twentieth Century* (New York and Oxford, 1985); Volodymyr Maruniak, *Ukrains'ka emigratsiia v Nimechchyni i Avstrii po druhii svitovii viini* (Munich, 1985); M. I. Pavlenko, *'Bizhentsi' ta 'peremishcheni osoby' v politytsi imperialistychnykh derzhav (1845–1949 rr.)* (Kiev, 1979); Nikolai Tolstoy, *The Minister and the Massacres* (London, 1986), and his *Victims of Yalta* (London, 1978), and *Stalin's Secret War* (London, 1981).
2 Elliott, p. 243; Marrus, p. 311; Proudfoot, p. 169.
3 On the evolution of the repatriation policy and agreement with various governments, see Proudfoot, pp. 120–57. SHAEF, Supreme Headquarters, Allied Expeditionary Force was terminated on 13 July 1945 and replaced by new organizations discussed below.
4 Proudfoot, pp. 212, 228, table 12; Maruniak, p. 37, states that the official Soviet figure was 2,229,552 to September 1946.
5 Proudfoot, p. 210, and p. 211, table ii.
6 Elliott, p. 2; Maruniak, p. 37, states that official sources reveal that 2,886,157 Soviet citizens were repatriated from the end of the war to 1 September, 1946, from the Soviet-controlled zones of Germany and Austria. Proudfoot, p. 212, states that 2,946,000 were repatriated from the Soviet areas of Germany, Austria, Poland and elsewhere.
7 Elliot, p. 2; on the number of the other (non-Soviet) peoples, see: John George Stoessinger, *The Refugee and the World Community* (Minneapolis, 1956), pp. 55–6; Marrus, pp. 320, 323; Proudfoot, p. 237, states the number to be 1,888,000 by September 1946, and he includes those in Italy.
8 See, for example: 'Determination and Reporting of Nationalities', from Headquarters, U.S. Forces, European Theater, 16 November 1945, in which Major General C.L. Adcock states that: 'This group [Ukrainians] is not recognized as a nationality and will be dealt with according to determined nationality status as Soviet, nationals of other countries of which they may be citizens, or as stateless persons, in accordance with U.S. Forces, European Theatre Main S–16517 of 9 August 1945.' UNRRA Archives, UNRRA Germany, U.S. Zone, Office of the Director, Displaced Persons Camps, 1–31 December 1945. A circular from the UNRRA director of the French zone in Germany reiterated this position. See UNRRA Archives, Records of the Germany Mission, Central Headquarters Repatriation, PAG–4/3.0.11.0.1.4:03, 'Repatriation Information', General Bulletin no. 9 (26 April 1946). See also, Vasyl' Sofroniv Levyts'kyi, *Respublika za drotamy: (zapysky skytal'tsia)* (Toronto, 1983), p. 40.
    This citizenship criterion was very much a legacy of the prewar period, when Ukrainians were living in Poland, Czechoslovakia, Rumania as well as in the Soviet

Union. Although almost 23.5 million Ukrainians lived in Soviet Ukraine, another five million, commonly referred to as Western Ukrainians, resided outside the Soviet Union, mainly in these three countries. See Bohdan Krawchenko, *Social Change and National Consciousness in Twentieth-Century Ukraine* (London, 1985) p. 115; and Raymond Pearson, *National Minorities in Eastern Europe, 1848–1945* (London, 1983), p. 171.

9 On the division of Germany and Austria see: Department of State, *Occupation of Germany: Policy and Progress, 1945–46* (Washington, 1947); John Gimbel, *The American Occupation of Germany: Politics and the Military, 1945–49* (Stanford, 1968); and William B. Bader, *Austria Between East and West, 1945–55* (Stanford, 1966).

The most respected Ukrainian demographer estimated that there were between 150,000 to 210,000 Ukrainians left in Austria and Germany at the end of 1945. See Volodymyr Kubiiovych, 'Z demohrafichnykh problem ukrains'koi emigratsii (na pryklad taboriv u Mittenval'di)' in *S'ohochasne i mynule*, vols 1–2 (Munich, 1949), p. 15. Another source, compiled by the Ukrainian umbrella organization for DPs, found that there were 206,871 Ukrainians in Germany and Austria in March 1946. Most were in the U.S. zone of Germany (104,024); the others were as follows: 54,580 in the British zone of Germany; 19,026 in the French zone of Germany; and 29,241 in the three Western zones of Austria. See Vasyl' Mudryi, 'Nova ukrains'ka emigratsiia,' in L. Myshḥha and A. Drahan, eds., *Ukraintsi u vil'nomu sviti. Iuvileina knyha U.N.S., 1894–1954* (Jersey City, [1954]), p. 117. For more on the demographic and social composition of the DPs see, Kubiiovych and Mudryi.

The U.S. Zone in Germany, as well as the Bremen enclave and the U.S. sector of Berlin, was under the command of the United States Forces European Theater (USFET), with headquarters at Frankfurt. The functions of military government, at first exercised by USFET, were later undertaken by the Office of Military Government, United States (OMGUS), a separate organization with headquarters in Berlin. USFET retained jurisdiction only in matters relating to disarmament and demilitarization, security, displaced persons, and matters unrelated to civil control in Germany. OMGUS exercised a general surveillance over all German internal affairs, operating increasingly through approved German administrative agencies and personnel.

10 See Yury Boshyk, ed., *Ukraine During World War II: History and Its Aftermath* (Edmonton, 1986).

11 Proudfoot, pp. 167–9 and p. 236.

12 Proudfoot, pp. 162–91 and p. 170.

13 For discussions on the Yalta agreement see the sources given in endnote 1, especially Elliot, pp. 102–04; Proudfoot, pp. 152–7; Tolstoy (1978) and (1986). Apparently, the terms of the Yalta agreement were not made public by the State Department until a year later, that is, in February 1946.

14 According to Elliot, (*Death to Spies*), p. 139, the Soviet Repatriation Commission was under the control of SMERSH, the Soviet secret police, and some of its personnel came from the Main Administration of Counterintelligence (GUKR) of SMERSH.

15 Olexa Woropay, *On the Road to the West: Diary of a Ukrainian Refugee* (London, 1982), p. 33; Elliott, pp. 90–1; Iurii L. [avrynenko], 'Rodina' i 'Skryning': Damokliv mech taboriv,' in *S'ochochasne i mynule* (Munich, 1949), vol. 1–2, p. 65.

16 Proudfoot, pp. 214–7.

17 UNRRA Archives, Germany Mission, Office of the Chief and Deputy Chief, PAG-4/3.0.11.0.0:6, 'Forcible Repatriation of the Ruthenians', 28 November 1945.

18 See, for example, Elliot, p. 104; Ivan Bolekhivs'kyi Bilych, 'Moia zustrich z Vasylem Sofronym Levyts'kym', in *Vasyl' Sofronir Levyts'kyi'*, *Respublika za drotamy (zapysky skytal'tsia)* (Toronto, 1983), pp. 154–5, 159, and p. 15 of the memoir; Omelian Kushnir, ed., *Regensburg: statti, spohady, dokumenty. Do istorii ukrains'koi emigratsii v Nimechchyni pislia druhoi svitovoi viiny* (New York-Toronto, 1985), pp. 26, 34, 37, 38, 40–1. I am grateful to the late Illia Horodecky for providing documentary materials about the interventions of U.S. Lt. Colonel Jaromir Pospisil, QMC, Deputy Military Government Officer, Regensburg.

19 Proudfoot, p. 155, mentions that there were 200,000 British and American soldiers in Soviet-controlled territories who were awaiting repatriation.

20 Vera M. Dean, 'Tug of War over the DP's' (November 1946), as cited in Michael Palij, 'The Problem of Displaced Persons in Germany, 1939–1950,' in *Almanac of the*

Ukrainian National Association for the Year 1985 (Jersey City, 1985), p. 32. See also, Vasyl' Ivanys, *Stezhkamy zhyttia (Spohady)*, vol. 5 (Neu Ulm, 1962), p. 382.

21 UNRRA Archives, Germany Mission, U.S. Zone, Office of the Director, PAG–4/3.0.11.3.0:9, 'Confidential Report on the General Situation of DPs to the Director General of UNRRA, September 1946.' Published in Yury Boshyk, ed., pp. 224–32. See also, Joseph A. Berger, 'DPs Are People Too,' unpublished manuscript (July 31, 1946). I would like to thank Dr. Antony Berger for permission to use this source. The author served as a director in the Displaced Persons Operations in the Freising area of Germany from June 1945 until July 1946. The area he directed was the largest of any UNRRA team.

22 Ibid., 'Confidential Report', in which is cited an anti-refugee article that appeared in the newspaper *The Go-Devil*, 60th Infantry Weekly, Ingolstadt, March 23, 1946.

23 Boris Shub, *The Choice* (New York, 1950), pp. 46–7, 49, 51, 69; *Ukrains'ki visti* (November 25, 1945), p. 7, and Lavrynenko. Shub was assigned by SHAEF to interview DPs and Soviet POWs.

24 In a Soviet radio broadcast to the DPs, the following appeal and warning was made: 'The fascist animals drove you by force into German slavery, they treated you cruelly and with ridicule, starved you and tortured you. Your motherland awaits you, the Party of Lenin, Stalin, Marx and Engels . . . Those who do not show up by 10 November 1945 . . . will be arrested and sent on the road to the police.' From V. Ost, *Repatriatsiia* (Germany, 1945–6), p. 5.

25 For a detailed discussion on the fate of the returnees, see Elliott, pp. 190–216.

26 Ibid., p. 171. Through those who had escaped during the Soviet repatriation process, the DPs learned about the treatment of Soviet DPs. A few DPs also managed somehow to travel between the zones, and some even made several trips to the Ukraine and back to the Western zonal camps. See Berger; V. Martynets', *Shliakhom taboriv DP* (Winnipeg, 1950), pp. 276–314; Shub, pp. 33–45, 163–5; Ost, p. 89.

27 Mudryi, p. 116; Zynovii Knysh, *Na porozi nevidomoho (spohady z 1945 roku)* (Toronto, 1963), pp. 95–107; Kushnir, ed., pp. 33–42; and *Dokumenty. Memorandum* (n.p., n.d. (December, 1945). Four requests were made to American authorities at that time: (1) to establish the legal status of Ukrainians as refugees of a distinct nationality and grant them political asylum; (2) appoint a Ukrainian representative who would defend their interests; (3) grant Ukrainian professionals permission to work in their fields; (4) permit Ukrainian religious, cultural and educational life to develop under the supervision of American authorities. On 1 November 1945 Ukrainian refugees and DPs formed the Central Representation of the Ukrainian Emigration in Germany, headed by Vasyl' Mudryi.

28 UNRRA Archives, Germany Mission, U.S. Zone, Office of the Director, Displaced Persons Camp, General, July-November 1945, PAG–4/3.0.11.3.0:10.

29 Swiss efforts are best described in the Ievhen Batchinsky archive, Carleton University, Ottawa. An example of the Ukraino-Swiss Relief Committee's interventions can be found in UNRRA Archives, Austria, Chief of Mission, PAG–4/3.0.1.0.0:7. For the activities of Ukrainians in America, see Ostap Tarnavs'kyi, *Brat-bratovi. Knyha pro ZUADK* (Philadephia, 1971); and for Canada, Gordon R. Bohdan Panchuk, *Heroes of Their Day: The Reminiscences of Bohdan Panchuk* (Toronto, 1983). Numerous interventions by the Vatican can be found in the National Archives, Civil Archives Division-Diplomatic Branch, RG 59, U.S. Department of State, Decimal Card Index, 'Displaced Persons'.

30 Elliott, pp. 92–6, 173.

31 Mykhailo Mandryka, *Ukrainian Refugees* (Winnipeg, 1946), p. 39.

32 Mudryi, p. 117; Pavlenko, p. 70; Ivanys, p. 384; Elliott, p. 173, and Berger.

33 Proudfoot, p. 217.

34 Elliott, p. 172; Milda Danys, *DP: Lithuanian Immigration to Canada after the Second World War* (Toronto, 1986), p. 36; interview with Luba Dyka, Cambridge, Mass., August 5, 1983.

35 F. Pihido-Pravoberezhnyi, *Velyka vitchyzniana viina* (Winnipeg, 1954) p. 207; National Archives, RG 59, State Department, 860.20231, Berlin, on the infiltration of Soviet and 'satellite' agents posing as DPs.

36 On the OUN, see John Armstrong, *Ukrainian Nationalism* (New York, 1963) and articles in Y. Boshyk, ed.

37 Levyts'kyi, pp. 21, 40, 46, 105. He recorded the views here of Western military officials.

38 Ivanys, p. 382; Levyts'kyi, p. 106.

39 Interview with Professor Myroslav Labunka, 10 August 1983, Cambridge, Massachusetts. He was the former secretary to Stepan Bandera. Individual Soviet Ukrainians and others were also 'terrorized' by the Bandera faction when not enough money was contributed during fund raising collections, according to Ivanys, p. 378. See also Levyts'kyi, pp. 107, 120.

40 Levyts'kyi, pp. 88, 111.

41 As cited in Semen Izhyk, *Smikh kriz slozy* (Winnipeg, 1961), p. 184. Ironically, the differences in political outlook and this intolerant treatment stimulated Ukrainians from the Soviet Union to form their own political organizations in the camps.

42 Levyts'kyi, pp. 104, 120.

43 See, for example, Eduard Bakis, 'D.P. Apathy', in *Flight and Resettlement*, edited by H.B.M. Murphy (Paris 1955), pp. 76–88; Edward A. Shils, 'Social and Psychological Aspects of Displacement,' in *Journal of Social Issues*, 1946, pp. 3–18.

44 On the evolution of the American policy, see Elliott, pp. 108–14. On the United Nations' change in policy on January 29 1946, see Penrose, pp. 142–3. On the French government's dissatisfaction with the Soviets, see Alfred J. Rieber, *Stalin and the French Communist Party, 1941–1947* (New York, 1962), pp. 200–1.

45 UNRRA Archives, Germany Mission, Office of the Chief and Deputy Chief, PAG–4/3.0.11.01.4:1, USFET Directive to Commanding Generals, 4 January 1946. See also Elliott, p. 111.

46 Ibid., UNRRA Archives, point 2.

47 Mykola Korol'ko, 'Pereselennia ukraintsiv na radians'ku Ukrainu,' in *Ukrains'kyi kaliendar na 1985 rik* (Warsaw, 1985), pp. 159–62. The pro-Soviet Polish government was 'interested only in persons of true Polish Nationality [sic] and not in Polish Ukrainians'. It also requested that Poles and Polish Ukrainians be separated into different camps. See, for example, UNRRA Archives, Austria, Chief of the Mission, Repatriation: Conditions Affecting Poland, PAG–4/3.0.1.0.0:19, 'Polish Mission for Repatriation in Austria', 4 April 1946.

48 Proudfoot, pp. 283–4, 290.

49 Elliot, p. 115.

50 UNRRA Archives, Germany Mission, Office of the Chief and Deputy Chief, PAG-4/3.0.11.01.4:1, USFET to Commanding Generals, 4 January 1946.

51 Ibid.

52 UNRRA Archives, Austria, Chief of Mission, Repatriation Policy, PAG–4/3.0.1.0.0.:19, 'Repatriation Reports from Camp Kuftein and Landeck,' 16 April 1946.

53 UNRRA Archives, PAG–4/3.0.11.01.4:1, 'Paraphrase of Restricted Cable, 15 March 1946 received by USFET from U.S. War Department'.

54 See, for example, Resolution 92 passed 29 March 1946, Atlantic City, 4th Session of UNRRA Council. UNRRA Archives, Germany Mission, Central Headquarters, Repatriation, PAG–4/3.0.11.0.1.4:2.

55 Ibid., 'Report on the Repatriation Poll of Displaced Persons in UNRRA Assembly Centres in Germany, Period 1–14 May 1946'; Ivanys, p. 378; the full analysis of the poll is reproduced in Y. Boshyk, ed., pp. 209–22.

56 Ibid.

57 The screening process was so infamous that it received a special place in the Ukrainian language of the time: 'skryning' and 'vyskryninguvaty'. See Lavrynenko, p. 66.

58 See Proudfoot, pp. 203–48, on the differences between UNRRA and military responsibilities for refugees.

59 UNRRA Archives, Germany Mission, Central Headquarters, Repatriation, PAG-4/3.0.11.0.1.4:2, 27 April 1946.

60 Ibid., 3 January 1947.

61 Ibid., 4 June 1946.

62 Ibid.

63   Ibid. 3 January 1947.
64   Maria Iurkevych to Ievhen Batchinsky, 23 February 1947, Ievhen Batchinsky Archive, Carleton University, Ottawa.
65   Lavrynenko, p. 67; H.B.M. Murphy, 'The Camps', in Murphy, ed., p. 58.
66   UNRRA Archive, PAG14/3.0.11.0.1.4:2, 3 January 1946.
67   Ibid., J.H. Whiting, Zone Director to General Brown, Deputy Director German Operations, UNRRA Central Headquarters, Arolsen, 22 August 1946. See also Lavrynenko, p. 67; see also the report from Ellwangen, in M. Kushnir, ed., *One Year in Ukrainian DP Camp Ellwangen* (Odyn rik v tabori Ellwangen) (Ellwangen, 1947) p. 3.
68   Stoessinger, p. 52; Proudfoot, pp. 252, 284.
69   UNRRA Archives, Germany Mission, U.S. Zone, Displaced Persons Camps, 1 February – 31 March 1946, 'Privileges of Soviet Liaison Officers in Displaced Persons Camps Other Than Wholly Soviet,' 8 March 1946.
70   UNRRA Archives, Austria, Chief of Mission, Repatriation Policy, PAG–4/3.0.1.0.0:19, 'Repatriation Reports from Camp Kufstein and Landeck,' 16 April 1947.
71   Ivanys, p. 373.
72   Judging by the primary source materials available to us, Allied Intelligence carefully followed Ukrainian refugee activities in the camps, especially because frequent Soviet accusations necessitated investigations and replies. See, for example, UNRRA Archives, Germany Mission, Central Headquarters, Repatriation, PAG–4/3.0.11.01.4:1, 'Report on Charges by Delegates at Special Session of the Committee of the Council for Europe [C.C.E.],' 20 August 1946.
73   See, for example, ibid., USFET Directive, 4 January 1946; ibid., 1 August 1946.
74   Ibid., PAG–4/3.0.11.0.1.4:3, 'C.C.E 23rd July 1946'; Pavlenko, pp. 56–79.
75   Vasyl' Svystun, *Ukraina i skytal'tsi* (Toronto, 1946), p. 17; John Kolasky, *The Shattered Illusion: The History of Ukrainian Pro-Communist Organizations in Canada* (Toronto, 1979), pp. 88–107.
76   See, for example, National Archives, RG 59, State Department Decimal Card Index, 25 June 1946, from the Ukrainian-American League, and 21 November 1945 from the Ukrainian-American Fraternal Union; and the introduction to, D.Z. Manuil's'kyi, *Ukrainsko-nimets'ki natsionalisty na sluzhbi u fashysts'koi Nimechchyny* (New York, 1946).
77   Interview with Mrs Timoshenko, nee Sadovs'ka, Toronto, Canada, November 1983.
78   *Ukrainian Bulletin* (New York) no. 3, 1948 (June 1), p. 2.
79   UNRRA Archives, PAG–4/3.0.11.0.1.4:2, 'Screening of DPs,' 2 May 1946.
80   *Ukrainian Bulletin*, no. 4, (1948), p. 4.
81   Lavrynenko, p. 67; on resistance to the last UNRRA screening, March 1947, see Levyts'kyi, p. 120.
82   Pavlenko, p. 48; Elliott, p. 122.
83   On the economic reasons for allowing resettlement see: Danys; Leonard Dinnerstein, *America and the Survivors of the Holocaust* (New York, 1982), pp. 159–60. This argument is central to a recent Soviet work by Pavlenko, cited above.
84   *Economist*, 9 June 1945, p. 762.
85   Numerous raids and searches were carried out by armed German police and U.S. military police, in the camps. This caused great resentment and fear among the refugees. See the Berger memoir and the UNRRA document, 'Confidential Report', cited above and printed in Y. Boshyk, ed., pp. 227–8.
86   *Emigratsiia* (Ellwangen, 1948), pp. 18–30. For a recent example of this criticism of the West by a former displaced person, see: S.Iu. Protsiuk, 'Taborovi chasy v bezposeredn'omu nasvitlenni,' *Narodnia volia* (Scranton, Pennsylvannia) (14 June, 1984), p. 5.
87   On cultural and other organizations in the camps, see Maruniak; for an example of the prolific publishing activity of the Ukrainian refugees, see Yury Boshyk and Wlodimierz Kiebalo, comps., *Publications by Ukrainian 'Displaced Persons' and Refugees, 1945–54* (Edmonton, 1988).

13 Polish refugees as military potential: policy objectives of the Polish government in exile

ANITA J. PRAZMOWSKA

At the end of the Second World War the British government found itself faced with a formidable problem posed by the fact that Britain appeared to have acquired approximately a quarter of a million Polish Displaced Persons. These were soldiers who had been enlisted into the Polish Fighting Forces and who had fought with the British in Africa, Italy and France, in addition to smaller numbers of Polish seamen and airmen. Britain had also undertaken to care for the dependents of these ex-combatants.

A puzzling feature of this situation is that large numbers of displaced people had not been attracted to Britain by any natural movement of populations when fleeing from hostilities or in search of safety. Geographically Britain does not lie directly on the route of those who fled from German occupied Poland. These Polish people found themselves in Britain as a result of a premeditated and primarily politically motivated decision of successive Polish governments in exile. These governments had decided to form an army with the aim of obtaining political leverage in negotiations with the Allied powers during and after the war. In other words the Polish governments in exile from the outset had sought to make a direct military contribution to fighting Germany primarily in order to secure for itself the right to participate in post-war decision making concerning not merely Poland, but also the whole of Europe.

It is necessary to distinguish the policies of two successive governments. The Sikorski government of 1939–43 was to all intents and purposes dominated by General Wladyslaw Sikorski and, in spite of differences of opinion about the wisdom and desirability of establishing relations with the Soviet Union, was united on the issue of the Polish Fighting Forces. The later government of Stanislaw Mikołajczyk was not dominated by its Prime Minister to the same extent its predecessor had been by Sikorski, and therefore decisions concerning the army tended to rest in the hands of General Kazimierz Sosnkowski, the Commander in Chief, and later General Władysław Anders, Commander of the Polish units in the Middle East and Italy, and acting Commander in Chief after Sosnkowski's dismissal.

There was one thing which these governments did have in common and that was a belief that the Polish government in exile's only strength and advantage in political terms was the army it could provide. Therefore the raising of an efficient and numerous Polish army was always considered to be an issue of vital and unquestionable importance. Where the politicians and military leaders differed was on the question of where to make these soldiers available (the eastern or the western front) and by what route they would return to Poland.

Throughout the war the Polish governments in exile sought to find sources of manpower in order to form the army, replace casualties and finally to continue the army's constant expansion. This was never an easy problem as, for obvious reasons, access to Polish manpower was restricted to those who were outside occupied Poland. Until the fall of France, there were two recruiting areas. One was the Polish community in France, mainly the earlier immigrants into the French mining industry, secondly, a steady trickle of Poles who made their way through Rumania, Hungary and Greece, and who, with the co-operation of the British, were transported to France and Britain. These were predominantly air crews. Some Polish naval units were able to escape from the Baltic. After the fall of France, and the loss of the majority of Polish units, which had earlier been formed there, the problem became an acute one and efforts were made to recruit in Canada and the USA.

The German attack on the Soviet Union in the summer of 1941 opened a new source of manpower. These were Poles who had lived in the Eastern regions, which were incorporated into the Soviet Union in September 1939, and who were deported by the Soviet authorities into the Russian interior. Polish-Soviet relations were normalised by Sikorski's signing of the Polish-Soviet agreement in July 1941, which provided for the raising of Polish troops in the Soviet Union. By the middle of 1942 relations had deteriorated and the Soviet authorities blocked earlier successful recruitment drives. The units which had been formed in the Soviet Union were moved in several stages to the Middle East and came under British command.

The opening of the European front, primarily in the west, meant that the Poles were once more able to restart a period of impressive expansion of their armed forces. This recruitment was from POW Poles who had been pressed into the Wehrmacht and who were now willing to fight against Germany, from liberated inmates of concentration camps, German POW camps, and from vast pools of Polish forced labour.

Thus throughout the war the Polish governments in exile were able to continue the expansion of the armed forces and, as will be shown below, did so with clear political aims in mind. The result was that at the end of the war numbers of Poles found themselves in Western Europe and under pressure from the exile government to stay there. The Polish fighting units had been the government's main political card. With the collapse of the exiled government, and the US and British recognition of the Soviet backed government of National Unity in Poland, they became the casualty of the failure of that policy.

The position of the Polish soldiers and their dependents who at the end of the Second World War refused to return to Poland was unusual. This was not a classic case of people displaced by war activities and seeking to return to their country of origin. The government in exile had made the decision to prevent the return of the fighting units to Poland in order to retain them as a military force with which to continue the fight against the one remaining enemy, the Soviet Union.

There are, therefore, legitimate doubts in labelling these people as displaced persons, as more accurately they were political refugees who believed that the fight for a free Poland could be better and more successfully pursued if they remained outside Poland.

I

With the collapse of Poland and its occupation by Nazi and Soviet troops in September 1939, a first government in exile was formed, in France. General Sikorski became Prime Minister, Minister of Defence, Minister of Justice and subsequently also Supreme Commander.[1] His proposals for the creation of a Polish army in exile on the whole reflected the aspirations of other Polish politicians and military leaders.

In a conversation which Sikorski had with the British Foreign Secretary, Lord Halifax, on 14 November 1939, he stated clearly that he hoped to raise not merely a nominal army, but a force which he expected to number 100,000 men.[2] Instructions to the Ministry for Foreign Affairs dated 30 December 1939 acknowledged that the Polish army, which was being raised in the west, was aimed at securing for Poland a position of equality with the other Allies in post-war negotiations.[3] Having outlined the undesirability of allowing a Versailles type peace to be again imposed on Poland it was stated:

1 The first and most important aim of the Polish government is the establishment and increase of its influence with the Allies so as to prevent their negotiating a premature compromise peace, which could be at Poland's expense.
2 Military cooperation on land, on sea and in the air at the side of the Allies and on the Western front is an urgent matter and an essential one, not only in order to create a well equipped Polish army . . . but also to maintain Polish prestige so Poland is seen as an effective ally cooperating with France and Britain.

Poland's territorial desiderata were defined at this stage as the return to the September 1939 borders and the creation of defensible borders and ones which would accord with Poland's national and state requirements.

It is apparent that the Polish government was anxious lest its contribution to the war effort be taken for granted. From the outset it was decided to seek rights of participation in all military and political debates. On several occasions the Poles pushed for the right to be represented in the Supreme War Council, something the British were not prepared to consider.[4] Poland's contribution to Allied war efforts (then still in the stage so aptly described as the Phoney War) was seen as inextricably tied to the problem of obtaining recognition of Poland's political importance in Europe. In a memorandum dated January 1940 entitled 'The State of Political-Military Affairs connected with the Recreation of the Army' the top priority was defined as 'the necessity of clearly stating on a diplomatic level the question of Poland's contribution to the present war . . . This should give us a direct right to obtain aid now and should guarantee satisfactory compensation after the war.'[5] The issue was summarised as 'the army and questions of strategy are an element of politics. At this moment the outcome of our fate will depend primarily on political achievements.'

Proposals for a Polish army were subsequently developed to define not only the desired area of operation but also its role in establishing in Poland a Western-orientated government of a preferred political persuasion. This was outlined in papers found in the personal archives of Professor Kot, General Sikorski's close collaborator and subsequently ambassador to Moscow.[6] In a memorandum entitled 'The Aims of the Polish Army' it was stated that at the end of the war the army should be of approximately one million men (in view of the very limited access to Polish manpower at this stage, this was a very audacious ambition), and that this was 'in order that we should have the right of dictating peace conditions and have the opportunity to outline our borders'. Difficulties concerning access to adequate sources of manpower were recognised: It was presumed that recruitment would continue as the army would come closer to Polish territories. Because of this and for strategic reasons it was considered advantageous that the Polish forces should operate in two groupings. The first, broadly heading from France and the Balkans eastwards, and the second from the British Isles as an expeditionary force, to secure the Baltic states, East Prussia and Pomerania.

In view of the army's involvement in inter-war politics the question of unity, and ideological unity in particular, had been foremost in Sikorski's mind. He avowedly sought consensus on national grounds, but as has been recently shown Sikorski did not distance himself from the old regime. On the contrary, he sought cooperation with the old military team.[7] This is confirmed in the above mentioned memorandum, where it was presumed that a revolution was likely to break out in Germany and in the Soviet Union and therefore it was considered necessary to give the army 'moral-political training'. It was further stated:

'It is in the military interest of our allies that the cadres of the Polish Army . . . should enter Poland in strength in order to back up a civilian uprising against the occupying forces and in order to organise a government which would politically orientate Poland towards cooperation with the Allies. It is in the interest of peace that Poland should become the centre of political alliances opposed to German expansion eastwards and Russian westwards.'

The German defeat of France temporarily appeared to shatter Polish hopes as the Polish army formed there was scattered and few units, amounting to 30,000 in all, were evacuated to Britain. Nor were hopes for obtaining the US government's consent to recruit among the Polish communities in the US realised. What Sikorski had hoped for was what he had already obtained from the British government and that was the right to call up Polish citizens into the Polish army. The US government allowed its Polish community to choose to join either US military formation or Polish ones, when called up. In view of the higher allowance and vastly preferable material conditions in the US army few Poles from the USA joined Polish units. In December 1942, the Minister for the National Defence, General Marian Kukiel openly admitted that the strength of patriotic feeling among the Poles living in the USA had been overestimated and few volunteered for the army, choosing instead to remain in civilian life and enjoy the high standard of living in the USA.[8] The German attack on the Soviet Union focussed Sikorski's attention on the Poles in Russia. There was an opportunity once more to obtain access to unlimited numbers of Polish citizens and many ex-officers of the Polish army. Thus Sikorski's determination to sign an agreement with the Soviet Union was not based on his willingness to ignore the fact that the Soviet Union had not been prepared to renounce the acquisitions of September 1939, but on his realistic appraisal of the Soviet Union's future role in the war and the need to gain access to Polish manpower. The man appointed to form the Polish army in the Soviet Union was General Władysław Anders. To him Sikorski wrote on 1 September 1941 outlining his political aims in creating Polish military units in the Soviet Union. Thus Sikorski wrote:

'The army presently being formed and led by you must retain total moral health; it must become an absolutely reliable instrument of the Polish state. It must be ideologically united. Because of this it must stand apart from all politics . . . I attach the highest priority to the military use of our army as one . . . Our prestige demands this and also operational considerations, which means that the army should not be broken up and wasted.'[9]

In his determination to treat the Soviet Union as one of the main allies, and thus a partner in a common struggle, Sikorski was to face considerable opposition from within his government. It is not possible to reiterate the course of debates on this problem and therefore the question of the use of the army remains the only issue which will be briefly highlighted.

While facing opposition in London, Sikorski was to realise that General Anders, the Commander of the Polish forces in the Soviet Union, had come to differ greatly in his evaluation of what should be the direction of Poland's political and military orientation. One is dealing here not only with the earlier stated high degree of political involvement on the part of the Polish officers, but also with the fact that most, if not all, those in the army in the Soviet Union came from the eastern regions of Poland, more specifically from areas of strong anti-Russian traditions. Secondly, all these people had experienced great hardships in Russia, had suffered in labour camps and were therefore committed anti-Communists. Sikorski found it impossible to persuade them of the need to cooperate with the Soviet war effort.

During his visit to London in April 1942, Anders took part in military discussions dealing with the question of the build-up of Polish forces. The British military authorities in the Middle East were pressing the Poles to transfer some of their reserves from Russia to replace casualties in the Polish units under British command, which were fighting in North Africa.[10] At the same time, the Soviet authorities were limiting the numbers of Poles recruited and were increasingly trying to prevent the expansion which the Poles felt that they could achieve.

The Polish military leaders in London were split on the subject of the front on which to concentrate the Polish war contribution. Anders favoured withdrawing troops from the Soviet Union and employing them in the Middle East from where he presumed the Poles would move to liberate Poland in advance of the Soviet troops. Sikorski still hoped to be able to obtain territorial and political concessions by cooperating with the Soviet troops in the eastern theatre as well as the British in the west.[11] Anders based his recommendation on the belief that the Soviet Union was not likely to withstand the German attack, while Sikorski believed the Soviet Union would defeat Germany and Polish units fighting with the Soviet Union would move west in the wake of a Soviet victory and thus Polish military cooperation would be symbolic of the joint effort and would lead to a peaceful territorial settlement.

In this dispute Sikorski was not able to prevail. He was outmanoeuvred by Anders' direct negotiations with Stalin and the British command in the Middle East. All Polish troops were withdrawn from Russian territory via Iraq, accompanied by dependents and as many Polish civilians as the Polish army could take out of Russia. The bulk of the evacuation was completed by 26 August 1942. In due course the Soviet authorities announced the closing down of the remaining recruiting stations. But by the end of 1942 the Polish government had been able to recreate a considerable army once more. In December 1943 General Kukiel calculated that he had under his command 97,000 trained infantrymen, 9,600 airmen and 2,400 seamen.[12] The infantry was stationed in two areas, one in the Middle East and the other in Scotland. Sikorski felt that this would allow for the Poles to participate in two presumed future operational theatres in Europe. In November 1942 he wrote a memorandum to Roosevelt, Churchill and General Brooke stating that in the east the Polish units could be used in the forthcoming military action in the Balkans and in Italy, and in the west in a continental landing from Britain.[13] Sikorski urged the Allied leaders to take the initiative against the German forces in the continent and himself hoped to move his operational command to the Mediterranean to be in the main area of fighting. Polish insistence that the summer of 1943 was the best moment for the opening of a Mediterranean and western front was being reinforced by drawing attention to the existence of plans for a major national uprising in Poland which would, in the Poles' estimation, make a major contribution to continental fighting. The latter point was never taken up by the western politicians and military leaders.

Worrying to the Poles were rumours that the Soviet authorities had embarked on establishing a 'Red Polish Division' to fight alongside the Soviet army. By the end of 1942 the London Poles believed they had irrefutable evidence of this.[14] The political advantage which Sikorski hoped to obtain from military cooperation with the Soviet Union, allowing him to lead the entry of Polish troops (and thus asserting Polish authority) into Poland together with the liberating Soviet armies, was lost. The estrangement in Polish-Soviet relations was confirmed by the break in Polish-Soviet diplomatic relations when information was received of the Katyń graves in April 1943.

On 4 July 1943 Sikorski died in an air accident off Gibraltar.

II

Sikorski's death sealed the fate of Polish-Soviet relations. These had already deteriorated but Sikorski had been unique among the exiled Polish politicians for his determination to negotiate with the Soviet Union. He had never underestimated the extent of Soviet demands for Polish territory but appreciated that the liberation of Poland was most likely to take place as a result of military activities from the east or at least combined operations from the east and south east.

Sikorski's death was followed by a battle for political influence and, in consequence, for a new orientation in Poland's foreign policy. Stanislaw Mikolajczyk became Prime Minister of the new government. His relations with the British never became as close or as cordial as they had been when Sikorski had been in power, nor did he retain such total control of Polish politics and military affairs as his predecessor had. The Prime Minister's prerogatives over military decisions were limited, in line with the accusation that Sikorski had used the army in defence of narrow party interests. Thus the two personalities which came to dominate Polish military affairs were Generals Sosnkowski and Anders. The first became Commander in Chief in July 1943 until his dismissal, when he was succeeded by General Bór-Komorowski on 30 September 1944. As Bór-Komorowski was in Poland until May 1945, General Anders became acting Commander in Chief. Both Generals Sosnkowski and Anders had strong views on the future course of Polish foreign policy and, in spite of claims to represent purely national interests, saw the army and its military potential as the main bargaining point to be used against the Soviet Union.

The death of Sikorski came at a time when the Soviet Union was achieving decisive victories over Germany (Stalingrad, February 1943, and the Kursk Salient, July 1943). Poland's importance in Allied, but particularly British, politics was gradually but decisively waning. In an interview with the Polish President on 26 July 1943, Churchill warned that 'it was more likely that it was the Russians rather than the Anglo-Saxon armies which would chase the Germans out of Poland and Rumania'.[15] Churchill asserted what the Poles already knew but were unwilling to accept, namely that the British were not prepared to support the Polish government's claim to a frontier beyond the Curzon line.

Polish politicians and military leaders believed that they had a strong card to play against the Russians, and that was the Polish Fighting Forces, notably the army in the Middle East. Scenting the possibility of a swift Italian withdrawal from the war, and with that the likelihood that the war was entering into its final stages, Polish leaders tried to take the initiative in relations with the Western Allies. Sosnkowski, writing to the Minister of National Defence on 3 August 1943, urged that attention should once more be paid to the possibility of the opening of a Balkan front, and simultaneously urged that pressure should be put on the British and the USA so that they demand of the Soviet Union that it clarify its attitude towards Poland.[16] Sosnkowski considered a Soviet-British conflict to be inevitable and in August 1943 wrote to Tadeusz Romer, the Polish Minister for Foreign Affairs, that 'after the defeat of Germany only Britain will stand in the way of Communist Russia taking over Europe, Middle East and Asia'.[17] He urged that pressure should be put upon the British to commit them to an uncompromising policy towards the Soviet Union. But the major issue was how was the Polish government to exert influence on the British? Then there was the problem of forcing the Big Three to recognise Poland as an ally of equal stature and with this obtaining recognition of Polish political aspirations in Europe and furthermore securing British and US support against the Soviet Union. Poland's only strength was its potential military contribution to the Allied effort, and clearly this was the only vehicle for the introduction of Polish desiderata into inter-allied discussions. Sosnkowski wrote to Romer in September 1943 that an attempt to present Polish proposals for a general uprising in Poland to the Combined Chiefs of Staff, and an attempt to have this action accepted as a major Allied military operation requiring supplies and coordination with other operations had failed.[18]

It was the Polish government, therefore, which pressed the British to commit them to putting the Polish soldiers into battle in the autumn of 1943. But in the autumn of 1943 the British were having doubts about the need to use Polish troops as it briefly appeared likely that Italy could be induced to abandon Germany.[19] In any case a great deal of confusion on the political front was matched by the lack of clear orders concerning the use of Polish troops. While numerous enquiries were being made between the War Office, the Foreign Office and British and US commands in the Mediterranean, the Poles appear to have been equally divided as to how to maximise the political benefits to be derived from the Allies' use of Polish forces in the west.

In October Allied military authorities in the Mediterranean communicated with the Chiefs of Staff in London to obtain elaboration of several points raised by the Poles. The Poles were demanding the right to establish military missions in Italy, ostensibly to identify and continue recruitment of Polish citizens who were found there. On political grounds it was felt undesirable to grant such concessions as this had far reaching political implications.[20] It was feared that the Soviet Union might object to this proposal, but also that it would oppose the future use and stationing of Polish troops in France. The British Foreign Office was also informed of Polish attempts to establish themselves in Yugoslavia as General Sosnkowski had approached General Mihailovic with the aim of attaching

Polish fighting units to his. The Special Operations Executive expressed its total opposition to this plan.[21]

The British were suspicious that these attempts to commit the Allies to using Polish troops, and subsequently to obtain the right to establish recruiting missions and various Polish units in strategic areas, were essentially political in their aim. Polish hopes of obtaining political leverage with the Allies were doomed to failure, as by 1943 the Polish question was not viewed through the prism of the need for Polish fighting units, but nearly exclusively as an aspect of Allied relations with the Soviet Union. Thus by the middle of 1943 the question of the Polish Fighting Forces was not likely to influence the Allies in their appraisal of Poland's future role in Europe.

The Polish government was either not aware of the failure of its policy or did not accept the full extent of its own negotiating weakness, and continued to behave as if it had obtained considerable political credit in its relations with the British through having allowed the use of Polish troops. This is evident from the content of the messages sent by the government in exile to its ambassador in Washington on the 5 October 1943, in which instructions were given to present a memorandum to the State Department on the eve of the conference of Foreign Ministers.[22] The message contained references to the undesirability of allowing the Soviet Union entry into Polish territory without the explicit permission of the government. If Soviet troops did so whilst fighting the Germans, they were to be allowed to have right of access only if the British and American military missions were present on Polish territory to prevent conflicts arising between the Soviet troops and the Polish population and to stop Communist propaganda being disseminated. The Poles also insisted on being included in talks concerning post-war Europe, in particular in those which were to deal with issues concerning Germany and the Mediterranean. The justification offered for inclusion on decision making concerning the Mediterranean was that Polish military units were to be used in Italy. The Poles correctly assumed that while military action was taking place, numerous and undoubtedly long-term in their consequences, decisions would be made by the military authorities and not the politicians, and therefore they insisted on being included in inter-Allied staff organisations.

Again, their rationale for putting such a demand was 'because of the numbers of Polish military forces involved, but also because the subjects of discussion in reference to Polish issues included the use made of the Polish Fighting Forces, access to Polish territory and the rearming of the Polish underground army'. Therefore using the fact and pretext of Polish troops being used in western Europe, the Polish government claimed a say not only in matters directly affecting the disposition of these units but also in decisions regarding the future of territories on which Polish soldiers were engaged.

The Poles were to be successful in none of these demands. They nevertheless persisted in their determination to increase the numbers of fighting Poles in the western front, still hoping to place Polish troops in strategic theatres of war and thus to force political concessions by sheer weight of their effort. In that aim the Polish government was not united. General Sosnkowski hoped to increase the numbers of Polish units stationed in Britain, and which it was planned to use in the forthcoming landing in Europe, and approved of the use of Polish troops in the Italian campaign.[23] The Prime Minister, Mikołajczyk, opposed this, fearing the dissipation of Polish troops, thus delaying their entry into battle. This would, in turn, weaken the political aspirations which relied on the argument that the Poles were of vital importance to the Allied war effort.[24]

In January 1944 Soviet troops entered Polish territory without having made prior agreements with the government in exile, thus rejecting the authority of the London Poles. There remained, therefore, only one way of forcing the Soviet Union to be more conciliatory: Britain and the USA must espouse the Polish cause. This they were not likely to do in 1944, when the Soviet war effort was at its most successful and the western Allies still sought to obtain Soviet cooperation in the forthcoming war with Japan. The European perspective of the British was bluntly stated in a Foreign Office memorandum on 26 March 1944,[25] stressing that 'Our policy is based on Anglo-American-Soviet cooperation. We may have no US troops in Europe within a year of the armistice. We can only control Germany with Soviet cooperation. Poland is no substitute for the Soviets.'

The Polish dilemma was startlingly apparent when General Sosnkowski was approached by the War Office to permit the use of the Polish Independent Parachute Brigade in an attempt to establish a bridgehead in Europe in 1944. This was the elite commando unit which it was hoped to parachute into Poland to assist a general uprising in the wake of German withdrawal and to establish Polish authority in advance of Soviet entry. Sosnkowski was, therefore, reluctant to consider this disposition at a time when its Polish objective appeared imminent. But similarly he did not want to miss an opportunity to see Polish soldiers being associated with a major military success. He therefore permitted the brigade's use but qualified this by presenting complicated conditions, all of which were rejected.[26] Ultimately Sosnkowski was forced to agree to place the Polish Parachute Brigade at the disposal of the Allies without any pre-conditions.[27]

As the European war drew to a close, the Polish government sought to retain and increase the only element of its contribution to the Allied effort, in order to regain lost ground in its political dealings with the Allies. At the same time a new strategy emerged from the Polish government's deliberations. If it could not force Britain and the USA to wring concessions out of the Soviet Union it would try to retain in the west a large and politically united Polish army for possible future action. Thus, far from planning for the disbandment of Polish fighting units, the Polish politicians in London suggested new means of utilising the Polish soldiers and continued to recruit into the Polish army.

The Poles continued to work on their earlier stated assumption that Soviet aggression would lead it into conflict with Britain after the end of the war with Germany. Polish military leaders, confident that Britain would win in such a confrontation believed that the Polish Fighting Forces could be retained until the inevitable moment of conflict occurred. They thus hoped that Britain, after a period of appeasing the Soviet Union, would come to its senses and when finally galvanized to fight the Soviet Union, would be desperately in need of manpower. This was the moment when the Polish army would be seen as of vital importance. A memorandum by the Operational Section of the General Staff dated 11 August 1944 outlined future plans for the Polish army. Basing itself on the accepted axiom that a British-Soviet conflict was inevitable (if possibly delayed by 10-15 years) it was considered vital that:

- the material situation of the armed forces be secured during this transitory period.

- all fighting units be brought together in one theatre of operation, preferably north France.

- the development of the Polish Fighting Forces in exile to be pursued to the maximum, holding in mind that its size is and will always remain the strongest argument in our relations with the Allies.[28]

If it was to be successful, such policy towards the army required a high degree of unity and internal cohesion, as there was the obvious fear that some of the Polish soldiers would seek to return to Poland. Thus in a secret order to the officers of the Polish army dated 20 August 1944 General Sosnkowski warned against allowing any discussion of alternatives. He in particular warned against suggestions that Poland should break with the Allies and join forces with the Soviet Union. He felt that such ideas could appeal 'to those of weak character, mentally unbalanced, who might be exploited by those acting as tools of foreign agencies, or by those who lacked any moral accountability'.[29]

On 26 August 1944 the War Office reported that it had formally received from the Polish Commander in Chief a plan for the future expansion of Polish Land Forces.[30] This was to be done in three phases. The first was to bring up to strength the navy, air force and the merchant navy. The second aimed at expanding the present army by additional units and the third would have led to an increase of the army by 100 per cent, taking place over a period of three years. The British thought that the Poles were unlikely to have access to sufficient Polish manpower, but soon reports came in of a very determined recruitment campaign in all areas where the Poles were based. In France this conflicted with the French Government's determination to allow no release into the army of men employed in vital industries.[31] But equal apprehension surfaced in Britain where the long term consequences of allowing the creation of a vast Polish army based outside Poland were to be faced.

By the beginning of 1945 it was known that the Polish soldiers were unlikely to return to Poland. This was clearly the aim of the Polish politicians and military leaders, and the wish of the soldiers. In February Churchill had a conversation with Anders in which the latter stated openly that the oath of allegiance which had been taken by the Polish soldiers bound them to the government in exile and therefore 'practically no Poles whatever in the Polish army would be able to return to Poland'.[32] Simultaneously, a demand was made by Anders that in view of the determination not to recognise the Yalta conference decisions, the Polish soldiers and their families should be allowed to remain in Britain. General Anders was not indifferent to the hardship this would impose on soldiers and when discussing with the British authorities proposals for the future, he stressed that on the one hand the expansion of the forces should continue, but on the other he also demanded that in the event of demobilisation taking place they should be assured of employment or possibly of territory for colonisation.[33]

As has been shown the political nature of a Polish army was not the result of an accident, it had emerged as a result of a consistent attitude on the part of its leaders, their refusal to accept the decisions of the Yalta conference, and their rejection of the government of National Unity which was formed in Poland. Their aim was that the army should stay in the west pending a future war with the Soviet Union.

The Polish government's plans for the army were communicated to the British in March and it became known that what they had in mind was to be retained as a foreign legion manning the British zone in Germany and ultimately to obtain some bases or trading concessions in the British Empire.[34] Churchill was very supportive of the idea of using the Poles as a foreign legion. But the Chiefs of Staff considered the Poles as an unruly element, having already seen them in action in Italy and having concluded from this that they would make a very bad occupation force. Mikołajczyk, who reluctantly accepted the creation of the Polish Government of National United noted General Anders' influence upon the army. The latter was reported as 'determined to insist that, since Poland had now been "sold" to Russia, the Polish army must be preserved intact to support the policy of the present Polish government in the confident hope and expectation that it would eventually be able to take part in a war of liberation against Russia'.[35]

In July 1945 the British government officially forbade further recruitment into the Polish forces and by August plans were made for the repatriation to Poland of those individuals who chose to do so. The army as a whole was not returned to Poland and the problem of the responsibility for their disbandment, dispersal and employment fell upon the British.

III

The emergence of a great number of Polish Displaced Persons in Europe, but most notably in Britain, was therefore not the result of a spontaneous population movement precipitated by war activities. It was the consequence of a policy on the part of the successive governments in exile, which planned to place Polish manpower at the disposal of the Allies in order to obtain political leverage in post-war decision making. While General Sikorski was aware of the possibility of Poland falling within a Soviet sphere of influence, and while he sought to place Polish troops on the eastern front to cooperate with the Soviet Union, his efforts were not successful. The team which took over after his death concentrated predominantly on building up a debt of gratitude in the West which they hoped to use to facilitate their confrontation with the Soviet Union.

Unfortunately, their major miscalculation was that the Western Allies would, at the time of war, or immediately after its conclusion in Europe, seek such a confrontation in order to aid Poland. By 1945 their actions had resulted in the creation of a Polish army based in Italy, France and Germany. But this initial miscalculation concerning the degree of support which they could expect from the West was compounded by their subsequent determination to continue opposing the *fait accompli*. This led to the army being given orders to remain outside Poland. This had been an army raised for political reasons, a pawn in a political game between the exiled politicians and the Allies. In consequence, the soldiers and their families became victims of the failure of the very policy which lay at the root of its creation.

Notes: Chapter 13

1 Walentyna Korpalsa, *Wladyslaw E. Sikorski, Biografia polityczna* (Warszawa, 1981), p. 204.
2 Polish Institute and Sikorski Museum, London (henceforth PISM), PRM. 3/8a. 14 November 1939.
3 Archiwum Akt Nowych, Warsaw, (henceforth AAN), Archiwum Paderewskiego 3087. 30 December 1939.
4 PISM. A.IV. 1/1. January 1940.
5 PISM. A.IV. 1/1. January 1940.
6 Zjednocznone Sronnictwo Ludowe, Warsaw (henceforth ZSL), Archiwum S. Kota, 119. 28 Febuary 1940.
7 W. Korpalska, pp. 206–207.
8 PISM. A.XII. 3/80. 11 December 1942.
9 PISM. 1/56. 1 September 1941.
10 PISM. KG.A.7.e. 24 April 1942.
11 PISM. KGA. 7.e. 24 April 1942.
12 PISM. A.XII. 3/80. 11 December 1942.
13 PISM. A.XII. 4/80. 17 November 1942.
14 PISM. A.XII. 3/23. 18 December 1942.
15 Public Records Office, London, (henceforth PRO) F.O. 371. 32485. C9006/258/G55. 26 July 1943.
16 PISM. A.XII. 3/82. 3 August 1943.
17 PISM. Archiwa T. Romera, McGill University, Canada, microfilm Kol. 5. Film. 5. 5 September 1943..
18 PISM. Archiewa T. Romera, Kol. 5. Film. 5. 30 September 1943.
19 PRO. F.O. 371. 34594. C101411/335/G55. 9 September 1943.
20 PRO. F.O. 371. 34561. C11625/23/G55. 5 October 1943.
21 PRO. F.O. 371. 34594. C14145/335/G55. 19 November 1943.
22 PISM. A.12. 52/8. 5 October 1943.
23 PRO. F.O. 371. 34594. C13793/335/55. 6 November 1943.
24 PRO. F.O. 371. 34589. C13865/258/G55. 22 November 1943.
25 PRO. F.O. 371. 39397. C4175/8/G55.

26 PRO. W.O. 32. 10107. 18 March 1944.
27 PRO. W.O. 32. 10107. 6 June 1944.
28 PISM. A.XII. 11 August 1944.
29 PISM. A.XII. 30 September 1944.
30 PRO. F.O. 371. 25933. C11506.1506/55. 26 August 1944.
31 PRO. F.O. 371. C12328/7937/55. 15 September 1944.
32 PRO. F.O. 371. 47579/N1884/6/G55. 21 February 1945.
33 PISM. A.XII. 10 March 1945.
34 PRO. F.O. 371. 47579. N1906/6/G55. March 1945.
35 PRO. F.O. 371. N2122/6/G55. 3 March 1945.

14 The absorption of Poles into civilian employment in Britain, 1945–1950

KEITH SWORD

I

Britain emerged from the Second World War in an unprecedented economic state. The country was, in the words of one prominent historian, 'financially insolvent for the first time in its modern history'.[1] Not only had a quarter of its wealth been expended on the war effort, but debts had accumulated which approached £3,500 million.[2] The economy had been twisted out of shape by the requirements of prolonged armed conflict; demands for both manpower and materials had made large inroads into key peacetime industries.[3] In the aftermath of war, and particularly with the shock withdrawal of American 'Lend-Lease' credits in August 1945, the economy had to be turned around once again to cater for peacetime needs. There was a desperate need (a) to accelerate the export drive; (b) to check unnecessary imports and reduce as much as possible overseas expenditure arising out of the war; and (c) to reconvert British industry from war to peace and demobilize our armed forces.[4]

Demobilisation of British forces began almost immediately under the 'age and service' scheme. However the Labour administration which came into power in July 1945 was faced with a very different problem in the form of almost a quarter of a million *Polish* servicemen – members of Polish forces in the West.[5] Loyal to the wartime Polish Government in London, these troops had served under British operational command. When, on 6 July 1945, Britain transferred recognition to the *de facto* (and Soviet-backed) Polish Provisional Government in Warsaw, she also assumed direct responsibility for these forces. In the course of this paper, I shall be outlining the way in which these servicemen and women were demobilized and a majority resettled into civilian employment in this country. For reasons of space I shall not be dealing with the relatively small number of civilian Poles – members of the exiled Polish Government and its administrative apparatus, as well as civilian refugees – who managed to resettle in Britain without official sponsorship. Nor shall I be touching on the recruitment of European Volunteer Workers (many thousands of whom were also Polish) who arrived during this same period.

The Poles formed the first large influx of immigrants to arrive in these shores during the postwar period. Their resettlement was distinctive for a number of reasons. In the first place they constituted a political refugee settlement rather than a traditional labour migration. Following on from this, they had expected to return to their homeland at the end of hostilities and could be said to have arrived here unwillingly. They were not exclusively, as is so often the case with labour migration, from poor rural or peasant backgrounds, but represented all classes of prewar Polish society. Unlike the gradual 'chain' process by which labour migration so often takes place, the Poles arrived in large numbers within a relatively short space of time. Furthermore they were members of a highly trained and disciplined military organisation. Finally, as one would expect from such a military formation, the settlement of Poles was predominantly male; evidence suggests that the sexual imbalance may have been as high as 4 or 5 to 1. Despite these factors, and despite the enormous administrative effort that went into the institutional resettlement of these Poles, the subject has rarely been thought worthy of further study by academics. Zubrzycki's 1956 study remains the only full-length work on the subject.[6]

II

Early expectations on the part of British politicians and administrators were that the majority of Poles could, and should, be induced to return to Poland. There was, therefore, a clear policy on the British side during 1945 and the early part of 1946 *not* to allow Polish servicemen already in Great Britain to demobilise in order to take up civilian employment. In September 1945 H.H. Eggers of the Treasury wrote to a Home Office official,

> As you are no doubt aware, it is the policy of the Interim Treasury Committee[7] not to do anything to encourage Poles not to return to their native land. The prospect of permanent employment in this country – or indeed of any employment without a definite time limit – might be regarded as encouragement in this sense.[8]

However, with the growing realisation that large numbers of Poles would not opt to return to a homeland in the throes of sovietisation, steps were taken by the government to ease the heavy financial responsibility involved in maintaining these forces under arms.[9] In February of 1946, the Prime Minister, Clement Attlee, called a Cabinet Foreign Labour Committee into being under the chairmanship of the Lord Privy Seal, Arthur Greenwood. In its terms of reference, the Committee was instructed to examine the possibility of the increased use of foreign labour in Britain, particularly in those essential industries which were finding difficulties in recruiting labour. Foremost among the topics to be discussed was the use of Poles in coal-mining and agriculture. Subsequently Attlee created a Cabinet Polish Forces Committee, chaired by the Chancellor, Hugh Dalton, to oversee general problems arising from the resettlement of Polish troops.

Moves to resettle and employ Poles in Britain were taken grudgingly. It is clear from the departmental correspondence of the period that, far from being regarded as an asset, they were looked on as something of a nuisance. Officials wrote of Britain 'being saddled' with the 'burden' of the Poles. One Foreign Office mandarin wrote that they should be 'encouraged to take their blessings elsewhere'[10] and to this end an exhaustive enquiry looked into the emigration possibilities for Poles. In all this officials were only sharing the views of their political masters. Even as members of the Polish Forces Committee discussed, at their third meeting in August 1946, plans for absorbing Poles into civilian life, the mood was that 'everything should be done to ensure that as few Poles as possible remained in this country'.[11]

This reluctance to extend hospitality to former allies might seem ungrateful given the Poles' fine war record under British command. It certainly seems illogical given the labour needs of the British economy at the time. As Stadulis has made clear, fears about the manpower situation in postwar Britain were based upon expectations of a declining population (lower fertility and a renewal of overseas migration) as well as the loss of certain categories of worker (large numbers of married women, elderly persons and those juveniles affected by the raising of the school-leaving age in 1947).[12] At the time the Foreign Labour Committee was being established the government was so concerned about the manpower shortage that it was contemplating importing 118,000 German prisoners of war from the U.S. and Canada, and 185,000 from Germany and Norway 'as transport and accommodation permitted'. (This would have been in addition to the several tens of thousands already in the country.) In the Cabinet's view, 'all possible steps should be taken to make available an adequate supply of prisoners to meet the needs of Scottish Agriculture'.[13] From late 1946 onwards the Ministry of Labour embarked upon the European Volunteer Worker scheme, by which Displaced Persons from the refugee camps of liberated Europe were recruited to specific areas of the British economy. Why, then, were the Poles initially viewed in such a negative light?

Apart from any political embarrassment that arose from the refusal of large numbers of Polish Troops in the west to be repatriated, there was a clear qualitative distinction to be drawn between POW or EVW labour, and that provided by former comrades in arms. In the first place, the Poles could not be directed into specific areas of the economy, nor employed in labour gangs with the same freedom as that exercised over German and Italian prisoners. Secondly, as free men they could hardly be prevented from mixing with the local population, risking friction and civil disorder on a wide scale. Thirdly, we have seen (p.234) that to admit the Poles to civilian employment was felt to be a first step towards granting permanent right of settlement. They could not, as was the case with POW labour, be sent home again when current manpower needs had been satisfied. Indeed, the key to an understanding of government ·thinking on the matter is contained in the summary to the Polish Forces Committee meeting mentioned above, at which there was 'general support for the view that the possibility of making *temporary* use of foreign labour to relieve the present manpower shortage should be explored as a matter of urgency'. At this early stage foreign labour was seen as an interim measure, a short-term expedient to aid the economy through its immediate difficulties. Where avoidable, no long-term commitments were to be entered into.

III

On 17 May 1946 a special meeting of the Joint Consultative Committee was held at the Ministry of Labour to discuss the employment of Polish troops. The Committee, which included representatives of both the British Employer's Confederation and the Trades Unions Council, heard that resettlement plans would involve some 160,000 Poles, more than half of whom were still in Italy. There was general agreement that, of the options available for dealing with the Polish Armed Forces, the most preferable was the creation of a resettlement corps under British military control, into which the Poles would be enlisted after disbandment of their own units. In this they would remain until arrangements for their orderly transfer into civilian employment in Britain, or their emigration to a third country, could take place.

After talks with Polish commanders a few days later, the Foreign Secretary, Ernest Bevin, outlined on 22 May in the Commons, plans for the creation of a Polish Resettlement Corps. The PRC, although nominally a military unit and under British military discipline would be an unarmed, non-combatant formation. Its primary function would be to ease the Poles' transition to civilian life by providing instruction in the English language, and vocational training where necessary. Each Pole would sign on for two years' service and, once enlisted, might be allocated to employment in one of two ways. Firstly, he could be allocated to an employer 'on loan' in a group – to carry out work of national importance such as harvesting or clearing bomb-sites. (British troops were also used on such work during this period.) In this case, the Poles would still be members of the Corps, and still under military discipline, but they would only be so used if no suitable British civilian labour was available. Polish troops employed in this way would receive their fixed pay as members of the Corps, but the employer would pay the Government the real rate for the job.

The second method of transfer to civilian employment was through individual release to a job which the Ministry of Labour considered suitable. Although there was a good deal of unease and even irritation among Poles that 'suitability' in this context meant directing them to the most difficult and least rewarding jobs, it is clear that there were attempts on the Government's part to avoid (a) unscrupulous employers exploiting Polish labour and, (b) too great a concentration of Polish workers in any one industry. A Pole employed in this way would not be discharged from the Corps, but would be relegated to the Reserve. In theory, if for any reason he left his civilian employment before service in the Corps was completed, he could be recalled to 'active service'. It was thought possible in this way to provide the Poles with an extra form of social insurance and give them time – a breathing space – during which to adjust to conditions of life in Britain.

On the same day as Bevin's Commons statement, the TUC General Council met to consider a secret document (JCC 173) on the resettlement of the Polish Forces and agreed to nominate members to a Polish Employment Sub-committee of the Joint Consultative Committee. The General Council decision to assist the Government in this matter was made provisional upon four conditions being satisfied:

a) before the introduction of a group of Poles into any industry, there should be appropriate consultations with the trade unions directly concerned.

b) in any case, no Poles should be employed in any grade in any industry where British labour was available.

c) where Poles require further training for filling posts in industry, the conditions under which such training would be provided should be comparable to those applying to British ex-servicemen.

d) if any Pole was placed in a suitable occupation and for any reason left it, subsequent employment should be secured only through the Ministry of Labour.[14]

IV

Although the first enlistments into the Resettlement Corps were not due to take place until mid-September 1946, negotiations with the unions began much earlier. Indeed, as early as February of that year, the Minister for Fuel and Power, Emmanuel Shinwell, had been asked by the Cabinet to determine the degree of willingness of the National Union of Mineworkers to accept Poles into the coal-mining industry. By June 1946 a working party under the chairmanship of Shinwell's Parliamentary Secretary, Hugh Gaitskell, had identified several hundred skilled miners among Poles based in Scotland and interviews were to begin with a view to their recruitment. Vacancies were known to exist for some eight hundred miners in Scottish collieries, the employment of Poles had been cleared with the local lodges of the NUM, and plans for the accommodation of the Poles were well advanced. However, there had been no formal consultation with the union at national level, and this omission was to prove the stumbling block to Government hopes to introduce large numbers of Poles into the collieries.

Government concern was understandable. Coal stocks were low and production was still below its prewar level (which it was to match only in 1950). Indeed, production had been dropping during 1945 and early 1946. Estimated production for October 1946 was 11 million tons, compared with 13 3/4 million tons for the same month in 1945.[15] Undoubtedly some of this fall was due to the labour situation in the mines. Although, by the summer of 1946 the mining industry was experiencing a weekly labour intake of 1,500 men – approximately 600 of whom were former miners returning from service in the forces – this gross figure did not take account of a continued outflow.[16] In his memorandum to the Cabinet of 10 June 1946, Herbert Morrison, Lord President of the Council, pointed out that ' . . . wastage from the industry would again exceed intake in the absence of further measures'.[17] He recommended a target of 2,000 miners per week be recruited. There were mixed feelings therefore when statistics collected by the War Office of the past employment record of Polish servicemen in Britain and Germany were made available. Although they showed that there were some valuable trade skills to be tapped, the number who admitted to coal-mining experience was disappointingly low:

Table 1:   *Figures of Poles with Trade Skills*[18] *1 May 1946*

	U.K.	BAOR	ALL
Skilled craftsmen			
in heavy industry	3,571	2,560	6,131
Building Trades	1,710	872	2,582
Miners	910	448	1,358
Textile workers	244	78	322
Agricultural workers	4,662	3,394	8,056
Clerical and Commercial	3,323	1,209	4,532
Technicians, scientists			
and engineers	1,732	197	1,929
Miscellaneous	9,184	4,395	13,579
	25,336	13,153	38,489

Hugh Gaitskell wrote,

The number of experienced and willing workers among the Poles in this country so far identified are very few. If the proportion among the Poles in Italy and elsewhere is no higher it must be recognised that the total yield of experienced miners is unlikely to exceed a few thousand at most. In confirmation, the proportion of the population employed in mining in prewar Poland was 1.2%. Applying the same percentage to the total Polish Forces under British command suggests that the number of experienced miners among them may not exceed 2–3,000 in all.[19]

While ministers began to give consideration to plans to recruit and train Poles inexperienced in mining work, the whole question remained entirely abstract. Talks with the miners over the introduction of Polish labour remained deadlocked. The NUM executive remained resolutely opposed to the employment of even experienced Polish miners and had, by the end of July 1946, extended the ban to those Poles previously accepted by local lodges in Scotland. Historical and external factors played a part in hardening attitudes. Miners' suspicion was in no small measure due to the legacy of economic insecurity that had plagued the industry under private ownership. The NUM insisted that agreement must be reached to implement the 'Miners' Charter' before they would accept Poles in the coalfields. This called for a five-day week as well as improved amenities and conditions of work. Negotiations with the miners were further complicated by the Labour Government's pending nationalisation of their industry, and the creation of the National Coal Board (which the Government argued would have eventually to take over such negotiations).

When, in September 1946, Mr Shinwell informed the NUM that 200 Polish miners were available for work immediately and the union remained intransigent, *The Times* commented acidly in a leader,

> If the nation shivers next winter it will at least have the satisfaction of knowing that such coal as it is possible to burn in British grates has not been touched by foreign hands, except by a couple of hundred pairs of Polish hands, if the Mineworkers' Union decides one day to permit it.[20]

George Orwell had earlier anticipated *The Times* leader-writer in ridiculing the contradictory nature of some of the views being put forward by union leaders opposed to the employment of Poles. On the one hand, there were complaints about 'wastage' of labour from the mines; on the other, protests that the introduction of Polish or German labour might lead to unemployment in the coal industry.[21] (In fact, the situation was to become even more bizarre than *The Times* leader-writer appreciated when, in May 1947, with many thousands of Poles in Britain still without work, the Government signed a three year trade agreement with Warsaw which provided for the import of Polish coal.)

Like the miners, the farmworkers recognised implicitly that an influx of labour to their industry was necessary, On the land productivity was only being maintained by the use of large numbers of German POWs who were, by September of 1946, shortly due to be repatriated at the rate of 15,000 a month. Like the miners, however, the farmworkers argued that conditions of work in their industry deterred native labour from seeking employment there. The National Union of Agricultural Workers pointed to the shortage of accommodation available (only 55 farm cottages existed for every 100 adult workers) and demanded a more realistic structure of hours and wages to compare with workers in urban areas.[22] Despite several appeals to the NUAW executive during August 1946, the Agriculture Minister, Tom Williams, was unable to gain the Union's acquiescence to the introduction of Poles into agriculture. Finally, he decided that their employment on the harvest would have to go ahead without prejudice to the general question of their employment in industry.[23] By mid-September it was reported from Scotland that all Poles available for work were busy on the potato harvest. Similar arrangements were made in England and Wales, although the effectiveness of these plans had been limited by the need to ensure that Poles did not mix with German POWs.

Controversy over the employment of Poles flared up again in October at the TUC Annual Congress in Brighton, when both NUM and NUAW representatives were among delegates opposed to the General Council's recommendations to support government efforts to employ the Poles in British industry. In an acrimonious debate, during which reference was made to the fact that many of the Poles arriving in Britain had served under British command only after deserting from the *Wehrmacht*, much hostility and a great deal of colourful language was aired. An attempt to refer back to the General Council's recommendations on a card vote produced astonishing scenes as delegations without a prior mandate huddled in groups to discuss how their votes should be cast. Eventually, the vote produced a majority *against* a reference back, but not before the government had been given notice of the strength of anti-Polish feeling that existed in sections of the trade union movement.[24]

Not all trade unions were opposed to the employment of Poles. Early agreements had been reached in the Gas Industry and in Building and Civil Engineering. The Transport and General Workers' Union set about actively recruiting Poles in the resettlement camps from 1947 onwards. By 1949 it had established three all-Polish branches with a combined membership of some 6,000.[25] (It is not known how many Poles may have joined local branches, since the TGWU keeps no nationality statistics of members.) The General and Municipal Workers' Union was similarly helpful. It had early (1943) established links with the Union of Polish Workers and Craftsmen in Britain (*Związek Rzemiéslnikòw i Robotnikòw Polskich w Wielkiej Brytanii*) and under the terms of an agreement between these two bodies, Poles could possess dual membership.[26] GMWU membership enabled many Poles to find employment at a time when other unions were opposing their introduction. Indeed, the support of the two largest unions in the country did much to help the Poles resettle at a time when the more publicised union reactions were ones of hostility.

Where it did exist, union opposition to the introduction of Poles was not entirely without justification, and in some cases their suspicion met with the sympathy of Ministry of Labour officials. Memories of the unemployment of the 1930s were still strong among working people, with all the uncertainties and fears that these engendered. Despite the assurances of a Labour administration that full employment would be the norm for the foreseeable future, trade unionists were wary. There was a natural feeling that the introduction of large numbers of foreign workers would hold down wage levels at a time when workers were seeking to improve their standards of living after years of wartime austerity.

An additional factor was the concerted propaganda campaign conducted against Poles by the pro-Moscow extreme left. It was true that some Poles had been forced into service with the German forces (and had deserted at the first opportunity to Allied lines). But to brand all Poles as 'landlords' and 'fascists' – particularly in view of their fine war record under British command – was plainly ludicrous. The Poles also made no secret of their dislike for Soviet Russia and for the particularly repressive style of state socialism that was being enforced upon their homeland. These views were not popular at a time when pro-Soviet sentiment, which had reached fever-pitch during the later years of the war, still influenced the British public's attitudes.

The lack of progress in negotiations with key unions brought considerable pressure to bear on the Minister of Labour, George Isaacs. In early October 1946, just prior to the stormy TUC Congress, an exchange of letters had taken place between Isaacs and Tom Williams. Isaacs pointed out with some impatience that the concept of the Resettlement Corps as a means of absorbing the Poles into civilian employment had been accepted by the TUC subject to *consultation* with the separate industries concerned; there was no understanding that the *consent* of each industry would have to be obtained. The purpose of consultation was to consider whether the basic conditions were satisfied, as they clearly were in agriculture. Isaacs went on to point out that if the farmworkers' union held out, the other unions would not play their part.[27]

V

In fact the problems experienced in placing Poles were not all caused by union intransigence, nor (as Foreign Office officials were wont to claim) by Ministry of Labour 'pussyfooting'. Several other factors played a part. Perhaps foremost among these was the problem of accommodation. When the decision had been taken to demobilise the Polish Forces in Britain, bringing in thousands of troops and their dependants from overseas theatres, it had seemed obvious that they should be housed, at least temporarily, in vacant service camps. This would avoid any further pressure on an already depleted housing stock, and the adverse publicity that might arise as a result. The expectation was that as many Poles were repatriated, or emigrated to third countries, space in the camps would become available for others. Unfortunately, partly due to shipping difficulties, the outward movement of Poles who did not want to remain in Britain could not take place with the speed that had been envisaged. In any case, it soon became clear that the numbers remaining and seeking civilian employment would be larger than at first anticipated. Urgent attention had to be given both to the extent of camp accommodation available, its quality (especially where families were to be housed), and importantly, its siting in relation to areas of labour shortage.

By October 1946 close to 120,000 Polish troops were quartered in 265 camps in Great Britain – most of them former British or Allied service camps.[28] These were well dispersed and largely in rural areas. Some 3,500 Poles had been located in Anglesey, 2,800 in Cumberland, 5,000 in Northumberland, as well as large numbers in isolated areas of Scotland.[29] However the very remoteness of such camps – and the absence of suitable accommodation in key areas of labour need – proved a major problem. In Gloucestershire, for example, a manufacturer of agricultural machinery had agreed to take up to 1,000 Poles. But apart from RAF camps in the area, there was no possible accommodation for them.[30] Similar reports came from Cornwall (where there was work in the china clay industry) and other parts of the country. At a relatively early stage, therefore, attention was turned to the reaccommodation of PRC members in areas where there was most chance of placing them in employment. Minister of Labour, George Isaacs, was keen to build new accommodation for the Poles near centres of population such as London, Birmingham and Coventry. There was strong opposition to this proposal, however, from Isaacs' colleagues Aneurin Bevan (Minister of Health) and George Tomlinson (Minister of Works). In the first place, they argued, the government had stated its wish to encourage *dispersal* from large urban areas. Secondly, Isaacs' scheme was politically unacceptable, since it would mean great expenditure and diversion of badly needed resources – materials and manpower – for Polish needs. Where it was necessary to reaccommodate Poles he was advised to look into the possibility of converting existing vacated camps, several hundred of which had been made available by the War Office to local authorities. In extreme cases, it was suggested that the Poles be transported from the camps to their place of work.[31]

In the course of 1947 the accommodation situation began to improve as more camps were made available. The Assistance Board and the National Service Hostels Corporation began to take over responsibility for camps previously administered by the War Office. Rumblings continued though, both at the departmental level, where the NSHC was thought to be dragging its feet in assuming responsibility (and the claims of EVW labour soon began to challenge those of the Poles) and from the Polish side, where complaints were made that much of the accommodation was unsuitable. There is no doubt that many such complaints were justified.[32]

VI

The initial rate of placement in civilian employment was slow. By 25 November 1946 – some two and a half months after the first enlistments into the Resettlement Corps had begun – only 342 members had been found jobs, as compared with 25,171 who had registered.[33] The Foreign Office, taking a keen interest in proceedings, thought this 'pretty rotten' and R.M.A. Hankey, chiefly responsible for Polish affairs in the FO Northern Department, lamented, 'This is going very badly. It really is ridiculous that we can't even get agreement to take on Poles to deal with the Xmas parcels traffic!'[34] The number placed had risen to over 2,000 by January of the following year, but the rate of placement was still not rapid enough for the departments concerned and the Ministry of Labour had decided upon a new initiative. In order to get things moving faster they proposed to open employment bureaux within the resettlement camps.

A breakthrough in the government's efforts came in January when, after long negotiations, agreement was finally reached with the NUM executive. Poles were to be admitted to the mining industry in return for the introduction of a 5-day week from 5 May 1947. Indeed there was much pressure on both sides to reach agreement as the bitterest winter for years gripped the country and the fuel crisis caused blackouts and temporary shutdowns in industry. The NUM concession had a sting in the tail however. Not only would the Poles have to agree to join the union and agree to be first to be released in the event of redundancies; their recruitment was also made subject to the approval of local miners' lodges.[35] Resistance from individual pits and lodges seriously hampered government plans to introduce Poles into the mines at the rate of 300 per week. Although by the end of July 1947 some 2,288 Poles had been absorbed into the industry, there were more than 1,000 others for whom jobs and accommodation were waiting, but who were kept idle because of local opposition.[36] It was in any case a fraction of the overall labour shortage of 100,000 in the mines, but the government was expecting that between 15,000 to 20,000 Poles could eventually be recruited towards making good this deficit.

Whether due to the establishment of the employment bureaux in the camps or to the breakthrough in negotiations with the miners, the overall rate of placement began to speed up considerably in the course of 1947, as figures in Table 2 show.

Table 2: *Progress in the resettlement of Poles in British industry from 1 January 1947 to 1 November 1947*[37]

January	2,764
February	4,639
March	4,829
April	7,716
May	13,164
June	22,099
July	27,146
August	33,746
September	37,000
October	43,340

(A further 3,200 Air Force personnel were also placed during this period)

By May *The Times* was reporting that Poles were being accepted 'in most industries' and that some 9,000 Poles had been absorbed into industry and agriculture. About 2,000 men had registered for work on the land, 'enlistment being tardy because the minimum wage of £4 a week compares unfavourably with the higher wage attainable in mining and other industries'.[38] Isaacs confided his hopes to Bevin that as many as 35,000 Poles would be placed in agriculture, but confessed that they were not volunteering in anything like the numbers required.[39] By early June when almost 20,000 Poles had been found jobs, the rate of placement was running at a very healthy 1,800 per week.[40]

A minor, but well-publicised, set-back to the government's efforts occurred in the last week of July, when the Amalgamated Union of Engineering Workers decided that Poles should be withdrawn from their industry. Of 30,000 Poles placed in employment at that stage, no more than 4,500 were in engineering and shipbuilding. Of these, less than 2,000 were AUEW members, so the problem was not a large one. However the principle was felt to be important. The union side argued that there had not been 'full consultation' before the Poles were employed and added, gratuitously, that they should return to Poland. Subsequently it advanced the flimsy rationale that British labour was available. But cases of 'availability' involved men who, although qualified and without work, were refusing to move from their homes to the areas where vacancies were available. The union executive promised that for Poles who had joined the union, their membership fees would be refunded. As a *reductio ad absurdum*, union branches even began contacting their headquarters to ask whether circularised instructions applied also to Poles who had arrived in Britain before the war.[41]

The *Manchester Guardian* drew attention to the difficult position in which the union's action placed employers and warned that if the Poles *were* dismissed they would be once again a charge on public funds. It was 'lamentable' that Mr Isaacs should again need to persuade the unions to accept Poles.[42] *Tribune* likewise attacked the AUEW decision to bar Poles from Employment in the engineering industry as 'painful to Socialists and altogether deplorable'.[43] Isaacs did embark on talks with both the union and the Employers' Federation but was unable to make progress. Eventually, the Ministry of Labour resolved to continue placing Poles in jobs in engineering without AUEW approval or membership. The union's opposition was eventually relaxed in February 1949 largely due to the fact that Poles entering the industry were gaining membership of other unions.[44]

By the end of 1947 it was clear that the back of the problem had been broken. Of 108,000 registrations to the PRC by December of that year, only 38,000 remained to be placed,[45] although there was a keen awareness at the Ministry of Labour and other interested departments that it was primarily the young and healthy who had been settled. The process was bound to slow down as the hard core of elderly, invalids, professional workers and recalcitrants were reached. Indeed the rate of placing slowed down to 1,000 per week by the end of 1947 and by March 1948 was running at 600 per week.[46]

VII

A significant number of Polish professional people, members of the prewar 'intelligentsia' – arrived in Britain during or just after the war. War Office statistics show that as many as 11,000 officers and 9,000 other ranks who joined the Resettlement Corps belonged to this category.[47] Some of these – engineers and scientists in particular – had been employed by the British in crucial war industries from an early date, and for such people finding openings in civilian life was not on the whole difficult. But other professionals, with inadequate mastery of the English language and unfamiliar with British work methods and organization, were handicapped.

These included, apart from engineers and scientists, lawyers, economists, bankers, doctors, teachers, university lecturers, former civil servants, and those career army officers with little or no professional experience outside army service.

A large proportion of these people, particularly of the officer group, were over 40 years old (3,000 were holders of Russian, German and Austrian diplomas and certificates issued before the First World War), and despite the value of much of their training and work experience, it proved extremely difficult to find appropriate openings for them. There was a strong reluctance by British employers to employ such aliens. In part this was due to fear of trade union and employee reactions, but there was also a marked suspicion of unfamiliar qualifications.

Towards the end of 1947 the War Office made an attempt to tackle the problem by establishing prevocational courses for officers in various parts of the country. These included courses ·in deep-sea fishing (Aberdeen), farming and forestry (Perthshire), mechanical trades, building, electrical skills and draftsmanship (all at Kinross), and assorted skills such as tailoring, watch-repairing, upholstery, etc. (Hereford).[48] Further inducement schemes were introduced in early 1948 enabling Polish officers to receive a gratuity and a grant in return for relinquishment of their commission. These were linked with the decision to allow officers who had their own means and were suitably qualified to establish their own enterprises.[49] (This relaxed one of the earliest conditions of settlement imposed upon the Poles that they should not open up in business on their own account.)

The concentration of resources on schemes for officers began gradually to show results. By February 1949, the number of officers who had opted for such schemes was 8,369 (of which 2,869 had relinquished their commissions). By the spring of 1950 many officers had set up in business – although of a type which owed more to British retraining schemes than to former professional skills. The most popular were farming (including dairy and poultry) – 177, watch and clock repairing – 128, furniture trade (including repairs and upholstery) – 78, leather and fancy goods - 70, photography – 67, boot and shoe making – 67, and hotels and boarding houses – 50.[50]

A report completed in October 1947 for the Foreign Secretary had described the question of the Polish officers as 'one of our worst problems' in the resettlement scheme.[51] The author of the report pointed out that it was difficult to insist on a man who was, for example, a lawyer or a professor in Poland before the war taking on a job as an unskilled labourer. Yet many of those who did not have the resources or expertise to set up in business were forced to take low paid employment as night watchmen, hotel kitchen hands, nursing orderlies or gardeners. *The Times* described the fate of such older officers and professional workers as a 'tragedy'.[52]

VIII

Although the movement of Poles into civilian employment had gathered pace during 1947, criticism was still heard from press and parliamentary sources that Poles were being maintained in idleness in the Resettlement Corps. Pressure mounted in the autumn when control of engagement, and limited powers of direction, were reintroduced for British workers – a move designed to encourage the inflow of labour to essential industries. The Cabinet invited the Ministry of Labour to work out 'detailed proposals for ensuring that men in the Polish Resettlement Corps should not be allowed to remain in idleness on military pay when work was available for them which they declined to take'.[53] Implicitly this indicated that sanctions should be devised for members who persistently refused offers of employment.

In a War Office report the Administrator of the Polish Forces, General Thomas, rejected these criticisms as unfair. The PRC could not be regarded as a pool of immediately available labour; any drastic steps to accelerate the numbers being released might result in an administrative breakdown. (Many Poles were employed on camp duties and administration of the PRC.) Furthermore, significant numbers of Polish troops had only recently begun to be transported from overseas theatres to the U.K. These movements would not be finished until early 1948. There was no foundation for the suggestion that Poles were turning down offers of employment on all sides. Throughout the country Anglo-Polish boards reviewed individual cases of men refusing offers of employment. The total number of these was 16 for September 1947 and 10 for October – figures which represented an 'infinitesimal' percentage of the Corps' total membership. The Control of Engagement Order as it applied to British citizens was no true analogy, since the Polish soldier had an 'assured status' as a member of the PRC until he could be released and offered employment.[54]

Ministry of Labour regulations governing placement of PRC members extended to Poles what officials regarded as very generous consideration. As encapsulated in Ministry Circular 58/34, the policy had been to steer Poles into essential work, while leaving them free to choose jobs in non-essential occupations should they so choose (and for which the majority of British workers were now ineligible). A possible advantage to this apparently quixotic approach to the problem was that it offered every encouragement to the Poles to leave the PRC and thus save the British taxpayer the heavy costs of keeping them in idleness. Nevertheless concern remained that Polish workers were in effect being treated more favourably than their British counterparts.

In April 1948 however, an appeal was circulated to the remaining unplaced members of the Resettlement Corps requesting their help in tackling the current economic crisis.[55] While acknowledging the part played by the 57,000 Poles who had already been placed in British industry (and had 'earned high praise from both their fellow workers and from their employers'), the document called for more volunteers and warned that stronger measures would have to be introduced against 'persistent refusers'. (The definition was generally applied by the War Office and the Ministry of Labour to cases where four or more reasonable offers of employment had been refused.) Where persistent refusal occurred, the person concerned would be subject to compulsory discharge from the Corps. Once discharged, he or she would be liable to be directed into employment if a British subject in similar circumstances would have been so directed.

IX

In March 1948 the period of service for new entrants to the Resettlement Corps was reduced to one year. Some 500 Poles were still eligible for the Corps but remained in overseas theatres. At this point the rate of placement in civilian employment was running at 600 per week and only 30,000 were left in the Corps. With the rapid rundown of the PRC the Foreign Labour Committee directed that plans should be made to wind up its activities in the course of the year. This meant the transfer of all remaining responsibilities from the War Office to the other departments concerned – as provided for under the 1947 Polish Resettlement Act. In fact, the winding up of the PRC proved practicable only in September of 1949 and it was July 1950 before all those capable of, and available for, work had been absorbed into the working population. Expenditure on resettlement – and on associated matters such as repatriation and onward migration had been considerable, as official figures illustrate:

Table 3: *Expenditure on Polish Resettlement 1945-1950 according to (a)Department*[56] *(b)Year*[57] *(War Office only)*

(a)	£000,000	(b)	£000,000
War Office	95.00		
Air Ministry	13.00	1945-46	29.00
Admiralty	2.50	1946-47	32.75
Foreign Office	0.50		
Home Office	0.61	1947-48	21.75
Ministry of Health	1.54	1948-49	10.25
National Assistance Board	3.00		
Ministry of Pensions	0.78	1949-50	1.25
Ministry of Education	4.54		
Ministry of Labour	0.85		
Total	122.32	Total	95.00

By early 1949 there is evidence that, despite the earlier misgivings about the prospects of large-scale Polish resettlement, and the heavy burden incurred by the Exchequer in the process, government departments were well pleased with the results of their efforts. Figures released by the Inspectorate General of the PRC showed that, of 140,200 Poles in Britain (at December 1948 – and excluding Polish European Volunteer Workers).

(a)   96,000 (68.5%) maintained themselves.
(b)   16,400 (11.7%) were dependants being maintained by heads of families.
(c)   27,800 (19.8%) were maintained on funds provided by the Treasury.

The latter figures, however, included some 9,000 Poles still employed in the administration of the PRC and by the Assistance Board. Had this group been categorised under (a) as maintaining themselves, then the number being wholly maintained by public funds would have dropped to 18,800 or 13.4%.[58]

The Pole was described in general terms as being 'an efficient and willing worker, ready to work overtime'. On the whole his technical qualifications were higher than those required for the jobs on which he was employed. This was an inevitable consequence of union measures to preserve entry into the skilled grades for native workers, but resulted in bad feelings and disillusionment on the part of many Poles. Only 29% of the Poles in employment had jobs corresponding to their qualifications; 16% (15,400) were professional and clerical workers employed on manual work, while 55% (52,800) were qualified workers employed as unskilled labour.[59]

Table 4: *Main occupations into which ex-members of the Polish Resettlement Corps were absorbed, 1947-1950*[60]

A. Manual Workers		B. Non–manual workers	
Agriculture	8,200	Local Government	1,000
Building	9,000	National Government	
Brick-making	3,100	Service	1,000
Coal-mining	7,300	Professional Services	2,000
Civil engineering	3,000	Students	2,000
Domestic service	1,300	Miscellaneous non-	
Food manufacturing	1,500	manual, including	
Hotels, catering	6,200	business on own account	8,000
Iron and steel	2,500		
General engineering	3,500		18,000
Textiles	6,400		
Miscellaneous	14,000		
Total	66,000		

The statistics in Table 4 show the main occupations in which Poles maintaining themselves were placed from the Resettlement Corps. Although agriculture, building and coal-mining, the three industries into which the government had hoped to see large numbers of Poles move, were indeed the largest employers of Polish labour, nevertheless the overall numbers engaged there were probably a disappointment.

By the end of the decade a great many Polish businesses had grown up – many to cater for the needs of the sizeable Polish community itself. In an article for the *Anglo-Polish Review* (June 1950) a contributor wrote,

About 1,000 Polish firms came into existence after the war, but only the exceptional ones have managed to prosper . . . the majority of them are condemned to limiting their commercial relations to Poles only, as they cannot win the confidence of the British buyer.

Yet a handbook produced in 1950 by the Union of Polish Traders and Businessmen contains some 104 pages and its list of businesses includes estate agencies, building firms, chemists, cafes, restaurants, travel bureaux, hotels, bookshops, printing firms, and, almost inevitably, import-export agencies.[61] Most of the concerns listed were in the London area, reflecting the heavy concentration of Poles in the capital even at this early date. The handbook itself provides further evidence of the speed with which the Polish community established itself, following resettlement, and of its economic vigour.

The PRC report pointed to a number of further benefits which absorption of Poles into British industry had provided. Since the Poles were mostly living in camps and hotels, they did not aggravate the local housing situation. They constituted a mobile reserve of manpower, easily transferable owing to the high percentage of single men and the lack of material or other ties with their place of present residence. Being newly recruited and starting generally from the level of unskilled work they were in the lowest pay groups. Nevertheless, owing to the proportion of single men, the percentage of Poles liable to income tax was probably higher than in the case of the normal working population. Indeed, taken as a whole, there was a higher proportion of worker-earners than was the case in 'normal' immigrant groups.

This fact (the report concluded) represents an advantage which should in the long run offset the disadvantages of the initial cost of resettlement and of the necessity of maintaining on assistance from public funds a part of the non-earning members of the Polish group.[62]

What of Polish views? Today there is a widely-held recognition among Poles that the British resettlement provisions were enlightened and even generous. A typical comment is that the British behaved 'decently'. There is particular praise for the farsightedness which led to the continued support of educational provisions. As a result many hundreds of younger Poles were able to complete vocational courses in further and higher education, and to play a valuable role in the economic and social life of the community.[63] Nevertheless, there is also a residue of bitterness to be found in some quarters. For some the Polish resettlement scheme was an opportunity lost when, in the interests of short-term labour needs, qualified and experienced workers were employed as unskilled labour; when Poles with professional skills were compelled to take menial and mentally undemanding work. The 'declassment' which this brought about was traumatic for many.

In 1951 *The Times* warned that if the discouragement and disappointment felt by foreign labour generally at their poor prospects were not remedied, there was a danger that many of the country's best foreign workers would decide to leave their important work, and even the country itself.[64] Unfortunately, by that time many thousands of disillusioned Poles had already made the decision either to return reluctantly to their homeland, or to emigrate further afield.

Notes: Chapter 14

1   F.S. Northedge, *Descent from Power* (London, 1974), p.38.
2   Ibid, 39; Also J. Frankel, *British Foreign Policy* (London, 1975), p. 82.
3   According to the *Labour Party Year Book, 1947-48*, over 5 million men and women were under arms at the end of the war, requiring the ancillary services of a further 4 million civilians. Government targets were aimed at reducing military manpower by 80% and defence costs accordingly, by the end of 1946. (p.119)
       Other sources state that at June 1945, Britain still had forty-five per cent of its workforce in the Services and munitions industries. (W.K. Hancock and M.M. Gowing, *The British War Economy*, (1949), p. 549)
4   These were the essential points put by the Chancellor of the Exchequer, Hugh Dalton, to the Cabinet on 17 August 1945. See H. Dalton, *High Tide and After. Memoirs 1945-60*, (London, 1962), p. 70.
5   I am relying here on statistics provided by J. Zubrzycki, *Polish Immigrants in Britain*, (The Hague, 1956) p. 57, who gives the strength of the Polish armed forces in July 1945 as 228,000. With the further recruitment on the continent of former prisoners of war, this figure rose to 249,000 by December 1945.
6   Ibid.
7   The Interim Treasury Committee for Polish Affairs was established in July 1945 to supervise the orderly liquidation of the London Polish Government and its administrative apparatus. It was chaired by Sir Wilfred Eady.
8   FO 371/47756 (N11797/1938/55). H.H. Eggers (Treasury) to H. Care (HO), 9 September, 1945.
9   In an influential Cabinet Paper on the Overseas Deficit prepared in early 1946, Lord Keynes stated that the Polish Army was costing £2 1/2 million pounds a month to maintain. His opinion was that 'The Polish Army should be disbanded immediately'. (C.P. (46) 58. 8 February 1946).
10   FO 371/56387. Letter from Ball to Treasury, June 1946.
11   FO 371/56631. (N10257/2615/55).
12   E. Stadulis, 'The Resettlement of Displaced Persons in the United Kingdom', *Population Studies*, vol. 5 (1952), no. 3, pp. 207–237.
13   Cabinet Papers. CP 15 (46) 6. 14 February 1946.
14   TUC 78th Annual Congress Report, 1946. Para 238.
15   Cabinet Papers. CP (46) 242. Memorandum by the Lord President of the Council on Employment in the Coalmining Industry.
16   Ibid.
17   Ibid.
18   FO 371/56627 (N5747/2615/55). Letter from Lt. Col. J.C. Daukes (War Office) to P.F. Hancock (Foreign Office), 1 May 1946.
19   FO 371/56566 (N8735/658.55). Report by H. Gaitskell on the Employment of Poles in the Coalmining Industry 3 July 1946.
20   *The Times*, 2 September, 1946.
21   G. Orwell, *Collected Essays, Journalism and Letters* , vol. 4, 1945–50 (1968), p. 122.
22   *Observer*, 29 September 1946.

23 FO 371/56634 (N13617/2615/55). Employment of Poles in Agriculture. Memorandum by the Minister of Agriculture and Fisheries for the Cabinet Polish Forces Committee, 19 October 1946.
24 TUC 78th Annual Congress Report, 1946, pp. 357–364.
25 Zubrzycki, *Polish Immigrants*, pp. 99–102. Also Stadulis, *Resettlement of Displaced Persons*, pp. 219 and 225.
26 See article 'Polski Ruch Zawodowy w Anglii' in *Orzeł Biały*, 8 May 1948. However Stadulis points out that the Polish Union subsequently ceased to be recognised as a legitimate body after some abuses regarding payment of dues came to light (*Resettlement of Displaced Persons*, p. 225).
27 FO 371/56635 (N13617/2615/55).
28 Written answer by Mr Bellenger, Secretary of State for War, to a question from Mr. Piratin, 19 October 1946, *Hansard*, (Commons), vol. 428, p. 79.
29 FO 371/56633 (N12126/2615/55). Memorandum by the Parliamentary Secretary to the Minister of Labour for the Cabinet Foreign Labour Committee (FLC), 19 September 1946.
30 FO 371/56636 (N15364/2615/55). Minutes of the 7th meeting of the Cabinet FLC, 27 November 1946.
31 FO 371/56635 (N14466/2615/55). Minutes of the 6th meeting of the Cabinet FLC, 7 November 1946.
32 A War Office report by General Thomas, Administrator of the Polish Forces, stated:

Accommodation for civilianised Poles in the working hostels is very appreciably below any standard which would be accepted by the British working man.

FO 371/66145 26 November 1947
33 FO 371/56673 (N15619/261/55). Second Report of the Official Committee for the Employment of Poles for the Cabinet FLC.
34 Ibid.
35 Cabinet Papers CP 9(47)2, 17 January 1947. Also *The Times*, 3 May 1947.
36 *Financial Times*, 18 August 1947.
37 FO 371/66145 (N13308/86/55).
38 *The Times*, 17 May 1947.
39 FO 371/66145 (N6366/86/55).
40 FO 371/66145 (N7423/86/55). Fifteenth report of the Offical Committee on the Employment of Poles for the Cabinet FLC, 23 June 1947.
41 FO 371/66145 (N9277/86/55). Memorandum by the Minister of Labour for the Cabinet FLC, 9 August 1947. See also LAB 8/1490 and the contemporary press.
42 *Manchester Guardian*, 29 July 1947.
43 *Tribune*, 1 August 1947.
44 *Manchester Guardian*, 18 February 1949.
45 FO 371/71538 (N415/57/55). Statistics on the Strength and Distribution of the Polish Resettlement Corps prepared by the Official Committee on the Employment of Poles, January 1948.
46 FO 371/71539 (2721/5755). Monthly report on Polish repatriation and the Polish Resettlement Corps for the Foreign Secretary, 5 March 1948.
47 FO 371/71540 (N12058/57/55). The employment of PRC members and ex-members with qualifications for intellectual workers. (Four page discussion document prepared for the fifth meeting of the Resettlement Committee for Poles.)
48 General Sikorski Historical Institute Archive. AXII. 1/83. War Office memorandum APF1/BM/195, 23 September 1947.
49 LAB 8/1488.
50 Ibid.
51 FO 371/66162 (N12077/147/55).
52 *The Times*, 21 May 1951.
53 Cabinet Papers, CP(47)248, 9 September 1947.
54 FO 371/66145 (13308/86/55). Note by General Thomas, 26 November 1947.
55 FO 371/71539 (N4784/57/55). Appeal to members of the Polish Resettlement Corps issued by the War Office, 20 April 1948.

56   J. Isaac, *British Post-War Migration*, (London, 1954), p.173.
57   Fourth Report of the Select Committee on Estimates, Session 1948–49. Polish Resettlement.
58   AST 18.1. Note on the number and source of income of Poles residing in Great Britain, January 1949.
59   Ibid.
60   These statistics are drawn from United Nations sources and are quoted in Zubrzycki (op. cit., 66). However they need to be treated with care, (a) because they are incomplete (the Federation of Poles in Great Britain gave the number of Poles in employment at July 1950 as 117,500) and (b) because they give evidence only of placement from the PRC, masking subsequent changes of employment.
61   'Informator Handlowy' printed by and for the *Związek Kupców i Przemysłowców Polskich w Wielkiej Brytanii*, London, 1950.
62   AST 18.1.
63   Owing to limitations of space it has not been possible to adequately deal with education and training in this paper. For an account of the work of the Committee for the Education of Poles in Great Britain, see the Ministry of Education Booklet 'Education in Exile', London, HMSO, 1956.
64   *The Times*, 21 May 1951.

(The official documents cited in the above footnotes are from the following collections: FO 371 – Foreign Office General Correspondence; LAB – Ministry of Labour; AST – Assistance Board; CP – Cabinet Papers. All documents are from the Public Records Office, Kew.)

15 The initial absorption of the Palestinian refugees in the Arab host countries, 1948–1949

BENNY MORRIS

The First Wave

The Palestinian Arab exodus began in December 1947, within days of the UN General Assembly passage of the Partition Resolution for Palestine and the start of Arab-Jewish hostilities around the country. The first wave of exiles, who numbered several tens of thousands over December 1947 – March 1948, was largely drawn from the urban middle classes – relatively wealthy families from Jaffa, Haifa and Jerusalem, some with second houses in Lebanon, Nablus or Amman, who preferred to be out of harm's way for the duration of the conflict. In most cases, they were not compelled to emigrate by Jewish order, pressure or victory in the field; often, as in Haifa and Jaffa in the first months of the war, the hostilities were relatively minor and these families, if at all, were only remotely threatened. Exile promised enhanced comfort and safety. Few of them thought that exodus would turn into refugeedom, and that their towns, houses and lands would be conquered and permanently occupied by the Jews; most probably expected the armies of the Arab states to intervene, make short shrift of the Haganah and the emergent Jewish state, and restore them to their towns and property, which, as the months passed, gradually fell under Jewish control.

The arrival in Sidon and Beirut, Ramallah and Nablus, Amman, Cairo and Alexandria of this first wave of refugees apparently passed without excessive difficulties; the numbers were relatively small, the influx stretched out over months and the exiles' money oiled the proceedings. There were no major problems of accommodation or sustenance; most had relatives to stay with, second houses or money to pay for hotel rooms and keep. And the hosts, like the exiles, never conceived of the influx as permanent; within weeks or months, they would be returning to Palestine. It occurred probably to no one on the Arab side at this stage that the war would definitively and radically transform the demography of Palestine to the detriment of the Arab population.

Hosting the Second Wave

But things changed dramatically during the end of March, April and the first half of May, with the Haganah switch to the strategic offensive and the Jewish conquest of most of the Arab-populated areas allotted to the Jewish state in the partition plan. Jewish pressure on the Arab villages of the Coastal Plain, and the Haganah conquest of parts of Arab Jerusalem and the Jerusalem Corridor, Tiberias, Haifa, the Hula Valley in the Galilee Panhandle, Jaffa and its environs, Beisan and Safad sent some 200,000–300,000 urban and rural Palestinian Arabs fleeing to the safety of the surrounding Arab states (Lebanon, Syria, Egypt and Transjordan) and the Arab population centres of Gaza, Nablus, Ramallah and Hebron. These refugees – driven by panic, fear of injury or death in the hostilities, wartime economic privation and Jewish pressures and expulsion orders – also did not conceive of exile as anything but a temporary expedient or condition. But this second and major wave of refugees, by sheer weight of numbers and chronological concentration, posed a new and radical problem for the Arab host governments, municipalities and local inhabitants.

Lt. General Gordon MacMillan, the British GOC Palestine, already before the fall of Arab Haifa wrote of the 'suffering' of the Arabs of Samaria (the Jenin-Tulkarm-Nablus-Ramallah area) from the 'enormous influx of refugees from Galilee'. The locals (as well as the refugees) were hit by shortages of food and petrol.[1]

Tens of thousands of the Galilee (and Haifa) Arabs had fled to Lebanon, where the influx, in May, was reported by the British Legation to be 'aggravating the shortages existing in certain essential commodities, especially cereals and oil products'. Petrol was in short supply and the Lebanese Government stopped the fuel ration to Palestinian-registered cars; Palestinian car-owners were forced to use the black market. In June, much was made in the Lebanese press of the suffering and death of refugees on the roads to Lebanon and, according to one French agent (who doubled for Israel), the refugees in Lebanon wanted to end the war at any price 'as they had reached the limit of their endurance'.[2]

The arrival in Egypt during April of what were the first major batches of refugees gave rise to problems, solutions and attitudes which were soon to characterize most of the host countries. More than 1,100 reached Port Said from Jaffa and Haifa between 25 and 29 April, arriving mostly in 'small steamers, fishing smacks, rowing boats and caiques'. About 270 of these, many of them women and children, arrived in 'open rowing boats, without sails' and without food. The Egyptian authorities placed them in quarantine and Port Said inhabitants took up a collection of funds and food for them.

A 'special quarantine camp' was set up to accommodate some of the refugees at Port Fuad (across the Suez Canal from Port Said), but 'a considerable number' were taken in by local Egyptian families. According to the American Consulate in Port Said, 'many' of the refugees had come with quantities of Palestinian banknotes 'and some of them have been found in possession of narcotic drugs (hashish) which they intended to sell in Egypt'. But there were more serious problems. 'The fact that many of the Arab refugees are of military age and able to bear arms tends to have a dampening effect on the enthusiasm of prospective Egyptian volunteers for military service with the Arab Legion. "Why should we go to Palestine to fight while Palestine Arab fighters are deserting the cause by flight to Egypt?" some of them have been heard to remark,' reported the consulate. Moreover, 'anti-British feeling' had increased in Port Said as a result of the influx, because the refugees were charging 'that the British are supporting the Jews and neglecting the defence of the Arab population in Palestine.'[3]

The problem of the refugees generating anti-British feelings among Arab host populations was to crop up increasingly through 1948, causing serious concern in Whitehall about Britain's position in the various host countries. Already in February 1948, the High Commissioner for Palestine, Sir Alan Gordon Cunningham, reported to London that Transjordan's King Abdullah – with whom he had lunched that week at Shuna – had complained about the 'exodus of Palestine Arabs into Transjordan [saying] . . . they were all arriving thoroughly anti-British and, hence, might give him trouble'.[4]

Egypt's Moslem religious leaders, meeting as the *Ulema* in Cairo on 26 April, called on the Arab governments to 'take action' (i.e., to go to war) to liberate Palestine and, meanwhile, 'to give asylum to Arab refugees from Palestine.' In Egypt, two new camps were readied for the absorption of refugees, at Kantara and Abbassia, on the banks of the Suez Canal; most of the 1,600 refugees who had arrived by sea at Port Said between 2 and 8 May were sent there. Local Egyptian relief organisations were still supplying food and clothing, but 'they do not appear to be as enthusiastic now as they were with the first arrivals'. Quarrels had erupted between the refugees and the local population. And a rumour had surfaced that the relief organisation officials intended to visit the camps and ask the able-bodied among the refugees to join volunteer units to 'fight the Jews. If the men refuse, the Committee [of representatives of the relief organisations] will request the Government [of Egypt] to send them back to Palestine.' Some middle class Egyptians had reportedly threatened that if the Government did not send them back, 'they will place them on caiques and send them back by force . . .'[5]

Similar sentiments surfaced in Transjordan. 'Some rich [refugees] have come to Amman and the fact that they are seen frequenting the banks is causing trouble and ill feeling, the Transjordan folk seeing no reason why their men should go to Palestine to fight for the Palestinians, who got their wealth by selling their land to the Jews,' wrote one British observer from Transjordan in mid-June. She also remarked that money and relief workers were urgently needed to take care of the mass of poor refugees.[6]

Palestinian leaders tried to combat this ill-feeling towards the refugees. Suleiman Tukan, a pro-Hashemite dignitary from Nablus, on 11 June on Amman Radio comprehensively defended the refugees by charging that the Arab states were 'responsible' for the plight of the Palestinians as they had not heeded the Palestinians' cries for help. The essence of Tukan's defence was that the Arabs had not fled the country of their own free will. Be that as it may, Tukan appealed to the refugees of the Samaria and Hebron districts to return to their homes; the appeal may have been the price Tukan had had to pay the Transjordanian authorities for allowing him to broadcast his 'defence' of the refugees.

The start of the First Truce between Israel and the Arab States on 11 June also apparently spurred the Syrians to try to 'push' their refugees back across the border, back to the abandoned Arab villages in the (Galilee Panhandle) Hula Valley. Israeli military intelligence assessed that Damascus had adopted this policy 'to remove from itself the economic and organisational burden [of their upkeep]' and 'to introduce a Fifth Column [back] into the Jewish areas cleared [of Arabs]'. Meanwhile, the Syrians were providing at least some of the refugees with food supplies.[7]

The IDF, of course, had received orders – stemming from both tactical military and strategic-political considerations – to halt with fire the return of refugees back into Israeli-held territory.[8] Local IDF intelligence officers in various sectors of the country believed that Arab refugees were infiltrating back into Israeli-held territory mainly to harvest the summer crops rather than to permanently resettle in their former villages. The refugees were driven by 'real hunger'. The situation of the refugees along the Israeli-Syrian border was so desperate that they braved IDF bullets to foray into the fields in the Galilee Panhandle during the nights. Some refugee farmers even returned at night to water their fields 'in the hope that they will manage to plant vegetables on [for?] their return to their village with the [start of the] truce'. IDF Intelligence Branch warned that the process, if allowed to go on, would eventually result in the refugees indeed permanently resettling in Israel.[9] The IDF duly barred the refugees from returning to Israeli-held territory.

The Third Wave and the State of
the Refugees During the Summer of 1948

The majority of the 300,000 refugees who had left Israeli-held territory by the 15 May invasion of Palestine by the Arab armies fell under the control, and became the immediate responsibility of King Abdullah and his government; his army, the Arab Legion, had occupied the Nablus-Tulkarm-Ramallah-Jericho-East Jerusalem-Hebron area (today known as the West Bank). Sir Alec Seath Kirkbride, the British Minister to Amman, grasped the significance of the events and sensed what was to come in terms of the refugees. 'It is not even possible to foresee how the Transjordan authorities are to provide food and shelter during the coming winter' for the thousands 'now living in destitution,' he wrote to Foreign Secretary Ernst Bevin. The refugees themselves, he added, were 'becoming increasingly vocal' in demanding an end to the war 'at all costs'. Their demand, he thought, was 'based on the assumption that if hostilities cease, they will be able to return to their homes in the Jewish areas. [But] why the Jews should permit them to do so, now that events have solved the most difficult problem which originally faced the Jewish state, that of a large Arab minority, it is difficult to see. In fact, the Arab world is likely to be faced with the resettlement of these refugees and not with their repatriation . . .' The Arab leaders had never 'anticipated' the mass flight of the Arab population, 'often without there being any imminent threat,' from their homes in the areas allocated to the Jews under the partition plan, he added as an afterthought.

Kirkbride's letter to Bevin sparked the first major internal Foreign Office debate about what could be done for or about the Palestinian refugees. Lance Thirkell thought that the International Refugee Organisation, which, he said, had 'done so much to help Jews to get into Palestine', could help the 'unfortunate Arabs who have been pushed out incidentally. Singularly little has been heard of the fact that the Jewish incursion into Palestine has produced an exodus of 300,000 refugees. I should have thought that this would have had some [anti-Israeli] propaganda value.' David Balfour also thought the IRO could help. But A.W. Wilkinson minuted: 'The IRO has insufficient funds to take on any more refugees and doesn't deal with "internally displaced" people.' She rejected Thirkell's and Balfour's comments that the IRO had helped Jews get to Palestine and said that, in fact, the organisation had assisted in the resettlement of European Moslem refugees. H. Beeley commented that in Palestine the issue was not really one of 'internal displacement'.[10]

The '10-day's fighting' (between the end of the First Truce and the beginning of the Second Truce) in mid-July both highlighted and exacerbated the plight of the refugees. A further 100,000 Palestinians joined the ranks of the exiles, the bulk of them expelled by the IDF from Lydda and Ramle to the Transjordanian-held part of Palestine (Latrun-Ramallah-Qalqilya-Jericho). The massive, concentrated influx (on top of the defeat administered to the Arab Legion) shook Abdullah's kingdom. The British colony in Amman considered evacuation, but rejected the idea after Legion commander General John Glubb said he was 'not pessimistic' about keeping order in the city: ' . . . it may be possible to keep Amman Suk [marketplace] and Palestinian refugee elements under control.' Abdullah and Glubb wanted to 'end hostilities' but were 'frightened' of the reaction of the other Arab states and of 'public feeling'. There had been several anti-British and, implicitly, anti-Abdullah demonstrations in Amman and elsewhere in the country.[11]

Transjordan's refugee problem had 'become acute' and the government was unable to cope. A rough idea of the situation in July in Ramallah, a town of about 10,000 and the first major way-station of the Lydda-Ramle refugees, is provided in a message from the municipality to King Abdullah, transmitted via the Arab Legion's radio communications system and monitored by Israeli intelligence. '. . . seventy thousand people are scattered in the streets, the great majority of them impoverished [and] suffering from a major lack of basic goods and water, constituting a serious health hazard,' reported acting mayor Hanna Khalaf. 'The municipal council beseeches Your Highness to issue [an order] to the city of Ramallah to evict [the refugees] as the city cannot cope.' Abdullah answered unsympathetically that the city must display 'patience towards your brothers', and that relief would soon be on its way. A graphic description of the situation in the town was provided by an English-language Ramallah radio broadcast: 'The smell is beginning to be bad, in so many places,' said the reporter-observer, 'and what can the girls do with small brooms of twigs, in classrooms now holding three hundred people? Look at the dignified families in the [olive] groves and rooms, attempting to make privacy for themselves with stretched out blankets and dresses . . . Look at the women washing clothes and baking some precopis flour for their hungry families . . . There won't be a drop of flour left in Ramallah in three days . . . There are seventy thousand people to feed . . . Transjordan rushed over dates, flour and bread, but it is a drop in the ocean . . .' Seen from Tel Aviv, the refugees constituted a major burden for the Transjordanian authorities, particularly the military, clogging roads, requiring food and shelter, diverting Arab Legion resources and energies, as well as undermining the morale of the local population in the towns north and west of Jerusalem.[12]

Towards the end of July thousands of Lydda-Ramle refugees moved from Ramallah, eastwards, into Transjordan, to Amman. There, too, most were housed in school buildings (the schools were recessed for the summer vacation) or camped out in olive groves and private gardens. One British observer, Winifred Coate, a school headmistress, found them 'lying on old sacks and rags', destitute. They lacked bedding and cooking utensils. 'Life out of doors like this does not seem unnatural to many of them who were accustomed to go out and camp in their vineyards at this time of year, but this is in the middle of Amman and is most unsuitable in a town,' she commented.[13]

The U.S. vice-consul in Amman, Wells Stabler, towards the end of July reported that the Transjordanian estimate of Palestinian refugees in Transjordan (east of the Jordan River – in Amman, As-Salt, Zarka and Irbid) stood at '80-100,000', and Abdullah had felt obliged to close the kingdom's frontiers to additional refugees. The British estimate at this time, based on figures provided by Glubb, was about 56,000 refugees in Transjordan proper and some 70-100,000 in the areas west of the Jordan River occupied by the Arab Legion.[14]

How were the Transjordanian authorities coping with the refugees? Coate thought that 'the people of T.J.[Transjordan] had risen to the occasion rather better than might have been expected, as they have no experience of the kind of organisation needed'. In Amman, two ladies' welfare societies had raised funds. In Zarqa, a 'Ladies Committee' had doled out to each family 'a small packet of rice and sugar and tea and a piece of soap; also the most destitute had been given one blanket per family'. But this order of voluntary assistance, as Coate realized, was 'only a drop in the bucket of the great need'.

Coate, friendly with the Transjordanian finance minister's wife, appears to have been well-informed, at least as regards the refugees east of the river. They were getting, at the end of July, two small loaves of bread per head per day from the government. In addition, pregnant women and some children were getting milk. The government planned, she said, to hand out 300 mils (about six shillings) per month per head to cover other necessities; but she probably treated this information skeptically in light of Transjordan's poverty.[15]

The skepticism of the British consul in Amman, Pirie Gordon, was more comprehensive and far-seeing. 'I doubt whether Transjordan Government is capable of preparing any plans for organizing the future relief, and in any case the main difficulty lies in the burden imposed on the country's minute financial resources,' he wrote. The local authorities foresaw starvation and the outbreak of epidemics if nothing substantial was done, quickly. And he was not particularly impressed by the level of public generosity displayed. In one Transjordan district, with 16,000 refugees, he wrote, the local authorities had managed to raise by public subscription only PL1,800. 'In Amman suggestion that merchants should contribute has been flatly rejected and an offer of funds of the Supreme Moslem Council and of the Ramle municipality approximately a total of [PL]90,000 has so far come to nothing because the Arab banks who hold these accounts prefers [sic] to have no funds available.' Meanwhile, prices had shot up, and the refugees themselves had quickly run out of savings and were begging or hungry; 'there has been a marked increase in crimes against property,' Pirie Gordon added.

In short, 'being idle, homeless, bereft of all their possessions and discontented with the relief efforts made on their behalf[,] the refugee communities in Amman and Salt at least, are fertile breeding grounds for embittered and opposed sentiments . . . Britain is accused as usual of being mainly responsible for their plight. The Arab rulers are held guilty of misleading them and involving them in the loss of their farms and settled lives. Local authorities regard them as a menace to the peace and security of the country and believe that communists are at work amongst them agitating against established order here,' wrote Pirie Gordon.[16]

In the Transjordanian-occupied part of Palestine, the situation was no better. Sir Hugh Dow, the British consul-general in Jerusalem, reported that 'local efforts to deal with the problem are largely uncoordinated and limited to bare emergency measures by local authorities and social committees . . . The main requirements of Arab refugees still inside Palestine are food, water, blankets and clothing. As the autumn approaches, the need for the two last named will increase and also for temporary or permanent housing . . .' Dow was thoroughly disgusted with the Arab governments' attitude to the refugees: they appeared less concerned with providing relief than getting rid of the 'refugee incubus'.

Dow suggested that the 'best' solution for the problem of the refugees from the Jewish areas would be their resettlement in Arab countries. Israel would pay for the abandoned Arab lands and other property in Palestine, and the money would go towards compensating individual refugees and towards 'the resettlement of the poorer refugees'. At the same time, fund-raising in Britain ('a Lord Mayor's Fund') could cover the cost of repatriating Palestinians to Arab or Jewish-held areas of Palestine ('though they should not be encouraged to do so', commented Dow). Dow said that the Lord Mayor's Fund should be administered by Britain rather than the Arabs (a suggestion with which Pirie Gordon concurred). He added, however, that one should expect Arab League opposition to the scheme 'since it will have a purely humanitarian and practical object and will not fit in with their political desire to rid themselves of refugees in their territories in the first place . . . and to send large Arab populations back into Jewish areas as a nucleus for future trouble'.[17]

Dow was reacting to a cable from W.E. Houstoun-Boswall, the British Minister in Beirut, who on 21 July had proposed the establishment of a Lord Mayor's fund as 'a spontaneous act on the part of the British public to show their sympathy and friendly feelings for the Arabs' and to counter the trend in the Arab countries of vilification of Britain as a betrayer of the Arab cause. Houstoun-Boswall, like many other British diplomats in the Middle East at the time, was at best dismissive of the Palestinians, who had chosen 'to run away rather than fight'; by their 'general exodus,' he had written, the Palestinians had 'shown themselves to be rather contemptible and perhaps not so deserving of sympathy . . .' But Britain must act charitably, to show that the British remain the Arabs' 'best friends'.[18]

The American assessment of the state of the refugees west of the Jordan River was at first somewhat more sanguine – 'Condition . . . not yet desperate'; it forecast complete destitution 'shortly', followed by 'hardship and danger to health' with the onset of winter. But an on-the-spot inspection by consular officials a fortnight later, in mid-August, produced a far darker picture. The Ramallah area was flooded with some 100,000 refugees, or almost twice the number of the normal local population. 'Condition refugees appalling . . . Live along sides road under trees . . . Housing facilities or even tents not available . . . Nights become very cold mid-September and rains start soon after . . . Water supply . . . precarious . . . water probably contaminated . . . Definitely possible that water supply may give out completely before end August.' The Transjordanian Government was daily distributing 250 grams of bread per day per refugee (half the amount east of the Jordan). The doctor accompanying the consular officials ruled that this represented about 600 calories per day and was 'insufficient [to] sustain life for long'. Moreover, 'sanitation practically nonexistent . . . no hospital beds available,' little vaccine left for immunization against typhoid, and none at all against typhus, smallpox, diphtheria and cholera. While 'good weather and good luck', to date, had left the adult death rate normal, and only 20 suspected cases of typhoid, one of diphtheria and one of meningitis had been reported, the worst was to be expected health-wise during the following weeks. The consul-general summed up the situation thus: 'Complete lack of organisation apparent. Local authorities overwhelmed by magnitude problem and admit own inability cope with situation. No funds or qualified personnel available for organizing camps, food distribution, sanitation and immunization programs etc.'[19]

The situation was no better north of Ramallah. Major Hacket-Paine, a former British liaison officer with the Transjordanians, in mid-August toured the Iraqi-controlled Samaria District (the Nablus-Tulkarm-Jenin 'triangle') and found the state of the refugees – whom he was told numbered in the District between 100,000 and 120,000 – 'very bad' and their morale 'very low'. Most lived in the open, under trees, in caves and in unfinished houses; few had blankets and there was insufficient food. A major health problem was expected when the rain came. Most blamed the British for their plight 'and their hatred for us plus America and the Arab League is unbelievable'. As well, since the fall of Lydda and Ramle, 'Abdulla's name is just plain dirt'. Hackett-Paine, too, pleaded for British relief aid (to be channeled not through the Arab League).

The Foreign Office's Lance Thirkell thought the major's report 'ungrammatical and over-emotional' but that it conveyed well the 'acute misery' of the refugees in Samaria. Another Foreign Office official minutes: 'We may be hated now but that is nothing like the hatred which the Jews are laying up for themselves in the future if they don't allow these people back.'[20]

The great majority of the Palestinian refugees at this time – as in future decades – were concentrated in Transjordan and in the Transjordanian-held eastern areas of Palestine; smaller groups had moved to Egypt, Lebanon, Syria and Iraq.

In Egypt, according to Jefferson Patterson, the U.S. charge d'affaires, there were some 14,000 refugees, dispersed in private homes and in the makeshift camps along the Suez Canal and in Cairo. 'All are reported to be in great need,' he reported. He had been informed that Egypt was considering expelling its Jewish community and confiscating their property 'in order to provide aid and houses for the Palestine Arab refugees'; Egyptian officials denied this. The Egyptian press, he reported, was 'indignant' at the world's silence about the plight of the refugees. There were another 50,000 refugees in Egyptian-occupied Palestine, mainly concentrated in the Gaza area.[21]

In Lebanon, mainly concentrated in camps outside Sidon, near Lake Kar'oun in the eastern Bek'a Valley and at Bint Jbail, just north of the Israeli border, were some 50,000 refugees. The government was providing each with 10 kilograms of flour and three Lebanese pounds per person. Part of this was covered by a grant to the Lebanese Government of 100,000 Egyptian pounds from the Arab League. The Lebanese were pressing UN Mediator for Palestine Count Folke Bernadotte to obtain Israeli permission for their repatriation. The Lebanese Christians viewed this massive influx of Moslems as a serious threat and 'would resist any attempt to [permanently] resettle refugees in Lebanon,' reported the British Minister, Houston-Boswall. He agreed with Dow's assessment that the solution to the refugee problem would ultimately have to be resettlement in the Arab countries, 'but Lebanon for obvious reasons would have to be excluded from any such scheme', he thought.[22]

By the end of July, only some 200 Palestinian refugees had reached Iraq. But Iraq, according to its prime minister, was about to receive another 5,000 (mainly from the 'little triangle' of Jaba, Ein Ghazal and Ijzim, an originally Iraqi-controlled Arab enclave in Palestine's coastal Plain conquered by the Israel Defence Forces during the Second Truce).

The Iraqis, according to the British Legation in Baghdad, had made no provision for the refugees and had raised no public funds on their behalf. Another 70,000 refugees were camped out, in poor condition, in Syria, mostly along the border with Israel. Both Iraq and Syria were already being targeted by senior British diplomats in the Middle East (as by Israeli officials) as the most appropriate sites for the permanent resettlement of most of the refugees. As a senior official in the British Middle East Office in Cairo put it, 'in Iraq and Syria . . . there are sufficient latent resources . . . to support a population several times the present numbers. In fact, in Iraq rapid progress in development is to a considerable extent dependent on an increase in population.' Of course, such argumentation was presented most forthrightly by British representatives in precisely those countries – such as Egypt and Lebanon – on which the burden of the refugee influx, be it for political, economic or demographic reasons, weighed most heavily.[23]

Two major factors emerged from the cursory British and American diplomatic investigations in late July and early August 1948 of the Palestinian refugee situation. The conditions of their existence were, by and large, 'appalling' – 'worse than anything he had ever seen,' according to Bernadotte – and that most of the Arab states were doing little, if anything, for their relief. As the Transjordanian prime minister told Kirkbride, Abdullah's appeal to his fellow Arab leaders for aid had secured only 'unfulfilled promises of money from Saudi Arabia and the Yemen'. Abdullah and his prime minister agreed, according to Kirkbride, that 'some of the Arab states best able to bear a heavy burden . . . are doing the least of all . . .'[24]

The Start of International Relief Efforts

Something obviously had to be done. British Foreign Secretary Bevin felt that the key lay in the hands of the Arab states themselves. On 13 August he sent a forceful cable to Britain's posts in the Middle East stating: 'I am by no means convinced that the Arab States, and particularly those who can best afford it, are using their resources to the best advantage for the relief of Arab refugees.' He instructed the British diplomats to inform the Arab governments that 'more could and should be done by the Arab States themselves. His Majesty's Government realise that the main concern of the Arab States is that the refugees should be allowed to return to their homes and that they wish to do nothing to prejudice this possibility.' But even if this became possible, much time would elapse before implementation could conceivably take place; meanwhile the refugees were living in misery. Bevin particularly feared the outbreak of major epidemics. He called on the Arab states to supply funds and equipment for the relief of the refugees, a course which might persuade the powers outside the Middle East also to come forward with assistance; and he proposed that a local, Middle Eastern refugee relief organisation be set up, to coordinate the efforts on behalf of the refugees.[25]

A similar feeling surfaced during July, August and early September among Bernadotte and his staff, as it gradually became clear to them that Israel had no intention of allowing a return of the refugees to their homes. Bernadotte had the UN secretary general send Sir Raphael Cilento, the Australian director of the Division of Social Activities in the UN's Department of Social Affairs, to investigate the situation of the refugees. Cilento toured Transjordan and in early August reported on their condition. Bernadotte subsequently formulated a three-stage plan for refugee relief: (1) Immediate relief of absolute basic needs, (2) relief from September to December, in conjunction with a thorough study of the problem, and (3) a long-range programme, covering January-September 1949. At the same time, he began personally to solicit assistance for the immediate relief of the refugees from dozens of governments and international bodies, asking for funds from the wealthier states, cereals from cereal exporters, and so on. Within his administration, a Disaster Relief Project (later called Refugee Relief Project) was set up, headed by Sir Raphael Cilento, to coordinate these efforts and to oversee the distribution of the contributions. But Bernadotte was assassinated in Jerusalem by Jewish terrorists on 17 September, and Cilento's organisation proved substantially ineffective, given the lack of any major contributions from the wealthier Western states and the lack of effective organisation and generosity by most of the Arab states. Britain, for example, had supplied thousands of tents. For weeks these remained unopened and unused in a warehouse in Beirut, where the major relief supplies bottleneck existed, due to a mixture of corruption and inefficiency. Money was not forthcoming and basic foods, water, medicines, doctors and medical facilities, tentage, clothing and bedding all remained in very short supply or nonexistent through August and September in most of the refugee communities.

In late September an official of the International Committee of the Red Cross toured the refugee centres in Lebanon, Syria, Transjordan and Palestine and reported that, despite the 'hullabaloo' surrounding international contributions, the 'tragic fact is that substantially nothing in food or goods have reached refugees up to October 1' apart from the direct aid proffered by the Arab governments and local communities. Stanton Griffis, the U.S. Ambassador in Cairo, found the situation 'extremely delicate' in view of the almost complete absence of any U.S. government or private contributions. Such aid was 'vital', said the ambassador, as the refugee issue had moved to the top of the Arab agenda in negotiations about a possible solution to the Middle East conflict.[26] Griffis felt very strongly about the refugees, not only within the context of American vulnerability and U.S. interests in the Middle East. In December 1948, he was appointed by the UN secretary general the first director of UN Relief for Palestine Refugees in the Near East, effectively replacing Cilento. As his adviser, Griffis appointed Dr Bayard Dodge (former president of the American University of Beirut).

A similar message reached the State Department from Amman, where Stabler reported that, with the onset of rain, the condition of the some '200,000' refugees in Transjordan proper and in Transjordanian-occupied

Palestine was 'severely deteriorating'. Transjordanian resources were too meagre to cope and, thus far, the only relief supplies to have arrived through the UN was a 'small amount [of] powdered milk for children and pregnant women . . . Immediate relief is not only of importance from humanitarian standpoint, but also as essential factor in arriving at satisfactory solution Palestine problem based on Bernadotte's conclusions [in his Interim Report and 'plan' of mid-September]. This running sore of refugees will make Arab acquiescence therein [i.e., in the plan] more difficult and odious as it will remain evidence of UN inability cope with complicated yet urgent problem.' Stabler warned that further delay in the provision of relief 'can only result in appalling number of deaths'. He strongly urged the State Department to pressure the UN to begin providing the necessary supplies.[27]

The sense of urgency and pressure from the field culminated, for the U.S. Government, with the cable of 17 October to the President and the Secretary of State from the new U.S. Special Representative to Israel, James McDonald. Of the 'approximately 400,000 refugees,' he wrote, an estimated '100,000 old men, women and children who are shelterless and have little or no food' would die when the rains came. The refugee problem was reaching 'catastrophic proportions and should be treated as a disaster'. The UN relief machinery was 'both inappropriate and inadequate' and had led to 'gross inefficiency and wastefulness'. Immediate action, guided by a comprehensive program of relief, was needed to 'avert horrifying losses'. The present system of getting the relief from the contributor through the UN machinery to the countries and then the individual refugees was a failure, with wastage *en route* estimated at as high as '90 per cent'. McDonald recommended the immediate transfer of the whole relief operation to the hands of the Red Cross. McDonald believed the UN administration, Israel and the Arab states could be persuaded that such a change would be in everybody's interest.[28]

The obvious anarchy in the relief efforts and the growing suffering of the refugees, issuing in increased international (mainly American) pressures, prompted the UN General Assembly resolution of December 1948 setting up the United Nations Relief for Palestine Refugees in the Near East (UNRPR). The UNRPR coordinated with and acted through the International Committee of the Red Cross, the League of Red Cross Societies and the American Friends Service Committee in the distribution of the relief supplies. The Red Cross was given 'jurisdiction' over the refugees in Israel and the Transjordanian-occupied parts of Palestine; the League of Red Cross Societies, over Transjordan, Syria and Lebanon; and the American Friends Service Committee, over the Egyptian-occupied Gaza District. The UNRPR effectively replaced the Disaster Relief Project. In turn, in December 1949 the UNRPR was succeeded by the United Nations Relief and Works Agency for Palestine Refugees in the Near East (UNRWA), which took over and ran the refugee camps during the following decades.[29]

Hosting the Fourth Wave,
the Winter of 1948/49 and Organizing the First Camps

The refugee situation took a major turn for the worse towards the end of 1948, with the successful Israeli offensives of October and December 1948 – January 1949, resulting in the expulsion and flight of a further 150,000–200,000 Palestinians, most of them to the Gaza area.

The Gaza District turned overnight into the worst hit area. According to a senior American Red Cross Official, R.T. Schaeffer, 'thousands of refugees have fallen by the roadside from starvation' and most of the survivors suffered from dysentery. There were only 900 tents in the area. An Egyptian doctor had refused to treat some serious cases, saying: 'After all, this is the season for dying'. The Gaza representative of the Red Cross estimated that 120 refugees were dying each night, mostly from starvation and dysentery. A UN official, F. G. Beard, who visited the Gaza area in mid-November, said the condition of the refugees defied description: There were some 230,000 refugees there, he said, living in the open and receiving no regular rations. '. . . Whenever he came near a group [of refugees], they practically smothered him with entreaties for food.' Beard found no 'sanitary facilities' anywhere among the refugees 'and conditions of horrifying filth exist'. He charged that the Egyptian Army, which controlled the Gaza area, and the Cairo-based Arab Higher Refugee Council, both had been 'grossly negligent'. The hard-pressed Egyptian army, maintained that the 'refugees . . . [were] not their responsibility'; one captain dealt with the refugees, occasionally handing out food to 'needy cases'.[30]

Although the refugee concentrations in Transjordan and Transjordanian-held parts of Palestine had not been substantially increased by further fighting after the summer of 1948, conditions there too had deteriorated, mainly because of the advent of winter. The commander of the Arab Legion, General Glubb, in December wrote from Amman to J. Baker-White, MP, that 'many died in the night', after the first rain of the season. Down the road from his house 11 refugees were living in a quarry. Glubb had sent them blankets 'but their little boy of about four . . . during the night died all the same'.

The Transjordanian authorities, in concert with the UN refugee officials, had during the autumn moved tens of thousands of refugees from the Ramallah-Hebron hill-country, where snow occasionally fell in winter, to the warmer Jordan valley; about 30,000 were living in refugee camps (and another 5-6,000 elsewhere) around Jericho by December.

Glubb complained at the start of December that the Jericho area refugees were getting 'no food'. This was inaccurate. According to British officials on the spot, the Transjordanian Government was distributing flour sufficient for 225 grams of bread per refugee per day, and food was arriving from the UN relief agency. More than 1,000 half-pints of milk were being prepared from powder and distributed daily for infants and nursing mothers. Two kilograms of potatoes and chunks of cheese had been distributed to each person, and a shipment of olive oil, tinned meat and margarine had been received and was to be distributed. A shipment of 1,000 blankets had also arrived and largely had been distributed.

The Jericho camps, according to British officials, were being run efficiently by a Belgian Red Cross official, Dr. Depage, but suffered from a basic lack of funds to cover such expenses as 'milling of wheat, sanitation, water supply, warehousing . . . and transport'. A Danish field hospital unit – with staff – was due to arrive, but meanwhile Depage suffered from lack of medical personnel. There were Arab doctors in Jericho but 'they were not willing to work without some form of payment' and Depage had no money.

Depage had probably created the first major experiment in organised camp life for the refugees in Palestine, a model camp. An attempt had been made to place people from the same villages together, in blocks. Arabs were given various jobs in the camp administration and cleanliness was enforced. And it appeared to work, as far as it went. But in January 1949, lack of supplies from the Disaster (Refugee) Relief Project, which had employed Depage, administrative changes, including Depage's removal, and unemployment resulted in major violence. Discontented refugees ransacked Jericho's Jordan Hotel, killed an Arab Legion officer and wounded several people. The refugees had heard that relief money was being used to throw a party at the hotel. The camp was then cordoned off by Legion armoured cars, searched and placed under curfew. Dow, the British consul-general in Jerusalem, pressed for funds to employ and pay at least some of the camps' male population, 'paid employment [being] a most important psychological factor in maintaining the morale of male refugees and preventing them from lapsing into anarchy and Communism'. The Red Cross, which had taken over the camps from the UN organisation, apparently preferred bringing in its own staff to using local workers.[31]

The situation in the Nablus area, controlled by the Iraqi military remained unchanged. 'To turn to Nablus from Jericho is to sink from Day No. 1 of the creation back into chaos,' wrote Dow. The refugees in the Nablus-Tulkarm area refused to move to warmer Jericho. The consul-general believed that they were being encouraged in this course by local officials and merchants, who stood to gain by their continued presence (charging those with money exorbitant prices and siphoning off some of the relief money destined for the refugees). The local authorities maintained that there were 128,000 refugees in their area; Dow thought the figure inflated, and implied that the inflated figure stemmed from a desire to receive more relief. At least three refugees were dying each day in the immediate vicinity of Nablus, according to the mayor. There was only haphazard local distribution of food and milk and there were no tents. 'The Iraqi army with . . . 1 line of [Communications] of 1,500 miles are unwilling and probably unable to do anything about them. There is flour in the Bazaar but the refugees cannot afford it.' The municipal authorities wanted the Transjordanian Government to administratively take over the Nablus area but the Iraqis, 'for reasons of prestige', refused to relinquish any authority. The consul-general recommended that a refugee camp be set up east of Nablus and that relief supplies only be given to those refugees who agreed to move to the camp.[32]

But the whole concept of the refugee camps (whether run directly by a UN agency or by the Red Cross), almost from the start was understood to be politically dangerous and insufficient. Cilento, who more or less supervised the establishment of the camps, told a gathering of representatives of voluntary relief organisations in Beirut in early December that the 'camps are not a good idea if their establishment leads to permanency or to an intensification of the feeling of isolation and frustration, which is the tendency of many of the refugees; nor are they good if they remain merely areas for the distribution of goods without any purposive trend towards a final solution'. The outbreak in Jericho in January 1949 had illustrated the danger the camps constituted to law and order, and perhaps to government, as well, in the Hashemite kingdom. A permanent solution, all understood, was possible in one of two ways: Repatriation to Israel or resettlement in the Arab states. A third possibility, of combining the two, was in fact a variation on the idea of resettlement in the Arab countries as, if Israel refused to accept and adopt the principle of repatriation (as was the case), it would certainly not accept more than a very small number of repatriates as part of any political deal with the Arabs.[33]

'The Refugee Threat' and the Possibility of Organised Resettlement in the Arab States

By the start of 1949, most U.S. diplomats in the Middle East understood that repatriation was out of the question as Israel, simply, refused to take back the refugees. And some, such as James McDonald, had come around to the Israeli view that the alternative, of organised resettlement in the Arab countries, was indeed preferable. As William Burdett Jr., the new U.S. Consul-General in Jerusalem (who was generally unfriendly to Israel), put it: 'Political-security best served by settling refugees in Arab states. Return refugees [to Israel] would create continuing minority problem and form constant temptation both to uprisings and intervention by neighbouring Arab states.' It was the height of the Cold War and Burdett, like most other American officials, was keenly aware of the revolutionary, 'pro-Communist' potential of the hundreds of thousands of disgruntled, ill-fed, ill-housed and stateless refugees: 'USSR may capitalize on opportunity,' he wrote. Unlike most of his peers, Burdett thought that the organized resettlement of the refugees could focus on Transjordan and the Arab occupied parts of Palestine (Samaria, the Nebron Hills and the Gaza district). His thinking was based primarily on his knowledge or intuition that the other Arab states – principally Syria and Iraq – would not agree to absorb any more refugees than they already had. But permanent absorption in Transjordan and the Arab-held parts of Palestine, he argued, would necessitate large scale development schemes, including irrigation projects in the Jordan Valley, road construction, fisheries, phosphate production and potash plants, which would provide employment. All this could be done only if the Western states poured in a lot of money.[34]

But Israel and most American officials preferred to focus on Iraq and Syria, rather than Transjordan and Palestine, as the best sites for the resettlement of the refugees. The head of the U.S. Legation in Jidda, Saudi Arabia, wrote that while, under Arab League pressure, the Saudis might accept 'a token number of Arab refugees,' the kingdom would refuse to take any substantial number. There were both economic and political reasons, the latter weighing the more heavily. Saudi agriculture could absorb none and the oil industries could absorb only a handful. But more important, 'the entry of a significant number of Palestinians . . . could not help but have far-reaching political implications . . . [because] the Palestinians, under British tutelage, grew accustomed to at least a semi-free press and other beginnings of democratic institutions. They would doubtless find it most difficult to accept the situation in Saudi Arabia where the rule is absolute . . .' Hence, the senior American diplomat felt that it was neither in the Saudi's nor America's interest to press the king to take in more than a token number of refugees. As repatriation to Israel was to be ruled out, resettlement in Arab countries, 'principally Iraq and possibly Syria', should be planned. The U.S. would have to foot the bulk of the bill, he felt. In the absence of an organized resettlement scheme, the refugees would 'remain a canker in the Near Eastern states and [a threat to] American relations with them for some time to come'.[35]

Similar resistance to the permanent absorption of Palestinian refugees was expressed by Lebanon, which by the start of 1949 had 90-120,000 on its soil. Economically, they were an 'unbearable burden'; Lebanon suffered from 5 per cent unemployment and could offer almost no employment to the Palestinians. The U.S. Beirut Legation concurred: 'It is difficult to see how present economic conditions in Lebanon will permit any significant absorption of refugees'. But even more important was the political aspect. 'The absorption of an alien population amounting to as much as 10 per cent of the native population . . . would create a Moslem majority and turn the entire political complexion of the country.' The Beirut Legation also pointed to Iraq and Syria, after appropriate agricultural investment and development, as the best sites for the refugees' relocation.[36]

A similar focus on Syria and Iraq for the refugees' permanent resettlement was to be found in Israeli planning at this time for the refugees' future. The proposal of the 'Transfer Committee' (set up by the government to smooth the path of the Palestinians' permanent relocation outside Israel), submitted to the Israeli Government at the end of November 1948, contained long sections detailing the absorptive capacity of the two countries. For months thereafter, committee members Ezra Danin, a senior Foreign Ministry official, and Yosef Weitz, director of the Jewish National Fund's Lands Department, promoted schemes for the absorption of the refugees in Syria, Iraq and, to a lesser extent, Transjordan and for their employment by foreign companies with interests in the Middle East, primarily the oil corporations.[37]

The problem, however, was that Syria, with some 80,000 refugees, and Iraq, with 4-5,000, wanted no more. Those already in Iraq could be employed in road construction, if funds were found for such projects, wrote the American Embassy in Baghdad; their continued presence would have only a 'negligible effect' on the country. But Iraq's policy was that even these 'should be returned to Palestine'. As to additional refugees, economically – with appropriate international investment in agricultural development schemes – it was 'conceivable'. But socially and politically, it would be extremely problematic. 'Despite their common Arab culture, Palestinians would be regarded as foreigners and an influx of them would not be welcome either in the towns or in the agricultural areas of Iraq. They would be likely to form another unassimilated, discontented minority group,' wrote the American Embassy. The Embassy, in short, reflecting Iraqi Government opinion, thought that 'the presence in Iraq of many thousands of victims of the clash between Arabs and Jews would be certain to keep the Palestine issue burning alive for generations. In the interest of long-range security in the Middle East, the Embassy recommends therefore that every effort be made to ensure . . . that refugees who so desire be returned to their homes [in Palestine] . . .' The Iraqis, then, wanted no more refugees, for economic and social-political reasons. Neither did the Syrians.[38]

But it went deeper than that, and this applied to Iraq as well as all or most of the Arab states, as the American representative to the Palestine Conciliation Commission, Mark Ethridge, understood. A major reason for the Arab unwillingness to properly absorb and resettle the refugees at this time was rooted in their struggle against Israel rather than in internal political or economic and social considerations. The Arabs saw in the '700,000 or 800,000' refugees a 'political weapon against the Jews. They feel they can summon world opinion [against Israel] even if some refugees die in the meantime.' The Arabs sought the refugees' repatriation, both as a demand of justice and as a means to subvert the Jewish state. Hence, it was better to leave the refugees for the time being in squalor and living impermanently than to support and implement resettlement schemes in Arab countries which would neutralize, and perhaps ultimately solve, the problem. Moreover, the refugees camped along Israel's borders (rather than in faraway Iraq), the Arab leaders told Ethridge, would provide the 'core of [an] irredentist movement that will plague all Arab states and provide basis for continual agitation to the point that there will be no possibility of having anything more than [Arab-Israeli] armistice in the Middle East'.[39]

So it was that the Palestinian Arab refugees, numbering between 600,000 and 800,000 remained *in situ*. Unwanted as repatriates by Israel and unwanted as new immigrants by the larger Arab countries, the refugees remained by and large where they had initially come to semi-permanent rest – mainly in and near the main Arab towns of Samaria and the Hebron Hills, Jericho and Transjordan, and the Gaza District, and, in smaller numbers, in Lebanon and Syria, near Israel's frontiers. And a handful were absorbed in Iraq.

Through 1948 the refugees suffered; hundreds, perhaps thousands, died. Their initial absorption by the Arab states and by the eastern Palestinian and Gazan communities, and the Iraqi, Transjordanian and Egyptian armies that controlled these areas, was anarchic and thoughtless. As most of the refugees reached these areas in the spring and summer of 1948, the need for reasonable, rain-proof accommodation was not immediately apparent. Life in olive groves, caves, private gardens and unfinished buildings and garages was possible, given the temperate climate. Moreover, for months most of the refugees and the Arab local and national leaders continued to believe that the refugees' lot was temporary, and that they would soon be returning to their homes, either in the wake of victorious Arab armies or as a result of international pressure on Israel. Few were able to think of non-return as a realistic prospect, or to suit their thinking and actions to what was and would be needed if the Palestinians' refugeedom was to become permanent. Lastly, the Arab states – poor, corrupt and highly disorganised, by Western standards – throughout 1948 were involved in a major war with Israel, their main energies and thinking focussing on the war effort rather than on the alleviation of the refugees' misery. The refugees were a side-issue, and were regarded mainly as an added burden for the Arab armies and states. The alleviation of their physical plight was left largely in the hands of local Arab authorities and voluntary committees, though in Transjordan, Transjordanian-occupied territory and in Lebanon, the state provided a basic quantity of food for daily sustenance, but little else. There was unhappiness about the influx of refugees in various localities; they brought filth, disease and demorali-sation. Why should Egyptian and Transjordanian boys fight for the rights of Palestinians who had fled without a fight? some argued. Good ladies organised to give aid, blankets, food, money. But local merchants and, apparently, officials exploited the refugees, hiking prices and siphoning off a proportion of the international and local relief contributions.

Attempts by Arab governments, such as Syria and in some areas, Transjordan, to get the refugees to go back were not pressed home. And, in any case, Israel was firmly resolved, from June 1948, not to allow the refugees to return, either in dribbles or *en masse*. Attempts by refugees to return were repulsed by fire. Moreover, many of the refugees, during the summer and autumn of 1948, preferred to stay put for some of the same reasons that had prompted them to leave Israeli-controlled areas in the first place – fear of the Jews and unwillingness to live as a minority in a Jewish state. Some, at least for a time, expected to return to their homes in the wake of conquering Arab armies.

International relief efforts on behalf of the refugees were slow off the mark, partly also because of a belief that the refugees would soon be repatriated. But as winter approached and everyone grew to accept that repatriation was not on the cards, tent camps were set up to accommodate the refugees. From the first, these were regarded – by the international relief bodies and the Arab host countries – as a temporary arrangement; the danger of the presence of hundreds of thousands of disgruntled, poorly-fed and poorly-housed refugees to the Arab host regimes was clear to all. By the winter, and only just, the UN and the other international agencies had overcome the bureaucratic muddle and the bottlenecks in Beirut and elsewhere, and a minimal if sufficient amount of relief aid began reaching the refugees. The UN managed to put its act together with the belated formation of the UNRPR, and the Arab states, armies and municipalities during the winter of 1948–49 were almost completely relieved of the burden of care for the basic physical necessities of the refugee communities.

But this was seen by the international community as merely a temporary situation, which required a major political initiative and solution. Pressures on Israel to allow back all or a large number of the refugees increased over the winter and spring; but, given its victories over the Arabs, so did the new state's strength, and its ability to resist such pressures successfully. Repatriation was just not on. But neither, it turned out, was its alternative, organised resettlement in the larger (and largely underpopulated) Arab countries – the solution by the start of 1949 favoured by Israel and most senior American and British officials (who also wanted to see Israel take back some refugees, if only as a political gesture of conciliation towards the Arabs). In the course of the summer and autumn of 1949, Iraq, Syria and the other major Arab countries resisted the dangled bait of large economic aid linked to readiness to absorb large numbers of refugees. There were economic, social-demographic and internal political reasons, the latter – the threat of revolutionary destabilisation – apparently predominating. But also, as Ethridge perceived, there was a need born of the context of conflict with Israel – to use the refugees as a weapon against the Jewish states. The hundreds of thousands of refugees, if left in misery, would continue to demand repatriation, and would find support for this in the international community. If allowed back, they could destabilize the Jewish state. If not allowed back, their existence would eat at world support for Israel and would ignite an endless and violent irredenta, which would leave the Arabs and Israel in permanent conflict. Ethridge pressed for American pressure on Israel to allow back some 250,000 of the refugees to neutralize this irredentist-political threat and to do at least partial justice to the Palestinians. But Israel, having won the war and got rid of its potentially destabilizing, large Arab minority was in no mood for compromise on the matter, a compromise seen by almost all of Israel's security-minded leaders as in itself a mortal threat to the country's well being. The refugees remained in the camps.

Notes: Chapter 15

1　Sir Alan Cunningham Papers V/4/9 (in St. Antony's College, the Middle East Centre, Oxford); *The General Position in Palestine* by Lt. General MacMillan, 21 April 1948.
2　Public Record Office (London) (PRO), Colonial Office Papers (CO) 537-3986, *Beirut [Legation] Summary for the Month of May, 1948*; and Israel State Archives (Jerusalem) (ISA), Foreign Ministry Papers (FM) 2408/16, *An excerpt from information given by Yosef Sabagh, an agent of the French Consulate in Tiberias and Safad, who had just returned from Lebanon*, 24 June 1948.

3 The National Archives (NA) (Washington), Record Group 84, Jerusalem Consulate, Classified Records 1948, 800 – Refugees, John P. Robertson, Vice Consul, U.S. Consulate, Port Said, Egypt, to State Department, 29 April 1948.
4 PRO, Foreign Office Papers (FO), 371–68537 (E3291/4/31), Sir A. Cunningham to J. M.Martin, Colonial Office, 2 February 1948.
5 PRO, FO 371–68371 (E5528/11/65), Sir Ronald Campbell, Cairo (British Middle East Office), to Foreign Office, 30 April 1948; and NA, Records Group 84, Jerusalem Consulate General, Classified Records 1948, 800 – Refugees, Philip Ernst, U.S. Consul, Port Said, to U.S. Embassy, Cairo, 13 May 1948.
6 Jerusalem and East Mission Papers (JE&EM), Box LXXIII/1, Winifred A. Coates, El Husn, Transjordan, to 'Mabel' (Jerusalem), 15 June 1948.
7 Kibbutz Meuhad Archive (EFAL, Israel), Palmah Archive (KMA-PA) 100/MemVavDalet/1 – 9, *Batziburiut Ha'aravit* (in the Arab public), Foreign Ministry Middle East Affairs Department, 11 June 1948. Copy also in ISA, FM 2570/6; and ISA, FM2408/16, 'An Excerpt from Information Given by Yosef Sabagh', op. cit.
8 See Benny Morris, 'The Battle for the Harvest of 1948 and the Creation of the Palestinian Refugee Problem,' forthcoming in *International Journal for Middle East Studies*.
9 KMA-PA 100/MemVavDalet/1 – 9, *Batziburiut Ha'aravit*, Foreign Ministry Middle East Affairs Department, 11 June 1948; and ISA, FM 2570/6, 'Tsur' (the code name of a local intelligence officer) to Hagawah Intelligence Service, 7 June 1948. The IDF duly barred the refugees from returning to Israeli-held territory.
10 PRO, FO 371–68570 (E9239/4/31), Sir A. Kirkbride, Amman, to E. Bevin, Foreign Office, 2 July 1948 and attached minutes by FO officials.
11 PRO, FO 371–68575 (E9723/4/31), C.M. Pirie Gordon, Amman, to Foreign Office, 18 July 1948; and NA 501 BB. Palestine/7–1548, Amman to Secretary of State, 15 July 1948.
12 NA 501 BB. Palestine/7–1548, Amman to Secretary of State, 15 July 1948; ISA, FM 2569/13, 'From Monitoring the Legion Wavelength', 21 July 1948; PRO, FO 371–68578 (E10440/4/31), Sir H. Dow, British Consul-General, Jerusalem, to Foreign Office, 19 July 1948, enclosing text of Ramallah Radio broadcast, undated; and ISA, FM 2569/13, the Research Division (the Foreign Ministry's intelligence department), to Y. Shimoni, acting director of the Foreign Ministry Middle East Affairs Department, 19 July 1948.
13 J&EM LXXIII/1, Winifred Coate, principal, C.M.S. Girls School, Amman, to 'Mabel' Jerusalem, 30 July 1948; and ISA FM 2569/13, 'Hiram' to Foreign Ministry Research Division, 19 July 1948.
14 NA, Record Group 84, Jerusalem Consulate General, Classified Records 1948, 800 – Refugees, Amman (Stabler) to State Department, 26 July 1948; and PRO, FO 371–68576 (E10219/10006/4), Amman (C.M. Pirie Gordon) to Foreign Office, 29 July 1948.
15 J&EM LXXIII/1, Winifred Coate, Amman, to 'Mabel' Jerusalem, 30 July 1948.
16 PRO, FO 371–68576 (E10219/10006/4), Amman (Pirie Gordon) to Foreign Office, 29 July 1948.
17 PRO, FO 371–68576 (E10235/4/31), H. Dow, Jerusalem, to Foreign Office, 29 July 1948 and (E10219/10006/4), Amman (Pirie Gordon) to Foreign Office, 29 July 1948.
18 PRO, FO 371–68575 (E9992/4.31), Houstoun-Boswall, Beirut, to Foreign Office, 21 July 1948.
19 NA Record Group 84, Jerusalem Consulate General, Classified Records, 1948, 800 – Refugees, John MacDonald, U.S. Consul-General, Jerusalem, to Secretary of State, 27 July 1948 and John MacDonald to Secretary of State, 12 August 1948.
20 PRO, FO 371–68677 (E11504/10748/31), copy of Hackett-Paine's report covering note from HM Consulate General, Jerusalem, to Eastern Department, Foreign Office, 25 August 1948, and minutes by several FO officials.
21 NA, Record Group 34, Jerusalem Consulate General, Classified Records 1948, 800 – Refugees, Patterson (Cairo) to Secretary of State, 7 August 1948.
22 PRO, FO 371–68576 (E10232/4.31), Houstoun-Boswall (Beirut) to Foreign Office, 28 July 1948.
23 PRO, FO 371–68576 (E10234/4/31), Richmond (Baghdad) to Foreign Office, 31 July 1948; (E10235/4/31), minute by Lance Thirkell, 4 August 1948; and FO 371–68578 (E10456/4/31), BMEO (Cairo) to Foreign Office, 3 August 1948.

24 PRO, FO 371–68677 (E1088/4/31), Chapman Andrews (BMEO, Cairo) to Foreign Office, 16 August 1948; and FO 371–68677 (E11025/10748/31), A. Kirkbride (Amman) to Foreign Office, 18 August 1948.

25 PRO, FO 371–68578, Foreign Office to Cairo, Baghdad, Beirut, Jidda, Damascus, Amman, BMEO, etc., 13 August 1948.

26 NA 501. BB Palestine/10–648, Cairo (Griffis) to Secretary of State, 6 October 1948.

27 NA 501. BB Palestine/10–148, Amman (Stabler) to Secretary of State 10 October 1948.

28 NA 501. BB Palestine/10–1748, Tel Aviv (McDonald) to Secretary of State (and President), 17 October 1948.

29 See Don Peretz, *Israel and the Palestine Arabs*, The Middle East Institute, Washington D.C., 1958, pp. 8–13.

30 NA 501. BB Palestine/11–1648, Cairo (Patterson) to Secretary of State, 16 November 1948 and 501. BB Palestine/12–748, Cairo (Patterson) to Secretary of State, 7 December 1948.

31 PRO, FO 371–68633 (E16038/10748/31), Glubb Pasha (Amman) to J. Baker-White, MP (London), 2 December 1948; FO 371–68683 (E16264/10748/31), R.A. Beaumont (Consulate-General, Jerusalem to B.A.A. Burrows, Foreign Office, undated, c.15 December 1948; FO 371–68683 (E16344/10748/31), Sir H. Dow (Jerusalem) to Foreign Office, 21 December 1948; FO 371–75417, Sir H. Dow (Jerusalem) to Foreign Office, 16 January 1949; and NA 501. BB Palestine/12–2748, 'Minutes of Fifth Meeting with Voluntary Agencies,' Beirut, 3 December 1948.

32 PRO, FO 371–68683 (E16344/10748/31), Sir H. Dow (Jerusalem) to Foreign Office, 21 December 1948.

33 NA 501. BB Palestine/12–2748, 'Minutes of the Fifth Meeting with Voluntary Agencies,' Beirut, 3 December 1948.

34 NA 501. BB Palestine/2–949, Burdett (Jerusalem) to Secretary of State, 9 February 1949. Already in August 1948 U.S. diplomats were warning of the 'Communist' revolutionary potential of the Palestinian refugee communities. On 24 August, Keeley, the U.S. Minister in Damascus, after a tour of camps in Syria wrote that the refugees were unquestionably 'ripe for Communist indoctrination.' See NA Record group 84, Jerusalem Consulate General, Classified Records 1948, 800 – Syria, Keeley (Damascus) to Secretary of State, 24 August 1948. See also NA 501. BB Palestine/3–2849, Beirut (Mark Ethridge, U.S. representative on the Palestine Conciliation Commission) to Secretary of State (and, at his discretion, to the President), 29 March 1949, for Ethridge's assessment of the refugees as a threat to the stability of the Arab host regimes.

35 NA 501. BB Palestine/1–2149, American Legation, Jidda, to Secretary of State, 21 January 1949.

36 NA 501. BB Palestine/2–449, American Legation, Beirut, to Secretary of State, 4 February 1949.

37 For details see Benny Morris, 'Yosef Weitz and the Transfer Committees', 1948–49,' forthcoming in *Middle Eastern Studies*, 1986.

38 NA 501. BB Palestine/2–749, Baghdad to Secretary of State, 7 February 1949.

39 NA 501. BB Palestine/3–2849, Beirut (Ethridge) to Secretary of State, 28 March 1949.

16 Palestinians in Lebanon: insecurity and flux

ROSEMARY SAYIGH

During the 1st Arab/Israeli war of 1948, some 100,000 Arab inhabitants of Palestine fled or were expelled into Lebanon, where, clustered in the South, they awaited the end of the fighting to return to their homes in Galilee and the coastal cities. As the scale of the exodus became apparent, emergency relief organisations were set up in Lebanon and elsewhere, leading in 1950 to the establishment of a special UN management agency, UNRWA. Although the exact size of the Lebanese population at that time is not known, a generally accepted estimate of the ratio of 'refugees' to host population is that it was 1:10, a heavy burden for any country, particularly one with Lebanon's unbalanced economy and delicate sectarian 'balance'.

Though the Arab states readily adopted the term 'Arab refugees' used by the UN and the Great Powers to denote the displaced indigenous population of Palestine, the refugee label is misleading, suggesting as it does control by host governments over ingress, and transfer across clear national boundaries. None of these conditions obtained in the case of the Palestinians. Before 1917, Palestine, Syria, Lebanon and 'Jordan' were closely linked administrative units within the Ottoman Empire; thus the borders between them were recent ones produced by Anglo/French occupation, and had no historic depth for the people of the area. In moving across them, the Palestinians had no premonition that flight could lead to permanent exile. Both they and their involuntary hosts understood their movement as an emergency measure, not as an abandonment of residence and national rights in Palestine/Israel.[1] A central element in the Palestinians' first struggle after exile was to reject the Arab refugee designation, and re-define themselves as exiled Palestinians.

From the outset, the situation of the Palestinians in Lebanon differed from that in the other host countries, and this difference has increased with time. The decisive factor in this divergence has been the inability of the Lebanese state, rooted in its sectarian origins and structure, wholly to control the refugee population, or prevent it forming political and social relations with segments of the Lebanese population. Erosion of state power combined with regional pressures to give the refugee community under the leadership of the Palestinian Resistance Movement (PRM) a degree of autonomy unparalleled elsewhere, encouraging close ties with some segments of the Lebanese, while arousing violent hostility from opposing segments. The appearance of anti-Palestinian militias and vigilante groups is a phenomenon not entirely confined to Lebanon,[2] but pushed further here than elsewhere.

The history of the Palestinians in Lebanon falls into three distinct periods. The first, from 1948 to 1969, was one of a developing system of state control mainly directed at the camp population. Little overt hostility was expressed by the host population towards the refugees; attitudes ranged from sympathy to indifference or latent antagonism. The second period, from 1969 to 1982, was ushered in by a revolt of the camps against Lebanese control, with the PRM emerging as a power centre within the Lebanese political system; transformed from 'refugees' to 'revolutionaries', Palestinians felt able to interact with Lebanese on a basis of equality tinged with pride; a sharp polarisation of the Lebanese into pro- and anti-Palestinian segments took place, articulated by political formations and reflected in mass sentiment. The third period, beginning with the Israeli invasion of 1982 and PRM withdrawal, has brought a higher level of threat and uncertainty for Palestinians who remain. New sources of hostility have appeared, notably the Amal Movement, the Shi'ite militia formed in 1974 by Imam Moussa Sadr, which before 1982 was an ally of the PRM; yet the origin of Palestinian insecurity lies not so much in specific parties (apart from long-term antagonists such as Israel and the Lebanese Force[3]), as in the sectarian nature of the Lebanese crisis, deepened by regional and international interventions. Palestinians cannot but be involved in the Lebanese conflict, as enemy or ally of factions in continual flux. Yet, as a self-defined *national* movement, they are fundamentally alien to a sectarian system, bound to be viewed as an obstructive element in any new sectarian arrangement. This study deals mainly with the first period, since it was then that the major 'givens' were laid down; it constitutes for the Lebanese a basic point of reference in discussing Palestinian status and rights, as well as their mutual obligations.

Israel's theory about the 'refugees' (accepted by much of the Western scholarly community) was that they should melt readily into the surrounding Arab peoples, with whom they shared language, history, culture and religion. As in other instances where population transfer has been proposed as a solution to a 'minority problem', the theory of Palestinian absorbability was self-interested, based on a colonialist disregard for indigenous peoples, and unconcerned with the real obstacles to assimilation. Of these, the primordial one was the question of national will and interests, both those of the Palestinians and the Arab peoples. Second, the Israeli case suggests that powerful state mechanisms are necessary to promote the integration of new immigrants (e.g. through accommodation, schooling, military service, etc.), as well as an externally aided economy able rapidly to absorb immigrant labour: conditions that did not obtain in the case of Lebanon and the other Arab host countries. Comparison with Israel's 'ingathering' further suggests that even when migration is voluntary (rather than coercive, as in the Palestinian case), and takes place within the common ideological framework provided by Zionism, yet the absorption of new migrants has met formidable obstacles. Third, the theory takes no account of the status cleavage between 'nationals' and 'refugees', or between old and new citizens, in regard to privilege, power and access to resources. Palestinian alienation in the Arab diaspora was not a quantity fixed by any political or cultural specificity they may have possessed in 1948, stateless amidst the interests and identities that were crystallizing around newly established states (Lebanon, Jordan, Syria, etc.). The development of the concepts 'citizen' and 'national' (non-existent in the Ottoman Empire), accentuated provincial specificities, giving them a national tinge, and discriminating between groups with well-established claims on state patronage and those, like the Palestinians, whose claims were marginal. Part of the usefulness of the history of the Palestinians in Lebanon arises from the clarity with which it illustrates this dynamic, interactive aspect of their alienation, and the interplay of political, economic, social and cultural factors in producing it.

In spite of its specificity, the situation of the Palestinian refugees in Lebanon must not be viewed as *sui generis*, unable to illuminate their situation in other regions of the diaspora, nor other refugee situations. On the contrary, the Lebanese case is useful in illustrating two possibly universal principles: that the refugee label directs a group into subordinate positions in host political and economic structures, even while designating them as 'outside' them, and inessential to their functioning; and second, that once a refugee group has been created by a particular power imbalance, it will be reproduced in a new environment. In other words, the production of refugees is seldom a one-time historical event, with consequences limited to the immediate victims, but rather a continuing process of power asymmetry which is liable to lead to further victimization. When Bashir Gemayel described the Palestinians as 'a people too many' in Lebanon,[4] he offered a striking example of what may be termed the 'institutionalisation of the refugee', whereby the victims of one displacement become targets for another if the conditions that favoured their reception by the host economy and policy change.

This study does not deal systematically with the politics of the Palestinian presence in Lebanon, though politics is the decisive sphere that has shaped in its development. The question of Lebanese-Palestinian relations is too complex and too polemical to be summarised briefly. Further, this subject has been well dealt with by a number of other writers, whereas economic, social and cultural aspects have hardly been touched on. It focuses on the first reception of the refugees, since this reveals both contemporary understandings of their status, as well as dispositions that were to have long lasting effects. The initial framework of laws, definitions and management agencies is outlined for the same reason, while official zoning policies are shown to be a basic arena of struggle between the authorities and the refugees. The position of Palestinian labour and capital in the Lebanese economy sheds light on the camp uprisings of 1969, and contributes to Lebanese anti-Palestinian feeling. Finally, social relations between Palestinians and Lebanese throughout the three periods are sketched in, with discussion of the role of sect[5], class, political orientation and historical period in generating solidarity or hostility.

First Reception

Initial Lebanese reception of the refugees is generally reported to have been sympathetic, certainly more welcoming than that given in Britain and the US to refugees from Nazi persecution. There was an outpouring of aid from many sources, public and private; even before the arrival of the International League of the Red Cross, a number of local social institutions were at work distributing food and organising shelter.[6] President Bishara al-Khoury assured the refugees that 'our house is your house', and he and Premier Rashid al-Solh toured refugee concentrations in the South. This warm reception was spontaneous and popular, arising out of a mood of Arab fraternalism generated by anti-colonialist struggle, and from the traditional practice of sanctuary-giving. It took many forms, from donations and voluntary work, to free accommodation, loans, and help in finding employment. Within this overall welcome, however, certain patterns of discrimination can be discerned that 'sorted' the refugees on a sectarian and class basis. At the same time, a mixture of motivations underlying the government's 'open door' policy pointed to future problems.

It has been suggested that the decision to allow unrestricted entry to the refugees was part of President al-Khoury's policy of attracting Lebanese Muslim support.[7] The move seems to have been a popular one, and though research into unpublished official documents might reveal evidence of misgivings within the government or sectors of the state, no open opposition was expressed at the time. Yet the President's calculations indicate the extent to which Palestinians were involuntarily involved in Lebanese politics even before their settlement, and foreshadows the polarising effect their presence would have on inter-sect relations.

Lebanese sectarianism was also quickly evident in the distribution of aid: Christian charitable associations helped Christian Palestinians, while Muslim associations, more recently formed and less well-endowed, helped the far more numerous Muslim Palestinians.[8] This sectarian 'sorting' led to the setting up of three small Christian camps in Beirut and Metn, with religiously endowed schooling.[9] With many middle class Christian Palestinians settling in Lebanese Christian areas, there was some sectarian divergence in what had been until then a strongly national struggle. Most visible in residence patterns, this divergence was expressed socially in efforts to assimilate, and politically in some support for Maronite leaders and parties. Later, acutely anti-Palestinian Lebanese would appear, such as Etienne Sacre, founder of the Guardians of the Cedars. But for the majority, such assimilationist trends were terminated by the Civil War of 1975/6.

Set apart, the reception of urban middle class Palestinians differed widely from that of the rural and poor urban strata. This was not so much due to difference in income levels, since many rural notables brough money with which they were able to rent accommodation. The difference lay in the connections formed before 1948 between Lebanese and Palestinians of similar class background, through trade, travel, inter-marriage, educational and work migration. Such connections were a form of capital helping urban refugees to tide over the first years of exile, linking them to accommodation, jobs, government officials and politicians, and familiarising them with the workings of the host system. Deprived of such connections, and without easily marketable skills, the rural and poor urban masses swarmed on streets and in public places; even after their partial segregation in camps, their destitution was a source of embarrassment and irritation. Such class-based sorting led to a dichotomy in the refugees' initial experience of the Lebanese: whereas middle class Palestinians recall many acts of kindness, camp Palestinians encountered the treatment accorded to vagrants and strangers. They remember having to pay for water, being treated as thieves if they gleaned fields or picked wayside fruit, and being avoided as carriers of bad luck, or as polluting.[10] Such differences help to account for the almost universal support given by camp Palestinians to the PRM, compared with the more cautious attitudes of the middle classes.

Given that 80% of the incoming Palestinians were Muslims, the size of the influx threatened the political ascendancy of the Maronite sect, who with the other Christian sects had held a slim majority over the Muslims at the time of the 1932 census. Lower Maronite birthrates and high rates of emigration added weight to fears that they would lose the demographic margin that supported their claims to political ascendancy. Even though the Palestinians were, as refugees, outside the polity, over the long-term their presence was likely to tip the demographic and political balance towards the Muslims. This likelihood struck Western diplomats stationed in Beirut;[11] but, as long as the refugee presence appeared temporary, it aroused no open Maronite protest, whatever fears may have been expressed privately.[12] As debate over repatriation in the UN dragged on and return appeared ever less likely, Maronite opposition to 'implantation' became as sharp as that of the Palestinians, without, however, leading to any project of alliance or co-operation such as that between German anti-Semites and the Zionist movement. Among other Lebanese sectors, except for a small politicised minority, the first fraternal sympathy for the refugees soon faded, to be replaced by indifference or irritation.

With continuing deportations from Israel and some transfer from other host countries, the number of Palestinians in Lebanon was estimated to have reached 116,000 by the end of 1951.[13] The subsequent demographical development of the exile community cannot be charted precisely because the original registration carried out by UNWRA was not complete, being based on an economic definition of a 'refugee' not a national one;[4] and second, because the number of Palestinians taking Lebanese nationality, or migrating from Lebanon, has never been registered. A demographer's estimate for the size of the community by 1970, based on an annual growth rate of 3.9%, is 247,000;[15] by 1982, the total is estimated to have reached 350,000. The much higher figure of 600,000 given by some rightist Maronite sources around this date is politically inflated.

The Legal and Management Framework

One of the basic problems of Palestinian existence in Lebanon is that no clear definition of their status and rights, no comprehensive body of law governing their residence, was ever drawn up.[16] Arab League resolutions advocated that the host governments should not offer nationality to the refugees since this could weaken their right to repatriation, but that all other civic rights should be given them, including the right to work. Though the League's resolutions were supposed to be binding, each host government interpreted them according to its own interests. Lebanon ignored the advice concerning the right to work, just as Jordan did concerning naturalisation. While many Lebanese admitted that Palestinians should not be classified as 'foreigners', failure to create a category for them with specific rights meant that, in practice, laws applied to foreigners were applied to them. This was most damaging in relation to work rights, since, to protect national workers, there were several kind of employment from which foreigners were excluded, particularly the public sector, banks, concessionary companies, and transport.[17] Foreign workers are further required to obtain permits for all types of work except in agriculture and construction. A second aspect of Lebanese law applied to Palestinians with adverse effects is the principle of reciprocity, which rules that foreign workers are to be treated as Lebanese workers are treated in their country. Applied retrospectively to Palestinians, this ruling was used to exclude them from social security benefits, even though contributions are deducted from their salaries.

Restrictions on professional workers and businessmen were intially less penal than those affecting manual and clerical workers. The practice of the 'free professions' (medicine, law, engineering, pharmacy) is conditional on membership in syndicates that are limited to Lebanese nationals, but middle class Palestinians could obtain nationality relatively easily until the mid-70s.

The law governing naturalisation made this conditional on presidential decree. Under President Chamoun (1952-8), naturalisation was greatly facilitated for Christian Palestinians, but by the mid-60s the authorities were becoming more restrictive. However, it has generally been possible even for Muslim Palestinians to gain nationality if they have connections and can pay lawyers' fees. Ease of naturalisation was one element in rousing Maronite hostility not only towards Palestinians, but to a state they increasingly saw as corrupt, and unable to defend 'national' (i.e. Maronite) interests.

In relation to ownership of property and businesses, Lebanese law was initially extremely liberal, in line with its policy of encouraging foreign investment. Unlike most Gulf countries, where the state facilitates capitalist enterprise, in Lebanon there is no obligation on foreign businessmen to seek a Lebanese partner; there is, however, a legal obligation to employ a majority of Lebanese workers. Thus, though the majority of Palestinian businessmen chose to come to Lebanon, the laws operated a separation between Palestinian capital and labour. Land ownership by foreigners began by being unrestricted, and increasingly came under limitation caused by political fears. In any case, it was deteriorating political conditions rather than legal restrictions that pushed Palestinian capital out of Lebanon from the late 1960s onwards.

The general point to be noted concerning refugee rights in Lebanon is that whatever laws existed were less important then ministerial decrees and the goodwill of important officials, both of which reflected the political conjuncture. Palestinians officially designated as *lajji'een* (refugees) depended on the issuing of official documents such as work permits and *laissez-passers* and this dependence became the basis for financial exactions and political control.

As official management agency, the government set up a Central Committee for Refugee Affairs in 1950, which was upgraded into a Directorate in 1959. This body, which issued identity cards and *laissez-passers* and registered refugee life events, was a section within the Ministry of Interior. A second main government controlling institution was the Ministry of Labour and Social Affairs, which issued work permits. However, after the Civil War of 1958, real control of camp Palestinians passed into the hands of the Directorate of General Security and the Army's Intelligence Branch. This change began under President Chehab (1958-64), a period which saw the rise of the *mukjabarat* (intelligence agents), and growing concern of the political elite about the potentialities of the Palestinians for 'de-stabilisation'.[18] The camps began to be kept under oppressive surveillance.

While the state controlled all aspects of refugee life related to 'national security', UNWRA (established in May 1950) took charge of their maintenance. Issuing from the US-inspired Clapp Mission of 1949, UNWRA's original mandate went beyond the immediate relief of the refugees to their ultimate integration in the host countries, an objective that was rejected by the Arab League, the host governments, and the refugees themselves, who expressed their refusal in numerous demonstrations and memoranda. Thus UNWRA's role was limited to the provision of basic maintenance, and social services. One of the Agency's first tasks was a 'final' registration of legitimate refugees, aimed at eliminating false and double registrations. After 1953, registration required exceptional procedures, even for new deportees, a point that acquired significance later when registration with UNWRA came to be viewed as the only legitimate basis for Palestinian residence in Lebanon. A second primary task for UNWRA was the organisation of camp sites, many of which were already in *de facto* existence. Refugees were divided into several categories, according to which rights to rations, medical and educational services or special hardship allowances were allocated. Such categories not only created inequalities and resentments between the refugees, they also became a basis for a patronage system among Agency employees.

Although UNWRA was a large employer of Palestinians (1200 in 1951, excluding daily paid labourers)[19] refugee demands were not represented at the Agency's decision-taking levels until 1973, when the UN General Assembly recognised the PLO as representative of the Palestinian people.

Before then there was no official channel of communication. Further, UNWRA's structure closely reflected colonial models, being composed of two separate hierarchies, one 'international', the other 'local', each with different status, conditions and pay levels. Thus the Agency served to reproduce colonialist attitudes towards the refugees, the more so in that it initially employed a number of former Mandate Government officials. Some local staff reflected such attitudes; a number used their position for personal advantage.

Lebanon was the scene of a major Palestinian attempt to ameliorate their civic status, the Cairo Agreement of 1969, negotiated under the auspices of President Nasser.[20] The Agreement did more than legitimise *feda'yeen* operations from South Lebanon, it acknowledged the national identity of the Palestinians, and affirmed their rights to residence, work and movement. For the population of the new autonomous camps, the Cairo Agreement marked a new epoch, marked by renewed national struggle and consciousness, a weakening of the power of the state, and lessening of dependence on UNWRA. Though the Cairo Agreement should have led to clarification of work rights, no progress was made on this point by PLO negotiators, and it was through the expanding structures of the PRM that camp Palestinians found new employment possibilities. Similarly it was the *de facto* power of the PRM rather than the (contested) Cairo Agreement that gave camp Palestinians normal rights to change residence, repair their homes, and enter or leave the country.

Zoning

Little initial effort was made by the authorities to control the distribution of the refugees. The majority stayed clustered near the border for the first two years, in expectation of imminent return. Even the eventual siting of camps was decided less by government policy than the availability of cheap or donated land, abandoned barracks or earlier refugee installations. Refugee clustering near the coastal cities (mainly Tyre and Sidon, and to a lesser exent Beirut and Tripoli) was probably due to the location of relief centres, but also to the eagerness of Lebanese employers for cheap labour.[21]

Eventually, however, two main lines of government zoning policy appeared. The first in time was to reduce refugee concentrations near the Southern border, viewed as dangerous because it encouraged 'infiltration' and smuggling. Thinning out concentrations in the South was implemented in the early years by forcible transfer to the Beka'[22] and in the 60s by declaring the South a military zone, and restricting Palestinian entry to it. Eventually, lack of employment in the Tyre region produced its own pressure towards northward migration; yet even as late as 1983, 48% of all registered refugees were still living in the southern provinces of Tyre and Sidon.[23]

The second government zoning principle was to reduce refugee concentrations around the capital city of Beirut. Until the construction boom of the late 50s, there was little refugee pressure to settle in the Beirut area, nor had the siting of seven camps within a 16-kilometer distance of the capital roused opposition, except in one case.[24] But by the early 60s the authorities began to be concerned by the build-up of population in the Beirut camps, caused partly by greater employment and educational openings. At the same time, a flood of poor, mainly Shi'ite Lebanese rural migrants added to the spread of slums around the capital. The authorities feared a revolutionary symbiosis between Palestinians, poor urban Sunnis and Shi'ite rural migrants.[25] Traditional Sunni and Shi'ite leaderships began to feel the challenge to their influence, as sectarian boundaries began to be eroded by new political formations, aided by common residence in Beirut's 'poverty belt'.

A sign of the authorities' fears is the plan to transfer the populations of two Beirut camps, Tell al-Za'ter and Chatila, to some other area. The plan was discussed by UNWRA and the government in the early 60s, and money set aside, but the move never took place, probably because cheap land was not available, possibly also for fear of political repercussions. However, other methods were found to reduce migration, such as instructing UNWRA not to transfer ration rights, combing the camps for illegal residents and arresting Palestinians found far from the zone of their original registration. Building homes outside camp boundaries was forbidden; fines were imposed for home expansion or repair; water and electricity supplies were withheld.[26] Surveillance was applied more oppressively to the Beirut camps than elsewhere.

The fears of Maronites and the inter-sect dominant elite concerning a Palestinian 'take-over' of the capital were exaggerated. Migration from the rural camps was held in check by fear of loss of shelter rights, and by housing shortages in Beirut. Moreover, migration was selective, affecting mainly young people seeking employment or education, and was offset by high rates of emigration from the Beirut camps to Europe or the Gulf. Indeed, Palestinians formed a small proportion of migrants to the 'poverty belt', the large majority being Lebanese Shi'ites,[27] while others were migrant workers from Arab and non-Arab countries.[28] But, especially after 1969, the camps formed the political and defence shield to this migratory mass. For the elite, the camps were a 'choker around our necks'[29], a 'string' set close to strategic routes joining Beirut to the provinces, as well as to the International Airport.[30] The Beirut camps thus formed the main target of Maronite militia attack during the Civil War of 1975/6, leading to the mass expulsion of Palestinians and Lebanese Muslims from East Beirut and Metn. Over time Palestinians have been 'sorted' into areas of Sunni and Shi'ite predominance, around the major coastal cities (including the western and southern parts of Beirut), south of the Awali River, and in the Beka'.

The Position of the Palestinians in the Lebanese Economy

Three factors have conditioned the impact of the refugees on the Lebanese economy. The most important is the nature of the Lebanese economy, the particular form of dependent capitalism taken by it in 1948 and afterwards.[31] Second, the legal and political/sectarian rigidities that have pressed the Palestinian labour force into particular sectors and levels of the economy. The economic characteristics of the refugee community, whether initially or as they have developed, are of lesser significance.[32]

The economic policy of all Lebanese governments since the establishment of the state has been one of extreme *laissez-faire*, marked by openness to world market forces, low taxation, minimal spending on infrastructure and public services, and neglect of the primary sectors of the economy in favour of banking, trade and services. The crisis-proneness of such an economy was already evident to foreign and local economists by the mid-'60s.[33]

State neglect of the sectors that could have generated employment for Palestinian as well as Lebanese workers – agriculture, industry, and public construction – meant low growth rates for these sectors between 1948 and 1975, with war-caused recession afterwards. The only expanding sectors of the economy – trade, banking, and services – offered little scope to Palestinians, except for a brief period between 1948 and 1966. Lebanon has been an exporter of labour for the whole period under consideration, a trend affecting Lebanese workers, but even more Palestinians. Yet even though unemployment and labour migration have remained high, the Lebanese economy traditionally encourages the entry of non-national workers – Syrian, Kurdish, Egyptian, Indian – who have fulfilled special economic functions, particularly in construction and domestic services. As well as building up pressure towards migration, the structure of the Lebanese economy has pushed both marginal Lebanese workers and Palestinians into the informal sector that proliferated in the wake of the rapid growth of Beirut, and of the services centred on it.

The Palestinian workforce was restricted in regard to employment by two kinds of law, that those exercising certain professions be members of syndicates, and that non-nationals apply for work permits. Palestinian professionals were not initially much impeded by these laws, but the work permit requirement pushed unskilled Palestinian workers into the sectors where permits were not required, i.e. agriculture and construction. From the beginning, the Ministry of Labour, under its 'Lebanist' director Emile Lahoud, restricted the issue of work permits to Palestinians.[34] The highest number ever issued, in 1968, was 2448, at a time when the number of economically active Palestinians was around 19,000.[35] After this date, the number and proportion relative to other foreign workers dropped.[36] It is therefore not surprising that in 1971 the majority of camp-based workers were paid daily (11,145 compared to 2,715 on contract), while nearly a quarter (3,585) were self-employed.[37] As late as 1980, a report estimates that 'the occupational distribution of the camp labour force exhibits overwhelmingly "blue-collar" characteristics'.[38]

Political/sectarian rigidities played little role in restricting the employment of Palestinians in the early period. Maronite employers were as ready as others to employ cheap refugee labour. If there was opposition, it came from segments of the Lebanese labour force threatened by the effect of low refugee wages on their own employment and wages. Increasing discrimination against Palestinian labour is attributable to a number of factors: economic crisis and unemployment, rising educational and technical/professional qualifications of formerly 'backward' segments of the Lebanese labour force, hostility towards the PRM, and a general intensification of sectarianism. Of the sectarian-based parties, the Maronite militias were the first to campaign against the employment of Palestinian workers, expelling them from East Beirut and the industrial zone of Mkalles during the fighting of 1975/6. The LF also used violence in the Sidon area and West Beirut after the Israeli invasion of 1982 to prevent the employment of Palestinians. Political tension between the Shi'ite-based Amal movement and Palestinians since 1982 has had a similarly disrupting effect on economic relations.

The sectoral distribution of the Palestinian workforce just before 1948 indicates the skills and resources brought by the refugees into Lebanon: two-thirds were rural-based, directly engaged in agriculture, or in crafts and trades based in agricultural production; 19% were employed in government or municipal administration; 11% were in industry (including construction and artisanal production); 9-10% were engaged in commerce, finance or tourist-related activities; 5% were in transport and communications, and 4% in the armed forces.[39] It is evident that the Lebanese economy offered much better employment possibilities to urban educated Palestinians than to the rural and poor urban masses, even though Palestinians played a role in the post-1948 development of citrus plantations in South Lebanon. Further, Lebanon offered the children of middle-class Palestinians excellent educational facilities for career advancement, whereas the education and training of camp Palestinians was greatly restricted. Free schooling provided by UNRWA (from 6 to 16 years), enabled a small proportion of camp youth to enter 'white-collar' occupations (e.g. as accountants, teachers, and clerical workers), while UNRWA's vocational training programme produced an even smaller number of highly skilled technical workers who mainly emigrated. But the structural limits to occupational mobility are demonstrated by the fact that, as late as 1979, 25% of the camp workforce was illiterate and 35.9% semi-literate, while only 23.8% had finished primary school and 0.4% had a vocational training diploma.[40]. Thus, while the Palestinian workforce in Lebanon has lost its predominantly agricultural skills (11% of camp workers were still employed in agriculture at the time of the PLO census of 1979), it has not acquired technical and professional skills to replace them. The profile is clearly one of an 'ethnic proletariat'.

If we break down the Palestinian labour force into three main components – businessmen, professional workers, and unskilled workers – we find that each has a somewhat different history in terms of the receptiveness of the economy over time, and in terms of reactions from the Lebanese population. Taking capital and businessmen first, we find that no obstacles were placed to the transfer of capital from Palestine, nor to the establishment of businesses. Beirut attracted the largest number of medium-sized Palestinian businesses, and though the total value of capital transfers is not known, it is estimated to have been considerable.[41] As well as capital, Palestinian entrepreneurs brought their stock of foreign contacts, and forms of business organisation new to Lebanon, such as auditing.[42] They rapidly entered into banking, tourism (hotels, bathing establishments), new types of manufacture and imports (e.g. chemical fertilizers), as well as cultural institutions (publishing, film-making). The adventurousness of Palestinian capital gave it a conspicuousness out of proportion to its real power. One venture in particular, Intra Bank, exemplified its brashness and ambition, extending its operations to the Gulf, Europe and the US, and thus arousing 'the envy and hostility of the older-established Lebanese political and financial bourgeoisie'.[43] In 1966 Intra Bank crashed in circumstances that have remained mysterious, but which were widely believed to have been the result of Central Bank manipulation. The crash marked the end both of Palestinian businessmen's confidence, and the economy's boom phase. From this date, political and economic crisis fed into each other, creating a hostile climate for Palestinian business. Many enterprises were destroyed during the Civil War of 1975/6; others moved out of Lebanon, fearing further insecurity. Legislation put new obstacles in the way of non-nationals buying land or property; establishing a business required higher-priced permits and heavier guarantees. By 1982, those businesses that remained were mainly small, without the capital or contacts needed to establish themselves elsewhere.

Beirut also attracted a high proportion of Palestine's professional workforce. They arrived at a moment when many large new foreign and national companies were being launched, requiring skills in English language and administration that Palestinians possessed more than their Lebanese counterparts. The number and level of Palestinian appointments in what constituted an elite sector of the economy irritated Lebanese nationalists, and the practice of hiring Palestinians came under attack in the National Assembly in 1953. Adoption of Lebanese nationality did little to protect Palestinian professionals from resentment caused by their too rapid success, and as economic crisis intensified in the 70s, such resetment became one strand in a generalised anti-Palestinian feeling not limited to Maronite regions. Rising professional qualifications among disadvantaged Lebanese sects (Sunnis, Druzes, Shi'ites), combined with increasing sectarianism to restrict the employment of Palestinians. As an example, whereas the main Sunni cultural institution, the Maqassad, had readily offered employment and training to Palestinians in the early period, this policy was reversed in the mid-70s. Palestinian employees increasingly encountered hostility in the workplace, often expressed in terms of criticism of the Resistance Movement, but undoubtedly owing much to their originally favoured position in the job market. With the rise of the sectarian militias, the practice of sectarian appointments became even more strongly entrenched.

The emergence of the PRM after 1969 slowly gave rise to a 'separate' Palestinian economy, based on a sizeable administrative apparatus which, along with social and productive institutions, is estimated to have employed around 65% of the Palestinian workforce. While Palestinian support for the PRM was primarily political and national, there was a substratum of economic motivation arising from exploitation and discrimination. There was also, by 1969, a certain convergence in the interests of the three main sectors of the Palestinian workforce, due to the worsening climate for business and professional workers described above. While the PRM-based economy primarily benefitted those whose position in the Lebanese economy had been most marginal, i.e. camp Palestinians, it also attracted a substantial number of skilled workers, whether out of nationalism, or because they were meeting discrimination in the Lebanese private sector. The PRM also generated openings for Palestinian capital, especially in construction, and the provision of supplies, from arms and equipment to medicines and raw materials for PRM workshops.

Potential conflict between Lebanese and Palestinian labour was thus reduced by the disadvantaged position of the latter, and by the tendency towards sectoral and regional segregation. Nevertheless, in the early period, some tension arose from Palestinian workers' readiness to accept low wage levels made possible by UNWRA rations and services. Shi'ite agricultural labourers are reported to have protested against the employment of Palestinians on citrus plantations in the 50s,[44] and some of the animosity behind Shi'ite attacks against Palestinians after 1982 arise from a perception of them as a *privileged* sector. A study of Koura in the 70s notes clashes between Palestinian and Lebanese workers in Tripoli.[45] However, such incidents seem to have been relatively rare, probably because pressures towards political alliance between disadvantaged sectors intervened. Another reason may be found in the exclusion of Palestinians from the public sector, which constitutes for Lebanese (especially Shi'ites) an important source of jobs and income.

The emergence of the PRM after 1969 slowly gave rise to a 'separate' Palestinian economy, at first limited to a small number of political cadres and fighters, but developing after 1976 a large administrative apparatus, along with social and productive institutions employing an estimated 65% of the Palestininan workforce.[46] From the preceding review, it will be seen that while Palestinian support for the PRM was primarily political and national, there was also a substratum of economic motivation arising from exploitation, discrimination, and bad life and work conditions. There was also, by 1969, a certain convergence in the interests of the three main sectors of the Palestinian workforce, due to the worsening climate for business and professional workers described above. While the PRM-based economy primarily benefitted those whose position in the Lebanese economy had been most marginal, i.e. the population of the camps, it also attracted into its ranks a substantial number of skilled Palestinian workers, e.g. doctors, engineers, journalists, academics. Whether out of nationalism, or because they were meeting discrimination in the Lebanese private sector, many highly qualified workers preferred to work for lower salaries in the institutions of the PRM. The PRM also generated openings for Palestinian capital, especially in the sector of building, real estate, and the provision of a wide range of supplies (arms, equipment, medicines, foodstuffs, clothing and raw materials for PRM workshops). Many fortunes were made out of 'national work'.

To what extent can Lebanese anti-Palestinian feeling be attributed to economic causes? No simple answer can be given, since much depends on the period and on which segment of the Lebanese and Palestinian population is in question. Further complexity arises from the fact that a single phenomenon, say PRM affluence, has generated contradicatory reactions in the same population segment. On the one hand, many Lebanese benefitted from the PRM economy, whether as suppliers of goods and services, employees, or receivers of welfare. Collective and individual Palestinian property during the era of the PRM removed the stigma of poverty, and encouraged normal social relations. On the other hand, stories of ill-gotten wealth generated reactions of envy and indignation, especially among Shi'ites from South Lebanon who had borne the brunt of Israeli devastation.

Not only Maronites blamed the Palestinians for Lebanon's economic ills, and for the destruction caused by Israeli attacks. The accusation *kharabu beladna* (they have ruined our country), the most serious ever brought against the refugee community by the host population, spread from the Maronites to other sectors from the time of the Civil War of 1975/76. However, this accusation is aimed less at the Palestinians' role in the economy than at the PRM's use of Lebanon as a base of struggle against Israel. In general we can say that political motives predominated in Lebanese anti-Palestinianism, but that economic competition played a role not expressed at the level of public discourse, but nonetheless real, and intensified by deteriorating economic conditions that made it natural to make a scape-goat of a non-national group.

Further study would probably show that the economic status of the camp Palestinians had different effects for different segments of the Lebanese people. For some, it was the *poverty* of the camps that formed a strand in anti-Palestinian feeling, rousing fears of crime and communism, while for others, particularly for poor Shi'ites, it was their relative privilege and prosperity that fuelled hostility. In common with other refugee communities, Palestinians in Lebanon have been seen by the host population predominantly as recipients (of aid, free shelter and schooling) rather than as producers. Their real contribution to the economy, whether in the form of labour, savings or consumptions, is seldom taken into account.

Social Relations

Both the early Arab and later Ottoman empires built strong states upon highly heterogeneous populations, without any drive to create a 'national' popular base, leaving groups of different origin scope to order their internal affairs and inter-relations. Further, the frequency from ancient times of population movement has produced cultural practices for establishing social relationships between 'strangers'; (clientship, fictive kinship, alliance, etc.) without any pressure towards ending group specificity. The question of Palestinian 'integration' in the Arab diaspora needs to be put into this historical and cultural framework before coming to specific regions or periods.

In Lebanon the refugees entered a 'stratified mosaic society'.[47] The threat posed by the Palestinians was immediately obvious. Less obvious was the threat the refugees posed as a pauperised mass. Lebanon's sect/class structure provided an innate pressure towards politicising the Palestinian presence even before the emergence of the Resistance Movement, and it is through this lens that we must look at the question of social relations between Palestinians and Lebanese.

In spite of the importance of sect in Lebanese politics and relations between people, there is little evidence of homogeneity within sects in attitudes towards, or dealings with, the refugees. Even in the case of the Maronites, the sect with the highest degree of internal organisation and of mobilisation against the Palestinians, we find diversity. Social relations have been influenced by other factors as well as sect: period, political orientation, class, educational level. Evidence from the early period suggests that sect was less important than it became later. Where Palestinians and Maronites shared the same neighbourhood or workplace, normal relations were established; it was only later that Palestinians living in Maronite milieus were ostracised, and eventually expelled. As to Sunnis, Palestinians recall that their initial welcome was not much warmer than that of the Maronites, in spite of their common sect; it was later, in response to Nasserism, that Sunni attitudes became more enthusiastic, and even then there was a difference between the Sunni bourgeoisie and the 'street'. Social relations between Palestinians and Druzes were slow to develop, less because of sect *per se*, than as a result of Israel's recruitment of Palestininan Druzes during and after the war of 1948. Lebanon's other major sect, the Shi'a provides the strongest evidence of fluctuation over time in stands towards the Palestinians and of intra-sect polarities. Sect is always an important factor in Lebanon, but generalisation based on sect about Lebanese attitudes towards Palestinians are misleading.

Evidence of change in the degree of mobilisation of sects for or against the Palestinians makes clear how much social relations are influenced by particular periods, and by developments outside Lebanon. The strongest illustration is offered by Nasserist Arab nationalism, which laid a basis for political alliance and social exchange between Palestinians and 'nationalist' Lebanese,[48] mainly Sunni. The Maronites' search for external allies (Israel, the US) emerged out of their antagonism to the Palestinians, and became an implicit condition for these allies' support. The rise of Khomeynist Iran has influenced Shi'ite stands towards the Palestinians, though in less clear-cut ways. Since most external support has been directed towards sectarian leaders and parties, it has had the effect of strengthening sectarianism, and weighting the sectarian factor in attitudes towards the Palestinians.

Political orientation and party membership have probably had a stronger influence than sect on Lebanese-Palestinian social relations. Palestinians remember that Lebanese with Arab nationalist leanings were initially more welcoming than others, regardless of sect or class. Membership in any of the secular, anti-imperialist parties (PPS, Ba'th, LCP, ANM)[49] encouraged support for the Palestinian struggle; political support built social relations. This trend was carried forward by the formation of the Lebanese National Movement which grouped all the opposition parties and sects except Amal.[50] It was during the period of the LNM/PRM alliance, from 1969 to 1982, a period of daily confrontation with Israel or the Lebanese Forces, that social relations between Palestinians and Lebanese were least disturbed by barriers of sect or nationality. Different types of parochialism certainly existed both within the PRM and allied Lebanese parties, but the slogan of *Sha'b waheid* (one people) was given reality at the mass level, especially in the areas of greatest residential mixing, the popular quarters of Beirut and Sidon. All forms of social exchange could be found, from routine visiting to matters requiring basic trust and respect, such as marriage, which in most social strata is still negotiated by families, and is thus the strongest indicator of good relations. Though marriage between Palestinians and Sunnis was the most frequent, intermarriage with Druzes and Shi'ites also occurred.

Though most writers on Lebanon see class structure and consciousness as weak in comparison with that based on sect, yet class needs to be invoked to explain intra-sect differences in stands towards the Palestinians. If we exclude the Maronites, among whom anti-Palestinianism is strongest at the working class and *petit bourgeois* levels, we find that with the other sects social relations with Palestinians are stronger at the base of the class pyramid than at other levels.[51] Middle and upper class Sunnis were as disturbed as Maronites by the squalid refugee camps around the coastal cities that form their demographic/political base. Landowning and mercantile Shi'ites have never supported the PRM as the Shi'ite masses did after 1967/8.[52] Traditional Sunni and Shi'ite leaders have feared the radicalising effects of the Palestinian presence even while supporting the Palestinian cause. Further study may show a connection between the degree of development of a middle class inside each sect and attitudes toward the Palestinians, based on this class's interest in a Lebanese entity and a strong state. It is equally likely that a common sense of class deprivation *vis-à-vis* the Lebanese ruling elite and the Maronite sect cemented relations between camp Palestinians and lower Sunni, Druze and Shi'ite strata.

Between 1948 and 1969, camp residence, poverty and dependence on UNWRA rations had a ghettoising effect, and there was little contact with surrounding Lebanese. In the early days of Bourj al-Barajneh camp, youths from the neighbouring suburb used to walk through the camp making loud comments on women, the clearest indication of the Palestinians' status loss. The fact that some women from camps were forced to work as domestic servants (a type of work never undertaken in Palestine), added to barriers of class level before 1969. Several changes broke down such barriers: camp Palestinian income levels improved; geographic overlapping increased as better-off Palestinians moved into near-camp suburbs; the PRM became a source of influence, jobs and subsidies, so that Palestinians could now offer *waasta* (connection to a source of power) to Lebanese friends and neighbours.

Just as social relationships between Palestinians and Lebanese have flourished under certain conditions, and in certain periods, they have also been very vulnerable to sectarian mobilisation. A Palestinian teacher from a mixed neighbourhood near Tell al-Za'ter camp became accustomed to daily visiting and mutual help with Maronite neighbours; yet it was these neighbours who looted his home during the siege of the camp in 1975/6. Close ties with Shi'ite neighbours in Beirut's southern suburbs were similarly disrupted by clashes with Amal in 1985/6. The speed with which social relations change in Lebanon, a product of factionalism and crisis, differentiates this from other regions of the diaspora, where relations with host populations have been more stable, and adds a special quality to Palestinian insecurity here, summed up in their saying, '*Sadiq hal-yawm, bukra adu*' (The friend today is the enemy tomorrow).

The Israeli invasion and PRM withdrawal of 1982 ushered in a new phase of insecurity for the Palestinians remaining in Lebanon. The Habib Accords negotiated between the US and Lebanon governments during the invasion supposedly guaranteed their status as 'law-abiding noncombatants',[53] but the massacre of September 16-18 in Sabra/Chatila demonstrated the hollowness of this guarantee. With Lebanon divided into zones controlled by different armies and militias, Palestinians have been subjected to arrest, kidnapping and intimidation, forcing them back into the relative security of the camps. Movement between one zone and another, involving passage through militia roadblocks, has become hazardous. Civilian PLO institutions that remained have been closed, harassed or blown up. To insecurity was added unemployment through the loss of PRM-generated jobs and the deterioration of the Lebanese economy. The slight improvement in conditions produced by the Lebanese Army withdrawal from West Beirut in February 1984, and Israeli withdrawal from most of South Lebanon in 1985, was offset by deterioration in relations between Amal and the Palestinians, and attacks on the Beirut camps.

Amal and Shi'ite hostility has more serious implications for Palestinians than that of the Maronite militias, since all but a few remaining camps are situated in areas of Shi'ite predominance. Amal casualties from the attacks on the Beirut camps have left a heavy residue of blood vengeance, leading to acts of individual retaliation in the margin of the fighting, breaking pre-1982 political and social ties. Caught in a system of fighting, sectarian militias, the insistence of the camps on keeping defensive weapons is understandable; without them, they risk repetition of the 1982 massacres. Yet armed, they present an obstacle to Amal's aim to control West Beirut and the southern suburbs, as well as to Syrian-sponsored steps to solve the Lebanese crisis. Thus the situation of the community is more alarming now than at any time since 1948.

The insistence of the Palestinians on carrying on their struggle against Israel has been seen by some observers as the primary cause of their insecurity in Lebanon. It is argued that if they had remained inconspicuous and untroublesome as refugees, they would have avoided the hostility and attacks to which they have been exposed. While no one would deny that the PRM had a de-stabilising effect on the Lebanese political system, the Lebanese problem was brewing long before the armed presence of the PLO became a factor in Lebanon's delicate sectarian balance...What the armed presence of the PLO did was to accelerate an already existing process and bring it to explosion point earlier than would otherwise have been the case.[54]

The close focus required to present the complexities of the Lebanese arena introduces its own kind of distortion, blurring the dominant role of external powers in producing events, and influencing the reactions of local actors and groups. The point to be stressed in conclusion is that refugee situations do not originate in the countries where we examine them, but in wider regional and international asymmetries. The Palestinian refugees were produced, and have been maintained, by such an asymmetry between Zionist and indigenous Palestinians, and between the United States and the Arab states. It is this power asymmetry, unparalleled even in the case of South Africa, that permits Israel to refuse solutions based on Palestinian national rights, to attack the Palestinians in host countries and to attack host populations as well. Such a regional/international power imbalance has its own dynamic, and cannot be abstracted from discussion of the fate of Palestinians in individual host countries. It is especially important to recall this point in the case of Lebanon, where the combined playing out of internal and external crises has caused immense losses and suffering to both Lebanese and Palestinians.

Notes: Chapter 16

1 The Palestinians' right to return was consecrated in their eyes by UN Resolution 194, which specified that 'the refugees wishing to return to their homes and live in peace with their neighbours should be permitted to do so at the earliest practicable date, and that compensation should be paid for the property of those choosing not to return'.

2 A comparative case is offered by the occupied West Bank where intimidation of Palestinians is carried out by armed Israeli settlers rather than by the authorities.

3 The Lebanese Forces, formed in August 1976 under the leadership of Bashir Gemayel, combined several Maronite militias: the Kata'eb, Chamoun's Tigers, The Organisation and The Guardians of the Cedars were the largest.

4 Randall, 1983, p. 17.

5 For a good account see H. Cobban, *The Palestinian Liberation Organisation* (Cambridge, UK, 1984); H. Cobban, *The Making of Modern Lebanon* (London, 1985); R. Khalidi, 'L'impact du mouvement national palestinien sur la politique et la societe libanaises', *Revue d'Etudes Palestiniennes*, no. 12, Summer 1984; R. Khalidi, 'External Paper' no. 65, Wilson Centre, Washington, June 1985; W. Khalidi, *Conflicts and Violence in Lebanon* (Cambridge, US, 1979); B. Odeh, *Lebanon: Dynamics of Conflict* (London, 1985); J. Randall, *Going All The Way* (New York, 1983); K. Salibi, *Crossroads to Civil War* (New York, 1976).

6 Some writers distinguish between 'sects' and 'minorities' when discussing religious-based groups in Lebanon. I follow Joseph (1978, p. 4) in using 'sect' to denote any group

organised on a religious basis. S. Joseph, 'Muslim-Christian Conflicts: A Theoretical Perspective' in S. Joseph and B. Pillsbury, Eds., *Muslim-Christian Conflicts: Economic, Political and Social Origin* (Boulder, 1978). An early account on local voluntary aid lists the Lebanese Red Cross, the Permanent Office for Palestine, the Kata'eb, the Najjadeh, the Federation of Scouts, the YMCA, and an official Central Committee for Assistance to the Refugees: F.Karam, 'Témoignage sur les Réfugiés Palestiniens', *Les Conférences du Cénacle*, IIIe année, no. 3-4, Beirut, March 1949.

7 Khalidi, 1979, p. 37.

8 The ratio of Christians to Muslims was higher among refugees to Lebanon, at 19.6: 80.4%, than it was nationally at 7.6:92.4%; Y. Sayigh, *Implications of UNWRA Operations*, MA thesis, American University of Beirut, 1952.

9 The Christian camps were Mar Elias (Greek Orthodox) in West Beirut, and Jisr al-Basha and Dbeyeh (both Catholic) in Metn. A secondary school was donated to Dbeyeh Camp by the Papal Mission.

10 Sayigh, 1979, p. 104.

11 The US Legation in Beirut reported, in 1949: 'The absorption of an *alien* population amounting to as much as 10 per cent of the native population...would create a Moslem majority and turn the entire political complexion of the country' (author's italics), B. Morris, 'The Initial Absorption of the Palestinian Refugees in the Arab Host Countries, 1948-49', paper for the Workshop on European and Middle East Refugees in the 20th Century, Oxford, August 1985, included in this volume.

12 Morris, op.cit. quotes the British minister in Beirut as reporting in 1948 that Lebanese Christians 'would resist any attempt (to permanently) resettle refugees in Lebanon'. However, according to *The Legal Status of the Palestinians in Lebanon* (Beirut, xerox, n.d.), the only Maronite figure openly to protest against free entry of the Palestinians was Bishop Mubarak. Among politicians, only a minor figure, Naim Mghabghab, deputy and member of Chamoun's National Liberal Party, publicly expressed anti-Palestinian views in the 1950s.

13 Sayigh, 1952, p. 11.

14 UNWRA's definition of a refugee was 'a person whose normal residence was Palestine for a minimum of two years preceding the conflict...and who as a result of this conflict lost both his home and his means of livelihood...'(UNWRA, *A Brief History* 1950-1982, Vienna, n.d., p. 66).

15 Kossaifi, 1970, p. 28.

16 *The Legal Status of the Palestinians in Lebanon*, nd.

17 TEAM, 1983, p. 8A.

18 Salibi, 1976, pp. 10 & 28.

19 Sayigh, 1952, p. 65.

20 Khalidi, 1979, p. 185.

21 This motive was raised in a discussion between three leading Maronites in 1975, one of whom remarked, 'It is we who deliberately put them near urban areas and not on frontiers, in response to the wishes of our businessmen for cheap labour.' (In 'Arab Reports and Analysis', *Journal of Palestine Studies*, no. 17/18, Autumn 1975/Winter 1976, p. 221).

22 Sayigh, 1979, p. 106.

23 *Map of UNWRA's Area of Operations*, 30 June 1983 (Public Information Division, UNWRA, Vienna, 1983).

24 This was Tell al-Za'ter, which became one of the largest, poorest and most heterogenous of all the camps, according to H. Mundus, *Work and Workers in a Palestinian Camp* (Arabic), (Beirut, 1974).

25 Writing of Chehab's 'strict police control' over the camps Salibib comments that though the authorities feared a 'natural symbiosis' between the Palestinian refugees and 'Muslim slum-dwellers', they were not at first concerned that this would spread to Shi'ites, whom they regarded as 'natural allies' of the Christians. This was before the rise of Imam Moussa Sadr: *Crossroad to Civil War* (New York, 1976), p. 10.

26 Arson is reported to have been used to remove squatters (Lebanese and Palestinian) from Church property in Karanteena and Maslakh in East Beirut in the 60s. These areas were razed by the Maronite militias in early 1976.

27 In 1948 only 10% of Shi'ites lived in cities. By 1974, two thirds were urban, with more than 45% living in Greater Beirut. S. Nasr. 'Roots of the Shi'i Movement', *MERIP Reports*, no. 133, June 1985. A 1983 estimate of the population of the predominantly Shi'ite southern suburbs was 500,000.

28 Until 1982, when many foreign workers were deported, the 'poverty belt' included: Syrians, Egyptians, Jordanians, Bangladeshis, Sri Lankans, as well as stateless persons.

29 Randall, 1976, pp. 9-10.

30 Salibi, 1976, pp. 9-10.

31 The Lebanese economy is a striking example of what neo-Marxist economists have called 'dependent capitalism'. Even after the end of the French Mandate, the banking sector continued to be dominated by foreign share-holders; public facilities (water, electricity, the port), as well as the monopoly of salt and tobacco production, were foreign-owned; most exports were primary products, and the political clout of the merchants effectively stifled industrial growth.

32 Consensus on the weaknesses of the Lebanese economy includes non-Marxist scholars. See, for example, M. Hudson, *The Precarious Republic* (Boulder, 1985) pp. 61-70, on three types of strain characterising the economy: dependence on outside investment; uneven distribution of prosperity; unemployment, especially in the industrial and agricultural sectors.

33 The French IRFED (Institut International de Recherches et de Formation en vue de Developpement) Mission predicted crisis in its report, *Besoins et Possibilités de Développement du Liban*, Beirut, 1960-61. See also Y. Sayigh and M. Atallah, *A Second Look at the Lebanese Economy* (Arabic), Beirut, 1966.

34 In 1951 UNWRA reached an agreement with the Government to employ refugees on construction projects. Lahoud immediately protested, even though Lebanese workers avoided such labour, for long left to Syrian migrant workers. *The Legal Status...*p. 18.

35 An unpublished Lebanese Manpower Survey carried out by the Ministry of Planning in 1971, gives a camp-based labour force of 20,580, TEAM, *Characteristics of the Palestinian Labour Force in Lebanon*, unpublished report, Beirut, 1983.

36 TEAM, 1983, p. 11.

37 See Table 9, B. Sirhan, 'Palestinian Refugee Camp Life in Lebanon', *Journal of Palestine Studies* no. 14, Winter 1975, p. 101.

38 TEAM, 1983, p. 76.

39 Sayigh, 1952, pp. 17 & 20.

40 Percentages calculated from Table VII/13, *Palestinian Statistical Abstract 1980* (PLO-PNF, Central Bureau of Statistics, Damascus), p226. TEAM, *Characteristics of the Palestinian Labour Force in Lebanon*, unpublished report, Beirut, 1983.

41 Sayigh, 1952, pp. 22-28

42 Limited share companies were required by commerical law in Palestine in the case of banking, insurance and auditing, but not in Lebanon where most local businesses, including banks, were individually owned, and not required to produce strictly audited accounting. Arabia Insurance, founded in Palestine in 1944, was one of the largest insurance companies in the Middle East in terms of capital, which was entirely Arab. Lebanese insurance firms were mainly subsidiaries of foreign firms.

43 Salibi, 1976, p. 29.

44 K. Salibi, interview, Sept 15 1985.

45 Mailloux, 1982, p. 113.

46 This estimate was given by an experienced Palestinian researcher who worked with PLO research and planning institutions before 1982, and on the TEAM Survey.

47 Barakat, 1977, p. 24.

48 The term 'nationalist' (*watanee*) is used to denote Arab nationalist Lebanese. I have used 'Lebanese nationalists' to denote those whose primary loyalty is to Lebanon, usually termed 'rightists' or isolationists' by 'nationalist' Lebanese.

49 The initials stand for: Parti Populaire Syrien, Lebanese Communist Party and Arab Nationalist Movement.

50 W. Khalidi, in *Conflict and Violence in Lebanon* (Cambridge, USA, 1979) gives a useful list of the member groups of the LNM. Amal Movement took form as a militia

in 1974, growing out of the earlier Mouvement des Désherités, both founded and led by Imam Moussa Sadr.

51   A study of Lebanese University students carried out in the early 70s found that upper and middle class Muslims (including Druzes) were more likely to be pro-Palestinian than Maronites of any class. When a sect is aggregated, the findings also show a significant difference between classes: See H. Bakarat, *Lebanon in Strife* (Austin, 1977), pp. 116-118.

52   When the camp of Nabatiyeh was badly damaged in an Israeli air-raid in 1973, it was not rebuilt because of opposition from the nearby, mainly Shi'ite city.

53   Cobban (1984, 0123) quotes a PRM leader as saying, 'Habib presented a written undertaking guaranteeing the security of the international forces'. The actual document (quoted p. 124) is more ambiguous: 'Law-abiding Palestinian noncombatants left behind in Beirut...will be subject to Lebanese laws and regulations. The Governments of Lebanon and the United States will provide appropriate guarantees of safety...': H. Cobban, *The Palestinian Liberation Organisation* (Cambridge, UK, 1984), p. 123.

54   Khalidi, 1979, p. 145.

17 Palestine refugees, economic integration and durable solutions

HOWARD ADELMAN

I Durable Solutions and Economic Integration

The United Nations High Commissioner for Refugees convened a meeting of experts on August 29-31, 1983, at Mont Pelerin in Switzerland to study questions of refugee aid and development. The report begins with these general considerations:

> Refugee problems demand *durable* solutions . . . A genuinely durable solution to a refugee problem means integration of the refugee into society: either reintegration in the country of origin after voluntary repatriation, or reintegration in the country of first asylum or country of resettlement.

There are three forms of durable solutions to refugee situations: repatriation to the country from which the refugees fled, resettlement in third countries which have the capacity and the willingness to take in the refugees, and settlement in the country of first asylum. Settlement in a country of first asylum is a matter of degree. Integration may imply the elimination of the distinctive identity of the refugees as a group – then it is *social* integration. It may entail elimination of their refugee *status* by *integrating them politically* into the state where they found refuge so that they become citizens of that state. Or integration may simply entail elimination of their *material condition* as refugees and their dependence on aid by integrating them *economically* into the society in which they found refuge.[1] For some, this last option is a *de facto* durable solution, though not a *de jure* one.

In contrast to these durable solutions, there are three forms of interim assistance provided to refugees: relief, works and economic integration. Relief entails the provision of emergency food rations, housing, health and sanitary services in the areas to which refugees have fled. Works is a more expensive effort which provides gainful employment to the refugees on projects useful to the country of first asylum; at the same time, the refugee achieves a degree of dignity through becoming self-supporting through labour, thereby inhibiting the development of a welfare mentality. The third form of interim solution, economic integration, is usually linked to development schemes to enable refugees to find long-term employment and become fully self-supporting and thereby integrated into the economic life of the countries where the refugees have found asylum. This is, by far, the form of interim assistance requiring the greatest initial capital outlay, though the intention in the long term is to save money. It is viewed as tantamount to a durable solution – settlement in the country of first asylum *in practice* without necessarily providing the protection of citizenship.

II   Beliefs about the Original Mandate of UNRWA

This article focuses on the analysis of the overlap of the long-term solution of economic integration and settlement in the country of first asylum as a durable solution. In particular, the article argues that the United Nations Relief and Works Agency for Palestine Refugees[2] (UNRWA) was created to use economic integration as a method of settlement in the country of first asylum, and to provide a long term interim solution which would, in effect, be a durable solution, even if in many or most cases, political integration into the country of asylum count not be achieved.

The phrase 'durable solution' can have an ironic, equivocal meaning. The accepted meaning is that a refugee *problem* can be solved permanently, that is, a particular group of refugees will no longer continue to exist as *refugees*. But the phrase could also mean 'enduring' *solution*, that the means used to solve the problem go on and on whether the problem itself is or is not solved.

UNRWA provides a case study of an agency set up to provide a durable solution in the ordinary meaning of that term – to eliminate the Palestine refugee problem – which later became a durable solution in the ironic, second sense of the term, where the solution applied continued on and on but the refugee situation was perpetuated.

There are two other interpretations of the original goals of UNRWA. The most predominant belief ascribes the most modest goal to UNRWA – to provide *only* interim assistance. UNRWA's contribution was not intended to provide a *solution* to the problem of the Palestinian refugees, only stop-gap measures to provide relief and works, as the name implies. The solution to the Palestine refugee problem was to come from the Palestine Conciliation Commission.

This interpretation comes from both defenders and opponents of UNRWA. The former Commissioner General of UNRWA, Olof Rydbeck, in a letter to me dated September 11, 1984, contended that the Agency's mandate was *always* '*simply* to provide services' until a durable solution could be found, a premise reiterated in the annual reports of UNRWA.

Professor Jack Garvey, in the publication *Refugee Aid and Middle East Peace*, published by WOJAC – the World Organization of Jews from Arab Countries – in an outright attack on UNRWA agrees that the UNRWA mandate was an interim one, premised on a durable solution, but, in his interpretation, the durable solution was repatriation (or compensation).

> The 'Temporary' institute of UNRWA was premised on the alternative long-term solutions to the Palestinian refugee problem, compensation and repatriation. (p.5)

The defenders of UNRWA deliberately separate its interim role from any specific political outcome; UNRWA efforts were without prejudice to the rights of repatriation. Professor Garvey's interpretation – that repatriation was the specific goal – is consistent only with the wording of the 1948 resolution but inconsistent with all the subsequent actions and words, including the 1949 resolution on UNRWA which was set up to implement the results of the Economic Survey Mission, which did not focus on repatriation as a solution. Trygve Lie's (Secretary General of the United Nations at the time) understanding of the problem was unambiguous.

In theory, there was every reason for their return; in practice, repatriation was impossible and most of them would have to be settled where they were. (Trygve Lie, *In the Cause of Peace*, p. 196).

There is a second interpretation of the goals of UNRWA when it was formed. The Heritage Foundation, an outspoken critic of UNRWA and the United Nations, in a United Nations Assessment Project Study on UNRWA published on May 28, 1985, describes UNRWA as, 'Originally intended as a temporary agency to carry out a relief works program,' (p. 2) and in that sense seems to agree with the apologists for UNRWA. But it adds that the interim relief would contribute to a solution of integrating refugees in their countries of first asylum, to prepare for the 'absorption of the displaced Arabs into neighboring states'(p. 2). UNRWA's goal was not to provide a durable solution; UNRWA was a necessary condition for preparing for a durable solution by economically integrating the refugees into the countries of first asylum.

The interpretation of this paper is that the *original goals* of UNRWA (even if the original plans for the first year were as the Heritage Foundation depicts them) were much more ambitious than in either of these two interpretations. Relief and works were not the end for UNRWA. Nor were they simply the means for some other organization to accomplish economic integration of the refugees. Relief and works were interim measures until UNRWA could introduce and implement economic development projects in conjunction with other large scale economic development plans so that the refugees could be integrated into the local economies. Further, this would, in effect, provide a durable solution. In other words, a durable solution was interpreted to mean economic integration. Political and, even more ambitiously, social integration was not the goal.

The critical factor to facilitate economic integration was the provision of economic development aid through UNRWA. Further, it was understood that the development assistance for refugees would have to go hand in hand with aid to the host population through other projects.

III   Historical Research and Its Current Application

The issue over the original goals of UNRWA is not just one of curiosity about the historical truth but has a present application quite separate from UNRWA and the issue of the Palestinian refugees, though it may indeed help us understand more about the factors contributing to their present plight. The issue is applicable to current United Nations policy, for there are other areas in which economic development is linked to economic integration of refugees in order to provide what would in effect be a durable solution, as in some of the programmes in Central America and Africa.

The problem of Palestinian refugees bears remarkable resemblances to many of the contemporary refugee situations. Palestine was a third world area before the term 'third world' was invented. The region was replete with developing countries recently emerging from political and economic colonial situations. The numbers of refugees were large. Resettlement into third countries abroad and repatriation to the country or area which they left seemed to be ruled out, even though the rhetorical goal of repatriation became part of the political bargaining process. Settlement in countries of first asylum seemed a possibility only if combined with economic development. In other words, all the ingredients of many contemporary situations – large numbers, low-income countries, and a lack of durable solutions suggesting refugees would be left in limbo for a long time – were all present in this situation almost forty years ago. What is more significant is that solutions that are being promoted now were tried then, and in a situation where the host countries shared the same language, culture, and, by and large, religion of the refugees. Further, although the refugee situation arose in countries recently emerging from colonialism, the refugees were not a result of the colonial struggle *per se*. The problem emerged from conflict over the successor regime, which was in turn rooted in an ethnic conflict – a characteristic prevalent in many third world refugee-producing situations today.

UNRWA, in its original vision, as we interpret it, was a prototype of an attempt to integrate aid with long-term development and to avoid treating refugees in isolation from the local population and economy.

The issue is not development aid as an approach to the refugee problem or suggestions that development aid might solve a refugee problem. It might, but it might not. The *goal* (as distinct from its achievement) of economic integration facilitated by development aid might help transform a refugee problem into a deeper and more long-lasting level of conflict and suffering. I believe the Palestinians are an abject lesson of the latter consequences of one attempt to link economic development and refugee integration as a durable solution to a refugee problem.

But we must first establish that, in the case of UNRWA, the linkage did exist in the minds of those who formulated UNRWA. And that requires historical research. Historical research into past attempts to solve refugee problems is invaluable if mistakes are not to be repeated. In that sense, refugee research shares a kinship with the refugees themselves. For refugee assistance has little if any sense of its own history. Milan Kindera, the famous Czech exile writer, in *The Book of Laughter and Forgetting*, describes the function of forgetting or repressing one's history. It allows the past to be invented and old solutions to be 'reinvented'.

Historical material or research on durable solutions for refugees is available in the early archives of UNRWA. The *Guide to the Archives of International Organizations: the United Nations System*, published by UNESCO in 1984 (France, ISBN92-3-102090-0), includes the following listing on p. 231:

Archives of the United Nations Relief and Works Agency for Palestine Refugees in the Near East (UNRWA) (ROA 6-4)

Volume: one linear metre. No finding aids.

In fact, there are over a thousand metres – by and large ignored, neglected and invaluable.

Refugee research must be rooted in history. The historical material exists to provide those roots. What is most important is that, in current discussions, UNRWA is usually held up as an example of the futility of founding an agency to provide band-aid solutions. The historical material indicate the reverse; UNRWA was not set up to provide temporary service. The historical material reveals that the intention in setting up UNRWA was to find a durable solution through economic integration into countries of first asylum. Those early attempts to solve the problem of refugees by economic means failed – not simply because of resistance to such solutions by the host countries. The causes of failure are complicated, but they are not part of this article.

One should note that even when the refugees do become economically integrated, economic integration does not necessarily provide a durable solution to the refugee problem. The situation and plight of the refugees may be alleviated, but the original ethnic and national conflict may be escalated, or at least perpetuated, rather than solved. By *institutionalizing* the economic solution, the political debate and conflict may also be institutionalized.

IV Background

Following the United Nations partition resolution of Palestine in November of 1947, refugees started to flee from the areas of conflict between Jews and Arabs in Palestine. This flight, particularly by Palestinian Arabs, accelerated dramatically for a number of causes in May of 1948 when the British formally ended their rule over the mandated territory, the Jewish Agency declared Israel an independent state, Arab armies invaded the nascent state and the civil war became an international conflict.

Initially, the countries to which the refugees fled provided shelter and interim relief to many of the homeless who were in need. With the understanding that the relief effort was beyond the economic and structural capacity of the countries in which the refugees found asylum (a questionable assumption in historical retrospect, but not an issue for this paper), a United Nations relief effort was mounted in November of

1948 and became operational in January of 1949. A new co-ordinating agency, the United Nations Relief for Palestine Refugees (UNRPR) was set up, and three voluntary non-governmental agencies (the International Red Cross, the League of Red Cross Societies and the American Friends Service Committee) were appointed as operating arms to deliver the relief in different areas where the refugees were located.

One year later a new organization, the United Nations Relief and Works Agency for Palestine Refugees in the Near East (UNRWA) was formally set up, ostensibly to integrate the programmes and assume direct responsibility for the relief work, and it relieved UNRPR and the three voluntary agencies of their responsibilities in May of 1950.

The archives of UNRWA and UNRPR, supplemented by those of other United Nations agencies, non-governmental agencies and national governments, provide a unique and untapped resource for a case study which throws a great deal of light on a number of contemporary issues concerned with interim and durable solutions to the plight of the refugees.

V   The Actual Original Goal of UNRWA

As stated earlier, UNRWA is usually viewed as an international organization set up to provide an interim solution of relief and works. The explanations for the restriction of UNRWA to such limited interim measures are:

(a) this was the only assistance route available for Palestinian refugees until a more durable solution was found;
(b) the assistance was urgent if the refugees were not to face extreme privation and even starvation;
(c) a political solution to the problem would be found within a reasonably short period;
(d) assistance to the refugees was crucial to fostering a peaceful solution; and
(e) a durable solution would follow the establishment of permanent peace through a political resolution of the problem.

We know the third assumption based on a quick political solution was incorrect. There are also many who suggest that UNRWA assistance helped to prolong the uncertain status of the refugees *and* the conflict rather than facilitate a peaceful solution as presumed in the fourth assumption. Whether or not that was true, there is no evidence that the assistance to the refugees helped foster a peaceful outcome of the conflict between Israel and the Arab states. We still wait to learn whether the fifth assumption is correct – that a durable solution for the refugees will follow a political resolution of the problem.

Were the first two assumptions correct? Was the UNRWA the *only* assistance route available for Palestinian refugees until a more durable solution could be found? Did the Palestinian refugees face extreme privation or even starvation without this interim solution? The answer to these two questions awaits a longer, separate article, but the answer appears to be that both these assumptions were also incorrect, since aid might more beneficially have been given directly to the host countries.

Whether or not any of these five assumptions were or were not correct, were they *believed* to be correct and, if so, did they constitute the motives for setting up UNRWA?

We will take them in reverse order. Was UNRWA founded on the belief that a durable solution to the refugee problem would follow a political resolution? Or was UNRWA expected to be involved in facilitating a political solution by resolving the refugee part of the problem. Would that durable solution follow a peace agreement or would it form *part* of the political resolution of the conflict? Specifically, was the idea to focus primarily on settlement in the countries of first asylum, largely fostered by development schemes which assisted the refugees to integrate into the local economies, supplemented by some repatriation?

The belief that there was a division of responsibility between the Palestine Conciliation Commission, set up to find durable solutions, and UNRWA, as a temporary relief organization, seems to be belied in early UNRWA documents. A memorandum, for example, dated January 25, 1950, reads as follows:

NOTE ON THE REINTEGRATION PLAN AND THE DIVISION OF COMPETENCE BETWEEN UNRWA AND THE PCC

I. *Conflict of Competence with the PCC*

In paragraph 11 of the Resolution of December 1948 on which the PCC bases its claim to competence in the domain of integration, the PCC is instructed to 'Facilitate the repatriation, resettlement and economic and social integration of the refugees.' At the time when this resolution was approved, the political atmosphere was such as to permit the hope that there would be mass repatriation, without any serious obstacles. It was estimated that compensation would only be paid to those refugees (tacitly understood to be only few in number) who *'chose not to return to their country.'*

The words 'repatriation, reinstallation and economic rehabilitation' in the second sub-paragraph were obviously, in the minds of the authors, the logical order for the various stages of the return to Palestine. Nor was there in existence any organization or financial allotment which would have enabled the United Nations to take an active and positive part in the reinstallation and economic rehabilitation of refugees. So the mandate given to the PCC (the vague and indefinite nature of the word 'facilitate' is sufficient proof of this) was, in a way, 'outside' the real reintegration competence permitted, a natural process of reabsorption left to the good offices of the Israeli Government.

These hopes having been shattered, there appeared a completely new problem, that of the prolonged maintenance of the refugees in the host countries. It was then decided to take stronger measures of conservation than direct relief. Consequently, Resolution 302 (IV) of 8 December 1949, established UNRWA with the following duties:

a) 'To carry out in collaboration with local governments the direct relief and works programmes as recommended by the Economic Survey Mission;
b) To consult with the interested Near Eastern Governments concerning measures to be taken by them preparatory to the time when international assistance for relief and works projects is no longer available.'

The memo makes clear that UNRWA believed that the PCC's primary task with respect to refugees was to facilitate their repatriation and the payment of compensation to those not choosing to repatriate. (Whether or not this was in fact a correct interpretation of what the PCC saw as the resolution of the refugee problem is not the subject of this paper.) The goal of repatriation, whether a real goal or merely a rhetorical one, was clearly a dead letter by the beginning of 1950. No state, including the Arab states, believed that the repatriation was a realistic solution to the problem of the bulk of the refugees, though many refugees hoped for that solution. In UNRWA's own eyes, UNRWA was set up because peace was no longer a realistic prospect and the solution to the refugee problem would not be found *as part of* that peace agreement.

But the above memo only *implies* that UNRWA would now assume the task of finding a durable solution to the refugee problem independent of any peace agreement and as a follow-through to the very temporary relief and works measures (clause (b)).

The following statement on the Reintegration Policy of UNRWA dated December 30, 1950, is much clearer. It begins,

The Agency must make preparations to use the reintegration fund for the financing of as many varieties of projects as possible including not only direct reintegration projects (agricultural or urban) but also general economic development projects the realization of which would lead to an increase in the absorbtive capacity of the host countries, thus facilitating indirect reintegration.

This confidential note and others refer to 'the *permanent re-establishment of refugees* and the removal from relief'. (January 19, 1951, their italics.)

Trygve Lie makes clear that this was not just the UNRWA policy and intent but that of the top United Nations officials.

A final settlement in the Middle East hinged largely on the question of refugee reintegration on a large scale. (Trygve Lie, *In the Cause of Peace*, New York: Macmillan, 1954, p. 196)

This was to be done with the *de facto*, though not the *de jure*, concurrence of the Arab states through formal and open agreements.

It would be unrealistic to expect the Arab states to agree to the principle of resettlement at that stage, and the *de facto* settlement of the bulk of the refugees was all that could reasonably be arrived at. (op. cit.)

This clearly suggests that the integration of refugees into their host countries would be part of larger development schemes. There is a great deal of documentation which overwhelmingly supports the view that: (1) the original goal of the UNRWA officials was to foster economic integration as in effect a durable solution to the refugee problem; (2) that many Arab states were interested in encouraging these development schemes in their own self-interest and, (3) that works programmes were directly linked to economic integration and long-term development.

For example, in General Kennedy's report, 'Assistance to Palestine Refugees: Interim Report of the Director of the UNRWA PRNE' to the General Assembly, fifth session (Supplement No. 19. A/1451/Rev. 1, N.Y. 1951), Kennedy cites the Economic Survey Mission's interim report (which was the basis for UNRWA in November 1949) which 'recommended the creation of a new agency, which would not only carry out relief *on a diminishing scale* (my emphasis), but would inaugurate a works programme in which able-bodied refugees could become self-supporting and at the same time create works of lasting benefit to the refugees and the countries concerned'(p.2).

Clearly, Kennedy is not describing a relief works or a winter works programme in terms of the experience of the depression of the 1930s. For temporary or interim works programmes do not make anyone *self-supporting*. What was envisioned can be grasped in a note from the Ministry of Foreign Affairs of Egypt to UNRWA (No. 117-48-4) dated September 5, 1950, on a discussion of possible works programmes in the Gaza Strip and the 'transformation of the refugees from a class depending on relief, to a class living from the products of its own work'. The memorandum notes 'that there is a very close connection between the economic development programme for the Near East and the refugee problem'.

In that note and again in a letter dated April 9, 1951, the Egyptians made it clear that they had no objections to the reintegration of the refugees, provided only that the reintegration schemes did *not* compromise the right of return of the Palestinians. 'Reintegration should not make us forget the principle problem of the Palestine question in general and that of the refugees in particular.'

In a letter dated November 22, 1950, from the Minister of Foreign Affairs of Jordan to Mr Herbert Kunde at UNRWA headquarters (then located in Beirut), UNRWA is solicited for the provision of technical experts for a petroleum scheme, cement plant and a railway project 'to benefit from the facilities provided by the Resolution 304(IV) adopted by the United Nations General Assembly of the 16th November 1949'. A memo of November 18, 1950, on Refugee Reintegration explicitly states that, 'Faced with the problem of securing cooperation from National Governments the larger works undertaken were those of national importance which created national benefits'. In other words, refugee integration was to be accomplished by providing works and development assistance which would benefit the host country generally as well as help settle the refugees.

Technical assistance in development schemes were not the only economic input UNRWA provided to benefit the host countries. The indigent poor also benefitted, though some senior UNRWA officials protested. For example, Colonel Ali Buriny, General Supervisor of Refugees, wrote on August 30, 1950, to the Chief District Officer of UNRWA in the Gaza Strip that 'some members of your staff are registering the names of some poor families of Gaza for the purpose of issuing them with rations'. This occurred in Jerusalem and the West Bank as well and was encouraged by the host states. This evidence, however, only suggests that the officials of UNRWA at the beginning set themselves on a course of economically integrating the refugees as a means of providing a durable solution to the refugee problem, and that host countries – at least, Egypt and Jordan in the quotes cited, with the largest numbers of refugees – conspired in that solution. Other Arab countries – Syria under Zaim and Selo and Libya, for example, at different periods, contrary to current beliefs, accepted that goal.

Perhaps, however, the officials conspired with the Arab states to exceed their mandate and their mandate was simply to provide temporary relief and works. After all, General Assembly resolution 302 (IV) paragraph 5 seems clear enough. As stated in UNRWA's own statement of its history,

> The General Assembly therefore decided to establish a temporary organization – the United Nations Relief and Works Agency for Palestine Refugees in the Near East (UNRWA) – which would assume the operational responsibility for providing relief services and, concurrently, implement 'constructive measures . . with a view to the termination of international assistance for relief.' The constructive measures were to be 'works programmes' designed to employ or provide gainful employment for large numbers of refugees. (UNRWA, *Past, Present and Future* p. 2)

The original text reinforces the point in clause 6 by explicitly dividing the allocation of $33.7 million into $20.2 million for direct relief and $13.5 million for works. However, clause 7 suggests a much more ambitious goal. For, in addition to relief and works, UNRWA was mandated, 7(b),

> to consult with the interested Near Eastern Governments concerning measures to be taken by them preparatory to the time when international assistance for relief and works projects is no longer available.

What measures? They were not to be works and relief, since these were referred to in the previous clause. Secondly, they were measures to be taken *prior to* the termination of relief and works assistance. I contend they were plans for economic development conjoined with refugee integration.

Clearly a book, not an article, is necessary to establish convincingly that behind the rhetoric of Resolution 302 of the United Nations, the funders and those involved in implementing the resolution, including most Arab States, had in mind developing economic programmes for the host nations which would foster the economic integration of the refugees, to provide, in effect, a durable solution.

However, additional evidence to reinforce this interpretation would be helpful here. The United States was the major funder of UNRWA. Ambassador George McGhee, who had been conscripted by Dean Rusk in February of 1949 to act as U.S. Coordinator on Palestine refugee matters, had been told in his terms of reference that 'the bulk of these refugees must be resettled in Arab-Palestine and in neighboring Arab States' (cf. Ambassador George McGhee, *Envoy to the Middle World: Adventures in Diplomacy*, New York: Harper & Row, 1983, p. 29). McGhee goes on to quote his own memorandum of March 15, 1949 to Secretary Dean Acheson that, 'a plan be developed . . . including proposals for relief, rehabilitation and long-range *resettlement* projects' (my emphasis) (p. 30). Economic development was the key to resettlement and a durable solution for the Palestine refugees.

The plan developed was the Clapp Plan of the Economic Survey Mission. Clapp was taken from the Tennessee Valley Authority so that similar solutions could be applied to the problems of refugees in the Near East. The Clapp Plan was the basis of UNRWA.

Our first thesis was that a durable solution was not intended to follow or even be coincident with a political resolution of the conflict, but, at the time UNRWA was set up, was considered to be a precondition of a peaceful solution. The desirable solution was to be fostered by economic integration of the Palestinian refugees in the countries of first asylum.

Was that assistance seen as *directly* connected to a peaceful solution? Only in a sense. Resolution 302 (IV), paragraph V, which authorized the creation of UNRWA, only connected relief, but not works or other long term measures, 'to further conditions of peace *and stability*'. I believe the relief measures were seen as preventing riots and domestic discontent among the refugees and between the refugees and the local population. The role of UNRWA and the use of economic development was *not* primarily to foster a peaceful solution between Israel and her Arab neighbours, but to enhance the chances of peace and stability within the Arab countries and in the Gaza strip where the refugees were located, although, indirectly, this stability might foster peace between Israel and her Arab neighbours as well. After all, this was part of the American ethos at the time.

> The positive effort of American diplomacy . . . has been directed both toward the restoration of stability in the world and toward the achievement of an international order that should make world peace more secure than it has been in the past . . . organized recovery efforts of great magnitude were necessary to obtain world peace and security. (John C. Campbell, *The United States in World Affairs, 1948-9*, Council on Foreign Relations, New York: Harper, 1949, p. vii.)

That the reference is the internal security of the Arab states as a bulwark against communist subversion in the eyes of the United States and not establishing peace between the Israelis and the Arabs is made clear by the pessimistic view of Americans towards the prospect of peace in that arena.

> The immediate struggle for Palestine was between two intense national-isms, Zionist and Arab, which could admit of no workable compromise. (ibid., p. 375)

If a peace of any sort between the Arab states and Israel was now seen as a long and protracted matter, the Western powers had a quite separate goal – preserving the stability of the Arab states. The mandate of UNRWA was established to that end and not directly to foster peace between Israel and the Arab states. Virtually everyone knew at the time UNRWA was set up that a political solution to the Arab/Israeli conflict would not be found in a reasonably short period. This in itself lends greater credence to the necessity for local integration, as repatriation in any significant numbers would be ruled out without a peace treaty, and the Western countries showed no inclination to resettle the Palestine refugees.

Was the assistance necessary 'to prevent conditions of starvation and distress' among the Palestinians? Again, this is a subject for a much longer study and not a critical factor to my argument about the original mandate of UNRWA. But there is evidence to suggest that starvation was *not* imminent in 1950. For unlike 1948 when the spectre of starvation did loom up by the end of that year, the problem was largely caused by the United Kingdom's refusal to order basic food supplies for the area since it was giving up its mandate.[3] There would of course have been the additional problem of distributing the food if it had been ordered, but the more basic danger came because it had not been ordered in the first place.

The Jewish Agency took steps to prevent a shortage of foodstuffs from affecting the partition area they would control, but no legitimate authority existed to assume this responsibility for the Arab population on either side of the partitioned territory. In 1950, Jordan annexed the West Bank and Egypt controlled Gaza. Both countries had sufficient resources *and backing* to feed the refugees. Their efforts in 1948, when the situation was more difficult, gave proof that they were both able and *willing* to do so, especially if their resources were supplemented by outside aid.

(This is, however, a separate story. The importance here is that the absence of any imminent starvation would reinforce the point that the alleged imminent starvation was used as a rationale, but not a reason for setting up UNRWA, and that the function was to foster stability within the Arab states while working to integrate the Palestinian refugees.)

Even if the willingness of the Arab states to help cannot be established definitively, UNRWA was not the only assistance route available for Palestinian refugees; to establish that it would be necessary to establish that the Arab states were definitely *unwilling* to help. Further, voluntary agencies, such as the International Red Cross, the League of Red Cross Societies, and the American Friends Service Committee, or substitutes for them, could have been used to continue a relief and works programme, just as they are used in UNHCR projects to this day. But long range regional development plans to foster refugee integration required much greater financial and political clout than UNRPR, the predecessor of UNRWA, possessed. Just to give some glimpse of what clout that $33.7 million would provide, that money in 1987 purchasing power would provide well over half the current budget of UNHCR which has a mandate to help and *protect* (which was not part of UNRWA's mandate) over 10 million refugees today. And the Palestinian refugees constituted less than 8% of current numbers.

UNRWA is a prototype of an attempt to integrate aid with long-term development and to avoid treating refugees in isolation from the local population and economy. This mode of assistance was attempted by UNRWA, and it did not work. The present apologists for UNRWA deny that original goal existed. Kundera's maxim will haunt us – 'If we forget our past, we are bound to repeat it,' with all the mistakes and suffering. The prolonged suffering, dependency and extremely high costs to the world community, as well as the possibility that the proposed solution actually hindered the realization of a solution, may be rooted in the original goals of UNRWA.

The attempt to promote productivity and stimulate employment through self-help enterprises, and large scale agricultural development based on the model of the TVA, were all part of the UNRWA effort. The premiss that the only alternative to long-term relief and dependence was large scale economic development to produce income-generating activities was the premiss of UNRWA. But the result was long-term relief and international involvement, and no attempt to learn from this precedent. Nothing is learned because when the Palestinian refugee case is discussed as an example, it is in terms of open-ended care and maintenance programmes and not in terms of a failed attempt at economic integration connected with development aid.

The failure was not a result of a failure to direct development at the host community as well as the refugees, since aid was provided to the host community as well as some of the indigenous poor who were included on the relief rolls.

Perhaps the reason for not using the Palestinian refugee case as a lesson, whatever the original goal was, is to be found in the particularities of the local situation. The uniqueness of the Palestinian refugee case and UNRWA does not arise, as one of the commentators on a preliminary version of this paper suggested, because '. . . Palestinians were to be officially defined as refugees until that day when they got their homeland,' a problem 'not found . . . in any other situation that the post-war refugee system has been involved in'.

But there is *no*, absolutely no, evidence that I have seen or read connecting the solution of the Palestinian refugee problem with their own homeland in the 1948-52 period. The issue was not the refugees having their own homeland but *either* getting back political control of the land the Zionists obtained (a remote prospect) *or* getting back to their homes even if control was kept by the Zionists *or* locally integrating *or* resettlement abroad (for a few). The real options were integration or repatriation. A Palestinian homeland was just not part of the lexicon of the time. This suggests how later problems and proposed solutions are used to read back into history problems which were not there at the time.

There are differences of course. Development aid was then in its infancy. The goals and the time-scale of development plans are at present far more realistic and modest. Now we talk of additionality – not taking away from existing development programmes. But whatever differences are found, the similarities are too remarkable to be ignored.

For example, one similarity is a concentration on agricultural schemes and increasing the quantity and quality of cultivable land. 'Absorptive capacity' was the phrase used then to indicate the number of refugees that could be settled in relationship to the productive land that could be developed, and in the spill-off effects for tradespeople and often non-agricultural workers. (It did not mean, as the phrase currently connotes, the psychological, sociological and political readiness of the host community to absorb the refugees.) The plans were based on the estimates of the quality of actually or potentially productive land that could be made available to make the refugee self-supporting.

UNRWA's concentration on agricultural schemes was a direct product of the Report of the United Nations Economic Survey Mission for the Middle East which estimated that a majority of the refugees had agricultural backgrounds and could be absorbed in agricultural pursuits. However, since relief was *mandated* to cease in December of 1950, none of the agricultural schemes could possibly have resulted in economically settling the refugees in such a short time span. Suggestions that agricultural schemes were adopted to meet the goal of making the refugees self-supporting have no basis in fact, any more than the assumption that 'only large scale agricultural development schemes – offered the prospect of absorbing large numbers of refugees'. (John Defrates, comment on an early version of this paper.) The reality proved otherwise.

The information seems to indicate that in spite of the efforts and the failures, the refugees did become self-supporting, but largely by *non-agricultural* economic activity. Yet little of the development effort seems to have been directed at the non-agricultural sector. The amount that was – education for example - was a byproduct of other, later efforts and not part of an initial plan to end dependence. Further, the small efforts to encourage non-agricultural manufacturing sectors encountered great difficulties.

VII   Additional Research

Though no two refugee situations are comparable, there are some modest lessons we can learn from the Palestinian refugee situation. Once we understand that UNRWA was set up to integrate and settle the Palestinian refugees we are in a position to examine a number of issues. The impact of outside aid, in whatever form and however substantial, is still marginal; though important in some situations, it is rarely the critical factor. Nevertheless, we must learn how to best use aid. Large-scale economic aid programmes – whether in the form of education or the more costly development aid – however beneficial, have other anticipatable (though not necessarily anticipated) consequences when acting in combination with the local political brew of the first asylum host country. New aid assistance perhaps has its own momentum; once started, aid may be perpetuated in spite of greater needs elsewhere. In both Jordan and the territories controlled by Israel, where the largest numbers of Palestinian refugees are to be found and where you have a highly educated population with very high levels of employment, the international community continues to fund UNRWA with the bulk of its budget being spent on education. One third of Canada's aid to all refugees goes to the Palestinians even though less than five per cent of the world's refugee population is made up of Palestinians who lack protection or the support of a country that can provide it.

There are also other historical issues that need to be clarified. There is a widespread belief that countries in Western Europe and North America continue to fund UNRWA (1) because Palestinian refugees are effectively wards of the United Nations, because it was the United Nations which decided to partition Palestine (against their wishes) and they became refugees as a result of that decision and (2) because withdrawal of aid to UNRWA is politically volatile and might exacerbate instability in that area.

With respect to the latter point, that was precisely the argument used in setting up UNRWA, but the volatility in the area has continued, and perhaps increased at times, in spite of, and some would say, in part because of, UNRWA's involvement. With respect to the first point, there is a widespread (and incorrect) belief that UNRWA originated in response to the United Nations' direct responsibility for the refugees since the United Nations, or its predecessor the League of Nations, had assigned the mandate to Great Britain. When Great Britain declared its intention to vacate the mandate, the responsibility fell back on the United Nations (though Britain was sure that the United Nations, in its inability to resolve the problem, would once again call upon the United Kingdom). The United Nations was not only the responsible forum for refugees in general, and the institution best prepared to facilitate a solution, but, because it had decided on partition, the United Nations had a unique responsibility for the Palestinians that it did not have with other refugees.

Professor Jack Garvey, no friend of UNRWA, in *Refugee Aid and Middle East Peace* (cited earlier) adopts this interpretation.

UNRWA originated in December, 1949, as a response to the legal-political argument that the United Nations as trustee of the former mandated territories had to assume continuing responsibility for the resolution of the conflict in Palestine and the refugee problem that had resulted under its trusteeship, as a consequence of the Palestine partition resolution of 1948. The establishment of UNRWA. . . proceeded on the basis that the United Nations was the 'responsible' forum, firstly, as the supervisory authority under which the refugee and peacekeeping problems had arisen, and secondly, as the international forum and organization in the best position to facilitate a peace process and eventual resolution of the conflict. (pp. 4-5)

I find *no* evidence, not one quote or comment, in the archives of Great Britain or the U.S.A., who were major players in the setting up of UNRWA, to suggest that the partition resolution legally obligated the United Nations to initiate UNRWA or that the United Nations had a unique responsibility to Palestinian refugees because of the outcome of the partition resolution. There were those who clearly wanted to assume responsibility, but not because the United Nations were legally responsible or had a unique moral responsibility, though these arguments may have been used as a rhetorical device to argue for a perpetuation of a United Nations role. Assuming such a legal or moral responsibility was inconsistent with the stubborn intransigence and non-cooperation of Great Britain and the consistent insistence of the United States that the United Nations lacked *legal authority* in the area whatever the other inconsistencies in the American approach to the United Nations role in the area. Neither these states nor Israel suggested that the United Nations was legally obligated to play a role. The United Nations was merely an instrument to be used when convenient, and ignored and discarded when in conflict with their own interests.

In any case, I suggest the explanation for the continuation of UNRWA follows Ockham's rule requiring a simpler explanation. I suggest it is simply inertia, the unwillingness to change gears, a factor in the continuation of many government programmes, which in this case is helped by the fear (unwarranted, I believe) that it would exacerbate the conflict in the area. Further, this need not be an argument for funding UNRWA, but for directly funding the Palestinians to run their own educational programmes.

Long-term economic assistance programmes will not necessarily solve refugee problems. The vision of a durable solution to problems may foster the willingness of donor countries to increase assistance, but the vision may also sow seeds of disillusion. Further, a problem which is in essence political will remain political. A political solution is required for Palestinians. Some economic solutions will defuse the intensity of the political problem and others will enhance it, especially when combined with the particular political brew of the local host country. Thus, development assistance must be applied in a way that is sensitive to both anticipatable consequences of the aid on the refugees, and the combinant reactions in the host country. Finally, durable, that is, lasting solutions to alleviate though not solve problems, should not be set up so they become self-perpetuating, and funds cannot or will not be shifted to help alleviate problems and situations in other parts of the world or to deny or limit the autonomy and self-determination of the refugees.

Notes: Chapter 17

1 John Defrates, who authored the volume on *UNRWA, Past, Present and Future* (Vienna, May 1986) argued in a commentary on an earlier version of this paper that 'economic integration' is not 'a form of interim assistance to refugees. It is normally an essential part of a permanent (i.e. durable) solution.' In my depiction, economic integration is the point at which the concepts of durable and interim solutions overlap. Nevertheless, Defrates' interpretation only strengthens my argument that the economic integration of the Palestinian refugees through UNRWA was intended to foster a durable solution to their problem.

2 The term 'Palestine refugee' refers to all refugees who lost their homes and means of livelihood in Palestine in the 1947-48 war. Jews and non-Arabs were included. Current parlance ignores this original technical use and a *Palestinian* refugee refers only to Arab refugees from the Palestine area and their descendants.

3 This was just one of the more inhumane decisions of Great Britain, even if it was prompted by Britain's understandable concern with its depleted foreign reserves. The fact, however, is that in this and all other areas, 'The British approach proved to be not in accord . . . with either the letter or the spirit of the partition plan'. (Trygve Lie, *In the Cause of Peace*. p. 164). Trygve Lie was being very diplomatic. The United Kingdom's policy was made very clear in a telex to Troutbeck in the British Middle East Office on March 19 1948. 'It is not (repeat not) our view that we shall in any judicial sense be handing over the administration of Palestine to the United Nations Commission on the 15th of May. If the U.N., in fact, succeed (sic!) supreme authority in Palestine, they will do so by virtue of the Assembly resolution and not by any formal transfer or succession from H.M.G.'

18 Bureaucratization and political commitment: challenges for NGO refugee assistance

C. MICHAEL LANPHIER

I

The creation of the High Commission for Refugees as a central arm of the UN with a continuing mandate for post-World War II refugees at once highlighted the complexity and long-range nature of refugee assistance. Not only would attention be focussed centrally by this office, it would be directed to ever wider theatres: not only Africa, but the Middle East, Southeast Asia and ultimately every continent.

Despite increases in the annual budgetary allocations of UNHCR to a level of approximately US$500 millions until the mid-1980s, the organizational apparatus does not provide enough assistance to refugees in quantity or kind. NGO relief operations have grown commensurately and have taken a form which reflects the same scale of operations as that undertaken in governmental organizations, even though any individual NGO is smaller and more focussed in its undertakings.

It is no accident that activities of non-governmental organizations (NGOs) have grown in number and complexity during the same period. Overall, the number of NGOs has seen a nine-fold increase since 1940: from 500 NGOs to about 1,500 in 1960. That total rose to some 4,300 NGOs in 1980 (Jacobson, 1984: 51). This increase is due to the number and complexity of problems which have not been addressed by international or national governments. States are often unwilling to accuse other states directly of human rights violations. It is left to NGOs to provide services to these victims, *faute de mieux*.

II The Church-Affiliated NGO

The church-affiliated NGO is constituted separately from ecclesiastical activities, as a general advocate for human rights and dignity, and provider of emergency aid to people in distress. As an example of an international NGO, reference is made specifically to ICMC (International Catholic Migration Commission). The ICMC attempts in the first instance to coordinate and promote such services with emphasis upon long-term assistance (ICMC *Annual Report*, 1984: 3–4). Throughout its 35 years of operation it has excluded the provision of direct services to refugees. Rather, it has maintained a coordinative role which is not only perceived as complementary to services directly provided by other NGOs, but also, as noted above, allows it pre-eminently to appear distinctive among NGOs.

Assistance to local settlement projects is interpreted in the following way by ICMC:

1) Fortification of the local infrastructure by promoting self- sufficiency and eventual independence of the local agency from outside administrative and logistical aid.

2) In order to reach this objective the NGO attempts to augment the expertise of the local agency or supporting personnel and to increase the local agency's credibility in the eyes of the donor community.

3) Specifically, the NGO undertakes the following organizational tasks:

  1) underwriting expenses for equipment and office maintenance;

  2) formal training programmes for officers;

  3) acquiring vehicles for the exclusive use of the local agency (even if excluded from the terms of a donor's specification);

  4) assisting local missions to 'assess the needs of uprooted populations in consultation with field representatives and undertake surveys that serve as the basis for specific project responses';

  5) undertaking fact-finding missions to ascertain local perceptions and needs '...and in turn communicate donor attitudes and procedural framework of international project funding'. An important objective of such missions is to enable local agents 'to learn in more detail how the project funding process operates, and what auditing and reporting requirements are stipulated by donor sources' (ICMC Annual Report 1984, 19–21).

In recent years, the centralized criteria have incorporated increasingly localized indicators for success i.e., as the development of local control, including control by refugee group, figure importantly as an element of a successful project.

The following evaluation criteria were recently announced by ICMC

1) Feasibility of implementation of the project, in addition to need of recipient group.

2) Potential independence in terms of funding, personnel, and materials from continuous outside support.

3) Utilization of existing resources, institutions and technologies.

4) Long-run potential for integration of the project into the ongoing life of the community through reliance upon active local input.

5) Involvement of both the local and refugee-recipient communities in decision-making concerning the implementation of the project, with incorporation of their needs and views (ICMC Annual Report, 1984: 23).

The specifically religious or confessional value structure of NGOs may be attractive to refugees, even though it differs from their own traditions.

The symbolic status of an established Western church signals a service organization which is universal and widely accepted in the Third World. Emphasis falls more upon the distinctiveness of the religious from the political than upon the nature of the authoritative ecclesiastical structure. However tenuous they may appear, religious auspices confer a certain trustworthiness and credibility upon the NGO personnel.

It is important to signal the transnational status of most church-based international NGOs (Jacobson, 1984: 10). Buttressed by their own religious hierarchical structure, they are capable of providing service deliveries and assistance to refugees in more than one state and often to oversee resettlement activities which move refugees across continents from origin through first asylum ultimately to third countries (Winkler 1981: 95–6).

III   Dynamics of NGO Service Delivery: Buffering and Legitimation

Service delivery occurs within the context of operation of a multi-layered bureaucracy of at least two types: 1) NGO's own bureaucracy; 2) the bureaucracy of the host country (first asylum or third-resettlement). While the role of the NGO is manifestly the delivery of goods and services, it is expected that the NGO's important latent function be the buffering of bureaucratic governmental and administrative control from the refugee group.

Buffering involves at least the four following functions

1. Explanation: The requirements, demands, restrictions, obligations and rights imposed upon the refugee group by the host government has to be made interpretable and comprehensible.

2. Paperwork: Innumerable forms and ancillary information are required by the host government for intake, asylum, and re-establishment of the refugee group.

3. Regularization: The NGO regularizes the status of the particular refugee group to that which is administratively recognizable to the host government; intentions of the refugee group have to be made explicit. The severity and urgency of their case has to be explained as an exception to the standard operating procedure for treatment of immigrants.

4. Legitimation: The NGO performs a two-way legitimation. For the refugee group, the NGO identifies its own organization and attendant prestige as advocate for the refugee group. For the host government, the NGO appears to be its representative (and interpreter, as outlined above) to the refugee group. For both, it serves as a legitimation of the other's status, up to and through the normative/organizational aspect of action.

Legitimation is an important and pertinent function which applies to the viability of the NGO itself. As the NGO delivers its resettlement services, the same legitimacy which it confers upon the reciprocal parties: refugee and host government, is itself reaffirmed as a cardinal attribute of the NGO. This conferral of legitimation upon the NGO goes well beyond the routine exchanges and recognition of official status of NGO personnel.

Rather, governments permit (or sometimes, tolerate) the NGO's assumption of tasks of re-socialization that would be otherwise undertaken by their own citizens and officialdom. Despite difficulties of access and in financing the work, the NGO still strives to maintain a certain 'organizational territory' which is unique to the NGO. Moreover, the refugee clientele is repeatedly reminded, not only by NGO personnel, but by members of the host government, that the NGO is responsible for attending to certain if not most of their (refugees') requests for assistance.

By the same token, NGOs assure their own organizational legitimacy by providing a conduit of resocialization. The results of resocialization are perceived to be instrumentally useful to the (government of the) host society. The correlative interests of NGOs for institutional recognition are thereby reinforced: the streaming of a (refugee) clientele assures public recognition, donor funding and organizational continuation (if not continuity).

These important functions themselves bring a re-cycling of administration and bureaucratic organization to NGO operations. The very organizational continuity which permits the NGO to fulfil these functions depends upon having established an international visibility (size, scale, budget, extra-organizational legitimator for the NGO itself). Of necessity, therefore, larger NGOs will resemble in organizational infrastructure the very governmental organization which they buffer! Consequently, a confusion may (unintentionally) appear between organization of governmental and non-governmental units in the eyes of the refugee group. The confusion may be compounded in the operational work of the NGO, as the buffering function implies the NGO serving as the organizational substitute for the government.

In contradistinction to traditions in other Western nations, U.S. refugee resettlement activities have in the first instance been the responsibility of church-based and some ethnic and secular NGOs. Their responsibility included primary voice as governmental advisory in selection as well as recruitment of sponsors and determination of resettlement service deliveries. With massive intake of the Southeast Asian wave, the escalated scale of NGO activity assumed increasingly a more bureaucratic form in agency structure and routinized operations (Nichols, 1988).

The quasi-autonomous activities of NGOs in refugee resettlement during the '60's and '70's resulted in an elaborate organization within each of the agencies. Each NGO differentiated both regionally and hierarchically; coordinating agencies were created for liaison across NGOs, especially for assignment of intake quotas to individual NGOs. Yet, after a wide-ranging governmental review, the Refugee Act of 1980 subordinated this complex NGO organizational structure to federal governmental control over allocation of tasks and evaluation of performance of NGOs. Although NGOs vigorously protested this move, they effectively became operational implementors of government refugee policy of the day (Zucker and Zucker, 1981).

In an effort to overcome any perceived confusion of unit (government vs NGO), NGOs have to adopt various forms of resolutions in their operational relationship with refugee groups. While the options for assertion of NGO distinctiveness differ according to type of service: local assistance vs resettlement, the identity is often distinguished by a longer-term association with the refugee group. The NGO delivers a succession of different services which reinforce this distinctiveness by their degree of specialization and/or transnational character (Gordenker, 1983; Lanphier, 1983a, 1983b; ICMC, 1984). For the NGO, the goal of appearing distinctive in the eyes of the refugee group goes hand-in-hand with that of service delivery.

No less important to the NGO is the assertion of political neutrality from the policies and practices of the host government of the day. This task is by no means easy or self-evident. Most international NGOs have local affiliates as front-line service delivery agents in the host country. The very continuity of the local organizational unit depends to some extent upon governmental co-operation. Compromise may be required in order to ensure the operational efficacy of the local delivery unit. Correspondingly, the local agency reasserts its affiliation with the international character of the NGO. It depends, for example, upon visits from officers from the distant central administration (often with photographs prominently displayed) for visible reminders.

The organizational problems of the church-based NGOs reflect the nature of their organizational environment more than their affiliation. Yet the organizational base differs profoundly from those of the governments, home ('sending') or receiving. In addition to the fact that the religious auspices grant a certain neutrality to the NGO's operations, its independence allows the NGO to be a critic of the very refugee assistance plan which they are implementing. They may serve either as a lobby to the government or as advocate of the refugees' requests, having been legitimized by both groups. By comparison, NGOs built upon ethnic backgrounds identical or similar to that of the refugee group are oriented more toward political concerns. It is to this comparison that our inquiry now turns.

IV   NGOs Sponsored by Members of Same Ethnic Origin as Refugees

Although NGOs directly connected ethnically or culturally to the refugee group are acquainted with the systematic and long-range quality of the refugee conditions for their people, the point may not be as quickly or thoroughly seized for maximum service to refugees.

A certain camaraderie develops in the operation of the NGO with its refugee clients. The organization of refugees in ethnic organizations highlights a dependence upon recollection of life and traditions in the home country. To the extent that the NGO re-creates these traditions, it receives the support of the refugee group over a sustained period of time.

If, however, advocacy or other activities on behalf of the refugees should be in conflict with the organizational principles of the parent ethnic group, the activities will be revised or curtailed (Luciuk, 1985). It is important to signal that refugee aid is perceived as an integral part of advocacy for the ethnic group. To the extent that such aid furthers the organizational goals, it will be supported and continued. Nevertheless, in cases of conflict between the organizational principles of the NGO and the demands of the incoming wave of refugees, the former will prevail.

Refugees' experience in camp may seriously affect and alter earlier (home-country) experiences. Among certain refugees, struggles during the camp experience to return home, or to develop quasi-militaristic organization may have irreversibly affected their future resettlement activities in the (future) host country. Leaders of incipient insurgent movements in the camp may have a determinative influence upon future resettlement, as they serve a dual function of providing a conduit of refugees to the receiving society as well as politicizing the cohort of refugees resident in camps. In certain instances, especially the Ukrainian exodus as a result of World War II displacements, adherence to the insurgent activities may be a precondition for exit from the camps (Luciuk, 1984, 1985).

Consequently, after arrival in the host country, certain activities of the ethnic NGO will be oriented to restore as many forms of home-country culture in as many media as possible: oral, written and electronically-reproduced folk, literary and artistic traditions. This activity proceeds normally unless or until effects of incipient social movements are experienced within the ranks of the NGO. Thereupon, the NGO may become factionalized, with contending leaders vying for organizational control (Luciuk, 1984, 1985).

Several organizational implications for ethnic NGOs follow upon the development of dissident factions. First, control of the NGO becomes divided. As refugees arrive, some will become part of the organizational apparatus for staffing and service to future incoming refugees. As there may be no other source of personnel at the moment, the ethnic NGO has little choice but to include the (politically committed) refugees in their ranks. Alternatively, if it is large and powerful enough, it may be able to exclude persons for whom the organization only months previously served as advocates and (organizational) sponsors. Generally, however, organizational dependence upon these recruits compromises the NGO in its activity.

Secondly, various interruptions in the NGO operations such as the following may occur

1) Rupture of relations with parent ethnic group: disruptions of the normal operating procedures of the NGO may cause the sponsor to overview the type of affiliation with the NGO which it founded. Ultimately, the NGO may have to re-institute its organization if the sponsors remain dissatisfied with the operational activities.
2) Rupture of relations with government of host country: the host government may find the behaviour of NGO members on behalf of incoming refugees to be embarrassing if it appears to involve activities which may affect the foreign relations of the host country either with the sending country or its allies.

3) Distortion of public image: such distortions may alter the image of the refugees. The NGO itself is impaired by the failure of the projected image of the refugee group to square with that given by the behaviour of the refugee group.

4) Change in relation of NGO to other community agencies: Other agencies may be cautious about receipt of referrals of refugee clients. Not only might refugees appear less desirable referrals, but the basis for referral would itself be organizationally dubious: it could be taken as an attempt to shift responsibility onto another agency.

The ethnic NGO attempts to provide a continuity with the homeland culture which emphasizes the political aspect of adaptation. This approach contrasts with that predominantly offered by church-based NGOs, whose services emphasize technical and administrative aspects of adaptation. Several implications follow from this difference in orientation as compared with the church-based NGO. First, longer-range interests are emphasized in services offered to refugees. These concerns may take precedence over the technical and adaptive problems which surface immediately upon arrival. Secondly, the assumption of the ethnic community leadership of the operations of the NGO severely limit the alternatives in its operational activities. The close working relationship between the NGO and its parent ethnic organization allows the newly-arrived refugee group members to become organizationally active and to participate politically in the host society. Quite likely, however, the refugees may resist making contact with organizations in the wider society if the activities are to some extent duplicated within the ethnic organization.

The ethnic NGO assumes therefore a dual role *vis-à-vis* the refugees: it provides the instrumental means of adaptation (orientation, new language, friendship and organizational referrals), while also providing a political sub-culture which may effectively replace that of the host society, at least initially.

V   Status of Refugees in the Host Society

Although the matter of the social position occupied by refugees upon entry to the host society is of persistent concern to all NGOs serving refugees, neither church-based nor ethnic-based NGOs directly intervene in the internal stratification process of the host society. As social status is largely determined by the occupation of the main breadwinners (usually the family head), the degree of intervention of NGOs is usually confined to assisting the refugee in the initial job search. That process may coincide with language classes and skills training arranged by the NGO (Neuwirth, 1985; Mignot, 1984).

Overall, the position assumed by incoming refugees is largely determined by social process within the host society. It is a variation of the *Unterschichtung*, process characterized by Hoffman-Nowotny (1981) with respect to immigrants. The process allocates positions to immigrants in the social status structure, including employment vacancies, which are inferior to that of long-term residents. Although the job vacancies are entry-level positions which appear to permit eventual upward mobility, they are embedded in a context which designates the job-holder as one whose position was either vacated or rejected by the resident population. Opportunities for social mobility are foreshortened, partly due to the nature of employment, and partly due to the lack of access to other instrumental resources (inadequate language facility, insufficient knowledge of activating organizational alternatives). The types of organized intervention by the host society (e.g., welfare schemes) may reinforce the ad hoc but no less obvious *Unterschichtung* status, even though it is the manifest role of such schemes to alleviate the effects of this status.

Nevertheless, NGOs are often perceived both by refugees and by wider society as the possible change agent in an otherwise unchanging environment. In the first instance, the NGO is expected to improve the social condition of refugees as individuals by means of upgrading skills and providing enriched language training. In the second instance, there are collectivity implications. NGOs are expected to serve as advocates for refugees in search of a wider set of rights and privileges. Yet the organizational status of the NGOs which fosters such expectations on the part of refugees and others may inhibit such direct and short-range intervention.

In the case of church-related NGOs, such inhibition may be attributable to the status of the international organization which inhibits such activity, as they are guests of the host government. While the local NGO personnel are usually nationals, their role represents a 'division of labour' with other national and community agencies. The church-based NGO may specialize, therefore, in certain activities of resource allocation which effectively short-circuit attention from the status problems of the refugee client. Advocacy is limited as well by the resources at the disposal of the NGO. The highly efficient division of labour may leave no single agency either with scope or responsibility to give attention to the collective status occupied by the incoming refugee group.

In France, two church-based NGOs, *Secours catholique* and *CIMADE* (ecumenical Protestant), have respectively assumed the highly differentiated and complex tasks of resettlement assistance to refugees opting for individual (i.e., not governmentally organized) resettlement arrangements, and French-language training. These services are integral to the national, highly centralized resettlement plan, with the active collaboration of the government and in co-ordination with at least two other large NGOs (*SSAE* and *Terre d'lAsile*). The demanding nature of these specialized tasks leaves little time, energy, or resources for systematic attention by NGOs to conditions fostering the creation of refugees or to deliberation over strategies of resettlement (Lanphier, 1983a; 1983b).

Ethnic NGOs may indeed form part of this same division of labour. Their interests lie, however, more with the collective aspects of the social position of the refugees. While these political interests may arouse the NGO to call attention to invidious status differentiation affecting refugees, the organizational infrastructure of the ethnic NGO may be no more capable of making effective alterations than church-based NGOs. They lack organizational power to effect social changes outside the general activity pattern which it sponsors. Nevertheless, these NGOs may affiliate with organizations which may have wider access to publicity or to instrumental resources permitting which in turn widen certain channels of mobility.

Throughout this process the NGO may experience a certain strain in advocating collective change within the existing social structure of the host society while reaffirming its manifest interest in upholding the constitutional features which allocate resources and power in that society. Nevertheless, there may be no advocate of collective status improvement other than the ethnic NGO.

In an effort to improve the status of their constituent refugee group, ethnic organizations often foster activities which establish a status system parallel to that of the host society. These activities may be wide-ranging – from ethnic commercial and occupational networks through programmes which reinforce a cultural presence in the diaspora. The establishment of an institutionally-complete set of services for the incoming group may be attempted. Whatever the degree of success, such attempts imply an interest in replacing the wider social structure of the host society with a near-ghetto alternative: goods and services, mobilization of personnel and incipient normative organization provided by or with the assistance of the ethnic NGO.

It is important to signal that however extensive these activities, they do not penetrate the stratification system of the wider social structure in most cases. Not only are the services more restricted in number and scope, but there is no obvious transferability of services offered by the ethnic NGO network to those of the wider society. Lacking the legitimacy conferred by the host society upon its own institutions and services, the ethnic NGO can offer access to services possibly at the expense of the refugees' participation in the wider society (Wiley, 1967).

This paper inquires into the type of role played by NGOs in refugee assistance by focussing on two general types of institutional control: church-based and ethnically-based organization. Church-based NGOs represent a differentiated part of an ecclesiastical hierarchical organization which awards unusual organizational longevity and scope to its activities, one among which is assistance to refugees. Ethnically-based NGOs are organizational outgrowths of mutual assistance networks developed from earlier migrations. They represent a formalization of locally-based assistance which has become an important feature of most refugee assistance programmes.

It is argued that the orientation of the church-based NGOs may or may not be distinctive in operational performance. Of importance is the type of tasks which the church-based NGO chooses to undertake: the delivery of goods and resources, as well as work on the problem of family reunification and re-establishment of family and kin structure in the host country.

The emphasis upon the more technical-adjustive and kinship problems provides full agenda for day-to-day operations. However consistent this agenda may be with wider church ministry, it de-emphasizes other features of refugee service. In particular, the political and integrative aspects of resettlement are addressed only indirectly and often as incidental to the primary activity. While this orientation has been criticized from within the church structure, the bulk of the operational activity is expressly directed otherwise.

While ethnic-based NGOs attend to these matters as well, they direct concern for the collective political problems of organization among refugee groups, both in the host country as well as in the home (sending) country. These activities may involve mobilization for various types of political action on behalf of the refugee group. Less attention falls upon the status of the refugees within the host society in the earlier stage of resettlement. These two organizational types, religious-based and ethnic NGOs, highlight two principal organizational dilemmas: bureaucratization and political involvement or partisanship.

If any change in orientation of church-based NGOs should occur, it will happen only by means of one of three alternative pathways. Each bears implications for organizational change and the minimizing of bureaucratic complexity in its delivery of services to refugees:

1. Incorporation of local affiliates with autonomously initiated and managed projects. This innovation reflects an internal form of organizational change. Many such ventures are already in operation, as previously discussed. Emphasis falls upon 'autonomously initiated', to highlight the importance of assistance to refugees in all phases of their adaptation to the local culture and social arrangements. In addition to technical-adjustive and kinship matters, the NGO undertakes sustained attention to any and all other problems, including political and social integration of refugees, either in formation of a sub-culture within the larger community or in a pervasive assimilation with the host society, according to the wishes of the refugee group themselves. As such arrangements cannot be directed internationally other than by the most programmatic of guidelines to this effect, a maximum of local autonomy is required to implement such a service orientation over a long-range plan.

2. Development or co-optation of ethnic organizations which assume project management and later aspects of resettlement. This alternative has also been implemented in many host countries, but only rarely systematically so. Such an arrangement requires mutual consent of two existing NGO structures. Invariably a certain compromise of visibility and independence has to be acknowledged in the interest of a single programme of refugee adaptation. For the church-based NGO, a series of such agreements would have to be made, as each refugee group served by a single NGO requires alliance with the appropriate ethnic organization. No less complex, from the perspective of the ethnic group in question is that several church-based NGOs (as in France) are

necessarily involved in refugee assistance to any single group. Despite the attractiveness of such a model, it is likely that such alliances occur on an *ad hoc* basis, under conditions which NGOs can serve a refugee group advantageously without much sacrifice of autonomy in the course of their respective organizational agendas.

3. Development of increased political awareness of social conditions which give rise to refugee movements, especially those with successive waves. This awareness may involve sensitizing not only the members of the NGO but more importantly may require diffusing this awareness among officials in the NGO's parent (church-ecclesiastical) structure.

The latter alternative of increasing sensitization brings the ecclesiastical structure more directly into a political involvement with refugee groups and their home state (sending country). This involvement has to occur at a level higher than the operational activities of the NGO: it is related both to the value position of the church and to established ecclesiastical authority.

Recommendations forthcoming from conferences on the church and refugees in Africa have repeatedly enumerated an agenda of programmatic steps for increasing sensitivity of the church to problems of refugees. These include episcopal conferences for surveying needs of refugees, the promotion of service deliveries on a regional basis, the development of secretariata for publicizing needs of refugees, the training of women for the pastoral ministry of refugees, a theological study of moral issues involving the church and liberation movements, a greater dialogue between local churches and liberation movements prior to involvement of international NGO activities, and the development of training and educational programmes uniquely keyed for local needs (Arrupe, 1981).

While such involvement is uncommon for Western churches in connection with refugee movements, it may be an implicit commitment.

Preliminary indications indicate changes in a limited number of avenues: greater local autonomy, co-optation of ethnic organizations or a more centralized political involvement. Each alternative bears an important organizational cost which may hinder implementation. Each no less bears a political 'risk', the ultimate advantages of which have to be carefully weighed in deliberations within and without non-governmental organizations in the late nineteen-eighties.

Bibliography

Arrupe, P., 'The Refugee Crisis in Africa: Opportunity and Challenge for the Church,' Conference paper, VI SECAM General Assembly, Yaounde, Cameroon, 1981.

Gordenker, L., 'Refugees in Developing Countries and Transnational Organization,' *The Annals of the American Academy of Political and Social Science*, 1983, 467, pp. 62–77.

Hoffman-Nowotny, H.-J., *et al.*, 'A Sociological Approach Towards a General Theory of Migration,' in Kirtz, M., *et al.*, eds., *Global Trends in Migration*, Staten Island, N.Y., Center for Migration Studies, 1981.

ICMC, (International Catholic Migration Commission), *Annual Report*, Geneva, 1981a.

ICMC, *Newsletter*, Vol. 6, 1981b.

ICMC, *Annual Report*, Geneva, 1982.

ICMC, *Newsletter*, Vol. 7., 1983b.

ICMC, *Annual Report*, Geneva, 1984.

Jacobson, H.K., *Networks of Interdependence: International Organizations and the Global Political System*, New York, Knopf, 1984.

Keely, C., *Global Refugee Policy: The Case for a Development-Oriented Strategy*, New York, Population Council, 1981.

Lanphier, C.M., 'Recent Resettlement of Southeast Asian Refugees in France.' *Refuge*, Vol. 2, February, 1983a.

Lanphier, C.M., 'Refugee Resettlement: Models in Transition, *International Migration Review*, no. 17, pp. 4–33, 1983b.

Luciuk, L., *Searching for Place: Ukrainian Refugee Migration to Canada after World War II*. Unpublished Ph.D. dissertation, University of Alberta, Edmonton, 1984.

Luciuk, L., 'Unintended Consequences in Refugee Resettlement: A Case Study of Ukrainian Refugee Immigration to Canada After World War II,' Research Committee on Migration, International Sociological Association, Dubrovnik, Yugoslavia, 1985.

Neuwirth, G., 'The Settlement of Southeast Asian Refugees in Canada: Sponsor and Refugee Perceptions.' conference paper, Research Committee on Migration, International Sociological Association, Dubrovnik, Yugoslavia, 1985.

Nichols, Bruce, 'Religion, Refugees and the U.S. Government' in this volume, 1988.

Paludan, Anne, 'Refugees in Europe,' *International Migration Review*, 15. pp. 69–73. 1981.

Paludan, Anne, Personal Communication, 1983.

Parsons, T., *Structure and Process in Modern Societies*, New York, Free Press of Glencoe, 1960.

Parsons, Talcott, *et al.*, *Working Papers in the General Theory of Action*, New York, Free Press of Glencoe, 1953.

Smelser, Neil, *Theory of Collective Behavior*, New York, Macmillan, 1962.

Wiley, N., 'The Ethnic Mobility Trap and Stratification Theory,' *Social Problems*, 15, pp. 147–159, 1967.

Winkler, E., 'Voluntary Agencies and Government Policy,' *International Migration Review*, 15, pp. 95–98.

Zucker, N.L. and Zucker, N.F., *The Voluntary Agencies and Refugee Resettlement in the U.S.: A Report to the Select Commission on Immigration and Refugee Policy*, Kingston, R.I., University of Rhode Island, 1980.

19 The refugee determination procedure in Belgium and the role of the United Nations High Commission for Refugees

JOHAN CELS and GIL LOESCHER

For the past thirty-five years an elaborate institutional mechanism has developed which offers protection to refugees. It includes receiving nations, international organizations and private voluntary agencies. At the core of this mechanism is the Office of the United Nations High Commission for Refugees (UNHCR). Its central role is attributable to several factors, not least of which is the fact that its mandate is the protection of refugee rights as laid down in the 1951 Refugee Convention and the 1967 Protocol[1]. Over the years, a growing number of states have acceded to the Convention and Protocol, incorporated all or part of these two instruments into their domestic law, and even in a few instances accepted a diminution of their sovereignty by granting the UNHCR a role in the determination of refugee status.

Despite its growing influence, the UNHCR acts within a framework of constraints. Above all, the success of the activities of the UNHCR depends on the willingness of national governments to co-operate with the office. National governments do not give up their sovereignty easily and are prone to put national interests before humanitarian concerns. The Convention and Protocol define the obligations of states to refugees but do not mandate the adoption of particular procedures. The determination of refugee status remains the right of sovereign states, and the role of the UNHCR is limited to advising and assisting applicants for refugee status and participating in an advisory or voting role in the decision-making process. Its powers of intervention are clearly limited, and in most countries the UNHCR representative fulfils only an advisory role, maintaining liaison with government officials and voluntary agencies. The selection of refugees for resettlement depends on a variety of factors, which include domestic support for particular refugees in the receiving country, the publicity afforded to particular instances of persecution, the financial strain likely to be incurred, and foreign policy concerns. Practically all refugee admission decisions are influenced by considerations of public opinion in the host country, and foreign policy.[2] This is particularly the case in recent years during a period of economic recession, high levels of unemployment and rising xenophobia among the Western public.

The institutional arrangements for implementing the Convention and the Protocol vary widely among Western nations.[3] Each government has adopted its own institutional arrangement, according to its particular constitutional and administrative structure. In many countries the UNHCR has an active role in the asylum decision-making process. In Belgium and France there is a formal institutionalized role for UNHCR, and in Great Britain and the Federal Republic of Germany there is informal access for UNHCR. Thus, UNHCR has a more significant role in Europe than in the United States where, apart from the possibility of contacting U.S. government authorities to express its views, the UNHCR has no role in the refugee determination process.

Unlike other European countries the importance of Belgium for the study of refugee problems lies not in the large number of applicants, nor its practices toward refugees, but in the unique arrangement Belgium has had with the UNHCR. Belgium has been the only country in the world which has given up an important aspect of its sovereignty, the right to determine refugee status, and has transferred it to an international organization. Since 1928 an international organization has determined refugee status more or less continuously.

In general, the literature on asylum practices praises the role of the UNHCR in Belgium. Atle Grahl-Madsen has observed,

'Over the years the Belgian authorities have got used to the idea that an international civil servant, appointed with the *agreement* of the Government . . . may exercise the function of certifying – and, implicitly, determining – refugeehood, just as trustworthily as any Government agency.'[4]

A report published by the Council of Europe expresses a similar opinion:

'Procedures for the determination of refugee status should indeed be harmonised among member states, . . . Belgium has in this context set an example: the procedure for granting refugee status is not handled by the Belgian authorities but by UNHCR itself. In this way, there is a guarantee of a standard application of the eligibility criteria.'[5]

The central role accorded UNHCR was of considerable value up to the early 1970s. Since then, that role has come under increasing criticism from different sides, including voluntary agencies and lawyers, but more importantly from the UNHCR itself. Since mid-1985 the government has been renegotiating its arrangement with UNHCR so that responsibility for the examination of asylum requests will eventually be transferred to the Ministry of Justice. Dissatisfaction with the role of the UNHCR centres on the lack of certain legal guarantees in the procedure, i.e. lack of an appeal procedure, no motivation of decisions and limited access for lawyers to the applicants' files. UNHCR no longer wants to remain the decision maker because, first, it is uncomfortable with the position of being both the judge and defender of refugees and believes that the political and foreign policy responsibility of asylum decisions should rightfully belong to the Belgian government and not to UNHCR as it does with other European countries. Second, the increase in the refugee flow from the Third World, which began in the 1970s, has resulted in a larger workload, more difficult and politically sensitive decisions, and a decline in recognition rates. Third, the refugee eligibility procedure in Belgium conflicts with the recommendations of the Executive Committee of the UNHCR and the Council of Europe, and fourth, the decisions of the UNHCR have recently been challenged in Belgian courts because they do not conform to the provisions in Belgian domestic legislation. It is generally expected that Belgium will eventually adopt a refugee determination procedure similar to the one in France, with the UNHCR having an advisory role in the appeals procedure.

I   The Refugee Determination Procedure and the Role of the UNHCR

Belgium is signatory to the major international and regional instruments dealing with refugees. The 1951 Convention was adopted by the law of 26 June 1953, and the law of 27 February 1969 adopted the 1967 Protocol.

Belgian law does not provide a specific definition of the term 'refugee'. Article 49 of the law of 15 December 1980 refers to the international agreements to which Belgium has acceded and defines a refugee as an alien who meets the requirements of the UN definition as outlined in the Convention and the Protocol.[7] Although the Convention and the Protocol are implicitly referred to in the law, there is no reference to any specific international agreement. This approach permits Belgium a certain flexibility toward any future expansion of the definition in international refugee law.

Belgian law is also somewhat unclear on the right to asylum. Article 48 does not recognize a right to asylum.[8] The word 'can' (*peut*) implies that even if all conditions are met, asylum is not automatically granted. Article 49, however, recognizes a subjective right of asylum under certain circumstances.[9] Article 49 also stipulates three different categories of refugees. If the refugee belongs to any of these categories, he will be admitted to sojourn or to establish himself in Belgium. The right to sojourn implicitly means a right to asylum. The first category refers to those aliens who are recognized as refugees by the Minister of Foreign Affairs or by the international authority to which the Minister has delegated his authority. This implies that once an alien has been recognized as a refugee by the UNHCR representative, he is granted the right to sojourn or to establish himself in Belgium. The second category refers to aliens who were recognized as refugees before the adoption of the law of 26 June 1953, approving the 1951 convention. The third category refers to aliens who were recognized as refugees by another state, which is a contracting party to the 1951 Convention, and on the condition that his/her refugee status is confirmed by the UNHCR.

The 1951 Convention and the 1967 Protocol do not contain any provisions about eligibility procedures, and it is left to states to develop their own procedure for the granting of refugee status. In Belgium, the Law of 15 December 1980 states that the Minister of Foreign Affairs alone is competent to decide the eligibility of persons who claim the benefit of the Convention. The Law authorizes him to delegate this authority to an international body under the auspices of the United Nations. A similar provision was included in the law on the Aliens Police of 28 March 1951. By the Ministerial Decree of 2 February 1954 the Minister of Foreign Affairs delegated this authority to the UNHCR representative in Belgium.[10]

The law of 1980 guarantees that an alien has the right to enter Belgium if he asks for refugee status. An alien who has entered Belgium in a regular way may ask for refugee status as long as he resides in a legal manner, and submits his application for asylum before the expiration of his visa, or when no visa is required, within a period of three months. A person entering Belgium illegally may apply for refugee status at the border or within 15 days of his arrival by reporting to the UNHCR delegate or certain public officials. After filing his application, the asylum seeker receives a form allowing him to remain in Belgium for the time it takes to decide on his application.

The applicant is interviewed by the Aliens Office of the Ministry of Justice (the *gendarmerie* does the actual interviewing) in order to determine if the applicant has: 1. registered with the municipal administration of the place where he is residing within eight working days; 2. not resided in a third country longer than three months after having left his country of origin (Article 52); 3. not filed an asylum application (or was granted asylum) in a third country; and 4. not submitted his request for asylum with undue delay.[11] During the interview, an interpreter is available, but the applicant may not be assisted by a lawyer. In the meantime, the Justice Ministry confirms the identity of the applicant and checks whether he has been accused of a criminal offence. On the basis of the interview and other information, the Aliens Office decides if the application is receivable or not.

If the application is non-receivable, the applicant is issued a 'Refusal of Sojourn and the Order to leave the Country'. He may appeal the refusal of sojourn and the order to leave the country. The appeal procedures have suspensive effect, and the Justice Minister must reconsider the file and seek the advice of the Aliens Consultative Commission.[12] The UNHCR delegate is allowed to attend the meetings of the Commission as an observer and can submit an opinion in writing. The Justice Minister is not bound by the advice of the Commission. If the Minister reaffirms the negative decision, the applicant can appeal the decision before the Council of State. When the applicant has exhausted all review possibilities, he must comply with the order to leave the country. If he refuses, he can be prosecuted for illegal sojourn, detained and forcibly expelled. If the application is declared receivable by the Aliens Office, the UNHCR representative is notified that the file can be examined as to its substance. There are no clear criteria or stated procedures for reaching a decision.[13]

It largely depends on the representative's interpretation of the Convention and the submitted information. It is assumed that the delegate follows the guidelines by the UNHCR as stated, for example, in the Handbook on Procedures and Criteria for Determining Refugee Status.[14]

The decision is made by the UNHCR delegate after consultation with the staff. The decision is based upon an interview of the applicant, the report of the Aliens Office, the submitted materials, and information gathered by the UNHCR. The applicant is interviewed by a UNHCR official in order to ask for his reasons for leaving the country of origin and to ascertain specific knowledge about his activities, among other things. During the interview, he is assisted by an interpreter. Lawyers are allowed during the interview, but UNHCR officials prefer that they are not present because it is their contention that the presence of lawyers at this stage of the procedure often prevents asylum seekers from revealing their 'real' reasons for leaving the country of origin.[15]

If the UNHCR representative recognizes the applicant as a refugee, the Minister of Justice is informed, and the latter grants a residence permit to the refugee. Once recognized, refugees are given extensive rights. They are guaranteed all the civil, economic, social and cultural rights provided for by the 1951 Convention. The law explicitly recognizes the principle of *non-refoulement*. Article 56 states that under certain circumstances a refugee may be expelled, but under no condition may the refugee be expelled to the country of origin.[16]

If the UNHCR delegate reaches a negative decision, the applicant is informed and invited to submit new evidence that might strengthen his case and lead to a revision of the preliminary decision within three weeks. It is only at this stage that most applicants consult a lawyer.[17] The applicant is not informed of the reasons for the UNHCR decision, but it is possible to have an oral explanation of the refusal. The oral explanation outlines any contradictions in the statements, the lack of proof, and any false statements which he is alleged to have made. The lawyer is allowed to see the applicant's file which contains all the statements of the client, the eligibility form, and the submitted proof. However, all UNHCR's internal documents are removed from the file. In a recent decision, the Ministry of Justice permitted UNHCR to pass on the reports from the Aliens Office to the lawyers, but no copies of the documents are allowed to be made.[18]

After three weeks, the UNHCR representative informs the Ministry of Justice of its final decision. Upon a negative decision, the applicant loses the protection offered by Belgian law and receives an order to leave the country. As in the case of a negative receivability decision the order to leave the country is subject to appeal.

There is no appeal against a negative decision of the UNHCR, however. Under certain circumstances the UNHCR representative can reopen the file and review the decision. Files are only reopened when new elements are submitted by the applicant, such as elements that were not available during the first examination, changes in the country of origin and when errors or misunderstandings have occurred.[19] On rare occasions, a file can be reopened for a second or a third time, but, according to the UNHCR, this has not happened for several years.[20]

During the period that the application is examined, the asylum seeker enjoys some important rights. According to Article 53: 'As long as an application is not refused or rejected, the asylum seeker may not be removed from the territory nor prosecuted on account of irregular entry or sojourn.'[21] Only in exceptional cases if he is a threat to the public order or to national security can the Minister of Justice expel or detain an asylum seeker. During this period the asylum seeker receives a certificate of registration, a work permit (which must be requested by the employer), and social welfare benefits.

In addition to examining the mechanics of the eligibility procedure in Belgium, it is important to determine the extent to which this procedure fails to follow the guidelines and the recommendations of the UNHCR's Executive Committee and of the Council of Europe regarding harmonization of procedures for the determination of refugee status.[22] The Executive Committee recommends that the procedures should satisfy certain basic requirements: 1. The border officials must act in accordance with international provisions; 2. There must be a single centralized authority capable of determining refugee status; 3. The applicant must be informed of the procedure, his status and his rights, and be given an interpreter; 4. And more importantly: 'If the applicant is not recognized, he should be given a reasonable time to appeal for a formal reconsideration of the decision, either to the same or to a different authority,....'[23] As is shown later in some detail, the UNHCR representative in Belgium does not follow these recommendations.

There exists in Belgium two special groups besides the Convention refugees: the assimilated and the quota refugees, and the receivability and the eligibility procedures differ for each of them. The law of 15 December 1980 provides the status of *assimilé* for a special category of refugees:

'The alien who fulfills the conditions of the present law for being recognized as refugee and who adduces serious reasons which prevent him from claiming this status may, at his request, be declared *assimilé* to a refugee by the Minister of Justice.'[24]

Assimilated refugees fulfil the conditions of the 1951 Convention, but they do not seek formal refugee status for certain special reasons, e.g., fear for the safety of remaining family in the country of origin. The determination procedure is similar as for other asylum seekers, except that the eligibility decision is taken by the Minister of Justice instead of by UNHCR. The assimilated refugees receive the same benefits accorded other refugees, except that they cannot receive the travel documents provided by the international instruments. An additional right for assimilated refugees is that, in case of a negative decision by the Minister of Justice, the applicant can appeal the decision before the Council of State. From a procedural viewpoint this is important, as the eligibility procedure by the UNHCR does not provide for an appeal process.

Recent crises in international politics have also led to the development of special programmes for refugee resettlement, generally called quota programmes. Since the early 1970s, the Belgian government responded to the appeals of the UNHCR and the voluntary agencies by recognizing large groups of Chileans (and other Latin Americans) and Indochinese as refugees. The quota refugees have the same rights as other refugees. The recognition procedure is simplified; refugee status is granted not upon the merits of each individual case, but to the group as a whole under the assumption that every person fulfils the criteria of the refugee definition.

II   Reasons for the Delegation of the Refugee Determination Authority

There are a number of reasons why Belgium delegated the refugee determination authority to an international organization. Belgium has a long history of treating aliens in a humanitarian manner. The large influxes of displaced persons after both World Wars resulted in the adoption of tolerant legislation toward aliens. Hand-in-hand with humanitarian motives, however, was the need to attract economic migrants, particularly to work in Belgium's coal mines.

The initial aim of the UNHCR was to show how institutional arrangements in Belgium demonstrated a way in which the international instruments might be implemented. From a humanitarian perspective, it was perceived to be beneficial for the asylum seeker to have his status determined by an independent international organization. The mandate of the UNHCR stressed the non-political nature of its activities, and it was assumed that the UNHCR representative would apply the refugee definition in a fair and neutral way, placing the interests of the refugee above political considerations.

For the Belgian government there have been important foreign policy and budgetary advantages to this institutional arrangement. It is estimated, for example, that were the government to assume the determination of refugee status today, the cost would be between 20 to 30 million Belgian francs yearly.[25] In a period of economic stagnation and high domestic unemployment, Belgian authorities have found it difficult in the past to justify these expenditures on aliens. From a foreign policy perspective, there have been additional advantages for Belgium in maintaining the UNHCR representative as the decision maker. For example, the granting of refugee status to a political opponent of a friendly or economically important regime can jeopardize relations between Belgium and the country of origin. Thus, Belgian authorities can use UNHCR as a shield, claiming not to be responsible for an unpopular or politically difficult decision. As a result, protests are directed towards UNHCR and not the Belgian government, and normal diplomatic and economic relations can be maintained with the country of origin.

For years, the decision to delegate the authority to UNHCR was motivated by a wish to continue previous generous asylum policies. Belgium in the 19th century provided refuge for a number of political activists and intellectuals and treated aliens liberally. After the First World War, Belgium adhered to most international agreements adopted to regularize the situation of the large numbers of refugees and stateless persons arising from that conflict and its aftermath.[26] In 1928, the Belgian and the French governments reached a special agreement with the League of Nations High Commissioner for Refugees to exercise consular functions regarding the recognition of refugees,[27] and in the late 1930s, due to an increasing outflow of refugees from Germany and Austria, the Belgian Ministry of Justice with the assistance, first of an interministerial commission and then of a ministerial commission, determined refugee status and treated refugees for the first time as a separate administrative category.

After the Second World War, the Belgian government delegated its authority to determine refugee status to this Committee. An Inter-governmental Committee had been set up in 1938 to assist refugees coming from Germany and Austria. The Committee's mandate was extended to all refugees under the Draft Constitution of the International Refugee Organization (IRO).[28] The IGCR concluded agreements with the occupation authorities in Germany and the Belgian government to resettle refugees and displaced persons from Germany, especially miners, a category of workers who were in great demand in Belgium.[29]

The IRO took over the responsibilities of the IGCR in 1947 and continued the task of resettling and repatriating Europe's refugees and displaced persons. Belgium was a member of the IRO, but it did not conclude an explicit agreement with the organization. Their mutual relations were regulated by oral agreements and a series of '*procès-verbal*'. The outcome of the mutual agreements, however, was that the IRO determined refugee status in Belgium.[30]

In the beginning of the 1950s the IRO was phased out and was succeeded by the UNHCR. In 1951, the IRO representative contacted the Belgian government in order to determine whether it wanted to take over the refugee determination procedure under the 1951 Convention and defray costs in connection with these activities.[31] The Belgian Minister of Foreign Affairs responded 'that the protection of refugees was a matter for an international organization and declined to defray costs in connection with protection activities'.[32] In a separate memorandum to the High Commissioner, the Belgian authorities stressed the fact that international organizations had traditionally determined refugee status in Belgium and urged the High Commissioner to continue this arrangement. Initially, UNHCR was reluctant to accept this responsibility, because its Statute limited 'the work of the High Commissioner ... to groups or categories of refugees and ... the High Commissioner should facilitate the tasks of governments'.[33] However, the High Commissioner subsequently adopted the view that his office should carry out protection functions in regard not only to groups but also to individuals because '... the High Commissioner has ruled that one cannot speak properly of the eligibility of a group. There can only be a *prima facie* assumption that a group is within or outside the Mandate. For the purpose of eligibility determination, such a ruling constitutes only a presumption and the eligibility of individuals belonging to this group has still to be determined individually on *the merits of the particular case.*[34]

On 27 December 1951 the High Commissioner agreed that its representative in Belgium was prepared to determine refugee status. In response, the Belgian authorities stressed that 'the recognition of refugees should only be granted to persons who *fully* met the condition which define the word refugee'.[35] UNHCR directives to its branch office in Brussels in January 1954 stated that the basis of its activities were to be Articles 1,2, and 8 of the Statute. UNHCR expressed the view that it would be the duty of the representative to see to it 'that refugees are admitted to the territory of the state in order to allow them to seek asylum' and that the representative should work in close co-operation with the government.[36] It was the view of the UNHCR at that time 'that the role bestowed upon the Branch Office of the High Commissioner in Belgium with regard to eligibility determination confers on the refugee the *maximum* of guarantees as to the recognition of their refugee status'.[37]

In some respects, the confiding of responsibility to the UNHCR was perceived as a mark of confidence in the international agency whose task it was to protect refugees. It was also a clear continuation of the tradition of leaving refugee decision-making authority in Belgium in the hands of a neutral international body. Although this institutional arrangement has continued for over three decades, it has come under increasing criticism in recent years. Before discussing the extent of this criticism, however, it is necessary to gain some awareness of the numbers of asylum applicants in Belgium, which countries they come from, and the recognition rates.

III Some Statistics Regarding the Refugee Determination Procedure

It is extremely difficult to present an overall picture of the number of asylum applicants, the number recognized and their distribution over time and countries of origin. Belgium is one of the few countries which is unwilling to provide asylum statistics, apparently for technical and diplomatic reasons. Currently there are approximately 36,400 refugees.

With the paucity of reliable data, it is difficult to categorize Belgium as being unduly liberal or unduly restrictive. What can be said is that given the percentage of asylum seekers recognized, the adoption of quota programmes and a special programme for handicapped refugees, Belgium is probably one of the more liberal European states. However, in recent years the recognition rate has dropped significantly and this is a matter of concern to voluntary agencies and potential refugees.[38].

Table 1 gives the number of persons applying for refugee status through 1981.[39] Most of the Latin Americans and Indochinese arrived under special government quota programmes. Three major trends are demonstrated in the table. The number of applicants increased significantly from 1977 to 1981. This is the result of the arrival of quota refugees from Indochina, and a large increase in applications from other Third World countries, mainly from Africa. The last two columns refer to the number of cases still under consideration as of 1982 and give an indication of the backlog at that time. Since then, the number of asylum seekers has increased to the following: 1982: 3,057; 1983: 2,948; 1984: 3,693; and 1985: 5,255.[40] The backlog has also increased considerably and in early 1986 was proximately 5,000 cases.[41] According to the UNHCR, the backlog has been largely caused by the increase in applications and too few personnel at the UNHCR office and the Justice Ministry to deal with the larger number of cases.[42]

Table 2 gives the number of persons who have obtained refugee status during the period 1977-1981. The last column indicates the number who did not receive refugee status, that is, those whose cases were declared unfounded by the UNHCR or non-receivable by the Justice Ministry, and those whose cases were closed because the applicants withdrew their applications or voluntarily left Belgium. The number of applicants recognized has declined in recent years. In the 1970s the recognition rate was on average between 57% and 63%. In 1983 the recognition rate declined to 48% and has further dropped to about 30% in 1985.[43] According to the UNHCR in Belgium, the decline is partly caused by an increase in unfounded applications,[44] but critics maintain that it is also the result of a more strict interpretation of the refugee definition by the UNHCR representative in Belgium.[45] In recent years, the largest group of applicants has been Christian Turks.[46] During 1982-83, there were also large influxes of applicants from Ghana, India and Pakistan.[47] The Belgium government and the UNHCR maintain that the majority of the claims by these national groups are unfounded,[48] and that asylum applicants from these countries are economic migrants. Not only has there been a significant decline in the recognition rate but, since the passage of the refugee law of 1980 only two persons have been granted the status of *assimilé*.[49]

Since 1972, Belgium has admitted a relatively large number of refugees from Latin America and Southeast Asia via quota programmes. These groups benefitted from intense media and press coverage describing the desperate plight of refugees from places like Chile and Vietnam. They were also the object of intensive lobbying efforts by broad coalitions of interested politicians, voluntary agencies, labour unions and the churches. Thus in the wake of the September 1973 coup that overthrew Salvador Allende in Chile, the Belgian government, responding to the public outcry over repression following the coup, pressures from the voluntary agencies, and resettlement appeals from the UNHCR, adopted an admission programme for Chilean political prisoners.[50] The 1973 coup in Chile also led to the establishment of the Association for the Reception of Refugees from Chile (COLARCH) which played an important role in the establishment, implementation, and extension of the quota programme. Since 1973, the Council of Ministers has organized eight programmes of 150 visas each. Initially limited to Chileans, the programme was extended in 1976 to political prisoners from Argentina, Uruguay, Bolivia and El Salvador. The candidates have been selected by the voluntary agencies who also helped to integrate the refugees into Belgian society.

Table 1:   *Number of Asylum Applicants*

	1977	1978	1979	1980	1981	**TOTAL**	1976	1981 (1)
1) Originating from Eastern Europe (including Yugoslavia)	325	233	236	322	637	**1.753**	162	570
2) Originating from Latin America and Indochina	353	484	1.562	1.156	1.191	**4.746**	87	99
3) Others	276	399	629	1.250	617	**3.171**	143	406
TOTAL	**954**	**1.116**	**2.427**	**2.728**	**2.445**	**9.670**	**392**	**1.075**

(1)   Under consideration on 31 December 1981.

Table 2:   *Number of Persons Recognized as Refugees*

	1977	1978	1979	1980	1981	**TOTAL**		differ–ence (2)
1) Originating from Eastern Europe (including Yugoslavia)	83	70	68	60	207	**488** (1)	**1.345**	857
2) Originating from Latin America and Indochina	343	480	1.476	1.254	1.118	**4.671** (1)	**4.734**	63
3) Others	151	115	833	316	981	**2.396** (1)	**2.908**	542
TOTAL	**577**	**665**	**2.377**	**1.630**	**2.306**	**7.555**	**8.987**	**1.432**

(1)   Total (table 1) of the number of asylum applicants under consideration at the end of 1976 minus the cases still under consideration at the end of 1981.
(2)   This column points out the number of persons who have not received refugees status (including applications judged to be unfounded, non-receivable according to the Belgian legislation or the cases closed because the applicant withdrew his application or voluntarily left Belgium).
Source: Belgian Ministry of Justice

In 1979, the Belgian government, responding to special UNHCR appeals to the international community to accept a large number of Vietnamese boat people and the public outcry over the drownings at sea which dominated nightly television viewing, agreed to provide 2,000 visas in 1979 and 300 in 1980. An umbrella organization for several voluntary organizations, the Belgian Committee for Aid to Refugees, played an active role in the Indochina quota programme by co-ordinating policies between the government, UNHCR and the voluntary agencies. These programmes were relatively short-lived, however. After public interest in both the boat people and Chile waned in 1980, the government announced that for budgetary reasons it was discontinuing the quota programmes.[51]

It is important to note that the numbers applying for political asylum in Belgium far fewer than those applying in neighbouring Germany or France. Despite the relatively small number of asylum applicants, the Belgian government, like other European governments, has recently instituted a number of new restrictive measures to deter the arrival of refugees. At the same time, UNHCR has been criticized for conducting the evaluation of asylum claims in Belgium without basic safeguards on procedure and evidence.

IV   Criticism of the Refugee Determination Procedure

1   *Criticism of the admissibility procedure*

The law of 1980 guarantees that an alien expressing his desire to seek asylum has the right to enter the country and have his case heard by the relevant authorities. Critics of Belgian policy contend that the right to enter is abridged in a number of instances. In particular, the border police limits access to the country,[52] and there have even been several unpublicized instances at the national airport where applicants have been expelled or compulsorily repatriated.[53] Refugee advocates complain that the police handling refugee claims are often young and inexperienced, have no knowledge of the country from which the claimant hails and frequently do not advise asylum applicants of their rights. It is alleged that the authorities actively discourage the entry of some nationalities. At one point an unofficial advisory note was posted at the airport stating that Turks were not political refugees, but economic migrants, so they should not be allowed to enter.[54] Other national groups, such as Ghanaians, Indians, Pakistanis and Zairians have similarly been regarded as economic migrants and have been refused permission to enter the country.[55] Thus despite the law of 1980, which is supposed to protect refugees from such abuses, it seems that the border police have taken the initiative to summarily reject people who they feel have manifestly unfounded applications.

In recent years the Belgian government has adopted a series of other measures to limit or deter the influx of aliens. In early 1983, the Ministry of Justice announced plans to cut immigration from outside the European Community and crack down on what is termed 'a growing traffic in self-styled refugees from India, Pakistan and Ghana'.[56] During the past three years the number of border posts for entry by non-EEC migrants has been reduced, visa requirements have been imposed on the citizens of refugee-producing countries, and there has been increased pressure on the airlines to check visa documents before entry into Belgium. In some cases, the airline companies have been held responsible and must bear the repatriation costs of illegal aliens. Occasionally, airport officials have refused entry to asylum seekers arriving in transit, returned them to the airplane and urged them to ask for asylum in the country of final destination.[58] Belgian embassies in refugee-generating countries have been urged to apply a more restrictive policy towards the issue of visas, and have, on occasion, required the visa applicant to sign an affidavit declaring that he will not ask for political refugee status while in Belgium.[59] Belgium has also recently initiated a programme of voluntary repatriation or emigration of asylum seekers and aliens.[60]

These restrictive practices have made it difficult for some *bona fide* refugees to reach Belgium. These measures permit the Aliens Office to follow a discriminatory policy towards certain groups and, in effect, give the Belgian authorities a pre-screening ability. The UNHCR has no control over the influx of asylum seekers at the border or the airport, and can only determine refugee status of applicants who have been declared receivable by the Aliens Office.

For those asylum applicants who are allowed entry into Belgium there are also problems regarding the receivability procedure. According to government officials and critics of Belgian policy, the police does not limit itself in the initial interview to determining the identity of the applicant and whether his application is receivable, but also inquires about the motivation of the applicant.[61] In particular, the police look for false declarations or contradictory statements.[62] According to the Ministry of Justice, the inquiries about motivations have no implications for the granting of refugee status, but are made in order to determine whether Belgium is the first country of asylum and whether any delays in the asylum requests are justified.[63] Another advantage of the procedure for the Ministry of Justice is that with a number of different interviews false applications can more readily be detected. The UNHCR receives copies of all the applicant's statements, including a transcript of the original interview. If, in the course of further interviews, the applicant's motivation changes considerably from that expressed in the initial interview, the credibility of his claim will be questioned and the asylum request will likely be denied.[64] Critics claim this is unfair and that contradictions in the statements made during the admissibility and the eligibility interviews, which are often six months or more apart, can occur easily. Furthermore, because of the language barrier and inadequate translations of interpreters, the asylum applicant is often misunderstood and misquoted during the interview and therefore the contradictions are more apparent than real.[65]

One of the most serious problems is that during the admissibility procedure, the Aliens Office can pre-screen all asylum applicants. This is possible because the UNHCR representative, as a result of the increase in the number of asylum applicants and the shortage of staff in recent years, cannot give a preliminary review of all the files of asylum applicants. According to one observer, 'as long as the UNHCR has not looked at the file, it does not know whether the person, although not receivable in Belgium, is a true refugee or not'.[66] Thus, even if the Justice Ministry respects the autonomy of UNHCR, it can still influence (or pre-select) the cases upon which the UNHCR has to decide.

2   Criticism of the eligibility procedure

The principal criticism of the eligibility procedure in Belgium is that the granting of refugee status is not regulated by a clearly established procedure. The major shortcomings of the present procedure are: the absence of a written motivation of the UNHCR decision, the limited access to the files by lawyers and applicants alike, and the lack of any appeal procedure. Moreover, the eligibility procedure does not conform to the provisions in Belgian legislation concerning the right of defense, motivation of decisions, and right of appeal.[67] Nor does the decision-making procedure of the UNHCR representative follow the recommendation of the Executive Committee.

Although it is difficult to determine how the UNHCR representative interprets the refugee definition and what criteria are used to reach a decision, most government and non-governmental agency officials believe that the UNHCR applies a liberal interpretation of the Convention.[68] A UNHCR internal study on the eligibility decisions in 1973 concluded that the Belgian practice at that time 'seem(ed) to be rather liberal,'[69] but that 'the general tendency, notably in most Western European countries, on presumptions about the political conditions in certain countries is valid in Belgium as well'.[70] According to some lawyers, the characterization by UNHCR in Belgium of certain nationalities, in particular Pakistanis, Zairians, and Ghanians, as economic migrants and applicants with 'manifestly unfounded claims' continues today.[71] Thus, according to one critic, the benefit of the doubt is hardly ever given to the asylum applicant in Belgium.[72]

One of the problems with the eligibility procedure is that in the case of a negative decision, the applicant is not informed of the reasons for the denial. Although the applicant and his lawyer can obtain an oral explanation of the decision and can have limited access to the file, some lawyers argue that without full written explanation of the reasons for the denial the *defense* of the applicant is hindered.[73]

Another fault with the procedure is that there is no appeal against decisions of the UNHCR. Only if the applicant submits new evidence, can the representative reopen the file and seek an advisory opinion from UNHCR headquarters in Geneva. Not only critics but the UNHCR itself recognizes the faults of the present arrangement and in principle favours the establishment of an appeal procedure. In 1974 the UNHCR representative wrote:

> 'This procedure (of appeal) does not respect the principle, generally accepted in administrative practice, that a review should be undertaken by a body different from the one that took the first decision. It is worthwhile underlining the fact that this is an aspect that should be borne in mind for future action.'[74]

Indeed, the basic procedural requirements outlined by the UNHCR Executive Committee clearly state that 'if the applicant is not recognized, he should be given a reasonable time to appeal for a formal reconsideration of the decision, either to the same or to a different authority'.[75]

Decisions of the UNHCR have been challenged on several occasions before the Council of State.[76] Each time the Council of State has refused to rule on the issue, arguing that the delegate of the UNHCR is an official of the United Nations, that no Belgian minister has authority over the representative, and that it is not an administrative authority within the context of the Belgian law.[77] This conclusion by the Council of State has been criticized by a number of lawyers arguing that the decision of the UNHCR is an administrative decision and that Belgium must carry the responsibility of the representative's decisions.[78]

Lack of procedural safeguards, such as right of appeal, steps to limit the admissibility of certain groups of asylum seekers, and the introduction of deterrent measures, such as visa requirements, are cause for alarm. Yet these developments are not the only factors which influence asylum decision making in Belgium. Such decisions do not occur in a political vacuum, but have serious political implications both at home and abroad. Therefore, domestic and foreign policy factors also influence who becomes a refugee in Belgium.

3 Domestic and foreign policy pressures

a: The domestic pressures upon the refugee determination process

In recent years there has been a trend toward adopting increasingly restrictive attitudes and policies toward asylum seekers. During the 1950s and the 1960s, Belgium, like other growing economies in Europe, recruited large numbers of economic migrants to work in the industrial and mining areas, but with the oil crisis of 1973, guest workers were no longer needed and the government officially ended its immigration policy a year later. According to the 1981 population census there are 841,177 aliens (excluding EEC nationals) in Belgium, or about 8.91 percent of the total population.[79] In comparison with other West European countries this is a relatively high percentage. The largest group of aliens are Italians, followed by Moroccans. There are also a considerable number of Turks, Algerians and Tunisians. There are about 8,575 Zairians.

By the 1980s, recession and unemployment resulted in increased hostility towards immigrant workers in Belgium.[80] In early 1986, the rate of unemployment is approximately 14 percent of the population of working age, and the majority of the unemployed are unskilled workers, a large percentage of whom are foreigners. Many Belgians believe that foreigners take away their jobs, and receive extensive social benefits from the public assistance budget.

The increasing number of asylum seekers causes various reception problems. In certain communities of the Brussels region the number of aliens exceeds fifty per cent of the local population. The increasing level of unemployment poses a heavy burden on the social welfare office (CPAS), and has led a number of communities to refuse to register refugees despite the fact that this policy violates the law of 1980. The government has failed to respond adequately to this challenge and in fact has legalized this practice. The Royal Decree of 1985 forbids aliens from non-EEC countries to reside in certain communities around Brussels because 'it is not in the public interest'.[81]

The refusal by local communities to register refugees is used as a justification by certain Public Welfare officials to deny social benefits to aliens. In certain communities, the CPAS has been unable to meet its financial obligations because the Ministry of Social Welfare has been extremely tardy in reimbursing funds spent by the local public welfare offices. Consequently a large number of asylum seekers have been without even the minimal subsistence allowance and have had to apply for help to the non-governmental refugee agencies (NGOs). Initially, the NGOs took over the welfare responsibility, but these activities seriously drained the financial reserves of these organizations. Consequently, certain agencies, e.g. Caritas, refused to provide aid to new asylum seekers.

Bowing to the welter of criticism by the CPAS and the voluntary agencies, the government has subsequently provided the *Comité Belge*, the principal national refugee assisting organization with the necessary financial means to fulfil the tasks of the local CPAS. However, several agencies have criticized this arrangement because the voluntary agencies now fulfil a role which rightfully belongs to the local communities. Nevertheless, the government appears unwilling to alleviate the situation in the short term because it fears that changing the reception policy might create an undesirable 'pull effect'.[82]

The impact of press, media and public opinion upon Belgian refugee policy is generally regarded as minimal, although there have been occasions when the press has exaggerated the number of refugees applying for political asylum and has thus contributed to the rising xenophobia against certain nationalities. The public has very little specific knowledge about the refugee problem, and makes no distinction between economic migrants and refugees.[83] Clearly, however, the media played a major role in dramatizing and in securing strong public support for both the Latin American and the Indochinese programmes.

b: Foreign policy pressures upon the refugee determination procedure
Foreign policy considerations play an important role, despite the fact that UNHCR is the decision maker on asylum matters in Belgium. Since the delegation of the eligibility authority to the UNHCR in the early 1950s, the refugee problem has changed radically. Up until the 1960s, there were few political problems involved in the refugee determination procedure as most of the refugees in Belgium came from Eastern Europe. Those fleeing communist regimes were almost universally presumed to be persecuted and were recognized as refugees relatively easy. Before Belgium signed the 1967 Protocol, the UNHCR representative could only grant refugee status within the 1951 Convention applicable to events occurring in Europe before 1 January 1951. For individuals coming from outside Europe and due to events after 1951, the Ministry of Justice could grant asylum. This procedure became important when asylum seekers started to come from Algeria and Zaire.[84] In 1954, several Algerians fled to Belgium because of persecution by France during the Algerian War. They were the cause of strained relations with France, because they requested political asylum and claimed the protection of the political offense exception.[85] Due to French pressure, no Algerians were granted asylum and several were extradited to France.

The political problems associated with the granting of refugee status became more serious after Zaire became independent in 1960. Political relations with President Mobuto have been extremely sensitive, and political refugee status has been given to only approximately 200 Zairians, despite the repressive nature of the Mobuto regime.[86] Given Belgium's special relationship with Zaire, UNHCR has been sensitive to the interests of both countries. For example, an early 1970s internal UNHCR study recounted the case of an individual who was granted political asylum and subsequently became the cause of strained relations between Belgium and Zaire:

'In one case the applicant was recognized because of his personal relations with President Mobuto. But the fact that he was granted refugee status in Belgium became the direct cause of severe disturbances between the Belgian and the Zairian Governments, and as a result all ships of a Belgian shipping company (Compagnie Maritime Belge) were blocked in Zaire. This blockade was not waived until the person in question left Belgian territory and after the personal intervention by the Belgian Minister of Justice.'[87]

After this controversy, the Belgian authorities seem to have reached a tacit understanding with the UNHCR that 'Zairians are not recognized as refugees, but are also not expelled'.[88] However, according to several voluntary agencies, Zairians are the target of Belgian government's deterrent measures. A high number of Zairians are not allowed to enter Belgium, and some are refouled at the airport. In particular, some voluntary agencies accuse the Aliens Office of applying a stricter interpretation of the receivability criteria for Zairian applicants than for other nationals.[89] The presumption that most Zairians are not *bona fide* refugees is also prevalent at UNHCR. According to UNHCR officials, all but a few of the applicants are either students who are unwilling to return home after finishing their studies,[90] or are economic migrants. [91] A voluntary agency official in Belgium maintained that there exists a bias against African applicants and that Zairians, in particular, have to provide 'three times the amount of proof' that an East European does to be recognized as a refugee in Belgium.[92] Many Zairians recognize the situation in Belgium and cross the border to France where they have a better chance of receiving refugee status.

After Belgium signed the 1967 Protocol which removed the geographical and time limits in the 1951 Convention, the UNHCR representative was granted authority to determine the refugee status of all asylum applicants. The signing of the 1967 Protocol coincided with the arrival of larger numbers of Third World nationals fleeing politically repressive and desperately poor regimes and seeking refuge in Europe. At the same time, fewer communist bloc nationals were permitted to flee to the West as the countries in Eastern Europe consolidated their rule. Unlike the treatment accorded Eastern Europeans, no presumptive refugee status was granted Third World applicants in Belgium or elsewhere in Europe.

Rather, as the number of Third World asylum applicants grew in the late 1970s, Belgium became increasingly restrictionist in its admissions policy, particularly as economic recession took hold in much of the West. There were important exceptions which included Chileans, other 'Southern Cone' Latin American refugees and the Vietnamese. The admission of these groups, however, depended to a large extent on the formation of broad coalitions of interested politicians, church representatives and voluntary agencies. Most Third World entrants were not the beneficiaries of this kind of sentiment and support. Part of this resistance can be explained by economic pressures and xenophobic attitudes in Belgium, but foreign policy considerations also played an important role. Nationals from Eastern Europe (with the exception of Yugoslavs) have generally had little difficulty making their persecution claims credible. Discrimination at the hands of local communist authorities or repeated interrogation by the police will usually suffice as reasons for granting refugee status. However, Yugoslavian applicants, since the early 1970s, have generally only been recognized in instances where the person in question has been an active opponent of the regime and has taken part in political propaganda against the Yugoslavian authorities. Evidently, as an internal UNHCR study pointed out, economic considerations, such as preventing the flow of further migrant labour from Yugoslavia, influenced the UNHCR decisions.[93] Currently, the large number of Turkish applicants pose a political problem as Turkey is a member of NATO, and has concluded an Association Treaty with the European Communities (which includes provisions for the free movement of labour).[94] Even the treatment of Poles has been influenced by foreign policy factors. After the imposition of martial law, the Poles were allowed to stay in Belgium under certain conditions without having to apply for refugee status.[95] This solution provided flexibility and prevented the Aliens Office and the UNHCR from being confronted with a large number of asylum applicants. At the same time, it enabled the Poles to return home after the repeal of martial law, without being questioned by the Polish government about their application for refugee status.

Despite the politicizing of some aspects of refugee decision making, the principal shortcomings of the Belgian refugee determination system and the role of UNHCR within it relate to procedure. There is increasing dissatisfaction expressed by UNHCR, by some quarters of the Belgian government, and by many voluntary agencies and lawyers with the present institutional arrangements. Thus, proposals and discussions about possible reform on the refugee determination system in Belgium have proliferated in recent years.

V The Reform of the Refugee Determination Procedure

Negotiations for reforming the refugee determination procedure in Belgium have been in progress for some time. During the parliamentary discussion of the law of 1980, special attention was given to the shortcomings in the refugee determination procedure. The report by the Senate Committee on the Judiciary urged the Minister of Foreign Affairs to negotiate a procedure with the UNHCR which would not be in conflict with the national legislation:

'La Commission se préoccupe de la possibilité d'un recours contre la décision du Haute Commissaire. Le rapporteur, resumant les souhaits de la Commission et constatant qu'en vertu de ce texte, l'autorité internationale est mandatée par le Ministre des Affaires Etrangères, estime que cette subdélégation est conditionnée par ce qui est prévu en droit interne. En outre, le Ministre compétent doit requérir de cette autorité internationale que ses décisions soient soumises au recours prévu par notre droit interne. La subdélégation doit être subordonnée aux guaranties assurées par le droit belge en matière de droit de défense, de motivation et de recours.'[96]

A 1984 court decision in Liege, upheld by an appeals tribunal, underlined the need for change. The decision involved the case of an asylum seeker who, upon receiving an order to leave the country after a negative decision by the UNHCR, claimed that the expulsion order was illegal. He argued that the expulsion order was based upon the decision of the UNHCR, and was not taken in accordance with internal Belgian law which requires that there be a right of motivation of decisions, of defense and of appeal:

'Pour les cas d'espèce, la loi belge décide, conformément à une principe général de notre droit en matière juridictionnelle, que les décisions administrative, relatives aux étrangers, doivent être motivées (Art. 62 de la loi du 15 décembre 1980). En doit en déduire apparemment, que la prise de position non motivée du H.C.R., qui n'a pas estimé pouvoir reconnaître au demandeur la qualité de refugié, n'est pas une decision au sens de consultation. Dés lors, on peut penser raisonnablement que l'Office des Etrangers, agissant dans notre ordre juridique interne, ne peut faire à une décision administrative déclarant la demande nonfondée (Art. 53 in fine de la loi du 15 dec. 1980). En conséquence, l'ordre de quitter le pays pris sur une pareille base est un acte en apparence illégal qui peut donner lieu à référé civil.'[99]

UNHCR's opposition to the continuation of its present role in the Belgian procedure dates back to the tenure of Sadruddin Aga Khan as UN High Commissioner for Refugees.[98] An internal UNHCR study of that period commented:

'While it appears that there is some legal justification to be found in Article 8(b) of the Statute of the High Commissioner's Office for accepting the tasks which delegated to UNHCR in Belgium, bearing the responsibility for all eligibility decisions puts the Office in a delicate position. Moreover, there are other legal considerations such as there expressed in Article 100, paragraph 1, of the UN Charter and in Article

35 of the 1951 Geneva Convention, the provisions of which might be conflicting with the present state of eligibility in Belgium.'[99]

The study continued that although Article 8(b) of the UNHCR statute urges the promotion of special agreements with the governments, the 'delegation, however, has the main characteristic of the Contracting State saddling the High Commissioner with a burden extending beyond the limits of co-operation.'[100] Within UNHCR there is great frustration with the Belgian procedure. The official view is that:

'The High Commissioner believes...that it is neither necessary nor in line with the traditional functions of his Office for the UNHCR to assume alone the decision-making responsibility, but that a meaningful participatory role is essential to meeting existing concerns.'[101]

Moreover, officials within UNHCR resent the fact that the Belgian government does not assume responsibility for UNHCR decisions. According to one UNHCR document: '... the High Commissioner ... has duties towards all members of the international community. Accepting delegation of power from one state in eligibility matters might lead him into difficulties with the legitimate interests of other States. It is also clear that the present system in Belgium – if it became a general practice – would be a source of a great number of conflicts, the more so as there is a tendency on the part of the State delegating its power to hide behind the High Commissioner's decision and not to recognize that decision as its own.'[102]

During the preparations for the refugee law of 1980, the UNHCR expressed its dissatisfaction with the institutional arrangement and pressed the government to adopt a new eligibility procedure. It did so discreetly, however, because it believed that 'It is not appropriate for UNHCR to press for a legislation to introduce such a procedure, since this could be considered as an indirect attempt to relinquish (our) responsibilities for the present procedure'.[103] In 1980, it was the view of the UNHCR representative that because the final authority belonged to the Belgian government, the government had to take the initiative for changing the system and in particular for instituting an appeals procedure.[104]

For the past few years, negotiations to change the refugee determination procedure have been taking place within a working group of the Ministries of Justice and Foreign Affairs and the UNHCR.[105] At the end of 1985 the government agreed to take back the authority delegated to UNHCR.[106] The majority of the voluntary agencies are concerned that Belgium's refugee admission policy may now become more restrictive and politicized. In order to prevent this, all the lawyers and the agencies insist that the UNHCR should continue to play an important role in the new procedure.

In early 1986, the government made public the general outline of the new procedure. The new draft law is scheduled to be discussed in Parliament in late 1986. The government plans to adopt an arrangement similar to the French procedure consisting of independent decision-making and appeals bodies. The Ministry of Justice will take over the responsibility to determine refugee status. Within the Ministry a special administrative unit will be established which will simultaneously decide on both the receivability and the eligibility of the claim. It is expected that this unit will take speedy decisions in cases of manifestly unfounded claims. Upon a negative motivated decision at the first instance, the applicant will be able to file and appeal before a specially established Commission which will be chaired by a judge and in which UNHCR will have an advisory role. The strengths of the French refugee determination procedure are: the existence of a clear developed procedure, the autonomy of both OFPRA and the Appeals Commission, and UNHCR participation.[107] There are a number of advantages to Belgium adopting a procedure similar to France's. First, the establishment of a clear procedure and motivation of decisions will avoid the impression that the decision making procedure is arbitrary. Second, in the appeals procedure the UNHCR could fulfil its role as defender of refugee interests, instead of judging refugee status. According to the UNHCR Executive Committee, UNHCR could:

> 'exercise a meaningful participatory or advisory role. While the exact nature of this role would depend upon the form of the particular procedure, it could involve the possibility for UNHCR to express its views before a negative decision is taken or to participate as an observer in the deliberation of advisory boards at the first instance of appeal level.'[108]

Third, the new procedure could also be an important step towards further harmonization of the determination procedures in Europe. Some have argued, however, that the adoption in Belgium of institutional arrangements similar to those that exist in France could be hampered by the lack of autonomy of the decision making bodies and possible increased politicizing of the decisions.[109] It is also argued, though, that the appointment of experienced and independent magistrates and a continued strong role for the UNHCR could strengthen the autonomy of the decision making and the appeals commissions.

Notes: Chapter 19

The manuscript for this article was completed in early 1986 and therefore does not take into account legal, political and social developments in Belgium refugee policy since that time. We would like to acknowledge the support and the enthusiasm of a large number of people who agreed to be interviewed and who helped in providing documentation. In our meeting with officials at every level we found a high degree of concern about the protection of refugees in Belgium. Our critique of the system is not a critique of persons who are involved in the process. Part of the research was made possible by a grant from the Zahm Travel Fund, the Jesse Jones Faculty Travel Fund, the Institute of Scholarship in the Liberal Arts, and the Kellogg Institute for International Studies of the University of Notre Dame.

1 Convention relating to the Status of Refugees, 28 July 1951, 189 United Nations Treaty Series 137, as amended by the Protocol relating to the Status of Refugees, 26 July 1967, 606 U.N. Treaty Series 267.

2 For a recent analysis of the political considerations in U.S. refugee admissions policy see: Gil Loescher and John Scanlan, *Calculated Kindness: Refugees and America's Half-Open Door, 1945 to the Present.* (New York and London: The Free Press, Macmillan, 1986).

3 Recent comparative studies of asylum policies are: Christopher Avery, 'Refugee Status Decision Making: The Systems of Ten Countries,' *Stanford Journal of International Law* 19, no. 2 (1983); T. Alexander Aleinikoff, 'Political Asylum in the Federal Republic of Germany and the Republic of France: Lessons for the United States,' *Journal of Law Reform* 17, no. 2 (1984), 183-241; M. Boerlage et al., *Asylum Policy and Family Reunification: Policy in Ten European Countries*, (Vienna, International Helsinki Foundation for Human Rights, 1985).

4 Atle Grahl-Madsen, *The Status of Refugees in International Law* (Leiden, Sijthoff, 1966), 343; cited in Avery, Ibid., 252.

5 Council of Europe, Parliamentary Assembly, *Report in Reply to the 21st. Report on the Activities of the Office of the United Nations High Commissioner for Refugees*, 4204, (1978) op. cit. 8.

6 Law of 26 June 1953, adopting the 1951 Convention (*Moniteur belge*, 4 October 1953); Ministerial Decree of 22 February 1954 relating to the competence to determine refugee status of the Representative in Belgium of the United Nations High Commissioner for Refugees; Royal Decree of 18 June 1964 (*Moniteur belge*, 25 April 1961), relating to the conditions of entry, residence and establishment of foreign nationals in Belgium; Royal Decree of 21 December 1965 (*Moniteur belge*, 31 December 1965), amended by Royal Decree of 11 July 1969 (*Moniteur belge*, 14 August 1969); Law of 27 February 1969 (*Moniteur belge*, 3 May 1969); approving the 1967 Protocol; Law of 15 December 1980, on access to the territory, sojourn, establishment and removal of aliens (*Moniteur belge*, 27 October 1981, Errata *Moniteur belge*, 28 October 1981).

7 Article 48 of the Law of 15 December 1980: 'Peut être reconnu comme réfugié l'étranger qui réunit les conditions requises à cet effet par les conventions internationales liant la Belgique.'

8 Catharina Dehullu, 'Ontwikkeling van het Vluchtelingenrecht in Theorie en Praktijk op Internationaal en Nationaal Vlak sinds het Verdrag van Geneve (1951): een Kritische Analyse en Evaluatie' (Dissertation, University of Louvain, Belgium, 1982), 390.

9 Pierre Mertens, 'Le Droit d'Asile en Belgique a l'Heure de la Révision Constitutionelle', *R.B.D.I.*, (1966), 218.

10 The authority is delegated to the UNHCR representative in Belgium, and not to UNHCR in general. The UNHCR headquarters can act as an adviser, but not as an instructor to its representative in Belgium. Thus, it is assumed that the representative acts independently from UNHCR headquarters on eligibility decisions falling within the 1951 Convention. Refugees recognized by the representative are Convention refugees. Under certain circumstances, the representative can recognize a refugee under the UNHCR mandate, but the latter decision falls outside the authority delegated.

11 European Consultation on Refugees and Exiles, *Asylum in Europe: A Handbook for Agencies assisting Refugees*, (Amsterdam: ECRE, 1983), 81.

12 The Commission Consultative des Etrangers is composed of a magistrate, a barrister and a representative of a voluntary agency.

13 Interview Ms. Badiani, ex-UNHCR representative in Belgium, Brussels, on 2 August 1984.

14 UNHCR, *Handbook on Procedures and Criteria to determining Refugee Status*, (Geneva, UNHCR, 1979).

15 Interview Ms. Badiani and Mrs. Declerk, eligibility officer, UNHCR, Brussels, on 2 August 1984.

16 Article 56 of the Law of 15 December 1980: 'Dans aucun cas, l'étranger reconnu comme réfugié ne peut être éloigné vers le pays qu'il a fui parce que sa vie sa liberté y était menacée.'

17 Interview Mrs. Declerck and Ms. Badiani.

18 Letter Minister of Justice to the macebearer of Brussels, 5 February 1985.

19 Guy S. Goodwin-Gill, 'Entry and Exclusion of Refugees: The obligations of States and the Protection Function of the Office of the United Nations High Commissioner for Refugees', in Michigan Yearbook of International Legal Studies, *Transnational legal Problems of Refugees*, (New York: Clark Boardman Co., 1982), 309.

20 Interview Mr. Desmet and Mr. Potter, UNHCR, Brussels, 11 January 1985.

21 European Consultation on Refugees and Exiles, (1983), op. cit. 78.

22 Council of Europe, Recommendation No. R(81)16, Committee of Ministers, 5 November 1981; and UNHCR, Report of the Twenty Eigth Session of the Executive Committee of the High Commissioners Programme, Geneva, 4-12 October 1977, General Assembly Document A/32/12 Add.1.

23 UNHCR, Report of the Twenty Eigth Session of the Executive Committee of the High Commissioner's programme, ibid. 12-6.

28 European Consultation on refugees and Exiles, op. cit. 68; and Law of 15 December 1980, Article 57: 'L'étranger qui remplit les conditions de la présente loi pour être reconnu comme réfugié et qui justifie de raisons sérieuses l'empêchant de demander cette qualité peut, à sa demande, être déclaré assimilé au réfugié par le Ministre de la Justice. Il beneficie dans ce cas du statut accordé aux réfugié par la loi belge, mais ne peut pretendré aux titres de voyage prévus par les traités internationaux.'

25 Interview Anne Sunde, Aide belge aux personnes deplacées, Huy, on 12 January 1985.

26 Belgium adhered to the following agreements: Arrangements of 31 May 1924, 12 May and 30 June 1928, related to the issue of Identity Certificate to Russian, Armenian and Assimilated Refugees; the Convention of 1933 relating to the International status of Refugees; the Convention of 1938 concerning the status of refugees coming from Germany; and the London Travel Document Agreement of 1946.
   For a discussion of these agreements and the situation in Belgium see: Louise W. Holborn, *Refugees: Problem of our Time*, 2 Vols., (Metuchen, N.J.: The Scarecrow Press, 1975); Louise W. Holborn, *The International Refugee Organization*, (London: The Oxford University Press, 1956); Jacques Vernant, *Les Réfugiés dans l'après-guerre, Rapport Préliminaire d'une groupe d'étude sur le Problème des Réfugiés*, (Geneva: ONU, 1951); M.P. Herremans, *Personnes Déplacées,*, (Brussels: Ed. Marie-Julienne); Betty Garfinkels, *Belgique, Terre d'Acceuil, problème du Réfugié 1933-1940*, (Brussels: Labor, 1974); Belgische Vereniging voor de Verenigde Naties. *Verslag over de Toestand van de Politieke Vluchtelingen in Belgie*, (Brussels, 1950); A. Bekaert, *Le Statut des Etrangers en Belgique* (Brussels: Larcier, 1940).

27 Arrangement relatif au statut juridique des réfugiés russes et armeniens, signed at Geneva, 30 June 1928. Société des Nations, Recueil des Traités, Vol. LXXXIX, No. 20005; the Belgian agreement, ratified on 2 May 1928; the French agreement, ratified on 21 May 1928.

28 Holborn, (1975), ibid. 18.

29 Vernant, (1953), ibid. 306-7.

30 Vernant, (1951), ibid. 111. '...il existe un accord verbal pour les réfugiés arrivant après le 15 Octobre 1949, qui a été mis en vigueur par une circulaire du Ministre de la Justice du 10 Decembre 1948. Le transfert, de l'OIR au Governement belge, des responsibilités de l'entretien matériel des réfugiés a fait également l'objet d'un procès verbal en date du 13 Février 1980 adressée par le Directeur Général de l'OIR au Ministre des Affaires Etrangères, les réfugiés du groupe résiduel qui se trouvaient en Belgique à la date du 30 Juin 1950 resteront leur vie durant à la charge du Gouvernement belge.'

31 UNHCR Document, Confidential.

32 Ibid.

33 Ibid.

34 Ibid.

35 Ibid.

36 Ibid.

°37 Ibid.

38 Interview UNHCR officer, Bonn, June 1985. According to this source, in some cases the UNHCR in Brussels is more restrictive in its decision making than the Federal Agency for the Recognition of Refugees in Zirndorf, West Germany.

39 Figures provided by Ministry of Justice.
40 European Consultation on Refugees and Exiles, letter from the Vereniging Vluchtel-ingenwerk Nederland, 19 May 1982. UNHCR General Report, Year 1984-5, Doc. no. A/AL96/639, 242. *Le Soir*, 30 January 1986.
41 Interview Mr. Desmet and Mr. Potter, and *De Standaart*, 15 January 1986.
42 Interview Ms. Badiani.
43 Ibid. and note Cabinet of Prime Minister 'Proposition du Groupe de Travail Candidats réfugiés politiques', 17 January 1986.
44 Ibid.
45 Interview Mr. Gillet, Amnesty International Belgique Francophone, Brussels, on 11 January 1985; Interview Mr. Sbolgi, Service Social des Etrangers, Brussels, on 11 January 1985; Interview Mr. De Kock, Lawyer, Brussels, on 4 January 1985; this is also the view of some UNHCR personnel (see note 38).
46 Interview Mr Beeckman de West Meerbeeck, Ministry of Justice, Aliens Office, Brussels, on 11 January 1985.
47 Note 'Proposition du Groupe de Travail Candidats réfugiés politiques', 17 January 1986.
48 Ibid.
49 Interview with Ms. Badiani; Question et reponse no. 103 du 14 mars 1986 de Mr. Dejardin au Ministre de Justice, unpublished.
50 Anne Sunde and Mauro Sbolgi, Pratique et Evolution des Procedures de la Recon-naissance du Statut de Réfugié Politique en Belgique, (Brussels, 1982).
51 Interviews Ms. Badiani and Mr. Beeckman de West Meerbeeck.
52 Association belge des Juristes démocrates, Association pour le droit des Etrangers, Collectif d'Avocats de Bruxelles, Onthaalcentrum voor Gastarbeiders van Brussel, Service Social des Etrangers, Vlaams Overlegcomite Opbouwwerk Migratie, Con-férence de presse sur les carences de la procédure de reconnaissance de réfugiés, la reconnaissance de la qualité de réfugié par le délégué en Belgique du Haut Commissariat des Nations Unies pour les Réfugiés, 23 March 1983.
53 Interview at the Airport, Zaventem, name withheld on request; World Council of Churches, West European Consultation on the Role of Churches in Helping Refugees at International airports, Frankfurt am Main, 13-14 February 1984.
54 Interviews Mr. Sbolgi and Mr. de Moffarts, Onthaalcentrum voor Gastarbeiders van Brussel, Brussels, on 24 January 1985.
55 Interview officials at the airport, name withheld on request; *De Standaard*, 6 July 1978; *De Standaard*, 22 January 1980.
56 Reuter Newsservice, 3 January 1983.
57 Note of the Minister of Communications and Foreign Trade to Airline Companies operating on Belgian civil airports, 6 February 1986.
58 Interview with Belgian officials at the airport.
59 *La Libre Belgique*, 12 April 1983.
60 'Programme pour le rapatriement volontaire des candidats réfugies et de certaines categories de migrants residant en Belgique', *Revue des Droits des Etrangers*, no. 2, (1983).
61 Mauro Sbolgi, 'Le Double Interrogatoire des Candidats Refugies,' *Bulletin d'informa-tion ADDE*, (Avril, Mai, Juin 1979); Interview Mr. Beeckman de west Meerbeeck.
62 Thierry Beeckmans de West Meerbeeck, Les Refugies et la Police des Etrangers, Rapport de Stage, (unpublished, 1976), 19:

'déclarations mensongères ou motifs apparaissant sans rapport avec les crit per-sécution prévus par la loi: la P.E. *Aliens Police* procède a un examen sommaire a ce sujet. Et si des eleménts suspects ou contradictions apparaissent, l'interéssé est réin-terrogé et si des contradictions subsistent ou si les motifs invoqués lui paraissent sans rapport avec la Convention, l'appréciation du H.C.R. tout en attirant son attention sur les points de faiblesse ou de contradiction de la demande. Dès lors, en pratique il ne s'agit plus de question de recevabilité, mais des questions examinées avec le fond par le H.C.R.'

63 Interview Mr. Beeckman de West Meerbeeck.
64 Ibid.

65   Interview Ms. Sunde; Sbolgi, ibid., 1-4. Critics argue that because the Aliens Office does not reread the interview back to the asylum applicant in his own language, many errors occur in the translation.
66   Interview Ms. Sunde.
67   Alain P. Couturier, 'Problèmes relatifs a la procédure de reconnaissance du statut de réfugie politique', *Journal des Tribunaux*, (1978), 308.
68   Interviews Mr. Rijkmans, Amnesty International Flemish Section, Louvain, 3 January 1985, and Mr. Jaeger.
69   UNHCR Document, Confidential.
70   Ibid.
71   Association Belge des Juristes Démocrates, Les carences de la procedure de reconnaissance du statut de réfugié, Conference de presse, 23 Mars 1983.
72   Interview Mr. De Kock.
73   Couturier, ibid., 308.
74   Stanley Wright, Report on problems of refugees and Exiles in Europe, (1974). Quoted in Dehullu, ibid., 510.
75   UNHCR, Report of the Twenty Eight Session of the Executive Committee of the High Commissioners Programme, Geneva, 4-12 October 1977, General Assembly Document A/32/12/add. 1.
76   Council of State, 25 September 1970, Kare Merat and Kaboza; Council of State, 21 September 1978, Lusnjani.
77   Ibid., 'Le délégué de Haut Commissaire n'est pas une autorité belge..., il convient de constater l'incompétence du Conseil d'Etat, le Haut Commissariat des Nations Unies pour les Refugies n'étant pas une institution belge.'
78   L.P. Seutens, Noot onder Raad van State, 21 September 1978, *Rechtskundig Weekblad*, (1978-79).
79   *Bareel*, no. 25, p. 10, and 'Operation fermees', *Jeune Afrique*, 14 March 1984.
80   Council of Europe, Parliamentary Assembly, *On Xenophobic Attitudes and Movements in Member Countries with regard to Migrant Workers*, Thirty-fifth Ordinary Session, Doc. 5107, order no. 420, (1983).
81   Arrêt royal du 7 mai 1985 interdisant à certain étrangers de sejourner ou de s'établier dans les communes d'Anderlecht, de Forest, de Molenbeek-Saint-Jean, de Saint- Gilles, de Saint-josse-ten-Noode, et de Scherbeeck, (*Moniteur Belge*, 15 May 1985).
82   Sources: *De Standaard*, 6th May 1986, 15th January, 1986, *Le Soir*, 30th January 1986.
83   Interviews Ms. Sunde and Ms. Badiani
84   Interview Mr. Sbolgi; P. Vermeylen, Conferénce sur l'évolution de la protection de réfugiés, (Brussels, A.S.B.L., 1980), 13.
85   Ch. Van Den Wijnaez, *The Political Offence Exception to Extradition*, (Deventer: Kluwer, 1980), 169-173.
86   *Knack*, 15 January 1986 and *Neue Zurcher Zeitung*, 16 November 1985.
87   UNHCR Document, Confidential.
88   Interviews Mr. De Kock and Mr. Sbolgi.
89   Statement by Mr. Krenz: Ligue belge pour la Defense des Droits d'Homme. Compte rendu pour la réunion au Commissariat pour le Statut des Réfugiés, mars 1980, (Brussels, 1980), 2.
90   Interview Mrs. Toscani, UNHCR Headquarters, Head of European Bureau, Geneva, on 15th January 1985.
91   Interview Mr. Mbaidjol, UNHCR Headquarters, Geneva, 15 January 1985.
92   Interview Ms. Sunde.
93   UNHCR Document, Confidential.
94   Commission of the European Communities, *The EEC and the Developing Countries: Outside the Lomé Convention and the Southern Mediterranean*, European Documentation, (Brussels: The European Communities, 1979).
95   Ministère de la Justice, Circulaire a MMs. et MM. les Bourgemestres relative a la régularisation de la situation de séjour de certaines ressortissants polonais, *Moniteur belge*, 20 May 1983.
96   M. Moureaux, Projet de loi sur l'accès au territoire, le séjour, l'établissement et l'eloignement des étrangers, Rapport fait au nom de la Commission de la Justice,

Sénat de Belgique, Session de 1980-81, Parlementaire Bescheiden 521, no. 2, (1980).

97 L'état belge répresenté par le Ministre de la Justice, Tribunal Civil Liège (Ref.) 13 Janvier 1984.
98 Interview with Dr. Paul Weis.
99 UNHCR Document, Confidential.
100 Ibid.
101 UNHCR, Follow-up on earlier Conclusions of the Sub-Committee – The Determination of Refugee Status, inter-alia, with Reference to the Role of UNHCR in National Refugee Status Determination Procedures, Sub-Committee of the Whole on International Protection, Executive Committee, 3 September 1982, Doc. EC/SCP/22 Rev. 1.
102 UNHCR Document, Confidential.
103 Ibid.
104 Ibid.
105 Questions et réponses, Chambre, Question No. 122, 22 February 1985.
106 Questions et réponses, Chambre, Question No. 13, 27 January 1986.
107 In France, refugee status is granted by OFPRA (Office français de protection des réfugiés et apatrides). The office is connected with the Ministry of Foreign Affairs, but it is legally, financially and administratively autonomous. The OFPRA director is appointed by the Minister of Foreign Affairs. He is assisted by a Council, which advises him on various issues, including on the determination of refugee status. The Council. does not discuss individual cases. The members of the Council are representatives of the Ministries of Justice, Interior, Labour, Finance, Health, and a delegate from a non-governmental organization dealing with refugees. During the Council's meetings, the UNHCR representative can express observations and formulate proposals.

The tasks of OFPRA are to provide legal and administrative protection to refugees, and to determine refugee status within the framework of the Convention and the Protocol. Upon a negative decision by OFPRA, the asylum seeker can appeal it before the Appeals Commission (Commission de Recours). The tasks of the Appeals Commission are 'to decide on appeals against refusal to recognize the status of refugees, and to advise on the application to refugees of measures such as expulsion and 'assignation a residence' in the light of Article 31, 32, and 33 of the 1951 Convention.' Members of the Appeals Commission are a member of the Council of State, a representative of OFPRA and a UNHCR delegate. The decisions of the Appeals Commission must be given in public and be motivated. After a positive decision of the Appeals Commission or OFPRA, the refugee is not automatically granted asylum. The residence permit is granted by the local *prefecture de police*, who can refuse it in certain cases. Guy S. Goodwin-Gill, *The Refugee in International Law*, (Oxford: Clarendon Press, 1983); European Consultation on Refugees and Exiles, ibid., pp. 119-50.
108 UNHCR, Follow-up..., ibid., p. 9.
109 Interview Mr. Beeckman de West Meerbeeck.

Selected List of Interviews:

1 Interviews in Belgium

Ms. Badiani, ex-UNHCR Representative in Belgium.
Mr. Potter, protection officer UNHCR.
Mrs Declerck, eligibility officer UNHCR.
Mr. Desmet, eligibility officer UNHCR.
Mr. Jaeger, ex-UNHCR Head of Protection and currently Chairman of Comité belge d'aide aux réfugiés.
Mr. Janssens, Aliens Office, Ministry of Justice.
Mr. Beeckman de West Meerbleck, Ministry of Justic.
Mr. Gillet, lawyer and Amnesty International Belgique Francophone.
Mr. De Kock, lawyer and Ligue belge pour la defense des droits de l'homme.
Mr. Rijkmans, Amnesty International Nederlandstalige afdeling.
Mr. Sbolgi, Service Social des étrangers.

Ms. Sunde, Aide belge aux personnes déplacées.
Mr. de Moffarts, lawyer and previously with Onthaalcentrum voor Gastarbeiders van Brussel.
Mr. De Brand, Caritas Catholica.

2   *Interviews in Geneva:*

Mr. Moussalli, Director Protection Division UNHCR.
Mr. Jackson, Deputy Director Protection Division UNHCR.
Mr. Krenz, ex-UNHCR representative in Belgium and currently Deputy Director Protection Division UNHCR.
Mr. Coles, Conferences and Promotion of Refugee Law Section UNHCR.
Mr. Bari, General Legal Section UNHCR.
Mr. Kalumiya, Senior Legal Research Officer UNHCR.
Mr. Mbaidjol, Associate Protection Officer for Central and West Africa Section UNHCR.
Mrs. Toscani, Chief European Section UNHCR.
Mr. Peterson, Protection Officer European Section UNHCR.
Mr. Goodwin-Gill, Senior Protection Officer Americas Section UNHCR.
Dr. Paul Weis.

Index

see also non-governmental agencies, US
  religious agencies
Vratusa, Anton   136

Wagner–Rogers Bill   89, 93
War
  crimes   15, 22
  Prisoners Aid, Inc.   99
  Refugee Board   99, 107
  Relief Services   98–9, 105
Warthegau   120–1, 126–7
Weimar Germany   51–63
West Bank of Israel   256
Wiener, Dr Alfred   159
Wilkinson, A. W.   257
William of Brandenburg   3, 16
Williams, Tom   239, 241
Wilson, President   23, 33
Winckler   115
Winton, R. W. L. de   146
Wise, Stephen   95
Wolff-Metternich, Count von   42
Wolhynian Germans   112, 117–18, 121–5

Workers' Welfare Association of the Jewish
  Organisations in Germany   60
World Council of Churches   105
World Organization of Jews from Arab
  Countries   296
World Relief   104

Yalta Conference   26, 168–71, 173, 200,
  202, 230
Young Turk   39, 41–2, 45
Yugoslavia   133, 140, 142
  Communists   135–6
  invasion of Italy   135–7
  occupation of Trieste   138–9
  population exchange   27
  refugees in Belgium   341
  rule of Istria and Fiume   141–4, 148
  resistance to   144–7
  see also Italian–Yugoslavian dispute, Tito

Zair   340
Zara   137, 144
zoning   281–2